Making and Unmaking Intellectual Property

Making and Unmaking
INTELLECTUAL PROPERTY
Creative Production in Legal and Cultural Perspective

Edited by

MARIO BIAGIOLI, PETER JASZI, *and*
MARTHA WOODMANSEE

The University of Chicago Press
Chicago and London

MARIO BIAGIOLI is professor of law and science and technology studies at the University of California at Davis.
PETER JASZI is professor of law at Washington College of Law, American University.
MARTHA WOODMANSEE is professor of English and law at Case Western Reserve University.

The University of Chicago Press, Chicago 60637
The University of Chicago Press, Ltd., London
© 2011 by The University of Chicago
All rights reserved. Published 2011
Printed in the United States of America

20 19 18 17 16 15 14 13 12 11   1 2 3 4 5

ISBN-13: 978-0-226-90708-6   (cloth)
ISBN-13: 978-0-226-90709-3   (paper)
ISBN-10: 0-226-90708-2   (cloth)
ISBN-10: 0-226-90709-0   (paper)

Library of Congress Cataloging-in-Publication Data

Making and unmaking intellectual property : creative production in legal and cultural perspective / Edited by Mario Biagioli, Peter Jaszi, and Martha Woodmansee.
      p. cm.
   Includes index.
   ISBN-13: 978-0-226-90708-6 (cloth : alk. paper)
   ISBN-10: 0-226-90708-2 (cloth : alk. paper)
   ISBN-13: 978-0-226-90709-3 (pbk. : alk. paper)
   ISBN-10: 0-226-90709-0 (pbk. : alk. paper)   1. Intellectual property—United States. I. Biagioli, Mario, 1955–   II. Jaszi, Peter. II. Woodmansee, Martha.
   KF2979.M32 2011
   346.7304'8—dc22

                                                            2010052460

⊗ The paper used in this publication meets the minimum requirements of the American National Standard for Information Sciences—Permanence of Paper for Printed Library Materials, ANSI Z39.48-1992.

CONTENTS

ACKNOWLEDGMENTS

The majority of the papers collected in this volume grew out of a conference sponsored by the Society for Critical Exchange, "Con/texts of Invention: Creative Production in Legal and Cultural Perspective," which took place April 20–23, 2006, at Case Western Reserve University. The editors wish to acknowledge the generous contributions of the CWRU Department of English and Center for Law, Technology, and the Arts; the Washington College of Law at American University; the History of Science Department at Harvard University; and the Morris Fishbein Center for the History of Science and Medicine at the University of Chicago. We are grateful to Brigid Quinn of the U.S. Patent and Trademark Office and to Kelly Guseman of the Chamber of Commerce of Milan, Ohio, home of the Edison Birthplace Museum, for broadening and enlivening the conference inquiry into our modern institutions of invention. We also wish to thank Nicholas Petzak, Dawn Richards, Joshua Palmer, Kimberly Peterson, and Linda Schneider for the exceptional administrative support they provided at various stages of this project, and we especially wish to thank the editorial staff at the University of Chicago Press, in particular editors Susan Bielstein and Ruth Goring, and freelance copyeditor George Roupe for their help and encouragement in bringing the project to fruition.

INTRODUCTION

Scenarios

Once an area of the law populated only by a technical subculture of attorneys and scholars, intellectual property (IP) has become a focus of vital concern and remarkably intense inquiry across an expanding range of disciplines and constituencies. Along with the "information society," the "knowledge economy," and "innovation," IP has also become a household term. The World Intellectual Property Organization (WIPO) would like it to enter the classroom as well—the sooner the better. To that end, WIPO has recently published a colorful comic book (featuring games like "Spot the Infringement") to instill respect for copyright in children's minds—a concept that might already be lost on their older, file-sharing siblings.[1] And as IP tries to enlist the preadult, it is also expanding into the silicon world and the indefinitely large realm of virtuality. Those who build alternative lives and design virtual clothing and artifacts in Web-based games like Second Life may need sophisticated counsel to negotiate the legal boundaries between real and second life, between their real-world copyrights and trademarks in their virtual designs, their "virtual property rights," and the Second Life Patent and Trademark Office.[2]

In more mundane, carbon-based environments the ubiquitous reliance on IP across industries and the corporate world is generating a steady stream of new legal, technical, and cultural questions. Legal scholars, courts, and law-makers engage questions over the expansion of criteria of patentability (genetic sequences, business models, etc.), copyrightability (software, databases, etc.), the length of copyright protection (the Sonny Bono Copyright Term Extension Act), and the exceptions to those rights (the research exception in patent, fair use in copyright). At the same time, concerns with the escalation and justifications of IP and with the conceptual difficulties posed by key legal distinctions such as between tangible and intangible property, idea and expression, and invention and discovery as well as the difficulties underlying other fundamental notions of IP law (originality, novelty, utility, authorship, inventorship, etc.) are fueling debates that exceed the bounds of policy and legal discourse. For example, the way copyright, patent, and trademark law codifies cultural and knowledge production (as well as the history of such legal codifications) are attracting ongoing and mounting attention from disciplines like anthropology, science studies, history, communication and cyberculture studies, political science, literary and postcolonial studies, the arts, and education.

Informed by critiques of the figure of the author in copyright law that initiated, in the mid-1980s, the historical and theoretical study of IP outside the policy-oriented discourse of legal practitioners, much of the current literature continues to operate in the critical register.[3] The early critical scholarship was the work of literary theorists and historians, while other disciplines participated in the subsequent debates generated by the advent of the 'information society,' which cast knowledge in terms of information, texts, and media products rather than material objects. The effect was to place copyright (and the contentious history of its key concepts) at the center of the critical discourse about IP.[4] Increasingly, however, other branches of IP also have been subjected to scrutiny.

In that vein, current scholarship (produced both within and without the legal profession) is concerned not only with the power of the dominant metaphors and tropes of IP but also with the gaps between the law's normative description of the production of culture and knowledge and the evidence brought up by empirical studies of such processes. That evidence tends to highlight the role of collaboration and borrowing at the expense of individual authorial agency as well as the cultural specificity of IP—a specificity that is at odds with other notions of property, object, cultural production, and the relation or kinship between people and things from other parts of the world.[5] As part and parcel of this scholarly trend, the history of IP (now a specialty with its own professional organization) has reconstructed much of the law's detailed documentary trail, showing the discontinuities and sociopolitical contingencies in its genealogy and the frequent whiggishness of lawyers' comforting narratives about the history of their doctrines.[6]

Scholarly critiques of intellectual property, however, have not prevented it from becoming central to the university's research policies and practices. (Its terms and concepts also have crept into the classroom itself, where plagiarism is often construed in overly broad terms and then incorrectly conflated with copyright violation.)[7] Once presented as an ivory tower independent from the world of commerce—an image it really never matched—the university now collaborates more frequently and intensively with public and private sponsors, especially since the Bayh-Dole Act and related legislation.[8] The university is also slowly but steadily reconceptualizing its faculty as providers of IP—from patentable research down to copyrightable course syllabi to be used in distance learning programs. These developments have triggered debates over the pros and cons of patenting publicly funded scientific university research; the relation between academia and the private high-tech start-up companies developed by its faculty; the so-called anticommons produced by the patenting of scientific research and research techniques; the IP-related constraints imposed by private funding on faculty publications and access to their research; and questions about who owns internally funded academic work and how it should be archived or made public.[9] Many decry the privatization of academic work, fearing that academic research will turn into "work for hire," literally or figuratively. One specific response to this trend has been the rise of the "open journal" movement, with its insistence on making scholarly results in a wide range of disciplines broadly available using electronic tools.[10]

On the other hand, many academic practitioners of the technosciences welcome the opportunities provided by the so-called privatization of knowledge and see no problem in keeping one foot in the world of "open" academic science while planting the other foot in patent-based start-up companies often financed by venture capital, often with the encouragement of university technology transfer offices.[11] As part of this trend, the distinction between industry and academia (or between research and development or pure and applied science) has been further blurred, especially in the biotech area, with many scientists finding the new high-tech industrial environments more open and amenable to intellectual risk taking than peer-review-bound academia and its numerous committees.[12] Instead of casting the privatization of scientific knowledge as "impure," some have gone as far as to present its epitome—emergent biotech industry—as "countercultural."[13]

Opposition to and transgressions of IP are almost as visible and varied as its simultaneously global and microscopic presence. From the stereotypical

"Asian pirates" burning away cheap DVDs (often with subtitles that transgress grammar as much as the recordings may infringe IP)[14] we have moved to file-swapping high-schoolers, scientists who nonchalantly ignore the restriction on patented research tools, and artists and musicians who take IP as one of their subjects, whether by turning infringement into an art form (Negativland), grounding creative practice on the exploitation of recognized IP exceptions like fair use (Girl Talk), or, still less defiantly, developing initiatives to place art directly in the public domain (Free Art & Technology, Graffiti Research Lab).[15] While the figure of the pirate has always been romanticized in some quarters even as it is vilified by the defenders of law and order, it is now interesting to see that some probusiness voices are recasting the pirate as a "rogue innovator" whose practices may actually have something useful to teach to industry.[16] Also changing is the stereotypical identification of developing countries with the figure of the freebooting infringer. Often perceived as dens of organized piracy, these regions are now in some cases reflecting those accusations back on developed countries, as they protest foreign misappropriation of local cultural resources and the inadequacy of existing IP regimes to address it. Since the Agreement on Trade-Related Aspects of Intellectual Property Rights and the Convention on Biological Diversity, intellectual property has become inextricably woven into global politics—hailed as either a solution for or a contributing factor to poor economic development and loss of biodiversity. However, its application to non-Western contexts is creating political and intellectual frictions around notions of traditional knowledge and cultural heritage (disputes that affect, among other things, the labeling of traditional foods in supermarkets as well as the handling of cultural artifacts by museums).[17] In opposition to dominant narratives of global economic development structured around the uniformity of treatment produced by equally global IP agreements, some scholars and activists now argue that the very logic of IP—its foundation in the dichotomy between the (unprotectable) public domain and (protected) private intellectual property—is making legal a very specific and costly form of piracy. When the public domain is defined as the opposite of IP and is taken to include traditional knowledge, pharmaceutical plants, seeds, artifacts, and cultural imagery, IP can be seen as permitting the West to appropriate these valuable resources from the Third World, all the while abiding by international IP treaties.[18] The political economy of the "public domain" is shaping up into a fascinating postcolonial puzzle: the very same concept can be a progressive tool to curb the excesses of IP in the West while also functioning as the prime justification for the West's appropriation of non-Western knowledge and culture.[19] The A2K ("access to knowledge") movement is running into similar problems.[20]

That the public domain can appear as a progressive, left-leaning concept in the West while assuming distinctly nonleftist meanings in developing countries illustrates a more general pattern: the traditional alignments of the supporters and critics of IP are changing in unpredictable ways, thanks to the emergence of a remarkable diversity in the uses and articulations of IP as well as to the effects of its geographical and cultural migrations. In these new scenarios familiar descriptions of IP interest-group conflicts can lose much of whatever clarity they previously had. For instance, the commons-based models put forward by the free software (FS) and open source (OS) movements make possible collaborative frameworks in which knowledge and information can be developed, provided, and used by individuals who, at different times, may act variously like creators, distributors, or simply consumers of knowledge.[21] But while this knowledge and information is "free" (in the sense of being accessible and collectively modifiable), it still operates fully within a regime of intellectual property. Such collaborative frameworks, in fact, are made possible by creative licensing based on the default allocation of rights that the law provides. It is by licensing their contributions to the collective project that these individuals promote access while expanding the overall size of knowledge commons.

Because in this case copyright operates as a tool to provide free access to works, whether the FS/OS model amounts to a critique or just a rearticulation of IP is very much in the eye of the beholder. While it is quite possible to see FS/OS as revolutionary—a radical inversion of the original aims of copyright, which turns it into a tool enabling a cascade of share-alike licenses and an expanding commons—it is equally possible to say that, with all the good intentions and progressive politics of its proponents, these models rest on the very figure—the possessive individual author—at the root of the problems they are trying to redress.[22] The partial decoupling of property from access effected by FS/OS models is a challenge to traditional critiques of IP that view a systematic exposure of the conceptual and political problems underlying property in intangibles (and subsequent legislative changes) as the best way to make knowledge and cultural expression freely available.

For better or for worse, the meaning of "criticism" is changing—a trend that also can be detected in the logic of "cultural environmentalism," perhaps the most popular progressive discourse about IP in the United States today.[23] By analogizing the public domain to the environment and IP to human uses of natural resources, cultural environmentalism does not cast intellectual property as inherently problematic (or at least no more problematic than building dwellings and cultivating the land) but rather as something that needs to be done in a way that maintains a sustainable ecological balance between human activity and a healthy environment. What cultural environmentalists criticize is not IP per se but its overuse—an overuse that they believe will lead to depletion of the public domain and, ultimately, to the impossibility of any new IP objects being produced. In sum, both the FS/OS models and the cultural environmentalism movement eschew the most fundamental criticism of intangible property in order to focus on the ways in which the production of knowledge, art, and culture can be sustained in collaborative settings within IP regimes. And, much as the FS/OS movement accommodates leftist, libertarian, and corporate interests (as shown by IBM's support of Linux), it is difficult to pin cultural environmentalism to a specific location on a traditional political spectrum.

One trend notable in this new discursive setting is the remarkable visibility and value now attached to the notion of "innovation."[24] It is not easy to criticize innovation, a concept put forward as being about the new but without the ideological baggage of more traditional terms like "progress." Cast as a process of emergence, innovation attaches value to the new but does not posit what shape the new should assume or in what direction it should be pursued. This flexibility is reinforced by the frequent characterization of innovation as "open"—a remarkably broad adjective that refers both to the collaborative character of its processes and to the nonteleological nature of its outcomes.[25] Innovation is presented as politically neutral and, unlike the equally broad notion of the "knowledge economy," it does not explicitly frame the new within a monetary economy. As a result, the concept of innovation can be applied equally well to the production of new scientific knowledge, new art, and new business models, to what hackers do as much as to the R&D activities of a corporate giant.

Some who call for promoting and sustaining innovation would probably have little problem acknowledging the unsolvable conceptual tensions at the foundations of IP, or the fact that the law misrepresents the actual processes of cultural production, especially collaboration. Generally, they prefer to avoid a radical conceptual critique of IP and focus instead on pragmatic workarounds like FS/OS collaborative frameworks for innovation. What matters are the results, not the theory. It is telling, in fact, that much of the criticism voiced by champions of innovation focuses not on the theory or even the doctrine of IP, but on its *institutions*. These critics are distinctly probusiness and do not view properly issued patents as monopolies. What upsets them is that the functioning of the patent *system*—how the Patent and Trademark Office evaluates and processes applications and how courts, particularly the specialized Court of Appeals for the Federal Circuit, handle their jobs—appears to have serious distortive effects. They argue that indiscriminate patenting may actually chill innovation, but they also contend that the patent system generally works well for some industries (chemical and pharmaceutical) but is a potential hindrance to others (software), thus effectively privileging one kind of innovation enterprise over another.[26] Advocates of innovation-based IP policy also put considerable weight on the importance of limitations and exceptions as a way of creating space within potentially over-restrictive doctrines.[27]

FS/OS platforms are very popular among the proponents of innovation, but their interest in collaborative forms of knowledge making (an interest that is shared, for different reasons, by scholars in the humanities and social sciences) extends to the study and elaboration of forms of knowledge production based on group customs and norms rather than IP law. In turn, this has created an interest in "economies" that hinge not on property but on prestige, visibility, and other forms of nonmonetary reward often associated with "open" platforms. Until recently, the best-known examples were found either in so-called traditional knowledge or in science, where researchers build careers primarily from the recognition they receive from their peers for the claims they publish, often in elaborately multiauthored papers.[28] Because their work is placed in the public domain through publication, not protected by IP, scientists do not receive rights but rather rewards in the form of professional recognition that can be turned into financial resources in the form of jobs, grants, etc. There are obvious—if somewhat misleading—analogies between scientific authorship and FS/OS economies of recognition and prestige[29] as well as between these two forms of collaboration and so-called gift economies.[30] What we are now seeing, however, is an expansion of the range of norm-based forms of knowledge and culture making being studied by legal scholars, anthropologists, and social scientists—chefs, comedians, magicians, as well as all sorts of communal forms of material resource management, from fisheries to grazing land and water.[31]

Technology is obviously crucial to all of the developments discussed here. But while patent, copyright, and trademark law has always evolved, in part, in relation to technological changes, today we are witnessing a different mode of interaction between technology and IP. Early patents tended to be about technologies of production but soon shifted to focus more on the consumer products made possible by those technologies. And as the very meaning of technology has changed and expanded, so have the subject matter requirements for patentability—from the *Diamond v. Chakrabarty* (1980) decision to allow the patenting of genetically modified organisms to the *Diamond v. Diehr* (1981) ruling about the patentability of software and the more recent acceptance of patent applications relating to "purified" genetic sequences.

Similarly, the subject matter of copyright has expanded from book texts to include printed images and then music, art, software, and a range of other products deriving from the "fixation" of authors' personal expression in material media. Although it is a truism of copyright that the law protects "expressions" and not "ideas," doctrinal evolution has put that familiar distinction under real pressure. For example, as more and more variants of a literary text (the movie rights, the translation rights, the video game rights, and so forth) have come to be comprehended under a single copyright, the focus of protection has inevitably shifted from the highly particular toward the relatively general. These shifts were, of course, strongly abetted by the presence of the author figure as the central organizing concept in personalist copyright discourse. They also owe much to technological changes that have increased the range of expressive options available to culture makers. Likewise, the development of biotech, digital technology, and the latter's articulations in infrastructures like the Web have profoundly changed the nature of the game, not only its size. For example, the patenting of human cell lines and, more generally, of the human genome is challenging traditional notions not only of property but of personhood itself.[32] Similarly, the use of geographical indications to protect traditional manufactures and local cultures (of products such as champagne, parmesan cheese, and possibly also Darjeeling tea, Mysore silk, and traditional *sarees* from specific Indian villages) shows that IP is becoming actively involved not only in the protection of goods and craft knowledge but also in the construction of local cultural identities.[33] Perhaps in the not so distant future the notion of "cultural imagery" will become subsumed under "branding."[34]

New information technologies are having other, even more far-reaching effects on the configuration of rights in intangible property. Digital technologies make the copying, manipulation, and distribution of texts, images, and music much easier and remarkably cheaper. But they also allow rights holders to take the law into their hands, so to speak, with wired-in functions that prevent copying or reproducing independently of the context of use. Digital rights management does this for digitized copyrighted material, while the "terminator genes" embedded in patented genetically modified seeds may be seen as the biological analog.[35] But in so doing, these technologies do not simply implement IP but effectively expand it in a way that is blind to context. This occurs (for example) when DRMs (interference with which is, in turn, prohibited by the 1998 Digital Millennium Copyright Act) effectively prevent actions and uses that, in some cases, could be lawful copying protected by fair use doctrine.

Finally, as these new technologies extend the production, enforcement, and expansion of IP down to a capillary level, they have turned millions of people into "authors." This means not only many more authors *but more different kinds* of authors occupying social niches that authors had not traditionally inhabited before. Even more important, technology has profoundly changed the conditions of possibility for collaborative production of knowledge and culture. While many kinds of collaborations are only marginally affected by the possibilities provided by cyberinfrastructure (like all those involving material objects and processes that cannot be digitized), there is no doubt that digital information technologies are creating collaborative spaces that never existed before. These technologies are putting great pressure on traditional notions of IP not only by making copying cheap and easy but also by making possible *new ways of producing new things* through the formation of new productive networks and forms of sociability.

Ubiquitous digitally enabled authorship has foregrounded some of the most basic tensions in copyright by highlighting the extent to which all new cultural production is inevitably not only collaborative but derivative. One result has been a new interest in limiting doctrines in IP, including copyright exceptions like fair use. In a world where accusations of infringement fly around videos posted on YouTube and other DIY media platforms, questions about when and how it is appropriate to make use of existing materials as resources for one's own creativity assume new importance. New technologies make it inevitable that more and more of us will be authors, whether or not we desire that status. They also remind us that we are all also users and that, as a result, we depend on the porosities of IP for the accomplishment of our own expressive projects.[36]

Rationale and Relevance

No single master narrative can account for the extraordinarily broad range of issues, positions, participants, and proposals that make up the conversations and disputes about IP, or for their intensity. And while the courts of law and IP attorneys have, and will retain, a key role in these processes, IP discourse is now fully "out of the bag" and has been taken up and acted on by a huge array of different stakeholders. In some contexts (as with policies about the protection of traditional knowledge) much of the action no longer takes place solely within the legal institutions of the state but is framed by international treaties and articulated through local negotiations and arrangements, often involving nongovernmental organizations. The overall trend in both developed and developing countries is not unlike what we see in biomedical research, where patients are increasingly assuming a key role in funding and directing research, as well as in lobbying the state for related policy.[37]

Those who have developed stakes in IP are not now just more vocal and proactive than their predecessors but have also made very tangible, specific contributions to both the practice and theory of IP. FS/OS models, for instance, were not invented by legal scholars, attorneys, or legislators, but by the hackers themselves as a solution to pressing problems about the governance of their collaborations. They wrote licenses the way they wrote code, as if these were two kinds of "instrument." While it is difficult to find many other examples as striking as this, there is no doubt that the previously tight divide between the law and its users and subjects has become a permeable membrane. Not everyone can successfully lobby Congress to change IP law, but there are obviously different ways to use and articulate and recombine it without having to call for legislative change or even go to law school. Analogously, the remarkably broad range of disciplines that now engage with IP should not be viewed as yet another academic exercise in interdisciplinarity but rather as the result of the actual migration of IP (both as a body of research topics and as matters of practical professional and political concern) into all these disciplines, further eroding the distinction between those whose lives have been affected by IP and those who are attracted to study it as a wonderfully complex bundle of problems.

We envisage a comparably broad readership: students and scholars across the disciplines as well as law students and scholars who want or need to look beyond the necessarily tight boundaries of IP textbooks—anthropologists familiar with issues of IP relating to traditional knowledge but seeking exposure to the cultural and conceptual dimensions of patents and copyright; literary and cultural historians; historians of the book and of print culture more generally; historians of science and technology; and scholars and practitioners working in music and the visual arts.

Accordingly, this book seeks to identify and interrogate a constellation of IP discourses and objects from the work of legal scholars, anthropologists, indigenous rights advocates, literary scholars, art historians, science studies and communications studies practitioners, musicologists, historians, folklorists, and economists. While related to legal definitions of IP, these discourses and objects do not necessarily match them. We are especially interested in these mismatches, as also in the arrangements that emerge at the margins of IP law. Not only can these mismatches and emergent scenarios suggest directions for saner future articulations of IP law, but they also provide excellent material for both understanding and producing culture. In this book, in fact, "intellectual property" is typically used under erasure. Many of the chapters show that the production of things, practices, and texts is not reducible or ascribable just to the "intellect" (and certainly not to the intellect of one individual) and that "property" rarely captures the relations between people and the things they produce, try to use, gain access to, or simply control.

Unlike the genre of general popular critiques of IP doctrine, the contributions to this volume are rooted in the specifics of material as well as legal practice. They engage the legal details without privileging the viewpoint of the legal profession. We avoid both general critical pronouncements about IP and the normalizing discourse of policy around "balancing" or "optimizing" IP doctrine. However valuable these may be, they fail to confront the root problems of the scenarios we are all facing. We want to make IP "strange," and we do so by engaging it very closely. Our contributors look at the writing and reviewing of patent applications, the rules about patent drawings, the reasons for granting IP protection to asexually reproduced plants but not to their sexually reproducing cousins, the intense discussions among hackers as they craft licensing agreements, and the practices of IP "educators," enforcers, and "pirates." It is only through this kind of attention to cultural production in the shadow of IP that one can find and analyze the interesting slippages between practice and its legal conceptualization.

Organization

Because of the web of questions that crisscross all these chapters, we have structured the volume around five argumentative clusters. Obviously the boundaries of these clusters are mutually overlapping, making the resulting map viable only as an introduction to the more complex networks of topics and arguments that can emerge only from a detailed engagement with the texts.

The first cluster, "High and Low: IP Practices and Materialities," is predominantly historical in nature, focusing on the daily practices of IP and the materials through which the law operates, with a focus on the often overlooked domain of patent law. It looks at the practices of patent writing, drawings, and examination, and how these frame and often shape the very content of legal doctrine. For instance, Mario Biagioli's "Patent Specification and Political Representation: How Patents Became Rights" relates the transformation of patents from monopolies to rights in France and the United States around 1790 to the emergence of representative politics. The new notions of citizen and "public" that emerged through these political transformations made it possible to think of the "patent bargain"—the modern conceptualization of patenting as a contract between the inventor and the state involving the inventor's disclosure of the invention in exchange for a temporary monopoly on that invention. Such a radical reconceptualization of the meaning of *patent* was propelled by large macroscopic sociopolitical trends but was utterly dependent on something very small and mundane: the introduction of a new piece of paperwork—the patent specification. This chapter argues that, in many ways, the introduction of patent specifications provided the conditions of possibility of modern patent law. Also focused on the materialities of the law, Kara Swanson's "Authoring an Invention: Patent Production in the Nineteenth-Century United States" reconstructs how patent applications were written, crafted, and evaluated in the nineteenth-century United States before and after the emergence of the professional patent examiner. The patent sanctions inventorship and the rights attached to that notion, but the patent itself is a text that is peculiarly cast as authorless while being obviously produced through an increasingly complex chain of bureaucratic "collaborations." Swanson traces the early history of the peculiar authorial status of the patent. Moving from texts to images, William Rankin's "The 'Person Skilled in the Art' Is Really Quite Conventional: U.S. Patent Drawings and the Persona of the Inventor, 1870–2005" shows that the changing standards of patent drawings can be related to the changing assumptions about the skills of the typical reader of such drawings. Although the typical reader turns out to be only a legal fiction—the "person skilled in the art"—the role this figure is assigned within patent law, and the skills and knowledge it is assumed to have, informed the development of the visual genre of patent drawings.

The second section, "Before and after the Commons and Traditional Knowledge," explores the notions of commons, public domain, and traditional knowledge—among the most ideologically charged categories in contemporary IP discourse. In "Cultural Agencies: The Legal Construction of Community Subjects and Their Properties" Rosemary Coombe critiques the naïve mobilization of "community" as a conceptual hinge on which to attach expanded notions of IP rights or other forms of rewards or resources connected to "traditional knowledge" or "cultural traditions." But she also challenges, with comparable energy, critiques of the notion of community as a "mere construction"—a politically and economically advantageous fiction covering up for the endemically leaky and mobile boundaries of any social group and for the instability inherent in any tradition. Her proposal is to look at invocations of communities, identities, and traditions not as a mobilization of claims about stable, traditional knowledge and social entities but as a "work in progress," that is, as evidence of the productive (but not necessarily positive) interaction between new, emergent collectivities and the framework of international treaties, conventions, international customary law, and human rights norms that have been articulated and circulated by global players and agencies. The fact that "community" is always already constructed does not prevent it from being a powerful tool for the further articulation of vernacular practices, obligations, commitments, and aspirations. Marilyn Strathern's

"Social Invention" opens with another key legal dichotomy—that between tangible and intangible properties—and shows that from a non-Western perspective this distinction is as problematic as the one between IP and the public domain. But despite all their problems, such dichotomies can also create the conditions of possibility for alternative bricolages. For instance, when confronting the problems posed by the application of both material and intangible property to traditional knowledge and artifacts, some "indigenous people" find the notion of right underlying these legal constructs quite attractive, because they are conducive to the creation of local alternatives such as, for example, the use of tangible property rights to cover objects that might otherwise fall into the domain of IP, or the articulation of hybrid forms of authorship. In "From 'Folklore' to 'Knowledge' in Global Governance: On the Metamorphoses of the Unauthored" Marc Perlman follows some of the issues discussed by Coombe and Strathern by mapping the metamorphosis of the concept of folklore into "traditional cultural expressions." Tracing how the discourse around rights in old local arts has shifted over the past thirty-five years, he insists on the importance of rhetorical structures in shaping the way in which all stakeholders—including culture makers in the less developed world—think about the issue. In particular, Perlman argues that today's master concept of "traditional cultural expressions" emerged in response to several intellectual forces, including an increased awareness of threats to biodiversity and the rise of the concept of "the indigenous."

Chris Kelty's "Inventing Copyleft" offers a detailed genealogy of what is arguably the mother of all such legal hybrids: the general public license (GPL) that either underpins or frames the vast majority of today's "information commons." Reconstructing the communications and disputes among Richard Stallman and the early hacker community, Kelty shows that the first free software license emerged bit by bit as a grassroots instrument for managing a viable community of collaborating code writers threatened by changing trends in software accessibility and ownership. Yochai Benkler's "Designing Cooperative Systems for Knowledge Production: An Initial Synthesis from Experimental Economics" looks at the other end of the trajectory laid out by Kelty. He takes for granted that the networked information economy has already proved that, as a class, commons-based models are not only sustainable but indeed more efficient than IP when applied to peer production and other collaborative practices. His question, therefore, is how to come up with better-informed guesses about what kinds of arrangements foster collaboration and knowledge production and which ones constrain it. While not dismissing the grassroots and make-it-as-you-go philosophy underlying some of the best recent success stories (like the GPL analyzed by Kelty), Benkler evaluates some of the tools that experimental economics could offer to the modeling and simulation of future frameworks for collaboration.

The third cluster, "IP Crimes and Other Fictions," looks at both the positive and negative imaginaries of IP. Much like the "commons," "piracy" and "plagiarism" are ideologically charged topoi in IP discourse. Cast as the "other" of proper IP practices, they are also fictional constructs—a fictionality they share with the heroic figures of the "author" and the "inventor." In "Beyond Representation: The Figure of the Pirate" Lawrence Liang explores the challenge that the figure of the pirate poses to the IP system. His focus is this figure's "irredeemability" even in critical theory and practice—that is, in the public domain advocacy of Lawrence Lessig and FS/OS movements. Exposing the diverse investments they share with IP fundamentalists, most notably in their privileging of innovation and creativity, he urges the advantages of shifting attention from what piracy is to what it does—of pursuing more nuanced investigation of the Asian "economies of recycling" that are being disparaged in all of our Western discourses. This is the thrust of Martha Woodmansee's essay, "Publishers, Privateers, Pirates: Eighteenth-Century German Book Piracy Revisited." She teases out some of the important cultural and economic contributions of the unauthorized reprinting activities of the eighteenth-century Viennese publisher and bookseller Johann Thomas Trattner, who has gone down in history as the scourge of Germany's great literary renaissance. The source of Trattner's vilification, she shows, was a cartel of ambitious publishers centered in the north German city of Leipzig, whose prices put their coveted books out of the reach of readers in the underdeveloped south where Trattner was active. Adrian Johns's "The Property Police" traces the history of the enforcement industry that has grown up to discourage activities like Trattner's. Johns is interested in the body of hybrid institutions that operate in alliance with police forces, governments, international bodies, and multinational trade groups not only to detect and deter IP infringements but to measure their scale and scope and in this way, as it were, to define them as "piracy." Tarleton Gillespie's "Characterizing Copyright in the Classroom: The Cultural Work of Antipiracy Campaigns" takes up the pedagogical infrastructure that is emerging to assist this industry—or rather, ideally, to obviate a need for it. His essay treats the antipiracy educational materials that are being distributed to K–12 teachers and administrators across the United States and Canada free of charge by traditional content providers. Gillespie focuses on the representational strategies deployed in these colorful materials, showing how their privileging of user obligations over user rights (which are simplified or altogether ignored) is operating to instill "good" IP-compliant values in the next generation. In "An Economic View of Legal Restrictions on Musical Borrowing and

Appropriation" Peter DiCola analyzes scenarios in which acts of borrowing are openly acknowledged and presented as absolutely necessary to the creative process—cases where borrowing is cast as a tribute to a tradition and author or as a way to further develop a cultural genre. However, unable to comprehend these practices and relations, copyright law constrains or prohibits them. For instance, sampling was part and parcel of the musical genres of jazz, blues, reggae, and early rap, but recent copyright decisions concerning musical compositions and recordings have transformed musicians' practices as well as the relationships among them. After mapping these changes in detail, DiCola proposes an uncanonical model of the economics of "intellectual property crime." His claim is that the legal and financial costs a musician would face by infringing copyright—what economists term "constraints"—may actually be less than what the musician could gain in terms of creativity and that such a "crime-related" gain should become part of the economic modeling.

The fourth set, "Old Things into New IP Objects," looks at the ongoing mismatch between things and the categories of IP law and at the movement of a given object across those categories. From the patenting of plants and animals and the recent use of race in pharmaceutical patents to the attempted application of open source models to yoga, we witness things and practices being turned into legal objects, but we also see the dramatic reconfiguration (if not subversion) of legal categories. Daniel Kevles's "New Blood, New Fruits: Protections for Breeders and Originators, 1789–1930" opens the section with a reconstruction of the business practices that, beginning in the eighteenth century, were developed by breeders and nurseries to protect their living products well before the application of IP law to plants and animals. Also looking at the early applications of IP law to living organisms, Alain Pottage and Brad Sherman's "Kinds, Clones, and Manufactures" analyzes how the traditional notion of invention from the industrial revolution (when most inventions were machines or machine-made products) was challenged by the attempt to cast plants as inventions. They do so by tracing how notions of the inventive step and of agency were redistributed between the inventor and nature itself in the first U.S. Plant Patent Act of 1930. Cori Hayden's "No Patent, No Generic: Pharmaceutical Access and the Politics of the Copy" moves outside of European and U.S. contexts to study the paradoxical construction of the notion of a "generic drug" in Mexico and Argentina, where different regimes of compulsory licensing question the notion of "original" from different angles and yet succumb to market interests and patients' desires to hold on to some marker of originality, even when there is seemingly none to be found. In "Inventing Race as a Genetic Commodity in Biotechnology Patents" Jonathan Kahn discusses a recent but growing trend in pharmaceutical patenting involving drugs marketed to specific ethnic groups. He shows that race not only enters into the marketing strategy but is actually employed as part of the patent claim, leading him to argue that this may be a rare case in which race (a category that has little or no genetic relevance) is actually endorsed by a federal document—a patent—granting a title based on the race-based claims put forward in the application. Pamela Samuelson's "The Strange Odyssey of Software Interfaces as Intellectual Property" concludes this set by adding a new angle to these discussions of objects that move in and out of IP with an example of an artifact—the software interface—that is hard to conceptualize as clearly belonging to either the category of patent or copyright. This is, in some ways, a contemporary high-tech replay of the dilemma between idea and expression that she dissected in her analysis of the Supreme Court's 1880 *Baker v. Selden* decision,[38] demonstrating the remarkable longevity of both IP concepts and their problems.

The final section, "Doing and Undoing Collaborative IP," focuses on the collaborative practices that grow around IP but also shows how close studies of collaborative work can deconstruct foundational IP notions such as "author," "inventor," or even "work." In "Invention, Origin, and Dedication: Republishing Women's Prints in Early Modern Italy" Evelyn Lincoln looks at the serial copying, purchase, and adaptation of printing plates and prints, primarily by early modern Italian women engravers. Through careful retracing of the serial metamorphoses of some of these prints, Lincoln makes the striking claim that, contrary to current views that construe the function of the author as the point of origin of the work, these early printers' practices indicate that authorship was instead tied to tailoring a print to a patron through a process of re-elaboration and dedication. Authorship (or what these printers called "invention") was therefore explicitly connected to the destination of the work rather than to its origin. Tracing the impact of this shift on the role of the authors' names inscribed on plates and prints, Lincoln argues that these should not be viewed as signatures—marks of authorial origin—but rather as "signature effects." Looking at radically different forms of collaboration, Tim Lenoir and Eric Giannella's "Technological Platforms and the Layers of Patent Data" uses patterns of coauthorship and co-inventorship as a tool to literally chart the emergence of technological platforms. Their case study of the development of microarray technologies in the San Francisco Bay area shows that networked infrastructures of innovation are reframing not only the divide between the university and the private sector but also the very notions of "inventor" and "invention."

Dotan Oliar and Chris Sprigman's "Intellectual Property Norms in Stand-Up Comedy" looks at joke-stealing prevention among U.S. comedians, from vaudeville to the present. Copyright law protects original expression, but jokes are closer to ideas than expressions. Furthermore, while in principle jokes can be expressed and staged in indefinitely many ways, the options actually tend to boil down to well-known life scenarios, thus casting doubt on the usefulness of costly infringement suits. However, the tightly knit community of comedians has managed to substitute a system of social norms for formal copyright protection, keeping copyright infringement suits virtually unknown among them. Moving from comedians to scientists, Fiona Murray's "Patenting Life: How the Oncomouse Patent Changed the Lives of Mice and Men" looks at a different but equally complex set of collaborative norms developed around or in response to IP. Her essay treats the patenting of a cancer-developing mouse—oncomouse—not within the debate about the patenting of life but as a powerful example of how patented research tools modify traditional collaborative practices among scientists. Taking a more nuanced view on the "anticommons" effect of patenting, she argues that while patents do constrain some traditional modes of scientific collaboration, they may also provide additional resources that scientists can exchange as they build new and different networks of collaboration. Peter Jaszi's "Is There Such a Thing as Postmodern Copyright?" concludes the volume by reassessing the status of a figure—the "romantic author"—that has been central to most of the critical literature on copyright of the last two decades. As he analyzes the role of collaboration as a juridical concept rather than a practice, he argues that the days of copyright law's fixation on the romantic (or modern) author construct may be numbered and that such a change is evidenced in several areas of contemporary copyright jurisprudence, like the recent turn in fair use case law toward a "transformativeness" standard that explicitly foregrounds the experiences and practices of copyright users to decide how far owners' limited monopoly should reach.

NOTES

1. WIPO, "Learn from the Past, Create the Future: The Arts and Copyright" (available at http://www.wipo.int). See also Tarleton Gillespie, this volume.

2. Second Life Terms of Service (http://secondlife.com/corporate/tos.php); Benjamin Tyson, *Virtual Law: Navigating the Legal Landscape of Virtual Worlds* (Washington, DC: American Bar Association, 2008); Jack Balkin and Beth Simone Noveck, *The State of the Play: Law, Games, and Virtual Worlds* (New York: New York UP, 2006).

3. Michel Foucault, "What Is an Author?" in Donald Bouchard (ed.), *Language, Counter-Memory, Practice: Selected Essays and Interviews* (Ithaca, NY: Cornell UP, 1977), 113–138; Roland

Barthes, "The Death of the Author," *Image, Music, Text* (New York: Hill & Wang, 1977), 42–48; Walter Benjamin, "The Author as Producer," *New Left Review* I/62 (July–August 1970): 83–96; Bernard Edelman, *Ownership of the Image: Elements of a Marxist Theory of the Law* (London: RKP, 1979); Martha Woodmansee, "The Genius and the Copyright: Economic and Legal Conditions of the Emergence of the 'Author,'" *Eighteenth-Century Studies* 17 (1984): 425–448; Mark Rose, "The Author as Proprietor: *Donaldson v. Beckett* and the Genealogy of Modern Authorship," *Representations* 23 (1988): 51–85; Carla Hesse, "Enlightenment Epistemology and the Laws of Authorship in Revolutionary France, 1777–1793," *Representations* 30 (1990): 109–137; Peter Jaszi, "Toward a Theory of Copyright: Metamorphoses of 'Authorship,'" *Duke Law Journal*, April 1991, 455–502; Jane Gaines, *Contested Culture: The Image, the Voice, and the Law* (Chapel Hill: U North Carolina P, 1991); David Saunders, *Authorship and Copyright* (London: Routledge, 1992); Martha Woodmansee and Peter Jaszi (eds.), *The Construction of Authorship: Textual Appropriation in Law and Literature* (Durham, NC: Duke UP, 1994).

4. James Boyle, *Shamans, Software, and Spleens: Law and the Construction of the Information Society* (Cambridge, MA: Harvard UP, 1996) epitomizes the translation of the "romantic author" from previous primarily historical studies to the problems of IP in the contemporary information society.

5. Rosemary Coombe, *The Cultural Life of Intellectual Properties: Authorship, Appropriation, and the Law* (Durham, NC: Duke UP, 1998); Peter Jaszi and Martha Woodmansee, "The Ethical Reaches of 'Authorship,'" *South Atlantic Quarterly* 95 (1996): 948–977; Peter Jaszi and Martha Woodmansee, "Beyond Authorship: Refiguring Rights in Traditional Culture and Bioknowledge," in Mario Biagioli and Peter Galison (eds.), *Scientific Authorship: Credit and Intellectual Property in Science* (New York: Routledge, 2003), 195–223; Marilyn Strathern, *Property, Substance, and Effect* (London: Athlone Press, 1990); Michael Brown, *Who Owns Native Culture?* (Cambridge, MA: Harvard UP, 2003); Eric Hirsch and Marilyn Strathern (eds.), *Transactions and Creations: Property Debates and the Stimulus of Melanesia* (New York: Berghahn, 2004); Rishab Aiyer Ghosh (ed.), *CODE: Collaborative Ownership and the Digital Economy* (Cambridge, MA: MIT Press, 2005).

6. International Society for the History and Theory of Intellectual Property at http://www.ishtip .org, and the "Primary Sources on Copyright, 1450–1900" project at http://www.copyrighthistory .org.

Among the many works on the history of early modern European and U.S. patenting, see Giulio Mandich, "Venetian Origins of Inventors' Rights," *Journal of the Patent Office Society* 42 (1960): 378–382 and "Venetian Patents, 1450–1550," *Journal of the Patent Office Society* 30 (1948): 166–224; Rob Iliffe, "In the Warehouse: Privacy, Property, and Priority in the Early Royal Society," *History of Science* 22 (1992): 29–62; Christine MacLeod, *Inventing the Industrial Revolution* (Cambridge: Cambridge UP, 1988); G. Doorman, *Patents for Inventions in the Netherlands during the 16th, 17th, and 18th Centuries* (The Hague: Nijhoof, 1942); Roberto Berveglieri, *Inventori Stranieri a Venezia, 1474–1788* (Venice: Istituto Veneto di Scienze, Lettere ed Arti, 1995); Pamela Long, *Openness, Secrecy, Authorship: Technical Arts and the Culture of Knowledge from Antiquity to the Renaissance* (Baltimore: Johns Hopkins University Press, 2001); Doron S. Ben-Atar, *Trade Secrets: Intellectual Piracy and the Origins of American Industrial Power* (New Haven, CT: Yale UP, 2004); Mario Biagioli, "From Print to Patent," *History of Science* 44 (2006): 139–186; Luisa Dolza and Liliane Hilaire-Perez, "Invention and Privileges in the Eighteenth Century: Norms and Practices," *History of Technology* 24 (2000): 21–44; Myles Jackson, "Can Artisans Be Scientific Authors?" in Mario Biagioli and Peter Galison (eds.), *Scientific Authorship: Credit and Intellectual Property in Science* (New York: Routledge, 2003), 113–132; Christine MacLeod, *Heroes of Invention* (Cambridge: Cambridge UP, 2008); Brad Sherman and Lionel Bently, *The Making of Modern Intellectual Property Law* (Cambridge: Cambridge UP, 1999); Harold Dutton, *The Patent System and Inventive Activity during the Industrial Revolution, 1750–1852* (Manchester: Manchester UP, 1984); Liliane Hilaire-Perez, *L'Invention technique au*

Siècle des Lumières (Paris: Albin Michel, 2000); Zorina Khan, *The Democratization of Invention* (Cambridge: Cambridge UP, 2005); Bruce W. Bugbee, *The Genesis of American Patent and Copyright Law* (Washington, DC: Public Affairs Press, 1967); Edward Walterscheid, *The Nature of the Intellectual Property Clause* (Buffalo: Hein, 2002) and *To Promote the Progress of Useful Arts* (Littleton, CO: Rothman, 1998); Oren Bracha, "Owning Ideas: A History of Anglo-American Intellectual Property," dissertation, Harvard Law School, 2005, at http://www.obracha.net.

On the history of copyright, see Horatio Brown, *The Venetian Printing Press* (New York: Putnam, 1891); Evelyn Lincoln, "Invention and Authorship in Early Modern Italian Visual Culture," *DePaul Law Review*, 52 (2003): 1104–1111; Elizabeth Armstrong, *Before Copyright: The French Book-Privilege System, 1498–1526* (Cambridge: Cambridge UP, 1990); Adrian Johns, *The Nature of the Book* (Chicago: U Chicago P, 1998); Roger Chartier, *The Order of Books: Readers, Authors, and Libraries in Europe between the Fourteenth and Eighteenth Centuries* (Stanford, CA: Stanford UP, 1994); Martha Woodmansee, *The Author, Art, and the Market: Rereading the History of Aesthetics* (New York: Columbia UP, 1994); Mark Rose, *Authors and Owners* (Cambridge, MA: Harvard UP, 1993); Ronan Deazley, *The Origin of the Right to Copy: Charting the Movement of Copyright Law in Eighteenth-Century Britain, 1695–1775* (London: Hart, 2004); Bugbee, *The Genesis of American Patent and Copyright Law*; Sherman and Bently, *The Making of Modern Intellectual Property Law*; Bracha, "Owning Ideas: A History of Anglo-American Intellectual Property"; Meredith McGill, *American Literature and the Culture of Reprinting, 1834–1853* (Philadelphia: U Pennsylvania P, 2002).

The historical literature on trademarks is, unfortunately, very limited, but see Franz Isaac Schechter, *The Historical Foundations of the Law Relating to Trade-Marks* (New York: Columbia Legal Studies, 1925), as well as the relevant chapters in Sherman and Bently, *The Making of Modern Intellectual Property Law*.

7. Martha Vicinus and Caroline Eisner (eds.), *Originality, Imitation, and Plagiarism: Teaching Writing in the Digital Age* (Ann Arbor: U Michigan P, 2008); Rebecca Moore Howard and Amy Robillard (eds.), *Pluralizing Plagiarism: Identities, Contexts, Pedagogies* (Portsmouth, NH: Boynton/Cook, 2008); Marilyn Randall, *Pragmatic Plagiarism: Authorship, Profit, and Power* (Toronto: U Toronto P, 2001); Lisa Maruca, "The Plagiarism Panic: Digital Policing in the New Intellectual Property Regime," in Fiona Macmillan (ed.), *New Directions in Copyright Law*, vol. 6 (Cheltenham: Edward Elgar, 2006), 248–261.

8. The literature is vast, but good starting points are Rebecca Eisenberg, "Public Research and Private Development: Patents and Technology Transfer in Government-Sponsored Research," *Virginia Law Review* 82, no. 8 (1996): 1663–1727; and David Mowery, Richard Nelson, Bhaven Sampat, and Arvids Ziedonis (eds.), *Ivory Tower and Industrial Innovation: University-Industry Technology Transfer before and after the Bayh-Dole Act* (Stanford, CA: Stanford UP, 2004).

9. Michael Heller and Rebecca Eisenberg, "Can Patents Deter Innovation? The Anticommons in Biomedical Research," *Science* 280, no. 5364 (1998): 698–701; John Walsh, Ashish Arora, and Wesley Cohen, "Science and the Law: Working through the Patent Problem," *Science* 299, no. 5609 (2003): 1021; John Walsh, Charlene Cho, and Wesley Cohen, "View from the Bench: Patents and Material Transfers," *Science* 309, no. 5743 (2005): 2002–2003; Fiona Murray and Scott Stern, "Do Formal Intellectual Property Rights Hinder the Free Flow of Scientific Knowledge? An Empirical Test of the Anti-Commons Hypothesis," NBER Working Paper no. W11465 (Cambridge, MA: National Bureau of Economic Research, 2005); Wesley Cohen and John Walsh, "Real Impediments to Academic Biomedical Research," in Adam Jaffe, Josh Lerner, and Scott Stern (eds.), *Innovation Policy and the Economy*, vol. 8 (Chicago: U Chicago P, 2008), 1–30.

10. A suggestion of the range of activities that make up this movement can be found at the Web site of the Scholarly Publishing and Academic Resources Coalition (SPARC), http://www.arl.org/sparc/.

11. The work-for-hire doctrine applies to work done "by an employee within the scope of his

or her employment" (17 U.S.C. sec. 101). In such cases, the copyright passes automatically to the employer. While faculty publications have typically been exempt from this rule, the reasons for this have a long and peculiar history but not a particularly strong legal standing (Todd F. Simon, "Faculty Writings: Are They 'Works Made for Hire' under the 1976 Copyright Act?" *Journal of College and University Law* 9 [1983]: 485–513). It now seems that the determination of whether the work-for-hire doctrine applies to academic faculty depends more on university policy than on copyright law. For instance, the copyright policy adopted by Harvard University in February 2008 states: "Recognizing *long-held customs* that have evolved concerning academic Copyrights, the Policy generally recognizes a right of Authors to retain copyright in their content-based scholarly works. . . . The University is the copyright owner of copyrightable works created as works made for hire by non-teaching staff. Under the Policy, Harvard also has ownership rights in copyrightable works that it commissions, whether from faculty, students or third parties" (Harvard University's Intellectual Property Policy: A Concise Guide, our emphasis). On the broader context of these discussions, see Corynne McSherry, *Who Owns Academic Work?* (Cambridge, MA: Harvard UP, 2001); and Marilyn Strathern, *Commons and Borderlands: Working Papers on Interdisciplinarity, Accountability, and the Flow of Knowledge* (London: Sean Kingston, 2003).

12. Paul Rabinow, *Making PCR: A Story of Biotechnology* (Chicago: U Chicago P, 1996); Arthur Kornberg, *The Golden Helix: Inside Biotech Ventures* (New York: University Science Books, 1995); Craig Venter, *A Life Decoded: My Genome, My Life* (New York: Viking, 2007).

13. Eric Vettel, *Biotech: Science, Politics, and the Birth of Industry* (Philadelphia: U Pennsylvania P, 2006).

14. Andrew Mertha, *The Politics of Piracy: Intellectual Property in Contemporary China* (Ithaca, NY: Cornell UP, 2005).

15. A more ambivalent, rather than openly negative, view of the pirate emerges in John Gantz and Jack Rochester, *Pirates of the Digital Millennium: How the Intellectual Property Wars Damage Our Personal Freedoms, Our Jobs, and the World Economy* (New York: Prentice Hall, 2005); Giselle Fahimian, "How the IP Guerrillas Won: ®TMark, Adbusters, Negativland, and the 'Bullying Back' of Creative Freedom and Social Commentary," *Stanford Technology Law Review* 1 (2004); Negativland, "Two Relationships to a Cultural Public Domain," *Law & Contemporary Problems* 6, nos. 1 & 2 (Winter/Spring 2003): 239–262; Negativland, *Fair Use: the Story of the Letter U and the Numeral 2* (Concord, CA: SeeLand, 1995). See also http://fffff.at/ and http://www.Graffitiresearchlab. com. On scientists' frequent disregard of IP in using patented research techniques, see John Walsh, Charlene Cho, and Wesley Cohen, "View from the Bench: Patents and Material Transfers," *Science* 309, no. 5743 (2005): 2002–2003.

16. Matt Mason, *The Pirate's Dilemma: How Youth Culture Is Reinventing Capitalism* (New York: Free Press, 2008).

17. Michael Ryan, *Knowledge Diplomacy: Global Competition and the Politics of Intellectual Property* (Washington, DC: Brookings Institution Press, 1998); Graham Dutfield, *Intellectual Property, Biogenetic Resources, and Traditional Knowledge* (London: Earthscan, 2004); Rosemary Coombe, Steven Schnoor, and Mohsen Ahmed, "Bearing Cultural Distinction: Information Capitalism and the New Expectations for Intellectual Property," *UC Davis Law Review* 4, no. 3 (2006): 891–917.

18. Peter Drahos and John Braithwaite, *Information Feudalism: Who Owns the Knowledge Economy?* (New York: New Press, 2002); Madhavi Sunder and Anupam Chander, "Romance of the Public Domain," *California Law Review* 92 (2004): 1331–1374.

19. Madhavi Sunder, "The Invention of Traditional Knowledge," *Law & Contemporary Problems* 70 (2007): 97–124.

20. Another point of contention is the very broad notion of "access" used in the recent and quite successful A2K initiative (http://www.access2knowledge.org). Because access is treated as a naturally positive notion (as opposed to the perceived constraints imposed by IP within developed countries),

it tends to make invisible the politics of the concept. Seen from the point of view of developing countries that are struggling to protect their traditional knowledge and cultures within the framework provided by IP, a celebration of "access" sounds like yet another neocolonial project.

21. The conceptual novelty of these developments and their relevance to both IP policies and to the future of collaborative practices have emerged as a key topic in legal scholarship since the late 1990s, starting with the work of Yochai Benkler.

22. Niva Elkin-Koren, "Exploring Creative Commons: A Skeptical View of a Worthy Pursuit," in Lucie Guibault and Bernt Hugenholtz (eds.), *The Future of Public Domain: Identifying the Commons in Information Law* (Boston: Kluwer Law International, 2006): 325–345.

23. The books of Lawrence Lessig—*The Future of Ideas* (New York: Random House, 2001) and *Free Culture: How Big Media Uses Technology and the Law to Lock Down Culture and Control Creativity* (New York: Penguin, 2004)—have created a popular buzz around cultural environmentalism, but it is James Boyle who has articulated the logic of this movement most fully, building on the work of David Lange and Jessica Litman on the public domain (David Lange, "Recognizing the Public Domain," *Law & Contemporary Problems* 44 [1981]: 147–181; Jessica Litman, "The Public Domain," *Emory Law Journal* 39 [1990]: 965–1011) and the work of Peter Jaszi and Martha Woodmansee on cultural sustainability ("Beyond Authorship: Refiguring Rights in Traditional Culture and Bioknowledge," in Mario Biagioli and Peter Galison [eds.], *Scientific Authorship: Credit and Intellectual Property in Science* [New York: Routledge, 2003], 195–223). On the conceptual framework of cultural environmentalism see James Boyle, *The Public Domain: Enclosing the Commons of the Mind* (New Haven, CT: Yale UP, 2008); Boyle, "The Second Enclosure Movement and the Construction of the Public Domain," in Boyle (ed.), special issue of *Law & Contemporary Problems* 66, nos. 1 & 2 (Winter/Spring 2003): 33–74; Boyle, "A Politics of Intellectual Property: Environmentalism for the Net?" (http://www.law.duke.edu/boylesite/Intprop.htm); and Lawrence Lessig (ed.), "Cultural Environmentalism @ 10," special issue of *Law & Contemporary Problems* 70 (Spring 2007). The relationship between Yochai Benkler's *The Wealth of Networks* (New Haven, CT: Yale UP, 2007) and cultural environmentalism is discussed in Brett Frischmann, "Cultural Environmentalism and *The Wealth of Networks*," *University of Chicago Law Review* 74 (2007): 1083–1143.

24. The trend was probably started by Eric von Hippel, *The Sources of Innovation* (Oxford: Oxford UP, 1988), but see also his recent *Democratizing Innovation* (Cambridge, MA: MIT Press, 2006) and Suzanne Scotchmer, *Innovation and Incentives* (Cambridge, MA: MIT Press, 2006).

25. Henry William Chesbrough, *Open Innovation: The New Imperative for Creating and Profiting from Technology* (Cambridge, MA: Harvard Business School Press, 2005), and Chesbrough et al. (eds.), *Open Innovation: Researching a New Paradigm* (Oxford: Oxford UP, 2008).

26. Adam Jaffe and Josh Lerner, *Innovation and Its Discontents: How Our Broken Patent System Is Endangering Innovation and Progress, and What to Do About It* (Princeton, NJ: Princeton UP, 2006); Jonas Bessen and Michael Meurer, *Patent Failure: How Judges, Bureaucrats, and Lawyers Put Innovators at Risk* (Princeton, NJ: Princeton UP, 2008); Brian Kahin, "Patent Reform for a Digital Economy," November 2006 (Computer and Communications Industry Association, http://www.ccianet.org).

27. See, for example, the 2010 update of Thomas Rogers and Andrew Szamosszegi, *Fair Use in the U.S. Economy: Economic Contribution of Industries Relying on Fair Use* (Washington, DC: Computer and Communications Industry Asociation), at http://www.ccianet.org/CCIA/files/ccLibraryFiles/Filename/000000000354/fair-use-study-final.pdf.

28. Mario Biagioli and Peter Galison (eds.), *Scientific Authorship: Credit and Intellectual Property in Science* (New York: Routledge, 2003); Mario Biagioli, "The Instability of Authorship: Credit and Responsibility in Contemporary Biomedicine," *FASEB Journal* 12, no. 1 (1998): 3–16.

29. Rishab Ghosh, "Cooking Pot Markets: An Economic Model for the Trade in Free Goods and Services on the Internet," *First Monday* 3, no. 3 (March 1998), http://www.firstmonday.org/issues/

issue3_3/ghosh/; Yochai Benkler, "Coase's Penguin, or, Linux and the Nature of the Firm," *Yale Law Journal* 112, no. 3 (2002): 369–446.

30. Eric Raymond, *The Cathedral and the Bazaar* (Sebastopol, CA: O'Reilly, 1999), 80–82; Warren Hagstrom, "Gift Giving as an Organizational Principle in Science," in Barry Barnes and David Edge (eds.), *Science in Context* (Cambridge, MA: MIT Press, 1992), 21–34; Yochai Benkler, *The Wealth of Networks* (New Haven, CT: Yale UP, 2006), 116–122. However, there is a tendency within the applications of the "gift economy" to FS/OS or creative commons scenarios to emphasize the alleged generosity of gift giving while downplaying the contractlike reciprocity and even competitive dimensions of the gift as studied by ethnographers. Furthermore, the licensing arrangements behind FS/OS platforms prevent actual gifts of property and allow only for "gifts of access" or "gifts of use."

31. On norm-based authorship see Kal Raustiala and Chris Sprigman, "The Piracy Paradox: Innovation and Intellectual Property in Fashion Design," *Virginia Law Review* 92 (2006): 1687–1777; Emmanuelle Fauchart and Eric von Hippel, "Norms-Based Intellectual Property Systems: The Case of French Chefs," MIT Sloan Working Paper 4576-06, January 2006 (available at http://ssrn.com/abstract=881781); Jacob Loshin, "Secrets Revealed: How Magicians Protect Intellectual Property without Law," in Christine Corcos (ed.), *Law and Magic: A Collection of Essays* (Durham, NC: Carolina Academic Press, 2008): 123–142. On resources held in common and managed through local, custom-based rules, see Elinor Ostrom, *Governing the Commons: The Evolution of Institutions for Collective Action* (Cambridge: Cambridge UP, 1990); and Carol Rose and James Acheson, *The Lobster Gangs of Maine* (Hanover, NH: University Press of New England, 1988).

32. Paul Rabinow, "Severing the Ties: Fragmentation and Dignity in Late Modernity," *The Anthropology of Reason* (Princeton, NJ: Princeton UP, 1996), 129–152; Hannah Landecker, *Culturing Life: How Cells Became Technologies* (Cambridge, MA: Harvard UP, 2007), esp. 68–106.

33. For a critique of the notion of "place" underlying the law of geographical indications, see Bronwyn Parry, "Geographical Indications: Not All 'Champagne and Roses,'" in Lionel Bently, Jennifer Davis, and Jane Ginsburg (eds.), *Trade Marks and Brands: An Interdisciplinary Critique* (Cambridge: Cambridge University Press, 2008), 361–380. More positive readings may be found in Madhavi Sunder, "The Invention of Traditional Knowledge," *Law & Contemporary Problems* 70 (2007): 97–124; and Rosemary Coombe, Steven Schnoor, and Mohsen Ahmed, "Bearing Cultural Distinction: Information Capitalism and the New Expectations for Intellectual Property," *UC Davis Law Review* 4, no. 3 (2006): 891–917.

34. On this trend, see Rosemary Coombe, *The Cultural Life of Intellectual Properties: Authorship, Appropriation, and the Law* (Durham, NC: Duke UP, 1998).

35. Lawrence Lessig, *Free Culture: How Big Media Uses Technology and the Law to Lock Down Culture and Control Creativity* (New York: Penguin, 2004); Tarleton Gillespie, *Closed Shut: Copyright and the Shape of Digital Culture* (Cambridge, MA: MIT Press, 2008); Alain Pottage, "Fiction Science and Proprietary Effect," in Jean Paul Gaudillière, Daniel Kevles, and Hans-Jörg Rheinberger (eds.), *Living Properties: Making Knowledge and Controlling Ownership in the History of Biology* (Berlin: Max Planck Institute for the History of Science, 2009), 225–239.

36. The growing importance of fair use is reflected in initiatives like the "Statement of Best Practices in Fair Use for Online Video" (Center for Social Media and Project on Intellectual Property and the Public Interest, American University, June 2008), at http://www.centerforsocialmedia.org/sites/default/files/online_best_practices_in_fair_use.pdf.

37. Vovolona Rabeharisoa and Michel Callon, "Patients and Scientists in French Muscular Dystrophy Research," in Sheila Jasanoff (ed.), *States of Knowledge: The Co-production of Science and Social Order* (London: Routledge, 2004), 142–160.

38. See Pamela Samuelson, "Why Copyright Excludes Systems and Processes from the Scope of Its Protection," *Texas Law Review* 85 (2007): 1921–1977.

I

High and Low: IP Practices and Materialities

MARIO BIAGIOLI

Patent Specification and Political Representation
How Patents Became Rights

In colonial America and early modern Europe, patents were gifts the sovereigns could grant or withhold from their subjects. Today, instead, we are entitled to intellectual property rights in our inventions, provided we fulfill certain legal requirements. The transition from patents as privileges to patents as rights parallels the demise of political absolutism, the emergence of the modern political subject, and the development of liberal economies. I want to look at such large-scale changes through the genealogy of a mundane document of patent bureaucracy: the specification of the invention. This is the section of the application in which the inventor describes the invention in sufficient detail to enable a third party to repeat it—a requirement central to patent law in the United States and virtually every country in the world. A key reason for the ubiquity of this requirement is that specifications make the modern patent system politically acceptable by distinguishing it from traditional monopolies.

The differences between patents and monopolies were central to the founding document of anglophone patent law, the 1624 English Statute of Monopolies. While outlawing most monopolies, the statute made an exception for patents of *new* inventions. Patents for new inventions were seen as harmless because they took nothing away from the public which it had before.[1] They were still monopolies, but monopolies on techniques that the public had not known or practiced—grants, so to speak, of newly discovered and uninhabited lands. But if patents of inventions could be cast as *harmless* because they did not take anything away from the public, today it is not uncommon to hear that patents are *good* and that they should be understood not as monopolies but as publications—tools for the public disclosure of new and potentially useful knowledge. The real enemies of public knowledge, we are told, are not patents but trade secrets.

It is the specification that, by making the invention known to the public, has allowed a "harmless monopoly" to be recast into the win-win situation that William Robinson, the renowned U.S. jurist, described in 1890: "A patent is a contract between the inventor and the public, by which the inventor, in consideration that the exclusive use of his invention is secured to him for a limited period of time, confers upon the public the knowledge of the invention during that period and an unrestricted right to use it after that period has expired. . . . The specification is the instrument in which the terms of these mutual considerations and promises are declared, and on its completeness and accuracy depends the validity and the value of the contract itself."[2]

This contract—the "patent bargain"—was alien to early modern inventors and their rulers.[3] While inventions were often described to state officials, those descriptions were not required to be either public or sufficiently detailed to enable the replication of the invention.[4] During the eighteenth century, especially in England, the descriptions included in the body of the patent grew in size, but they never approached the length and detail of a modern specification.[5] Enabling specifications became necessary in England only toward the end of the century—a requirement that was then codified in U.S. and French patent law around 1790 when, with the introduction of new political regimes, patents became rights. Inventions, I argue, gained specifications when people gained political representation.

Galileo to Jefferson

Two examples, two hundred years apart, capture this dramatic transformation. The first dates from September 1594, when the senate of the Republic of Venice granted Galileo a twenty-year privilege for a water pump.[6] The entire description of the invention in the application and final text of the privilege boils down to two lines in which the pump is said to "raise water and irrigate land, [and] with the work of a single horse it will keep twenty water spouts

connected to it going at the same time."[7] In Venice—but also in early modern
Florence, Germany, France, England, the Netherlands, as well as colonial
America—state officials expected inventors to provide basic descriptions and
models of their devices but seemed to use that information primarily to assess possible overlaps between a new application and preexisting patents or
to develop an archive of prior art to adjudicate possible future infringement
disputes.[8] These summary descriptions were not meant to enable the reproduction of the invention after the patents' expiration—a function that was
typically taken up by provisions about the training of workers and artisans to
build and operate the invention *in loco*—a "disclosure" through bodies rather
than texts.[9] In securing a patent, the invention's local utility was vastly more
important than its detailed description. Terminally swampy Venice had a soft
spot for water pumps, and Galileo was granted a patent for a design he promised to be a particularly efficient one.[10]

It is therefore striking that, when we fast-forward two centuries to the first
U.S. Patent Act of April 1790, we find that applicants had to

> deliver to the Secretary of State a Specification in Writing, containing a descrip-
> tion, accompanied with drafts or models . . . of the thing or things by him or
> them invented or discovered, and described as aforesaid in the said Patents,
> which *specifications shall be so particular, and said models so exact, as not only to
> distinguish the invention or discovery from other things before known and used,
> but also to enable a Workman or other person skilled in the Art or Manufacture . . .
> to make, construct, or use the same*, to the end that the public may have the full
> benefit thereof after the expiration of the Patent term.[11]

Interestingly, the first French Patent Law of 1791 introduced comparable specification requirements.[12] Also striking was the U.S. 1790 Patent Act's provision
that the newly required specifications could be accessed and studied by any
interested citizen even while the patent was valid, not just after its expiration.[13]
The invention itself could not be copied while protected by the patent, but the
knowledge included in the specification became public at the time the patent
was issued—a change found in the French Patent Law of 1791 as well.

What changed radically between 1594 and 1790 were not just the *standards*
of patent descriptions but their *political economy*. Patents did not simply become more descriptive, but, together with their inventors and their users, they
entered a brand new legal regime that hinged on representation. The transformation of the subjects of political absolutism into a politically sovereign
"public" set the conditions of possibility of the patent bargain—the contract
between inventors and citizens. At the same time, it was the introduction of

patent specifications that made that contract politically defensible by distancing it from the "odious monopolies" of the ancien régime.

More stark differences emerge when we compare privileges and modern patents. Like most privileges, Galileo's was to expire within a year unless the invention was put to work.[14] So strict reduction to practice requirements fit well the logic of the privilege and are found, in fact, in many other early modern countries.[15] Privilege-granting authorities wanted to maximize local utility, not to disclose knowledge about the invention. (In the absence of international patent agreements, public disclosure of an invention could facilitate easy and undesirable transfer to nearby countries.)[16] What mattered was that inventions worked, not how they worked. If inventors could show that they had reduced their devices to practice or could provide working models for them, why would the king or the state care about how they worked?

The 1790 Patent Act turned this upside down. It specified no reduction to practice requirements but stated that a patent would be voided if the specification "does not contain the whole of the truth concerning his invention or discovery; or that it contains more than is necessary to produce the effect described."[17] This does not mean that the reduction to practice requirement had disappeared but rather that it was being reconceptualized in relation to the newly introduced specification requirements. By 1841 in *Hildreth v. Heath*, the court stated that "if a machine be invented and *described* in such a manner that it may be made and used . . . the invention may be said to be *reduced to practice*."[18] It appears, then, that specification requirements entail reduction to practice requirements in the sense that the applicant is either asked to show evidence of an actual embodiment of the invention (actual reduction to practice) or to describe in detail what she/he takes to be the best way to construct his/her invention (constructive reduction to practice).[19] In the patents-as-privileges regime, reduction to practice or working requirements performed the role we now give to specifications. But in the patents-as-rights regime reduction to practice requirements have been logically subsumed under specification requirements to the point that they may be fulfilled not by showing an actual device but a detailed *textual and pictorial description* of a *possible* device. Reduction to practice has gone virtual.

That specifications were absent in the colonial period but began to emerge after the Declaration of Independence to become eventually codified in the first U.S. Patent Act reinforces a correlation between political representation and patent representations.[20] The hypothesis gains further strength when we notice that while the 1790 act marked a sharp departure from both earlier European and colonial American patent practice, its provisions were closely matched by the first French postrevolutionary patent law. Passed in January

1791, that law stated that the applicant had to provide a complete, enabling disclosure of the invention; the disclosure was to be accessible to the public; and the patent would be voided if the specification was found wanting.[21] Comparable specification requirements were eventually adopted throughout Europe.[22]

Introducing Originality, Reinventing Novelty

Together with the shift from reduction to practice to specification came an equally drastic reframing of what it meant for an invention to be new. While related in practice, originality and novelty are logically distinct: the former concerns the authorship of the invention, while the latter refers to the differences between an invention and others that preceded it. One may be the original inventor of a device (in the sense of inventing it oneself), but that does not rule out the possibility that someone else might have already invented an equivalent device.

In 1790, U.S. patent law linked patentability to originality, saying that a patent would be void if it was proven that the patentee was not the "first and true inventor or discoverer" of the invention.[23] But it also added a novelty requirement: an "Art, Manufacture, Engine, Machine, or Device, or any improvement therein" could be patented only if "not known or used before." Although the act did not specify where the invention was supposed to be unknown and unused prior to its patenting, legislative history indicates that the lawmakers meant "anywhere in the world."[24] Two important consequences followed from these requirements. First, no U.S. patent could issue for an invention previously patented somewhere else. Second, an invention could be rendered unpatentable in the United States not only by operating it prior to the application, but also by making it publicly known. Though not always applied, the originality and novelty requirements of the 1790 Patent Act represented a sharp break from previous doctrine. Until then the granting of privileges (in England, continental Europe, and colonial America) had been utterly independent from the determination of whose mind had first produced the idea of the invention. Privileges went to the first person to put a certain invention to work in a certain country. It was quite reasonable to focus on novelty relative to a place (rather than on originality or absolute novelty) because privileges were initially aimed at obtaining useful manufactures that were previously unavailable in a specific country.[25] It was therefore immaterial whether the inventor had extracted the invention from his/her mind or from the country next door—"whether it is learned by travel, or by study it is the same thing."[26]

Seen against this background, the shift inscribed in the first U.S. Patent Act was literally categorical: it substituted a geographical construct (local novelty) with a mentalistic one (originality). It also turned novelty (a notion that had been previously local and relative) into an absolute one—novelty anywhere. Thus it changed the very referent of novelty, not only its geographical scope. While the patents-as-privileges regime was primarily concerned with the novelty of an *invention in a certain place*, early U.S. patent law started to conceive of novelty in terms of the difference between *a patent and another that preceded it*. It looked at the relationship between patent and prior art, not at whether a material invention had or had not been brought to a certain place. The shift was so radical that the notion of geographical novelty central to the patents-as-privileges regime has become oxymoronic in modern patent law. Modern patent law construes novelty in strictly temporal, not spatial, terms.[27]

Authors in Space, Not Things in Place

The introduction of specifications redefined the notion of invention in textual terms.[28] Specification requirements mandated that the inventor write down the invention in order to describe it in a way that could be understood and made replicable by the public as represented by the "person of ordinary skill in the art." This created the conditions of possibility for treating the actual material invention (the entity that used to be protected by early modern privileges) as separate from its "idea" (the entity protected by modern patent law). It was a paper item—the specification—that put the "intellectual" into "intellectual property."[29] Creating a space for the idea as distinct from its material embodiment, specifications made it possible for that idea to become the immaterial "essence" of the invention. This in turn recast the material invention (which had previously been the sole instantiation of the invention) as just one of the possible (and therefore inessential) embodiments of such an idea. This was not a process of abstraction from particular to general but rather one of separation between form and matter—a process discussed by Pottage and Sherman in chapter 15 of this volume.

Like the 1790 Act, modern patent law does not allow for the patenting of ideas or principles in and of themselves.[30] Much as in copyright, where the author is granted IP rights in his/her "personal expression" conceived not as a free-standing abstract entity but as something fixed in a medium, modern patents protect "inventive ideas" only when they are embodied in something material. This view was implicit in the specification requirements introduced in 1790 but became explicit in the 1793 Patent Act: "in the case of any machine, he [the inventor] shall fully explain the *principle and the several modes* in which he has contemplated the application of that principle or character."[31]

The invention becomes neither the abstract idea of the philosopher nor the immanent material device of the early modern engineer but rather a principle with various possible embodiments. Its two halves, however, began to lead separate lives. Inscribed on a piece of paper, the "inventive idea" moved into the halls of soon-to-be-established patent offices to become the primary focus of patent law and practice, while its material embodiments stayed outside, in the world of manufacture and commerce.

Not only did the introduction of specifications change the very concept of invention, but it also made possible the geographical expansion of the patents' protection. Without patent specifications, it would have been impossible to develop the international patent treaties that, starting in 1883, have led toward the globalization of intellectual property that we see today.[32] How could different countries compare, exchange, and cross-register patents without a specification, without a piece of paper one could put on a desk and check against other specifications of inventions from other countries?[33] If it was the recasting of invention from thing to text that allowed its transformation from privilege to right, then it was its newly acquired status as right that in turn allowed its legal protection to travel in space through international treaties about patent rights.

In this context, the idea of the invention did not emerge through a process of abstraction but through one of inscription—not by thinking it up but by writing it down. In time, the law came to focus less on how the actual invention looked, how it was built, and what it did here and now and more on how it was described on the surface of the application.[34] While the relationship between invention and privilege had been one between a machine and a document that regulated its use, modern patent law has come to construe the patented invention itself as a text.

The changing use of models may epitomize this shift. The early modern privilege regime treated models as the most important descriptions (or, rather, simulations) of the invention because of their ability to give an impression of its functioning in practice—the feature that the privilege system was most concerned with. But the modern patent system cared little, or not at all, about models. Only the United States continued to require models after 1790 and eventually phased them out in the 1870s. Between 1790 and 1870, models seemed to function as material supplements to textual and pictorial specifications—inscriptions whose language was still very much a work in progress. The law mandated enabling specifications, but judges and juries struggled to grasp an invention by looking at texts and drawings alone. However, as the language of patent claims became more stable, its inscriptions ceased to be buttressed by the "reality effect" of the model.[35] Modern patent disputes rarely engage the materiality of the invention because they have become, in effect, contests of textual interpretation over competing patents.[36] Similarly, issues of patent priority are settled by going back to dates and signatures in laboratory notebooks and written affidavits but only rarely to things. In the few cases in which the invention is still presented and archived (as in modern genetic sequences), its role is only that of the supplement to the specification, not the other way around (as was the case in the early modern period).

I am not saying that people did not have ideas about their inventions prior to 1790 but rather that whatever went on in the inventors' minds (or in the books they wrote about their inventions) was perfectly irrelevant to the working of the privilege system. Privileges rewarded working machines in specific places, period. They were technology transfer tools, not instruments of intellectual property. I mean this not only in the historical and empirical sense that privileges were introduced to facilitate the immigration of machines, manufactures, and skilled labor into the confines of the privilege-granting nation, but also in the logical sense that, as a regime, the privilege had no need for the idea of the invention (as a legal category), nor did it have a conceptual or legal space to represent it even if such an idea were to be found in the inventor's mind. In this sense, there was nothing intellectual about the privilege. It was all about locality, materiality, and utility.

It was the reconceptualization of the invention from actual machine to inventive idea that enabled the emergence of the notion of inventors' rights—at least in France and the United States. Such a transformation does not appear to have stemmed from an attempt to develop legal tools to match the emergence of new technological objects and activities or from the pressure of the inventors lobbying to get their rights recognized. With an overwhelmingly agrarian economy at the end of the eighteenth century, the United States had little pressing concern for patents—a fact reflected in the near absence of debate prior to the inclusion of the clause about inventors' rights in the Constitution.[37] My hypothesis is that the reframing of the inventor as a right-bearing author stemmed from changes that developed from inside the law in response to the introduction of a brand new political regime. It was the direct result of the introduction of two new legal requirements—disclosure and originality—that were correlated (in a formal sense) with the conceptual framework that went with the new political regime.

Giving Space to Time

The invention was at first conceived of as a material and locally operating manufacture but subsequently became an idea that, while inscribed in a patent application, did not need to hinge on one specific material embodiment—at least not in the United States. But without an essential connection to one "body," the invention was no longer attached to a specific place either. Once specification requirements turned the invention into an increasingly complex and lengthy text, it also began to circulate in space—generic spaces that were unrelated to the site where the invention would be put to work.

This shift reframed the temporal dimension of the invention. The role of time was barely visible in the privilege system, where transactions around inventions were either instantaneous or marginally extended in time. Inventors offered working or soon-to-work manufactures to kings, republics, and cities, and received privileges and rewards there and then. But the patent system and the switch to specification turned the invention into a forward-looking entity, something that existed in the present in a potential state that may be actualized in an unspecified future. The inventor's author function changed too. It moved from artisan and importer to author, but a peculiar kind of author. While artists and writers can point to their work as something existing in the present, the invention exists between the present and the future, between potentiality and actuality. In this sense, the inventor is an author who, while having already rights in his/her invention here and now, is also an author waiting to happen.

A comparable fate awaited utility. It started out as a straightforward notion connected to the benefits an invention could provide to the public or the state in a specific place at a specific time. But with the introduction of specification, utility requirements turned more indeterminate. The 1790 Patent Act stated that patent officials had to consider the patent's general utility but did not specify any threshold for it.[38] The stipulation, in a 1792 patent bill, that inventions should "not be injurious to the public" to be patentable also suggests that, unable to either maintain an early modern notion of utility or to develop a new stable and enforceable one, Congress was defensively rewriting utility as mere harmlessness.[39] That trend was confirmed by Justice Story in an influential 1817 case: "All that the law requires is that the invention should not be frivolous or injurious to the well-being, good policy, or sound morals of society. The word "useful," therefore, is incorporated into the act in contradistinction to mischievous or immoral. For instance, a new invention to poison people, or to promote debauchery, or to facilitate private assassination, is not a patentable invention. But if the invention steers wide of these objections, whether it be more or less useful is a circumstance very material to the interests of the patentee, but of no importance to the public."[40] Utility requirements reappeared in the 1836 Patent Act together with the reintroduction of patent examination but were applied rarely and inconsistently.[41] Utility has since become even more notional, deferred to an indefinite future and often related to beneficiaries that may not exist yet.[42]

Like the diminishing role of reduction to practice, the turning of utility into a vestigial notion is, I believe, a direct consequence of specification requirements. Utility and reduction to practice rose and fell together. In the privilege system, they constituted the two sides of the same concern: the local operation of the invention. The demise of locality and materiality under the patent regime took utility and reduction to practice down with them. The modern notion of the invention is about opportunity and potentiality rather than locality, materiality, and stability. The invention is now construed as emergent. It is attached to rights from the very moment of its "origin," but the value of those rights will accrue in the future, if at all.

To say that privileges provided local protection while patent protection is increasingly global misses much of what's interesting about the transition between the two regimes. Privileges were local because their coverage did not extend beyond the political jurisdiction of the privilege-granting authorities but, more important, because their granting hinged on the invention's perceived utility, that is, its contribution to the local economy and the revenue of the prince or state that issued the privilege. Within the regime of the privilege, utility had specific temporal and geographical features: it was local and short term. As protection expanded in space under the patent regime, utility became unhinged from the local. But rather than being relocated elsewhere in space, utility ended up displaced into the future.

Presentation to Representation

Perhaps one way to encapsulate several of the shifts discussed above is to say that both people and inventions moved from a regime of presentation into one of representation. This can be seen by the way the various categories of the patents-as-privilege regime dovetailed with each other but clashed with the categories of the patents-as-rights regime. Table 1.1 shows how the two regimes were coherent within themselves but nearly opposed to each other. Because of space constraints, I will focus only on the last row. I argue that, in the early modern period, inventions were not *represented* but literally *presented* by the inventor directly to the prince or his officials. The latter assessed the local merits of the invention by themselves, without reference to the fictional "person skilled in the art" that the patent-as-rights regime instead needs as the persona "elected" to represent the state of the knowledge in the invention's field. Furthermore, their deliberations concerned an actual material invention, not representations of its inventive idea. While drawings and sketches might

Table 1.1. Early privileges compared with modern patents

Early privileges (ca. 1450–1790)	Modern patents (ca. 1790 to present)
Privileges were gifts to subjects	Patents are rights of citizens
Privileges provided local protection only	Patent protection has been growing global
Novelty as a geographical category	Novelty as chronologically priority
Local novelty requirements	Global novelty requirements
Local and present utility	Temporally deferred and geographically unspecified utility
Reduction to practice	Specification requirements
Actual reduction to practice	Constructive reduction to practice
Training of local users	Textual and pictorial disclosure to anybody, anywhere
Marginal disclosure requirements	Virtual reduction to practice requirements
Invention as material object	Invention as embodied inventive idea
Invention as practice	Invention as knowledge
Inventor as artisan and importer	Inventor as author
Prior art as prior operation in a given jurisdiction	Prior art as earlier use, operation, or public knowledge, anywhere
Presentation	Representation

be used when the invention could not be produced or exhibited with the application, they did not function as representations. They were not (and could not be) copies of a preexisting object simply because such an object did not exist yet. Their referent could not be represented because it was deferred into the future.

Tridimensional models did not function as representations either, for at least two reasons. First, a model was not a copy of an invention. The distinction between model and machine was not one of copy to original but only one of scale. Models do not have originals. We cannot say whether the "original" was the machine or the model—whether the model was scaled down or the machine scaled up.[43] When a model was entered as evidence of the claim to be covered by the privilege, it functioned as the invention itself—it *presented* the invention. Furthermore, models were used not so much as static boundary markers of the invention's claim but rather as a way to demonstrate the functioning of the invention—a kind of scaled-down reduction to practice.

Similarly, we do not need to invoke representation to make sense of the processes through which early modern inventions were replicated. Early inventors were not required to provide specifications but to train local workers and artisans to operate and produce them. The invention was "worked" but not represented. Training involved the transmission of skilled bodily practices but not of knowledge as representation of the invention.

In the realm of politics, the privilege was not a contract involving people acting as political representatives. Patent officials may have "represented" the prince or sovereign power that hired them, but those political powers did not represent the people. As a result, the privilege was not a contract between the inventor and the public (through an elected government) but rather a material gift from one person (the prince or a *persona ficta* like a city) to another person (the inventor). The very notion of the modern patent bargain would have been unthinkable outside of a political regime based on representation. Today's contract between the inventor and the public is predicated on the fact that the public—through its elected officials—is committed to enforcing that contract. But the privilege could not be construed as such a bargain because the entity in charge of enforcing it was not the public or a government elected by the public. The very conditions of possibility of such a bargain are rooted in a regime of political representation.[44]

Because the problems of today's intellectual property regime share the same political genealogy with cherished notions of individual rights and property, it is difficult to believe that they will be controllable through clever, ad hoc policy adjustments. The possibility for a better solution may come instead from understanding the radical shift that happened around 1790 and how that made possible what we now call intellectual property. Knowing that we once moved from privileges to rights should help us grasp that we can move again—this time beyond the notion of intellectual property rights.

NOTES

1. "An Act concerning Monopolies and Dispensations of Penal Laws, and the Forfeitures Therof" (21 Jac. I. c. 3.) in Charles Loosey, *Recueil des lois publiées dans tous les Etats de l'Europe, les Etats-Unis d'Amerique et les Indes d'ouest de la Hollande sur les privileges et les brevets d'invention* (Paris: Bossange, 1849), p.117.

2. William C. Robinson, *The Law of Patents for Useful Inventions*, vol. 2 (Boston: Little, Brown, 1890), p. 70. The earliest appearance of the image of the patent bargain in the United States is probably in Joseph Barnes, *Treatise on the Justice, Policy, and Utility of Establishing an Effectual System of Promoting the Progress of Useful Arts by Assuring Property in the Products of Genius* (Philadelphia:

Bailey, 1792), p. 25. See Harold Irvin Dutton, *The Patent System and Inventive Activity during the Industrial Revolution, 1750–1852* (Manchester: Manchester University Press, 1984), p. 22, for English examples.

3. Thomas Fessenden, *An Essay on the Law of Patents for New Inventions . . .* (Boston: Mallory, 1810), p. 49.

4. The literature on early patent specification is sparse: D. Seaborne Davies, "The Early History of the Patent Specification," *Law Quarterly Review* 50 (1934): 86–109, 260–274; John Adams and Gwen Averley, "The Patent Specification: The Role of *Liardet v Johnson*," *Journal of Legal History* 7 (1986): 156–177; E. Wyndham Hulme, "On the Consideration of the Patent Grant, Past and Present" *Law Quarterly Review* 13 (1897): 313–318; *idem*, "On the History of Patent Law in the Seventeenth and Eighteenth Centuries," *Law Quarterly Review* 18 (1902): 280–288; and Allan Gomme, *Patents of Invention: Origin and Growth of the Patent System in Britain* (London: Longmans, 1946), pp. 25–39. While in France and in the United States we find an abrupt shift in specification requirements around 1790, Seaborne Davies, Hulme, Adams, and Averley present a much less drastic pattern for England. While showing the same transition from virtual absence of specifications around 1600 to "modern" enabling specifications toward the end of the eighteenth century—*Liardet v. Johnson* (1778) being the landmark case—the English trajectory is more complicated, perhaps because the country did not experience the same kind of revolutionary political change that affected France and the United States. There is, however, consensus that even in England, "throughout the [eighteenth] century, specifications were enrolled which could in no way have enabled those skilled in the art to carry out the invention, and which would have been valueless in an infringement action" (Adams and Averley, "The Patent Specification," p. 160). Similarly, Christine MacLeod, *Inventing the Industrial Revolution: The English Patent System, 1660–1800* (Cambridge: Cambridge University Press, 1988), p. 50, argues: "Since official and judicial guidance was lacking for most of the eighteenth century, it is doubtful whether patentees had any clear idea what the function of specifications was or how full and accurate it ought to be. Like most other things about the system, it was left to the patentee's discretion."

5. Davies, "The Early History of the Patent Specification," pp. 269–271.

6. Galileo Galilei, *Opere*, vol. 19, Antonio Favaro (ed.) (Florence: Barbera, 1907) (hereafter *GO*), p. 126.

7. *GO*, p. 128. We know that applicants might be asked for descriptions, drawings, and models of their devices, but the sparseness of this material in the Venetian archives indicates an inconsistent demand for such information (Roberto Berveglieri, *Inventori Stranieri a Venezia (1474–1788)* [Venice: Marsilio, 1995], pp. 26–27, 38).

8. Models were typically kept out of the public's reach as well (Hansjoerg Pohlmann, "The Inventor's Rights in Early German Law," *Journal of the Patent Office Society* 43 [(1961]: 126).

9. Davies, "The Early History of the Patent Specification," pp. 104–105; Dutton, *The Patent System*, p. 39.

10. Unlike "private" patents, inventions of military interest, or inventions for whose development the inventor was requesting state funding were often tested, as shown by the Venetian patent rolls.

11. US Patent Act of 1790, sec. 2, in Edward Walterscheid, *To Promote the Progress of Useful Arts: American Patent Law and Administration, 1787–1836* (Littleton, CO: Rothman, 1998) (hereafter *WT*), p. 465 (emphasis mine). An equivalent requirement is found in the very first Copyright and Patents Bill (June 23, 1789) that failed to pass (*WT*, p. 436).

12. *Loi Relative aux Decouvertes utiles, & aux moyens d'en assurer la propriété à ceux qui seront reconnus en etre les Auteurs. Donnée à Paris, le 7 Janvier 1791* (Paris: Imprimerie Royale, 1791), articles 4 and 16.

13. U.S. Patent Act of 1790, sec. 3, in *WT*, p. 466. The first director of the Patent Office read this

provision to mean that specifications were to be made public only in court or upon authorization by the patentee but was rebuffed by the secretary of state (Kenneth W. Dobyns, *The Patent Office Pony* [San Diego: Sergeant Kirkland's Press, 1997], pp. 76–78).

14. *GO*, p. 128.

15. Mario Biagioli, "From Print to Patents," *History of Science* 44 (2006), p. 154, note 144; Wyndham Hulme, "On the Consideration of the Patent Grant," p. 314.

16. Dutton, *The Patent System*, pp. 41–42.

17. U.S. Patent Act of 1790, sec. 6, in *WT*, p. 468. The only reference to something like a working requirement clause is found in a draft of the 1790 act that was dropped.

18. 47 *ARCP* 804, cited in Kendall J. Dood, "Patent Models and the Patent Law: 1790–1880 (Part II)," *Journal of the Patent Office Society* 65 (1983): 245n10 (emphasis mine), but see also Stephen D. Law, *Digest of American Cases Relating to Patents for Inventions and Copyrights from 1789 to 1862* (New York: Law, 1870), p. 424.

19. Dood, "Patent Models and the Law"; Sheldon W. Halpern, Craig Allen Nard, and Kenneth L. Port, *Fundamentals of United States Intellectual Property Law* (The Hague: Kluwer, 1999), pp. 188, 205–207.

20. The specification requirement started to emerge between the Declaration of Independence and the ratification of the Constitution in patents issued by individual states (Bruce Bugbee, *Genesis of American Patent and Copyright Law* [Washington, DC: Public Affairs Press, 1967], pp. 85–88, 94–95).

21. *Loi Relative aux Decouvertes utiles*, articles 4, 11, 15, and 16.

22. Loosey, *Recueil des lois publiées*, pp. 58, 332, 341–342, 357, 392–395, 415, 430–433, 443.

23. U.S. Patent Act of 1790, sec. 5, in *WT*, p. 467.

24. *WT*, p. 373. The wording of the 1790 act is not accidental, as previous drafts include more restrictive provisions—"not before known or used *within the United States*"—which were then dropped.

25. Biagioli, "From Print to Patents," pp. 147–152.

26. Fessenden, *An Essay on the Law of Patents*, p. 48.

27. I take the articulation of the notion of nonobviousness in *Hotchkiss v. Greenwood* (1851) to represent the next step in the logical evolution of the notion of novelty.

28. Oren Bracha's "Genius and Owners: The Construction of Inventors and the Emergence of American Intellectual Property" (paper circulated at "Con/Texts of Invention" at Case Western Reserve University, April 2006) has provided much inspiration for my argument. Although Bracha does not single out the introduction of specifications as a primary cause for the transition from what he calls the image of the inventor as entrepreneur and craftsman to one as "genius-owner" and relates such a shift primarily to broad cultural and economic trends, he does suggest that there may be a link between the move from a conceptualization of inventions as things and inventions as ideas at the same time that we find a switch from privileges for devices to patents for disclosed inventions. While we deal with much of the same evidence and many of the same issues, my argument differs from his by effectively ignoring economic and cultural considerations, while focusing on the implications of the new political framework, the demands of the patent bargain, and the key role of patent specifications, in that I try to argue that most of the phenomena we are looking at are consequences of the introduction of enabling specifications.

29. Neither the U.S. Constitution nor the first (1790) Patent Act mentions the term "intellectual property." They only refer to the granting "for limited Times to Authors and Inventors the exclusive Right to their respective Writings and Discoveries." "Property" (but not intellectual property) is mentioned in the 1793 Patent Act (sec. 1) and in Fessenden, *An Essay on the Law of Patents*, p. 58.

30. The recent wave of patents involving business models would seem to contradict this. The opposition to this trend is, however, both vocal and widespread among legal scholars. The U.S. Court of Appeals for the Federal Circuit's decision against Bilksi suggests that the tide might be turning against the patenting of immaterial methods and algorithms (http://www.cafc.uscourts.gov/opinions/07-1130.pdf).

31. U.S. Patent Act of 1793, sec. 3, in *WT*, p. 480 (emphasis mine).

32. Yves Plasseraud, *Paris 1883: Genese du droit unioniste des brevets* (Paris: Litec, 1983).

33. Bruno Latour, "Drawing Things Together," in Michael Lynch and Steven Woolgar (eds.), *Representation in Scientific Practice* (Cambridge, MA: MIT Press, 1988), pp. 19–68.

34. Even the drawings commonly used in specifications are not treated as freestanding inscriptions but function only in relation to the textual specification.

35. William Rankin, "The Person Skilled in the Art Is Quite Conventional," (this volume); Alain Pottage, "Normative Engines: The Mechanical Manufacture of Modern Patent Law," forthcoming; and Dood, "Patent Models and the Patent Law," pp. 234–274.

36. Brad Sherman and Lionel Bently, *The Making of Modern Intellectual Property Law: The British Experience, 1760–1911* (Cambridge: Cambridge University Press, 1999), pp. 185–186. Sherman and Bently's argument is about how the problems of identification of intangible property change as a result of the systematic adoption of a registration system, but it is, I believe, quite parallel to the issues I am discussing here once one replaces what I mean by "idea" with what they mean by "intangible property."

37. Edward C. Walterscheid, *The Nature of the Intellectual Property Clause: A Study in Historical Perspective* (Buffalo, NY: Hein, 2002), p. 2.

38. U.S. Patent Act of 1790, sec. 1, in *WT*, p. 463.

39. *WT*, pp. 473–474.

40. *Lowell v. Lewis*, 15 F. Cas 1018 (C.C.D. Mass., 1817) (No. 8,568).

41. *WT*, p. 428.

42. Like originality, utility is a requirement that has to be kept on the books to legitimize the patent system despite the fact that, as a requirement, it is very difficult to uphold on empirical grounds. Some legal scholars have noticed this tension: "At first glance, the utility requirement in patent law appears to be somewhat superfluous. . . . However, there is a purpose behind the utility requirement in that it secures a quid pro quo for society" (Halpern et al., *Fundamentals of United States Intellectual Property Law*, p. 121). For similar trends in nineteenth-century Europe, see Yves Plasseraud and François Savignon, *L'Etat et l'invention* (Paris: Documentation Française, 1985), pp. 11, 60–61; and Dutton, *The Patent System*, p. 80.

43. For instance, the Venetian officials who considered Galileo's patent application for a water pump did not contrast his actual invention with the model but simply referred to its "large" and "small" forms (*GO*, p. 127).

44. I am thinking, for instance, about the pattern of shifts from the classical to the modern episteme described in Michel Foucault, *The Order of Things: An Archaeology of the Human Sciences* (New York: Pantheon, 1970).

KARA W. SWANSON

2

Authoring an Invention
Patent Production in the Nineteenth-Century United States

In modern patent systems, an invention achieves legal existence as a text, the official words of a patent.[1] The patent is a bureaucratic text, a product of multiple individuals linked in a faceless bureaucracy.[2] From the perspective of the legal system, a U.S. patent is not a "literary work" to be protected by copyright[3] but an inscribed verbal act that forms a different type of intellectual property, one that protects an idea rather than particular words. The distinction between authorship and invention is recognized in the U.S. Constitution, which grants Congress the power "to promote the Progress of Science and useful Arts, by securing for limited Times to Authors and Inventors the exclusive Right to their respective Writings and Discoveries."[4] The legal separation between "Authors," who generate "Writings," and "Inventors," who generate "Discoveries," is considered part of the development of the modern law of intellectual property.[5] This distinction, so doctrinally clear, blurs when one considers the actual process of creating patent texts, an act that might be considered authoring an invention.

A patent text is not the only legally cognizable text without an author.[6] But unlike other bureaucratic texts, such as statutes, which are considered anonymous government publications, the modern patent is an intensely personal text. As the U.S. patent system developed as the world's first formalized patent regime,[7] a double shift occurred. The production of the patent text moved from the inventor to third parties, while simultaneously the patent text came both legally and culturally to represent the creation of a modern self,[8] much as a literary work came to be seen as the product of an individual author through copyright law.[9] This chapter traces the development of the patent as a unique type of bureaucratic text by examining this transition in American patent practice. By the end of the nineteenth century, patents were authored in the sense that they described the "mental act" of an individual mind.[10] This mind was analogous to the "romantic author" who displayed creative genius in the production of literary works, but the text of patents, unlike literary works, were no longer the product of the inventor's pen. An inventor was a romantic author who did not write.

Learning to Author Patents: Early Patent Practice

When the U.S. Constitution was ratified in 1787, a patent did not necessarily signify an inventive act by the patentee. In the scattered, ad hoc colonial patent practice, a monopoly grant to make, use, and sell a new technology might be given to the first to *import* a new technology.[11] In passing the first federal patent statute, the Patent Act of 1790, Congress limited patents for the first time to those who had new ideas, as long as the ideas were "sufficiently useful and important."[12] The Patent Act also provided the first formal requirements for a patent petition, beginning the process of defining the text of patents by requiring a written description of the invention "so particular . . . as not only to distinguish the invention or discovery from other things before known and used, but also to enable a workman or other person skilled in the art or manufacture . . . to make, construct, or use, the same."[13] If the petition was approved, the result was a succinct document signed by President George Washington, establishing a monopoly in the manufacture, use, and sale of the invention for a set term.

The first U.S. patent, for example, was one paragraph with three parts. The text identified the inventor, "Samuel Hopkins of the City of Philadelphia." Then it described his invention, "an Improvement in the making of Pot ash and Pearl ash by a new apparatus and process," listing the four steps of the process in fewer than one hundred words, and briefly mentioning the advantage of the improvement ("leaves little Residuum; and produces a much greater Quantity of Salt"). It then recited the words of grant, which gave Hopkins for fourteen years the exclusive right "of using and vending to others the said

Discovery."[14] While this paragraph almost certainly drew upon the words of Hopkins's petition,[15] before a patent was granted in these early years of the republic, the claimant might be asked to appear before the secretary of state, the secretary of war, and the attorney general, the government officials charged with evaluating patent petitions, to demonstrate and discuss his invention.[16] As secretary of state, Thomas Jefferson on occasion asked respected men of science to join him in considering a new apparatus.[17] These early patents, then, comprised an amalgam of words provided by the inventor (the description), which may have been rewritten after the examining officials collected oral and visual information about the invention, and words provided by a government functionary (the grant), all written out longhand by the State Department clerk. While early patents probably had a very limited circulation, to at least the few Americans who came in contact with them, these documents provided the first generalizable vision of texts of invention in the United States. This amalgamated model was made explicit in a revision of the patent law in 1793, which specifically required that patents "recite the allegations and suggestions of the . . . petition,"[18] that is, the inventor's own words of description.[19]

The Patent Act of 1793 also heightened the importance of the text of the petition by abolishing any examination of the claimed invention for utility or importance. Without any face-to-face interaction, only the petition itself, with the accompanying drawings and model, mattered. The inventor became the certifier of his own invention in a registration system like that used for copyrights today. The act specified that the applicant should submit a signed, witnessed oath that he was the "true inventor," and that he was providing "a written description of his invention . . . in . . . full, clear and exact terms."[20] If the application met the formal requirements, it was granted. The patent law thus moved from indifference about the identity of the "true inventor" in the colonial period to reliance on a named individual to attest not only to the accuracy of the description but to the truth of his "mental act" of invention. The inventor's name served not only as an indication of the source of the inventive idea but as a locus for responsibility, just as did the author's name in early print culture.[21] An issued patent, instead of a paragraph that contained perhaps an excerpted or rewritten piece of the petition, became a formalized paragraph of grant, to which was attached the lengthier description in the words provided by the inventor.[22] Thus, when Cephus Thompson provided documents for the patent office to recreate its record of his 1806 patent after an office fire,[23] he certified that "the schedule referred to in these Letters Patent and making part of the same contain[s] a description in the words of . . . Cephus Thompson himself of his delineating machine."[24] The inventor was now the most important contributor to the text of a patent.

With the inventor's petition elevated in significance, all aspects of its form and content were important. The Patent Act of 1793 had left unspecified the details of how the patent application papers should look, how they should be delivered, how the government might communicate any insufficiencies or defects in the paperwork, and what might happen if errors in the description of the invention were discovered after a patent was granted. Inventors needed to learn how to prepare this crucial text. The federal government also needed help processing the increasing number of such petitions. Neither of the first two patent acts had created a formal patent office, and State Department clerks managed the patent paperwork in addition to their other duties. In 1802, Thomas Jefferson, now president, appointed William Thornton, a physician, architect, and technological enthusiast, who eventually obtained several patents himself, as the first federal employee dedicated to processing patent petitions.[25] As the sole person involved with all applications, Thornton dominated patent practice until his death in 1828. During his long tenure, Thornton and others developed the first patent how-to literature to instruct inventors how to draft petitions.

Thornton wrote and circulated "a few lines of information" for patent applicants by 1811.[26] He offered a form of a petition, which like the patents that he himself would write in longhand, had two parts. The first was the formal words of petition, a fill-in-the-blank paragraph, which when completed would identify the applicant and his invention and attest to his mental act in conceiving of an idea "not known or used before." The second part, the description or specification, was to be written by the applicant alone. Thornton could not provide any boilerplate language for this part, just advice that the words used must be "clear and specific," and that "as this specification . . . enters into, and forms part of the patent, it must be without any references to a model or drawing, and must be signed by the applicant or applicants, before two witnesses."[27] The applicant's words were crucial and must stand alone, irrespective of any nontextual parts of the application. These were rules of authorship, guidance in using the inventor's own personal knowledge of his invention to supplement the standard language of the form Thornton offered, with words that would then become part of the bureaucratic text, as it was amalgamated by Thornton.

Although uniquely powerful in his influence on early-nineteenth-century patent practice, Thornton was not alone in teaching Americans how to compose texts of invention. Thomas Fessenden wrote the first United States patent treatise in 1810, *An Essay on the Law of Patents for Invention*.[28] Fessenden directed his treatise to "those men of inventive powers, who are unacquainted with the niceties of legal distinctions."[29] To assist these "men of inventive powers," Fessenden offered a form for the patent petition very similar to Thornton's example and also provided would-be patentees with a form of a patent, showing just how the words they added to his forms would be included in similar blanks on the patent, to which their specification would be attached.[30] Between Thornton's advice pamphlet and Fessenden's book, which was issued in a second edition in 1822, the model of the standardized and amalgamated patent text was put into broad circulation, with its combination of government boilerplate and the "clear and specific" words of description chosen by the inventor.

Fessenden, a Dartmouth College graduate who was admitted to the Vermont bar around 1799, appears to have had little or no experience with patents as a lawyer.[31] His book was based on his personal interest in patents, first as co-owner and then as a patentee himself.[32] Like Thornton, who blended the roles of inventor and bureaucrat, Fessenden served both as inventor and lawyer. While these roles would be seen as distinct sources of expertise in patenting by the end of the nineteenth century, in antebellum America, each of these men considered the inventor to be the most significant participant in the creation of the patent text. A patent was acknowledged as a bureaucratic text, but it was also seen as a personal product of the inventor.

The persistence of this mode of proceeding can be seen in the longevity of Fessenden's *Essay*, which remained the only American patent law treatise until 1837, when Willard Phillips, a Boston lawyer, stopped the presses on *The Law of Patents for Inventions* in order to include the Patent Act of 1836.[33] Unlike Fessenden's volume, *The Law of Patents* was directed to lawyers who tried patent cases in the courts. Phillips, who himself appeared frequently in patent cases by the 1830s,[34] produced a truncated version of his treatise, called *The Inventor's Guide*, aimed specifically at inventors.[35] Phillips offered rules and forms to allow an inventor to add a "knowledge of the law of patents generally" to his existing "skill and knowledge of the subject of the invention."[36] Phillips's readers were expected to obtain a patent themselves and then to turn to a lawyer to defend or enforce the resulting text. Until 1836, the inventor was the key participant in authoring the words of his invention that would become the bureaucratic text of a patent.

Using Ghostwriters: Professionalization of Patent Practice

The Patent Act of 1836 did much more than threaten to make Phillips's treatise outdated before it was published. The act was a complete legislative overhaul of the patent system, which resulted in a dramatic change in patent practice and in the way patent texts were created.[37] It created a formal patent office staffed by examiners, men with scientific training who examined claimed inventions for novelty and usefulness. A patent petition was transformed from an inventor-certified document that was processed into an official patent if formalities were met and fees were paid into a contested and examined text, subjected to a process that might involve considerable exchange with one of the new examiners. The examiners became participants in the crafting of the words of patents in ways far beyond the fill-in-the blank rewriting of petitions into grants. They examined the words of the application, suggested new ones, required changes, and even rejected applications.[38] In response to this heightened scrutiny of their petitions, increasingly inventors turned to patent practitioners to prepare the paperwork, giving up personal participation in the process of textual generation.[39]

The statutory change sparked an explosion of patent advice literature in the second half of the nineteenth century, as patent practitioners strove to present the most up-to-date information to the public, and in so doing, increase the demand for their services.[40] The proliferating how-to literature demonstrated a growing consensus that any savvy inventor would use a patent practitioner as his agent in dealings with the patent office, leaving his "mental acts" to be described to the examiner by someone with experience in patent drafting, a specialized form of ghostwriting. The inventor was repositioned as someone who had inventive genius but lacked even the limited authorial genius to contribute to the bureaucratic text that would certify his "inventive powers."

While the concept of agency was new neither in patent practice nor in the publication of texts, the use of agents in the generation of patent texts became much more emphasized and much more popular after 1836.[41] This shift in patent practice was illustrated in the career of another prominent attorney, who began practice immediately after the Civil War. William Simonds graduated from Yale Law School in 1865. Just six years later, he described himself as specializing in patent law, both procurement and litigation, in his first patent publication, *Practical Suggestions on the Sale of Patents*.[42] This slim volume exemplified the new patent advice literature. Simonds's goal was not to empower the inventor to apply for a patent himself but rather to convince him to hire Simonds to prepare the application. After describing how to commercialize a patent once obtained, he warned that "it is advisable for almost all persons to avail themselves of the services of a faithful solicitor, in. . . . securing patents."[43] When Simonds later published traditional patent treatises for both inventors and patent practitioners, he again urged reliance on professional help: "Skilled counsel is very important in the preparation and prosecution of an application."[44]

Patent practitioners functioned essentially as ghostwriters, for even as they took over the writing tasks previously handled by inventors, the personal identification of the inventor with the patent text remained. The text, when finalized, was an expression of his "inventive powers," rather than any skill of his "faithful solicitor." The elegies to inventive genius as the basis for patent awards that had begun by the late eighteenth century continued as the nineteenth century advanced, perhaps most famously in the explanation by patentee and attorney Abraham Lincoln in 1859 that the patent law added the "fuel of interest to the fire of genius."[45] The common law relied upon and increasingly articulated this notion of individualized inventive genius in the second half of the nineteenth century through the judicial concern that inventors show "inventive faculty" in order to merit a patent. For example, after the Civil War, the legal emphasis on "non-obviousness" increased.[46] This requirement of patentability stressed the individual, personal genius of the inventor who saw something not obvious to the ordinary man.

Yet, as seen in Simonds's publications, outside the courtroom, in the daily practice of patent production, there was a competing discourse that distinguished the genius of the inventor as made manifest in a patent from the genius of a romantic author expressed in a literary work. While patent drafting required genius of a sort, such authorial genius was no longer expected to be found in the same individual who possessed the fire of inventive genius. John Kingsley and Joseph Pirsson, midcentury patent agents, offered a new description of where genius lay: "As persons having experience, we can truly aver, that there is no business or profession where greater ingenuity and skill are indispensable, even when coupled with the best judgment and experience, than that of 'Procuring Patents for Inventions.'"[47] The patent agents exercised a new sort of authorial ingenuity in the generation of this bureaucratic text, translating the mental act of the individual inventor into words that could be accepted and certified by the patent examiners. Through the development of patent law and the increasingly complicated patent practice, the author function of a patent became split: the ingenuity of choosing and negotiating the best words to protect an idea resided in the patent practitioner, while the modern self who was credited with the inventive act of generating the novel idea was the inventor, who swore to the veracity of the specification and the originality of the idea described in someone else's words.

This discourse emphasizing the separation of the individual mental act from wordsmithing served the professional needs of patent practitioners, who greatly increased in numbers during the second half of the nineteenth century. By the 1860s, the patent agency Munn and Company was among the most successful of the new agencies, claiming responsibility for about one-third of all United States patents issued annually.[48] Munn and Company published advice literature for inventors from at least 1849 onward.[49] Its 1861 pamphlet began by offering a free and confidential consultation, in person or by mail, based on "a pen-and-ink sketch and a description of the invention."[50] Then it described the process of application, promising a patent about six weeks after the inventor had provided the necessary model, fee, and written description to Munn, and signed the papers that Munn's employees would prepare.[51] Far from encouraging inventors to act directly for themselves, the pamphlet argued that "no inventor can possibly have facilities or influence superior to our own."[52] In its 1863 pamphlet, Munn and Company carefully corrected the impression that books such *An Inventor's Guide* might have created about the ability of inventors to participate directly in the texts of their inventions: "Many inventors suppose that by taking the forms of specification, petition, and oath here prescribed by the Patent Office, they will have no trouble in getting an official decision upon their applications. This is an erroneous impression, and has led many applicants into great trouble and expense."[53] Munn also included a testimonial letter from a satisfied client who had realized this point and articulated the separation of inventor and patent practice: "It is two things," noted Heman B. Hammon of Bristolville, Ohio, "to *invent* and to *secure a patent.*"[54]

By 1876, Munn described the minimal efforts at authorship required of the inventor: "Never mind spelling or grammar, but be very particular to give your ideas in full about the invention. Describe its intended working, and mention all the advantages that you can think of. This statement is always of assistance to use in preparing the specification and drawings. . . . We will then prepare the drawings and specification, and send the latter to you, with full instructions, for examination and signature."[55] In this proposed mode of authoring an invention, the inventor had an idea and explained the invention in ungrammatical prose, which was "of assistance" to the agent who actually prepared the specification.

This mode could fail. One of Munn's less satisfied clients was Thomas Edison, whose hiring of the agency to file a few patent applications resulted in specifications which, although signed by Edison, were reportedly incomprehensible to him.[56] Edison agreed, though, that inventing and securing a patent were two different things, and rather than assume authorial control after his poor experience with Munn, he hired attorneys more experienced in his areas of invention to translate his stream of inventive ideas into the commercial property on which he based his business success.[57]

Eventually, this shift in patent authorship gained even the support of the patent office, which in the antebellum era had resisted the splintering of the author function, clinging to the ideal of inventors petitioning for patents unaided as a way of distinguishing the democratic accessibility of patents in the United States from the more expensive and complicated British system.[58] By 1897, however, the patent office advised all applicants to employ an agent, and began to maintain an official registry of patent agents.[59] In a three-volume treatise that became a classic text on patent law for lawyers, William Robinson, a Yale law professor, summed up the turn-of-the-century view of the role of the inventor in patent production:

> The business between inventors and the Patent Office is usually transacted through attorneys. An inventor has the right to prepare his own application, and to appear and prosecute his claims in person; but in most cases by doing this he encounters great difficulties, arising partly from his ignorance of the requirements of the law, and partly from his inability to comply with them if they were known. A due regard for their own interests has led inventors to intrust such affairs to men trained for that purpose, and the practice has been encouraged by the Patent Office as tending to facilitate its own labors, as well as to render more secure the results of patentees.[60]

Perhaps even more telling than the opinion of a law professor was the opinion of his lay contemporary and sometime novelist Edmund Pearson Dole, who in a popular book, *Talks about Law*, described the drafting of a patent specification as "often requiring the highest degree of care and skill. . . . Inventors, as a class, have not the special training that renders men exact and accurate in the use of language; indeed, this is one of the rarest attainments."[61] It was the patent practitioner who was the man of rare attainment who could author the invention by generating and negotiating the patent text. The inventor was an author no longer.

The Heroic Inventor and the Authors of Inventions

By the time Robinson and Dole were describing the practice of patent generation, Thomas Edison, who was granted over a thousand patents in his lifetime, epitomized the heroic inventor as an American cultural ideal. Patents were crucial to Edison's carefully constructed public image as a "wizard" inventor. They were a frequently cited measure of his inventive genius—the number of patents he held was and is used as a stand-in for his stature as inventor.[62] Patents were also a key component of the financial and technological networks he carefully built to make his ideas socially and commercially successful.[63] Yet, while these texts were foundational to his reputation and success, it was Edison's wizardry in his Menlo Park laboratory that formed the basis for his public reputation as an inventor-hero. The process of translating his ideas into patents, with its protracted back-and-forth correspondence with the patent examiners,[64] was not in public view and not considered in the personal identity of Edison as inventor. But just as an individual acquired the status of romantic author through texts ascribed to her name, Edison's identity and fame were publicly evidenced through texts that represented Edison's cultural capital, the bureaucratic texts of issued patents. It was Edison, not the patent agents or bureaucrats, who received credit for these patents, as an author receives credit for her published work. He was the author of his inventions.

The history of nineteenth-century American patent practice reveals a self-conscious relationship between personality and text that differs both from the early modern fusion of text and modern self into the romantic author[65] and from the postmodern separation of authorship from text that results in the dissipation of any identified self within or behind the text.[66] By the end of the nineteenth century, all participants in the patent system acknowledged the role of patent practitioners, and indeed celebrated and encouraged their genius in drafting and negotiating the actual words of most patents. The inventor was not an author in that he was usually not involved in textual generation. Yet the depersonalization of the *production* of the patent, rendering it an unauthored bureaucratic text, did not eliminate the personal *significance* of the text as the manifestation of individual genius. The divided author function did not preclude a profound and indispensible sense in which inventors such as Edison authored inventions through the patent system.

At the end of the twentieth century, this sense of a romantic self embedded within the bureaucratic text of a patent remained sufficiently strong to allow a court to rule that the inventors who were granted a biotech patent had the same relationship with the patent text as they would with the text of a peer-reviewed scientific article published under their names. Despite the presence in the courtroom of the patent attorney who testified about choosing the words of the patent application himself, the court identified the inventors as the "authors."[67] In the construction of the patent text as an unauthored bureaucratic text that yet is interpreted in law and culture as an expression of a modern individual self, the practices of the American patent system illustrate that the "romantic author" is a powerful social, legal, and cultural role that is not limited to literary works and copyright law but that is also foundational to the formally distinct legal category of invention. The Inventor is the Author.

NOTES

1. The text can be supplemented by two- and three-dimensional representations. Until the late nineteenth century, patent models were more significant in the United States, and drawings remain an integral part of patents. See William Rankin, "The 'Person Skilled in the Art' Is Really Quite Conventional," this volume. Early modern European patents were also less text based. Mario Biagioli, "Patent Republic: Representing Inventions, Constructing Rights and Authors," *Social Research* 73 (2006): 1129–1172.

2. I employ the term "bureaucratic text" with reference to the work of Joseph Vining, who has considered "legal texts bureaucratically produced—texts that are not written by the person who signs them" in the context of his concern about the bureaucratization of the courts and the loss of a "legal mind" behind judicial opinions. Joseph Vining, "Law and Enchantment: The Place of Belief," *Mich. L. Rev.* 86:3 (Dec. 1987): 577–597, at 577; "Justice, Bureaucracy, and Legal Method," *Mich. L. Rev.* 80:2 (Dec. 1981): 248–258, at 253.

3. 17 U.S. Code Sec. 102(a)(1).

4. U.S. Constitution, art. I, sec. 8, cl. 8.

5. Oren Bracha, "Geniuses and Owners: The Construction of Inventors and the Emergence of American Intellectual Property," in Daniel W. Hamilton and Alfred L. Brophy, eds., *Transformations in American Legal History: Essays in Honor of Professor Morton J. Horwitz* (Cambridge, MA: Harvard Law School, 2009), pp. 369–390, at 381.

6. Michel Foucault, "What Is an Author?" in Paul Rabinow, ed., *The Foucault Reader* (New York: Pantheon Books, 1984), pp. 101–120, at 108.

7. For discussion of the early history of the U.S. patent system, see Frank D. Prager, "Trends and Developments in United States Patent Law from Jefferson to Clifford (1790–1870), Part II," *Am. J. Legal History* 6:1 (Jan. 1962): 45–62; Bruce W. Bugbee, *Genesis of American Patent and Copyright Law* (Washington, DC: Public Affairs Press, 1967), pp. 125–158; Edward C. Walterscheid, *To Promote the Progress of Useful Arts: American Patent Law and Administration, 1787–1836* (Littleton, CO: Rothman, 1998); and Oren Bracha, *Owning Ideas: A History of Anglo-American Intellectual Property*, SJD thesis, Harvard Law School (2005), pp. 401–518.

8. The late-eighteenth- and early-nineteenth-century development in the United States of the "genius inventor" is discussed in Bracha, "Geniuses and Owners." For the nineteenth-century rise of the "heroic inventor" in Great Britain, see Christine MacLeod, *Heroes of Invention: Technology, Liberalism and British Identity, 1750–1914* (Cambridge: Cambridge University Press, 2007).

9. Martha Woodmansee, "The Genius and the Copyright: Economic and Legal Conditions of the Emergence of the 'Author,'" *Eighteenth-Century Studies* 17:4 (Summer 1984): 425; David Saunders, *Authorship and Copyright* (London: Routledge, 1992); and Mark Rose, *Authors and Owners: The Invention of Copyright* (Cambridge, MA: Harvard University Press, 1993).

10. The use of the term "mental act" to describe invention arose out of case law and commentary during the nineteenth century. See, e.g., Henry Childs Merwin, *The Patentability of Inventions* (Boston: Little, Brown, 1883), p. 2, and William C. Robinson, *The Law of Patents for Useful Inventions* (Boston: Little, Brown, 1890), vol. 1, p. 116.

11. Bugbee, *Genesis of American Patent and Copyright Law*, pp. 57–103; P. J. Federico, "Colonial Monopolies and Patents," in P. J. Federico, ed., *Outline of the History of the United States Patent Office* (Washington, DC: Patent Office Society, 1936), pp. 35–42. This chapter uses the modern term "patents" for what were more accurately called "patents for invention" in the early modern period, to distinguish them from other types of "letters patent," such as land grants.

12. Patent Act of 1790, sec. 1.

13. Patent Act of 1790, sec. 2. For the significance of this requirement, which was not standard in earlier practice, see Biagioli, "Patent Republic."

14. U.S. Patent X1, July 31, 1790.

15. Because of a fire in the Patent Office in 1836, earlier patent office records are virtually nonexistent, and what issued patents are available are surviving inventor's copies, or re-created office copies. United States Patent Office, *An Account of the Destruction by Fire on 24th September, 1877 together with a History of the Patent Office from 1790 to 1877* (Washington, DC, 1877).

16. Patent Act of 1790, sec. 1.

17. Dumas Malone, *Jefferson and the Rights of Man*, vol. 2 of *Jefferson and His Time* (Charlottesville: University of Virginia Press, 1951), pp. 213–214; Walterscheid, *To Promote the Progress of the Useful Arts*, pp. 178–181.

18. Patent Act of 1793, sec. 1.

19. While it was usual for inventors to draft petitions themselves, it was not required, and even at this early stage, there is evidence that some inventors had assistance. Bracha, *Owning Ideas*, pp. 411–412, n. 34.

20. Patent Act of 1793, sec. 3.

21. Foucault, "What Is an Author?" p. 108.

22. A generic patent of this period is included in Thomas G. Fessenden, *An Essay on the Law of Patents for New Inventions*, 1st ed. (1810; reprint, Clark, NJ: Lawbook Exchange, 2003), p. 204.

23. See note 15 above.

24. U.S. Patent X657, issued Feb. 5, 1806.

25. For a discussion of patent practice during Thornton's tenure, and of Thornton himself, see Kenneth W. Dobyns, *The Patent Office Pony: A History of the Early Patent Office* (Fredericksburg, VA: Sergeant Kirkland's Museum and Historical Society, 1997), pp. 35, 39–57, 60–70; William I. Wyman, "Dr. William Thornton and the Patent Office to 1836," in Federico, *Outline of the History*, pp. 83–90; Daniel Preston, "The Administration and Reform of the U.S. Patent Office, 1790–1836," *Journal of the Early Republic* 5:3 (Autumn 1985): 334–351; and Beatrice Starr Jenkins, *William Thornton: Small Star of the American Enlightenment* (San Luis Obispo, CA: Merritt Starr Books, 1982).

26. "Patents," *Journal of the Patent Office Society* 6:3 (Nov. 1923): 97–103, at 97–98 (reprint); Levin H. Campbell, *The Patent System of the United States* (Washington, DC: McGill & Wallace, 1891), p. 26.

27. "Patents," p. 101–102.

28. Fessenden, *An Essay on the Law*, 1st ed.; Thomas G. Fessenden, *An Essay on the Law of Patents for New Inventions*, 2d ed. (Boston: C. Ewer, 1822).

29. Fessenden, *An Essay on the Law*, 1st ed., p. xxxviii; ibid., 2d ed., p. xxxii.

30. Fessenden, *An Essay on the Law*, 1st ed., pp. 202–205; ibid., 2d ed., pp. 401–405.

31. Porter Gale Perrin, *The Life and Works of Thomas Green Fessenden, 1771–1837*, University of Maine Studies, 2d series, no. 4 (Orono, ME: University Press, 1925), pp. 31–32, 142–144, 147; William T. Davis, *Bench and Bar of the Commonwealth of Massachusetts* (n.p.: Boston History Company, 1895), vol. 1, p. 245.

32. Perrin, pp. 32, 48–49, 166.

33. Willard Phillips, *The Law of Patents for Inventions* (Boston: American Stationers, 1837).

34. Charles Warren, *A History of the American Bar* (Boston: Little, Brown, 1911), pp. 457–458.

35. Willard Phillips, *The Inventor's Guide, Comprising the Rules, Forms, and Proceedings, for Securing Patent Rights* (Boston: S. Colman; New York: Collins, Keese, 1837).

36. Phillips, *Inventor's Guide*, p. 238.

37. For a discussion of the passage of the 1836 act, see William I. Wyman and Edwin W. Thomas, "The Patent Act of 1936," in Federico, *Outline of the History*, pp. 91–102; and Dobyns, *Patent Office Pony*, pp. 96–102.

38. See, generally, Robert C. Post, "'Liberalizers' versus 'Scientific Men' in the Antebellum Patent Office," *Technology and Culture* 17:1 (Jan. 1976): 24–54; see also Charles Bazerman, *The Languages of Edison's Light* (Cambridge, MA: MIT Press, 1999), pp. 240–245.

39. For the history of the patent practitioner, see Kara W. Swanson, "The Emergence of the Professional Patent Practitioner," *Technology and Culture* 50:3 (July 2009): 519–548.

40. See, for example, George Ticknor Curtis, *A Treatise on the Law of Patents for Useful Inventions in the United States of America* (Boston: Little, Brown, 1849, 1854, 1867, 1873); Merwin *The Patentability of Inventions* (1883); J. G. Moore, *Patent Office and Patent Laws* (Philadelphia: Henry Carey Baird, 1855, 1860); James B. Robb, *A Collection of Patent Cases* (Boston: Little, Brown, 1854); and Albert H. Walker, *Text-Book of the Patent Laws of the United States of America* (New York: L. K. Strouse, 1883, 1886, 1889, 1895).

41. Early patent agents are discussed in Post, "'Liberalizers,'" pp. 52–53; and Dobyns, *Patent Office Pony*, p. 73 and elsewhere. Early American literary agents are discussed in James Hepburn, *The Author's Empty Purse and the Rise of the Literary Agent* (London: Oxford University Press, 1968), pp. 67–75.

42. William Edgar Simonds, *Practical Suggestions on the Sale of Patents* (Hartford, CT: William Edgar Simonds, 1871), title page.

43. Simonds, *Practical Suggestions*, p. 74.

44. William Edgar Simonds, *A Manual of Patent Law* (Hartford, CT: William Edgar Simonds, 1874), p. 121. He also published *A Summary of the Law of Patents for Useful Inventions with Forms* (1883; reprint, Littleton, CO: Rothman, 1995).

45. Abraham Lincoln, "Second Lecture on Discoveries and Inventions," in Roy P. Baster, ed., *The Collected Works of Abraham Lincoln*, vol. 3, pp. 356-363, at p. 363 (New Brunswick, NJ: Rutgers University Press, 1953); U.S. Patent 6469, issued May 22, 1849.

46. Nonobviousness was applied as a criterion of patentability in *Hotchkiss v. Greenwood*, 52 U.S. 248 (1851). For its rise to prominence as a doctrine and judicial discussion of the "inventive faculty," see Bracha, *Owning Ideas*, pp. 504–517.

47. John L Kingsley and Joseph P. Pirsson, *Laws and Practice of All Nations and Governments Relating to Patents for Inventions* (New York: Kingsley and Pirsson, 1848), p. iv.

48. Dobyns, *Patent Office Pony*, p. 129.

49. *The Patent Laws of the United States* (New York: Scientific American, 1849); *Hints to Inventors, Concerning the Procuring of Patents* (New York: Munn & Co., Patent Solicitors, 1861); *United States Patent Law: Instructions How to Obtain Letters Patent for New Inventions* (New York: Munn & Co., 1863, 1867); *The Scientific American Reference Book* (New York: Munn & Co., 1876).

50. *Hints to Inventors*, p. 1.

51. *Hints to Inventors*, pp. 3–5.

52. *Hints to Inventors*, p. 7, italics and font changes omitted.

53. *United States Patent Law*, 1863, p. 23.

54. *United States Patent Law*, 1863, p. 34, emphasis in original.

55. *Scientific American Reference Book*, 1876, p. 10.

56. Paul Israel, *Edison: A Life of Invention* (New York: Wiley, 1998), p. 80.

57. For examples of Edison's work with patent attorneys, see Reese V. Jenkins et al., *The Papers of Thomas A. Edison* (Baltimore: Johns Hopkins University Press, 1989–), vol. 1, pp. 173, 497–498; vol. 3, p. 284 n. 5; vol. 4, p. 206 n. 16; vol. 6, p. 312.

58. United States Patent Office, *Annual Report of the Commissioner of Patents for the Year 1849*, 31st Cong., 1st sess., Senate Executive Document 15 (Washington, DC, 1850), pp. 514–515. See further discussion in Kara W. Swanson, "The Bureaucracy of Genius: Striking the Patent Bargain in the

Nineteenth-Century United States," as presented at the Harvard Legal History Colloquium, Harvard Law School, Cambridge, MA, October, 2008.

59. *Rules of Practice before the Patent Office*, sec. 17 (Dec. 1, 1897).

60. William C. Robinson, *The Law of Patents for Useful Inventions* (Boston: Little, Brown, 1890), vol. 2, p. 12.

61. Edmund P. Dole, *Talks about Law : A Popular Statement of What Our Law Is and How It Is Administered* (1887; reprint, Kansas City: Bowen, Merrill, 1892), p. 397.

62. For example, Israel begins his comprehensive and analytic biography by citing "Edison's re-cord of 1,093 U.S. patents" in his first sentence. Israel, *Edison: A Life*, p. vii. Edison's status as "wizard" is discussed in Bazerman, *Languages of Edison's Light*, pp. 29–33.

63. Bazerman, *Languages of Edison's Light*, pp. 86–90; Israel, *Edison: A Life*, pp. 208–212 and passim.

64. Bazerman, *Languages of Edison's Light*, pp. 86–90, 240–248; Israel, *Edison: A Life*, p. 42.

65. See references at note 9.

66. See Foucault, "What Is an Author?"; and Roland Barthes, "The Death of the Author," in Richard Howard, trans., *The Rustle of Language*, pp. 49–55 (1986; reprint, Berkeley: University of California Press, 1989).

67. *Hoffman-La Roche, Inc., et al. v. Promega Corporation*, 1999 WL 1797330 (N.D. Cal.), as discussed in Kara W. Swanson, "Biotech in Court: A Legal Lesson on the Unity of Science," *Social Studies of Science* 37:3 (June 2007): 357–384.

WILLIAM J. RANKIN

3

The "Person Skilled in the Art" Is Really Quite Conventional
U.S. Patent Drawings and the Persona of the Inventor, 1870–2005

Consider the drawing shown in figure 3.1. It shows a new and useful steam trap for discharging condensate from a pressurized steam system.[1] As pressurized water and steam enter from the left at C, the water fills the trap body A and eventually overspills into the cylindrical bucket E. When the bucket is heavy enough to pull the arm 9, a weight 30 rolls to the left, causing the pin 23 to be knocked forcefully enough to rotate the arm 19 around the pivot 22 and open the valve 18 at the bottom of the bucket. The pressure in the system forces water out of the right-hand pipe 13, but the valve closes before the bucket is empty, thus preventing the escape of steam. The 45-degree hatch lines indicate that this is a cross section, and that the cut is taken through metal. The thin vertical lines to the left of E show that this object is cylindrical; the shading and dashed lines of the various moving parts likewise make it clear how they interact. The overall effect is of a three-dimensional object cut and labeled to best display the complex workings of a steam trap, but it is certainly not a naturalistic view of an actual object: cutting metal does not reveal diagonal lines, and the lack of perspective distortion indicates that this view could never been seen in reality.

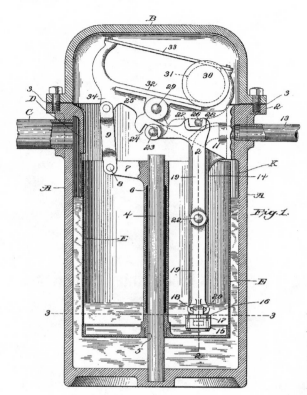

Figure 3.1. Drawing of a new and useful steam trap, from U.S. patent 583,064 (1897), granted to W. B. Mason of Boston.

The peculiar qualities of these kinds of drawings make them an important part of the patent system. They fulfill legal requirements, stabilize certain legal fictions, and even help define the idea of "invention" and the kind of person who can be an "inventor." Drawings very similar to figure 3.1 have been included with the vast majority of U.S. patents, not just for mechanical inventions like steam traps, but also for chemical, electrical, and even biological patents. Almost all these drawings, especially those issued between the early 1870s and the early 1980s, exhibit a similar tension between the abstract and the naturalistic and use conventions of light, shade, and hatch patterns quite different from standard engineering drawings. These conventions are powerful rhetorical devices that encode rather specific assumptions about intellectual property, and understanding how they work and how they change can help to reveal large-scale shifts in the patent system as a whole.

This chapter analyzes these drawings in two ways. First, patent drawings are important for reinforcing the dual status of a patent as something that both protects an idea and discloses it to the public, in line with the modern understanding of patents as a contractual exchange between inventor and society.[2] The holder of the steam-trap patent must enable others to learn from his work, but in order to guard against infringement it is in his interest to depict an invention as generically as possible so that it protects not just a particular steam trap but all steam traps that share certain characteristics. Patent drawings appear to refer to actual extant objects yet leave unanswered many questions of manufacture, assembly, or specific materials. The way this is accomplished is important for understanding the tensions inherent in the logic of modern patents.

Second, patent drawings provide great insight to the identity of the (fictional) person to whom the patent specification is addressed—the ideal "person skilled in the art" referenced in every patent act since 1790. Like the implied reader of a text, every drawing creates a rhetorical reader often quite different from its actual audience, and the selection of both conventions and content implies a viewer with a certain set of practical skills and reasons for consulting the drawing. And because in the United States the creative inventor is only defined negatively against the ordinary person who is merely skilled, analyzing the "person skilled in the art" is a useful way of analyzing the "inventor" as well.[3] For most of the twentieth century, the person skilled in the art was a self-contradictory jack-of-all-trades who had more in common with the (fictional) nineteenth-century "lone inventor" than any actual person. Patent drawings helped to stabilize the identity of this implied reader and smooth over legal contradictions.

This chapter ends by using patent drawings to examine some important shifts in the U.S. patent system from the last few decades, beginning in the late 1960s but manifest mostly since the 1980s. During that time, the traditional conventions of patent drawings were largely abandoned, and it is now relatively uncommon to find patents accompanied by drawings like the one in figure 3.1. At the same time, the patent system has changed in other ways as well: patent judges have become increasingly specialized, patent rights have been strengthened, and the criteria of patentability have been incrementally broadened to include software, biotechnology, and even "business methods." Contributing to this increasing patent-friendliness has been a legal change in the version of the "person skilled in the art" used to test for obviousness. Analyzing these changes alongside the recent shift in drawing standards helps us understand the larger stakes of these developments. Since drawings encode the ideal reader of patents—and thus the ideal inventor as well—they can be used to identify a larger shift in the idea of invention assumed by the patent system. Recent patent drawings show that both the inventor and the noninventor have become more specialized, and they now seem much more like typical corporate knowledge workers than mythical polymaths.

Reading Patent Drawings as Evidence

Nontextual material has been required in U.S. patents since the very first Patent Act in 1790. For most of the nineteenth century, patentees provided working models and color drawings, but these artifacts were often idiosyncratic, fragile, and difficult to disseminate. As a result, in the early 1870s the commissioner of patents changed official guidelines to require standardized black-and-white ink drawings reproducible using the new process of photolithography. The Patent Office shifted from being a central archive of mechanical knowledge to being more like a publishing house, with new drawings and specifications sent throughout the country on a weekly schedule.[4] Since this important change, patent drawings have remained remarkably stable, buttressed by technological momentum, bureaucratic inertia, and relative continuity in the role that they play in the patent system. Even given the changes in patent drawings (and patent law) in the last few decades, many of their most important characteristics have been unaffected. Their two major functions—disclosing a new idea to the public and guaranteeing intellectual property to a patentee—have remained the same.

From the point of view of the public, the primary function of a patent drawing is disclosure. For this, the law requires methodical, literal denotation, and the reader of the patent is guided by the visual analog of legalese. Usually, the multiplication of detail is commensurate with the complexity of the device, such as when an automatic card feeder requires 14 figures and 150 numerical labels (see fig. 3.2). But at times the assumed reader of a patent requires a visual prolixity that ranges from comically unnecessary to simply pathological. For example, a simple package for Camembert cheese requires three different views (fig. 3.3), while at the other extreme a 2001 patent for a pseudorandom number generator included 3,273 pages of flowcharts and circuit diagrams.[5] Long-standing legal precedent holds that drawings constitute a kind of disclosure distinct from text: intellectual property rights may not be granted to novelty which is claimed in writing but not shown in the drawing, and disclosure in a drawing can establish precedence even when not included in the text.[6] Thus drawings are often used as a final test of the claims of a patent, and if failure to draw the "plurality of separate portions of cheese" as in figure 3.3 is interpreted as lack of adequate disclosure, the patent may become worthless.

But this visual effusiveness is balanced by an ambiguity necessary for a patent's claims to be robust, and in general patent drawings do not specify

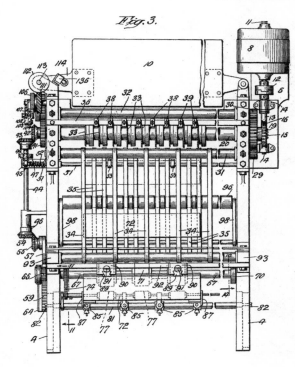

Figure 3.2. An automatic card reader (U.S. patent 1,594,883; 1923): a detailed drawing for a complex machine.

detail unless absolutely necessary. For example, in contrast to the visual redundancy required of engineering drawings, patent lawyers recommend that all duplication be avoided in patents, since inadvertent contradictions in different drawings may render all claims invalid. If the invention is a modification or improvement to an existing device, the parent object is shown dotted, and the connection between the old and the new is made clear but not explicit, lest the patent be invalidated for inaccurately depicting prior art. In order to make the broadest claims possible, verisimilitude is often completely abandoned. Monolithic parts are idealized for the sake of generality, and strict adherence to scale is not always important, especially for drawings of processes, assembly lines, or clothing (for an example, see fig. 3.4).[7] Likewise, individual parts are never shown on their own but as part of a working whole: the goal is to patent a set of relationships, not a particular object (see fig. 3.5 for an extreme case). Materials are labeled as generically as possible, often identified as simply "metal" or "wood." Dimensions, centerlines, and milling tolerances are omitted. When drafting a claim, patent lawyers begin by describing the drawing itself—what they call the "picture claim"—and then incrementally broaden

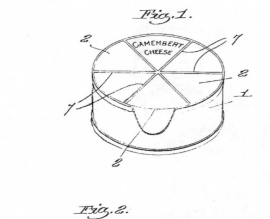

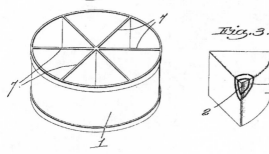

Figure 3.3. A new and useful way of storing Camembert cheese (U.S. patent 1,054,433; 1913): a detailed drawing for a cheese box.

subsequent claims to include as many similar ideas as possible. The original drawing must be ambiguous enough to allow these broader claims.[8]

The balance between prolixity and ambiguity in patent drawings is not an inherent feature of visual evidence. Most engineering drawings, for example, do not work this way: to a working engineer, no amount of ambiguity is acceptable. Likewise, these kinds of drawings are not used when patenting plants or designs, since for these patents, standards for both disclosure and protection are more narrowly circumscribed and the primary worth of the patent is to establish successful reduction to practice, as in a simple registration system (similar to copyright).[9] Not coincidentally, plants and designs are often accompanied by photographs, and photographs tend to provide only mimetic evidence; neither explanatory nor ambiguous, they are useful primarily for proving infringement.[10] Patent drawings should not be seen as just a more easily reproducible alternative to other visual sources. They are carefully calibrated to reconcile the conflicting interests of the public and the inventor.

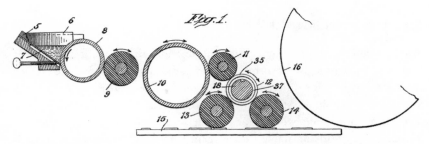

Figure 3.4. This drawing of a process for color offset printing (U.S. patent 2,189,073; 1940) shows idealized, monolithic parts: cylinders are shown floating in the air or incomplete, and a general sense of hierarchy is emphasized over precise dimensions.

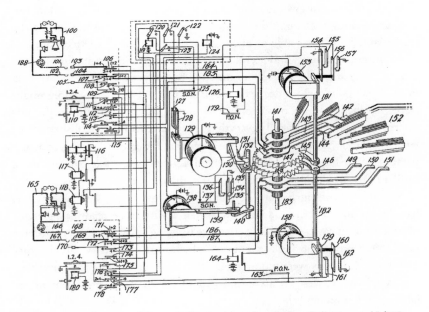

Figure 3.5. A combination of electric and axonometric drawing for a "selector switch" (U.S. patent 1,523,439; 1920). The space of the drawing does not correspond to any physical space that could be occupied by an actual object, and there are many ways that this set of relationships could be realized in practice.

Patent Drawings and the Person Skilled in the Art

Even though patent drawings fulfill legal functions that come from different sections of patent legislation and disparate judicial precedents, there are not separate drawings for different requirements. While perhaps unintentional, the reliance on a single set of drawings is a powerful device for creating a unified ideal reader—one who is not just the sum of conflicting legal requirements, but instead the stable Other against which the creative inventor is defined. Since the mid-nineteenth century, this reader—the "person skilled in the art"—has been asked to fulfill two functions: she/he must evaluate whether an invention has been adequately disclosed and, simultaneously, ensure that it is not just an "obvious" extension of the "ordinary skill in the art."[11] Until the late twentieth century, the person skilled in the art thus had a split personality, as the law defined these two roles in very different ways. A good set of patent drawings would enable him or her to replicate an invention, but in order to enforce adequate disclosure the reader was generally assumed to be thick-skulled and incapable of making inferences in unclear situations, thus requiring great prolixity and literalness. At the same time, testing for obviousness meant that she/he was also assumed to be perfectly aware of all prior art in any "analogous" field and able to understand how all past innovations might be recombined to solve a new problem. By the mid-twentieth century, this was interpreted to include literally everything that had ever been published in any language.[12] Drawing conventions were important for reconciling this apparent paradox and helped to establish the person skilled in the art as someone quite similar to the mythical lone inventor of the nineteenth century.

The distinguishing feature of patent drawings, as stressed by drawing handbooks and official guidelines, was their ability to be read "at a glance." Maintaining an easily readable at-a-glance drawing style, however, required a rather strict set of drawing conventions, which were policed by Patent Office examiners. Not only were requirements for the size and kind of paper specified exactly, but so were the margins, acceptable orientations, arrangement and labeling of figures, and the location of the inventor's and witnesses' names. In the drawing, all parts were to be called out with reference numbers no less than one-eighth-inch high and connected to the drawing with the shortest possible lead lines. Enclosing these references in quotation marks, brackets, or circles was not allowed. All characters were to be from the English alphabet, except for conventional mathematical symbols. All exploded views were to be placed in brackets, section lines shown clearly, and section-hatching drawn at 45 degrees. The patent office also published a set of standard hatch patterns for depicting materials and colors. Material could be distinguished in surface treatment and in cross-section, and guidelines were available for every-thing from metal and wood to cheese and human flesh. Hatch patterns were also used for the standard ROYGBV colors plus brown, black, and gray (see fig. 3.6).[13]

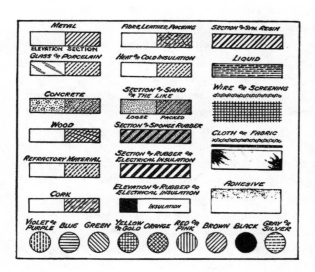

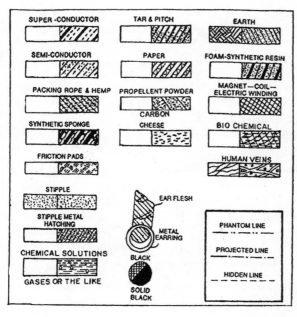

Figure 3.6. Standard hatch patterns from the Patent Office. This hatch-pattern chart has been published since at least the 1940s; these images are from the *Manual of Patent Examining Procedure* (Washington, DC: USPTO, May 2004), 600-99 and 600-100.

Perhaps the most important convention was a method for making nonperspectival orthographic drawings (such as in fig. 3.1 or 3.2) intelligible as views of three-dimensional objects. The drafter was told that "light should come from the upper left corner at an angle of forty-five degrees" to the surface of the paper.[14] Edges to the bottom and right should thus be made graphically thicker, to indicate a shadow. In combination with surface shading of curved parts, these shade lines can aid greatly in understanding an object three-dimensionally. Whereas modern engineering drawings will show an object in several standard views (front, side, top, etc.), patents will usually only show one such view, and shade lines might be the only way to differentiate between a hole and a protrusion, or a surface seam and a hard edge (see fig. 3.7 for examples; fig. 3.8 shows an actual patent drawing with shade lines). In a similar way, line weights on axonometric and perspective drawings were often used to add depth and eliminate optical gestalt shifts. Edges that point toward the viewer were made heavy, while all other lines were left light—figure 3.9 shows this convention in principle, while figure 3.10 shows it in a published patent. Together with hatch symbols and standardized reference labels, these visual effects gave patent drawings a surprisingly uniform flavor; after only a short time spent scanning the patents published in the weekly *Official Gazette of the U.S. Patent Office*, most drawings can indeed be understood (almost) at a glance.

This at-a-glance drawing style played an important rhetorical role in establishing the person skilled in the art as someone qualified to evaluate a new invention's obviousness. Having all drawings legible at a glance created a visual

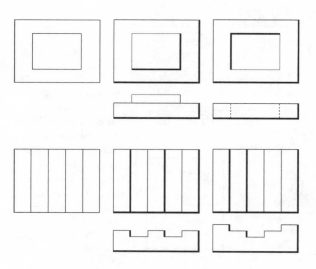

Figure 3.7. The two drawings in the left column have no shade lines. The middle and right columns show two versions of how the ambiguity of the left-hand drawings is resolved by shade lines (drawings by the author).

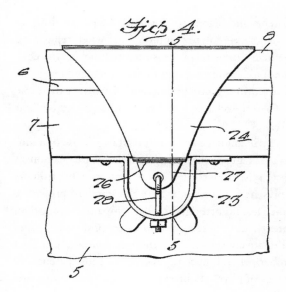

Figure 3.8. Shade lines in use on a "box wall securing means" (U.S. patent 1,523,479; 1924). The V-shaped surface is shown to protrude, while the lower half of the background surface is recessed.

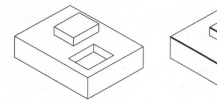

Figure 3.9. Shade lines in axonometric drawing are added to help resolve gestalt shifts (drawings by the author).

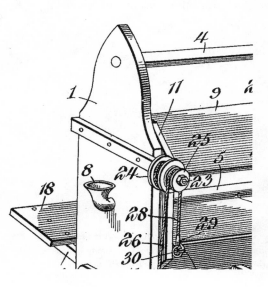

Figure 3.10. Shade lines used to show a sanitary drinking trough (detail from U.S. patent 1,054,462; 1913). In a complex drawing, thick lines can help greatly in properly reading three-dimensionality.

language that unified all patents and helped to construct the patent-drawing reader as someone who, while unable to use common sense when replicating an innovation, could nevertheless draw from ideas across all fields. The conventions of black-and-white lines, numbered figures, hatching, and reference numbers allowed atypical inventions to be understood visually in the same way as valves and engines. Even flowcharts were usually illuminated by light from the upper left (fig. 3.11).

The universality of this visual language was reinforced by the use of a limited number of drawing types. Figure 3.12 shows the relative proportion of different kinds of drawings published in the *Official Gazette*, roughly from its beginning in 1872 to the present.[15] At no point have the standard projective views (perspective, axonometric, and orthographic) accompanied fewer than 70 percent of all issued patents, and the relative popularity of different types of drawings has remained relatively stable. Even though chemical and electrical patents now outnumber general mechanical patents, most patents are still accompanied by drawings of physical objects that can be drawn in plane projection and understood in only one or two views. By using standardized conventions and relatively few drawing types to depict almost all inventions with reference to some kind of object, fields as disparate as chemistry, electrical engineering, and materials science could be united as a single discussion of machine technology.

Perhaps surprisingly, it is this same universal visual language that also establishes the person skilled in the art as the dimwitted reader who must evaluate disclosure requirements and potentially replicate an invention. This overlap can best be seen by analyzing the historical origins of patent drawings. The

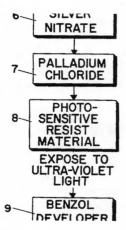

Figure 3.11. Detail of a flowchart showing a method of photo-plating electrical circuits (U.S. patent 3,006,819; 1961), with numerical labels and light from the upper left.

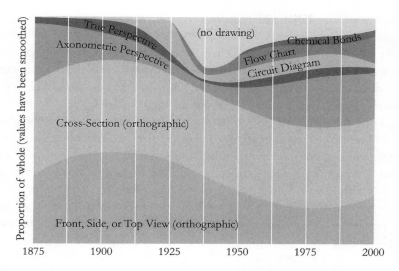

Figure 3.12. Types of patent drawings, as published in the *Official Gazette*, 1875–2000. Based on samples of 100 consecutive patents, every twelve years (1,100 patents total).

at-a-glance visual style was used throughout the nineteenth century, and for the most part, patent drawing standards can be understood as a translation of standard 1870s engineering drafting practice to the requirements of black-and-white reproduction; many of the features that today seem unique to patents are a preservation of the features of nineteenth-century drawing.[16] Nineteenth-century technical drawings were generally much less specialized than drawings today, and there was relatively little difference between the conventions used in an ideal working drawing and those used for promotional material. Three conventions typified these drawings: shade lines, shadows, and the use of color washes to differentiate between materials.[17] Before photolithography, most patent drawings used these same conventions. In the 1850s, a simple drawing of a washing machine attached to a patent application might look quite similar to a large cross-section of the Great Eastern steamship drawn to woo investors; both would show a nonperspective view, use blue coloring for steel and yellow for brass, and show light coming from the upper left.[18] In the transition to photolithography, patent drawings substituted hatch patterns for color washes, but they maintained almost all other conventions without modification.

These nineteenth-century conventions addressed problems of communication specific to a world in which engineers interacted on a daily basis more with nonspecialists than with other engineers. For example, three-dimensional shade effects had long played a role in the division of labor between engineers and unmathematical mechanics. Shade lines were used on the steam-engine drawings of inventor-engineers like James Watt and Richard Trevithick, who found that they increased a drawing's legibility for artisans, and pedagogues of technical drawing were explicit about the social role of shade and shadow. As Gaspard Monge—the patron saint of projective geometry and cofounder of the École Polytechnique—pointed out in his treatise on drafting, flattened orthographic drawings could be quite confusing to craftsmen who tended to communicate using nonprojective pictures, and the goal of shadow casting was to make precisely measured drawings look more like naturalistic views.[19] The convention of shade lines was a way to bridge both the social and epistemic gaps between tradesmen and those with mathematical training. The same logic also applied to the equally unmathematical audiences of industrialists and middle-class consumers. Nineteenth-century drawings did not differentiate between different kinds of nonspecialists, and no visual language was widely used for purely esoteric communication. The implied reader of a patent drawing which uses these conventions thus occupies a subject position similar to the various nonspecialists of the nineteenth century. Just like financiers, artisanal mechanics, and the interested public, the reader of patent drawing finds himself or herself contemplating an object which is comprehensible three-dimensionally even if she/he has had no prior exposure to its mechanical principles.

By implying universal accessibility, the visual language of patent drawings—at least from the 1870s to the early 1980s—constructs the person skilled in the art as someone sharing many qualities with the hopeful loners of the nineteenth-century ideal of American inventorship. This isolated inventor, a kind of aspiring Thomas Edison, was thought to interact with the patent system mostly through published specifications instead of the workaday world of industrial laboratories and corporate patent policies. She/he would likewise gain knowledge by reading patents, not through academic or professional training, and would not be limited to one specific area of interest.[20] This mythical inventor would have seen no contradiction between disclosure and obviousness requirements—she/he was indeed ignorant but did not see the world's knowledge divided into disciplinary fiefdoms.

The association between patent drawings and nineteenth-century visual communication was often made explicit in patent-drawing handbooks, if perhaps unintentionally. In the mid-twentieth century, patent drafters were told that the conventions of shade and shadow were intended to "disclose the invention so clearly that any skilled mechanic could successfully construct the device with the use of these drawings and the specification," even though actual mechanics had come to rely increasingly on the kind of precise dimensions, tolerances, and assembly instructions eschewed in patent specifications.[21] This admonition was doubly contrived, since patent drawings were generally only seen by lawyers, patent examiners, and judges. Even though the actual audience for patent drawings did not include (nineteenth-century) mechanics, these skilled but relatively unspecialized craftsmen remained important as rhetorical readers, and the social roles encoded and reinforced by early industrial drawings remained present until the end of the twentieth century.

The Abandonment of Conventions, and a New Concept of Invention

Since the 1980s, the use of shade and shadow conventions in patent drawings has plummeted. From 1875 until the mid-1970s, roughly four-fifths of all patent drawings used conventions of shade lines or axonometric line weights, while in the year 2000 only around one-quarter of projective drawings attempted to convey three-dimensionality.[22] In the last few decades, the typical patent drawing has come to resemble the drawing shown in figure 3.13. According to the earlier guidelines, this drawing would not be legible "at a glance": it does not use shade, material codes, or even line weights. Most likely, it is easily comprehensible only to those who are already familiar with the relevant art, and it is more visually aligned with drawings used by mechanical engineers than with other patent drawings—note in particular the use of centerlines, a standard feature of engineering drawing that had long been banned from patents.

Why did this shift occur? And what significance does it have for understanding patents more generally? It might be tempting to see the abandonment of at-a-glance conventions as the result of computer-aided drafting or the general decline of drafting as a profession. After all, drafters had faced de-skilling throughout the twentieth century, and by the 1970s responsibility for technical drawing had been decisively transferred to technicians and engineers.[23] Specialized patent drafters were similarly rendered obsolete.[24] But if the Patent Office could maintain a peculiar drawing tradition separate from engineering practice for one hundred years, it seems unlikely that it could not still be maintained in a different labor environment. Computers can draw shade lines just as easily as any other kind of line, and there seems no reason why technicians or patent-preparers could not have taken on tasks previously assigned to professional drafters.

It is also clear that the retreat from traditional conventions was not due to changes in official requirements. The old rules are still published; patent lawyers have simply found that they are no longer "strictly enforced.... As a practical matter, all the Patent Office now wants are drawings of sufficient

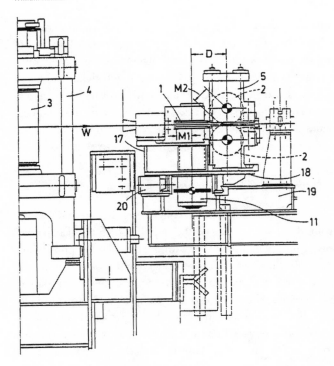

Figure 3.13. Drawing of a rolling mill train (U.S. patent 5,000,023; 1991): to the untrained eye, a jumble of lines with no shade, shadow, or hatch patterns.

quality to be ... suitable for reproduction."[25] The Patent Office's once rigid insistence on conventions that create a universal (nineteenth-century) visual language has simply withered—gradually and silently.

Rather than looking for external causes, I would suggest that the change in drawing conventions can best be understood in relation to other changes in the patent system: if drawing standards are no longer relevant, it is because many of the assumptions codified by traditional patent drawings have themselves been challenged. On the whole, the balance between the interests of the public and those of the inventor has been increasingly tipped in favor of the inventor. This is seen most clearly in the expanding range of patentable innovations. Some newly patentable ideas—such as computer software and biotechnology—seem just to track the changing state of the art, but a 1998 decision allowing the patentability of "business methods" suggested that even transformations of data were "a useful, concrete and tangible result" deserving of protection; this included patents for new financial instruments, Amazon.com's one-click purchasing, or Priceline.com's system of reverse auctions.[26] For activists against the patentability of data and software, patent rights are looking increasingly like a way to stifle competition instead of means of disclosing novelty to the public.[27]

Likewise, the 1982 creation of the Court of Appeals for the Federal Circuit has generally been beneficial to patentees. Previously, patent cases were adjudicated by the regional circuit courts, but the increasing complexity of patentable inventions had led to long case backlogs and somewhat arbitrary decisions.[28] Designed to replace the ignorance of regional court judges with a uniform system, the Federal Circuit has effectively centralized patent law and made other courts' opinions increasingly irrelevant. In the mid-1980s one of the Federal Circuit's own judges regretted its "eagerness to pronounce legal doctrines not immediately necessary to make our decisions," a fact he found doubly distressing because the creation of the court had also "reduce[d] the number of educated, intelligent people of the caliber of federal appellate judges who are thinking and writing about [patent] law."[29] As patent law has become the purview of an increasingly specialized (and usually pro-patent-rights) court, it is not surprising to find that since 1982 the number of patent holders having their claims upheld in court has doubled, from approximately one-third to two-thirds.[30]

The superhuman "person skilled in the art" used to test for obviousness has also been largely replaced by the humbler "person having ordinary skill in the art"—and the acronym PHOSITA is increasingly used in contrast to the older, less precise moniker.[31] A 1984 Federal Circuit decision indicated that the PHOSITA is "no longer presumed to have knowledge of all material prior art," and a 1986 decision explicitly stated that obviousness would be based on the "conventional wisdom in the art," not the allegedly subjective judgment of patent examiners applying analytical hindsight.[32] Since the late 1960s, "secondary conditions" like commercial success have also been allowed as tests for nonobviousness. These changes have real effects: judges have become more inclined to find that a complex patent is addressed to multiple PHOSITAs and have come to enforce different standards of disclosure and enablement for different fields. For example, in software patents, the courts are becoming less inclined to invalidate patents for inadequate disclosure, and less of the art of programming is required to be included in specifications: standard subroutines, firmware, and even unspecified work assumed to take as much as one year of programmer labor can be omitted.[33] Completely different guidelines are used in fields like biotechnology, where requirements for disclosure remain quite stringent, but almost no patents are invalidated due to obviousness.[34]

Taken by themselves, these changes seem like a somewhat piecemeal and incremental strengthening of intellectual property rights. But like a coal miner's canary, the concomitant change in patent drawings suggests that something larger is at stake, namely, the ideal audience of patents—and thus the identity of the inventor as well. If for most of the twentieth century the "person skilled in the art" had much in common with the aspiring (and mythical) lone inventor—a combination of machinist, engineer, and member of the general public, simultaneously uncreative and incredibly knowledgeable—the pretense of general accessibility has been increasingly dropped. Nonspecialist judges are no longer expected to understand patents, and machinists are no longer used as rhetorical readers. For the most part, patent drawings do not use traditional conventions, and they are directed to a reader who is well versed in the skills and assumptions of a specific field. Their visual tendency toward unity has been eliminated: disparate fields no longer share a universal visual language, and different drawings in the same patent can be directed to different audiences.

Patent drawings are now largely illegible to the public and are instead quite similar to the drawings that engineers use on a day-to-day basis. Gone, therefore, are the perhaps admirable goals of contributing to the universal amateur knowledge of the individual inventor and addressing the general public through a visual rhetoric designed for nonspecialists. But with the new emphasis on the "ordinary" skilled person, there is now greater correspondence between the patent system and the actual practice of innovation. For decades corporations have seen research as the product of interdisciplinary teamwork and long-term investment, not exceptional individual creativity—Monsanto's iconic "no geniuses here" is a fitting slogan for the PHOSITA.[35] In this environment, the creative inventor, visually as well as legally, is increasingly addressing ordinary colleagues and competitors, not some improbable savant simultaneously ignorant of common practice yet possessing encyclopedic knowledge of all prior art.

NOTES

1. I gratefully acknowledge the close readings and helpful comments of Kara Swanson, Daniel Margocsy, Mario Biagioli, Dan Kevles, Jimena Canales, and two anonymous reviewers.

2. See Biagioli, this volume. See also Harold Dutton, *The Patent System and Inventive Activity during the Industrial Revolution, 1750–1852* (Manchester: Manchester University Press, 1984). For comparison with systems of registration, see Christine MacLeod, *Inventing the Industrial Revolution: The English Patent System, 1660–1800* (Cambridge: Cambridge University Press, 1988), 43–54; or in the United States between 1793 and 1836, Edward Walterscheid, *To Promote the Progress of Useful Arts* (Littleton, CO: Rothman, 1998), 11ff, and U.S. Patent Office Society, *Outline of the History of the United States Patent Office* (Washington, DC: Patent Office Society, 1936), 19–55.

3. This connection is made clear in court opinions that distinguish "invention" and "skill." For example, see Amos Hart, *Digest of Decisions of Law and Practice in the Patent Office . . . 1886–1898* (Chicago: Callahan, 1898), 224–227.

4. I discuss the importance of these changes to questions of disclosure and the concept of invention in a separate article, forthcoming.

5. Patent 6,314,440, apparently the longest patent ever issued. The Patent Office does prohibit excess prolixity, which may serve to obscure more than it discloses.

6. Before the 1880s, drawings could be used to revise a patent's claims after it had been issued. This is no longer true, but unclaimed novelty shown in drawings still establishes prior art. For cases since the 1880s, see Ernest Lipscomb, *Lipscomb's Walker on Patents* (Rochester, NY: Lawyers Co-Operative, 1984), vol. 1, secs. 4:9 and 4:32.

7. Harry Radzinsky, *Making Patent Drawings* (New York: Macmillan, 1945), 21–26.

8. Jeffrey Sheldon, *How to Write a Patent Application*, release 14 (New York: Practising Law Institute, 2004), 6-74 to 6-78.

9. On the peculiarities of plant patents, or patents on life more generally, see Kevles, this volume, and Sherman and Pottage, this volume. Compare to the copyright registration process described in Adrian Johns, *The Nature of the Book* (Chicago: University of Chicago Press, 1998).

10. Early plant patents—the first was issued in 1931—were accompanied by color drawings or watercolors; I am grateful to Dan Kevles for bringing these drawings to my attention. In industrial patents, photographs (usually microscopic) tend to be used in similar ways, such as when the visual disclosure of a biological or metallurgical process would not necessarily establish reduction to practice or help identify the successful use (or infringement) of the patent.

11. As first laid out in *Hotchkiss v. Greenwood* (1850), all inventions were to be nonobvious to "an ordinary mechanic acquainted with the business," but this was expanded to the broader sense above in the Patent Act of 1952. See Cyril Soans, "Some Absurd Presumptions in Patent Cases," *IDEA* 10 (1966); Michael Ebert, "Superperson and the Prior Art," *Journal of the Patent and Trademark Office Society* 67 (1985); and John Tesansky, "PHOSITA—The Ubiquitous and Enigmatic Person in Patent Law," *JPTOS* 73 (1991). For a more general discussion of patent audience, see Greg Myers, "From Discovery to Invention: The Writing and Rewriting of Two Patents," *Social Studies of Science* 25 (1995).

12. Ebert, "Superperson," 657.

13. These guidelines have appeared in the semiperiodical *General Information Concerning Patents* (Washington, DC: USPTO) since 1922. For earlier—and similar—guidelines, starting in 1870, see E. J. Stoddard, *Annotated Rules of Practice in the United States Patent Office* (Detroit: Drake, 1920).

14. *Manual of Patent Examining Procedure* (Washington, DC: USPTO, May 2004), 600-94.

15. This graph is based on surveys of one hundred consecutive patents from the third week of January, every twelve or thirteen years, as published in the *Official Gazette of the United States Patent Office* (Washington, DC: USPTO). Before 1952, patent issues are not grouped by category, and drawing types are presumably randomly distributed. After 1952, weekly patent issues have been grouped into three categories: General and Mechanical, Chemical, and Electrical. For years since 1952, I sampled consecutive patents from these categories in proportion to the relative number of total patents in each category. Data before and after 1952 are thus not directly comparable, but given the overall continuity of this graph it seems reasonable to draw qualitative conclusions. Any residuals in post-1952 data will be consistent, and relatively small.

16. I discuss the convergence of patent and engineering drawings in a separate article, forthcoming. The later separation of patent and engineering drawing can be traced through textbooks. Compare Anson Cross, *Mechanical Drawing* (Boston: Ginn, 1898); Thomas French, *A Manual of Engineering Drawing* (New York: McGraw-Hill, 1941); and Frank Zozzora, *Engineering Drawing*

(New York: McGraw-Hill, 1958). For specialized manuals see Radzinsky, *Making Patent Drawings*; or the official *Guide for Patent Draftsmen* (Washington, DC: USPTO), published erratically between 1953 and 1989.

17. On color washes in working drawings, see M. Armengaud the Elder, *The Practical Draughtsman's Book of Industrial Design and Machinist's and Engineer's Drawing Companion*, trans. William Johnson (Philadelphia: Baird, 1871), 122.

18. For material coding in patent drawings, see "Official Rules and Directions for Proceedings in the Patent Office," reprinted in Munn & Co., *The United States Patent Law* (New York: Munn & Co., 1867), 21–34. Drawings of the Great Eastern are reproduced in Ken Baynes and Francis Pugh, *The Art of the Engineer* (Guildford, UK: Lutterworth, 1981). The ultimate reason that light comes from the left is perhaps only because most people are right-handed. In seventeenth-century Dutch studio painting, light always came from the left, since this arrangement of subject and easel allowed right-handed artists to paint without obscuring their work with their arm. The convention persisted in nonstudio painting. See Svetlana Alpers, "The Studio, the Laboratory, and the Vexations of Art," in *Picturing Science, Producing Art*, ed. Caroline A. Jones and Peter Galison (New York: Routledge, 1998).

19. For these examples, see Peter Jeffrey Booker, *A History of Engineering Drawing* (London: Chatto & Windus, 1963), 141. See also Wolfgang Lefèvre, "The Limits of Pictures," in *The Power of Images in Early Modern Science*, ed. Lefèvre, Jurge Renn, and Urs Schoepflin (Basel: Birkhäuser, 2003).

20. For the contradictions inherent in this persona with respect to text and authorship, see Swanson, this volume. This kind of inventor was explicitly the audience for the early *Official Gazette*, which might reach those without access to a large city library. See *Annual Report of the Commissioner of Patents for the Year 1871* (Washington, DC: USGPO, 1872), 10–11.

21. Radzinsky, *Making Patent Drawings*, 21.

22. Statistic based on the survey of patents described above, excluding electrical or chemical diagrams, flowcharts, and other miscellaneous drawing types.

23. Changes in textbooks make these changes especially apparent. See W. L. Healy and A. H. Rau, *Simplified Drafting Practice* (New York: Wiley, 1953); Thomas E. French and Charles J. Vierck, *Graphic Science and Design*, 3d ed. (New York: McGraw-Hill, 1970); and Frederick E. Giesecke, et al., *Technical Drawing with Computer Graphics* (New York: Macmillan, 1985).

24. Until recently the Patent Office published pamphlets like the *Guide for Patent Draftsmen*—a title which indicated that such a group existed—and maintained its own staff of drafters. The 1922 edition of *General Information Concerning Patents* states that "the office will furnish the drawings at cost, as promptly as its draftsmen can make them for applicants who can not otherwise conveniently procure them" (7). This line was omitted from the 1985 edition, and the *Guide for Patent Draftsmen* was discontinued in 1989. It has been replaced by privately published books such as Jack Lo and David Pressman, *How to Make Patent Drawings Yourself* (Berkeley, CA: Nolo Press, 1999).

25. Sheldon, *Write a Patent Application*, 5–21.

26. Computer software was held patentable in 1981 (*Diamond v. Diehr*), and guidelines were officially promulgated in 1995. Biotechnology was deemed patentable in 1980 (*Diamond v. Chakrabarty*) and business methods in 1998 (*State Street Bank & Trust Company v. Signature Financial Group, Inc.*).

27. This is a prominent theme in activists' comparisons between pending EU legislation and U.S. practice. See for example Richard Stallman, "Patent Absurdity," *Guardian*, June 20, 2005, or http://www.nosoftwarepatents.com (accessed May 2009).

28. The introduction to the "Act to Establish a United States Court of Appeals for the Federal Circuit" (April 2, 1982; 96 Stat. 25) discusses this rationale. Within the Seventh Circuit, for example,

it was said that "at the district level, patent cases would be decided by flipping a quarter. But the Appellate Court knew better—they'd use a half-dollar." (Communication of James Rankin, erstwhile Seventh-Circuit clerk, December 2004.)

29. Both quotes from Senior Circuit Judge Nichols, cited in Robert Harmon, *Patents and the Federal Circuit* (Washington, DC: Bureau of National Affairs, 1988), ix–x.

30. "Patent Wars," *Economist*, April 8–14, 2000.

31. The first use of the acronym seems to be in Soans, "Some Absurd Presumptions"; it was not in common use by 1991 (see Tesansky, "PHOSITA"), but since the mid-1990s it has become widespread.

32. Tesansky, "PHOSITA," 40–41.

33. Sheldon, *Write a Patent Application*, 7-22 to 7-27.

34. Burk and Lemley, "Policy Levers in Patent Law," *Virginia Law Review* 89 (2003): 1650, 1680.

35. Not all legal scholars see the shift in patents' implied audience—from machinists to professional researchers—as a good thing; see Jonathan Darrow, "The Neglected Dimension of Patent Law's PHOSITA Standard," *Harvard Journal of Law & Technology* 23 (Fall 2009).

Before and after the Commons and Traditional Knowledge

ROSEMARY J. COOMBE

4

Cultural Agencies
The Legal Construction of Community Subjects and Their Properties

New holders of intellectual properties and other rights in intangible cultural heritage are emerging to make distinctive claims under the auspices of international treaties, conventions, international customary law, and human rights norms.[1] These new collectivities and the social movements in which they figure often stress local priorities, needs, and place-based cultural values, but their activities are shaped by the activities of external actors, global networks of influence, and transnationally circulating documents, as well as by international norms and fields of publicity. To understand the relationships among these activities, we need to take the measure of a transnational, multiscalar politics in which diverse actors engage in practices of articulation that draw upon a range of legal and normative resources.

In these transnational processes, communities are in important ways imagined, "traditions" are often invented and "cultures" seem to be emerging everywhere in legal guise (Coombe 2005b, 2010). Nonetheless, simple assertions of social constructivism seem woefully inadequate as a form of critique in these contexts. There is little doubt that many new cultural collectivities making possessive claims do so as market actors for economic purposes (Comaroff & Comaroff 2009).

However, the recognition of collective identities and values has also become a means by which international agencies such as development donors as well as various nongovernmental organizations (NGOs) act transnationally to locate investments, invest energies, and demonstrate their progressive intentions. Simultaneously the assertion of collective values may enable peoples linked into larger social movements to express aspirations for distinctive livelihoods and alternative futures. Control over traditional knowledge, for example, has become a crucial nexus where development industry desires to locate social capital, and invest in market-based cultural goods come up against rights-based struggles for recognition and autonomy. Intellectual property policy is being forged to address both sets of interests.

New social movements struggle to incorporate traditional knowledge within the global frameworks of indigenous and human rights rather than the trade-based commodity logic of existing intellectual property regimes in the hope that the former will provide a normative counterweight to the market forms that states and transnational development agencies ask those who bear cultural distinction to embrace (Coombe, Schnoor, & Ahmed 2007). Critical explorations of emerging global politics with respect to intellectual property do need to address the interpellation of market-based subjectivities in which possessive relationships to culture become naturalized (e.g., Comaroff & Comaroff 2009), but they also need to attend to local values and aspirations as these are expressed in the ideals of transnational social movements that inspire rights claims to cultural goods (Coombe 2009).

Legal Subjects and Governmentalities' Agents

The anthropologist Clifford Geertz (1983) once observed that law creates the facts it purports merely to recognize. This includes the subjects it recognizes and the subject positions it affords. As Marxist theorists note, a possessive, rights-bearing subject is called forth by forms of capital accumulation as a matter of legal ideology, interpellation, and consciousness (Collier, Maurer, & Suarez-Navaz 2001, Frow 1996). These perspectives were also elaborated by poststructuralist attention to the force of legal policy in shaping ideals for modern selves (Miller 1993). Legal anthropologists have illustrated that identities are forged in accommodation and in resistance to law and that communities and localities are forged in relation to legal representations and their interpretations (Mertz 1994: 1243). Critical and constitutive theories of law (Greenhouse 1994) also recognize law's productive capacities—its provision of generative conditions for articulating social realities and resources for those seeking new forms of political recognition: "The law must be understood not simply as an institutional forum or legitimating discourse to which social groups turn to have preexisting differences recognized but, more crucially, as a central locus for the control and dissemination of those signifying forms with which difference is made and remade. The signifying forms around which political action mobilizes and with which social rearticulations are accomplished are attractive and compelling precisely because of the powers legally bestowed upon them" (Coombe 1998: 37). Critical theories of personhood and property, moreover, have increasingly shown that the relationships between the legal construction of persons and the natural realities of individuality and sociality are radically contingent (Pottage & Mundy 2004: 3). Rather than focusing on the degree of their correspondence, we might consider how the emergence and deployment of law's categories through distinctive technologies comes to constitute a world of opportunities as well as constraints, political options as well as foreclosures.

Some of the richest interdisciplinary scholarship on intellectual property has explored the law and society tenet that identities do not exist before the law but are forged in relation to law and the subject positions it affords. Work considering how both the subject position of the author and specific forms of authorial creativity are legitimated by copyright law (Gibson 2006, Rose 1993, Woodmansee & Jaszi 1993, Woodmansee 2000), how publicity rights enable celebrity personas (Gaines 1991, 2005, Lury 1993), and how early trademark laws worked to constitute national consumer subjects (Coombe 1998) has illustrated the constitutive character of intellectual property law. This recognition of intellectual property's productive capacities needs to be extended into the globalized contexts in which intellectual property and other related cultural rights are being extended.

Intellectual property laws are one means by which attachments and entitlements to "intangibles" such as expressive works and heritage goods are forged. Under neoliberal conditions, this work is done not only by states but by NGOs whose agencies validate new forms of knowledge held by newly empowered subjects, such as the traditional environmental knowledge recognized as being held by indigenous and local communities under the Convention on Biological Diversity (CBD). An "assemblage of legal practices, legal institutions, statutes, legal codes, authorities, discourses, texts, norms and forms of judgment" (Rose & Valverde 1998: 542) is now doing the work of interpellation in fields where new rights are negotiated and collective subjects are recognized and invested with new responsibilities for managing cultural goods.

Considerations of negotiations over new forms of intellectual property would be more fruitfully approached with these insights in mind. For example, international deliberations about the best means to protect traditional environmental knowledge, innovations and practices (hereinafter "traditional knowledge") have engaged governments, NGOs, indigenous peoples, the World Trade Organization, the Trade-Related Aspects of Intellectual Property Rights Council, the World Intellectual Property Organization (WIPO), the Conference of the Parties to the CBD, and numerous UN bodies over the past twenty years. So-called local and traditional communities as well as those politically acknowledged as "indigenous" are understood to make substantial contributions to the preservation and maintenance of biological diversity and, through their traditional knowledge, to biotechnology's inventions but are excluded from the benefits that accrue from the use of their knowledge and innovations in commerce. Whether one accepts this narrative as an objective truth (Mgbeoji 2005), insists that it is a romantic and dangerous fiction to be denied (Chen 2006), or understands it politically as one pillar of new social movements (Coombe 2005a), there is simply no denying the energies, hopes, and aspirations that attend to it or the years of deliberative effort that have been poured into resolving this perceived problem. Nor should we ignore the ways in which countries of the Global South have found in this narrative a new form of global intellectual property and trade policy leverage.

In any case, we need to move beyond the question of whether this new imposition of neoliberal rationality adequately describes or represents a society that preexists it, to critically consider how it operates to produce new forms of knowledge, expertise, and identity that govern new domains of regulation, such as environmentalist regimes of sustainable development with their valuations of biological diversity (Harvey 2001, Watts 2000) and heritage regimes with their registers of cultural diversity (Hafstein 2009). Moreover, as nature and "life itself" (Franklin 2000, Rose 2007) are drawn into the economic discourse of efficient resource management, and both genetic resources and traditional knowledge are represented as works and innovations to be exchanged under the logic of informational capital (Coombe 2003, Parry 2004), new subjects must be found to broker these transactions.

Although they are *not* uniformly popular and may indeed be inappropriate, variations on intellectual property rights are recommended as solutions to the problems that the historical lack of recognition and compensation for traditional knowledge has created (as means to ensure appropriate "access and benefit sharing," to secure practices of prior informed consent, to demand disclosures of origin and respect for customary law, and to prevent practices of corporate misappropriation). In these ongoing policy-making efforts, norms and subjects coevolve and are coproduced (to use the useful vocabulary of science and technology studies; see Reardon 2005).

WIPO has taken up these issues through an intergovernmental commit-tee (IGC) that has been convening regularly and developing new guidelines for intellectual property policy with respect to genetic resources, traditional knowledge, and traditional cultural expressions since 2001. Simultaneously, UNESCO steered the Intangible Cultural Heritage Convention to bring it into force in April 2006 and facilitated the passage of the Convention on Cultural Diversity, which went into force in 2007. These international instru-ments share legitimating narratives that proceed from recognition of distinc-tive values (biodiversity and cultural diversity), coupled with a presumption of their impending loss, to recognize new holders of rights in distinctive intan-gibles, who are thereby deemed to have an incentive to preserve, maintain, and develop these cultural resources in a sustainable fashion (or at least to prevent their misappropriation). The homology of purpose and plan across these in-struments is not insignificant. Governmental intervention takes place through the use of assemblages—abstractable, mobile, and dynamic forms that traverse and reconstitute society, culture, and economy (Ong & Collier 2005, Perry & Maurer 2003). Fact-finding missions, government recognition and compi-lation of best practices, material transfer agreements, inventories, and com-munity research protocols are all legal technologies in the area of intellectual property that constitute new forms of governmental intervention.

Under neoliberal conditions the devolution of the management of distinc-tive cultural identities and resources is arguably a distinct form of subjectifi-cation. Recognition of "indigenous and local communities embodying tradi-tional lifestyles relevant for the conservation and sustainable use of biological diversity," for example, might be considered as an interpellation of culturally objectivized collective subjects—new forms of collective personhood de-signed for state ends and overdetermined by international legal requirements and multilateral institutional demands. The UNESCO Convention on the Safeguarding of the Intangible Cultural Heritage also functions to constitute communities as new subjects while it locates the heritage resources they are now invited or enjoined to protect (Albro 2007, Blake 2009, Hafstein 2007). Population groups are "subjectified" as communities and their practices "ob-jectified" as intangible cultural heritage or as evidence of cultural diversity through these demands for their participation. To paraphrase Arun Agrawal's discussion of natural resource management (substituting "intellectual prop-erty" for "environment" and "cultural resources" for "forest resources"):

> It would be fair to say that changes in human subjectivities, as these occur
> concomitantly with changes in institutionalized governance of [intellectual

property], are the least well understood and investigated of all [intellectual property] related changes. Institutional strategies to govern [cultural resources]—to allocate, to monitor, to sanction, to enforce, to adjudicate—do not simply constrain the actions of already existing sovereign subjects. Nor is it the case that people's responses to new forms of regulatory strategies are exhausted by the continuum between resistance and conformity. Instead, it is important to recognize how these strategies and their effects on flows of power shape human subjects, their interests, and their agency. (2003: 258)

Community "Stakeholders"

Just as critical intellectual property scholars caution us against the "romance of the public domain" (Chander & Sunder 2004), critical social scientists caution us against the romance of community, most recently and relevantly through critical ethnographic studies of community-based natural resource management regimes (Agrawal & Gibson 2001, Brosius 1997, Brosius, Tsing, & Zerner 1998, 2005). Widespread preoccupations with mythic communities—small, harmonious, integrated, isolated groups using locally evolved norms to manage resources sustainably—may operate to blind policy makers to internal divisions, local politics, and multiscalar strategic alliances. Policies that insist upon locating a commons and a suitably "corporate" property-owning social group as the relevant designated community as a condition for extending rights and directing investments may exclude many of the world's poor (Li 2005). In many parts of the world, people indigenous to a region are not formed into bounded groups with a clear sense of territorial possession (Li 2000, Tsing 1999). Many peoples have been historically displaced and their migration to new areas encouraged; efforts by the World Bank and NGOs in such regions to map well-defined units of indigenous groups and associated territory may be misguided and, in the worst-case scenario, do new forms of social violence. A constitutive legal perspective, however, might be less concerned with ascertaining who the "natural" social actors for such policies are or should be and more concerned with the realities such mappings propound.

Rather than positing or refuting the positivity of communities, then, we might attempt to focus on community-making processes. Critical scholarship on the environmental politics of community-based natural resource management suggests that communities form in contexts and for purposes of engagement with other institutions; they will present themselves in the fashion that attracts powerful interlocutors at different levels of power (Li 2000). In this they are often assisted by other actors such as NGOs who may be adept at deploying the political rhetoric that enamors metropolitan audiences to their causes. In such engagements, communities draw upon available legal resources and subject positions to attract state resources and NGO investments, resist some capitalist development industries, and encourage others. We should keep this in mind when we consider the extension of collective rights to traditional knowledge, intangible cultural heritage, and the possession of traditional cultural expressions. The evocation of community in cultural resource management will be used to further diverse agendas, just as it did in the field of natural resource management (Brosius, Tsing, & Zerner 1998, 2005). There, "conservationists hoped to involve local people as a means of protecting biological diversity, development organizations [driven in part by past criticisms] aimed to promote local participation . . . activists hoped to empower local groups . . . [while] indigenous peoples' advocates aspired to new forms of recognition and political rights based on their cultural knowledge" (ibid.). A similar set of agendas is clearly at work in the principles animating the Convention on Intangible Cultural Heritage (Smith & Akagawa 2009), and the Convention on Cultural Diversity (Beat Graber 2008), both of which provide new rationales for transforming intellectual property protections.

Many early scholars of environmentalism ignored the diverse agencies and objectives at work in community-based management schemes. Instead, they scrutinized the "fictions" of community, territory, and tradition used to further these social and political agendas. If advocates used these concepts romantically, however, critical scholars glorified their own critical and ironic stance toward "social construction," thereby reducing genuine political dilemmas, environmental needs, livelihood struggles, and local aspirations to philosophical problems of essentialism (Brosius, Tsing, & Zerner 2005: 159–160) and its perceived dangers. We should strive to avoid the same reductionist forms of critique in our considerations of global intellectual property politics. Simple allegations of essentialism (strategic or otherwise), sitings of social construction, and accusations of romanticism reveal a profound lack of political sensitivity to the fields of power and leverage in which peoples struggle for recognition, resources, and opportunity: "Community is important because it is typically seen as a locus of *knowledge*; a site of *regulation* and management; a source of *identity* and a repository of *tradition*; the embodiment of various *institutions* (say, property rights), which necessarily turn on questions of representation, power, authority, governance, and accountability; an object of *state control*; and a theatre of *resistance* and struggle (of social movements and potentially of *alternative visions of development*)" (Watts 2000: 37, italics in original).

Given the intense density of its referents and connotations, community cannot be invoked as a unity—an undifferentiated political actor that speaks with a single voice of truth to a singular site of power. It is better assessed in terms of the forms of governance (quality of representation, democracy, transparency, and accountability) it enables. Certainly many anthropological studies of bioprospecting and alleged biopiracy (Berlin & Berlin 2004, Brown 2003, Greene 2004, Hayden 2003a, 2003b) illustrate the performative politics, strategic entrepreneurialism, and perverse consequences that may ensue when knowledge is objectified and community reified. In the shadow of national laws yet to be promulgated and obligatory norms of consent and benefit sharing, those groups with the greatest access to powerful external actors have had considerably more leverage to assume representative roles for cultural collectivities. To the extent that international treaties and emerging legal norms demand that communities provide consent for the use of their knowledge and resources, such communities must be found, and if they cannot be located on one scale, those bearing obligations to secure consent will inevitably find "communities" at another scale who are prepared to bargain.

Nonetheless, as Joshua Rosenthal (2006) points out in an exploration of collaborative biodiversity research projects, difficulties in locating appropriate communities are better understood in terms of the presence or absence of a clearly defined governance hierarchy that establishes consenting authority. Such authorities may change over time, different communities may share knowledge traditions, and national laws may fail to recognize indigenous governance structures, but these issues are far from insurmountable. Autonomous, established, credible, and politically representative indigenous governance systems with participatory processes exist in many parts of the world, if only at the village level; where political institutions do not exist to facilitate deliberations among and between such communities to provide consent, he suggests that activists and researchers have a responsibility to support their creation (126). This is a task that is increasingly taken up by diverse transnational agencies.

NGOs and Indigenous Politics

International institutions and NGOs clearly play important roles in the process of mobilizing communities to claim rights to resources and traditional knowledge. Indigenous peoples have strategically used their new role in biodiversity politics, for example, as a means to effect an institutionalization of their territorial and political rights while calling international attention to capitalist accumulation through their dispossession. For some scholars, it seems that the existence of foreign agents and external interventions in the political emergence of indigenous agencies and identities makes such politics automatically suspect. For example, geographer Raymond Bryant (2002) calls our attention to the role of NGOs in the politics of biodiversity governance where implementation of the Biodiversity Convention has enabled new forms of governance in which indigenous persons were positioned, first as "partners in parks management," and then as "custodians of ancestral domains." National indigenous rights NGOs secured ancestral domain claims and community forest stewardship agreements while tutoring indigenous groups in the political means of asserting claims and in the arts of negotiation.

The NGO effort to document ancestral domains by mapping natural resources and their local cultural usages in the Philippines, Bryant feared, constituted a voluntary provision of a large mass of hitherto little-known data that would inevitably enable greater state control and surveillance in these areas. Bryant cautioned that peoples might be tied to territories (particular, usually marginal environments) and their rights to resources frozen according to knowledge gleaned only at one particular point in time. Still, it is important to understand that the Ancestral Domain Program was a response to the perceived moral and political *shortcomings* of the previous (1985–2000) foreign-donor-led Integrated Protected Areas System (IPAS) conservation project. Under that system, local communities were seen as in need of education, and their capacities were "enhanced" by a range of third-party experts. Scientists specified which areas needed protecting, where priorities should lie, and what values sites should be accorded, while mapping and monitoring these areas using information technologies in which their own capabilities were valorized. Local residents' access to resources was dictated by outside evaluations of local livelihood activities as biodiversity-enhancing or biodiversity-endangering. Community leaders and sympathetic NGOs feared that resource-based livelihoods would be jeopardized by external agents unable to appreciate worldviews that sustained livelihoods based on fishing, hunting, agriculture, handicrafts production, or the collection of birds' nests.

The lack of opportunity indigenous peoples were afforded to influence the design of this system seems to have spurred a parallel effort to map traditional territories considered politically crucial to indigenous communities bent on establishing rights to ecosystems whose conservation they deemed their own accomplishment and responsibility. Given this history of environmental governance, the Ancestral Domain Program, which affirmed local people's knowledge and recognized local resource entitlements, was considered a big improvement. Such affirmations might have been especially welcome because they resonated with a global rights-based indigenous movement that was accruing adherents and political influence in this country by the early 1990s.

The Indigenous People's Rights Act of 1997 recognized those indigenous to the Philippines as distinctive peoples with distinctive traditions, laws, and practices. Still, the process of settling indigenous ancestral claims was a protracted one and "there were genuine concerns that protected conservation areas would be finalized prior to the settlement of ancestral claims" (Bryant 2000: 691). Although ancestral claims do not provide full legal control over resources, they are considered important milestones on the way to a comprehensive settlement of indigenous claims. For rural peoples in the Philippines, as elsewhere, conservation is only meaningful if it is part of a wider recognition of their occupancy of relevant territories and the ways in which they have lived within them. To the extent that people have managed historically to protect their ancestral domains, they have thereby also protected its biodiversity, and only if they can protect their livelihoods are any partnerships feasible. Conservation and protection, I suggest, are tropes that serve to marshal one set of social actors' concerns about pending resource scarcity to meet another set of social actors' anxieties about maintaining livelihood security.

It is not difficult, then, to see why landscapes become culturalized so that they bear the distinctive signature of a traditional community, whose livelihood practices, recoded as distinctive management systems, require recognition and conservation. Safeguarding local resource use is given a different priority and articulated with a larger movement of rights-based politics when it is recoded as recognition of an aboriginal cultural attachment to territory. Greater respect for local decision making—increasingly recoded as respect for customary law—is but one example of how neoliberal discursive resources are being politically shifted to serve the interests of local political autonomy. A full exploration of this phenomenon would need to be situated in a larger discussion about the increasing number of peoples with "substantive economies" (Nash 2001) who have embraced an indigenous identity and thus come, by invitation or otherwise, to reflect upon the nature of their cultures when resisting or negotiating their incorporation into new forms of "market citizenship" (Coombe 2010, Harvey 2001).

Biodiversity protection has always been coupled with new forms of capital accumulation (McAfee 1999). In the Philippines, as elsewhere, these included the promotion of bioprospecting and ecotourism projects as alternatives to logging and fishing (Bryant 2000: 684). As a consequence, the Ancestral Domain Program put the protection of indigenous peoples' intellectual property rights squarely on the table. The regime clearly tied biological to cultural diversity, promising that recognition of local knowledge would revitalize traditional customs and patterns of sharing knowledge. While the former IPAS regime used the crisis of species extinction to impose technical solutions, the new initiative focused on the cultural meaning surrounding specific socionatural activities, asserting an integrated and localized sense of "nature-culture" in which local cultural narratives about emplaced group history were central (ibid.). For peoples who have long been defined as objects for state intervention and management, the capacity to self-identify and to tell their own stories about the places in which they have lived—and to map their own histories of association with place—is politically significant. Bryant himself provides evidence that this process worked to build group identity and esteem and strengthened a sense of cultural community among some peoples who developed a new appreciation for their own knowledge (ibid.: 700). In short, even if they had no cultural identities as communities that preexisted this legal process, some empowered communities with a possessive relationship to their culture emerged as a *consequence* of this project.

Concessions wielded from the state in the form of self-governance rights, Bryant suggested (2002: 280–281), were primarily effective as means of incorporating indigenous peoples into the "normal" practices of Philippine political life. Recognition from the state, however, is hardly an insignificant matter for many indigenous peoples. Visibility may be politically preferable to invisibility but only if it is accompanied by voice. Ironically, it is precisely *as* "traditional" communities with unique contributions to make that many social groups are receiving state and international attention as full participants in "modernity" and in the alleviation of its crises (see also Coombe 2010). Admittedly the provision of extensive maps, the location and traditional usage of biodiversity resources, and other knowledge and information to the state is accompanied by certain risks, particularly if the state refuses to respect international principles of indigenous rights and opens up ancestral territories to exploitative encroachment. Arguably this becomes more difficult to accomplish under the increased international scrutiny that environmental and indigenous rights regimes invite. In their larger struggles for autonomy, moreover, indigenous peoples may inscribe their own forms of governance within neoliberal management schemes (O'Malley 1996) that resist and deflect state agencies. By virtue of alliances forged with other indigenous peoples in indigenist politics (Niezen 2003), they may also share these strategies in quests for new forms of sovereignty within and beyond the modern nation state.

Perhaps the real problem for peoples in the Philippines was not their sudden visibility but the lens through which they were viewed. To the extent that global environmental institutions constitute "communities," they have a tendency to view them "from above" based on a series of visualization methods or "state simplifications" designed to make communities "legible" (Brosius 2006). States and international organizations produce modern global templates that tend to "overwrite the specificities of location" (ibid.: 228) even when they attempt to validate knowledge that is traditional or local. As implemented, the Philippines Ancestral Domain Program, didn't merely misrepresent local political realities but fundamentally misrecognized the nature of the traditional resource use it purported to respect by assuming a simple relationship between a bounded territory and a bounded group. Indigenous notions of land tenure, however, appeared to be based upon practices and expectations rather than boundaries; they were dynamic and shifting rather than fixed or static, and they anticipated multiple contemporaneous uses rather than distinct and fixed zones of usage (Gatmaytan 2005: 463).

The irony is that legislation that "was supposed to be the state's answer to the indigenous people's demands for respect for their cultures" by demanding a monolithic national grid of group communal ownership in the face of local complexities and contingencies imposed uniformity in the face of cultural difference (ibid.: 468–469). For decades, peoples who identified as indigenous in the Philippines demanded state recognition of their rights to self-determination, an international concept that includes customary territorial and resource rights. The original political demand for self-determination, however, was reduced to a mechanistic legal procedure for determining who owned what lands; by linking simple notions of group recognition to specific parcels of land, communities and territories were indeed formed, but indigenous tenure systems were ignored as the basis of these distinctive substantive livelihoods. Moreover, recognition of the distinctive contribution of indigenous peoples to the national political community was avoided. Lawyers and NGOs who "interposed themselves between a state with little institutional cultural sensitivity and indigenous peoples and communities who are still developing their own links to the state, media, and other sources of power" (469) and thereby arrogated to themselves the task of translation were complicit in this process.

At first glance, it may appear that we have strayed a long way from intellectual property issues. However, I would suggest that the academic literature on community in environmental politics is important for a consideration of indigenous political and cultural rights struggles and their intellectual property interests. This is not simply because it provides cautions and homologies but because the agencies, institutions, and principles of environmental governance preexist those of intellectual property, intangible heritage, and cultural diversity protection in so many parts of the world. Environmental regimes may precede legal recognition of indigenous peoples and their rights and have occasionally been the pretext for them. The subjects, objects, and mappings these regimes have put into place provide templates that, for better or worse, are likely to shape expectations for and allocations of intellectual property rights. International policy makers ask governments, development agencies, and NGOs to consider cultural diversity to be as endangered as biological diversity and in need of similar kinds of intervention; biocultural diversity is a hybrid policy metaphor that acknowledges their interdependence (Zent & Zent 2007). The metaphor of sustainability, drawn from the environmental field, has also been promoted as a more sensitive means for approaching cultural resources than those provided by the dominant informational matrix (Jaszi & Woodmansee 2003).

To return to the Philippines as our example, maps of community territories demarcated for the purpose of natural resource management, then elaborated to make claims to ancestral territories, were presented by the Philippines to the 1999 WIPO IGC meetings as natural boundaries for access and benefit-sharing agreements with respect to genetic resources and for the recognition of traditional knowledge. The Philippines also delivered a Community Intellectual Rights Protection Act (2001 draft) to the WIPO IGC as a planned sui generis law for the protection of traditional knowledge in 2002 (Gibson 2006: 139), drawing upon these preexisting regimes of environmental governmentality. The Intellectual Property Office of the Philippines continues to assert the country's status as a megadiverse country with valuable and unique biodiversity to protect, decries biopiracy, regulates access to genetic resources, asserts the desirability of developing its genetic materials, encourages commercial research agreements with transnational institutions, and urges local scientists and inventors to apply for patents on innovations derived from the country's unique species (IP Philippines 2008). This is the neoliberal policy matrix in which the CBD principle of sharing benefits with local and indigenous communities as custodians of these resources becomes the rationale for further amending "the Indigenous Peoples Rights Act to clarify and enhance the indigenous peoples' intellectual property rights over their knowledge and various uses of genetic resources" (ibid.).

Over the past fifteen years, however, Philippines-based NGOs and intergovernmental organizations such as the Tebtebba Foundation and the South Centre have worked tirelessly in international policy fora, often in coordination with environmental advocates such as the Centre for International Environmental Law, to insist that intellectual property rights in traditional knowledge instead serve sustainable development objectives and further establish indigenous human rights principles (e.g., CIEL 2007). Their leaders have moved these concerns from environmental into indigenous policy-making fora, where they join forces with representatives of aboriginal peoples from Canada and Australia and forest-dwelling and pastoral peoples from Africa as well as highly organized indigenous peoples from Latin America—to assert their own alternative visions of development. Again, neoliberal governance structures are met with proposals for intellectual property articulated through the rhetoric of human rights.

Conversations about the interrelationship of biological and cultural diversity have also been ongoing in Colombia, where for two decades an insistence on going beyond intellectual property and rejecting trade-based models for understanding their resources and their knowledge have occupied the creative energies of legal, indigenous, and Afro-Colombian community activists (Correal 1998, Escobar 2008, Florez 1998, Hurtado 1998, Pombo 1998, Sertje 2003, Ulloa 2005, Valencia 1998, Wilshusen 2006). Despite increasing levels of violence and instability in the region, Afro-Colombian transnational advocates continue to stress the dangers of free trade agreements to rural communities and the continuing need for what they refer to as community intellectual rights (e.g., Murillo-Urrutia 2007).

Taking advantage of a new national constitution that stresses pluralism, cultural difference, and collective rights to land and cultural identity (Chaves 1998), Colombian activists seized upon perceived urgencies with respect to biodiversity preservation in the 1990s to forge collective "biocultural territories" through cultural mappings of local resource use that affirmed local livelihoods and values while asserting traditional knowledge as the basis for social reproduction, food security, and alternative development. Such "life projects" (Escobar 2008: 146–153, Blaser, Feit, & McRae 2004), as they were developed in the Colombian Pacific region, energized Afro-Colombian peoples who came to understand themselves politically as communities in this process. Alternative, community-authored representations of traditional practices of resource use have been prepared for environmental projects and planning purposes in many regions of the world. These community sustainability projects increasingly provide evidence for indigenous land claims, as well as territorial resource entitlements under national and international law (Colchester 2005, Poole 2005, Rocheleau 2005, Topatimasang 2005). We might anticipate that these "countermappings" (Peluso 1995) will also be used as evidence of and for the existence and authority of customary law with respect to traditional knowledge and practices and the vernacular forms of intellectual property that recognition of such law might establish.

Conclusion

Communities and their properties are evolving; intellectual property and other emerging cultural rights issues will shape that evolution. Bruno Latour (2004) cautions us against being satisfied with a critique that begins and ends with revealing the social construction of naturalized facts; the critic, he suggests, recognizes that "matters of fact are only very partial . . . and very polemical, very political rendering of matters of concern" (232). Further, "The critic is not the one who debunks, but the one who assembles. . . . The critic is not the one who alternates haphazardly between anti-fetishism and positivism . . . but the one for whom, if something is constructed, then it means it is fragile and in need of care and caution" (246).

The communities "empowered" by recognition of their traditional knowledge, their intangible cultural heritage, or their traditional cultural expressions may sometimes be artifactual, but they are still empathically real and have material and political consequence. In some areas of the world, they may map nicely onto historical forms of identity, solidarity, and communal attachments, but in others they may be constituted using borders that reiterate colonial divisions of power or further exaggerate local relations of social inequality. State powers may instantiate new forms of collective subjectivity for purposes of discipline and surveillance; NGOs may "discover" traditions in those communities where they are most comfortable working. We may, however, also find these newly "capacitated" communities making new demands on states, transnational movements, and international courts for constitutional recognition, political autonomy, and respect for customary law, to limit and enjoin extractive development projects and to demand new forms of citizenship as they have done in Amazonian and Andean regions of Latin America (Coombe 2010).

Intellectual property rights have conventionally been central to regimes of exchange and accumulation, but they also clearly figure as cultural rights within a wider range of human rights norms and (in emerging vernacular form) international indigenous rights regimes that provide normative resources that can be used to limit and shape neoliberal tendencies. States and corporations, NGOs, UN bodies, development aid institutions, and new social movements all have particular interests in "empowering" communities as entrepreneurs, owners, stewards, or custodians of what are perceived to be scarce and endangered forms of knowledge, difference, and distinction. While governmental practices may seek to attach groups to the kinds of heritage that can most easily be managed as commodifiable resources through a conventional intellectual property paradigm, they will not necessarily succeed in so doing. "It is important to look not just at the forms of collective and individual identity promoted by practices of government, but also at how particular agents negotiate these forms—how they embrace, adapt, or refuse them" (Inda 2005: 11).

Community intellectual property and sui generis rights may originally have been imagined and designed to incorporate so-called local communities more completely into regimes of market citizenship. However, to the extent that these subject positions have been encoded as indigenous, local communities thus subjected may reflect upon their historical practices and express their appeals in the normative discourses of right that global indigenist movements afford them. Processes of community formation are processes of political articulation. Diverse forms of sociality are engendered in relation to expectations for intellectual property; the communities located to serve the needs of neoliberal interventions may instead become involved in rights-based movements for livelihood security, political autonomy, territorial rights, and distinctive forms of citizenship. Situated in the friction (Tsing 2005) produced when neoliberalism flashes up against rights-based movements, the propriety of owning cultural resources as intellectual property promises to be the site of ongoing political struggle.

NOTE

1. The author would like to acknowledge the Stellenbosch Institute for Advanced Studies for time and support for this work and Nicole Aylwin for research and bibliographic assistance. Another paper using a similar framework but one more clearly situated within the Foucaultian analytic of governmentality that draws upon examples from Amazonian and Andean Latin America was published in 2010.

REFERENCES

Agrawal, A. (2003). Sustainable Governance of Common-Pool Resources: Context, Methods and Politics. *Annual Review of Anthropology* 32: 243–262.

Agrawal, A., and Gibson, C., eds. (2001). The Role of Community in Natural Resource Conservation. In A. Agrawal and C. Gibson, eds., *Communities and the Environment*. New Brunswick, NJ: Rutgers University Press, 1–31.

Albro, R. (2007). The Terms of Participation in recent UNESCO Cultural Policy Making. In J. Blake, ed., *Safeguarding Intangible Cultural Heritage: Challenges and Approaches*. Builth Wells, Wales: Institute of Art and Law, 109–128.

Beat Graber, C. (2008). Substantive Rights and Obligations under the UNESCO Convention on Cultural Diversity. In H. Schneider and P. Van de Bossche, eds., *Protection of Cultural Diversity from a European and International Perspective*. Antwerp: Intersentia, 141–161.

Berlin, B., and Berlin, E. P. (2004). Prior Informed Consent and Bioprospecting in Chiapas. In M. Riley, ed., *Indigenous Intellectual Property Rights: Legal Obstacles and Innovative Solutions*. Walnut Creek, CA: AltaMira Press, 341–363.

Blake, J. (2009). UNESCO's 2003 Convention on Intangible Cultural Heritage: The Implications of Community Involvement in "Safeguarding." In L. Smith and N. Akagawa, eds., *Intangible Cultural Heritage*. London: Routledge, 46–57.

Blaser, M., Feit, H., and McRae, G., eds. (2004). *In the Way of Development: Indigenous Peoples' Life Projects and Globalization*. London: Zed Books and the Canadian International Development Research Centre.

Brosius, J. P. (2006). Seeing Communities: Technologies of Visualization in Conservation. In G. Creed, ed., *The Seductions of Community: The Unintended Consequences of an Intellectual Romance.* Santa Fe, NM: School of American Research, 227–254.

———. (1997). Endangered Forest, Endangered People: Environmentalist Representations of Indigenous Knowledge, *Human Ecology* 25(1):47-69.

Brosius, J. P., Tsing, A. L., and Zerner, C. (2005). Introduction: Raising Questions about Communities and Conservation. In J. P. Brosius, A. L. Tsing, and C. Zerner, eds., *Communities and Conservation: Histories and Politics of Community-Based Natural Resource Management.* Walnut Creek, CA: AltaMira Press, 1–34.

———. (1998). Representing Communities: Histories and Politics of Community-Based Natural Resource Management. *Society and Natural Resources* 11: 157–168.

Brown, M. (2003). *Who Owns Native Culture?* Cambridge, MA: Harvard University Press.

Bryant, R. (2002). Non-Governmental Organizations and Governmentality: Consuming Biodiversity and Indigenous People in the Philippines. *Political Studies* 50: 268–292.

———. (2000). Politicized Moral Geographies: Debating Biodiversity Conservation and Ancestral Domain in the Philippines. *Political Geography* 19: 673–705.

Chander, A., and Sunder, M. (2004). The Romance of the Public Domain. *California Law Review* 92: 1331–1374.

Chaves, J. (1998). Toward a Proposal for the Protection of Traditional Knowledge of the Indigenous, Afro-American and Local Farming Communities: Perspectives from the Colombian Legal System. *Beyond Law: New Work on Law and Social Change from Latin America* 6 (18 & 19): 195–216.

Chen, J. (2006). There's No Such Thing as Biopiracy . . . and It's a Good Thing Too. *McGeorge Law Review* 37: 345–367.

CIEL (Centre for International Environmental Law). (2007). The Gap between Indigenous People's Demands and WIPO's Framework on Traditional Knowledge. Available at http://www.ciel.org/Publications/WIPO_Gap_Sept07.pdf.

Colchester, M. (2005). Maps, Power and the Defence of Territory: The Upper Mazaruni Land Claim in Guyana. In J. P. Brosius, A. L. Tsing, and C. Zerner, eds., *Communities and Conservation: Histories and Politics of Community-Based Natural Resource Management.* Walnut Creek, CA: AltaMira Press, 271–304.

Collier, J., Maurer, W., and Suarez- Navaz, L. (2001). Sanctioned Identities: Legal Constructions of Modern Personhood. *Identities* 2 (1–2): 1–27.

Collier, S. J., and Ong, S. (2005). Global Assemblages, Anthropological Problems. In A. Ong and S. J. Collier eds., *Global Assemblages: Technology, Politics, and Ethics as Anthropological Problems.* Malden, MA: Blackwell, 3–21.

Comaroff, J., and Comaroff, J. (2009). *Ethnicity, Inc.* Chicago: University of Chicago Press.

Coombe, R. J. (2010). "Possessing Culture": Political Economies of Community Subjects and Their Properties. In M. Busse and V. Strang, eds., *Ownership and Appropriation.* London: Berg, 105–127.

———. (2009). The Expanding Purview of Cultural Properties and their Politics, *Annual Review of Law and Social Sciences* 5: 493–518.

———. (2005a). Protecting Traditional Environmental Knowledge and New Social Movements in the Americas: Intellectual Property, Human Right or Claims to an Alternative Form of Sustainable Development? *Florida Journal of International Law* 17: 115–136.

———. (2005b). Legal Claims to Culture in and against the Market: Neoliberalism and the Global Proliferation of Meaningful Difference. *Law, Culture and Humanities* 1: 32–55.

———. (2003). Works in Progress: Indigenous Knowledge, Biological Diversity and Intellectual Property in a Neoliberal Era. In R. W. Perry and W. Maurer, eds., *Globalization Under*

Construction: Governmentality, Law, and Identity. Minneapolis: University of Minnesota Press, 273–314.

———. (1998). A Critical Cultural Studies of Law. In A. Sarat & T. Kearns, eds., *Law in the Domains of Culture*. Ann Arbor: University of Michigan Press, 21–64.

Coombe, R. J., Schnoor, S., and Ahmed, M. (2007). Bearing Cultural Distinction: Informational Capital and New Expectations for Intellectual Property. *University of California Davis Law Review* 40: 891–917.

Correal, I. G. (1998). The Public Interest in the Protection and Management of Genetic Resources. *Beyond Law: New Work on Law and Social Change* 6 (18 & 19): 173–182.

Escobar, A. (2008). *Territories of Difference: Place, Movements, Life, Redes*. Durham, NC: Duke University Press.

Florez, M. (1998). Treatment of Biological and Cultural Diversity: Regulations, Domains, Actors, and Dilemmas. *Beyond Law: New Work on Law and Social Change from Latin America* 6 (18 & 19): 25–38.

Franklin, S. (2000). Life Itself: Global Nature and the Genetic Imaginary. In S. Franklin and J. Stacy, eds., *Global Nature, Global Culture*. London: Sage, 188–226.

Frow, J. (1995). Elvis's Fame: The Commodity Form and the Form of the Person. *Cardozo Studies in Law and Literature* 7: 131–171.

Gaines, J. (1991). *Contested Culture: The Image, the Voice, and the Law*. Chapel Hill: University of North Carolina Press.

———. (1995). Reincarnation as the Ring on Liz Taylor's Finger: Andy Warhol and the Right of Publicity. In A. Sarat and T. Kearns, eds., *Identities, Politics, and Rights*. Ann Arbor: University of Michigan Press, 131–148.

Gatmaytan, A. B. (2005). Advocacy as Translation: Notes on the Philippine Experience. In J. P. Brosius, A. L. Tsing, and C. Zerner, eds., *Communities and Conservation: Histories and Politics of Community-Based Natural Resource Management*. Walnut Creek, CA: AltaMira Press, 459–476.

Geertz, C. (1983). Local Knowledge: Fact and Law in Comparative Perspective. In *Local Knowledge: Further Essays in Interpretive Anthropology*. New York: Basic Books, 183–234.

Gibson, J. (2006). *Creating Selves: Intellectual Property and the Narration of Culture*. London: Ashgate.

Greene, S. (2004). Indigenous People Incorporated? Culture as Politics, Culture as Property in Pharmaceutical Bioprospecting. *Current Anthropology* 45: 211–237.

Greenhouse, C. (1994). Constructive Approaches to Law, Culture and Identity. *Law and Society Review* 28: 1231–1240.

Hafstein, V. (2009). Intangible Cultural Heritage as a List: From Masterpieces to Representation. In L. Smith and N. Akagawa, eds., *Intangible Heritage*. London: Routledge, 93–111.

———. (2007) Sauvegarde du Patrimoine immaterial et gouvernance communautaire. In *60 Ans D'Histoire de L'UNESCO* (Paris: UNESCO), 308–348.

Harvey, N. (2001). Globalisation and Resistance in Post–Cold War Mexico: Difference, Citizenship and Biodiversity Conflicts in Chiapas. *Third World Quarterly* 22: 1045–1061.

Hayden, C. (2003a). *When Nature Goes Public: The Making and Unmaking of Bioprospecting in Mexico*. Princeton, NJ: Princeton University Press.

———. (2003b). From Market to Market: Bioprospecting's Idioms of Inclusion. *American Ethnologist* 30: 359–371.

Hirsch, S., & Lazarus Black, M., eds. (1994). *Contested States: Law, Hegemony, and Resistance*. New York: Routledge.

Hurtado, L. M. (1998). Access to the Resources of Biodiversity and Indigenous Peoples. *Beyond Law: New Work on Law and Social Change from Latin America* 6 (18 & 19): 143–150.

Inda, J. X. (2005). Analytics of the Modern: An Introduction. In J. X. Inda, ed., *Anthropologies of Modernity: Foucault, Governmentality, and Life Politics*. Malden, MA: Blackwell, 1–20.

IP Philippines (2008). Country's Biodiverse Resources Worth Billions of Dollars Most Threatened in the World. Available at www.ipophil.gov.ph/htm_doc/pressrelease01252008.html.

Jaszi, P., and Woodmansee, M. (2003). Beyond Authorship: Refiguring Rights in Traditional Culture and Bioknowledge. In M. Biagioli and P. Gallison, eds., *Scientific Authorship: Credit and Intellectual Property in Science*. New York: Routledge, 195–225.

Latour, B. (2004). Why Has Critique Run Out of Steam? From Matters of Fact to Matters of Concern. *Critical Inquiry* 30 (2): 225–248.

Li, T. M. (2005). Engaging Simplifications: Community-Based Natural Resource Management, Market Processes, and State Agendas in Upland Southeast Asia. In J. P. Brosius, A. L. Tsing, and C. Zerner, eds., *Communities and Conservation: Histories and Politics of Community-Based Natural Resource Management*. Walnut Creek, CA: AltaMira Press, 427–458.

———. (2000). Locating Indigenous Environmental Knowledge in Indonesia. In R. Ellen, A. Bicker, and P. Parkes, eds., *Indigenous Environmental Knowledge and Its Transformations: Critical Anthropological Perspectives*. New York: Routledge, 121–149.

Lury, C. (1993). *Cultural Rights: Technology, Legality, and Personality*. London: Routledge.

McAfee, K. (1999) Selling Nature to Save It? Biodiversity and Green Developmentalism. *Environment and Planning D: Society and Space,* 17 (2): 133–154.

Mertz, E. (1994). A New Social Constructivism for Sociolegal Studies. *Law and Society Review* 28: 1243–1265.

Mgbeoji, I. (2005). *Global Biopiracy: Patents, Plants, and Indigenous Knowledge*. Ithaca, NY: Cornell University Press.

Miller, T. (1993). *The Well-Tempered Self*. Baltimore: Johns Hopkins University Press.

Murillo-Urrutia, L. G. (2007). Contemporary Challenges in Colombia: An Afro-Colombian Perspective. *Journal of Pan African Studies* 1: 135–153.

Nash, J. (2001). *Mayan Visions: The Quest for Autonomy in an Age of Globalization*. New York: Routledge.

Niezen, R. (2003). *The Origins of Indigenism*. Berkeley: University of California Press.

O'Malley, P. (1996). Risk and Responsibility. In A. Barry, T. Osborne, & N. Rose, eds., *Foucault and Political Reason: Liberalism, Neo-Liberalism, and Rationalities of Government*, London: UCL Press, 189–207.

Ong, A., and Collier, S. J., eds. (2005). *Global Assemblages: Technology, Politics, and Ethics as Anthropological Problems*. Malden: Blackwell Publishing.

Parry, B. (2004). *Trading the Genome: Investigating the Commodification of Bio-Information*. New York: Columbia University Press.

Peluso, N. L. (1995). Whose Woods are These? Counter-mapping Forest Territories in Kalimantan, Indonesia. *Antipode* 27 (4): 383–406.

Perry, R. W., and Maurer, W., eds. (2003). *Globalization Under Construction: Governmentality, Law, and Identity*. Minneapolis: University of Minnesota Press.

Pombo, D. (1998). Colombia in Search of Options for the Defense of Biological and Cultural Diversity on the International Stage. *Beyond Law: New Work on Law and Social Change from Latin America* 6 (18 & 19): 53–72.

Poole, P. (2005). Ye'kuana Mapping Project. In J. P. Brosius, A. Tsing, and C. Zerner, eds., *Communities and Conservation: Histories and Politics of Community-Based Natural Resource Management*. Walnut Creek, CA: AltaMira Press, 305–326.

Pottage, A. and Mundy, M. (2004). *Law, Anthropology, and the Constitution of the Social: Making Persons and Things*. Cambridge: Cambridge University Press.

Reardon, J. (2005). *Racing to the Finish: Identity and Governance in an Age of Genomics.* Princeton: Princeton University Press.

Rhoades, R. E. (ed.) (2006). Linking Sustainability Science, Community, and Culture. In R. E. Rhoades, ed., *Development with Identity: Community, Culture and Sustainability in the Andes.* Boston: CABI, 1–16.

Rocheleau, D. (2005). Maps as Power Tools: Locating Communities in Space or Situating People and Ecologies in Place? In J. P. Brosius, A. L. Tsing, and C. Zerner, eds., *Communities and Conservation: Histories and Politics of Community-Based Natural Resource Management.* Walnut Creek, CA: AltaMira Press, 327–362.

Rose, M. (1993). *Authors and Owners: The Invention of Copyright.* Cambridge, MA: Harvard University Press.

Rose, N. (2007). *The Politics of Life Itself.* Princeton, NJ: Princeton University Press.

Rose, N., and Valverde, M. (1998). Governed by Law? *Social and Legal Studies* 7 (4): 541–551.

Rosenthal, J. (2006). Politics, Culture and Governance in the Development of Prior Informed Consent in Indigenous Communities. *Current Anthropology* 47: 119–142.

Sertje, M. (2003) Malocas and Barracones. Tradition, Biodiversity and Participation in the Colombian Amazon. *International Social Science Journal* 174: 561–571.

Smith, L., and Akagawa, N., eds., (2009). *Intangible Heritage.* London: Routledge.

Topatimasang, R. (2005). Mapping as a Tool for Community Organizing against Power: A Moluccas Experience. In J. P. Brosius, A. L. Tsing, and C. Zerner, eds. *Communities and Conservation: Histories and Politics of Community-Based Natural Resource Management.* Walnut Creek, CA: AltaMira Press, 363–390.

Tsing, A. (2005). *Friction: An Ethnography of Global Connection.* Princeton, NJ: Princeton University Press.

———. (1999). Becoming a Tribal Elder and Other Development Fantasies. In T. M. Li, ed., *Transforming the Indonesian Uplands: Marginality, Power, and Production.* London: Routledge, 159–202.

Ulloa, A. (2005). *The Ecological Native: Indigenous Peoples' Movements and Eco-Governmentality in Colombia.* New York: Routledge.

Valencia, M. (1998). Legal Pluralism: The Basis for Collective Intellectual Rights. *Beyond Law: New Work on Law and Social Change* 6 (18 & 19): 39–52.

Watts, M. (2000). Contested Communities, Malignant Markets, and Gilded Governance: Justice, Resource Extraction, and Conservation in the Tropics. In C. Zerner, ed., *People, Plants, and Justice: The Politics of Nature Conservation.* New York: Columbia University Press, 21–51.

Wilshusen, P. (2006). Territory, Nature, and Culture: Negotiating the Boundaries of Biodiversity Conservation in the Colombian Pacific Coast Region. In S. Brechin et. al., eds., *Contested Nature: Promoting International Biodiversity with Social Justice in the Twenty-first Century.* Albany: State University of New York Press, 73–88.

Woodmansee, M. (2000). The Cultural Work of Copyright. In A. Sarat, and T. Kearns, eds., *Law in the Domains of Culture.* Ann Arbor: University of Michigan Press, 65–96.

———. (1994). *The Author, Art, and the Market.* New York: Columbia University Press.

Woodmansee, M., and Jaszi, P. (1994). *The Construction of Authorship: Textual Appropriation in Law and Literature.* Durham: Duke University Press.

Zent, S., and Zent, E. L. (2007). On Biocultural Diversity from a Venezuelan Perspective: Tracing the Interrelationships among Biodiversity, Culture Change, and Legal Reforms. In C. McManis, ed., *Biodiversity and the Law: Intellectual Property, Biotechnology, and Traditional Knowledge.* London: Earthscan, 91–114.

5

Social Invention

The foundational notion of intellectual property, that certain immaterial or intangible aspects of material things can be the subject of
property rights, implies a distinction between such intangibles and
the tangible subjects of other rights.[1] The distinction vanishes when
one steps outside Euro-American property law, at least for much of
the developing world that is the field for this chapter. That does not
make IP irrelevant. Discussions about intellectual property may carry
on but feed different concerns, so protocols initially meant to promote
innovation hold promise for defenders of cultural tradition. The past
thirty years have seen the rise and fall of the potential of IP as a set of
international legal and policy instruments by which expression could
be given to culture itself. For the anthropologist, the issue becomes
what understandings of social life are created in such moves.

Following Rosemary Coombe's (1998) and Michael Brown's (2003)
lead, this chapter focuses on circumstances under which aspects of culture are treated as property. Precisely because property signals rights,
those who might criticize Euro-American property forms—especially self-styled indigenous peoples—may be attracted to the notions
of ownership and protection it also brings. One outcome has been

attempts to formulate laws for protection in deliberate antithesis to property. Such weaving between stimulus (ideas that catch the imagination) and detachment (putting ideas to purposes removed from their original locations) recurs over and again.

A Recent History

Modern IP developed as an adjunct of industry and commerce, investing intellectual creations with economic rights. One should not underestimate the extent to which, itself an intellectual creation, IP invites imaginative response. Competitive resource hunting uncovers new entities to which economic value is attached, and patents invite "prospecting" for future potential (Barry 2001; Hayden 2003). At the same time, value put on knowledge as a creative resource leads to reflection on talent already embedded in artifacts (such as designs) and practices (such as medical remedies revealed in ethnobotanical classifications), that is, already embedded in "culture."

IP flourishes in a social context energized by national aspirations to globalization and technocommercial advance. In the 1990s, international policy instruments such as the 1992 Convention on Biological Diversity (CBD) and 1994 Trade-Related Aspects of Intellectual Property Rights (TRIPS) invited the reevaluation of resources of all kinds. The World Intellectual Property Organization (WIPO) helped draw up, for national adoption, model laws for implementing IP legislation; for example, signatories to TRIPS would recognize one another's patenting procedures. World concern with the protection of intellectual rights also engendered organizations, including NGOs, and instruments, including soft law[2] promulgations, which encouraged communication (learning what others are doing) and regulation (international agreements) beyond the state. Human rights advocates singled out peoples likely to be underprivileged and identified interest groups. This all created possibilities for enfranchising local interests through a global identity such as "indigenous people." It also challenged the expectation, written into many international agreements, that national interests are people's interests. From this milieu came UNESCO's standard-setting convention in the area of "intangible cultural heritage."[3]

"Cultural property" had in effect moved from its location within the world of national monuments and heritage conservation to fuse with notions of "cultural rights" (Cowan, Dembour, and Wilson 2001). While there is "nothing unusual about communities mobilizing what power they can command to protect a valued resource . . . [w]hat does appear to be new is asserting such claims on the basis of culture" (Winthrop 2002: 116). As we shall see, the fusion of cultural property and cultural rights simultaneously engages with the application of IP to items of culture *and* with many objections to so doing. It also moves back and forth between different understandings of social forms.

UNESCO and WIPO had already joined forces in 1978–1979 to agree on an approach to the international protection of "folklore"; UNESCO was to concentrate on safeguarding intangible cultural heritage, WIPO to consider the application of IP to expressions of culture. But despite their best efforts the time was not right. Then came Erica-Irene Daes's 1993 study, the "Cultural and Intellectual Property of Indigenous Peoples" (Daes 1997), produced for the UN Working Group on Indigenous Populations. In 1998 WIPO set up a Global Intellectual Property Issues Division in order to include "indigenous peoples" within its purview (Roulet 1999: 129), and "traditional knowledge" began to take over from earlier understandings of cultural property as folklore. As Michael Blakeney (1999, 2000) remarks, this significantly changed the discourse. Folklore was typically discussed in terms of copyright; traditional knowledge points toward patent law.

Perceiving culture as encoding knowledge went hand in hand with recognizing biological, environmental, and other knowledge-sensitive assets. Indeed, the question of *protection* as a matter of sustainability, alongside that of exploitation with just reward, arguably arose from the association of traditional knowledge with natural resources that had figured in the CBD (Brush and Orlove 1996; Brush 1999). Indigeneity, originally tied to being of a place, now backed up people's claims as original owners of resources—and therefore appropriate guardians of them (Simpson 1997; Muehlebach 2001).

Biodiversity was a significant entry point for the academic discipline of social-cultural anthropology (e.g., Brush 1993; Posey 1996; Ellen and Harris 1997). Initially hopefully, but then with increasing doubt, anthropologists asked whether IP could acknowledge practices and values that other legal instruments could not (Greaves 1994; Brush and Stabinsky 1996; Patel 1996; Taylor 2000). Thomas Greaves's study was a pioneer here. As for tradition, under the impetus of anthropological critique a frequently cited position is that "tradition" refers less to the products of cultural life than to modes of transmission. Thus Graham Dutfield (1999: 105) goes back to a 1992 statement that the "social process of learning and sharing knowledge unique to every culture is at the heart of its 'traditionality.'"[4] Lawrence Kuna Kalinoe (1999: 35) writes of Papua New Guinea that "custom" need not have existed from time immemorial, and is "fluid, flexible and responsive to social change." There were other questions.

Whether *property* was ever an appropriate mode for the negotiation of interests was raised from the outset in relation to developing countries and indigenous groups. What kinds of relations do property rights imply? Then there is the appropriateness of conceiving of *intellectual* rights. Daes's formula, "intellectual and cultural property," had put the terms in parallel, but are the intangible resources gathered under the rubric of "cultural property" most usefully described as intellectual (Gudeman 1996)? As to *rights*, the very conditions under which rights are rendered claimable already belong to the international community. How applicable are they locally? All three offer a Euro-American commentary on the kind of social life being imagined. From a large literature I take an exemplar of each.

Property: Enthusiasm or Antagonism

Debates over IP regimes frequently turn on the very notion of "property." But while it is acknowledged that assumptions originating from Europe and North America inform many values that the international community takes for granted, fundamental opposition also comes from the same source. Euro-American ambiguity toward property fuels both enthusiasm for and antagonism against IP. Private property is a recurrent target of Euro-Americans' self-criticism: for three hundred years they have railed against its individualistic connotations, their idea of an alternative generally pointing to communal forms of ownership. In the specific case of intellectual property, nineteenth-century protesters resisted the notion of treating knowledge as property on both practical and moral grounds. One could not control the flow of ideas; equally, "ideas are in essence free goods and, therefore, common property" (Brush 1993: 655).

In the words of the Convention on Biological Diversity, intellectual property offers a route to publicly recognizing holders of "knowledge, innovations and practices of indigenous and local communities embodying traditional lifestyles relevant for the sustainable use of biological diversity" (CBD, article 8j). At the same time, the CBD cautioned signatory nations lest IP agreements run counter to rather than support their objectives (article 16.5). For what protects one person may exploit others. This contributes to the double-edged character of property as at once a highly moral and highly duplicitous construct. We find an equal equivocation in soft law regulations.

On one hand, rights are positively coupled with property. The 1994 UN Draft Declaration on the Rights of Indigenous Peoples saw it a strength to talk of "cultural, intellectual, religious and spiritual property" (Simpson 1997: 18; Roulet 1999); the right to own property is recognized in the Universal Declaration on Human Rights. Adding that such declarations "do not draw on the principles of indigenous customary law," Simpson (1997: 35) notes that they "assume that the sovereignty of the National State and the concept of exclusive possession lie at the heart of property rights, thereby denying the existence of collective ownership . . . central to indigenous property systems." On the other hand, rights are uncoupled from property. The UN Working Group on Indigenous Populations, participants at diverse WIPO Roundtables on Intellectual Property and Indigenous Peoples in the 1980s and 1990s, called for protection of the "traditional knowledge" and "cultural values" of indigenous peoples without presuming that the relationship was one of property ownership.

Cutting across this is the creative ambiguity at the heart of Euro-American ideas: property refers both to things and to social relations (Hann 1998). It is equally the thing in which a person holds rights and those rights themselves (claims made by persons in relation to others). Enthusiasm for and antagonism against IP pick up both senses and create property as a boundary object to be enrolled in support of different positions (e.g., Strathern et al. 1998). I caricature some of them as follows.

1. Enthusiasm
    1.1. *Things*: IP is seen as allowing indigenous communities to assert claims on the international stage in a manner hardly before possible. What helps technology also helps indigenous activists. "Indigenous knowledge, historically scorned by the world of industrial societies, has now become intensely, commercially attractive. . . . [I]ntellectual property rights consist of efforts to assert access to, and control over, cultural knowledge and to things produced through its application. . . . [And] the thought arises, why couldn't indigenous people *own* their cultural knowledge, and then, if they allow it to be used elsewhere, secure a just share of the money it generates?" (Greaves 1994: ix, 4; original italics).
    1.2. *Relations*: IP is premised on a two-way flow of knowledge and recompense. It does not just create a legal arena to protect rights; it gives power to new social actors, those identified as inventor or author in whom economic rights can be invested. Such persons are legal individuals, a concept that includes corporate bodies (government agencies, research institutes). Any social unit—individual, clan, village—could theoretically assert identity as a potential rights holder.
2. Antagonism
    2.1. *Things*: Not everything is appropriately turned into an object of property ownership and thus open to disposal to another (Gray 1991), for in Euro-American thinking, property implies the right of alienation. The question of what can and cannot be alienated is often answered in terms of the kind of thing at issue. Thus many people regard "nature"

as a common resource that should not be allocated to specific owners. The 1998 European Directive for the legal protection of biotechnological inventions, giving companies the right to patent organisms created through microbiological processes, was referred to by one opponent as a charter to enslave nature. In such thinking, organisms are not appropriately owned as property. This comes from Euro-American perceptions of things as inanimate objects of manipulation and of nature as a realm to be freely roamed.

2.2. *Relations*: The question of what can be alienated is answered in terms of people's relationships with one another. Opponents of IP may see it as asserting a form of private property that challenges the ethos of sharing they would attribute to collective ownership "typical" of indigenous communities. The counterpoint to private property is seen as the sharing of resources, and collective rights are assumed to be communal ones.

Such Euro-American positionings keep "property" open to perpetual appropriation by different parties.

Intellectual Input: Broad or Narrow

Broad and narrow claims to originality echo for copyright what has become a vigorous controversy over the breadth of patents.[5] New technologies have problematized distinctions that were once the basis of legal limits in patenting, primarily between invention and discovery. Critics note legal artifices (e.g., putting weight on the purified character of biological material takes it out of "nature"), which ignore the purpose of the original distinction to promote the innovation of products, not of abstractions (Drahos 1999). Or they observe doctrinal distinctions being used to disqualify political or ethical objections (Pottage 1998).[6] Brown (1998; 2003) voices criticism of "the moral alchemy" by which broad questions about fair use and expression turn into narrow disputes over commodification; property discourse displaces debate about the morality of, say, sequestering public domain information. Complex ethical issues are submerged in favor of competing claims to exclusive ownership. Here I comment on the breadth of claims to originality, taking a well-discussed example.

Terry Yumbulul's action against the Reserve Bank of Australia has been seized on for the relationship it reveals between an individual artist and the source of his creativity (Barron 1998; Blakeney 1995, 2000; Kalinoe 2001, 2004). Yumbulul granted an exclusive license, with respect to copyright he held in a decorated wooden pole, to an Australian collecting society administering reproduction rights in Aboriginal art. Through a sublicense from the collecting society, the bank reproduced the design ("Morning Star") on its ten-dollar note. Under pressure from his clan, who claimed that this reproduction was a desecration, Yumbulul went to court to dispute the original license, asserting that he did not really have copyright to transfer. The Morning Star configuration on his pole was clan heritage material. Kalinoe (2001) focuses on the fact that the capacity to carve the pole did not indicate original creative work but had been bestowed through initiation rites, among other things authorizing his production of the Morning Star design. The carving was meant to be a faithful reproduction of existing imagery. To comment on Euro-American ideas of communal ownership (see 2.2 above), this is not a general matter of "traditional knowledge" being owned by a "group": through the ritual Yumbulul had been placed into a specific relationship to clan ancestors, comembers, related clans, and other kin.[7]

Writing from a Papua New Guinean perspective, Kalinoe comments on the limits of IP rationality when individuals must seek authorization from others: those others become part of the reproductive act. Their sharing of sacred or heritage knowledge is not the same as the general sharing of mundane knowledge. He proposes that cultural property identified with heritage knowledge should be treated for legal purposes simply as property, albeit of a special kind in being inalienably identified with its owners, but emphatically *not* as intellectual property. More generally, the preservation of culture should be kept separate from the promotion of IP. One reason is that IP brings things into the public eye; the limited restriction guaranteed by initial protection is nothing compared to exposure when copyright expires (Kalinoe 2004: 50). The public domain aspect of IP causes as many problems as its private property aspect.

And originality? The Australian Federal Court hearing of 1991 upheld (against Yumbulul's will) the appropriateness of copyright as a property relation between the Aboriginal artist and his carving of the sacred emblem. How had this legal recognition happened? Anne Barron (1998) discusses broad issues in the air at the time. Aside from the newly discovered value of Aboriginal art were general Euro-American assumptions about individual creativity and the genius of the individual. Yet the law could satisfy itself with a narrow view. Copyright was allocated to the artist as the originator of the work (he and no other carved it), without invoking any stronger sense of creative input.

Now what in the law was an easily settled question about "breadth" of originality, on the Aboriginal side was a view on the "breadth" of creativity.

Creativity entails the capacity to (re)produce (life) forms. It engages issues of personhood, contingent for the courts, central for Yumbulul's kin. Euro-Americans equate sources of potency with an origin in the person as a singular indivisible entity. Imagining instead how copyright ownership maps onto Aboriginal concepts of clan ownership, Barron (1998: 72) notes *the distribution of relationships*: "The unification of copyright ownership in a single entity, albeit a collective one, would not mirror the distribution of rights among individual members of the clan." Such rights are neither public nor private. Rather, they show how the design authorizes the carver by its identification with persons embodied in it. A painting executed in reference to ancestral images contains its own conditions of reproduction: the design indexes who has the right to paint it. In this narrow view, artist belongs to painting rather than painting to artist.

Yet that narrow identification can entertain a broad view of relationships. Reproducing a design may involve sources of creativity apart from the owners—people who help bring forth what belongs to others.

The director of the Papua New Guinea National Cultural Commission (Simet 2000, 2001) has observed of the Tolai of New Britain (2000: 78): "One idea which might easily form part of a mechanism for protection of indigenous knowledge is the assumption that all traditional knowledge is communally owned." In fact, "people were very particular about acquisition, ownership, transfer, protection and use of knowledge. Only some kinds of knowledge belonged to the public domain, while the rest belonged to individuals and social groups." Tolai individuals and groups are enmeshed in diverse social relations with one another. Thus signs of a clan's identity are distributed between masks and the magic that makes the masks effective vehicles of power. A mask is held by a clan member who acts as manager for the clan; the magic is held by a nonmember, a custodian who animates it for them.[8] Clan members cannot manipulate their own magic themselves.

One might want to agree in a broad way with Darrell Posey and Graham Dutfield (1996: 220): "For indigenous peoples, life is a common property which cannot be owned, commercialised, and monopolised by individuals." But this becomes a narrow view when it overlooks how creativity channeled through artifacts and practices is also channeled through specific persons, multiple actors to whom acknowledgement is owed. These others may be ancestors or bush spirits or members of separate groups; very often the source of animation has to be paid for. Papua New Guineans are used to making payments against the flow of benefits. In this way intangible benefits (the power to reproduce forms) are rendered tangible (wealth given in return). Thus the circulation of "rights" over intangibles (knowledge, magic) is often bound up with "rights" over performance (exchange, ritual). The accompanying transactions cut across the logic of both patenting (sustaining the flow of ideas) and copyright (reproducing unique personal expressions). "Ownership" in these circumstances is not straightforward. People may wish to facilitate *both* the protection of items that belong to groups *and* the flow of exchanges guaranteeing that what is of value circulates and marks the value that circulation—keeping up relationships—confers (Araho 2000). And in a larger sense owners and nonowners together "own" the outcome of their collaborations.

Either protection or flow could be seen as broad or narrow, oscillating between how many relationships need be taken into account and the precise connections that confer precise privileges.

Holders of Rights: Communal or Multiple

The 1990s ended with attempts to replace IP by other formulations of rights. If "indigenous" systems everywhere are purportedly characterized "by transgenerational, non-materialistic, and non-exclusive or communal ownership of rights" that make IP rights inappropriate (Puri 2003), the relevant "property right," it is claimed, should accrue to those who own traditional knowledge and expressions of culture.

Kamal Puri was writing of the 2001 draft Pacific Islands Model Law that made its case for establishing protection mechanisms *outside* intellectual property regimes by insisting on the claims of "traditional owners." Collective interests were addressed in the opposites familiar to Euro-American property thinking: private versus "community" ownership. Thus explicit objection to certain Western formulae went along with the endorsement of others: the indigenous mode is held to be "communal" control over the reproduction of works vested in group, clan, or community. This overlooks equivocations such as Jacob Simet's contrast (2000: 74–75), and Kalinoe's (above) between a public domain in which certain types of knowledge circulate on a nonexclusive basis and clans or groups asserting exclusive claims. Moreover, exclusive access does not mean that the clan has authority over all it owns: as we have seen, aspects may be under the control of nonmember custodians. So what does Simet's contrast entail? It is clearly a certain view of social life.

Consider those Euro-American positionings over property that reveal (Euro-American) ideas of "community" in action. While the emphasis on originality and innovation in copyright and patent identifies individual persons as right holders, including publishers or employers enabling original work to take place, an *assertion* of property right may summon what is left out—what is imagined as the wider community. It is a truism that inventions are either new ways of producing something old or old ways of producing something new, every invention a "new combination of pre-existing knowledge" (Bainbridge 1999: 349). Nonetheless, the social context from which creations come does not itself create rights.

Particularly in relation to scientific knowledge, an issue arises over the propriety of acquiring rights in areas claimed for people ("the public," "humankind") in general. It may be argued that because "the building blocks of intangible work—knowledge—is a social product," no individual should have exclusive ownership (Moore 2000: 113). In this view, "the commons" designates resources that should be freely available.[9] Conversely, the "public domain" is reinvented by intellectual property regimes, as when modern copyright, in limiting the period of copyright monopoly, creates a "world" beyond, into which rights are released (Brush 1999: 541). However, in everyday usage these terms often converge. Thus it is asserted that knowledge created from common resources of benefit to everyone should be put "back" into the public domain. Once public, it cannot be subject to proprietary claims.

We return to Simet's contrast for Papua New Guinea. By "nonexclusive" he has in mind the field of mundane knowledge to which no one lays special claim. When people think of styles and practices with which they identify, the collective character of these items may seem inseparable from their general possession of themselves as a people. However, when people think specifically of items handed on from the custodians[10] of previous generations, where "heritage" held in trust cannot be disposed of nor collective interests extinguished, a further nuance arises. What could look like the Euro-American idea of "the commons," emphasizing inclusion by denying exclusion (no one can be excluded), overlooks the significance of one's social position: inclusion from an insider's viewpoint can mean exclusion for the outsider.

When exclusiveness is asserted in forms of "common property" implying a specified owner, as when rights in common are shared among a body of co-owners forming a corporate entity, clans and kin groups exercise rights to the exclusion of nonmembers (for a Papua New Guinea reading, Kalinoe 1999: 51, 297). Common property rights imply coequal ownership of the rights, not equal shares to resources, and members may hold differing (and individuating) rights to use the resources, but the point is that group ownership cannot be extinguished by the actions of individuals. In these terms corporate property emerges either as a kind of collective property (ownership rights shared among the members) or as a kind of individual property (the corporate groups acts as an entity in relation to others). Corporate claims to group emblems or signs (dances, carvings, myths) (Mosko 2002) are in practice "inalienable."

However, imagining rights in such terms may be put alongside other possible understandings of social life already sketched in the previous section. These understandings define interests as neither individual nor collective but as invested rather in sustaining relations. Here people act as parties to enduring relationships and act from obligations to specific others—they are always in a sense in transaction with them. Immaterial assets inhere in material forms: alliances between intermarrying kin groups from which flow gifts between them (artifacts, parcels of land); contracts between rulers and subjects (regalia, ceremony); obligations entailed in ritual duties (songs, magic). Exchanges or payments may be valued for their own sake, that is, keeping up the exchange itself. Such relationships may be significant precisely because they cut across group alignments. Value lies in the fact that access to display or performance exists because of their origination in another social entity. That is, the "rights" are specifically laid to something that must be recognized as coming from elsewhere.

Transactions that are part and parcel of keeping up relationships imply a social form we may call "multiple ownership" (see Coombe, this volume), where people have overlapping interests in one another's claims. Analytically speaking, I use "ownership" to subsume both relations among varieties of owners and relations between owners and nonowners. Multiple ownership determines both what is transactable and the parties to the transaction,[11] interested parties emerging at the time of the interchange itself (e.g., Hirsch 2001, 2004; Sykes 2001). So over what are rights owned? It is not property. The gaining and disposal of items does not extinguish the parties' mutual interest in the things or in one another: *in "owning" the flow of items, they "own" the relationship between them.* As a result, much indigenous knowledge is both embedded and transactable. There is no simple confrontation between communal and individual rights: specific interests are embedded in relations between persons, and things reify the relations. The transaction of tangibles thereby sustains a flow of intangible benefits—"life" or "well-being." Persons identified as the origins of such benefits may be said to "create" rather than produce them, so benefits are embodied in (the life of) persons who are thus created by others (Leach 2003). When benefits come from a particular social other, that source is part of the benefit.

Differing understandings of rights—and I have contrasted here those who think in communal terms with those who, thinking of diverse relationships, always keep alive a multiplicity of interests—reflect back differing understandings of social life.

NOTES

1. Work on which this chapter is based stems from the 1999–2002 project "Property, Transactions and Creations: New Economic Relations in the Pacific" (UK Economic and Social Research Council award R000237838, gratefully acknowledged). Texts on which it is based include the introduction to Hirsch and Strathern (2004) and Strathern's chapters in Whimp and Busse (2000) and especially in the *Handbook of Material Culture* (edited by Tilley, Keane, Kuechler, Rowlands, and Spyer, Sage Publications, 2005).

2. Declarations of principles, codes of practice, standards, and such, not legally binding but nonetheless prompting or inviting respect by the international community.

3. UNESCO (2002), Draft of an International Convention for the Safeguarding of Intangible Cultural Heritage. UNESCO's earlier Convention Concerning the Protection of the World Cultural and Natural Heritage (1972) was about demarcating sites and thus about conservation and not reproduction (Coombe 1993: 264).

4. From a submission to the 1992 CBD by the Four Directions Council, an organization of Canadian indigenous peoples.

5. For example, the "broad" and "narrow" readings that the European Patent Office gives to aspects of the European Patent Convention (Drahos 1999). The U.S. Patent Code defines standards for "novelty" and "nonobviousness" although courts are alleged to apply them loosely (Barton 2000).

6. Allegedly, a spokesman for the UK patent office said: "If you find something in nature, then finding some way to separate it and to make it into something useful can be an invention" (*Guardian* [UK] 18 Feb. 2000), citing a Maryland firm securing rights over a gene that allows the AIDS virus to settle in the body, since it can stake a claim to any AIDS medicine targeting the gene. (Such breadth is a position from which there has since been general retreat.)

7. Knowing (recognizing and caring for) the sacred evidence of ancestral Dreamtime carries obligations as well as rights. Yumbulul's entitlement was to paint and even sell artifacts with the designs but not to authorize reproduction by others (Barron 1998: 48–51).

8. The animating spirit comes from outside. In this matrilineal system the relevant nonmembers are "children" born to male members. Tolai land usage repeats the division, between "owners" of land and "custodians" of its history, nonowner children who keep it secure.

9. Popular Euro-American usage equivocates as to whether this refers to property that belongs to everyone (a common resource in which there can be no private property) or the property of no one (resources open to conversion into private property).

10. "Caretaker" is preferred in Garrity's (1999) review of Maori concepts of intellectual property ("stewardship" or "guardianship" assumes human beings can control the environment in ways at odds with Maori understandings).

11. IP categories point to multiple interests but not necessarily in a relational mode. English copyright recognizes joint authors who own the right severally, as "tenants-in-common," each being a full owner in relation to the part of the work that was theirs. The several owners of the patent may act as tenants-in-common, where an invention is the outcome of combined efforts, or as "joint tenants" entitled to exploit the product individually but unable to dispose of the right without permission from the others. Another potential for multiple ownership arises where the development of products depends on marshaling together elements that have been separately patented by different companies (Heller & Eisenberg 1998).

REFERENCES

Araho, N. 2000. Presentation, in K. Whimp and M. Busse (eds.), *Protection of Intellectual, Biological and Cultural Property in Papua New Guinea*, Canberra: Asia Pacific Press.

Bainbridge, D. 1999. *Intellectual Property* (4th edition), London: Financial Times Management & Pitman Publishing.

Barron, A. 1998. No Other Law? Author-ity, Property and Aboriginal Art, in L. Bently and S. Mariatis (eds.), *Intellectual Property and Ethics*, London: Sweet and Maxwell.

Barry, A. 2001. *Political Machines: Governing a Technological Society*, London: Athlone Press.

Barton, J. 2000. Reforming the Patent System, *Science*, 287: 1933.

Blakeney, M. 1995. Protecting Expressions of Australian Aboriginal Folklore under Copyright Law, *European Intellectual Property Review*, 9: 442–445.

Blakeney, M. 1999. The International Framework of Access to Plant Genetic Resources, in M. Blakeney (ed.), *Intellectual Property Aspects of Ethnobiology*, London: Sweet and Maxwell.

Blakeney, M. 2000. The Protection of Traditional Knowledge under Intellectual Property Law, *European Intellectual Property Review*, 6: 251–261.

Brown, M. 1998. Can Culture Be Copyrighted? *Current Anthropology*, 39(2): 193–222.

Brown, M. 2003. *Who Owns Native Culture?* Cambridge: Cambridge University Press.

Brush, S. B. 1993. Indigenous Knowledge of Biological Resources and Intellectual Property Rights: the Role of Anthropology, *American Anthropologist*, 95(3):653–686.

Brush, S. B. 1999. Bioprospecting in the Public Domain, *Cultural Anthropology*, 14: 535–555.

Brush, S. B., and B. Orlove. 1996. Anthropology and the Conservation of Biodiversity, *Annual Review of Anthropology*, 25: 329–352.

Brush, S. B., and D. Stabinsky. 1996. *Valuing Local Knowledge: Indigenous Peoples and Intellectual Property Rights*, Washington, DC: Island Press.

Coombe, R. 1993. The Properties of Culture and the Politics of Possessing Identity: Native Claims in the Cultural Appropriation Controversy, *Canadian J. Law and Jurisprudence*, 6(2): 249–285.

Coombe, R. 1998. *The Cultural Life of Intellectual Properties: Authorship, Appropriation, and the Law*, Durham, NC: Duke University Press.

Cowan, J., M.-B. Dembour, and R. Wilson (eds.). 2001. *Culture and Rights: Anthropological Perspectives*, Cambridge: Cambridge University Press.

Daes, E.-I. 1997. *Protection of the Heritage of Indigenous People*, New York: United Nations.

Drahos, P. 1999. Biotechnology Patents, Market and Morality, *European Intellectual Property Review*, 21: 441–449.

Dutfield, G. 1999. The Public and Private Domains: Intellectual Property Rights in Traditional Ecological Knowledge, Working Paper 03/99, *Oxford Electronic Journal of Intellectual Property Rights*.

Ellen, R., and H. Harris. 1997. "Concepts of Indigenous Environmental Knowledge in Scientific and Development Studies Literature: A Critical Assessment," Avenir des Peuples des Forêts Tropicales Working Paper 2, http://lucy.ukc.ac.uk/rainforest/publicationsg.html. Avenir des Peuples des Forêts Tropicales, http://lucy.ukc.ac.uk/rainforest/publicationsg.html

Garrity, B. 1999. Conflict between Maori and Western Concepts of Intellectual Property, *Auckland University Law Review*, 8: 1193–1210.

Gray, K. 1991. Property in Thin Air, *Cambridge Law Journal*, 50: 252–307.

Greaves, T. (ed.). 1994. *Intellectual Property Rights for Indigenous Peoples: A Sourcebook*, Oklahoma City: Society for Applied Anthropology.

Gudeman, S. 1996. Sketches, Qualms, and Other Thoughts on Intellectual Property Rights, in S. B. Brush and D. Stabinsky (eds.), *Valuing Local Knowledge: Indigenous People and Intellectual Property Rights*, Washington, DC: Island Press.

Hann, C. M. (ed.). 1998. *Property Relations: Renewing the Anthropological Tradition*, Cambridge: Cambridge University Press.

Hayden, C. 2003. *When Nature Goes Public: The Making and Unmaking of Bioprospecting in Mexico*, Princeton, NJ: Princeton University Press.

Heller, M., and R. Eisenberg. 1998. Can Patents Deter Innovation? The Anticommons in Biomedical Research, *Science*, 280: 698–701.

Hirsch, E. 2001. New Boundaries of Influence in Highland Papua: "Culture," Mining and Ritual Conversions, *Oceania*, 71: 298–312.

Hirsch, E. 2004 . Boundaries of Creation: The Work of Credibility in Science and Ceremony, in E Hirsch and M. Strathern (eds.), *Transactions and Creations: Property Debates and the Stimulus of Melanesia*, Oxford: Berghahn.

Hirsch, E. and M. Strathern (eds.). 2004. *Transactions and Creations: Property Debates and the Stimulus of Melanesia*, Oxford: Berghahn.

Kalinoe, L. K. 1999. *Water Law and Customary Water Rights in Papua New Guinea*, New Delhi: UBS.

Kalinoe, L. K. 2001. Expressions of Culture: A Cultural Perspective from Papua New Guinea, WIPO Sub-Regional Workshop on Intellectual Property, Genetic Resources and Traditional Knowledge, Brisbane, Australia, 2001.

Kalinoe, L. K. 2004. Legal Options for the Regulation of Intellectual and Cultural Property in Papua New Guinea, in E Hirsch & M Strathern (eds.), *Transactions and Creations: Property Debates and the Stimulus of Melanesia*, Oxford: Berghahn.

Leach, J. 2003. *Creative Land: Place and Procreation on the Rai Coast of Papua New Guinea*, Oxford: Berghahn.

Moore, A. 2000. Owning Genetic Information and Gene Enhancement Techniques: Why Privacy and Property Rights May Undermine Social Control of the Human Genome, *Bioethics*, 14: 97–119.

Mosko, M. 2002. Totem and Transaction: The Objectification of "Tradition" among North Mekeo, *Oceania*, 73(2): 89–110.

Muehlebach, A. 2001. Making Place at the United Nations: Indigenous Cultural Politics at the UN Working Group on Indigenous Populations, *Cultural Anthropology*, 16(3): 415–448.

Patel, S. 1996. Can the Intellectual Property Rights System Serve the Interests of Indigenous Knowledge? in S. B. Brush and D. Stabinsky (eds.), *Valuing Local Knowledge: Indigenous Peoples and Intellectual Property Rights*, Washington, DC: Island Press.

Posey, D. 1996. Traditional Resource Rights: International Instruments for Protection and Compensation for Indigenous Peoples and Local Communities, Gland, Switzerland: International Union for Conservation of Nature.

Posey, D., and G. Dutfield, 1996. *Beyond Intellectual Property: Toward Traditional Resource Rights for Indigenous Peoples and Local Communities*, Ottawa: International Development Research Centre.

Pottage, A. 1998. The Inscription of Life in Law: Genes, Parents, and Bio-politics, *Modern Law Review*, 61: 740–765.

Puri, K. 2003. Model Law for the Protection of Traditional Knowledge and Expressions of Culture, in *Working and Information Papers, 2nd Working Group on the Protection of Traditional Knowledge and Expressions of Culture, Noumea, New Caledonia, 2003*.

Rabinow, P. 1996. *Making PCR: A Story of Biotechnology*, Chicago: University of Chicago Press.

Roulet, F. 1999. *Human Rights and Indigenous Peoples: A Handbook on the UN System*, Copenhagen: International Work Group for Indigenous Affairs.

Simet, J. 2000. Copyrighting Traditional Tolai knowledge? in K. Whimp and M. Busse (eds.), *Protection of Intellectual, Biological and Cultural Property in Papua New Guinea*, Canberra: Asia Pacific Press.

Simet, J. 2001. Conclusions: Reflections on Cultural Property Research, in K. Sykes with J. Simet and S. Kamene (eds.), *Culture and Cultural Property in the New Guinea Islands Region: Seven Case Studies*, New Delhi: UBS.

Simpson, T. 1997. *Indigenous Heritage and Self-Determination: The Cultural and Intellectual Property Rights of Indigenous Peoples*, Copenhagen: International Work Group for Indigenous Affairs.

Strathern, M., M. Carneiro da Cuhna, P. Descola, C. A. Afonso, and P. Harvey. 1998. Exploitable Knowledge Belongs to the Creators of It: A Debate, *Social Anthropology*, 6: 109–126.

Sykes, K., with J. Simet and S. Kamene (eds.). 2001. *Culture and Cultural Property in the New Guinea Islands Region: Seven Case Studies*, New Delhi: UBS.

Taylor, M. Foreword, in K. Whimp and M. Busse (eds.), *Protection of Intellectual, Biological and Cultural Property in Papua New Guinea*, Canberra: Asia Pacific Press.

Whimp, K., and M. Busse (eds.). 2000. *Protection of Intellectual, Biological and Cultural Property in Papua New Guinea*, Canberra: Asia Pacific Press.

Winthrop, R. 2002. Exploring Cultural: Rights: an Introduction, in Cultural Rights and Indigenous Identity in the Americas, special issue, *Cultural Dynamics*, 14: 115–120.

MARC PERLMAN

6

From "Folklore" to "Knowledge" in Global Governance
On the Metamorphoses of the Unauthored

The latter decades of the twentieth century witnessed a pair of inter-national struggles over the intangible.[1] One was fought on the terrain of intellectual property law, where those who wished to expand the rights of "authors" were opposed by those who wished to protect the "public domain." The other struggle was fought over "unauthored" in-tangibles, historically referred to as "folklore." These materials had no clear authors in IP law. They had accordingly been viewed as lying in the public domain, until a movement arose to reconstruct this realm as a domain of intangible property—in effect, assigning ownership rights in folklore.

The history of this latter movement has attracted little attention, perhaps because it has been so far unsuccessful—it has made only des-ultory progress since the 1950s, with achievements at the domestic and regional levels but still no binding international instrument. Yet the history of the unauthored, though less eventful than the history of authorship, is equally interesting. For just as authorship has been de-scribed in quite different ways throughout the centuries of propertiza-tion, the unauthored too has been variously imagined in the struggles to make it an object of global governance.

In this chapter I inventory a few of these imaginings (these cognitive models, if you will) as they found expression in the institutions of global governance over four decades. I have chosen to present this inventory as a historical narrative, but neither this choice, nor my use of the metaphor of metamorphosis, should be taken to imply a monolinear, evolutionary account. Disparate visions of authorship have coexisted and clashed for centuries; we may expect that multiple cognitive models of the unauthored similarly share the historical stage.

In what follows, I focus on the period between 1967 and 2005. Such a brief account will necessarily be highly selective. I concentrate on one striking contrast, reflected in the difference between two sets of keywords: "folklore" / "authenticity" on one hand, and "traditional cultural expressions" / "traditional knowledge" on the other. I illustrate this contrast by examining two draft documents separated by two decades (*Model Provisions* 1985; *Revised Provisions* 2005). Fully contextualizing this contrast would require more space than is available, so I will single out two factors that have been especially influential in shaping the imagination of the unauthored: environmentalism and the indigenous peoples' movement.

Prelude: 1967

The first attempts to craft an international regime governing the ownership of folklore tried to find a place for the unauthored in copyright law. In 1967 the major copyright treaty, the Berne Convention for the Protection of Literary and Artistic Works, was due for revision. Early that year, the East Asian Seminar on Copyright, held in New Delhi, discussed a draft Model Copyright Law for Developing Countries. There were provisions in the model law covering folklore, but the delegates felt that it made more sense to protect the use of folklore internationally so that "the developing countries could benefit from the use of their folklore in other countries."

Thus they analyzed folklore from the point of view of the Berne Convention, deciding that works of folklore could be categorized as "anonymous works" and "joint works," which, under the convention, are entitled to fifty years' protection after publication. Under Berne, public performance does not constitute publication; therefore, since "most folklore in developing countries is either unpublished or, if published, not yet fifty years old," most folklore could be protected under Berne. True, the convention does not require its member states to protect works whose authors are presumed dead for more than fifty years, but since expressions of folklore are constantly being modified—hence constantly acquiring new "coauthors"—this condition might not apply. The convention need only be revised to clarify that sound recordings do not constitute publications, and to let the state (rather than the publisher) represent the anonymous author (*East Asian* 1967).

India presented this proposal to the Berne Convention meeting in Stockholm, and the question was referred to a committee, which decided that folklore was "extremely difficult to define" (*Stockholm 1967* 1971:876–878, 1173). They recommended that expressions of folklore simply be treated as anonymous works, and so a provision was inserted that allows each state to designate a "competent authority" to represent its anonymous authors. But this provision, it seems, was never utilized.[2]

Act I: 1973–1985

The next such attempt also started as a proposed revision of a copyright convention, though it led to something quite different. In 1973, Bolivia sent a memo to UNESCO suggesting that the copyright treaty it administered should be revised in view of the "invasion of the consumer market" by the folk arts. Bolivia wanted states to be able to claim copyright in their "cultural expressions of collective or anonymous origin which have been elaborated or acquired traditional character." UNESCO responded by convening a Committee of Experts, which issued a report on the protection of folklore in 1977 (*Aspects* 1977).

The committee members were particularly concerned to protect folklore's authenticity from commercialization. They did not think of folklore as static or frozen; when, however, it is "transplanted from its native soil" and used for commercial purposes, distortion may result unless there are "strictly applied regulations" to preserve its authenticity (p. 13). Not that the committee rejected all commercial exploitation; properly done, it could provide countries with a source of income. But how might this income be shared with the community of origin? Under copyright law, the author of a work can claim the financial benefits, but the "fragmentation of the notion of author" in folklore makes this solution unavailable. Yet the committee members were unenthusiastic about the obvious alternative, of paying the community: "While a community might conceivably be invested with a moral right exercised by a representative, it is more difficult to accept the idea of a pecuniary right" (p. 15).

In its deliberations, the committee introduced two concerns that had not been addressed in the 1967 initiative. The first was *authenticity*, which in various guises would reappear in virtually all future legal initiatives. The second— even more significant—innovation was the introduction of the *community* into a discourse that had previously acknowledged only the individual and the state. (In the published records of neither the Stockholm conference nor the East Asian Seminar do we find "community" mentioned.) Folklore was now assumed to be the product of a community, even if the committee members did not explore the legal ramifications of this idea. They did not see how a community could be treated as the owner of its folklore, assuming instead that the state would be the rights-bearing agent. Though they wanted the community to benefit from the use of its folklore, they did not contemplate letting the community decide how the profits should be spent. They did not foresee potential damage to the source community from noncustomary uses of its folklore; they certainly didn't mention the possibility that sacred folk expressions might be profaned even by noncommercial use or that some communities might want to restrict the use of certain expressions to particular families, sexes, or age groups. They seemed to fear more for the dignity and authenticity of the art than for the autonomy and integrity of the community.

UNESCO decided to pursue the "copyright aspects" of this matter further in collaboration with the World Intellectual Property Organization (WIPO) (*Report* 1985:15–16). This joint effort culminated in a series of meetings (1980–1983) to draft and implement what became its "Model Provisions for National Laws on the Protection of Expressions of Folklore Against Illicit Exploitation and Other Prejudicial Actions" (*Model Provisions* 1985) and a draft treaty constructed on similar lines.

With these Model Provisions, UNESCO and WIPO abandoned the attempt to fit folklore within the existing structure of copyright law, crafting instead a sui generis regime of protection (*Model Provisions* 1985:5). This regime covers only the "traditional artistic heritage" of a community (p. 9) and does not protect "traditional beliefs, scientific views (e.g., traditional cosmogony), substance of legends . . . or merely practical traditions" (p. 16). These provisions treated folklore both as the product of communities and as "the cultural heritage of the nation," to be protected in order to guard "the cultural and economic interests of the nation" (p. 9). They are also somewhat more solicitous of the community than the Committee of Experts had been: every user of an expression of folklore would be required to mention its community of origin, and deliberate distortions prejudicial to the cultural interests of that community would be forbidden. Nevertheless, the only uses that had to be preauthorized were ones that were both outside of the traditional or customary context and undertaken for commercial purposes. The national legislation could designate a "competent authority" (p. 10) to issue such authorizations (and collect any fees) or allow the community concerned to do so. Under the former option, the "competent authority" would be required to use the fees to promote or safeguard national folklore or culture (though the commentary to the provisions states it is "advisable" to allocate a certain percentage for the source community [p. 26]). Finally, some exceptions were allowed: educational use did not need approval, nor did the creation of a new work inspired by folklore.

While some of the Model Provisions influenced lawmaking in various states, this initiative did not lead to an international convention. UNESCO and WIPO concluded that a treaty to protect folklore would be "premature" (*Attempts* 2002:15), and, at least as far as WIPO was concerned, the enterprise went into virtual hibernation for a decade.

Interlude: Environmentalism and Indigenism

When the ownership of folklore reentered the agenda of international lawmaking in the 1990s, it did so in a context that was radically altered. The presence of two newly influential actors in global governance—the environmental movement and the indigenous peoples' movement—recast the arena and the terms of the debate.

Starting in the 1970s, conservationists became increasingly concerned about the erosion of the world's genetic diversity. Antihunger activists, who had been criticizing the political economy and ecological impact of the Green Revolution, saw these environmental concerns as compatible with their social-justice agenda. They saw corporate control of industrial agriculture as one source of increasing genetic uniformity. Since the profitability of an increasingly concentrated agribusiness sector depended on new and extended IP rights in plants, these activists mobilized against "plant breeders' rights" (Fowler 1994:134). In the early 1980s, they took this issue to the international level (1994:180–182), arguing that it was inequitable for the developed world to privatize the genetic riches of the developing world: "The North has been patenting the offshoots of this common heritage and is now marketing its new varieties, at great profit, around the world" (Mooney 1983:3).

Biodiversity was also important as a source of new medicines. Pharmaceutical companies were taking plants from the South and testing them for active ingredients, often guided by the ethnopharmacology—the traditional knowledge—of the local people. In legal terms, ethnopharmacological knowledge was as unprotectable as crop landraces, yet drugs developed using this knowledge, like newly bred cultivars, could benefit from IP protection. This legalized misappropriation (of plant germplasm and traditional knowledge) was what the activists attacked as biopiracy.

The other new actor on the international stage was the indigenous peoples' movement. Though it had roots extending back to the 1920s, the international phase of the movement effectively started with the 1971 Declaration of Barbados and the convening of the World Council of Indigenous Peoples in 1975. Originating in settler societies, where the concept of "indigenous peoples" could be tied to the historical injustice of dispossession, the movement spread to Africa and Asia, where there was not always a clear distinction to be drawn between "original" and historically belated populations. The concept was thus redefined to denote any systematically disadvantaged minority whose traditional lifestyle was culturally or ecologically distinctive.[3] Though the movement paid a great deal of attention to land rights, it was also concerned with cultural survival.

The International Union for the Conservation of Nature had spent much of the 1980s working toward a treaty that was to become the Convention on Biological Diversity (CBD) of 1992. The original intent was to reaffirm the status of the world's genetic resources as the common heritage of humankind, but by the time the convention was finalized at the Earth Summit at Rio de Janeiro, it awarded all states sovereignty over their genetic resources (McNeely 2004). Nevertheless, the interests of indigenous peoples were also recognized, if only indirectly. Each signatory state agreed to respect the traditional knowledge of "indigenous and local communities embodying traditional lifestyles" and committed itself to obtaining the "approval" of those communities before applying their traditional knowledge and to the "equitable sharing" of whatever benefits were produced by such application.

Thus, despite the fact that states had been seeking international protection of their *traditional arts* for decades, the first legally binding treaty to recognize unauthored entities concerned biological diversity, and protected *knowledge of the natural environment*. Moreover, states that benefited from this protection were obliged to respect the knowledge-holding communities, among whom *indigenous* communities were singled out for special mention.

These developments were to recast the debate over the protection of folklore in both substantive and conceptual ways. Substantively, lawmakers became aware that expressions of folklore could play a wider variety of social roles than the drafters of the Model Provisions had envisioned. In particular, some indigenous cultures considered some of their traditional expressions to hold spiritual power, and surrounded them with restrictions. Such expressions must not be used by—or even known to—certain groups of people, lest the forces they embody or control be deranged or lose their power. These kinds of restrictions were not unique to indigenous cultures, but they seem to have been brought to the attention of international governance institutions by Australian diplomats who had studied Aboriginal customary law.[4]

These examples suggested that indigenous societies might have distinctive interests in expressions of folklore, interests that required protection unavailable from the Model Provisions. But the indigenous peoples' movement also demanded that the legal community rethink the governance mechanisms for folklore. In particular, by linking folklore with other kinds of intangible as well as tangible heritage, the movement portrayed indigenous culture as an integral whole that defied the analytical scalpel of IP law.

In this view, IP rights could not provide appropriate protection for indigenous traditions for two reasons. First, they were rooted in an individualistic ideology that was antithetical to the communal nature of indigenous societies. But IP rights—offering different types and degrees of protection through copyright, patent, and trademark—were also insufficiently *holistic*: "Dividing intellectual, cultural, and scientific property into three separate areas is strange and unwelcome to indigenous peoples who see these as part of a whole, more like the Western concept of culture" (Posey & Dutfield 1996:1). For indigenous life was a unity, weaving together land, expressive culture, medical knowledge, and spirituality (Daes 1993:21–22):

> Indigenous peoples regard all products of the human mind and heart as interrelated, and as flowing from the same source: the relationships between the people and their land, their kinship with the other living creatures that share the land, and with the spirit world. Since the ultimate source of knowledge and creativity is the land itself, all of the art and science of a specific people are manifestations of the same underlying relationships, and can be considered as manifestations of the people as a whole.
>
> A song, for example, is not a "commodity," a "good," or a form of "property," but one of the manifestations of an ancient and continuing relationship between the people and their territory.

This inseparability can be illustrated by the example of some Australian Aboriginal cultures, where stories, songs, dances, designs, and the landscape are all considered to be perceptible forms of ancestral beings and their actions in a realm both ancient and timeless (Morphy 1998). But it is confirmed in many ways by representatives of indigenous peoples from many parts of the world.

Act II: 1996 and After

The Return of Folklore

The proximate trigger responsible for folklore's comeback at WIPO was the developed world's drive to extend IP rights. In part this was a response to digital technology: intent on enhancing the protection of databases, and worried by the ease of copying copyrighted works in a digital, wired environment, the developed countries sought to strengthen IP protection. They negotiated a pair of new treaties in 1996, the WIPO Copyright Treaty and the WIPO Performances and Phonograms Treaty. Some developing countries used this opportunity to remind the developed world of their demands for folklore protection; after all, technological advances left expressions of folklore just as vulnerable to exploitation as copyrighted works. WIPO addressed some of these concerns, expanding the definition of "performer" to include performers of folklore, but the developing countries asked for a special conference devoted wholly to folklore.[5]

In April of the following year (1997), WIPO and UNESCO held a World Forum on the Protection of Folklore at Phuket, Thailand. Many of the issues discussed there were familiar from the 1980s; there were, however, some notable differences in the tenor of the discourse. Indigenous members of the Australian delegation protested the nearly total "exclusion of Indigenous peoples" at the conference. They called for legislation that would address "the holistic nature of Indigenous cultural material" (Janke 1997:121). They argued that folklore was "narrowly defined"; it should not be limited to artistic expressions but should also include "knowledge systems and biological diversity." Furthermore, the word connotes inferiority. Hence they recommended dispensing with it, and substituting "Indigenous Intellectual and Cultural Property" (Janke 1997:110).

Facing the Challenge of Global Issues

About six months after the World Forum, WIPO elected a new director general, the Sudanese diplomat Kamil Idris. He felt that WIPO must "reach out to its partners in the United Nations family of organizations and to the World Trade Organization" to face the challenges of "global issues," among which he listed "indigenous technology, intangible heritage, folklore," and trade relations (*General Assembly* 1997:7). In early 1998, Idris founded the Global Intellectual Property Issues Division to carry out this work.

Meanwhile, the CBD's provisions on traditional knowledge, originally championed mostly by NGOs, had become of interest to many governments (Dutfield 2001:237). The CBD's Conference of the Parties resolved in 1998 to work with WIPO to integrate these provisions with existing IP conventions (Dutfield 2001:262).

Thus WIPO's new division started life working on both the newly resurrected folklore agenda and the issues of genetic resources and traditional knowledge that had been highlighted in the CBD. Besides four regional consultations on folklore, the Division arranged for two Roundtables on Intellectual Property and Indigenous Peoples, where the protection of traditional knowledge was discussed. And WIPO undertook a series of fact-finding missions in 1998 and 1999 to meet government officials and indigenous representatives in twenty-eight countries, listening to their concerns about folklore, traditional knowledge, and genetic resources.

In these activities, the Division started to merge the concern over folklore, inherited from the 1980s, with the new attention to traditional knowledge. The Regional Consultations on the Protection of Expressions of Folklore, for example, despite their name, each included one speaker on the protection of traditional knowledge. Three of the four consultations recommended the establishment of a standing WIPO committee to discuss both folklore and traditional knowledge.

Moreover, the Division combined these topics by using "traditional knowledge" as the superordinate term. The mandate of the fact-finding missions was phrased in terms of "traditional knowledge," now used as an umbrella category. In this choice of words the missions followed the lead of the CBD (*IP Needs* 2001:247; cf. Wendland 2002:486), though they expanded the concept to include folklore (fig. 6.1). As a result, "traditional knowledge" now acquired two senses: *stricto sensu*, it still referred to medical and environmental knowledge, knowledge of irrigation techniques or the healing properties of plants; *lato sensu*, it could refer to all these *as well as* songs, dances, or textile designs (*Composite Study* 2003:8).

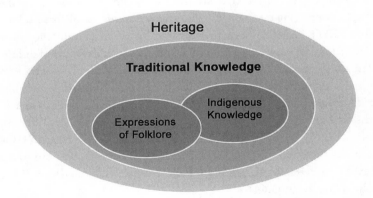

Figure 6.1. Graphic depiction of "expressions of folklore" as a subset of "traditional knowledge." From *IP Needs* (2001:26). Reproduced courtesy of WIPO.

The Birth of the IGCGRTKF

This conceptual conflation was soon embodied in an administrative conflation. Starting in 1996, some states had called for the revision of patent laws to
reduce the risk of biopiracy. While the CBD mandated benefit sharing, and
while developing countries could pass laws to require prior informed consent
for any genetic materials removed from the country, they could not prevent inventions derived from those materials from being patented in other countries.
So several parties proposed that patent applications for biological materials
should be required to state the geographical origin of the plants or animals
from which the invention was derived and certify that the materials were being
used in accordance with the source country's laws (Tobin 2001).

As WIPO's Standing Committee on Patents was finalizing its new Patent
Law Treaty in 1999, Colombia proposed that this disclosure requirement be
included. To prevent the debate on this issue from delaying the treaty, WIPO
proposed establishing a separate forum to discuss the question of genetic resources. Since traditional knowledge was considered relevant to bioprospecting, it was added to the committee's remit. And folklore, too, was added to the
list, since "the three themes are closely interrelated, and none can be addressed
effectively without considering aspects of the others" (*Matters* 2000:4). Thus
was born the Intergovernmental Committee on Genetic Resources, Traditional Knowledge, and Folklore (IGCGRTKF). After a hiatus of over a decade, there was a regular forum at WIPO for discussions of property rights
in folklore. But now the traditional arts would have to share the stage with
debates about biopiracy.

Separable, even disparate issues are often bundled together in international negotiations, for either administrative, technical reasons or strategic,
political reasons (Helfer 2004:12–13). The juxtaposition of three topics on
the IGCGRTKF agenda—whether technically or strategically motivated—
revealed a tension between demands for holistic consideration and differentiated treatment. Some delegations insisted that all of the elements of traditional
knowledge should be viewed in accordance with their "holistic, indivisible nature" (Andean Community, *Report* 2002:62), that "any attempt to break TK
[traditional knowledge] down into its component parts for separate protection is liable to destroy its very nature" (Venezuela, *Report* 2002:67). Other
delegations preferred to "establish a dividing line between TK and folklore"
and explore different legal options for each (European Union, *Report* 2002:52;
cf. China, *Report* 2002:64).

The secretariat staff presumably wished to avoid taking sides in this debate.

They did not want to appear to be forcing traditional knowledge onto what some indigenous advocates call "the Procrustean bed of patent and copyright" (Barsh 1999:41). Yet they constantly found themselves arguing for the need to separate the three topics, if only methodologically (*Overview* 2007:34). While "technical know-how and artistic expressions" may be integrated in "the daily life of indigenous peoples," they could be distinguished for analytical purposes (Wendland 2008:150). And court-ordered remedies for misappropriation would not need to embrace the totality of an indigenous worldview (Taubman & Leistner 2008:78–79). The secretariat staff noted that the yoking together of these three subjects made negotiation extremely difficult, though they admitted that respect for the holism of indigenous life might leave no alternative.[6]

This new source of tension was added to some long-standing points of contention, such as the respective roles of the state and the community. Already in 1985 there had been arguments over how much control should be vested in the local community and how much in a national administrative agency. In the IGCGRTKF, where many indigenous peoples were represented by NGOs, these disagreements resurfaced. Some of the representatives of indigenous peoples insisted that the state must not be recognized as the owner of folklore, nor should it be assigned any role in the management of the rights to folklore, since "the interests of the State were often quite contrary to the interests of indigenous people" (Saami Council, *Report* 2004:52). Against this, several delegations appealed to "the principle of national sovereignty of States over their resources" (Iran, *Report* 2004:97), arguing that "the State could be the beneficiary of protection" (Egypt, *Report* 2004:34).

The Difference Twenty Years Makes: The "Revised Provisions"

The IGCGRTKF met fifteen times between 2001 and 2009 but has yet to produce a draft convention. However, based on an interim benchmark document from 2005, it is possible to make a tentative comparison between the terms of the ongoing discussions and the Model Provisions of the 1980s.

First, however, a note on terminology: early in the IGCGRTKF process the term "folklore" showed signs of succumbing to the waves of suspicion that had buffeted it over the years. Some delegations reported that they considered it pejorative, and as we have seen, indigenous peoples had criticized it as insufficiently holistic and too narrowly focused on expressive culture. By 2002, WIPO was considering alternatives to "folklore" (or "expressions of folklore"), adopting the term "traditional cultural expressions" (TCEs).[7]

In several respects the "Revised Provisions for the Protection of Traditional Cultural Expressions/Expressions of Folklore" of 2005 resemble the Model Provisions. For example, in both of them the traditional and customary uses of TCEs are left unregulated. But there are also significant differences between these two drafts.

In the Model Provisions, folklore was defined as "productions consisting of characteristic elements of the traditional artistic heritage." In the Revised Provisions, TCEs are defined as "forms . . . in which traditional culture and knowledge are expressed" (p. 11).

In the Model Provisions, folklore was defined as the product of a community, but the productions of individuals were recognized as well, insofar as they reflected "the traditional artistic expectations of such a community" (*Model Provisions* 1985). In the Revised Provisions, both community and individual are likewise recognized. But the individuals who maintain, use, or develop TCEs are now described as those who have "the right or responsibility to do so in accordance with the *customary law and practices* of that community" (p. 11, emphasis added).

In the Model Provisions, the beneficiaries of protection are not expressly named; states may allow communities to control the uses of their folklore (and reap the benefits thereof), or states may appoint a "competent authority" to do so, in which case the revenue would be used to support "national folklore" or "national culture." In the Revised Provisions, the beneficiaries are stipulated: they are "indigenous peoples and traditional and other cultural communities." Such a formulation would seem to leave no role for the state, but in fact the state has not been expunged: "other cultural communities" is meant to include entire countries (*Revised Provisions* 2005:17).

No longer are distortions actionable only if they are willful; all potential users of TCEs must avoid uses offensive to the source community. The exception in favor of the creation of new works has been eliminated.

The single most striking change from the Model Provisions is a distinction between three types of TCEs: (1) secret TCEs, (2) TCEs "of particular cultural or spiritual value or significance to a community" (p. 19), and (3) TCEs *sans phrase*. To these three types correspond three "layers" of protection. Secret TCEs need not be registered to be protected. TCEs of particular cultural or spiritual value can be entered in a register, indicating that their use requires prior informed consent. TCEs not so registered can be used without prior authorization, as long as they are properly attributed; are free from distortion, mutilation, modification or other derogatory action with regard to the TCE; do not falsely suggest an association with or endorsement by the community; and (if for-profit) pay equitable remuneration.

Thus, in sum, the Revised Provisions differ from the Model Provisions in the way they regard folklore (not as artistic expressions but as expressions of "traditional culture and knowledge"); in the way they view community (as the express beneficiary of protection and as an independent normative realm whose customary law is to be respected); and in the recognition of the secrecy and "spiritual value" of some TCEs. And, of course, the Revised Provisions, unlike the Model Provisions, make explicit reference to indigenous peoples as one type of TCE-holding community (while affirming that an entire nation can also be a cultural community).

These differences seem to reflect the influence of the indigenous peoples' movement, in ways both relatively abstract and concrete. On one hand, the holistic view of unauthored intangibles seems to have given traditional cultural expressions a new intentional object. The term "expressions of folklore" implied that what was being expressed was folklore; "traditional cultural expressions" could be interpreted similarly to refer to expressions of traditional culture. But WIPO documents now describe TCEs as expressions *of traditional knowledge*.[8] In this way, the legal conceptualization of TCEs shifts away from an emphasis on their formal, affective, or aesthetic properties, instead describing them as carriers or embodiments of *information or beliefs*.

On the other hand, discussions of TCEs in legal scholarship increasingly treat indigenous TCEs as prototypical of all TCEs. It is not uncommon for such analyses to situate TCEs entirely within the context of indigenous peoples and indigenous heritage, with little or no mention of the TCEs that may be found among nonindigenous communities.[9] Furthermore, specific attributes of folklore that are characteristic of some indigenous groups have become increasingly central to the image of folklore. This is particularly true of secrecy and sacredness, which have now achieved a prominent place in many delineations of traditional cultural expressions.

For example, one survey of the legal questions raised by the efforts to protect folklore presents secrecy as paradigmatic for folklore: "Expressions of folklore . . . have not been created to reach as broad a public as possible. They were originally intended solely for the community from which they originate and whose traditions and beliefs they embody. *The majority of them are even of a secret nature* and are only transmitted from generation to generation through certain members of the community by virtue of their age, their sex or their status, i.e., the position they occupy within the community" (Lucas-Schloetter 2008:390, emphasis added).

Similarly, traditional cultural expressions are becoming associated with spirituality or religion. In a recent document produced by the WIPO secretariat, eight characteristics are given as typical of TCEs. Most of these correspond to elements of similar definitions dating back for decades, but there are also some new additions. One of these is that TCEs "are often primarily created for spiritual and religious purposes" (*Draft Gap Analysis* 2008:4).[10]

I suspect that this highlighting of the secret and spiritual aspects of TCEs is a response to the magnetic pull of indigenous culture, increasingly seen as prototypical for all traditional culture. Similarly, the assertion of the indivisibility of TCEs and traditional knowledge, though it may have been encouraged by WIPO's administrative conflation of the two topics, also echoes the holism espoused by many in the indigenous peoples' movement, given global resonance by the drive to conserve the world's biodiversity.

Conclusion

Over four decades, the diplomats, legal scholars, and activists who contemplated an international legal regime for folklore have imagined it in various ways: as the product of anonymous individuals or of communities governed by customary law; as the property of a nation or of an indigenous people; as artistic heritage threatened by commercialization or as traditional knowledge bound inseparably to spiritual beliefs, traditional medicine, and stewardship of the land. I have presented these cognitive models in historical sequence, but there is no reason to think that the new have entirely displaced the old. Indeed, some of the strategic ambiguities in the 2005 Revised Provisions (such as the very capacious understanding of "community") can be seen as designed to accommodate a range of these imaginings.

Some of these conceptualizations seem to be straightforward responses to social and economic change. In the early 1980s, the legal imagination had been dominated by unrestricted, secular, artistic expressions governed by no particular community institutions. With the increasing strength of the indigenous peoples' movement, the institutions of global governance gave customary law, secrecy, and sacredness increasing prominence in their characterizations of TCEs. Meanwhile, the growing importance of agribusiness and biotechnology in the world economy made genetic resources—and traditional knowledge of them—a valuable commodity, the rights over which WIPO needed to address.

It is less obvious why, when WIPO restarted its negotiations on folklore, this topic was folded in with genetic resources under the rubric of traditional knowledge. This may have been due in part to the prior example of the CBD, to indigenous peoples' assertions of holism, to the need to preserve a coalition of *demandeur* states (some of which were relatively poor in biodiversity), and perhaps even to the wish to attach an already much-discussed issue to a new agenda item that seemed to have more momentum.[11]

Legislation, like adjudication, may bear the marks of the particular circumstances that motivate it (Schauer 2006). But the law gazes at social life through its own thick spectacles, and even when it borrows terms from common use—words like "performance," "originality," or "publication"—it will bend their meanings to its own purposes. I have tried to explain how "folklore," when fed into the machinery of global lawmaking, emerged as "traditional cultural expressions," considered as a kind of knowledge. But there is no reason to suppose that the metamorphoses of the unauthored will stop here. New cognitive models may emerge, responding to future developments in technology, future political alliances, and future social movements—but always as they are refracted through the peculiar prism of the law.

NOTES

1. I wish to thank Martha Woodmansee for inviting me to participate in the Con/Texts of Invention conference, the Andrew W. Mellon Foundation for a New Directions Fellowship that allowed me to attend the Washington College of Law and the Boalt Hall School of Law, and all my teachers at those two institutions. I'm particularly indebted to Francis Gurry and Wend Wendland of WIPO, and to Lise McLeod, the librarian there. (None of them are responsible for any errors or for my interpretations in this paper.) Most of all, I owe an enormous debt of gratitude to Peter Jaszi, who welcomed me into the world of legal scholarship with exceptional generosity and warmth. My subtitle is an allusion to his "Toward a Theory of Copyright: The Metamorphoses of 'Authorship'" (1991).

2. As of 1985 no Berne member state had informed WIPO that it had designated such a "competent authority" (*Model Provisions* 1985:5).

3. "Indigenous" was thus often conjoined with "tribal" and "endangered," sometimes in effect equated with them. For competing views on the broadening (or blurring) of the notion of "indigenous," see Sissons (2005:23–24) and Kingsbury (1998). For an insightful comparative analysis, see Tsing (2007).

4. Robin Bell, the Australian delegate to some of the meetings on the Model Provisions, had served on a working party charged with developing legal measures for the protection of Aboriginal folklore (*IP Aspects* 1982:59; *Regional Committee Asia* 1983:198).

5. See, e.g., *Development Cooperation* (1994:20), and the statement of the Nigerian delegation in *Protocol/Instrument* (1996:8).

6. "It would promote clarity and an understanding of the issues if the three themes could be further disentangled from each other only to facilitate management of the discussion. In view of the holism with which indigenous peoples view their natural and cultural heritage, this may be politically unavoidable, however" (Wendland 2008:163).

7. The term appears in June 2002 in a report prepared for the third session of the IGCGRTKF (*Final Report* 2002:34). By the end of 2002, the secretariat was using the terms "expressions of folklore" and "traditional cultural expressions" interchangeably (*Systematic Analysis* 2002:3).

8. For example, "the protection of 'traditional cultural expressions' may be said to refer to the protection of expressions of traditional knowledge" (*Consolidated* 2003:21; cf. Wendland 2008:150).

9. See, for example, Lewinski (2009).

10. Interestingly, this clause attracted criticism from one of the WIPO member states. At the October 14, 2008, IGCGRTKF meeting where this document was discussed, a delegate from India objected to this definition, for it excludes many items by tying the concept to the spiritual heritage of a community.

11. I use "attach" here in the sense that Gray (2002) has given to "policy attachment" in his analysis of local government.

REFERENCES

Aspects. 1977. UNESCO Committee of Experts on the Legal Protection of Folklore (Tunis, July 11–15, 1977). "Study of the Various Aspects Involved in the Protection of Folklore." UN Document UNESCO/FOLK/I/3.

Attempts. 2002. WIPO International Forum on Intellectual Property and Traditional Knowledge. "Our Identity, Our Future: The Attempts to Protect Expressions of Folklore and Traditional Knowledge." WIPO Document IPTK/MCT/02/INF.5.

Barsh, Russel L. 1999. "How Do You Patent a Landscape? The Perils of Dichotomizing Cultural and Intellectual Property." *International Journal of Cultural Property* 8(1):14–47.

Composite Study. 2003. Intergovernmental Committee on Intellectual Property and Genetic Resources, Traditional Knowledge and Folklore (Fifth Session, Geneva, July 7–15, 2003). "Composite Study on the Protection of Traditional Knowledge." WIPO Document WIPO/GRTKF/IC/5/8.

Consolidated. 2003. Intergovernmental Committee on Intellectual Property and Genetic Resources, Traditional Knowledge and Folklore, Fifth Session (Geneva, July 7–15, 2003). "Consolidated Analysis of the Legal Protection of Traditional Cultural Expressions." WIPO Document WIPO/GRTKF/IC/5/3.

Consultations. 1999. "UNESCO/WIPO Regional Consultations on the Protection of Traditional and Popular Culture (Folklore)." *Copyright Bulletin* 33(4):35–60.

Daes, Erica-Irene. 1993. "Study on the Protection of the Cultural and Intellectual Property of Indigenous Peoples." UN Commission on Human Rights, Sub-Commission on Prevention of Discrimination and Protection of Minorities. UN Document E/CN.4/Sub.2/1993/28.

Development Cooperation. 1994. "Report on the May 24 to 27, 1994, Session of the Permanent Committee on Development Cooperation Related to Copyright and Neighboring Rights." WIPO Document WO/CF/XIII/1, Annex II.

Draft Gap Analysis. 2008. Intergovernmental Committee on Intellectual Property and Genetic Resources, Traditional Knowledge and Folklore, Thirteenth Session (Geneva, October 13–17, 2008). "Draft Gap Analysis on the Protection of Traditional Cultural Expressions." WIPO Document WIPO/GRTKF/IC/13/4(b), Annex I.

Dutfield, Graham. 2001. "TRIPS-Related Aspects of Traditional Knowledge." *Case Western Reserve Journal of International Law* 33:233–275.

East Asian. 1967. "East Asian Seminar on Copyright." *Copyright* 3(3):42–53.

Final Report. 2002. Intergovernmental Committee on Intellectual Property and Genetic Resources,

Traditional Knowledge and Folklore, Third Session (Geneva, June 13–21, 2002). "Final Report on National Experiences with the Legal Protection of Expressions of Folklore." WIPO Document WIPO/GRTKF/IC/3/10.

Fowler, Cary. 1994. *Unnatural Selection: Technology, Politics, and Plant Evolution*. Yverdon, Switzerland: Gordon and Breach.

General Assembly. 1997. WIPO General Assembly (Geneva, September 22–October 1, 1997). "Report." WIPO Document WO/GA/XXI/13.

Gray, C. 2002. "Local Government and the Arts." *Local Government Studies* 28(1):77–90.

Helfer, Laurence R. 2004. "Regime Shifting: The TRIPs Agreement and New Dynamics of International Intellectual Property Lawmaking." *Yale Journal of International Law* 29:1–83.

IP Aspects. 1982. Committee of Governmental Experts on the Intellectual Property Aspects of the Protection of Expressions of Folklore (Geneva, June 28–July 2, 1982). "Report." *Copyright Bulletin* 16(4):55–68.

IP Needs. 2001. *Intellectual Property Needs and Expectations of Traditional Knowledge Holders: WIPO Report on Fact-Finding Missions on Intellectual Property and Traditional Knowledge (1998–1999)*. Geneva: WIPO.

Janke, Terri. 1997. "UNESCO-WIPO World Forum on the Protection of Folklore: Lessons for Protecting Indigenous Australian Cultural and Intellectual Property." *Copyright Reporter: Journal of the Copyright Society of Australia* 15(3):104–127.

Jaszi, Peter. 1991. "Toward a Theory of Copyright: The Metamorphoses of 'Authorship.'" *Duke Law Journal* (April): 455–502.

Kingsbury, Benedict. 1998. "'Indigenous Peoples' in International Law: A Constructivist Approach to the Asian Controversy." *American Journal of International Law* 92:414–457.

Lewinski, Silke von (ed.). 2008. *Indigenous Heritage and Intellectual Property: Genetic Resources, Traditional Knowledge and Folklore*. 2d edition. Alphen aan den Rijn, the Netherlands: Kluwer Law International.

Lewinski, Silke von. 2009. "An Analysis of WIPO's Latest Proposal and the Model Law 2002 of the Pacific Community for the Protection of Traditional Cultural Expressions." Pp. 109–125 in Christoph Antons (ed.), *Traditional Knowledge, Traditional Cultural Expressions and Intellectual Property Law in the Asia-Pacific Region*. Alphen aan den Rijn, the Netherlands: Kluwer Law International.

Lucas-Schloetter, Agnes. 2008. "Folklore." Pp. 339–505 in Lewinski (2008).

Matters. 2000. WIPO General Assembly (Geneva, September 25–October 3, 2000). "Matters Concerning Intellectual Property and Genetic Resources, Traditional Knowledge and Folklore." WIPO Document WO/GA/26/6.

McNeely, Jeffrey A. 2004. "IUCN and the CBD." P. 5 in *The Convention on Biological Diversity: From Conception to Implementation*. CBD News Special Edition. Montreal: Secretariat of the Convention on Biological Diversity.

Model Provisions. 1985. "Model Provisions for National Laws on the Protection of Expressions of Folklore Against Illicit Exploitation and Other Prejudicial Actions." Paris and Geneva: UNESCO and WIPO.

Mooney, Pat. 1983. "The Law of the Seed: Another Development and Plant Genetic Resources." *Development Dialogue* 1–2:7–172.

Morphy, Howard. 1992. *Ancestral Connections: Art and an Aboriginal System of Knowledge*. Chicago: University of Chicago Press.

Overview. 2007. Intergovernmental Committee on Intellectual Property and Genetic Resources, Traditional Knowledge and Folklore (Geneva, July 3–12, 2007): "Overview of Activities and

Outcomes of the Intergovernmental Committee." WIPO Document WIPO/GRTKF/IC/11/9, Annex.

Posey, Darrell A., & Graham Dutfield. 1996. *Beyond Intellectual Property: Toward Traditional Resources Rights for Indigenous Peoples and Local Communities*. Ottawa: International Development Research Centre, 1996.

Protocol/Instrument. 1996. Committee of Experts on a Possible Protocol to the Berne Convention— Committee of Experts on a Possible Instrument for the Protection of the Rights of Performers and Producers of Phonograms (Geneva, February 1–9, 1996). "Report." WIPO Document BCP/CE/VI/16-INR/CE/V/14.

Regional Committee Asia. 1983. Regional Committee of Experts on Means of Implementation in Asia of Model Provisions on Intellectual Property Aspects of Protection of Expressions of Folklore (New Delhi, January 31–February 2, 1983). "Report." *Copyright* 19:195–200.

Report. 1985. "Report on the Proceedings of the Second Committee of Governmental Experts on the Safeguarding of Folklore and on the Joint UNESCO-WIPO Activities Concerning the Possible Adoption of Specific International Regulations Regarding 'Intellectual Property' Aspects of the Protection of Folklore." UN Document 121 EX/18.

Report. 2002. Intergovernmental Committee on Intellectual Property and Genetic Resources, Traditional Knowledge and Folklore (Third Session, Geneva, June 13–21, 2002). "Report." WIPO Document WIPO/GRTKF/IC/3/17.

Report. 2004. Intergovernmental Committee on Intellectual Property and Genetic Resources, Traditional Knowledge and Folklore, Seventh Session (Geneva, November 1–5, 2004). "Report." WIPO Document WIPO/GRTKF/IC/7/15.

Revised Provisions. 2005. "Revised Provisions for the Protection of Traditional Cultural Expressions/ Expressions of Folklore." WIPO Document WIPO/GRTKF/IC/8/4, Annex.

Schauer, Frederick. 2006. "Do Cases Make Bad Law?" *University of Chicago Law Review* 73:883–918.

Sissons, Jeffrey. 2005. *First Peoples: Indigenous Cultures and their Futures*. London: Reaktion Books.

Stockholm 1967. 1971. *Records of the Intellectual Property Conference of Stockholm: June 11 to July 14, 1967*. Geneva: WIPO.

Systematic Analysis. 2002. Intergovernmental Committee on Intellectual Property and Genetic Resources, Traditional Knowledge and Folklore (Fourth Session, Geneva, December 9–17, 2002). "Preliminary Systematic Analysis of National Experiences with the Legal Protection of Expressions of Folklore." WIPO Document WIPO/GRTKF/IC/4/3.

Taubman, Anthony, and M. Leistner 2008. "Traditional Knowledge." Pp. 59–179 in Lewinski (2008).

Tobin, Brendan. 2001. "Redefining Perspectives in the Search for Protection of Traditional Knowledge: A Case Study from Peru." *RECIEL* 10(1):47–64.

Tsing, Anna. 2007. "Indigenous Voice." Pp. 33–68 in Marisol de la Cardena and Orin Starn (eds.), *Indigenous Experience Today*. Oxford: Berg.

Wendland, Wend. 2002. "Intellectual Property, Traditional Knowledge and Folklore: WIPO's Exploratory Program." *International Review of Industrial Property and Copyright Law* 33(4):485–504.

Wendland, Wend. 2008. "'It's a Small World (after All)': Some Reflections on Intellectual Property and Traditional Cultural Expressions." Pp. 150–181 in Christoph Beat Graber and Mira Burri-Nenova (eds.), *Intellectual Property and Traditional Cultural Expressions in a Digital Environment*. Cheltenham, UK: Edward Elgar.

CHRISTOPHER KELTY

7

Inventing Copyleft

The question of invention in software is one riddled with curious philosophical mysteries: its dual efficacy and intangibility, the breakdown of the idea/expression dichotomy, and the tricky definition of what constitutes creativity or inventiveness in such a complex and technically arcane world.[1] It is safe to say that software, when crossed with intellectual property law, has troubled its users and creators since its very inception. This chapter explores one case—a central one—of invention and controversy in the world of free software: that of Editing MACroS (EMACS) and the general public license (GPL). The story of the controversy is well known among hackers and geeks, but not often told, and not in detail, outside these small circles.[2] Moreover, the details of context are rarely noted: the ways in which different actors mobilize distinct but overlapping interpretations of both IP law and the technical functions of software, in order to make *moral* claims. One implication of this ethnographic approach is to show how the so-called hacker ethic can be seen as the *outcome* of such controversy and negotiation and not something that precedes or determines the actions of people involved.[3]

The Software

EMACS is a text editor; it is also something like a religion. As one of the two most famous text editors it is frequently lauded by its devoted users and attacked by detractors (those preferring Bill Joy's vi, also created in the late 1970s). EMACS is more than just a tool for writing text—for many programmers it was (and still is) the principal interface to the operating system. EMACS allows a programmer to write a program, to debug it, to compile it, to run it, to e-mail it to another user, all from within the same interface. It allows users to quickly and easily write extensions to EMACS itself—extensions that automate frequent tasks and in turn become core features of the software. It can do almost anything, but it can also frustrate almost anyone. The name itself (Editing MACroS) refers to its much admired extensibility. Like all such projects, many people contributed to the creation and maintenance of EMACS (including Guy Steele, Dave Moon, Richard Greenblatt, and Charles Frankston), but there is a clear recognition that it had "'RMS' [Richard Stallman's handle] chiseled somewhere" on it.[4]

Around 1978, EMACS began to proliferate to different operating systems and user communities, a fact both pleasing and frustrating to Stallman, who urged people "to refer to a nonextensible imitation of EMACS as an 'ersatz EMACS.'"[5] Thus, while EMACS in its original form was a creation of Stallman, the *idea* of EMACS as a "real-time display editor" was proliferating. The phrase "nonextensible imitation" captures the combination of design philosophy and moral philosophy that EMACS represented. Extensibility meant that users could make their improvements easily available to all because EMACS had a clever way for users to both add extensions and learn how to use new ones (the "self-documenting" feature of the system). Thus the conceptual integrity of EMACS was compromised when it was copied imperfectly. EMACS has a modular, extensible design that by its very nature invites users to contribute to it and to extend it and to make it perform all manner of tasks—to literally copy and modify it instead of imitating it. For Stallman, this was not only a clever design; it was an expression of a moral order he knew from the small-scale setting of the AI Lab at MIT.

Not everyone shared Stallman's sense of communal order, however. So to facilitate the extension of EMACS through sharing, Stallman started something he called the "EMACS Commune." In a user's manual for EMACS (AI Lab Memo 554, 22 October 1981) Stallman gave a detailed and colorful explanation:

EMACS does not cost anything; instead, you are joining the EMACS software-sharing commune. The conditions of membership are that you must send back any improvements you make to EMACS, including any libraries you write, and that you must not redistribute the system except exactly as you got it, complete. (You can also distribute your customizations, *separately*.) Please do not attempt to get a copy of EMACS, for yourself or anyone else, by dumping it off of your local system. It is almost certain to be incomplete or inconsistent. It is pathetic to hear from sites that received incomplete copies lacking the sources [source code], asking me years later whether sources are available. . . . If you wish to give away a copy of EMACS, copy a distribution tape from MIT, or mail me a tape and get a new one.[6]

Because EMACS was so widely admired and respected, Stallman had a certain amount of power over this commune: he was not the only person who benefited from this communal arrangement. Two disparate sites may well have needed the same macro extension, and so users could see the social benefit in becoming a kind of codeveloper of EMACS by returning improvements. As a result, the demands of the EMACS commune, while unusual and autocratic, were of obvious value to the flock.

The terms of the EMACS distribution agreement were not quite legally binding; nothing compelled participation except Stallman's reputation, his hectoring or a user's desire to reciprocate. On one hand Stallman had not yet delved deeply into the world of copyright, trademark, and trade secrets, so the EMACS commune was the next best thing; on the other hand, the state of intellectual property law was in great flux at the time, and it was not clear to anyone, corporate or academic, exactly what kind of legal arrangements would be legitimate. Stallman's "agreement" was a set of informal rules that expressed the general sense of mutual aid that was a feature of both the design of the system and Stallman's own experience at the AI Lab. In the absence of legal threats over a trademarked term, there was not much to stop people from calling their "ersatz" versions "EMACS"—a problem of success not unlike that of Kleenex or Xerox. As time went on, EMACS was ported, forked, rewritten, copied, or imitated on different operating systems and different computer architectures in universities and corporations around the world; within five or six years, a number of different versions of EMACS were in wide use—and it was this situation of successful adoption that would provide the context for the controversy that erupted in 1983–1985.

The Controversy

In brief the controversy was this: In 1983, James Gosling decided to sell his version of EMACS—a version written in C for UNIX called GOSMACS—to a commercial software vendor called UniPress. GOSMACS was the second most famous implementation of EMACS (after Stallman's itself), written when Gosling was a graduate student at Carnegie Mellon University. For years, Gosling had distributed GOSMACS by himself and had run a mailing list on Usenet on which he answered queries and discussed extensions. Gosling had explicitly asked people *not to redistribute the program*, but to send people to him directly for new versions, making GOSMACS more of a benevolent dictatorship than a commune. Gosling maintained his authority but graciously accepted revisions, bug fixes, and extensions from users, incorporating them into new releases. Stallman's system, by contrast, allowed users to distribute their extensions themselves and have them included in the "official" EMACS. By 1983, Gosling decided he was unable to effectively maintain and support GOSMACS—a task he considered the proper role of a corporation.

For Stallman, Gosling's decision to sell GOSMACS to UniPress was "software sabotage." Though Gosling had been substantially responsible for writing GOSMACS, Stallman felt propriety over this "ersatz" version and was irked that no noncommercial UNIX version of EMACS now existed. So Stallman wrote his own UNIX version, called GNU EMACS, and released it under the same EMACS commune terms. The crux of the debate is that Stallman used (ostensibly with permission) a small piece of Gosling's code in his new version of EMACS—a fact that led numerous people, including the new commercial suppliers of EMACS, to cry foul. Recriminations and legal threats ensued, and the controversy was eventually resolved by Stallman's rewriting the offending code, thus creating an entirely "Gosling-free" version that went on to become the standard UNIX version of EMACS.

The story raises several questions about the changing legal context, and about copyright in particular. Three issues were undecided at the time: the copyrightability of software, the definition of what counts as software, and the meaning of copyright infringement. While the controversy did not resolve any of these issues (the first two would be resolved by Congress and the courts, the third is still somewhat murky), it did clarify the legal issues enough for Stallman to move from the informal EMACS commune to the first version of a free software (copyleft) license, the GNU general public license, in 1985.

Gosling announced his decision to sell GOSMACS in April of 1983. Prior to Gosling's announcement there had been quite a bit of discussion around different versions of EMACS—including an already "commercial" version called

Computer Corporation of America (CCA) EMACS, written by Steve Zimmerman.[7] Some readers of net.emacs (a USENET group) wanted comparisons between CCA EMACS and Gosling EMACS; others objected that it was improper to discuss a "commercial" version on the list. Gosling's announcement (April 9, 1983) was therefore a surprise, since it was already perceived to be the "noncommercial" version:

> The version of EMACS that I wrote is now available commercially through a company called Unipress. . . . They will be doing development, maintenance and will be producing a real manual. . . . Along with this, I regret to say that I will no longer be distributing it. This is a hard step to take, but I feel that it is necessary. . . . The alternative of abandoning it to the public domain is unacceptable. Too many other programs have been destroyed that way. Please support these folks. The effort that they can afford to put into looking after EMACS is directly related to the support they get. Their prices are reasonable.[8]

Gosling's work of distributing the tapes had become "unmanageable"— and the work of maintenance and porting (making it available on multiple architectures) is something he clearly believed should be done by a commercial enterprise. Gosling did not consider GOSMACS to be a communal creation, but he did incorporate the work and suggestions of others, contributions that arrived because of his commitment to keeping it free.

"Free" however, did not mean "public domain"—as is clear from his statement that "abandoning it" to the public domain would destroy it. The distinction is important: "free" means without charge—but Gosling clearly intended to be identified as the author, owner, maintainer, distributor, and sole beneficiary of whatever value GOSMACS had. "Public domain" by contrast, implied giving up all these rights.[9] The UniPress sale was a decision to transfer these rights to a company that would charge for the labor he had provided for free prior to that point. Such a distinction was not clear to everyone; many people considered the fact that GOSMACS was free to imply that it was in the public domain.[10] Not least of these was Richard Stallman, who urged people to avoid using the "semi-ersatz" UniPress version.[11]

To Stallman "free" meant something more than either "public domain" or "for no cost." The EMACS commune was designed to keep EMACS alive and growing as well as to provide it for free—it was an image of community stewardship, a community that had included Gosling until April 1983.

The disappearance of a UNIX version of EMACS also fed into Stallman's nascent plan to create a completely new, noncommercial, non-AT&T UNIX operating system called GNU ("Gnu's Not Unix").[12] At this point (1983–1984)

Stallman probably intended to require the same EMACS commune rules to apply to GNU—rules that he would be able to informally control by overseeing who was sent or sold what and by demanding that any modifications or improvements come in the form of donations. The GNU project initially received little attention except in the context of discussions of AT&T's UNIX licensing practices around the time of its divestiture.[13]

Stallman's original plan for GNU was to start with the core operating system, the kernel, but the controversy led him to start with EMACS. In 1984, and into 1985, he and others began work on a UNIX version of GNU EMACS. The two commercial versions of UNIX EMACS (CCA EMACS and Uni-Press EMACS) continued to circulate and improve in parallel. By March of 1985, Stallman had a complete version (version 15) of GNU EMACS running on the BSD4.2 version of UNIX. Stallman announced this software in a characteristically flamboyant manner by publishing an article in the computer programmers' magazine *Dr. Dobbs*, entitled "The GNU Manifesto."[14] The announcement caused some concern among the commercial distributors—principally because GNU EMACS 15.34 contained code marked "Copyright © James Gosling."[15]

The discovery was not so difficult, since Stallman always distributed the source code along with the binary, but it led to extensive discussion among EMACS users of issues such as the mechanics of copyright, the nature of infringement, the definition of software, the meaning of "public domain," the difference between patent, copyright, and trade secret, the mechanics of permission and its granting—in short a discussion that would be repeatedly recapitulated in nearly every software and IP controversy in the future.

The controversy began in early June, on net.emacs: "RMS's work is based on a version of Gosling code that existed before UniPress got it. Gosling had put that code into the public domain. Any work taking off from the early Gosling code is therefore also public domain."[16] This claim, clearly a false one, brought an extensive reply from Steve Zimmerman, the author of CCA EMACS:

> This is completely contrary to Gosling's public statements. Before he made his arrangements with Unipress, Gosling's policy was that he would send a free copy of his EMACS to anyone who asked, but he did not (publicly, at least) give anyone else permission to make copies. Once Unipress started selling Gosling's EMACS, Gosling stopped distributing free copies and still did not grant anyone else permission to make them; instead, he suggested that people buy EMACS from Unipress. All versions of Gosling's EMACS distributed by him carry his copyright notice, and therefore none of them are in the public domain. Removing copyright notices without the author's permission is, of course,

illegal. . . . What this all means is that unless RMS got written permission from
Gosling to distribute his code, all copies of GNU EMACS constitute violations of the copyright law. All those people making such copies, including those
people who allow them to be copied off their machines, could each be liable
for large sums of money. I think that RMS had better tell us if he has Gosling's
written permission to make these copies. If so, why has he not stated this earlier
(preferably in the distribution itself) and thereby cleared up a potentially major
point of confusion? If not, why has he gone ahead and made many, many people
liable for criminal prosecution by recommending that they distribute this code
without even warning them of their liability? . . .

Now, I have nothing against free software; it's a free country and people
can do what they want. It's just that people who do distribute free software had
better be sure that they have the legal right to do so, or be prepared to face the
consequences. (June 9, 1985)[17]

Stallman replied the next day:

Nobody has any reason to be afraid to use or distribute GNU EMACS. It is
well known that I do not believe any software is anyone's property. However,
for the GNU project, I decided it was necessary to obey the law. I have refused
to look at code I did not have permission to distribute. About 5% of GNU
EMACS is close to (though quite a bit changed from) an old version of Gosling
EMACS. I am distributing it for Fen Labalme, who received permission from
Gosling to distribute it. It is therefore legal for me to do so. To be scrupu-
lously legal, I put statements at the front of the files concerned, describing this
situation.

I don't see anything I should warn people about—except that Zimmerman is
going to try to browbeat them.[18]

Stallman's original defense for using Gosling's code was that he had permission to do so. According to him, Fen Labalme had received written permission
(whether to make use of or to redistribute is not clear) for the display code
in GNU EMACS 15.34. According to Stallman, versions of Labalme's version of Gosling's version of EMACS were in use in various places (including
Labalme's employer, Megatest) and that they considered this a legally defensible position.[19]

Over the next two weeks, a slough of messages picked apart the issues of
copyright, ownership, distribution, and authorship. Gosling clarified that
GOSMACS was never in the public domain but that "unfortunately, two
moves have left my records in a shambles," and he is therefore silent on the

question of whether he granted permission.[20] Gosling's claim could well be strategic: if he had given permission, it might anger UniPress, which expected exclusive control over the version he had sold; by the same token, he may have approved of Stallman's re-creation but not wanted to affirm this in any legally actionable way.

Stallman's legal grounds for using Gosling's code may or may not have been sound. Zimmerman did his best throughout to explain in detail what kind of permission Stallman and Labalme would have needed, drawing on his own experience with the CCA version of EMACS. Meanwhile UniPress posted an official message: "UniPress wants to inform the community that portions of the GNU EMACS program are most definitely not public domain, and that use and/or distribution of the GNU EMACS program is not necessarily proper."[21] The admittedly vague tone of the message left most people wondering whether the company intended to sue anyone. Strategically speaking, it may have wished to maintain good will among hackers and readers of net. emacs—an audience most likely composed of many potential customers. By contrast, if Gosling had given permission to Stallman, then UniPress would itself have been on uncertain legal ground—unable to firmly and definitively threaten users of GNU EMACS with legal action. In either case, whether or not permission was needed was not in question—there was only the question of whether it had been granted.

However, a more complicated legal issue arose: the status of code previously contributed to Gosling by others. Fen Labalme wrote a message to net. EMACS that did not clarify the legal status of his permission (which Labalme was also unable to find) but did raise a related issue: the fact that he and others had made significant contributions to Gosling EMACS, which Gosling had incorporated into his version and then sold to UniPress without their permission: "As one of the 'others' who helped to bring EMACS [GOSMACS] up to speed, I was distressed when Jim sold the editor to UniPress. This seemed to be a direct violation of the trust that I and others had placed in Jim as we sent him our improvements, modifications, and bug fixes. I am especially bothered by the general mercenary attitude surrounding EMACS which has taken over from the once proud "'hacker' ethic—EMACS is a tool that can make all of our lives better. Let's help it to grow!"[22]

The implications of Labalme's message is that Gosling may have infringed on the rights of others in selling the code to UniPress. A message from Joaquim Martillo confirmed that "these modules contain code people like Chris Torek and others contributed when Gosling's emacs was in the public domain. I must wonder whether these people would have contributed had they known their freely-given code was going to become part of someone's product."[23] The complicated situation was not without irony: Stallman was using code from Gosling, based on permission Gosling had given to Labalme, but Labalme had written code for Gosling that he had commercialized without telling Labalme. In turn, all of them were creating software that had been originally conceived in large part by Stallman (but based on ideas and work on TECO, an editor written twenty years earlier), who was now busy rewriting the very software Gosling had rewritten for UNIX. The "once proud 'hacker' ethic" appeared to be more a case of poor management than a noble enterprise.

By July 4, 1985, all of the legal discussion was rendered moot when Stallman announced that he would completely rewrite the display code in EMACS, "even though I still believe Fen and I have permission to distribute that code, in order to keep people's confidence in the GNU project. I came to this decision when I found, this night, that I saw how to rewrite the parts that had seemed hard. I expect to have the job done by the weekend."[24] And on July 4 Stallman was able to send out a message that said: "Celebrate our independence from Unipress! EMACS version 16, 100% Gosling-free, is now being tested at several places."[25]

The speed with which Stallman created this final bit of code was a testament to his widely recognized skills in creating great software—not any urgent (legal) threat. Though UniPress seems to have been concerned about its own reputation, it was a month before the company even responded, after the fact, that it had no intention of suing anyone using the Gosling-free EMACS, version 16 and higher.[26]

Both Stallman and UniPress received various attacks and defenses from observers of the controversy—many people pointed out that Stallman should get credit for "inventing" EMACS and that the issue of his infringing on his own invention was therefore ironic—others proclaimed the innocence and moral character of UniPress, which, it was claimed, was providing more of a service (support for EMACS) than the program itself. Some readers interpreted the fact that Stallman had rewritten the display code (whether under pressure from UniPress or not) as confirmation of the ideas expressed in the GNU Manifesto—that commercial software stifles innovation.[27] On the other hand, latent within this discussion is a deep sense of propriety about what people had created; many people contributed to making EMACS what it was—not only Stallman and Gosling and Zimmerman—and most people had done so under the assumption (legally correct or not) that it would not be taken away from them or, worse, that others might profit by it.

Gosling's sale of EMACS is thus of a different order from his participation in the common stewardship of EMACS. The distinction between creating software and maintaining it is a commercial fiction driven in large part by the structure of intellectual property laws. Maintaining software can mean improving it, and improving it can mean incorporating the original work and ideas of others. To do so by the rules of a changing intellectual property structure forces different choices than to do so according to an informal "hacker ethic" or an experimental "commune." One programmer's minor improvement is another programmer's original contribution.

The Context

The EMACS controversy occurred just after some of the largest changes to U.S. intellectual property law in seventy years. Two aspects of this context are worth emphasizing: (1) practices and knowledge about the law change slowly and do not immediately reflect the change in either the law or the strategies of actors; and (2) U.S. law creates a structural form of uncertainty in which the interplay between legislation and case law is never entirely certain. First, programmers who grew up in the 1970s saw a commercial practice entirely dominated by trade secret and patent protection, almost never by copyright; thus the shift to widespread use of copyright law (endorsed and facilitated by the 1976 and 1980 changes to the law) was a shift in thinking that only slowly dawned on many participants—even the most legally astute—since it was a shift in both strategy and statute. Second, the 1976 and 1980 changes to the copyright law contained a number of uncertainties that would take more than a decade to be worked out in case law—issues such as the copyrightability of software, the definition of software, and the meaning of infringement in software copyright, to say nothing of the impact of the codification of fair use and the removal of the requirement to register. Both aspects set the stage for the EMACS controversy and Stallman's creation of the GPL.

Legally speaking, the EMACS controversy was about copyright, permission, and the meanings of public domain and the reuse of software (and, though never explicitly mentioned, fair use). Software patenting and trade secret law were not directly concerned but form a background to the controversy. Many participants expressed a legal and conventional orthodoxy that software was not patentable—that is, that algorithms, ideas, and fundamental equations fell outside the scope of patent—even though the 1981 case *Diamond v. Diehr* is generally seen as the first strong case for patentability.[28] Software, this orthodoxy went, was thus better protected by trade secret law than patent.

By contrast, copyright law had been rare in software. The first copyright registration of software occurred in 1964, and some corporations, like IBM, routinely marked all source code with a copyright symbol. Others asserted it only on the binaries they distributed or in license agreements. The case of software on the UNIX operating system and its derivatives is particularly haphazard, and the existence of copyright notices by the authors varies widely. An informal survey by Barry Gold singled out only James Gosling, Walter Tichy (author of revision control system) and the RAND Corporation for adequately using copyright notices.[29] Gosling was also the first to register EMACS as copyrighted software in 1983, while Stallman registered GNU EMACS just after version 15.34 was released in May 1985.[30]

The uncertainty of the change from trade secret to copyright is clear in some of the statements made by Stallman about his reuse of Gosling's code. Since neither Stallman nor Gosling sought to keep the program secret—either by licensing it or by requiring users to keep it secret—there could be no claims of trade secret status on either program. Nonetheless there is frequent concern about whether one has "seen" any code (especially code from a UNIX operating system, covered by trade secret) and whether code that someone else has seen, rewritten, or distributed publicly is therefore "in the public domain."[31] Under trade secret rules, Gosling's public distribution of GOSMACS appears to give the green light to its reuse, but under copyright law (a law of strict liability), any unauthorized use is a violation.

The uncertainty over copyright was in part a reflection of a changing strategy in the software industry, an uneven development in which copyright slowly and haphazardly came to displace trade secret. This switch had consequences for how noncommercial programmers, researchers, and amateurs might interpret their own work, as much as that of the companies whose lawyers were struggling with the same issues. Of course, copyright and trade secret protection are not mutually exclusive, but they structure the need for secrecy in different ways, and they make different claims on issues like similarity, reuse, and modification.

The 1976 Copyright Act introduced a number of changes. It codified fair use rights, it removed the requirement to register, and it expanded the scope of copyrightable materials considerably but said nothing about software. In 1980, the presidential Commission on New Technological Uses of Copyrighted Works (CONTU) was charged with making suggestions for changes to the law with respect to software. It was therefore only in 1980 that Congress implemented these changes and explicitly added software to chapter 17 of the U.S. Copyright Statute as something that could be considered copyrightable by law.[32]

The 1980 amendment to the copyright law answered one of three lingering questions about the copyrightability of software: is software copyrightable? Congress answered yes. It did not, however, indicate what "software" meant. During the 1980s, a series of court cases helped specify what counted as "software," including source code, object code (binaries), screen display/output, look and feel, and microcode/firmware.[33] Nor did Congress specify how much similarity would constitute an infringement, and this is something the courts are still adjudicating.

The EMACS controversy confronts all three of these questions. Stallman's initial creation of EMACS was accomplished under conditions where it was unclear whether copyright would apply (i.e., before 1980). Stallman did not attempt to copyright the earliest versions of EMACS, though the 1976 amendments removed the requirement to register, thus rendering everything written after 1978 automatically copyrighted, registration representing only an additional effort to assert that ownership in cases of suspected infringement.

Throughout this period, the question of whether software was copyrightable—or copyrighted—was being answered differently in different cases: AT&T was relying on trade secret status; Gosling, UniPress, and CCA negotiated over copyrighted material; and Stallman was experimenting with his "commune." Although the uncertainty was addressed statutorily by the 1980 amendment, not everyone instantly understood this new law or changed their practices accordingly. There is ample evidence throughout the Usenet archive that the 1976 and 1980 changes were poorly understood—especially in comparison with the legal sophistication of hackers in the 1990s and 2000s.

Second, a tension emerged between the meaning of "source code" and the meaning of "software"—that is, the definition of the *boundaries* of software in a context where all software relies on other software in order to run at all. For instance, EMACS was originally built on top of TECO (written in 1962), which is referred to both as an editor and as a programming language; even seemingly obvious distinctions (application versus programming language) were not necessarily always clear. If TECO is a programming language and EMACS an application written in TECO, then EMACS should have its own copyright, but if EMACS is an extension or modification of TECO the *editor*, then EMACS is a derivative work and would require the explicit permission of the copyright holder of TECO.

Finally, the question of what constitutes infringement was at the heart of this controversy and was not resolved by law or by legal adjudication but simply by rewriting the code to avoid the question. Stallman's use of Gosling's code, his claim of third-hand permission, the presence or absence of written permission, the sale of GOSMACS to UniPress when it most likely contained code not written by Gosling but was copyrighted in his name—all of these issues complicate the question of infringement to the point where the only feasible option for Stallman was to avoid using anyone else's code at all. Barring new precedents in court, GNU EMACS 15.34 was the safest option: a completely new version that performs the same tasks but in a different manner, using different algorithms and code.

Even as it resolved the controversy, however, it posed new problems for Stallman: How would the EMACS commune survive if it wasn't clear whether one can legally use another person's code, even if freely contributed? Was Gosling's action in selling work by others to UniPress legitimate? Would Stallman be able to enforce its opposite—namely prevent people from commercializing EMACS code they contributed to him? How would Stallman avoid the future possibility of his own volunteers and contributors later asserting that he had infringed on their copyright?

Given the controversy and the context, by 1986 Stallman sent out a letter that recorded the formal transfer of copyright to the Free Software Foundation (which he had founded in late 1985), with equal rights to nonexclusive use of the software.[34] Having been accused himself of not having proper permission to use someone else's copyrighted material in his free version of GNU EMACS, Stallman took steps to forestall such an event in the future—ultimately resulting in the copyleft license and the free software movement. Far from representing the triumph of the "hacker ethic"—the GNU GPL represents the concrete, tangible outcome of a relatively wide-ranging cultural conversation hemmed in by changing laws, court decisions, practices both commercial and academic, and experiments with the limits and forms of new media and new technology.

The Conclusion

The rest of the story is quickly told: Stallman resigned from the AI lab at MIT and started the Free Software Foundation in 1985; he created a raft of new tools but ultimately no full UNIX operating system, and he issued a series of licenses, culminating with version 1.0 of the GPL in 1989. In 1990 he was awarded a MacArthur "Genius" grant and over the course of the 1990s was involved in various high-profile battles among a new generation of hackers—ranging from Linus Torvald's creation of Linux (which Stallman insists be referred to as GNU/Linux) to the forking of EMACS into Xemacs and his frequent participation in—and exclusion from—conferences and events devoted to free software.

The creation of the GPL and the Free Software Foundation are often understood as expressions of the "hacker ethic," but the story of EMACS and the complex technical and legal details that structure it illustrate how the GPL was more than just a hack: it was a novel, privately ordered legal "commune." It was a space thoroughly independent of but insinuated into the existing bedrock of rules and practices of the world of corporate and university software and carved out of the slippery, changing substance of intellectual property statutes. At a time when the giants of the industry were fighting to preserve and even strengthen existing relations of intellectual property, this hack was a radical alternative that emphasized the sovereignty not of a national or corporate status quo but of self-fashioning individuals who sought to opt out of that national/corporate unity. The creation of the GNU GPL was not a return to a golden age of small-scale communities freed from the dominating structures of bureaucratic modernity but the creation of something new out of those structures. It relied on and emphasized not their destruction but their stability.

EMACS is still widely used (version 23.2 was issued in 2010), the controversy with UniPress has faded into the distance, and the GPL has become the most widely used and most finely scrutinized of the legal licenses. The controversy over EMACS is by no means the only such controversy to have erupted in the lives of software programmers; indeed, by now it is virtually a rite of passage for young geeks to be involved in such a controversy. Not all such controversies end in the complete rewriting of source code, and today many of them concern the attempt to evangelize for the release of source code under a free software license. The EMACS controversy is in some ways a primal scene—a traumatic one for sure—that has determined the outcome of many subsequent fights by giving form to the free software license and its uses.

NOTES

1. A longer version of this chapter appears as chapter 6 of *Two Bits: The Cultural Significance of Free Software*, Durham, NC: Duke University Press, 2008. I would like to thank Mario Biagioli for his generous and careful reading of this piece and Martha Woodmansee, Peter Jaszi, and Adrian Johns for their organization of the "Con/text of Invention" conference and this volume. Gabriella Coleman, Hannah Landecker, and Lisa Gitelman also provided help and suggestions.

Two excellent starting points in the rapidly expanding legal literature on free software are Greg R. Vetter, "'Infections' Open Source Software: Spreading Incentives or Promoting Resistance?" *Rutgers Law Journal*, 36, no. 1 (Fall 2004): 53; and Greg R. Vetter, "The Collaborative Integrity of Open-Source Software," *Utah Law Review* 2004, no. 2: 563.

2. See Peter Wayner, *Free for All: How LINUX and the Free Software Movement Undercut the High-Tech Titans*, New York: Harper Business, 2000; Glyn Moody, *Rebel Code: Inside Linux and the Open Source Revolution*, Cambridge, MA: Perseus, 2001; and Sam Williams, *Free as in Freedom: Richard Stallman's Crusade for Free Software*, Sebastopol, CA: O'Reilly, 2002. All of the messages referenced here are cited by their "Message-ID," which should allow anyone interested to access the original messages through Google Groups (groups.google.com).

3. See Steven Levy, *Hackers: Heroes of the Computer Revolution*, New York: Basic Books, 1984; and Pekka Himanen, *The Hacker Ethic and the Spirit of the Information Age*, New York: Random House, 2001.

4. Eugene Ciccarelli, "An Introduction to the EMACS Editor," MIT Artificial Intelligence Laboratory, AI Memo 447 (1978), 2.

5. Richard Stallman, "EMACS: The Extensible, Customizable Self-Documenting Display Editor," MIT Artificial Intelligence Laboratory, MIT Artificial Intelligence Laboratory, AI Memo 519a (26 March 1981), 19. Also published as Richard M. Stallman, "EMACS the Extensible, Customizable Self-Documenting Display Editor," *Proceedings of the ACM SIGPLAN SIGOA Symposium on Text Manipulation* (June 8–10, 1981), 147–156.

6. Richard M. Stallman, "EMACS Manual for ITS Users," MIT Artificial Intelligence Laboratory, AI Memo 554 (22 October 1981), 163.

7. In January 1983, Steve Zimmerman announced that CCA had created a commercial version of EMACS (Message-ID: <385@yetti.UUCP>). Zimmerman had not written this version entirely, but he had taken a version written by Warren Montgomery at Bell Labs (written for UNIX on PDP-11s) and created a version for programmers at CCA. Zimmerman had apparently distributed it by FTP at first, but when CCA determined that it might be worth something, it decided to exploit it commercially. By Zimmerman's own account, this whole procedure required ensuring that there was nothing left of the original code by Warren Montgomery that Bell Labs owned (Message-ID: <730@masscomp.UUCP>).

8. Message-ID: <bnews.sri-arpa.865>.

9. The thread starting at Message-ID: <969@sdcsvax.UUCP> contains one example of a discussion over the difference between public domain and commercial software.

10. In particular, a thread discussing this in detail starts at Message-ID: <172@encore.UUCP> and includes Message-ID: <137@osu-eddie.UUCP>, Message-ID: <1127@godot.UUCP>, Message-ID: <148@osu-eddie.UUCP>.

11. Message-ID: <bnews.sri-arpa.988>.

12. Message-ID: <771@mit-eddie.UUCP>.

13. E.g., Message-ID: <6818@brl-tgr.ARPA>.

14. Richard Stallman, "The GNU Manifesto," *Dr. Dobbs Journal* 10, no. 3 (March 1985), http://www.gnu.org/gnu/manifesto.html.

15. The main file of the controversy was called display.c—a version that was modified by Chris Torek appears in net.sources: Message-ID: <424@umcp-cs.UUCP>. A separate example of something written by Gosling bears a note that claims he had declared it public domain but did not "include the infamous Stallman anti-copyright clause." Message-ID: <78@tove.UUCP>.

16. Message-ID: <11400007@inmet.UUCP>.

17. Message-ID: <717@masscomp.UUCP>.

18. Message-ID: <4421@mit-eddie.UUCP>.

19. Message-ID: <4486@mit-eddie.UUCP>; Stallman also recounts this version of events in a 1986 lecture at http://www.gnu.org/philosophy/stallman-kth.html.

20. Message-ID: <2334@sun.UUCP>.

21. Message-ID: <103@unipress.UUCP>.

22. Message-ID: <18@megatest>. Note here the use of "once proud 'hacker' ethic," which seems to confirm the perpetual feeling that the ethic has been compromised.

23. Message-ID: <287@mit-athena.UUCP>.

24. Message-ID: <4559@mit-eddie.UUCP>.

25. Message-ID: <4605@mit-eddie.UUCP>.

26. Message-ID: <104@unipress.uucp>.

27. Joaquim Martillo, Message-ID: <287@mit-athena.UUCP>: "Trying to forbid RMS from using discarded code so that he must spend time to reinvent the wheel supports his contention that 'software hoarders' are slowing down progress in computer science."

28. *Diamond V. Diehr*, 450 U.S. 175 (1981), the supreme court decision forcing the Patent Office to grant patents on software. Interestingly, software patents had been granted much earlier but went either uncontested or unenforced. An excellent example is patent 3,568,156, held by Ken Thompson, on regular expression pattern matching, granted in 1971.

29. Message-ID: <933@sdcrdcf.UUCP>.

30. Gosling's EMACS version 264 (not the version Stallman copied, which was number 84) is registered with the Library of Congress, as is GNU EMACS 15.34. Gosling's EMACS Library of Congress registration number is TX-3-407-458. The registration date is listed as 1992; Stallman's is TX-1-575-302, registered May 1985. The listed dates are uncertain, however, since there are periodic reregistrations and updates.

31. This is particularly confusing in the case of "dbx": Message-ID: <4437@mit-eddie.UUCP>, Message-ID: <6238@Shasta.ARPA>, Message-ID: <6447@Shasta.ARPA>, and Message-ID: <730@masscomp.UUCP>.

32. CONTU Report, http://digital-law-online.info/CONTU/contu1.html (visited Dec. 8, 2006).

33. The cases that determine the meaning of the 1976 and 1980 amendments begin around 1986: *Whelan Associates, Inc. v. Jaslow Dental Laboratory, Inc., et al.*, U.S. Court of Appeals, Third Circuit, August 4, 1986, 797 F.2d 1222, 230 USPQ 481, (affirming that "structure [or sequence or organization]" of software is copyrightable, not only the literal software code); *Computer Associates International, Inc., v. Altai, Inc.*, U.S. Court of Appeals, Second Circuit, June 22, 1992, 982 F.2d 693, 23 USPQ2d 1241 (arguing that the structure test in Whelan was not sufficient to determine infringement and thus proposing the three-part "abstraction-filiation-comparison" test); *Apple Computer, Inc., v. Microsoft Corp*, U.S. Court of Appeals, Ninth Circuit, 35 F.3d 1435 (9th Cir. 1994) (finding that the "desktop metaphor" used in Macintosh and Windows was not identical and thus did not constitute infringement); *Lotus Development Corporation v. Borland International, Inc.* (94-2003), 513 U.S. 233 (1996) (finding that the "look and feel" of a menu interface was not copyrightable).

34. Message-ID: <8605202356.AA12789@ucbvax.Berkeley.edu>.

YOCHAI BENKLER

8

Designing Cooperative Systems for Knowledge Production
An Initial Synthesis from Experimental Economics

The networked information economy has led to a significant increase in the efficacy and salience of social sharing as a modality of information, knowledge, and cultural production. From GNU/Linux to Wikipedia, from BitTorrent to citizen journalism, information and knowledge goods are being produced outside of the intellectual property system's expected incentives and institutional arrangements, sometimes in direct opposition to its commands. These and other commons-based efforts have come to present new sources of competition to traditional market-based organizations and new opportunities for businesses that have come to see servicing and interacting with these commons-based practices as market opportunities. Cooperation in these systems is organized through neither explicit prices nor hierarchical organization. Instead, they are anchored in social processes and motivations largely unexplored in the traditional intellectual property literature.[1] In parallel to what is happening in open networks, a significant literature of organizational sociology has explored how organizations seek to become more flexible, adaptive, and better at innovating and learning about their own processes and environment by flattening hierarchies,

instituting cooperation and communication, and seeking to create greater af‐
fective commitment. These changes have even been called a transformation of
the firm toward a model of "collaborative community."[2]

My purpose in this chapter is specific. I do not examine the reasons for the
turn to cooperation. I do not seek to reestablish the sustainability of social
production of information, knowledge, and culture. I take these as given and
ask how we can systematize our approach to designing cooperation‐based hu‐
man systems. To complement the case‐study method used by economic so‐
ciology and the trial and error of social software design, I try to synthesize a
series of midlevel abstractions, to which I will refer as "design levers," out of the
literature on cooperation in experimental economics. While this technique
cannot replace the richness of the other approaches, it offers a set of materi‐
als focused on delivering relatively tractable and parsimonious observations.
Abstraction from the experiments allows us to form provisional predictions
about how specific interventions may improve cooperation.

A word on how this chapter relates to the project of the volume as a whole:
the Anglo‐American view of "intellectual property" is largely based on the
core assumptions of possessive individualism. It assumes that individuals are
self‐interested and seek to serve their material interests. Innovators and cre‐
ators will not create without the ability to appropriate the material benefits
created by their work. Users—readers, listeners, viewers, and future innova‐
tors and creators—in turn will not pay the originators unless forced to do so.
On the background of these assumptions, IP serves as the legal mechanism
that forces self‐interested users to pay self‐interested creators to create. The
economic "quirkiness" is introduced because "information," in the broad sense
of the products of creativity and innovation, is a "public good" in the technical
economic sense, which leads to the standard understanding of the trade‐off
between incentives and access and between present innovators and future in‐
novators. My point here, however, is that a more foundational challenge to the
supposed necessity of IP at any level is the supposed robustness of the model
of universal self‐interest. Once we find ways of taking account of the actual dis‐
tribution and complexity of human motivations, we can design cultural pro‐
duction and innovation systems without being stuck in the conceptual cycle
that assumes that we must balance between incentives to innovate and create
in one generation and access to the products of innovation and the inputs for
new creation in the next. We can begin to get to a point where, if one wishes
to create a system for subtitling online videos, one's question would be "How
should I design a system to reliably harness contributions from online users so
that I can make the subtitles or closed‐captioning available for free?" rather

than "How do I clear the rights and make sure a subtitling/closed-captioning company can charge for implementing the subtitles so as to sustain the public good of subtitled videos on such a massive scale?"

I anchor the synthesis primarily in experimental economics, although I also rely on substantial work in experimental psychology, anthropology, and human evolutionary biology. Experimental economics of cooperation is anchored by the work of Ernst Fehr and his many collaborators: Samuel Bowles, Herbert Gintis, Colin Camerer, and others. The anthropology literature that interfaces with this more stylized approach is represented by work of Robert Boyd, Peter Richerson, and Joseph Henrich. The basic method is to use a well-understood game theoretical setup with theoretically determinate outcomes, play it under experimental settings, and observe how subjects play the game in fact and how they respond to discrete changes in the terms of engagement. Most, though not all, of these are social dilemma games like the prisoner's dilemma: behaviors and payoffs available to players are structured such that cooperation leads to higher payoff for all participants, but defection leads some or all to have a higher payoff at the expense of others. These games have been played, critiqued, and refined for over twenty years; they have been run with students as well as other types of subjects in many developed countries and among a range of small-scale societies in collaboration with anthropologists.[3] An excellent review of the basics is offered by Camerer and Ernst Fehr,[4] and an earlier excellent review of parallel work in political science is offered by Elinor Ostrom.[5] Throughout this period, participants in these conversations have also developed mathematical models to include other-regarding preferences into the utility function of agents.[6]

In this short chapter I do not offer even a brief review of this literature. I instead go to the task of synthesizing from it a series of design principles for human systems intended to achieve cooperation. Unlike much of what is called "behavioral economics," the study of cooperation does not challenge rationality. It does not involve cognitive biases but anchors in experimental and theoretical work the claim that rational individuals are diversely motivated and that many act in ways consistent with a range of preferences to cooperate under the right conditions.

These studies regularly show that human beings are diversely motivated and sort imperfectly into two basic groups. About 30 percent behave more or less like *homo economicus*. Another 50 percent cooperate. A majority of these are reciprocators, generous to those who are generous toward them, but do not cooperate with, and may even wreak vengeance on, free riders and selfish actors. A large number of cooperators, however, seem to continue to cooperate even if the other party is not cooperating—because they are completely self-less, or perhaps because they cannot be bothered to monitor what the other party is doing. The remaining 20 percent are insufficiently predictable to map. The experimental literature does not as yet provide a basis to tell whether individuals are stable "types" who behave as one or the other character or whether each of us has a distribution of probabilities to behave in a self-interested manner or cooperatively, depending on context. The experiments merely identify a distribution of behavioral patterns to be expected in a group at any given time rather than a distribution of stable types in the population. The experiments also do not tell us whether individuals change their behavioral profile over time and context. This distinction would be important if it were possible to design systems that, through habit or practice, were to lead more people to be more cooperative over time. But development of the "virtue" of generosity and cooperation is at this point speculative.[7]

Building on the details of various studies, I synthesize design elements that could make it easier for cooperators to find each other and cooperate, for reciprocators to police the defections of selfish actors, and for selfish actors to find that it is, ultimately, in their own best interest to cooperate. It is important to emphasize that this is an early essay. It is a first stab at creating a usable tool set out of the large experimental literature on social cooperation, a tool set that could then be used in any human systems design enterprise—be it the design of technical platforms, organizational practices, or legal frameworks.

Design Levers for Constructing Human Systems of Cooperation

Communication

The most powerful intervention in social dilemma game experiments is the introduction of communication. David Sally's highly cited 1995 paper used a meta-analysis of thirty-five years of prisoner's dilemma experiments to show that communication was enormously important in increasing cooperation.[8] Similarly, organizational sociology has focused on the shift from hierarchy and price signals to systems based on discussion and dialogue as the core shift that characterizes the current industrial divide. Many of the following design elements are folded into the overarching commitment to communication as a design principle. But the core insight is that cooperation is fundamentally an act of human communication. Its success relies on the possibility of practical dialog: about goals, process, implementation details, sensed obstacles and possible solutions, and the fairness of the cooperative relationship itself. In this, cooperation as a design approach is starkly opposed to the prevailing incentives-based or control-oriented design approaches, which try to specify the conditions of interaction in advance to cause "efficient" or desired behavior to emerge out of isolated individual action that is not based on continuous, repeated conversation.

Humanization

Studies suggest that communications are far more effective when conducted face to face than when conducted remotely. Because face-to-face communications are such a rich medium, it is difficult to parse whether what occurs is an assessment of trustworthiness, an exchange of at least emotional commitment, or something else. In a series of experiments, however, Bohnet and Frey showed that participants steadily increased their level of cooperation and generosity toward others as they transitioned from anonymity to silent recognition of the other's person (by seeing them or reading a short description) to direct communication.[9] Simple recognition of the counterparty as a human being led to greater cooperation and generosity, independent of anything else that might occur in actual communication. This interpretation finds some support in later neuroscience studies that show that areas of the brain associated with reward show greater activation when human subjects cooperate with other human subjects than when these same subjects "cooperate" with computers.[10]

Trust Construction

"Trust" is often used to describe the outcome of a system of constraints and affordances. This is particularly so in computer systems design but can also be used loosely to describe the state of a society that uses norms, monitoring, perhaps religion, etc., to achieve a state of trust, or a firm that uses a variety of levers to achieve affective commitments from employees. I use a narrower definition that can serve as input into systems design rather than a characterization of its output. By "trust" I mean an attitude people have toward other people, a belief participating agents hold about the likelihood that other participants in that system will cooperate above and beyond whatever the agent holding the belief can enforce or rely on the system to constrain. Trust therefore depends on risk, or the possibility of action that is not forced by the system into a cooperative model. Attaining it is therefore served by breaking up the cooperation process into smaller chunks, each involving lower risks in the event of defection and allowing the behavior of the other to be observed so that each can assess the other as a cooperator. Iterated, small-scale reciprocal cooperative efforts, defection from which imposes only a low price on the trusting party, can more readily be engaged in and can build trust.

Norm Creation

People seem to care about complying with norms—both with what they take to be right and with what they take to be simply "normal" behavior. In some cases, a "norm" is merely a coordination focal point on what everyone is expected to do. In other words, if there are several available cooperative paths, the first requirement of cooperation is coordination, assuming good faith. Here, a "norm" may be an unstated widely held assumption about what pattern of behavior would lead to a coordinate outcome (drive on the left, drive on the right; write many short stubs on Wikipedia, write fewer stubs but more complete skeletal articles, etc.). In other cases, the norm for proper behavior can be more substantive, or aimed at defining the content of the cooperative enterprise. Looking again at Wikipedia, the "neutral point of view" norm expresses a set of substantive commitments as to what counts as an encyclopedia entry and what counts as an opinion essay. It lays claim upon participants to direct their efforts toward the former and marks efforts of the latter type as noncooperative.

More generally we can say that once a statement is made about what counts as cooperation, it is easier for participants to reciprocate cooperation; to identify defection; to characterize the intentions of participants who act in ways that harm others, and, through intentions, to distinguish "defection," which calls for retaliation or departure from the interaction, from "just punishment or reciprocation for defection," which indicates the system is functioning well and the actor is cooperating even in the process of harming another.[11] Andrea McDowell's work on mining codes in California in the 1840s and 1950s,[12] as well as experimental work by Ostrom, Roy Gardner, and James Walker,[13] suggests that self-chosen norms, once set, tend to garner significant compliance with relatively little defection and therefore relatively little need for enforcement.

Fairness

Substantial experimental and game theoretical work focuses on fairness.[14] At the broadest level of generality, the literature suggests that in order for cooperation to be sustained, the outcomes, or distribution of benefits and burdens; the participants' intentions; and the process need to be seen as fair.

What is "fair," however, is weakly defined and can be affected by design and cultural context. Studies in market-based societies suggest that, absent a reason for deviation, participants have a strong focal point on equal division of gains. This focal point can be changed, however, when the game is modulated so that some players are perceived as having "won" the endowment in a lottery or "earned" it by solving a set of puzzles. It is perhaps not surprising that market and liberal society, which place such an important emphasis on individual worth and independence, would yield a fairness focal point on equal division of the surplus or the burden, absent reason to deviate.

No single theory of fairness is required for cooperation to be sustained. But distribution rules that are easy to understand and map onto widely accepted practices are easier to characterize, implement, and perceive and will support cooperative outcomes. This is probably why Ostrom found that common pool resource systems work better when participants have symmetric resources. The point is not that symmetry per se is important. The point is that when the invested resources are symmetric, the intuitive focal point is equal division of the burdens and benefits, which is easy to coordinate on and monitor. When resources are asymmetric, particularly when they are in different forms, such as labor, land, or financial capital, characterizing the respective values of what was contributed, what was divided, and the ways in which these divisions do or do not map onto a fair distribution is more complex. It requires a more complex theory of justice and more complex measurement for inputs and outputs. It is not impossible. It is just harder and, possibly, sufficiently harder that converting the various input contributions and outputs into money and managing the contributions and distributions through property and contracts rather than cooperative social relations may work better.

Work in economics has focused on defining theoretically and testing experimentally different theories of fairness that agents might hold that could explain their behavior in social dilemma games. The major division in this work is between theories that think of fairness in terms of distribution of outcomes and those that think of fairness in terms of intentions. Individuals seem to care about how well off they are from the interaction relative to others in the interaction, as well as relative to how well these others could have made them. They also care about the intentions of others—whether others have intentionally or unintentionally helped or harmed them. Despite long-standing commitment of rational actor models to focusing on absolute payoffs to individuals as the core motivation, the perception of fairness in the interaction turns out to be significant in affecting how people behave. Moreover, Tom Tyler's work on legitimacy and policing suggests that, over and above outcomes and intentions, the fairness of the process by which results are reached is possibly an even more important determinant of the psychological acceptance of outcomes, including negative punishing outcomes.[15]

Constructing Group Identity

The importance of group identity has long been the subject of psychological studies.[16] The degree to which group identification is important is hardly news to anyone. From sports teams to nations, from "our class versus theirs" in elementary school to corporate challenges or the teams formed on globally dispersed, practically anonymous projects like SETI@Home, people tend to identify with groups, to mark "us/them" distinctions, to be loyal to "us," and often to be belligerent to "them." Group identity appears to be not a fixed phenomenon but a culturally constructed and malleable phenomenon, even within short periods and in abstracted setting. One study showed that during the presidential primaries in the 2008 elections, supporters of Hillary Clinton and Barack Obama continued to treat each other as "outsiders" for purposes of dictator game experiments even six weeks after the primary was over. The public performance of unity in the Democratic convention, however, immediately expressed itself in the experiment as an elimination of the in-group/out-group bias between the two groups, even in such an anonymous, abstracted experimental setting.[17] There is some evidence, though not consistently, that increasing contributions "for the team" are a phenomenon driven primarily by the sensitivity of young males to competitive group identity priming.[18] Group identity is, in any event, a double-edged sword, as Samuel Bowles and Herbert Gintis emphasized in focusing on the parochialism and xenophobia it can breed.[19] It is important to understand in this regard that all of these cooperative platforms are available to solve all sorts of human collective action problems. The prisoners in the prisoner's dilemma may well be really bad crooks, and we (as society) may not want them to be able to solve their social dilemma. In this regard, close attention to what makes for successful cooperation can also be a guide to disrupting successful antisocial collaborations.

Discipline and Punishment

A consistent result in public goods games is that if participants can punish defectors, even when punishment is costly, contribution levels improve to near optimal over time. This was an important finding because self-costly punishment creates a second-order public good. If punishment is meted out, selfish actors cooperate, and the payoff to everyone in the group increases. Those who punish, however, bear the full cost of punishment but share the gains equally with all. The standard rational actor model predicts that punishment would therefore not occur, and selfish actors, knowing this, would not cooperate. Experimentally, punishment occurs, is robust, and drives selfish actors to act like cooperators.

Introducing punishment into a cooperative system is tricky business. First, it is possible that punishment crowds out trust and that these are two competing rather than complimentary levers.[20] Experiments that explored this problem suggest that enterprises likely to be homogenously populated by cooperators and reciprocators should be wary of introducing punishment as a prophylactic against potential invasion by selfish actors. For example, if self-selection is possible and participation is relatively costly with low material gains, these factors may be sufficient to exclude selfish actors without the added protection of a punishment system, whose introduction could reduce trust.

Second, introduction of punishment in public goods games with many players of unknown character is likely to be interpreted by participants as helpful to cooperation, and the exertion of punishment is likely to be seen as cooperation in the second-order public goods problem of disciplining defectors. On the other hand, work by Fehr and Bettina Rockenbach suggests that for platforms that are better characterized by bilateral trust games, where individuals can interpret the threat of punishment as a personal lack of trust in them, that threat of punishment for failure to cooperate actually *reduces* the degree to which trustees cooperate.

Third, punishment systems can be abused by defectors. Sometimes noncooperators punish, contrary to expectations, and in patterns that differ from those adopted by reciprocators.[21] Most significantly, they punish to reduce payoffs to others whom they seem to envy, and in some cultures they punish to take revenge on cooperators who punish them for their own defections. Usefully, however, the demand of selfish actors for punishment is elastic. Increasing the cost of punishing reduces destructive punishment by noncooperators more than it reduces helpful punishment by reciprocators.

Fourth, Elinor Ostrom's work suggests that sanctions should be graduated. In some communities of longer standing, this could take the form of gossip. In others, it might mean a series of graduated exclusions, "penalty box" provisions, or temporarily limited privileges. The details are not clearly derivable from the literature when applied outside of long-standing communities. What matters is that sanctions should begin so as to preserve cooperation and keep participants warned and "in" the cooperative sphere, without inducing retaliation. Only repeated violations or some other indicia of willful violation should be graduated toward higher penalties.

Transparency

Cooperative social systems need transparency. Most of the other important design levers depend on a degree of transparency about who is participating and what they are doing. For purposes of humanization, trust, monitoring and punishment, norm creation and fairness, it is important that participants be able to recognize each other, observe each other's actions, characterize them correctly, communicate with each other and about each other's actions and intentions. All these social interactions require transparency. Complete anonymity impedes cooperation as well as humanization. Inability to observe the actions or payoffs of specific others, as opposed to an overall pattern, makes it impossible to recognize cooperation and defection. But transparency is not an unambiguous good for people in social settings. Segmenting information flows is one way in which individuals control the various social spheres and interactions that constitute their lives. We use "privacy" as a broad umbrella term for this concern. This tension requires that identity be available, but not all interactions require perfect, stable, life-encompassing identification. Many online collaboration platforms, for example, depend on persistent pseudonymity rather than real identity. Cooperation systems also work better when they transparently render actions and outcomes. This need not imply a requirement for perfect information (à la perfect markets). Rather, it marks a looser requirement for opportunities for mutual observation and characterization of the others' action to the extent possible. Finally, transparency as to the system design itself is probably also necessary. When one designs systems anchored in the principle that human beings come to know their own ends and preferences through conversation with others and by treating each other as social beings, "expert" manipulation that is not transparent and truthful about its assumptions and interventions can be destructive. Understanding the system design, in particular whether the system is well designed to facilitate cooperators and reciprocators finding each other and cooperating, as well as identifying and punishing defectors, will lead participants to form a more robust belief that actions within the system will conform to cooperative outcomes and to take the cooperative enterprise as their own.

Self-Selection

One factor that is as much a design constraint as a design lever is the extent to which participation in a cooperative setting is voluntary, with relatively easy entry and exit. Several studies have shown that cooperation increases when entry and exit from a social context is available. Entry and exit are a design constraint because in many settings the ease or difficulty of entry will depend on circumstances external to the system whose design is being considered. An employee of a firm in a small town may be perfectly free to resign his or her job but have no alternative employment options. The difficulty of exit or of avoiding involuntary participation in the interaction, and the potential resulting difficulty presented by having not only employees who want to be an engaged part of the cooperative enterprise but also employees who experience themselves as being forced into this interaction by necessity, is unavoidable. One cannot design "easy exit" for the employees in this setting. Similarly, Wikipedia began as a purely self-selected collaboration. As its cultural significance increased, its contents became significant to people who did not care about coauthoring an encyclopedia but cared about how issues were represented in it. This led to a gradual shift from a purely communicative, norms-based, collaborative effort to one that includes technical and organizational processes designed to constrain uncooperative behavior and channel dissent into conversation and decision rather than unilateral destructive behavior. Recognizing that difficulty requires system designers to consider whether they are in a choice-based or necessity-driven interaction and to respond to the necessity-driven, lower-cooperation setting by using other levers to improve cooperation.

Cost

The cooperation literature models cooperation for rational actors operating within a beliefs, preferences, and constraints model. The more costly cooperating (or punishing defectors) is, the less the "demand" for it will be among those who have a preference for cooperation. In prisoner's dilemma games, for example, cooperation rises when the opportunity cost of cooperating is lower. Low cost is not an absolute precondition to cooperation. Some participants are willing to spend a lot to cooperate. But the relationship between cost of cooperation and levels of cooperation is still inverse. Field studies of cooperation systems also confirm that structures that lower the cost of cooperation—both in provisioning the primary public good and in provisioning the secondary public good of policing against defection—are common in successful cooperative enterprises.

Crowding Out

Systems, and elements within systems, interact with each other. Some add cumulatively to each other's effects. More importantly as a design constraint, some may conflict with each other and limit the efficacy of the system as a whole in achieving its goals.[22] This is called "crowding out." We can think of "crowding out" between systems or between elements within a system.

An example of crowding out between systems is presented by the case of Taiwanese irrigation associations. These voluntary associations were created and run by farmers and were considered highly successful at managing the common pool resource of the irrigation systems. In 1993 the Taiwanese government sought to appear "profarmer" by taking over the association fees the farmers were required to pay. In later studies, that benign intervention seems to have shifted the associations from participatory associations of farmers who knew their system well and volunteered to manage the association to a system that one gets from the government. The introduction of the state as system crowded out the community as system.[23] More controlled versions of the introduction of incentives and monitoring into a cooperative setting identified the same phenomenon.[24] Much of the work on crowding out between systems has occurred within the literature on motivation crowding out—a literature that has shown in many experiments and observations that introduction of monetary incentives crowds out social motivations for cooperation. By introducing a price or an organizational command and control system, one is likely to crowd out social cooperation *as a system*. Such interventions may be desirable when a social system is not functioning properly. But because systems are not necessarily cumulative, the overall effect of any given proposed intervention—be it introduction of a market mechanism or an administrative mechanism, governmental or private-organizational—must consider its impact on any existing social cooperation system or on social cooperation systems that could be created or improved.

A second aspect of crowding out is an effect among elements within systems. In the list that I have offered in this part we see, for example, that punishment crowds out trust. This is entirely consistent with the "motivation crowding out" literature but operates here as an insight not into the choice between, say, a market-based system and a social cooperation platform, but into the choice of elements within a given system. One may have to choose, for example, between providing opportunities for punishment and not doing so, or setting the levels and types of punishment. This choice may depend on one's expectations of the heterogeneity of participant types and the degree of self-selection involved, on the availability of face-to-face communications, or on whether the system is one that has been agreed upon by the participants in advance. In general, inter-element crowding out is one constraint on cooperative human systems design.

Leadership and Asymmetric Contribution

The final design lever comes not from the experimental literature but from case studies of online cooperation. "Leadership" ranges from active, charismatic leadership to the acts of the many who do the heavy lifting necessary to start a project and provide a foundation and scaffolding around which multiple contributions can develop. Leadership need not imply "organization" or control. Leadership does not necessitate separation of authority from capacity to act. That separation, the mark of control hierarchies, is a particular method of exercising leadership and suffers limitations in sensing and adapting to the environment in which the group functions. Leadership in cooperation settings is therefore best seen as covering diverse instances of asymmetric contribution tied to asymmetric voice in the direction of the collective effort. A leader at the platoon level may be its commander but may also be a forceful soldier who bears more than his fair burden. One of the mistakes made by some commentators on online peer production is the interpretation of lead users, or highly asymmetric contributions, as suckers carrying free riders on their back rather than as leaders. Leadership opportunities can be built into a cooperation platform. Distributed computing projects like SETI@Home purposely provide opportunities for showing "leadership," combining "Big Man" agonistic gift structures with nonagonistic forms of interaction. Being a leader, having a following, seeing the success of something one knows to have been disproportionately the outcome of one's own life plan through the coordinated contribution of others is its own reward for autonomous, planning individuals whose sense of self and worth is bound up with the success of their projects.

Conclusion

Patents and copyrights are thought to solve the public goods problem of information production conceived through a selfish model of human motivation and action. They give authors and inventors and the organizations that employ or finance them control over who uses their products and enables them to extract rents that fund the system and motivate everyone to create the knowledge. I have elsewhere explained why patents, copyrights, and similar exclusive rights provide an anchor for one business model, or organizational and social form of solving this public goods problem, but that there are many other models for which patents and copyrights merely raise the costs of information production without providing benefits. Most significant among these in the networked information economy has been the emergence of social production generally, and peer production in particular, as a major modality of information, knowledge, and cultural production.

After we recognize the stability and sustainability of peer production, it is time to dig deeper into cooperative systems design. Better microanalysis of what makes some systems succeed and others fail is important to the design of successful systems—by participants for themselves, and by other actors, in particular organizations—both commercial and nonprofit—as they try to find ways to coexist with and adapt to the presence of social production. In this chapter I offer a sketch of the design elements involved in designing systems for human cooperation. It is the product of analyzing the experimental economics literature on social cooperation. The design elements I offer here are an initial effort. Because the experimental economics work itself is dedicated to parsimony and tractability, of necessity it simplifies, and perhaps obscures, much of the dynamics of these systems. The next step will be to study in the field how cooperation enterprises use these or other levers to improve our ability to approach human systems design for enabling human cooperation. We have spent decades refining our mechanism design around the selfish rational actor model. We must now work to develop an equally robust approach to mechanism design, one based on the more realistic, experimentally verified, and more humane view of humanity.

NOTES

1. Yochai Benkler, Coase's Penguin, or Linux and the Nature of the Firm, 112 *Yale L. J.* 369 (2002); Yochai Benkler, "Sharing Nicely": On Shareable Goods and the Emergence of Sharing as a Modality of Economic Production, 114 *Yale L. J.* 273 (2004).

2. *The Firm as a Collaborative Community, Reconstructing Trust in the Knowledge Economy* (Charles Hecksher and Paul S. Adler, eds., 2006). In particular there, see Adler & Hecksher, Towards Collaborative Community, at 11–105; Charles F. Sabel, A Real-Time Revolution in Routines, at 106–156.

3. *Foundations of Human Sociality: Economic Experiments and Ethnographic Evidence from Fifteen Small-Scale Societies* (Joseph Henrich et al., eds., 2004).

4. Colin F. Camerer & Ernst Fehr, Measuring Social Norms and Preferences Using Experimental Games: A Guide for Social Scientists, in Henrich et al., *Foundations of Human Sociality*, chapter 3.

5. Elinor Ostrom, A Behavioral Approach to the Rational Choice Theory of Collective Action, 92 *Am. Pol. Sci. Rev.* 1–22 (1998).

6. Matthew Rabin, Incorporating Fairness into Game Theory and Economics, 83 *Am. Econ. Rev.* 1281 (1993).

7. Yochai Benkler & Helen Nissenbaum, Commons-Based Peer Production and Virtue, 14 *Journal of Political Philosophy* 394–419 (2006).

8. David Sally, Conversation and Cooperation in Social Dilemmas, 7 *Rationality and Society* 57–92 (1995).

9. Iris Bohnet & Bruno Frey, The Sound of Silence in Prisoner's Dilemma and Dictator Games, 38 *J. Econ. Behavior & Org.* 43–57 (1999).

10. James K. Rilling et al., A Neural Basis for Social Cooperation, 35(2) *Neuron* 395–405 (2002); James K. Rilling et al., Opposing Bold Responses to Reciprocated and Unreciprocated Altruism in Putative Reward Pathways, 15(6) *Neuroreport* 2539–2543 (2004).

11. Bohnet & Frey.

12. Andrea McDowell, Real Property, Spontaneous Order, and Norms in the Gold Miners, 29 *Law & Social Inquiry* 771 (2004).

13. Elinor Ostrom, Roy Gardner, & James Walker, *Rules, Games, and Common Pool Resources* (1994).

14. Ernst Fehr & K. Schmidt, Theories of Fairness and Reciprocity: Evidence and Economic Applications, in *Advances in Economics and Econometrics: Theory and Applications, Eighth World Congress* (M. Dwatripont et al., eds., 2001).

15. Tom R. Tyler, Procedural Justice, Legitimacy, and the Effective Rule of Law, 30 *Crime and Justice* 283–357 (2003).

16. Henri Tajfel & John Turner, An Integrative Theory of Intergroup Conflict, in *The Social Psychology of Intergroup Relations* (W. G. Austin & S. Worchel, eds., 1979); Toshio Yamagishi et al., Bounded Generalized Reciprocity: Ingroup Boasting and Ingroup Favoritism, 16 *Advances Group Processes* 161–197 (1999); J. H. Fowler & C. D. Kam, Beyond the Self: Social Identity, Altruism, and Political Participation, 69 *J. Politics* 813–827 (2007).

17. David G. Rand et al., Dynamic Remodeling of In-Group Bias during the 2008 Presidential Election, 106 *PNAS* 6187 (April 14, 2009).

18. Rand et al.; C. Efferson, R. Lalive, and E. Feh, The Coevolution of Cultural Groups and Ingroup Favoritism, 321 *Science* 1844–1849 (2008).

19. Samuel Bowles & Herbert Gintis, *Persistent Parochialism: Trust and Exclusion in Ethnic Networks* (2003); Samuel Bowles & Herbert Gintis, *Social Capital and Community Governance* (2001).

20. Toshio Yamagishi, The Provision of a Sanctioning System as a Public Good, 51 *J. Personality Social Psychology* 110–116 (1986); Ernst Fehr & Bettina Rockenbach, Detrimental Effects of Sanctions on Human Altruism, 422 *Nature* 137–140 (2002).

21. Armin Falk et al., Driving Forces behind Informal Sanctions, 73 *Econometrica* 2017 (2005).

22. Bruno Frey, A Constitution for Knaves Crowds Out Civic Virtues, 443 *Econ. J.* 1043–1053 (1997); Bruno Frey & Reto Jege, Motivation Crowding Theory: A Survey of Empirical Evidence, 15(5) *J. Econ. Surveys* 589 (2001); Samuel Bowles, Policies Designed for Self-Interested Citizens May Undermine "Moral Sentiments": Evidence from Economic Experiments, 320 *Science* 1605–1609 (2008); Yochai Benkler, *Beyond the Bad Man and the Knave: Law and the Interdependence of Motivational Vectors* (2009).

23. Elinor Ostrom, Policies That Crowd Out Reciprocity and Collective Action, in *Moral Sentiments and Material Interests: The Foundations of Cooperation in Economic Life* (Herbert Gintis, Samuel Bowles, Robert Boyd, and Ernst Fehr, eds., 2005), 253, 261–263.

24. Juan Camilo Cardenas, John K. Stranlund, and Cleve E. Willis, Local Environmental Control and Institutional Crowding Out, 28 *World Development* 1719–1733 (2000).

IP Crimes and Other Fictions

LAWRENCE LIANG

9

Beyond Representation
The Figure of the Pirate

It would seem almost paradoxical to suggest that there is a representational problem with respect to the figure of the pirate in contemporary discourse. If the mainstream media are anything to go by, then the figure of the media pirate is everywhere, and the problem would seem to be one of overrepresentation. We are, however, not concerned with the way in which the pirate is narrated as a figure of illegality by the likes of Jack Valenti or the Recording Industry Association of America (RIAA), both of whom argue for a more stringent enforcement of copyright.[1] My focus instead is on the challenges that the figure of the pirate poses to the various and even conflicting discourses that have emerged over the past few years to challenge the hegemonic account of intellectual property.

From political economy critiques of intellectual property to calls for a much stronger public domain, Free/Libre/Open Source Software (FLOSS) collaborative practices, and critiques of the figure of the author from literary and legal theory, the critical scholarship on intellectual property has been vital in the framing of an alternative paradigm to the study of IP in general. However, a quick survey of the range of these debates also reveals the relative absence of any serious engagement with the world of quotidian nonlegal media consumption and circulation or piracy. This is surprising, given that the everyday life of IP plays itself out through an extraordinary focus on the pirate.[2] What is it about the nature of piracy that creates this uncomfortable silence around it? Or is it possible that there is instead something about the way in which the critical responses to IP have been framed that makes it impossible for them to deal with piracy or for piracy to redeem itself?

Unlike those who operate in the public domain and have a clear visibility, the pirate always emerges as an abstract, spectral figure. With allegations of links to terrorism and the underworld and of being the cause for the decline of the entertainment industry and tax revenues to the state, the pirate as a criminal figure invites the legal attention of the state and of private enforcers. Piracy has also become the subject of media attention, and rarely a day goes by without some sensational account of a raid. At the other end of the spectrum—that is, within the critical work on the public domain—there is either an embarrassing silence about or a disavowal of the pirate.

Lawrence Lessig and others have responded to debates on IP by looking beyond the binaries of legality/illegality that are set up by traditional copyright, yet when it comes to piracy, they still confront a problem of accommodation. What exactly, then, is the problem of piracy, and why can it not be accommodated within the terms of public domain theorists? Surely, it cannot be just the fact that piracy is tainted by illegality, since other practices defended by these scholars (like downloading music) are also tainted by illegality. There must be more specific ways in which these acts find redemption, while the pirate simply cannot.

Piracy operates within the logic of profit and within the terms of commerce. For this reason, it cannot claim the same moral ground available to other nonlegal media practices. For critics of the copyright regime dominated by media conglomerates, it would be an embarrassment to admit support of any nonlegal commercial enterprise. Another reason for the inattention to commercial piracy among critical theorists of IP is that piracy pertains to the domain of pleasure. Unlike those nonlegal uses of IP that secure access to affordable medicines or learning materials, there is very little possibility of redeeming a practice that simply provides people with low-cost DVDs, MP3s, etc. Moreover, unlike the case of transformative piracy, commercial piracy is unable to redeem itself as an act of creativity. In an instance of transformative piracy, for example, a young musician might illegally download and then remix music to produce a new piece of music. But in commercial piracy there is a slavish making of copies without any transformative redemption.

Let us now try to understand the terms of representation that public domain scholarship establishes for itself. While the public domain has emerged
as the most viable alternative to the expansion of IP, the question remains
whether the public domain is the only way through which we can understand
contemporary conflicts around IP. More specifically, there are limits to the
public domain approach in providing an account of piracy. The public domain
deploys classical terms of representation, which borrow from either political or cultural theory; these include categories of citizenship, resistance, and
creativity.[3] Piracy often does not fit within any of these categories. There is a
positivity or excess in the body of the pirate that cannot be disavowed. The
only manner in which a copyright infringer is rescued from the accusation of
being an illegal pirate is through an act of redemption, for instance by showing that his acts of infringement actually result in an increase in creativity
through so-called transformative authorship. But what about the entire realm
of nontransformative authorship or "Asian piracy," which does not necessarily transform but merely reproduces? While one can understand that Lessig
would have to be careful about how he pitches a reform of copyright law in
the United States, it is also difficult to miss the linkages between his narrative
and older accounts of illegality in Asia, where urban experience has been typically narrated in terms of its preponderant criminality and illegality. While
the United States has always narrated itself through the tropes of constitution-
alism and the rule of law, a crisis arrived in the form of the Internet, where the
very language of criminality and illegality that has been applied to much of the
world hit home in the realm of the ordinary, in the form of the criminalization
of students downloading music. Clearly one cannot have an account of illegality in a country that prides itself on its constitutional tradition and rule of law.
One strategy, then, has been to redeem the acts of "ordinary" American citizens through the discursive construction of an "other," an "Asian" other. The
categories of the public domain serve as the neutral ground through which the
two kinds of pirates are pitted against each other, and the terms of reference
for this public domain are creativity and innovation.

Underlying copyright's mythology is the modernist idea of creativity, which
is shared by advocates of stronger copyright as well as advocates of the public
domain. The difference between public domain scholars and copyright advocates lies in their understanding of the idea of the creative, and the question
under debate is whether we arrive at the ultimate public good through the
route of more copyright or through more freedom. Public domain advocates
would argue that the realm of creativity is enabled by various acts of copying,
for it is through constant copying and additions that a regenerative culture of
production is achieved. Thus, if someone creates a parody or a remix, there

is no problem because they have added to the larger pool of raw ingredients available to all within the public domain. Public domain advocates also mobilize the idea of resistance. Transformative users are represented as producing an ideological critique of the original content they appropriate.

Here it becomes useful to connect to political theories that have looked at the conditions of representation, since many ideas of the public domain do derive from a larger political and constitutional base. The public domain, which imagines a particular kind of creative citizen-subject, is in many ways an extension of constitutional categories of representation in general, including citizenship. The public domain is bracketed as a space of equal participation in which everyone can participate as an equal, rights-bearing citizen. The linking of public domain theories to freedom of speech is not accidental, and the model of the public domain as the sphere of rational communication borrows from existing accounts of the public/private divide.[4] Many postcolonial scholars have seriously contested the category of the citizen as the universal bearer of rights, and the representative capacity of the citizen to participate in the public sphere as an unmarked individual remains mythical at best. In India, for instance, the creation of the citizen-subject category demanded a move away from the oversignified body of the individual marked by religion, gender, caste, etc., into an unmarked subject position—"the citizen"—based on equality and access and guaranteed rights within the constitutional framework. But the majority of people in India are only precarious citizens who often do not have the ability to claim rights in the same manner as the Indian elite. Instead, the most frequent manner in which they access institutions of democracy and "welfare" is through complex negotiations and networks, often marked by their illegal status.[5]

One way of understanding the place of the "illegal" in the Indian context is through Partha Chatterjee's notion of political society.[6] From the very beginning of the independent career of the Indian nation-state, Chatterjee argues, there was a contradiction between its modernizing aspirations and its commitment to democracy that was intended to be managed on the terrain of political society. Democracy was, then, a large and muddled field where compromises had to be made, from point to point, moment to moment. Political society constituted a field lacking the clarity of moral language and legal concepts that were supposed to define the relations between state and civil society. This meant bending the rules, recognizing that the legal fiction of equal citizenship did not always apply and that the laws of property and contract might sometimes need to be overlooked. It meant speaking in both languages, of rights as well as policy, often using the one to overcome the limitations of the other. Concession was thus the norm rather than the exception.[7]

Similarly, pirates who merely reproduce without producing are unable to shed their illegal excesses and thus play a role or become a part of the reconstituted public domain. Pirates allegedly contribute nothing because they cannot claim the representative status given to the transforming creator within the productive public domain. And yet a look at history and at the present seems to indicate that there is a certain stubbornness on the part of those who, in this fashion, do not find a representative space in the public domain—the trickster, the copier, the thief, the pirate—who inhabit a marginal site of production and circulation.[8]

Moving beyond the Impasse

The simplistic divide of legality and illegality that separates pirates and others renders almost impossible any serious engagement with the phenomenon of piracy. Let us take for granted the illegal status of piracy, but let us not stop there. It might be more useful to ask the question, not of what piracy is, but of what piracy does. Shifting focus from the discursive and moral representation of the illegal deed to the wider social world in which the deed is located allows us to bring into light the very nature of the law that names a particular act as an illegal one. What about the naming of the deed as an illegal one prevents us from reflecting on the nature of the act? When we look at the act of sharing, it is an act immediately invested with a sense of virtue. But the same act, when rendered through the prism of private property, becomes an act of infringement and a crime. The debate between morality and ethics is now a familiar one, and indeed it might even be argued that the law's monopoly over official definitions of morality does not render obsolete the question of whether an act can still be considered in terms of ethics. The shift away from what piracy is to what piracy does enables us to consider on the same plane its linkages to the normative considerations that public domain advocates argue for yet are often unable to achieve.

Rather than looking at the neat spaces of legal/illegal, it might be more fruitful to consider one space in which piracy plays itself out—the transforming urban landscapes—and the specific histories of nooks and corners rendering this space an illegal one, as well as the accumulated histories of regulation, tractability, and negotiation that render its topography intelligible.[9] In urban studies, the idea of an illegal city is familiar. One reads, for instance, that an average of 40 percent and in some cases 70 percent of the population of major cities lives in illegal conditions. Furthermore, 70 to 95 percent of all new housing is built illegally.[10] The primary reason for this state of illegality arises from the nature of land tenure forms in cities, where the twin tropes of ownership and title are clearly unable to account for the myriad ways through which people assert a claim on land and to the city more generally. The people who live in this perpetual state of illegality also engage in other networks of illegality, such as stealing electricity and water or bribing their way through Kafkaesque bureaucratic structures to access civic amenities that the legal city takes for granted. Thus, when we return to the piracy story and we are told that over 70 percent of the software used in India is illegal, we encounter this statistic with a sense of familiarity and not anxiety.[11] While the older illegal city has been in existence for a while, the proliferation of new nonlegal media practices (from pirated VCDs, DVDs, and MP3s to gray market mobile phones) has added another layer to its experience and narration.

A Peek into Life at Madipur, 29 June 2004

Text by: Bhagwati Prasad <bhagwati@sarai.net>
Translated by: Shveta <shveta@sarai.net>

The Madipur Village lies adjacent to the Madipur Colony. . . . The factories produce hosiery, shirts, trousers etc. Factory workers live in this village. . . . Sundays are off, and so the day for relaxing, roaming around. But Saturday nights have a different importance altogether. That's the time for watching films.

The cassette shops here rent out some cassettes, but mostly CDs. Every shop-keeper/owner possesses five to six video CD players. . . . A set-up comprising a VCD player, a colour television and four movies is rent out at rates between Rs. 120 and 150. There was a police raid here a few days ago. All the shopkeepers were apprehended and asked to pay up Rs. 5000. At first, the shopkeepers refused. But there was little they could do. The police simply stated that not only do you not have licenses to run video parlours, but moreover you rent out pirated VCDs. If you don't pay up, we'll confiscate all your material. What could the shopkeepers do? They all handed over the five thousand rupees without another moment's hesitation. Among the shopkeepers is Mohd. Faizal. He said, "At least this will get the policemen to leave us in peace. . . . Four to five rentals every night mean an earning of Rs. 600. And all the material returns to the shop by morning. Why would we want to close a business such as this?" This much is clear[:] that the police is aware of the weak links in this business, and uses them to its advantage to earn money. But the shopkeepers also know that if they have to continue their business, they will have to bear with these small injuries.

This simple and yet compelling description of a "place of piracy" locates it within larger rhythms of daily life common to many parts of South Asia, of the daily negotiations with law and power, and of survival and dreams and fantasies that also escape the normal grind of livelihood and survival. The lines that divide the legal and the illegal city are often blurred and intersect with each other in unpredictable ways, rendering any naïve belief in neatness redundant. Just as one cannot understand land tenure through the prism of liberal legality alone, any attempt to understand the complex networks of economic and social relations underlying the phenomenon of piracy will have to engage with the conflict over control over the means of technological and cultural production in this contemporary moment of globalization. The ways in which the illegal media city emerges and coexists alongside the vibrant, innovative, and productive debris of the older city, part of the more generally schizoid relationship between legality and illegality in postcolonial cities, suggests that the crisis of IP may not lie in legal/illegal relations, and we may need to turn the gaze of the law from the usual suspects of illegality to legality itself and the relations that underlie its existence.[12]

Piracy transforms the technological experience, which has traditionally been rooted either in monumental visions of development or in the aspirations of the Indian elites, and provides an entry point for a much wider array of people to experience on their own terms the "Information Age." The cheap CD or DVD supplements the experience of cyberspace while at the same time being rooted within diverse spaces in the city. Even as the urban landscape is being transformed and older media spaces like cinema halls give way to high-rise malls with multiplexes, and even as the spaces of traditional mass media begin to shrink because of their prohibitive prices, we see the emergence of a widely distributed chain of circulation of media commodities challenging the regime of IP. The critical difference between this world of everyday media and the celebratory approach of radical new media activists or public domain scholars is that the world of quotidian media experience does not articulate itself through the terms of resistance or appropriation. Piracy obviously does not stake a claim in the world of official creativity, either. It remains what it is: a culture of the copy that exists alongside livelihood and labor, profit and pornography.

Reading the New Cultures of the Copy through the Old

One objection to piracy is that it operates within the domain of slavish reproduction, without any transformative act of creativity allowing for its redemption from the status of an illegal object. We are therefore forced to reflect on the nature of the copy in contemporary culture: What is the precise cultural status of the duplicate CD or DVD in relation to the world of creativity and innovation? In the brilliant story "Pierre Menard, Author of the Quixote," Jorge Luis Borges narrates the efforts of an eclectic scholar, Pierre Menard (author of a range of scholarly and taxonomic works), who decides to rewrite Cervantes's *Don Quixote*. Menard does not want to write a version of *Don Quixote* but to reproduce the text. He completes it, and when he compares the two texts, he finds them to be identical, and yet Borges shows us that they are different texts.[13]

If we move to the contemporary and consider the ubiquitous pirate DVD, the prized commodity of pirate aesthetics, we may ask whether this new product of digital reproduction still allows for differences to be produced. After all, it is the machine instead of human hands doing the copying.[14] One of the strange things that people who have watched films on pirated DVDs will find is the phenomenon of the subtitles being different from the actual words spoken on screen. The reason for this is that the pirates usually get an early copy of the film, usually a screening copy, which does not yet have all the frills and extras eventually found on the "original" DVD.

For this reason a number of features, including dubbing or subtitling, have to be done by the pirates themselves. Brian Larkin's work on piracy in Nigeria similarly forces us not only to look at and listen to the onscreen content but also to consider the conditions under which texts are pirated and circulated.[15] Larkin demonstrates the critical importance of paying attention to infrastructures of production in developing countries where the very process of cultural production is tied to the relative lack of infrastructure, on the one hand, and also becomes the basis for the transformation of the conditions of production by generating a parallel economy of low-cost infrastructure. This economy of recycling, which Ravi Sundaram also describes as the "pirate modern,"[16] becomes the arena for all kinds of technological innovation and extends into experiments with cultural forms such as parodies, remixes, and cover versions. Larkin's invocation of the importance of infrastructure contrasts with the obsessive fixation on content one sees in most Western accounts of creativity. In this case the content also has to be filtered through the regime of its own production. Piracy imposes particular conditions on the recording, transmission, and retrieval of data. Constant copying erodes data storage, degrades image and sound, and overwhelms the signal of media content with the noise produced by the means of reproduction. Larkin notes that because pirated videos so often contain blurred images and distorted sound, they create a kind of material space "that filters audiences' engagement with media technologies and their senses of time, speed, space, and contemporaneity. In this way, piracy creates an aesthetic, a set of formal qualities that generate a particular sensorial experience of media marked by poor transmission, interference, and noise."[17]

Larkin uses the question of pirate infrastructure to open up the debate on intellectual property and foreground the importance of addressing the question of content while looking at a legal aspect of culture. If infrastructures represent attempts to order, regulate, and rationalize society, then breakdowns in their operation, or the rise of provisional and informal infrastructures, highlight the failure of that ordering and the recoding that takes its place. When the material operation of piracy and its social consequences are scrutinized, it becomes clear that pirate infrastructure is a powerful mediating force that produces new modes of organizing sensory perception, time, space, and economic networks.

Revisiting the Story of Creativity

The common ground bringing together copyright fundamentalists and public domain advocates is the presumption of creativity and innovation. The argument of those who argue for a stronger public domain approach to copyright is that copyright fails in fulfilling its self-appointed role as the guardian of creativity and that it would serve creativity much better to have a model allowing for greater access and less restriction. What remains stable, however, is the account of creativity as a value-neutral public good that we have to strive for and seek to protect. This is of course explicit in the justificatory theories of intellectual property, which are argued not only on the principles of exclusive rights and property but on the grounds of the promotion of creativity and progress.

In the previous section we undertook the task of expanding the terms of creativity to look at other sites of creativity, including the domain of the technological and infrastructure. Another means of framing contemporary transitions and conflicts might arise from revisiting the very idea of creativity itself. Thus, rather than translating a series of practices within the terms of creativity, we can start posing questions about the conditions under which terms such as creativity, public good, and progress become narrated as universals in copyright and in the alternatives proposed to copyright.

Critiquing the unquestioned value of creativity as the particular experience and story of history narrated as the universal imperative of mankind, John Mason argues we step back from our arrogant sense of our place in the world and consider creativity not merely as an impulse in itself but in relation to other values such as justice, harmony, sustainability, and equity.[18] In a world in which many forms of life (including our own) can only survive in controlled environments, we would esteem resourceful skills of reproduction as highly as (or more highly than) energetic and significant production. We would value the curator as much as (perhaps more than) the creator.

The Raqs Media Collective suggests that rather than speaking of end users of digital information, it would be more accurate to speak of custodians who nurture pieces of information when they receive them or to think of them as part of a networked community of receivers who are also always givers and as users who are also potentially, if not actually, producers. The epics, stories, songs, and sagas that represent in some ways the collective heritage of humanity have survived only because their custodians took care not to lock them into a system of end usage; instead they embellished them, adding to their health and vitality before passing them on to others.

Revisiting the History of the Commons and Dispossession

Recent scholarship on intellectual property and the public domain has been marked by the invocation of the metaphor of the commons and the threat that it faces from the limitless expansion of intellectual property. More often than not the commons is allegorized as a mythical ideal governed by principles of sharing, access, and collaboration, which was lost after the first enclosure movement. The argument proceeds to caution against a similar enclosure, the second enclosures movement, in the realm of the information ecology threatening to privatize every aspect of information and thereby creativity.

Social historians of crime, for instance, have rigorously alerted us to the intertwined histories of property and criminalization. It may therefore not be sufficient for us to invoke the commons only in allegorical terms; it may be more fruitful to look at current conflict within a wider historical continuum of the nature, definition, contours, and protection of property. The history of the commons is also a history of criminalization and the defining of ideas of trespass and encroachment.

The figure of the trespasser is common in the history of property, and in many ways the central imagination of property is founded on the prima facie denial of the trespasser. Emerging from the early history of the enclosure of the commons, the idea of the trespasser has shown remarkable resilience and adaptability to the changing ideas of property and value. The trespasser has resurfaced in the information era along with other familiar figures from the history of property such as the pirate, the copier, etc. As with the historical expansion of material property, the expansion of intellectual property relies on strategies by which various categories of illegality are mobilized both to justify IP and to argue for stronger enforcement regimes. And yet the resurfacing of the trespasser is complicated by the fact that it brings with it residual memories such as that of the commons. The debate on intellectual property has thus far been characterized as a predominantly legal debate and, within the legal field, as a debate specific to intangible property. But can the conflicts that have been raging for the past few years be confined within such terms alone? Can the invocation of the commons remain only within the world of allegory?

One way of opening up the debate on IP may be to throw it beyond the question of information and the intangibles alone and to instead work with the idea of "contested commons and trespassing publics" as a way of understanding and theorizing contemporary conflicts around the world of intangibles as property. By taking the history of exclusion, trespass, and encroachment not merely as linguistic inheritances from the history of the commons but as conceptual linkages that tie in the worlds of the tangible and intangible, historical and contemporary, we may be able to draw on conceptual resources unavailable to any singular entry point into the domain.

For instance, if exclusion has been the central fulcrum tying the histories of property's older avatars to its present forms, then the question is whether there can be such a straightforward application of the idea of exclusion/trespass when we deal with the world of the intangible. Fences, boundaries, and walls that once marked the binaries between the owner/trespasser, legal/illegal, and occupier/encroacher face many conceptual difficulties when translated into the domain of the intangible.

It is also pertinent to note the difference between the idea of the trespasser as an isolated spectral figure of deviance and the idea of the trespassing public. The sheer range of people and practices today that would be implicated within the idea of trespass is noteworthy, including the unauthorized artists who appropriate images, the pirate using low-cost technologies of reproduction to compete with media empires, the counterfeit passing itself off as genuine, and the medical patients demanding lower-cost medicines. There seem to be few safe spaces left where one is not identified and reprimanded as a trespasser. This range of offenders against the regime of property sounds uncannily similar to the "motley crew" in the social history of crime, where runaway slaves encountered condemned idlers, radical Anabaptists, and renegade sailors.

Peter Linebaugh and Marcus Rediker in their account of early piracy begin with an invocation of the twin myths of the many-headed hydra[19] and of its slaying by Hercules as a way of thinking about the challenges faced by the world of capital as it seeks to reproduce itself endlessly across borders and domains of life, having the sovereign authority of law as its eternal companion. Looking at the material organization of many thousands of workers into transatlantic circuits of commodity exchange and capital accumulation, Linebaugh and Rediker proceed to examine how the dispossessed translated their cooperation into anticapitalist projects. The first enclosures, which resulted in the expropriation of the commons, freed large territories for capitalist agriculture, logging, mining, and speculation in land, at the same time creating a vast army freed to become wage earners in new industrializing areas at home or abroad; otherwise, they were criminalized through harsh laws imposing penal servitude in the colonies. Those dispossessed from the land also became the bulk of the workforce for the new engines transporting commodities across continents. Sailors and ships linked the mode of production and expanded the international capitalist economy. The ship was also the site for the coming together of diverse forms of labor, from different ethnicities, bound together by a pidgin tongue. The solidarity of this motley crew was forged around a commonality of their dispossession and labor—a solidarity that would challenge the smooth flow of capital.

The first pirates were often the "outcasts of the land" who would mutiny against the conditions of their work, in doing so creating an alternative order challenging the division of labor and of capital. In fashioning their hierarchy, these buccaneers often drew from the memory of utopias created by pedants, in which work had been abolished, property redistributed, social distinctions leveled, health restored, and food made abundant.

Piracy's redistribution of wealth was considered by many to be a massive problem, and pirates were declared to belong to no nation. In fact, piracy emerged as one of the earliest crimes of universal jurisdiction in a time when nation-states were carving out their absolute sovereignty. But piracy was not merely a problem of the failure of implementation or enforcement; it also established an alternative ethic and mode of being. Piracy was democratic in an undemocratic age and egalitarian in a highly unequal age. Linebaugh and Rediker provide various accounts in which pirate ships inverted all rules of social hierarchy and the laws of private property were suspended to allow for experimentation with alternative social imaginaries, even if for very brief spells. It seems the contemporary landscape is marked by a similar constellation of ships, commodities, and valuables that travel on the information highway. While being the new symbols of capital, they are also as vulnerable as the ships of early maritime capitalism were to attacks of piracy. Just as the piracy of the past disturbed the division of labor and of spoils while also creating new utopian communities, contemporary piracy also makes the "whole enterprise of earning vast sums of money from the nothing of data and culture a difficult business."[20]

NOTES

1. For examples see Jack Valenti's statements at http://www.fact-uk.org.uk/general%20pdfs/valenti%20speech.pdf and John Stokes, "Kids, When You Buy a Bootleg DVD, You May Be Supporting People Who Might Sympathize with a Terrorist Group That Hasn't Actually Attacked Us," Ars Technica, May 29, 2005, http://arstechnica.com/news.ars/post/20050528-4952.html. A recent statement by the U.S. Department of Transportation states, "They run computer manufacturing plants and noodle shops, sell 'designer clothes' and 'bargain basement' CD's. They invest, pay taxes, give to charity, and fly like trapeze artists between one international venue and another. The end game, however, is not to buy a bigger house or send the kids to an Ivy League school—it's to blow up a building, to hijack a jet, to release a plague, and to kill thousands of innocent civilians," U.S. Department of Transportation, Office of Safety and Security, Transit Security Newsletter 36 (May 2003), p. 2. For a scathing critique of this trend, see Nikhil Govil, "War in the Age of Pirate Reproduction," in *Sarai Reader 04: Crisis/Media* (Delhi: Sarai, 2004) . This declaration has been similarly followed up by the Indian copyright enforcers (led by former commissioner of police Julio Rebiero), who have stated that music piracy funds Jihadi terrorists. See R. Rangaraj, "Music Piracy and Terrorism," Chennaonline, Sept. 28, 2003, http://www.chennaionline.com/musicnew/films/09musicpiracy.

2. See chapter 4 of Lawrence Lessig, *Free Culture: How Big Media Uses Technology and the Law to Lock Down Culture and Control Creativity* (New York: Penguin, 2004).

3. Rosemary J. Coombe, *The Cultural Life of Intellectual Properties: Authorship, Appropriation, and the Law* (Durham, NC: Duke University Press, 1998); Yochai Benkler, "Through the Looking Glass: Alice and the Constitutional Foundations of the Public Domain," 66 Law & Contemp. Probs. 173 (2003).

4. James Boyle, *Shamans, Software and Spleens: Law and the Construction of the Information Society* (Cambridge, MA: Harvard University Press, 1996); Diane Leenheer Zimmerman, "Information as Speech, Information as Goods: Some Thoughts on Marketplaces and the Bill of Rights," 33 Wm. & Mary L. Rev. 665 (1992); Yochai Benkler, "Siren Songs and Amish Children: Autonomy, Information, and Law," 76 N.Y.U. L. Rev. 23, 59 (2001).

5. Partha Chatterjee, "On Civil and Political Societies in Postcolonial Democracies," in Sudipta Kaviraj and Sunil Khilnani (eds.), *Civil Society: History and Possibilities* (Cambridge: Cambridge University Press, 2001), 165.

6. Partha Chatterjee, "Beyond the Nation? Or Within?" 32(1/2) Economic & Political Weekly 30 (1997); "Democracy and the Violence of the State: A Political Negotiation of Death," 2(1) Inter-Asia Cultural Studies 7 (2001).

7. Awadhendra Sharan, "Digital India: Remapping the Divide," paper presented at the Southern Voices and Global Order Conference, University of Warwick, July 7–9, 2004.

8. John Mason, *The Value of Creativity: The Origins and Emergence of a Modern Belief* (Aldershot, UK: Ashgate, 2003)

9. For an account of the everyday life of law and social relations, see Susan Silbey and Patrick Ewick, *The Common Place of the Law: Stories from Everyday Life* (Chicago: University of Chicago Press, 1998).

10. Alain Durand-Lasserve and Laruen Royston, *Holding Their Ground: Securing Land Tenure for the Urban Poor in Developing Countries* (London: Earthscan, 2002); Arthur J. Jacobson, "The Informal Economy: The Other Path of the Law," 103 Yale L. J. 2213 (1994).

11. Lawrence Liang, "Porous Legalities and Avenues of Participation," in *Sarai Reader 05: Bare Acts* 6 (New Delhi: Sarai/CSDS, 2005).

12. Ibid.

13. Jorge Luis Borges, "Pierre Menard, Author of the Quixote," in *Ficciones*, Anthony Kerrigan et al., trans. (New York: Grove Press, 1962).

14. Laikwan Pang, "Global Modernity and Movie Piracy," paper presented at Contested Commons/Trespassing Publics: A Conference on Inequalities, Conflicts and Intellectual Property, January 2005, New Delhi.

15. Larkin, *Signal and Noise*.

16. Ravi Sundaram, "Recycling Modernity: Pirate Electronic Cultures in India," 13(47) Third Text 59 (1999).

17. Brian Larkin, *Signal and Noise: Media, Infrastructure, and Urban Culture in Nigeria* (Durham, NC: Duke University Press, 2008), 14.

18. John Hope Mason, *The Value of Creativity: The Origins and Emergence of a Modern Belief* (Aldershot, UK: Ashgate, 2003).

19. Peter Linebaugh and Marcus Rediker, *The Many-Headed Hydra: Sailors, Slaves, Commoners, and the Hidden History of the Revolutionary Atlantic* (Boston: Beacon Press, 2000).

20. Raqs Media Collective, "Value and Its Other," in Armin Medosch (ed.), *Electronic Culture: Slave Ships and Private Galleons* (Liverpool: FACT, 2003), available at http://www.raqsmediacollective.net/texts6.html.

10

MARTHA WOODMANSEE

Publishers, Privateers, Pirates
Eighteenth-Century German Book Piracy Revisited

The Tr[attners], Sch[mieders], the W[althards]are certainly thieves.
JOHANN GOTTLIEB FICHTE

In Trattner's reprints eighteenth-century Austria encountered the great German literature. The literary education of Austria is rooted in his reprints. Austria's own great literature ripened in his reprints.
JOSEF NADLER

Hardly a week goes by that we do not read about the piracy besetting the U.S. entertainment industry.[1] Alarms are regularly issued by the Motion Picture Association of America (MPAA) and the Recording Industry Association of America (RIAA) about the billions in annual profits they are losing to peer-to-peer (P2P) file sharing on college campuses or to foreign CD and DVD bootlegging. In recent years the ante has been upped by industry-sponsored research that, by linking foreign piracy to organized crime and terrorism, is aimed at getting the U.S. government to pressure foreign powers to improve enforcement of their copyright laws and, indeed, to beef these up by criminalizing the piratical activity in their countries.[2]

This chapter seeks to provide historical perspective on present-day international piracy of this kind. It examines an episode of unauthorized book reprinting that disrupted the burgeoning book trade in the German-speaking states of central Europe during the final decades of the eighteenth century. In the eighteenth century this area, which today extends across Germany, Switzerland, Austria, and Hungary, consisted of over three hundred separate states linked by a more or less common language but little else, least of all by a common government and uniform codes of law.[3] The only legal mechanism capable of inhibiting unauthorized reprinting, the book *privilege*, did not extend beyond a state's borders, leaving interstate book commerce to be regulated by trade customs.

In addition to its political fragmentation, this area of central Europe was marked by an economic and cultural cleavage that gives the eighteenth-century German book trade there particular relevance to the globalizing trend that we are presently witnessing in information commerce. Its many independent states were divided *developmentally* down the line between north and south that marks our own world as well. The vibrant centers of book production were clustered in the Protestant north, in the states of Saxony and Brandenburg-Prussia especially. The Thirty Years' War had left the Catholic south a relative backwater in this regard. Music and the visual arts flourished in many a court like Vienna, but the key centers of learning were concentrated in cities in the northeast such as Leipzig, Halle, Jena, Hamburg, Dresden, and Berlin. It was here that the *Aufklärer* were living, writing and publishing—the first generation of the poets and philosophers who would create the national pantheon—Kant, Herder, Klopstock, Lessing, Wieland, etc.

This is where things get hazy. The story that has come down to us is that shortly after midcentury a vicious piratical assault took off that wreaked havoc in this burgeoning north German book trade, cheating its aspiring national authors out of the honoraria they deserved and debauching the nascent reading public. The assault is said to have stemmed chiefly from the south. The basis for this story is a substantial body of commentary—both public and private, occasional and systematic—by publishers, poets, jurists, and philosophers for and against unauthorized reprinting [*Nachdruck*]. I have written elsewhere about this "piracy debate"—which often took a wildly metaphysical turn.[4] Here I want to take a closer look at the phenomenon all this scribbling was grappling with by pursuing the kind of inquiry Lawrence Liang is advocating in his chapter in this volume when he calls attention to the "abstract, spectral figure" the pirate cuts in the whole spectrum of contemporary discourse about intellectual property, the critical discourse no less than that of industry enforcers. Might this spectral figure, which also haunts literary discourse, be fleshed out? This is the aim of the present chapter. It examines the career of one of the "pirate princes" [*Nachdruckerfürsten*] of the German book trade in this era, Johann Thomas Trattner (1717–1798), a Viennese publisher and bookseller whom the rising powers in the trade singled out for special vilification, with an eye to identifying the kinds of social, economic, and political investments that led to his vilification.

Born to poor peasants in Hungary and orphaned at two, Trattner was raised by an aunt outside Vienna and at eighteen apprenticed to the printer Samuel Müller. When he had completed the apprenticeship, four years later, Trattner joined the firm of the court printer, Johann Peter van Gehlen, to continue his training. There he worked for a further nine years as a pressman and compositor. In addition to a printing shop and type foundry, the firm had a bookstore and a good-sized library that was available for his use. Then, in 1748, when Trattner was thirty-one, he got an opportunity to set up independently when a printing shop, the Jahnische Druckerei in Schottenhof, went up for sale. From this point Trattner's rise was meteoric. Within two years he had become the university printer, a year later he was appointed court bookseller, and the following year he received permission to open a bookstore.[5] By 1754 he had also been named court printer, on the death of his former employer van Gehlen. This was an impressive achievement within so short a time, but it was just the beginning.

Trattner expanded his business at an astonishing speed by diversifying and adding branches. The trend at this time was toward specialization in one or another of the crafts involved in book production,[6] but Trattner began *adding* specialties to his printing business. By 1752 he had opened a type foundry. He also founded a workshop for copper engraving. In 1756 he added a bookbindery. A paper mill was added in 1774. The trained craftsmen for these additions to his business were still lacking in Vienna—and the south German lands generally—so Trattner's expansion necessitated his combing Europe for experts whom he could hire to train and supervise his workers. This so improved his production values that for the quality of its type, its paper, and its copper engraving the firm of Trattner rapidly gained recognition throughout Europe.

While expanding his Vienna business in this way, Trattner was simultaneously extending its reach throughout middle and southeastern Europe. He began already in 1756 to add branches. The first was a printing house in Triest. A year later in 1757 he opened another in Prague, to which in 1768 he added a publishing house. He got permission for a printing and publishing operation in Innsbruck in 1766. He expanded to Linz in 1782, first with a publishing house to which three years later he added a paper mill. In Vienna, meanwhile, he had in 1777 also opened a comprehensive lending library, open weekdays from eight until eight and from ten until six on Sundays. Memberships, payable by the month or by the day, entitled readers to browse, borrow, and in some cases, purchase from a wide selection of newspapers, periodicals, and old and new books on all subjects and in diverse languages. Foreign items were featured, and the library apparently became the place to see and be seen in Vienna (as the traveling Friedrich Nicolai observes in his journal).[7]

Many of the books available in the library would have been of Trattner's own making. He had been publishing books since 1752. The innovation for which he would have been best known at the time lay in the book series he produced. These were designed for middle-class readers of limited means and uncertain taste who, in Matthew Arnold's words, wanted to read "the best that had been thought and said" but had no idea what that might be. Trattner's series consisted of the works—in some cases selected works, in other cases the complete works—of those he considered the "best German writers" of the period. The series he announced to the world in 1765 included Gellert, Geßner, Hagedorn, Haller, Ewald von Kleist, Klopstock, Rabener, and Zacharia, with the promise that "Gleim, Cronegcks, Günthers, and the rest" were at press. Trattner used uniform paper and formatting so that books in the series could be conveniently and attractively displayed in the home, and he offered them at a price middle-class readers could afford.[8] The project was so well received that Trattner immediately began enhancing it. "The large duodecimo format was substituted for a handier medium duodecimo; good paper, high quality print, attractive vignettes, and exact proofing were promised. To assure customers that they wouldn't be overcharged at the retail shops, prices were to be printed 'clearly in raised letters' on the books' title pages. At an additional cost the books could also be had bound."[9]

Trattner undertook a much more ambitious project of this kind in 1785—a "Plan to Disseminate Literature throughout the Austro-Hungarian Lands through Inexpensive Delivery of Books in all Fields of Knowledge."[10] Whereas the 1765 series collected the best literary works, this series aimed to bring together all of the best works of theology, law, history, medicine, philosophy, and military science as well, in annotated editions available in diverse formats at diverse prices to suit diverse needs and budgets. In his detailed publicity for the series we learn that delivery will be free to subscribers in the cities in which branches or affiliates of his firm are located. Rural subscribers are assured that all they need to do is to contact the nearest affiliate to receive their orders postage free. An appendix listing these affiliates reveals the extent of Trattner's reach. His network includes 85 distributors in all, only 23 of which are, as it were, domestic (i.e., Austro-Hungarian). The other 62 span Europe, from Copenhagen to Zurich and from Cologne to St. Petersburg.[11] It would seem that in Trattner we have a veritable Amazon.com—with the customer profiling "from above" but also with free delivery.

In the interest of space and theme I focus on Trattner's most ambitious publishing projects. His other activities as a book dealer were many and varied.[12] Ursula Giese estimates that he was more involved than any other book dealer of the period in the publication and distribution throughout Europe of newspapers, magazines, and periodicals, broadsides, brochures, and catalogues—and not invariably just as a printer. He was regularly involved editorially as well.[13]

At its peak, in new premises acquired in 1759, Trattner's Vienna plant— which he dubbed the "Typographical Palace"—housed thirty-seven presses and employed two hundred workers. An innovative health and benefits plan he established for them in 1760 was adopted by the government eleven years later and made mandatory for all print workers.[14] This was but one of his many "services," which space does not permit me to recount in full here. Taken together, Trattner's accomplishments would seem to make him the very type— an early modern prototype—of the entrepreneur, and his firm a prototype of our present-day communication giants, which prosper from their success at bringing so many different facets of "content" production and delivery under a single umbrella.

I am obviously quite taken by this enterprising spirit—as were also many of Trattner's contemporaries, including many in high places. His enterprise and ingenuity resulted in his being knighted in 1747 by a grateful Maria Theresa, one of whose chief objectives as empress was to raise her lands developmentally to the level of the lands of her competitors in Versailles and Potsdam. The progress she was making owed much to the entrepreneurism of Trattner, the success of whose many ventures, in turn, owed much to the favor of his royal sponsor.

How could the legacy of such an enterprising figure have gotten inverted in transmission such that he has come down to us simply as the scourge of the emerging German classical literary tradition? Readers versed in German literature may be thinking that most of the titles in the impressive book series described above are piracies. But this would be incorrect. It is true that most had appeared previously in the north. But there existed as yet no legal accords prohibiting their being reprinted elsewhere. The German-speaking lands, as I noted, consisted of over three hundred independent states, and while many prohibited unauthorized reprinting of their own domestic produce, these prohibitions did not extend to books produced in neighboring states. And indeed in many, especially in the south, such reprinting was actively encouraged.

I noted that when Trattner began his career Austria was a literary back-water. Maria Theresa aimed to change this—her success is one of her chief legacies. In 1750, shortly after Trattner had set up as an independent printer, he obtained an audience with the empress, an audience that was to have an im-portant impact not only on his own career but on Austro-Hungarian cultural history generally. I will quote from the part of their conversation that has come down to us concerning the state of literacy. Maria Theresa is urging the need to improve literacy—the need for books that "reinforce morality, improve taste, and spread useful knowledge" throughout her realm. Trattner is reported to have responded, "But we lack authors. Only a few can write. Their German is atrocious." To this Maria Theresa observes: "That will change. Professor Son-nenfels [a trusted counselor] will see to it. . . . It's state priority: Books must be produced. There are practically none here. A lot of printing is going to be nec-essary. You'll have to reprint until original works appear. Reprint! Sonnenfels will tell you which ones."[15] Trattner's reprinting projects were sanctioned by the Austrian monarch herself. His career as a "pirate" began at his monarch's urging[16]—as part of a comprehensive scheme to kick-start Austrian develop-ment.[17]

Far from being prohibited, or disparaged as "piracy," the reprinting of for-eign-made books was state policy in Austria, as in many other jurisdictions of the German-speaking lands. It followed *politically* from the division of this area into governmentally independent, competing principalities and *eco-nomically* from the mercantilist economic policy they shared, which sought to prevent the flow of currency outside state borders, so discouraged imports generally. Despite its widespread sanction, reprinting on a large scale did not take off until the 1760s when publishers in the north imposed a new trading policy that had the effect of making south German trade with them virtually impossible.

For several hundred years the central European book trade had operated chiefly by barter. Publishers, who selected and financed the printing of manu-scripts, brought these—unbound printed sheets—to the biannual book fairs in Frankfurt and Leipzig and exchanged them for the goods of other publish-ers. This enabled them to return home with a more diverse inventory that they could go on to exchange at regional fairs; sell to retailers, itinerant booksellers or peddlers, and clients; and give as honoraria to their authors, etc.[18] Large capital outlays were unnecessary under this system, financial risk was spread out, and little money changed hands—which was a huge advantage, given the number of different currencies and the fluctuation in exchange rates in the German-speaking lands. In the south especially, the need for large cash outlays up front was further reduced by the development of a system of consignment that allowed booksellers to postpone payment until items were sold and also to return unsold items.

In the 1760s this traditional barter or exchange system began to give way. Northern publishers, concentrated in Saxony, began to eschew travel to the book fairs in Frankfurt, located in the southwest, in favor of doing their chief trading at the nearby Leipzig fairs. They also began to demand cash up front and in Saxon currency at the imperial exchange rate for their merchandise, they ceased to accept returns on unsold items, and they reduced the discounts that trading partners had traditionally granted one another to cover transportation costs. These changes, introduced unilaterally by the producers of what were rapidly becoming the most attractive books on the market, resulted in a long period of chaos in the German book trade—what the first major trade historian terms its "storm and stress."[19]

Smaller firms did not have the capital to continue trading with the Saxon publishers. Firms in the south were hit especially hard because of transportation costs. It is estimated that the cost of transportation of merchandise from the Leipzig book fairs to the south averaged 15 percent of a book's selling price. Trattner estimated it at 17 percent to Vienna. And overhead—the diverse costs of attending the fairs—added another 5 percent. Trade discounts aimed at covering such expenses had customarily been quite flexible, ranging from 25 percent to 40 percent of the selling price of books, depending on the relationship between trading partners. Under the new Saxon policy a standard discount of 25 percent was imposed. Given the unfavorable exchange rate, this reduced to around 16 percent for booksellers in the south. So from their point of view the numbers simply did not add up. These booksellers were 4 percent to 6 percent short of even covering their costs. As Reinhard Wittmann explains, booksellers in the south could no longer even hope to break even in trade with the Saxon publishers, much less make a profit.[20]

Trattner appealed these changes in a letter explaining that to make a go of it he needed and deserved a 33 1/3 percent discount at a minimum, but he was rebuffed. It was at this point, in 1765, that he announced the first reprint series I described. Other publishers, in the south especially, followed suit, resulting in the large-scale reprinting that has given the twenty-year period up until 1785 its name as the "age of piracy."

The architect of the new trade policy was Philipp Erasmus Reich (1717–1787), CEO of the Leipzig firm of Weidmanns Erben & Reich. Under Reich's leadership the firm had become one of the most prominent of the era. Generous honoraria had enabled Reich to attract and retain many of the leading authors across the entire spectrum of subjects, from belles lettres to philosophy, history, law, science, medicine, and political economy, and including many translations, especially from English—the most, indeed, of any publisher of the period.[21] "Names like Gellert, Wieland, Sulzer, Weiße, Ramler, Zollikofer, Lavater, Zimmerman, as well as the scholars Ernesti, Schröckh, Johannes von Müller, Spalding, and Heyne made the firm a mark of quality, guaranteeing the quality of the titles it released by unknown authors."[22] The firm's strong position in the burgeoning German book market made Reich a leader in and contributed to his becoming the chief spokesman for the major Leipzig publishing houses and the Saxon book trade generally.

By 1764 the Saxon publishers had already achieved a dominant position in the German book trade, and it seems likely that the new trade policy Reich announced was aimed at consolidating and increasing this market dominance. If so, his tactics misfired. They slowed trade with book dealers, in the south especially, who could not meet the new conditions so began to resort to reprinting, and Saxon sales declined. Perhaps in anticipation, Reich began simultaneously to take the reprinters on publicly, and over the next two decades he hounded them in pamphlets and essays, by organizing a trade association, lobbying the local and state legislatures, and filing lawsuits. The number and scope of his interventions made him his era's most famous opponent of reprinting, the prototype of our own era's Jack Valenti.

The rhetoric of vilification that empowers Reich's interventions is established in a 1764 pamphlet, "To Booksellers Visiting the Leipzig Fairs," urging his "legitimate" colleagues in the trade to "view and treat reprinters as robbers,"[23] and an anonymous self-published essay of 1773 singles out Trattner by name. By this time Reich had taken legal action against Trattner (as he would against many other publishers) for reprinting his "writings of Gellert and others";[24] and by singling him out in this essay, "Thoughts of a Bookseller on Herr Klopstock's Announcement of a Republic of Letters," Reich subjects the Viennese publisher to wider, public shaming: "Herr von Trattner claims to be helping spread the arts and sciences in his fatherland. But is [reprinting] the right way? ... Are good manners spread by robbing and plundering? Is reprinting anything other than theft and robbery?"[25]

Friedrich Gottlob Klopstock's announcement of a "republic of letters," which had appeared the previous year, was a devastating criticism by Germany's most revered poet of the publishing trade *generally*. Klopstock accused publishers of "getting rich at authors' expense" and called on his fellow authors to declare their independence—to actualize the profits they deserved from their intellectual labor by cutting out the middlemen and joining together to disseminate their work themselves by subscription as Alexander Pope had done in England with his Homer translation.[26] In his response to Klopstock, Reich defended his trade by detailing the crucial mediating role it played between authors and readers, a role, he submitted, that authors lacked the time or expertise to play effectively themselves, and he laid blame for the low royalties they were receiving at the feet of the pirates. If authors would just join "legitimate" publishers in lobbying governments to pass a "universal law against reprinting," he argued, "we would be able to afford to pay you appropriately for the fruits of your industry."[27]

Reich's untiring campaign against reprinting, only a few stops in which I describe here, had only modest success. The same year, and largely as a result of his lobbying, a "Mandat" was adopted in Saxony protecting any book printed there for ten years on the condition a publisher could demonstrate that he had gotten permission to publish from the book's author. The "Mandat" punished reprinting with confiscation and fines, and it also banned trade in reprints at the Leipzig book fairs.[28] But much as the old *privilege*, the "Mandat" did not extend to neighboring states (though in 1776 it did become the basis for an accord with Prussia).[29] Reprinting thus continued to flourish. No longer able to do business at the Leipzig fairs, the reprinters even began to mount their own "reprint fairs" in the state of Hessen.[30]

With the escalation of reprinting, which their new trade policies had precipitated, I noted that Saxon sales declined. The Saxon publishers adjusted by concentrating even more intently than before on the high-end market—on the narrow circle of relatively affluent and educated readers in the middle and north German court, university, and commercial cities.[31] By focusing their efforts in this way they could raise their prices. Wittmann estimates that between 1760 and 1785 the price of books produced in the north rose between 600 and 700 percent.[32] To attract and hold the elite audience able to afford the steep price increases, the Saxon publishers enhanced the quality of their merchandise both in form and content—by paying higher honoraria to attract the best authors, using higher-quality paper, better type, more and better engravings, and the like. And indeed, many of the writers we still today think of as the best poets and philosophers of this period emerged in this publishing milieu. So the Saxon publishers' profits held steady. But they did not increase, because by raising their prices so exorbitantly and imposing draconian trade policies, they priced themselves out of the emerging middle-class markets in the south where books were still an extreme luxury. They in effect ceded this huge market to the reprinters. This left book dealers like Trattner to their own resources, and liberated by Saxon greed from the trade ethic that had formerly kept poaching within reasonable bounds, these entrepreneurial individuals launched ambitious reprinting projects like those I've sketched to supply—and expand—the south German book market.

It would seem, therefore, that piracy did not produce any big losers in the eighteenth-century book trade. But what about the other stakeholders? Were authors and readers disadvantaged by reprinting? "Legitimate" publishers believed that they were, as Reich's plea to authors to ally with publishers in lobbying for legislation against the practice demonstrates. His rhetoric of the "poor author" whom the plague of piracy was cheating out of his just deserts may still be heard regularly today in the IP enforcement campaigns of the MPAA and RIAA. Is there any truth in Reich's claim?

In the 1760s there were still comparatively few writers who expected to earn a livelihood by the pen. Then—as indeed today—most made their livings in the employ of institutions such as the courts, churches, schools, and universities. Reprinting found wide acceptance among such writers, who viewed it as extending their reach to readers who would not otherwise have been able to afford to purchase their works. This was especially true of scholars in natural science and medicine, law and theology, but it also holds true of the growing number of writers across the disciplines who began over the next decades to attempt to pursue writing as a full-time occupation. In a report to a Viennese court commission on education, the Austrian physician Anton von Störck, for example, credits reprinting with disseminating useful knowledge and improving public health. It gets critical medical and surgical literature into the rural villages that scientific knowledge has not yet penetrated. By making books cheap it "puts students, the young doctors, physicians, and healers in a position to acquire essential works. Reprinting awakens a desire to read and boosts the sciences and medicine. Even the essential works of the immortal van Swieten [Maria Theresa's personal physician] would not be in the hands of so many physicians and surgeons were it not for reprinting."[33] Störck's take on book piracy anticipates that of the "open science" movement today. "Educated physicians don't complain about it," he reports, "because they don't write for profit but to improve human life, to spread knowledge, and to achieve status in the scholarly world."[34] Some of the same sentiments may be heard in the memoirs and correspondence of the smaller but growing number of authors by vocation. As outspoken an opponent of reprinting as the novelist Christoph Martin Wieland (1733–1813), for example, confides in a letter to his son-in-law that "reprints can only half displease us because they inevitably honor us and further our aims, enlarge our circle of influence and spread our fame."[35] Being pirated became an important mark of success for professional authors, something to brag about—albeit sardonically, for financially they did not profit from the reprints.

We know that in negotiating as low an honorarium as possible with writers, "legitimate" publishers like Reich often gave the excuse that the likelihood of piracy prevented them from paying more. Whether this was more than a convenient excuse is uncertain. But it is certain that when authors negotiated a price and delivered over their manuscripts, their works became the property of their publishers and that this arrangement disadvantaged authors financially. When the work sold, perhaps even warranted additional printings or editions, it was the publisher alone who profited (for the practice of paying authors "royalties" based on sales did not yet exist).[36] The injustice authors sensed in this arrangement was ill designed to ally them with "legitimate" publishers against the reprinters. Having received in the honorarium the only earnings they could expect, up front, their chief concern turned to circulation, and the reprinters could ensure this as well or better than their own publishers.

Were it not for the reprinters, many an author might never have seen a second edition of his writings or have enjoyed a "collected" or "complete" edition. Observing that therefore "many authors had to admit that they were better served by the reprinters than by their own publishers," Wittmann relates that the first collection of Goethe's works in 1775 was the inspiration of the Swiss pirate Christoph Heilmann. "And after Heilmann the pirates Himburg, Walthard, Schmieder, and Fleischhauer reproduced several runs of this collection before the first 'authentic' collected works [*Gesamtausgabe*] appeared with Göschen in 1787."[37]

Interestingly, the Himburg piracy of this work raises doubts about another of the charges that "legitimate" publishers leveled against piracy in their push to dominate the book trade—namely, that in addition to cheating authors out of fair profits on their labor, reprints disseminated their work in carelessly produced, even garbled, and sometimes expurgated editions. The charge certainly cannot be refuted completely—indeed, it could be turned back equally against the "legitimate" publishers of the period[38]—but it is noteworthy that evidence of enormous care has been found in the editorial practices of some of the era's most notorious pirates.[39] The reaction of Goethe to the first "authentic" edition of his collected works merits quoting in this context. "I cannot say that the sight of the first three volumes of my writings . . . gives me great pleasure," he wrote to his publisher Göschen. "The paper seems to be good printing paper rather than writing paper, the format is too small after the pages have been cut, the letters appear dulled, the color like the paper is uneven, so that these volumes look more like an ephemeral journal than a book that should last for a time. There happened to be a copy of the Himburg edition here—it looks like a dedication copy compared to yours."[40]

It was through the Himburg edition, or one of the many other reprints, that the majority of readers, in the south especially, became acquainted with the author of *Werther*. Like the important scientific and medical books mentioned by Störck, contemporary works of literature, philosophy, music, art, and social criticism streamed out across the distribution networks developed by pirates like Trattner into even the remotest rural villages in the provinces—in better and worse editions and at prices readers could begin to afford.[41] By the end of the eighteenth century reading was as widespread there as in the north, and nurtured on reprints, readers shared similar tastes.[42]

The German-speaking states remained as *politically* fragmented at the end of the century as they had been in the 1760s, but the *cultural* gap between the two regions had closed. As demand for books grew in the south, indigenous writers emerged, and an indigenous publishing industry developed.[43] Piracy subsided. It had ceased to be lucrative. With indigenous book trades to protect, states in the south began entering into bilateral accords—as the two northern powerhouses of publishing in this era, Prussia and Saxony, had done in 1776. The "universal law against reprinting" that Reich had lobbied so hard for did not begin to materialize until 1835. When it did, it merely codified publishing practices that had grown to seem mutually beneficial enough to be "universally" embraced.[44]

The law inevitably simplifies, stylizes the activities it is charged to treat, placing a heavy burden of responsibility on legal scholars to descry the complexities that may be effaced in this process. While important progress has been made with the trope of "authorship," this chapter suggests that much work remains to be done on the *other* of this linchpin of copyright law, "piracy."[45]

Examination of the activities that triggered eighteenth-century Germany's legendary intellectual property debate reveals that many of the activities that were vilified as "piracy" were not only lawful but morally justifiable and extremely efficacious. Reprinting was Austrian state policy when the "pirate prince" Trattner was active, his reprinting activities were necessitated by the impossible trading conditions imposed upon him by a greedy cartel of trading partners in the north, and his reprints spread literacy in the intellectual backwater of the south where he was most active, redounding by the end of the century in an indigenous Austrian literary renaissance.

Recent advances in book history are facilitating critical reassessment of important moments like this in the history of book piracy. A comparably nuanced understanding of the diverse instances of digital piracy with which the developing world is being charged today will require both sustained ethnographic research and a sharp eye for the rhetoricity of legal rhetoric.

NOTES

1. This chapter grew out of research supported by the Deutscher Akademischer Austauschdienst at the Herzog August Bibliothek in Wolfenbüttel, Germany. I wish to thank Paul Gehl, curator of the History of Printing Collections at the Newberry Library, for encouraging me to revisit this material for presentation to the Caxton Club, and the Adam Helms Lectures Committee at the University of Stockholm for offering me such a pleasant incentive to develop my work on it. Invitations by Sheldon Halpern to share the work at a conference on the normative role of copyright law, and by Will Slauter to share it with the Columbia Society of Fellows aided me in articulating its relevance to present-day policy deliberation.

2. See, for example, the 2008 report by Gregory F. Treverton et al. of the RAND Corporation, "Film Piracy, Organized Crime, and Terrorism"; and Andre Yoskowitz's coverage of U.S. Attorney General Michael Mukasey's 2008 speech to Silicon Valley executives, "U.S. Attorney General Claims Piracy Funds Terrorism."

3. Consisting of 314 states and 1,475 estates, making a total of 1,789 independent sovereign powers, Germany prior to 1800 was often described as a "carnival jacket" (Pinson, p. 5).

4. See especially "The Genius and the Copyright."

5. Giese, pp. 1028–1029, 1103. Giese's 1961 study of Trattner, on which I chiefly rely, remains the key source on his career.

6. Kiesel and Münch, p. 124; Selwyn, p. 59.

7. Giese, p. 1129.

8. Ibid., p. 1109.

9. Ibid., p. 1110.

10. Trattner, p. 136. For a reproduction of the proposal see Giese, pp. 1154–1158.

11. The "domestic" distributors Trattner lists are: Agram, Brünn, Clagenfurt, Cremsier, Grätz, Herrmannstadt, Innsprugg, Königgrätz, Laybach, Lemberg, Linz, Neusohl, Oedenburg, Ollmütz, Pest, Prag, Preßburg, Raab, Steyer, Temeswar, Teschen, Triest, Troppau. He lists these "foreign" distributors: Altenburg, Anspach, Augsburg, Bamberg, Basel, Berlin, Bern, Braunschweig, Bremen, Breslau, Carlsruh, Coblenz, Cohburg, Cölln, Constanz, Coppenhagen, Dresden, Eisenach, Erfurt, Erlangen, Jena, Königsberg, Lausanne, Leipzig, Lemgo, Liegnitz, Lübeck, Lüneburg, Magdeburg, Mannheim, Mietau, München, Münster, Nürnberg, Petersburg, Potsdam, Regensburg, Riga, Rostok, Salzburg, Straßburg, Stuttgard, Tübingen, Ulm, Upsal, Warschau, Weimar, Winterthur, Wittenberg, Wolffenbüttel, Würzburg, Zürich (Giese, p. 1159).

12. He was also one of the leading music publishers of the period, and had a personal relationship with Mozart, whose family lodged at the Trattnerhof in 1784. Mozart tutored Trattner's second wife, Theresia, in piano, and he dedicated the Fantasy and Sonata, K475 and K457, to her (Weinmann).

13. Giese, pp. 1190–1191.

14. Ibid., p. 1078.

15. Ibid., p. 1019; trans. mine.

16. Technically, the royal sanction of his activities makes Trattner a "privateer" rather than a "pirate"—a distinction with little more difference to his competitors in the contemporary book trade than to Spanish seafarers in the age of Sir Francis Drake. See Drahos and Braithwaite, pp. 22ff.

17. On the essential role played by book piracy in the European enlightenment more generally, see Darnton, "The Science of Piracy," and Lehmstedt, "Ein Strohm der alles überschwemmet," p. 176.

18. Kiesel and Münch, pp. 125–26.

19. Kapp and Goldfriedrich, vol. 3, pp. 50, 116.

20. Ibid., p. 116.

21. Rosenstrauch, p. 67.

22. Ibid., p. 68.

23. Kiesel and Münch, p. 136. In his next 1765 pamphlet Reich goes so far as to urge his "legitimate" colleagues to retaliate by cooperating to flood the market with reprints of "robber" reprinters' most valuable (original) titles.

24. The suit was filed in 1765 according to Lehmstedt, who has located "many thousands of pages" of materials relating to Reich's legal actions, which could "drag out for years, especially when they had to be adjudicated in the Reichshofrat in Vienna" (*Philipp Erasmus Reich*, p. 101). For a more comprehensive treatment of Reich's diverse actions against Trattner (and reprinting generally), see Lehmstedt, "'Ein Strohm der alles überschwemmet.'"

25. *Zufällige Gedanken eines Buchhändlers über Herrn Klopstocks Anzeige einer gelehrten Republik*, p. 27. For a visual salvo in the campaign against Trattner, see Daniel Chodowiecki's allegorical copper engraving of 1781 (rpt. in Woodmansee, *The Author, Art, and the Market*, p. 34) depicting him as a highway bandit stripping the clothes off of the legitimate publishers Friedrich Nicolai and P. E. Reich.

26. Klopstock's proposal of a republic of letters triggered the "piracy debate" that occupied scholars and intellectuals for two decades. See Woodmansee, "The Genius and the Copyright," pp. 440ff., and *The Author, Art, and the Market*, pp. 47ff.

27. *Zufällige Gedanken*, pp. 24–25. Five years later, in 1778, Reich would publish a German translation of the more systematic argument to the same effect by the French jurist and publicist Simon Nicholas Henri Linguet, *Des Herrn Linguets Betrachtungen über die Rechte des Schriftstellers und seines Verlegers*.

28. Kiesel and Münch, p. 139.

29. Vogel, *Deutsche Urheber*, pp. 82–83.

30. They were poorly attended, according to Kiesel and Münch, and in 1775 they were outlawed (p. 139). Cf. Kapp and Goldfriedrich, vol. 3, p. 66.

31. Wittmann, "Der gerechtfertigte Nachdrucker," p. 88.

32. *Geschichte des deutschen Buchhandels*, p. 118.

33. Giese, p. 1149.

34. Ibid.

35. To Reinhold, December 12, 1789, qtd. in Ungern-Sternberg, vol. 1, p. 157. Among professional writers the chief official apologists for reprinting were Heinrich Reimarus and Adolph Freiherr von Knigge.

36. The notorious case of the poet Christian Gellert living out his life in only modest comfort even as his publisher Wendler became a wealthy man occasioned Klopstock's subscription scheme, described above. See Woodmansee, "The Genius and the Copyright," p. 436.

37. Wittmann, "Der gerechtfertigte Nachdrucker," p. 85. Goethe's disparagement of reprinting is examined in Müller, "Goethes urheberrechtliche Gedanken."

38. Many of the liberties publishers in this era took with authors' texts were aimed at making them more marketable. However much some authors may have wished to retain control of their texts, few expected to once they had sold their manuscripts to a publisher.

39. A key example is Christian Gottlieb Schmieder. See Breitenbruch, "Der Karlsruher Buchhändler Christian Gottlieb Schmieder und der Nachdruck in Südwestdeutschland im letzten Viertel des 18. Jahrhunderts."

40. Goethe to Göschen, October 27, 1787, as qtd. in Unseld, p. 64.

41. Wittmann estimates that the annual book budget for middle-class readers could not have exceeded 10–20 talers, even less for students, court tutors, teachers, and pastors. So great was the price differential that such readers would have had to choose between buying 8–10 originals and 40–50 reprints annually. In other words, originals cost five times as much as reprints. The option for the lower economic orders was even simpler: it was a reprint or nothing ("Der gerechtfertigte Nachdrucker," p. 88).

42. The German reading public as a whole remained extremely small. Schenda estimates that in 1800 at most 25 percent of the population was truly literate, up from around 15 percent in 1770 (Kiesel and Münch, p. 162).

43. Austria is believed to have quadrupled its production of original works between 1810 and 1830 (Vogel, "Deutsche Urheber," p. 159).

44. On April 2, 1835, the Deutscher Bund, the loose confederation of thirty-nine states established by the 1815 Congress of Vienna, resolved: "The governments agree that reprinting should be forbidden throughout the whole of the confederation and the property of authors should be identified and protected according to uniform principles." The resolution's interpretation and codification into law in all thirty-nine states would take many more years.

45. On the trope of "authorship," see Woodmansee, "The Genius and the Copyright"; and Woodmansee and Jaszi, eds., *The Construction of Authorship*. For some important strides on "piracy," see Halbert, "Intellectual Property Piracy"; and Loughlan, "Pirates, Parasites, Reapers, Sowers."

REFERENCES

Bosse, Heinrich. *Autorschaft ist Werkherrschaft*. Paderborn: Ferdinand Schöningh, 1981.

Breitenbruch, Bernd. "Der Karlsruher Buchhändler Christian Gottlieb Schmieder und der Nachdruck in Südwestdeutschland im letzten Viertel des 18. Jahrhunderts." *AGB* 9 (1969): 643–732.

Darnton, Robert. "The Science of Piracy: A Crucial Ingredient in Eighteenth-Century Publishing." *Studies in Voltaire and the Eighteenth Century* 12 (2003): 3–29.

Drahos, Peter, and John Braithwaite. *Information Feudalism: Who Owns the Knowledge Economy?* New York: New Press, 2002.

Fichte, Johann Gottlieb. "Proof of the Illegality of Reprinting: A Rationale and a Parable." Trans. Martha Woodmansee. In Lionel Bently and Martin Kretschmer, eds., *Primary Sources on Copyright, 1450–1900* <http://www.copyrighthistory.org/cgi-bin/kleioc/0010/exec/showTranslation/%22d_1793_im_001_0001.jpg%22>

Giese, Ursula. "Johann Thomas Edler von Trattner. Seine Bedeutung als Buchdrucker, Buchhändler und Herausgeber." *AGB* 3 (1961): 1013–1454.

Halbert, Debora. "Intellectual Property Piracy: The Narrative Construction of Deviance." *International Journal for the Semiotics of Law* 10 (1997): 55–78.

Kapp, Friedrich, and Johann Goldfriedrich. *Geschichte des deutschen Buchhandels*. 4 vols. Leipzig: Verlag des Börsenvereins der Deutschen Buchhändler, 1886–1913.

Kiesel, Helmuth, and Paul Münch. *Gesellschaft und Literatur im 18. Jahrhundert*. Munich: C. H. Beck, 1977.

Lehmstedt, Mark. *Philipp Erasmus Reich (1717–1787): Verleger der Aufklärung und Reformer des deutschen Buchhandels.* Exhibition Catalog, Karl-Marx-Universität Leipzig. Leipzig, 1989.

———. "'Ein Strohm der alles überschwemmet.' Dokumente zum Verhältnis von Philipp Erasmus Reich und Johann Thomas von Trattner. Ein Beitrag zur Geschichte des Nachdrucks in Deutschland im 18. Jahrhundert." *Bibliothek und Wissenschaft* 25 (1991): 176–267.

Linguet, Simon Nicolas Henri. *Des Herrn Linguets Betrachtungen über die Rechte des Schriftstellers und seines Verlegers.* Ed. and trans. Philipp Erasmus Reich. Leipzig: Weidmanns Erben & Reich, 1778.

Loughlan, Patricia. "Pirates, Parasites, Reapers, Sowers, Fruits, Foxes . . . : The Metaphors of Intellectual Property." *Sydney Law Review* 28 (2006): 211–226.

Müller, Georg. "Goethes urheberrechtliche Gedanken." *Archiv für Urheber-Film-und Theaterrecht* 12 (1939): 1–38.

"[Nürnberger] Schlußnahme." *Neues Archiv für Gelehrte, Buchhändler und Antiquare.* Erstes Jahr 1795. Zwölfte Woche, 181–196.

Pinson, Koppel S. *Modern Germany: Its History and Civilization.* 2nd ed. New York: Macmillan, 1966.

Reich, Philipp Erasmus. *Der Bücher-Verlag in allen Absichten genauer bestimmt.* Leipzig: [Weidmanns Erben und Reich], 1773.

———. *Zufällige Gedanken eines Buchhändlers über Herrn Klopstocks Anzeige einer gelehrten Republik.* Leipzig: [Weidmanns Erben und Reich], 1773.

Reimarus, J[ohann] A[lbert] H[einrich]. *Der Bücherverlag in Betrachtung der Schriftsteller, der Buchhändler und des Publikums erwogen.* Hamburg, 1773.

———. *Erwägung des Verlags-Rechts in Ansehung des Nachdruks.* Hamburg, 1792.

Ricketson, Sam, and Jane C. Ginsburg. *International Copyright and Neighbouring Rights: The Berne Convention and Beyond.* 2nd ed., 2 vols. Oxford: Oxford UP, 2006.

Rosenfeld, Hellmut. "Zur Geschichte von Nachdruck und Plagiat." *AGB* 11 (1971): 337–372.

Rosenstrauch, Hazel. "Buchhandelsmanufaktur und Aufklärung. Die Reformen des Buchhändlers und Verlegers Ph. E. Reich (1717–1780). Sozialgeschichtliche Studie zur Entwicklung des literarischen Marktes." *AGB* 26 (1986): 1–129.

———. "Philipp Erasmus Reich—Bourgeois und Citoyen." *Karl-Marx-Universität Leipzig. Wissenschaftliche Zeitschrift.* Gesellschaftswissenschaftliche Reihe 1 (1989): 96–107.

Schmieder, Christian G. *Wider und Für den Büchernachdruk aus den Papieren des blauen Mannes.* [Karlsruhe]: Im Reich und für das Reich, 1790.

Selwyn, Pamela E. *Everyday Life in the German Book Trade. Friedrich Nicolai as Bookseller and Publisher in the Age of Enlightenment, 1750–1810.* University Park: Penn State UP, 2000.

Trattner, Johann Thomas. "Plan zur allgemeinen Verbreitung der Lektüre, in den k.k. Staaten, durch wohlfeile Lieferung der Bücher für alle Fächer der Wissenschaften." *Provinzialnachrichten aus den Kaiserl. Königl. Staaten* 9–13 (1785): 136–141, 153–158, 171–174, 183–188, 205–206.

Treverton, Gregory F., Carl Matthies, Karla J. Cunningham, Jeremiah Gouka, Greg Ridgeway, and Anny Wong. *Film Piracy, Organized Crime, and Terrorism.* Santa Monica, CA: RAND Corporation, 2008.

Ungern-Sternberg, Wolfgang von. "Schriftsteller und literarischer Markt. In: Rolf Grimminger, ed., *Hansers Socialgeschichte der deutschen Literatur. Band 3: Deutsche Aufklärung bis zur Französischen Revolution, 1680–1789.* 2 vols. Munich: Carl Hanser Vlg., 1980.

Unseld, Siegfried. *Goethe and His Publishers.* Trans. Kenneth J. Northcott. Chicago: U Chicago P, 1996.

Vierhaus, Rudolf. *Germany in the Age of Absolutism.* Cambridge: Cambridge UP, 1988.

Vogel, Martin. "Der literarische Markt und die Entstehung des Verlags- und Urheberrechts bis zum Jahre 1800." In *Rhetorik, Ästhetik, Ideologie. Aspekte einer kritischen Kulturwissenschaft.* Stuttgart: J. B. Metzler, 1973.

———. "Deutsche Urheber- und Verlagsrechtsgeschichte zwischen 1450 und 1850." *AGB* 19 (1978): 1–190.

Ward, Albert. *Book Production, Fiction, and the German Reading Public, 1740–1800.* Oxford: Clarendon, 1974.

Weinmann, Alexander. "Trattner, Johann Thomas, Edler von." In *Grove Music Online. Oxford Music Online,* <http://www.oxfordmusiconline.com/subscriber/article/grove/music/28282> (accessed August 6, 2009).

Wieland, Christian Martin. "Actenstücke zur Oesterreichischen Nachdruckergeschichte." *Der Teutsche Merkur* (May 1785): 154–172.

Wilcke, Christian Heinrich. *Der gerechtfertigte Nachdrucker.* Vienna and Leipzig: Weidmanns Erben und Reich, 1774.

Wittmann, Reinhard. "Der gerechtfertigte Nachdrucker? Nachdruck und literarisches Leben im achtzehnten Jahrhundert." In Wittmann, *Buchmarkt und Lektüre im 18. und 19. Jahrhundert.* Tübingen: Max Niemeyer, 1982.

———. *Geschichte des deutschen Buchhandels. Ein Überblick.* Munich: C. H. Beck, 1991.

Woodmansee, Martha. *The Author, Art, and the Market.* New York: Columbia UP, 1994.

———. "The Genius and the Copyright: Economic and Legal Conditions of the Emergence of the 'Author.'" *ECS* 17.4 (1984): 425–448. Rpt. in Woodmansee, *The Author, Art, and the Market* (New York: Columbia UP, 1994), 35–55.

Woodmansee, Martha, and Peter Jaszi, eds. *The Construction of Authorship: Textual Appropriation in Law and Literature.* Durham, NC: Duke UP, 1994.

Yar, Majid. "The Global 'Epidemic' of Movie 'Piracy': Crime-Wave or Social Construction?" *Media, Culture & Society* 27 (2005): 677–696.

Yoskowitz, Andre. "U.S. Attorney General Claims Piracy Funds Terrorism." Report on U.S. Attorney General Michael Mukasey's speech to Silicon Valley executives. 29 March 2008 <http://www.afterdawn.com/news/archive/13431.cfm> accessed 2 August 2009.

ADRIAN JOHNS

11

The Property Police

There is an increasingly evident gulf in our understanding of the issues raised by modern intellectual property systems. On the one hand, we now know a good deal about the legal doctrines to do with patenting, copyrights, and trademarks. We know both how they arose in relation to other branches of the law and how they drew upon, and in turn affected, ideas about authorship, property, and the common good. On the other hand, large literatures also now exist on the impact such legal doctrines have had on, for example, music and filmmaking. And the issues involved in extending legal doctrines from the developed world to the developing have also received a vast amount of attention. But all this work, impressive as it is, nevertheless leaves something important aside. What it has neglected is neither the formation nor the effect of intellectual property law, but the practice of implementation—of detection and enforcement—that links the two. That is, we lack a coherent history of the social and technological intermediation between law and culture. That lack is all the more regrettable at a time when the law itself seems to be relatively static, but an industry of detection and enforcement is changing rapidly and growing apace.

Self-evidently, laws do not apply themselves. They take effect, color perceptions, tinge conduct and change behavior to the extent that they are known, responded to, and appropriated. At the extreme, all legal systems have laws that are effectively dormant—laws that are on the books but never applied. Some statutes are actually passed with the conscious intention that they should be of this kind (the antievolution law of Tennessee that led to the Scopes Trial was one example), and in principle any law could fall into the category or emerge from it. The point is that it is not only the fact of a law's being passed or remaining on the statute book (or in the universe of precedents) that gives it its meaning and efficacy but also its continuous application—often outside legal institutions—by communities of knowledge, training, enforcement, and prosecution. To say this is to voice a commonplace, of course. But in the case of intellectual property it is a commonplace the import of which we have been slow to appreciate. For far longer than we tend to assume, communities of skill and expertise have devoted themselves to detecting pirates, deterring piracy, and embedding intellectual property laws into the very artifacts of creativity. The history of intellectual property, I submit, is substantially the history of these communities.

I want to sketch here a brief history of the mediation of intellectual property by cultures of detection and enforcement. My contention is that the principal issues we face today emerge from those cultures. In particular, they arise from the coalescence of two industries, the history of which is long but the alliance recent. The first is the industry devoted to the surveillance, interdiction, and policing of "pirates" themselves. This industry has become a powerful hybrid entity, combining private and public institutions and with worldwide reach. Its actions often determine the application, and hence the meaning, of laws. The second is an enterprise on which that first industry has come to depend. It is devoted to what may be called tracking technologies. These technologies depend on embedding and detecting "traces"—flags, watermarks, digital rights data, genetic markers, and the like—in creative products. Historically, the print industries pioneered the use of such traces in the Renaissance. Like the enforcement industry, this too has grown and diversified. Together the two endeavors have aspired to become global in scale and universal in scope.

Early Modern Europe: Participant Policing

The distant origins of today's intellectual property systems lie in early modern Europe. The earliest patents are usually said to date from the fifteenth-century Italian city-states. Prior to the development of statutory copyright, these privileges existed in an uneasy tension with various guild registration systems. The distinction between them was essentially political. Patents were manifestations of royal or state prerogative, each one being a bespoke utterance on the part of the ruler. By contrast, guild systems drew their legitimacy from the continuity of a craft, and their authority extended no further than the membership of the guild concerned. The two protocols were in tension and often clashed. For present purposes, however, what matters is what they had in common. In both cases the patentee or craftsman had to act to defend him- or herself against violators and therefore to sustain literary or creative property as property at all. Much of the history of IP mediation derives, directly or indirectly, from that fact.

As is well known, there were no professional police forces in early modern society. Each city had its own arrangements for keeping order and enforcing laws. In England, to cite the example I know best, what made lay enforcement practicable was a presumption of social circulation—the kind of thing given political articulation in the republican schemes of a James Harrington. Once his short term of office (typically a year) expired, a constable or guild official would return to live among the people he had just been responsible for policing. In practice, therefore, the boundary between acting on behalf of the public and acting on behalf of interest was never hard and fast. And perhaps it had to be so, because the knowledge on which officers relied came from personal acquaintances. Their effectiveness derived from the very fact that they were categorically indistinct from the people they oversaw.[1]

The pursuit of "pirates" (a name first given to thieves of literary rights in late-seventeenth-century London) partook of this culture of policing. Tracking them down was a matter initially for the printer or bookseller concerned. In the case of a property gained by registration, and if the piracy were being produced locally, then it was relatively straightforward. Guild officers had the right to search members' premises and did so regularly. An alleged pirate would be summoned to appear at a company court. The grandees of the trade would there decide upon some appropriate outcome, typically the destruction of stock. Very rarely did printers pursue conflicts into the broader courts system, and in fact they were enjoined not to do so. The practice of sustaining titles was thus invisible to authors and readers. What kept it honest, in theory at least, was an awareness that an officer who searched a given home was quite likely to be investigated by the target himself during that person's turn in office. The system rested order and a kind of property on the golden rule of "do as you would be done by."

Another option, however, was to treat a usurpation of authorship as a potential danger to church and state. This could be done by virtue of the licensing systems that all early modern polities upheld. While licensing was designed to restrain dangerous works, in practice an unlicensed book was unlikely to cause trouble for its producer unless some interested party decided to pursue it. In such a case an offended author or bookseller would encourage a state or church official—or, in Restoration London, the "Surveyor of the Press"—to prosecute the perpetrator before a court of law. But trade rivalries were still often the motors of such processes, and trade and politics remained hard to distinguish.[2]

Participant enforcement remained normal across Europe through the end of the seventeenth century, and it bore certain consequences. For example, literary property was assumed to be a matter of privy knowledge. It was a field notorious for informers and turncoats and attended with something of the disrepute that such antisocial types endured. And despite a lot of rhetoric about sedition, states were quite willing to recruit pirates as policemen.

Patents on machines, medicines, and the like involved similar issues. Here too enforcement rested on the initiative of the individual—in this case, the patentee, who might be the inventor or a gentleman rather than the tradesman—and on the use of inside knowledge, often gained from informers. In all cases it required money, expertise, patience, and constant attendance. Yet it was an essential activity, because a patent might not be regarded as conferring a right at all until it had been tested by a judicial process. Determining the identity of the thing patented and setting criteria for distinguishing that thing from other things were among the trickiest problems here. A very refined art developed of designing specifications, drawings, and models to reveal and conceal in just the right ways. As a result, calls for specialist tribunals to try patent cases arose in the late seventeenth century. They would persist until at least the late twentieth.

Nation, Space, and Enlightenment

In the eighteenth century the principle of participant enforcement fell into doubt and then into disrepute. Moral dubiety grew with the establishment of political theories of interest and reason of state, in the wake of Machiavellian and neoclassical republicanism. By the mid-eighteenth century the Fielding brothers were undertaking their famous initiative in establishing a paid force of Bow Street Runners to replace traditional constables. It is conventional to see in this initiative the first move toward a professional police force. In the same generations the practice of policing literary property and patents changed too, but in a rather different direction. Its proponents tried to extend participant policing to a national scale.

In 1710 Britain passed what is usually called the world's first statute of copyright. Yet that term, copyright, was not used in the act itself. It came into use as a result of controversies about practical policing. These controversies had to do with liberty and nation as much as with literary property per se. As is well known, the statute provided a limited-term protection for works. In the 1730s this protection expired for some very profitable titles, and Scottish booksellers began to reprint them. Faced with enforcing a literary property regime that had no statutory warrant, the London trade responded by extending the practices it was familiar with. The leading booksellers had long formed alliances to share risks on publications. It was these combines that secured the status of titles as properties—perpetual ones.[3] The Londoners tried to fix this practice in law by amassing injunctions against so-called pirates. But when a case finally went to trial, the attempt collapsed. Edinburgh's judges ruled against the Londoners, leaving Scottish publishers free to reprint anything outside the protection of the 1710 law. This drove the Londoners to enter into a "conspiracy" to eradicate piracy. It proved catastrophically counterproductive.

Some sixty metropolitan booksellers signed on to the scheme, subscribing £3,000 to deny the "pirates" a market. Every one of England's provincial booksellers was warned that "agents" would ride out from London to inspect their stocks. Anyone found harboring piracies would be prosecuted mercilessly, they were told, and all should take care "for fear you are informed against." Significantly, the Londoners did pursue legal action at the same time, but the case was a contrivance, and the high court disdained to hear it.[4] The extralegal campaign was the real heart of the initiative. It provoked enormous resentment. In particular, it galvanized an Edinburgh bookseller, Alexander Donaldson, into assuming the mantle of pirate in chief and mounting a counterattack. Donaldson got hold of a copy of the threat and reprinted it so that "the world may see how unjust their pretensions to an exclusive right are, and how oppressive, in these lands of liberty, their monopolising schemes have been." He contended that a property regime resting on trade combinations, monopolies, extortion, and battalions of agents intruding into private homes across the land was more of a threat than piracy could ever be. It was the so-called pirates who upheld the public sphere.

For the first time, a principled rejection of literary property on Enlightenment grounds found real purchase. Donaldson was not a simple libertine; he wanted, in effect, a patent system for literary inventions. But he triggered the long process that would culminate in the House of Lords as *Donaldson v. Becket*, which overthrew London's aspirations to a legal perpetual property once and for all. In its place came copyright. That epochal decision was a direct result, not of the letter of the law, but of an attempt to extend an older metropolitan practice of detection and policing across the land.[5]

The disastrous attempt to sustain a perpetual literary property had one other aspect worth noting here. The Scots argued not only that the purported right did not exist but that their own reprinting contributed to the economic and cultural development of the Scottish nation. They made theirs a struggle for industry and nation against a foreign monopoly. Henry Home—later Lord Kames—was the foremost proponent of this cause. Home noted that London's apparent determination to "crush this Manufacture in the Bud" had a specific meaning in the context of eighteenth-century political economy. It amounted to insisting that Scotland was a colony of England. After all, England sought to confine all its colonies to the furnishing of agricultural produce and raw materials. If the Londoners won their case for literary property, Home thought, then Scotland's book trade—and hence its public culture—risked being relegated to an equivalent colonial status. That would not only have disastrous effects for Enlightenment. It would also have disastrous political and economic consequences.[6] Arguments of this kind, relating literary property to mercantile political economy and to nationhood, began to be made explicitly in the context of enforcement attempts.

This made manifest something that has remained controversial ever since: the extension of literary property across political space. Prior to 1710, literary property regimes had usually been specific to particular cities. Now they became national. But there was of course no official policing agency of this scope, which was why the London trade had to create its own network. And it was also why, when the Londoners sought stronger statutory protection, what they got was a law decreeing all imported editions of works previously published in England to be contraband. The problem exemplified the centrality of cross-border "piracy" to Enlightenment in general. On a broader stage, as Robert Darnton has argued, Enlightenment depended on interregional and cross-border "pirates," and more particularly on their ability to evade countermeasures that were based locally and nationally.[7] And Martha Woodmansee's portrayal of Trattner's massive Viennese business confirms the point for the German lands (see chapter 10, this volume). Mercantilism, nationalism, and cosmopolitanism mixed in complex ways in such situations.

This applied not only, or even especially, to texts. It had long been accepted practice for regimes to give patents to individuals introducing new trades from other countries. Rival cities and states vied for the tacit knowledge possessed by skilled engineers and artisans, forbidding the expatriation of artisans or the export of machines (and designs of machines), while seeking to attract skilled personnel from other countries. The policing of patents now merged with that of copyrights, and both with the practice of great-power espionage. Associations of manufacturers sprouted up across Britain's heartland, determined to restrict strangers' access to plants, to encourage informers, and to promote the use of customs searches to weed out expropriators. They frankly confessed that their measures struck directly at ideals of the free exchange of knowledge.[8]

This is as much as to say that the relation between practices of intellectual property and political space was transformed in the Industrial Revolution. Early modern participant policing had been local to precinct and ward. Now, with the cosmopolitan ideologies of Enlightenment set against the incipient development of colonial empires and steam-powered industries (of transport as well as manufacturing), that had to change. The call went up for first regional, then national, then international regimes of oversight and policing. As they began to take shape, what had previously been broadly consensual practices arising from within increasingly came to be resented as impositions from without. Private agents, heavy-handed searching of houses, appeals for informers, the invocation of high principle (on all sides), and the resort to economic nationalism: these clashes fomented many of the passions that would continue to prevail around intellectual property policing in the modern era.

Spaces and Forces

Despite the convulsions in legal principle and industrial technology of the late eighteenth century, well into the nineteenth it remained conceivable that moral conventions within industries themselves might serve to limit the kind, extent, and scope of intellectual property conflicts. This was again clearest in the book trade. When Philadelphia publishers decided what to reprint, they and their rivals appealed to what they called "courtesies of the trade." These courtesies comprised a series of norms, generally uncodified, that together defined a kind of literary property regime independent of the law and enforced by moral peer pressure. For example, a newspaper advertisement that a publisher had an edition in hand of a British novel gave that publisher a claim to exclusivity—not only to the novel itself, but to subsequent productions by the same author. This principle had absolutely no basis in law but was nonetheless broadly honored in practice. Almost as significant, when it was *not* honored, the transgression was seen as such—as a scandal and a crisis.[9]

Courtesies had roots extending back to the early modern crafts. Indeed, in the early United States there were attempts to institutionalize them in the form of an American Booksellers' Company designed on professedly old-world lines.[10] But as the book trade became a publishing industry, with large-scale manufacturing and markets spread across the continent, so courtesies became more and more an anachronism. The shift of the publishing industry to strong support for international copyright tracked this agglomeration. By the end of the century, the Berne and Paris conventions were the basis of an internationalization process that has continued ever since, alongside similarly treaty-based universalizing trends: the internationalization of science, metrological standards, public health measures, arms agreements, and trade policies.

In terms of the history at issue here, however, an equally important innovation is exemplified by one of the last branches of publishing to retain older customs. Music publishers remained small operations into the 1900s, selling sheet music to be played on household pianos. In the first years of the twentieth century, piracy of these songs became rampant. One Frederick Willetts's People's Music Publishing Company distributed pirated music across Britain. It provoked the creation of one of the first private antipiracy police forces.

Legally, Willetts had no case; he was clearly infringing copyright. But at this time prosecution still fell to the victims, who found that taking offenders to court was time-consuming, expensive, and unrewarding. In the end, the publishers banded together and formed an alliance dedicated to fighting the pirates. They recruited a professional, dedicated antipiracy squad. Mainly comprising ex-police officers, its so-called commandoes traversed the country, tracking down street sellers, following them to their suppliers, and trying to gain entry to the houses where piracies were made and stored. Their activities were not merely distinct from those of the regular police but skirted illegality in their own right. One homeowner was confronted in his doorway by half a dozen men, for example, who barged into the house threatening to "drop" him if he resisted. The publishers' policy was one of "organized hooliganism," declared the magistrate at the resulting case, ruling the men guilty of assault. Another judge lamented that "the liberty of the subject is becoming of no regard at all." Assault and forced entry seemed an altogether more serious matter than piracy.[11] The attempt to employ an army of agents to stamp out music piracy thus raised constitutional complaints as serious as those of Donaldson's time. Yet unlike their predecessors, the publishers did in the end win their fight with the pirates. Faced with the prospect of private commandoes roaming the country, the government resolved to bring music piracy under the remit of the public police.

In effect, a new kind of entrepreneurship came into being around 1900—a business of intellectual property policing. It derived in part from the proliferation of private detective agencies and security companies in the mid-nineteenth century. The dubious activities of agencies like Pinkerton's were soon being put to use to guard creative properties in several fields. Daniel Kevles has discovered one of them: Pinkerton's was hired by seed companies to seek out farmers planting proprietary fruits—something which, Kevles points out, had no legal warrant whatsoever. The music publishers were but one example. But they stood out because they did not hire one of these new agencies but formed their own force. The subsequent history of intellectual property policing would see the growth and entrenchment of such forces across economic fields.

Building on this foundation, after World War II the private policing of intellectual property became an element in the biggest boom in private policing and military industries since at least the Renaissance. The large trade associations were the first to create permanent divisions devoted to the task, and a pattern emerged. The Motion Picture Association of America, for example, formed its group by 1975. Like the music publishers, it recruited its members from the public police (mainly the FBI), and the force again proved a spur to legislators: Congress soon imposed the first major criminal sanctions against movie pirates. In 1982, Britain followed with its Federation against Copyright Theft (FACT). Again, its chief investigator came from a background in the Serious Crimes Unit, the Fraud Squad, and the Flying Squad; he had also commanded the Anti-Terrorist Unit. And again, criminalization swiftly followed. Moreover, such groups took full advantage of the skills their officers learned in their days in the police. FACT hit on a strategy of recruiting video rental franchisees as informers, encouraging them to distinguish themselves from fly-by-night rivals by revealing information about piratical activities. The federation also found that it could get secret judicial authorization to enter and search the premises (including homes) of suspects. Hundreds of these actions took place in the late 1970s and early 1980s, and only when a Luton pirate had the gumption to object was the practice ended. At that point Britain passed a law giving the regular police search and seizure powers.

The enforcement business also emerged as semiautonomous divisions within major companies. It is hard to be certain—secrecy pervades this sector—but it seems likely that many prominent corporations in the digital and pharmaceutical realms created antipiracy and anticounterfeiting units in the generation after 1970. Many were spun off, becoming independent corporations marketing encryption devices, digital watermarks, and more ambitious detection and policing services. As freelancing pirate-hunters, they stood ready to answer companies' desire to outsource this vital service.

At the same time as expanding their reach inward, into homes, the intellectual property police also extended it outward, across the world. By the mid-1980s major trade associations had divisions dedicated to coordinating antipiracy measures in Asia, Africa, Europe, and the Americas. The Joint Anti-Piracy Intelligence Group, founded in 1984, became an intellectual property counterpart to Interpol, with the capability to track cargo vessels across oceans and tap local customs agents to intercept them when they made landfall. In some circumstances private antipiracy forces now rival or outstrip all but the most munificently funded police forces with which they cooperate. Such bodies have consolidated, becoming permanent players alongside governments, the United Nations, and indeed Interpol itself in a vast administrative and juridical machinery devoted to antipiracy actions. By now, a World Intellectual Property Organization conference on enforcement can expect to attract more than 500 participants, from governmental, NGO, and corporate bodies across the world.

In short, the policing of intellectual property has become a huge hybrid enterprise, in which the interests of states, private corporations, multinationals, and world bodies like the United Nations are intertwined. Its strategies and tactics, as well as its institutional character, have roots extending back to the origins of capitalism in the early modern period. This raises evident issues, not the least of which is that of public representation. There are real concerns related to privacy and cognate rights, and it is unclear how those concerns can be raised or addressed at present. A prominent example arises in the biotechnology industry. As is well known, biotech concerns came to view the distribution and reuse of patented genetically modified organism (GMO) seeds beyond rather narrow limits as what it called "seed piracy." Corporations devoted substantial resources to building antipiracy efforts. What this has involved in practice is contested. Monsanto alone acknowledges that it "investigates" about 500 "tips" about seed piracy every year, and the company has been reported to employ its own department of 75 employees with a $10 million budget to do so. It also hires private detective companies. For years Monsanto's agents have been accused of traipsing onto farmers' grounds, sometimes claiming to be engaged in mapping or some other civic job, and occasionally accompanied by regular police officers. There are even allegations that they have acted as *agents provocateurs*. How many of these allegations are well founded remains to be seen. But they do have precedents in the history of IP policing. At the very least, they make it worth asking once again the old question so central to all policing: *quis custodes custodiet?*[12]

Detectives and Detectors

What is new today is the coalescence of this antipiracy policing industry with an industry of tracking technologies. That too is an industry with deep historical roots. The alliance risks conferring an unwonted rigidity, and perhaps brittleness, on intellectual property. It changes the social nature of the concept.

The idea of using technology to combat piracy is an old one. In the West, at least, it is almost as old as the printing press. A favorite early device was the insertion of an individuating mark into manufactured objects to identify them as emerging from a particular source. This was easy to do as long as the number of such objects was not large. For example, authors could sign each copy of an edition by hand to distinguish authorized copies from piracies. But this kind of tactic became impossible for editions of more than a thousand or so. Above that threshold, some kind of machine had to be used. This was a far more difficult proposition, because the very quality of reproducibility threatened to make the verifying mark vulnerable to the same piracy as the objects themselves. The distinct but closely related world of currency minting, for example, took centuries to integrate printing with policing successfully. In the late seventeenth century, counterfeiting was a serious national concern, threatening the very value of the currency itself, and Isaac Newton and Edmond Halley devoted much time and effort to the problem as officers of the mint. The concern grew more serious still when the prospect arose of adopting paper money. The history of this adoption is extremely complex, but the fear of counterfeiting—in effect, of pirating money—was a major deterrent whenever the idea was considered.[13]

From such origins antipiracy technologies have proliferated in the modern era, at least as far and as fast as the varieties of media in which intellectual property exists. At risk of drastically oversimplifying the situation and of flattening its historical morphology, it may be helpful to display a taxonomy of the various types in terms of a pseudo-Ramist scheme (fig. 11.1).

In this scheme, technologies may be either "preventative," in which case they are designed to *prevent* piratical copying (and, all too often, *any* copying), or "detective," in which case they are intended to reveal when copying has taken place. Preventative technologies may be *overt*, like the encryption that satellite television broadcasters use, which requires that the end user have a decoder to access the signal. Another example of this was photocopy-proof paper, which was made in the age of analog photocopiers to resist being copied from (it had a background color that the machines were unable to distinguish from the black of type, producing copies that were illegible). But they may equally be *covert*, in which case the object itself—an LP, say, in the 1970s—is usable without any special decoding device, but contains some imperceptible signal that prevents its copying. Media companies invested large sums in the seventies and eighties in an attempt to create an anticopying signal of this kind. It should be inaudible, but would prevent a cassette recorder from producing a taped reproduction of a record. CBS came closest, but in fact no such technology was ever deemed viable. With digitization it revived as a real possibility, because the mark could definitively be distinguished from the recording

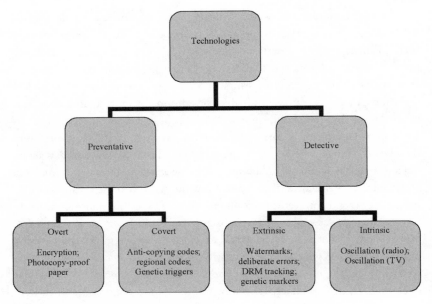

Figure 11.1. Typology of antipiracy technologies.

itself. The regional codes inscribed into modern DVDs are a simple and much-derided instance of this kind of device. Another example, in agricultural genomics, is the use of specific genetic triggers in GMO seeds, either to prevent their reproduction (the so-called terminator gene, so controversial that it has not been brought to market) or to prejudice them in some less severe way.

Other kinds of technology are designed to reveal when copying (or, in some cases, unauthorized access) has occurred. These depend on some kind of tell-tale but peripheral trace or signal, rather like an informational "clue" in a crime scene; they therefore fall into the history of such traces that has been outlined by Carlo Ginzburg.[14] I have distinguished here between *intrinsic* and *extrinsic* traces. Extrinsic ones—the vast majority in such technologies—are deliberately inserted into an object by its producer, to be revealed later either in the act of copying or in the resulting copies. Examples include watermarks, both in paper (dating back to the Renaissance) and in the various digital rights management (DRM) systems used in today's media. Another would be the use of radio frequency identification devices (discussed in chapter 20 of this volume by Tim Lenoir and Eric Giannella) to track pharmaceuticals from factory to pharmacy in a bid to prevent counterfeit drugs entering the medical system. Or, again, a peculiarly telling instance concerns mathematical tables: in the nineteenth century, printers of tables would sometimes insert a deliberate error in one entry and look for that as a tell-tale marker when rivals produced their own versions. The error was in principle perfectly visible, but in practice—given that some of these tables ran to numerous pages of closely printed numbers—undetectable. Today, the descendents of these techniques include the markers used for tracking digital rights and distinctive genetic marks in some GMOs.

There are, by contrast, few *intrinsic* revealers of piracy—traces that are in some sense essential to the medium or the act itself. One that has played an important role in the history of the media, however, is the resonant feedback phenomenon known as "oscillation." Oscillation was a major problem for early broadcasting. Early radio receivers, if imprecisely tuned, might begin to act as transmitters in resonance with the incoming signal, producing a "howl" that would drown out programming for a considerable area. Analogous problems occurred in telephone systems and in other kinds of electronic communications equipment (for example, sound systems in the early talkies). Oscillation was a complex phenomenon, hard to deal with both mathematically and technologically, because it involved a signal "feeding back" into itself. Attempts to deal with it consumed much time and investment in the 1920s communications industry. It has become well known that the origins of information theory lie partly in those attempts, pursued by figures like Claude Shannon at Bell Labs.[15] But what has been forgotten is that, amplification aside, oscillation had positive uses. In particular, it became the basis of the first modern pirate-detection device. The British Post Office made use of it to detect radios (and later televisions) being used by citizens who had not paid their license fee to support the BBC.[16]

What to Be Worried About

This account of the history of antipiracy strategies and technologies is necessarily sketchy. The intent is to provoke questions. It should be sufficient, however, to suggest that there is indeed a subject of inquiry here, and a consequential one. When, in the seventeenth century, searchers on behalf of a company of printers and booksellers claimed the right to enter citizens' homes and search for signs of piracy, it was a matter of fierce and impassioned controversy because it could be held to trample on the prerogatives of the subject. Nowadays, the polity, moral economy, and agency are all very different, but the ferocity and passion are no less evident, because access and surveillance remain among the most pivotal of political powers. It is all the more critical, therefore, to approach the issue historically, by looking at the development of skills, techniques, cultures, and technologies of antipiracy. In a sense, this is the counterpart of Lawrence Liang's call to look at what piracy does, not what it is (see chapter 9 of this volume).

Intellectual property law lives in its application. When, therefore, scholars and campaigners urge a need to revise the law, they may be better advised to look at the burgeoning industry of enforcement that puts statutes into effect. That industry has a long history. At this point it has become powerful and far-reaching—but remains almost unknown to the public. The appropriate divisions of responsibilities, powers, and resources to sustain it in a responsible society have not yet been made, let alone made clear. It is a basic requirement of an accountable, social-democratic polity that they should be. We have got used to hearing about the perils of excessive intellectual property rights; we have also heard a lot about the perils of piracy. Yet the questions raised by the antipiracy industry in action are modern versions of problems that history has made central to modern political order. Their terms—privacy, property, accountability, citizenship, freedom—are among what history has told us to recognize as the fundamental elements of a just society. There lies the moral implication of this history.

NOTES

1. C. B. Herrup, *The Common Peace: participation and the criminal law in seventeenth-century England* (Cambridge: Cambridge University Press, 1987), 59–61, 69–70.

2. E.g., J. Greene, *The trouble with ownership: Literary property and authorial liability in England, 1660–1730* (Philadelphia: University of Pennsylvania Press, 2005).

3. C. Blagden, *The notebook of Thomas Bennet and Henry Clements (1686–1719) with some aspects of book trade practice* (Oxford: Oxford Bibliographical Society Publications, n.s., 6, 1953 [i.e., 1956]), 67–100.

4. J. Feather, *Publishing, piracy, and politics: An historical study of copyright in Britain* (London: Mansell, 1994), 83–84; M. Rose, *Authors and owners: The invention of copyright* (Cambridge, MA: Harvard University Press, 1993), 74–78.

5. [A. Donaldson], *Some thoughts on the state of literary property* (London: printed for A. Donaldson, 1764), 3–4, 7–19, 24.

6. W. McDougall, "Copyright litigation in the Court of Session, 1738–1749, and the rise of the Scottish book trade," *Edinburgh Bibliographical Society Transactions* 5:5 (1988), 2–31, esp. 6–8.

7. R. Darnton, "The science of piracy: a crucial ingredient in eighteenth-century publishing," *Studies in Voltaire and the Eighteenth Century* 12 (2003), 3–29.

8. J. R. Harris, *Industrial espionage and technology transfer: Britain and France in the eighteenth century* (Aldershot, UK: Ashgate, 1998), 453–477; D. S. Ben-Atar, *Trade Secrets: Intellectual piracy and the origins of American industrial power* (New Haven, CT: Yale University Press, 2004).

9. E. Exman, *The brothers Harper* (New York: Harper and Row, 1965), 53–55, 393–396.

10. M. Carey, *Autobiography* (New York: E. L. Schwaab, 1942; orig. 1833–1834), 49–50.

11. J. Coover, *Music publishing, copyright and piracy in Victorian England* (London: Mansell, 1985), 88; British Library, Music Library, Ms. M.55 (Arthur Preston's scrapbook), fragment from Leeds, n.d.

12. The report on these practices by the Center for Food Safety (http://www.centerforfoodsafety.org/pubs/CFSMOnsantovsFarmerReport1.13.05.pdf, 23 June 2006), interested as it undoubtedly is, provides plentiful empirical citations and buttressing for its claims.

13. J. Craig, *Newton at the mint* (Cambridge: Cambridge University Press, 1946); S. Mihm, *A nation of counterfeiters: Capitalists, con men, and the making of the United States* (Cambridge, MA: Harvard University Press, 2007), 25–62.

14. C. Ginzburg, *Clues, myths, and the historical method* (Baltimore: Johns Hopkins University Press, 1989).

15. D. A. Mindell, *Between human and machine: Feedback, control, and computing before cybernetics* (Baltimore: Johns Hopkins University Press, 2002).

16. A. Johns, *Piracy: the intellectual property wars from Gutenberg to Gates* (Chicago: University of Chicago Press, 2009), chapter 13.

12

Characterizing Copyright in the Classroom
The Cultural Work of Antipiracy Campaigns

Before the Internet, there was little reason for the ordinary citizen to know much about copyright.[1] Outside of professional media producers and librarians, the rest of us could remain conveniently ignorant. Today, with recent developments (both technical and societal) in who makes, distributes, and consumes information, suddenly everyone is implicated. So how do citizens learn the law? And how do they learn about in a moment when the contexts to which it applies are in flux, when society's sense of how it should apply is under discussion? We depend on certain institutions to help us know the law: government agencies, schools, nonprofit organizations, and corporations whose product may be relevant. Each is working to inform citizens of the law and simultaneously to instill the social norm of obeying that law (Lessig, 1995; Sunstein, 1996). The risk, of course, is that some of these mediating institutions may have a vested interest in the law being understood in a particular way.

The rapid innovations in the material, economic, and social contours of information that have troubled copyright law have also troubled the major U.S. movie studios, record labels, and software makers. In response, the trade organizations representing these industries have worked against what they see as the promiscuous circulation of their products online, through lawsuits, technical copy protection mechanisms, and lobbying for new and stronger laws (see Gillespie, 2007). Some of these organizations have also developed public campaigns to inform ordinary citizens about copyright and change the "copynorms" (Schultz, 2007) around unauthorized downloading: PSAs on television and before movies, newspaper and magazine ads, and Web sites—sometimes all of these bundled into a single campaign. In addition to these public campaigns, many of these same organizations have also been providing antipiracy materials to K–12 schools.

Less visible than their public counterparts, these antipiracy educational materials have quietly proliferated in recent years. They range from games and comics available on organization Web sites, to multimedia presentations for school assemblies, to fully developed curricular modules to be taught in the classroom. These are either posted online as teacher resources or mailed directly to schools. Most target late elementary and early junior high school students, though some are aimed at even younger audiences. These classroom materials are generally made available free of charge or packaged with an established scholastic publication (such as *Junior Achievement* and *Weekly Reader*). Recently the Copyright Alliance, a trade organization of trade organizations, established the Copyright Alliance Education Foundation to push its own curriculum.[2] These industry-sponsored antipiracy campaigns are joined by a number of other copyright education programs from a variety of sources: government agencies, scholastic publishers, academic organizations, and grassroots activist groups (fig. 12.1).

These free teaching resources are not mere corporate altruism: they offer a powerful opportunity to speak directly to children about copyright and to frame the larger debate in terms most amenable to their special interests. They take advantage of the fact that students are a captive audience, and they lean on the authority and legitimacy of the teachers who deliver these corporate appeals. They are part of the proliferation of *sponsored educational materials*, materials produced and distributed by corporations for K–12 classrooms in order to wrap their brand or corporate message into an educational package (Schor, 2004, pp. 85–98; Calvert, 2008). Concern about the increasing presence of these materials surged in the late 1990s, particularly around the Channel One service. Yet despite the continued concern of a few (Molnar et. al., 2008), public attention to the issue has waned.

An obvious concern is how copyright and its violation are characterized in these campaigns—by stakeholders who have obvious economic and ideological investments in the law being understood in particular ways. These materials may be the first, possibly the only time schoolchildren learn anything about

Figure 12.1. From Join the © Team (Entertainment Software Association and Young Minds Inspired, 2007).

copyright law, how it works, or why it exists. In fact, the producers of these materials are counting on it. These organizations are not neutral conveyors of copyright law but interested interpreters of it. So it is of great importance that we consider how the law is being presented, or better, *represented*, by these or-ganizations—and to whom. (See Gillespie, 2009 for more; also Gates, 2006; Hetcher, 2004; Jensen, 2003; Yar, 2008.)

But the concern extends beyond what a particular child will end up think-ing or doing with regard to unauthorized downloading. These deliberate ef-forts to frame the law and its current challenges are strategic interventions into the broader public discourse around digital copyright, an effort to pick and choose the terms in which the problem will be understood. Just as the way copyright law is imposed depends on the careful rhetorical performance of its key concepts (Jaszi, 1991; Woodmansee and Jaszi, 1994), how the controversy is characterized has a great deal to do with how it will be resolved (Halbert,

1997; Litman, 2004; Logie, 2006; Loughlan, 2008; Reyman, 2009; Spitz and Hunter, 2005).

Portraying Piracy

These classroom antipiracy campaigns nearly all share a single rhetorical strategy—a concerted effort to simplify the rights and obligations of copyright law down to a clear equation: *piracy = theft*. This claim is common to the public campaigns as well, part of a broader and convenient demonization of piracy (Litman, 2000; see also Govil, 2004) effected in part through the regular emphasis on that word. In the educational context it is pervasive and fundamental: as copyright is "explained" to middle-schoolers, it is reduced in myriad ways to some version of this misleading platitude.

Quite often, the equation is made explicitly, as if it is an unproblematic fact about copyright and its obligations. The most explicit may be in the Wake Up to Illegal File-Sharing materials produced by the Motion Picture Association of America (MPAA) and Lifetime Learning Systems: question one of the "P2P Pop Quiz" is "Piracy is theft. True/False" (fig. 12.2).[3] The answer provided is unambiguous. In "How Harry Potter Was Born," part of its Copyright Awareness Week 2006 project, the Copyright Society notes that "making or downloading copies that you did not pay for means you infringe (steal) the rights of authors like J. K. Copyright infringement is just a fancy word for cheating and stealing by getting something for free that should be paid for."[4]

The parenthetical comment—and the entire document—elides important differences between copyright infringement and stealing material property and coating the former with a moral judgment by equating it with "cheating" a beloved author. The Join the © Team program developed by the Entertainment Software Association (ESA) in 2007 is more subtle, offering up what it calls a "simple axiom" as the key to copyright education: "The rules and laws reviewed here all rest on an ethical recognition that it is wrong to take the intellectual property of another person, just as it is wrong to steal material objects that don't belong to us. Reminding students of this simple axiom, guiding them toward this conscience-touching realization, may be the place to start instruction on the concept of intellectual property, and may be the most effective lesson in the end."[5]

A preferred trope among these materials is to compare copyright infringement to shoplifting, with the suggestion that there is no difference between the two. The Business Software Alliance's (BSA's) Play It Cybersafe poses and answers its own question: "What's the difference between copying software from a friend and stealing software from a store? Nothing" (fig. 12.3).[6] In the

1 **Piracy is theft.**

True   **False**

Figure 12.2. From Wake Up to Illegal File-Sharing (MPAA and Lifetime Learning Systems, 2006).

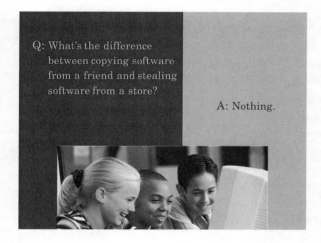

Q: What's the difference between copying software from a friend and stealing software from a store?

A: Nothing.

Figure 12.3. From Play It Cybersafe (BSA and Weekly Reader Corp., 2002).

Recording Industry Association of America (RIAA) and Close Up's *Face the Music* DVD, a moderator poses the question to a group of teens:

> Joe Geraghty, Close Up Foundation: "What really is the difference between shoplifting and illegal downloading?"
> Keith: "Legally . . . nothing."[7]

Keith's answer, though factually incorrect, is allowed to stand, and is reiterated immediately after by a music retailer who agrees because, completing the tautological circle, "theft is theft."

This more subtle approach reaches its fullest manifestation in a single, manufactured word, included now in four different curricula, to describe online copyright infringement: "songlifting." The term appears in Music Rules! produced by LearningWorks, and Whose Music Is It? and Face the Music, both produced by the Close Up Foundation. More recently it has appeared in passing, as if merely a term of art, in Microsoft's Teachers Guide to Intellectual Property Rights Education. The obvious resonance with the term *shoplifting* sustains the comparison liminally, while avoiding the harsher words *theft* and *piracy*. Music Rules! uses "songlifting" as its organizing term, and only once defines the word. In the assignments that follow, songlifting is simply the name for these activities. The equation to shoplifting is discursively sealed; students are then merely asked to document the many wrongs associated with an action that's already been defined as wrong. Whatever difference there may be between copyright infringement and shoplifting is set aside and forgotten (fig. 12.4).

Throughout these campaigns a complex legal bargain is portrayed as a clean, ethical distinction. "It is actually quite easy to tell a good guy from a bad guy when one of the guys is being called a thief" (Loughlan, 2008). And it's much more compelling to ask someone to be fair or good or just than to be law-abiding. This is most apparent in the pervasive emphasis on "respecting" copyright. The term "respect" here does a great deal of discursive work: while sometimes "respect" refers simply to obeying a rule, as in "respect the speed limit," it can also mean to hold in high regard, to appreciate something for its inherent value, as in "respect your elders." Here these two meanings are united; kids are asked to obey the law and to hold it in high esteem. In the instructions provided by the American Society of Composers, Authors, and Publishers (ASCAP) and i-SAFE, they use "respect" in their campaign's mission: "*The Donny the Downloader Experience* creates an assembly that teaches students a powerful anti-piracy message, empowers them to respect all intellectual property, and shows students appropriate and legal alternatives to illegal downloading."[8] How respecting copyright will be "empowering" is left unclear. This emphasis on respect is not exclusive to the industry-produced campaigns; it provides a powerful frame for nearly all of the lessons on copyright and antipiracy (fig. 12.5).[9]

This respect for the law is also extended to the creators of the content and to the content itself, with the suggestion that respect for artists and their work justifies respect for copyright law. The Copyright Society's Copyright Kids site answers the question "Why should I care about copyright?" by noting: "These talented musicians, authors, illustrators and screenwriters deserve our respect and appreciation—and they deserve to make a living from the hard work they

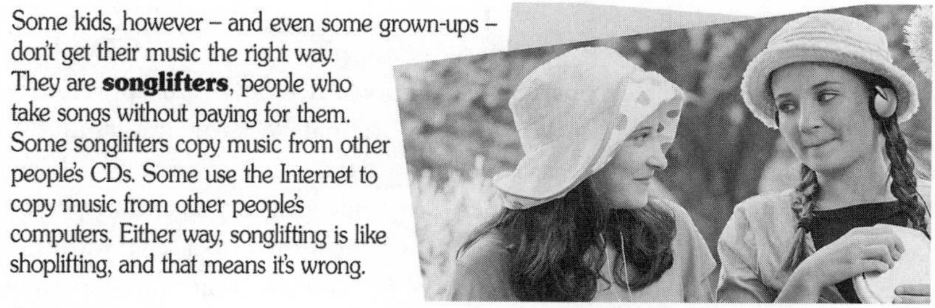

Some kids, however – and even some grown-ups – don't get their music the right way. They are **songlifters**, people who take songs without paying for them. Some songlifters copy music from other people's CDs. Some use the Internet to copy music from other people's computers. Either way, songlifting is like shoplifting, and that means it's wrong.

Figure 12.4. From Music Rules! (RIAA and LearningWorks, 2006).

Think First, © Copy Later...
Respecting Creative Ownership
Copyright protects the rights of authors, artists, composers, and other owners of creative works from the unauthorized use of their works. If you want to copy or use someone else's creative work, here are some tips to help you do it the right way!
Respect: Creative works are someone else's property and the creator has the right to decide how they are used.
Remember: Works are copyrighted whether in physical or digital form. Copying digital works like software, music, photographs, or video games is not permitted, the same way photocopying an entire book is not permitted.

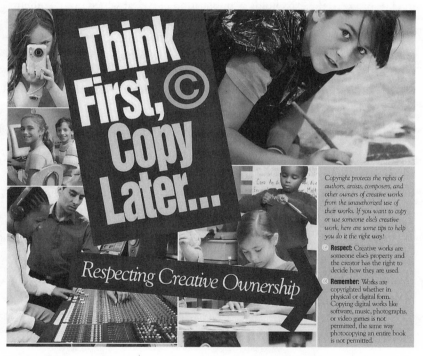

Figure 12.5. From Think First, Copy Later: Respect Creative Ownership (Copyright Alliance and Young Minds Inspired, 2009).

put into their creative works—otherwise most of them wouldn't be able to produce as many (or any) of the songs, books, plays, movies and TV shows that you like. That's what copyright is all about. It reflects our appreciation for all the hard work that goes into creating 'original works of authorship' and respect for the right of the creator of that work to control what people can and cannot do with it."[10] This link between respecting artists and respecting copyright can even allow a campaign to forgo the more direct legal warnings. The 2007 ESA's Join the © Team campaign is unique among these classroom materials in that it never once mentions piracy, downloading, or peer-to-peer networks. Billed as "An Educational Program Encouraging Creativity and Respect for Intellectual Property," its purported aim is to help kids "discover the natural connection between copyright and creativity." After completing in-class projects, the class holds a "publication party," at which point students are given a "You're part of the © Team" sticker (provided) to apply to their work. The sticker is a kind of gold star reward for their creative effort, and it also applies a boilerplate "all rights reserved" copyright statement to their work.[11] Piracy never appears as an explicit issue anywhere in the campaign; copyright is simply presented as the ultimate and natural expression of respect for creativity (fig. 12.6).

William Fisher (2001) has noted that copyright law has enjoyed a set of distinct and tangled philosophical justifications. European law emphasizes that authors deserve copyright privileges because of the effort behind or special value of their work; U.S. law depends more on the utilitarian perspective expressed in the Constitution that copyright serves the public and spurs intellectual progress for the greater good. U.S. courts have in a number of cases rejected the idea that copyright should merely reward creativity or effort. So it is significant that these materials, for U.S. classrooms, so regularly conflate the idea that artists "deserve our respect and appreciation"—though they arguably do—with the benefits of copyright that may accrue to them, though not exactly for that reason.

Conveying Copyright

Copyright law is a quite complex doctrine with exceptions, caveats, and deliberate ambiguities. It is reasonable to simplify such a complex phenomenon in order to suit the cognitive capacities of children at their particular developmental level. Deciding what children can comprehend is, of course, not an exact science. But the question is not *whether* these materials simplify the law in the process of explaining it but *how* it gets simplified.

The most common of these simplifications is to describe copyright in terms

Figure 12.6. From Join the © Team (ESA and Young Minds Inspired, 2007).

that turn the balance of rights into a more exclusive property regime. "As the
creator of your work, you should have the right to control what people can
and cannot do with your work."[12] Not only does the "should" in that sentence
shift this statement of fact into a normative claim, it also presents copyright
as a blanket control over what people can do with their intellectual property,
which the law does not in fact provide (Herman, 2008). This notion of copyright law as comprehensive right often appears in the form of advice: "*Never
copy someone else's creative work without permission from the copyright
holder*"[13] (fig. 12.7). A statement like this hides the fact that some copying is
actually acceptable, either because it does not infringe the owner's rights or
because it could qualify as fair use.

Fair use regularly falls victim to this simplification. In the "never" com-
mandment above, it is simply disregarded. Even when it is addressed, fair use
is often defined more narrowly than a reasonable reading of case law would
warrant. The RIAA's *Whose Music Is It?* explains it only in terms of the right
to time-shift or legitimately redistribute content, completely overlooking the
protection fair use affords to quoting or modifying copyrighted works. The
Join the © Team program narrows fair use by claiming that it exists only in the

Figure 12.7. From Music Rules! (RIAA and LearningWorks, 2006).

classroom and nowhere else. Under the subheading "Respecting Copyright," the teacher's instructions read: "Conclude this class discussion by reminding students that the special rules for respecting intellectual property in school don't apply outside the classroom. Students are allowed to copy short passages of copyrighted text, individual copyrighted images, and excerpts from other copyrighted material in their school work, as long as they credit their sources. This is called 'fair use.' But no one is allowed to copy copyrighted material outside the classroom for any reason without getting permission."[14] This mischaracterization entirely excludes fair use's long-standing application to journalism, criticism, and parody, all forms of expression that tech-savvy preteens might already be exploring. The Copyright Awareness Week 2006 materials suggest that fair use only applies if there is no commercial impact whatsoever: "These examples and others are fair to authors like J. K. Rowling, because they do not cheat authors out of royalties."[15]

In light of Aufderheide and Jaszi's (2007) evidence that fair use continues to be widely misunderstood by ordinary citizens, these mischaracterizations are problematic. Taken together, these caveats make fair use a risky proposition, a risk some of these campaigns are happy to use as cause for dismissal. Copyright Kids suggests that "unless you are absolutely sure, relying on the doctrine of 'Fair Use' to avoid seeking Permission to copy a work is risky. . . . The best course of action is simply to seek permission for all copied material you intend to use."[16]

These explanations of the law are not regulated by anything other than the producers' desire not to be caught egregiously misrepresenting a particular issue. We regulate advertisements for false claims, but it is unclear whether these materials are or are not advertisements. We regulate political advertising by third parties and tobacco, alcohol, and drug advertising through their producers, but we have no rules for the producers of culture. Yet "the culture industries have a central governing role to play in the process of producing cultural policy and governing cultural citizens, not simply in the representations that they circulate, but in the rationales for particular types of conduct that they instruct and prescribe" (Gates, 2006: 58–59). While there have been some efforts to present the balance of rights differently, both in the classroom (American Library Association, Electronic Frontier Foundation) and out (American University's Center for Social Media), these organizations do not have the power to distribute campaigns as widely as the content industry trade organizations can.

Reifying Roles

One of the most powerful ways these campaigns frame this issue is through the roles kids are offered in these lessons, activities, and narratives. This is a powerful technique in both education and advertising—and these campaigns are both. These campaigns traffic in a limited set of roles for kids to inhabit. Much of the ideological work they do is crafting those roles and then associating a particular perspective on copyright and piracy with them.

Let's consider more closely one classroom activity, part of the 2003 What's the Diff? A Guide to Digital Citizenship for Volunteers and Teachers program published by Junior Achievement and the MPAA. The campaign was distributed in the United States to approximately 900,000 kids in 36,000 classrooms, grades 5–9.[17] The activity, called "Living in a Fishbowl," is an awkward combination of role-playing and debate. Students are assigned one of six roles and provided with cards that suggest how someone in that role might feel about online piracy of movies. Students first meet in groups to talk through how to present that role's priorities to the class. Then one from each group meets in the "fishbowl," a circle of chairs in the center of the room, to engage in a kind of debate—the teacher or Junior Achievement volunteer poses a question, and each student attempts to answer as the assigned role. Six new volunteers then replace them in the fishbowl to respond to a different question. The roles they are asked to adopt are shown in figure 12.8.

Five of the six are professional roles inside the corporate movie and music industries as they are currently structured. Note the absence of, for instance, a struggling film student, or a team of documentary filmmakers, or a festival organizer, or a DJ.[18] In the five profiles, there is no mention of online production, distribution, or collaboration: these are archetypes that could just have

Producer

I am responsible for raising money and making the deals for a new film. I am responsible for hiring the writer, director, costumer, art director, editor, casting director and of course the movie stars. I am found on the set daily. I supervise the production of the movie. I am responsible for solving all of the problems on the set, so the director and actors can do their jobs. I make sure the movie stays within budget. I decide on the movie posters and television commercials for the movie. I work incredibly hard to make the movie a success. Copyrights protect all of my hard work. Illegal "file-swapping" makes it possible for people to steal my original work. If "file-swapping" continues, I will no longer be able to do my job. "File-swapping" is costing me big bucks. I'm not getting the money I have earned for making movies. "File-swapping" just isn't fair.

Actor

I am an actor. I make the characters come to life on the big screen. I memorize lines and rehearse with other actors to make sure that the scenes are as real as possible. I work with the director and producer to develop a realistic script. I provide ideas on the set and support other actors as they work. I promote the movie and attend lots of different functions to make sure that people know about the movie and are convinced they want to see it in the theaters. I put a lot of my time, talent and energy into making films. People need to respect me and stop illegally downloading my movies from the Internet. "File-swapping" means less profits for studios, less money available to make new movies, and fewer jobs for me.

Key Carpenter

I am responsible for all the carpentry work that is required to build the sets for the movie. I am a skilled craftsperson with tons of experience. I have an in-depth knowledge of carpentry techniques, materials and equipment. On the set I am responsible for hanging doors, setting windows and making the layout for any stairs used on the set. I work with the set director to read the blueprints and make sure that the set looks just right. I'm not one of the million-dollar employees that everyone sees when they watch movies. I only make money when I am working on a movie set. I can go months without work. People who buy tickets pay my salary. When people illegally download, they are stealing from my family and me. If studios can no longer afford to make as many movies because "file-swapping" has cut into their profits, that means less opportunities for me to work.

Singer

I am a young and talented singer. I am just getting started in the business and have created my first CD. I write all of my own music based on my personal experiences. I am working hard to get my name out to the public. I am starting to perform my music and have just signed on with a big record label. I am starting to experience the success I have hoped for since I started singing and writing music. Illegal "file-swapping" has turned my dreams into nightmares. All of my efforts and struggles are for nothing. My CD sales are poor because everyone is downloading my songs for free from the Internet. Now the recording company does not want to invest in producing a new CD of my latest songs. What people don't realize is that it is ruining my career. Just imagine working your whole life for a dream and having someone ruin it. Every time someone takes my music and file shares it, I lose money. Talk about unfair!

Director

I direct the movies people love to watch. I have the vision for how the written script will look on the big screen. I have to make sure that my vision is understandable to everyone. I make sure that everyone works together to create an amazing movie. I work with the producer on developing a script. I make sure that the actors understand their roles and help them develop their talents. Copyrights make sure that I receive the recognition I deserve for all of my hard work and energy. Just imagine if you put a lot of time and energy into a project you were working on and then someone else got the credit. "File-swapping" is the same thing. I do all the work to create a great movie, but I don't receive all the money I've earned. Every time someone "file-swaps" my movie, I lose money. It really isn't fair.

Computer User

There is nothing wrong with "file-swapping". It's just like borrowing a book from the library. It's not like I am selling the music and besides I'm just one person; how much harm can I cause? The technology is available on my personal computer. How could it possibly be illegal to download movies and music from the Internet? We are just swapping information. They call it peer-to-peer "file-swapping". Besides, don't you think the movie and music industry has enough money already? I say that if I bought the CD, it is mine to swap with my friends. And another thing, who is going to catch me? Last time I checked, Internet police didn't exist. It's really no big deal! I think everyone needs to relax.

Figure 12.8. From *What's the Diff? A Guide to Digital Citizenship for Volunteers and Teachers* (MPAA and Junior Achievement, 2003; used with permission of Junior Achievement).

easily been drawn from the heyday of the studio system as from our contemporary moment. And all five follow the same script: (1) I work hard to perform X valuable function in the production of movies, (2) copyright protects that hard work and rewards my effort, (3) piracy is hurting me economically, and (4) it is deeply unfair.

Then there's the sixth and final role, the "computer user." He is the only one who supports peer-to-peer file-sharing, so the "fishbowl" debate is very likely to be a pitched battle. He has no profession, so he offers no way to refute the economic imperatives repeated by the other five. His eyes are turned to the sky, his eyebrows are askew, his mouth is crooked, together producing a look of confusion and mild stupidity. He arguably looks younger than the others, suggesting a certain naïveté. He launches into his justifications for his use of peer-to-peer, which are written as a nearly incoherent rant: badly written, morally bankrupt, and full of obvious misstatements, a stitched-together series of rationalizations that do not hold up to scrutiny (though they are drawn from and continue to be deployed by existing peer-to-peer users). And finally, the top of his head is missing, and beams of starlight are streaming out of his open skull. It is not unreasonable to suggest this is a dismissive, even derisive representation.

This campaign and others offer a carefully circumscribed set of roles offered to kids, both explicitly in role-playing activities and more implicitly in the explanations and examples offered: fan/consumer, struggling artist, industry professional, pirate. These are not roles that the students may imaginatively explore, but proscribed roles they must simply accept. Though at the time an MPAA spokesperson described the What's the Diff? campaign as a means for "students to reach their own conclusions about being a good digital citizen" (Rich Taylor, quoted in Howe, 2004), the materials are quite clear about what being a good digital citizen entails, and they only leave open the "conclusion" of whether to accept or reject them.

But these campaigns have a further tactic: not just offering roles, but establishing ideological relationships between them. First, what kids are doing inside narrative examples or are addressed as doing in their own lives is overwhelmingly about the "consumption" of music, be it illicit sharing on peer-to-peer networks or purchasing content from legitimate content services (fig. 12.9). The traditional role of consumer, active in its zeal but passive in terms of subsequent creation or even interpretive freedom, is offered as a comfortable position from which to engage with copyright. The recurring imagery of headphones and air guitar is an ironic reminder: this uncanny absence of production marks how fanhood here is understood entirely as an act of consumption (fig. 12.10).

The emphasis on consumption is not absolute. Occasionally kids are presented as producers, most often in light of what they make in the classroom: reports, in-class presentations, term papers. Occasionally they are amateur producers, editors of the yearbook, hobbyist musicians. Rarely are they reusers and remixers, despite the emerging venues for such activities. Copyright Kids,

Figure 12.9. From Music Rules! (RIAA and LearningWorks, 2006).

Figure 12.10. From Music Rules! (RIAA and LearningWorks, 2006).

one of the earliest campaigns, is a curious exception; a Q&A asks students whether copyright allows them any latitude when "you just saw the coolest video clip on the internet. You want to download it and cut it into your own video" and is not entirely prohibitive in its answer. Blogging, social networking, online collaboration, wikis, and open source software design are rendered almost invisible by the incessant focus on mass culture consumption, seen only as sites of possible infringement when they do appear (Denegri-Knott, 2004).

In opposition to this fan/consumer stands the pirate, which is obviously never presented as a viable role to inhabit; rather, it is carefully circumscribed as a violation both of the law and of music fanhood and youth culture. Many of the campaigns construct a diametric opposition between fan/consumer and pirate to convince kids not only that they should want to be one rather than the other but that they cannot be both.

Second, many of these campaigns construct a career arc of fan/consumer—struggling artist—industry professional as a logical sequence, one that could conceivably happen for these kids some day. This positioning allows kids not only to envision stardom or a career in the entertainment industry in the future; it also justifies their identification with the professional perspective on copyright and piracy right now: You may be that famous artist tomorrow, so honor their rights today.

Several campaigns use teens struggling to make it professionally as their voice of reason; ASCAP's *The Donny the Downloader Experience* program makes it the central conceit, contrasting the animated exploits of Donny with videos chronicling Sonya Bender, a seventeen-year-old aspiring singer/songwriter, simultaneously preparing for open-mic night and interviewing music insiders about copyright. She is narrator and, even more, our stand-in, and her modest combination of starry dreams and teenage quirks make her a compelling dose of reality. Her interviews with music insiders represent a second strategy, common to several of these campaigns, where "behind-the-scenes" players in the entertainment production business are deployed as voices in the copyright debates. A Music Rules! exercise employs a third tactic, envisioning kids in these roles literally: in the pictures not only of the "diva" recording artist but also the talent scouts and studio producers who helped her get there, the faces are all of teenagers rather than the adults they would actually be (fig. 12.11).

Culture as Commerce

Kelly Gates (2006) describes these industry antipiracy campaigns as a kind of soft governance, like the "model citizen" instruction once a central tenet in K–12 pedagogy. William Patry goes further: "I find it misleading to describe such efforts as education: they are propaganda, albeit propaganda copyright owners in good faith believe in."[19] And Majid Yar (2008) suggests that they are just one example of the normative work of capital itself, to discursively establish the boundaries of what counts as violation of the market's needs.

I would say it a bit differently. By no means are these materials well coordinated, and by all means, this characterization of recent changes is endemic,

Figure 12.11. From Music Rules! (RIAA and LearningWorks, 2006).

extending well beyond them. Emerging sociocultural paradigms run up against the entrenched assumptions and the entrenched interests that feel it necessary to resist them. Classroom pedagogy tries to keep up with the changing technological and social world but does so with a conservative bent. This tension is exacerbated by the thorny issue of who produces the actual materials from which the students learn and what viewpoint those materials take.

Perhaps the most troubling assertion here is the way the distinction between illegal and legal online content gets perfectly mapped onto whether the content is free or not. Again and again, these campaigns conflate the theft of copyrighted works with not paying for them. In What's the Diff? the MPAA and Junior Achievement hit us with these bullet points:

- To legally own it, legally buy it.
- If you haven't paid for it, you've stolen it.[20]

The ESA makes it specific to the Internet: "Children who realize that few things on the Internet are free are less likely to become involved in trading illegally copied music, movies, games, and other software."[21] Elsewhere in the What's the Diff? campaign, the MPAA quotes a newspaper columnist suggesting that "you have to be awfully young, awfully naïve or awfully both to believe in free anything"[22]— not only another equation of free and illegal, but more generally, a pretty reprehensible sentiment to include in a classroom activity for fifth graders.

Again, simplification is a tricky thing. Helping kids distinguish between legitimate content services and peer-to-peer networks is a reasonable aim, regardless of your politics about the future of copyright. The distinction may not be an easy one to make, especially as peer-to-peer tools have grown increasingly user-friendly and professionally designed. Looking for shorthand ways to discern the difference is a part of this. But this particular equation, of free to illegal, has implications for our understanding of digital culture—at the very moment we are experimenting as a society with new arrangements for distributing culture that may not depend on direct sale (Anderson, 2008) and new arrangements for the production of information that may not depend on direct financial reward (Benkler, 2006; Shirky, 2008). The very innovations in distribution, pricing, and purpose that the Internet seems to allow are swallowed whole by the rhetoric of these campaigns.

The presentation of the Internet as a vehicle for the consumption of mass entertainment is certainly in the best financial interests of the trade organizations that produced most of these campaigns. But the equation of culture and commerce is not simply the strategic self-interest of major commercial content providers; it is also fundamental to the way copyright law was written: as a means of encouraging the production of culture by making it into a commodity. The law may in many ways have its intended effect. But it tends to install price as a mechanism not just for managing distribution but for measuring the value of culture (Bettig, 1992).

In ASCAP and i-SAFE's *The Donny the Downloader Experience*, Michelle, a professional songwriter, expresses her worries about piracy in precisely these terms: "I'm worried that songs will go away, I'm worried that songs will become—that making music will become a hobby for most people, that people won't take it as seriously. People value what they pay for, and if it's free, it'll be—it's like wallpaper, it's like air, it's like water that you dr[ink]—no one—it becomes disposable. It's not good for music, ultimately, to treat it like it's free, and out there—you know, treat it like it's worthless. Because it isn't. It—music brings a lot to people."[23] These campaigns traffic in particular interpretations of copyright and the Internet, and particular understandings of culture and technology more broadly, that fall back again and again on commercial, industrial, traditional arrangements and a measure of value that is entirely financial. As such, they may powerfully intervene in the ongoing dialogues spurred by the sway and churn of technologies, practices, and rules that students are just beginning to encounter. They aim to hold together the fragile equation of cultural participation, commercial value, and industrial production that could otherwise be productively in flux in this contentious moment.

NOTES

1. A longer version of this article appeared in *Communication, Culture & Critique* 2(3), in August 2009. It appears here with permission of Blackwell Publishing. That article includes a complete list of the campaigns I examined.

2. Copyright Alliance, "Copyright Alliance Launches New Educational Foundation," May 21, 2009: http://www.copyrightalliance.org/news.php?id=65.

3. MPAA / Lifetime Learning Systems, "P2P Pop Quiz!" Wake Up to Illegal File-Sharing, 2.

4. Copyright Society of the USA, "How Harry Potter Was Born," Copyright Awareness Week 2006, 3.

5. ESA / Young Minds Inspired, "Educator's Guide to Intellectual Property," Join the © Team, 6.

6. BSA / *Weekly Reader*, "Class Poster," Play It Cybersafe.

7. RIAA / Close Up, *Face the Music*, DVD.

8. ASCAP/i-SAFE, Instruction book, *The Donny the Downloader Experience*, 6.

9. See, for example, Maria Kardick, American Library Association / National Council of Teachers of English, ReadWriteThink, Exploring Plagiarism, Copyright, and Paraphrasing (Lesson 1062); WIPO, Learn from the Past, Create the Future: The Arts and Copyright.

10. Copyright Society of the USA, "Copyright Basics," Copyright Kids, http://www.copyright kids.org/cbasicsframes.htm.

11. ESA/YMI, Stickers, Join the © Team.

12. Copyright Society of the USA, "Copyright Basics," Copyright Kids, http://www.copyright kids.org/cbasicsframes.htm.

13. RIAA/YMI, "Classroom Poster," Music Rules!

14. ESA/YMI, "Let's C©py Right: 2–3," Join the © Team, 2.

15. Copyright Society of the USA, "How Harry Potter Was Born," Copyright Awareness Week 2006, 4.

16. Copyright Society of the USA, "Copyright Basics," Copyright Kids, http://www.copyright kids.org/cbasicsframes.htm.

17. Junior Achievement, "Film/TV Industry Launches Public Service Announcements as Part of Nationwide Awareness Campaign on the Impact of Digital Piracy," press release, July 2003. No longer available online.

18. One of the ALA-sponsored lesson plans has a similar role-based debate exercise, but a wider range of concerns and roles are offered. When the class is asked to debate the legality of peer-to-peer file-sharing, students are offered six roles: film producer, cutting-edge technology company, YouTube user, college student with limited budget, recording executive, and musician with a new CD out.

At least in this case the value of the distribution platform, both to its provider and its user, is up for discussion. Cassandra Love, ALA/NCTE/ReadWriteThink, Copyright Law: From Digital Reprints to Downloads (Lesson 1067).

19. William Patry, "Kopyright and Kids Continued," blog post, Oct. 10, 2007, http://william patry.blogspot.com/2007/10/kopyright-and-kids-continued.html.

20. MPAA/Junior Achievement, What's the Diff? A Guide to Digital Citizenship for Volunteers and Teachers, 12.

21. ESA/YMI, "Take Home Booklet: Online Resources for Parents," Join the © Team, 2.

22. MPAA/Junior Achievement, What's the Diff? A Guide to Digital Citizenship for Volunteers and Teachers, 3.

23. ASCAP/i-SAFE, video ~8:30, *The Donny the Downloader Experience.*

REFERENCES

Anderson, Chris (2008). Free! Why $0.00 Is the Future of Business. *Wired* 16(3) http://www.wired .com/techbiz/it/magazine/16-03/ff_free.

Aufderheide, Patricia, and Peter Jaszi (2007). *The Good, the Bad, and the Confusing: User-Generated Video Creators on Copyright.* Washington DC: Center for Social Media, School of Communication, American University.

Benkler, Yochai (2006). *The Wealth of Networks: How Social Production Transforms Markets and Freedom.* New Haven, CT: Yale University Press.

Bettig, Ronald (1992). Critical Perspectives on the History and Philosophy of Copyright. *Critical Studies in Mass Communication* 9(2): 131–155.

Calvert, Susan (2008). Children as Consumers: Marketing and Advertising. *The Future of Children* 18(1): 205–234.

Denegri-Knott, Janice (2004). Sinking the Online "Music Pirates": Foucault, Power and Deviance on the Web. *Journal of Computer-Mediated Communication* 9(4). http://jcmc.indiana.edu/vol9/ issue4/denegri_knott.html.

Fisher, William (2001). Theories of Intellectual Property. In S. Munzer (Ed.), *New Essays in the Legal and Political Theory of Property.* Cambridge: Cambridge University Press.

Gates, Kelly (2006). Will Work for Copyrights: The Cultural Policy of Anti-Piracy Campaigns. *Social Semiotics* 16 (1): 57–73.

Gillespie, Tarleton (2007). *Wired Shut: Copyright and the Shape of Digital Culture.* Cambridge, MA: MIT Press.

Gillespie, Tarleton (2009). Characterizing Copyright in the Classroom: The Cultural Work of Anti-Piracy Campaigns. *Communication, Culture & Critique* 2(3): 274–318.

Govil, Nitin (2004). War in the Age of Pirate Reproduction. *Sarai Reader 04: Crisis/Media.*

Halbert, Debora (1997). Intellectual Property Piracy: The Narrative Construction of Deviance. *International Journal for the Semiotics of Law* 10 (28): 55–78.

Herman, Bill (2008). Breaking and Entering My Own Computer: The Contest of Copyright Metaphors. *Communication Law and Policy* 13(2): 231–274.

Hetcher, Steven (2004). The Music Industry's Failed Attempt to Influence File Sharing Norms. *Vanderbilt Journal of Entertainment and Technology Law* 7(1): 10–40.

Howe, Jeff (2004). File-Sharing Is, Like, Totally Uncool. *Wired* 12(5): 274–318.

Jaszi, Peter (1991). Toward a Theory of Copyright: The Metamorphoses of "Authorship." *Duke Law Journal* 2: 455–502.

Jensen, Christopher (2003). The More Things Change, the More They Stay the Same: Copyright, Digital Technology, and Social Norms. *Stanford Law Review* 56(2): 531–570.

Lessig, Lawrence (1995). The Regulation of Social Meaning. *University of Chicago Law Review* 62(3): 944–1045.

Litman, Jessica (2000). The Demonization of Piracy. In *CFP 2000: Challenging the Assumptions; Tenth Conference on Computers, Freedom & Privacy.* N.p.: Toronto, Canada.

Litman, Jessica (2004). Sharing and Stealing. *Hastings Communications and Entertainment Law Journal* 27: 1–50.

Logie, John (2006). *Peers, Pirates, and Persuasion: Rhetoric in the Peer-to-Peer Debates.* West Lafayette, IN: Parlor Press.

Loughlan, Patricia (2007). "You Wouldn't Steal a Car": Intellectual Property and the Language of Theft. *European Intellectual Property Review* 29(10): 401–405.

Molnar, Alex, Faith Boninger, Gary Wilkinson, and Joseph Fogarty (2008). *At Sea in a Marketing-Saturated World: The Eleventh Annual Report on Schoolhouse Commercialism Trends: 2007–2008.* Boulder, CO: Education and the Public Interest Center (EPIC) & Commercialism in Education Research Unit (CERU).

Reyman, Jessica (2009). Property, Theft, Piracy: Rhetoric and Regulation in *MGM Studios v. Grokster.* In S. Westbrook (Ed.), *Composition and Copyright: Perspectives on Teaching, Textmaking, and Fair Use.* Albany: State University of New York Press.

Schor, Juliet (2004). *Born to Buy: The Commercialized Child and the New Consumer Culture.* New York: Scribner.

Schultz, Mark (2007). Copynorms: Copyright and Social Norms. In P. Yu (Ed.), *Intellectual Property and Information Wealth: Issues and Practices in the Digital Age.* Westport, CT: Praeger.

Shirky, Clay (2008). *Here Comes Everybody: The Power of Organizing without Organizations.* New York: Penguin.

Spitz, David, and Starling Hunter (2005). Contested Codes: The Social Construction of Napster. *Information Society* 21(3): 169–180.

Sunstein, Cass (1996). Social Norms and Social Roles. *Columbia Law Review* 96(4): 903–968.

Woodmansee, Martha, and Peter Jaszi, eds. (1994). *The Construction of Authorship: Textual Appropriation in Law and Literature, Post-contemporary Interventions.* Durham, NC: Duke University Press.

Yar, Majid (2008). The Rhetorics and Myths of Anti-Piracy Campaigns: Criminalization, Moral Pedagogy and Capitalist Property Relations in the Classroom. *New Media & Society* 10(2): 457–475.

13

PETER DICOLA

An Economic View of Legal Restrictions on Musical Borrowing and Appropriation

In 2006 two pop superstars, Shakira and Nelly Furtado, released songs that led to copyright controversies.[1] Both songs employ the musical technique of sampling, which involves incorporating portions of previously released recordings (and the underlying compositions) into new songs.[2] Shakira's "Hips Don't Lie," a collaboration with Wyclef Jean, includes a horn part from a recording by salsa star Jerry Rivera.[3] When Rivera complained that he had not granted permission for the sample, he caused a minor stir—which calmed down when it turned out that Rivera's publishing company and record label had in fact granted permission.[4] This illustrates how copyright holders, not necessarily creators, decide when to grant permission for samples. Furtado's "Do It," produced by studio wizard Timbaland,[5] presented a different issue. The song allegedly samples a keyboard line from a remix of a song by Finnish musician Janne Suni. The remix artist, Glenn Rune Gallefoss, and his label have sued.[6] This raises a frequent question: When does unauthorized sampling constitute copyright infringement?

While all musical creation builds sequentially on previous musical ideas, sampling represents a particularly direct form of musical borrowing—or appropriation, depending on one's point of view[7]—that often leads to controversy. Copyright mediates relationships among musicians,[8] giving it the power to affect creative choices directly. Thus, sampling concerns stories outside the headlines—the songs that musicians choose not to create. Has copyright deterred musicians from using particular sound fragments in new songs? Has the music industry's implementation of copyright foreclosed the commercial release of collage-based music because the licensing burden would be too great? The less visible effects of legal constraints on sampling could have large aggregate effects on musical creativity. Economics provides a way to examine these effects systematically. This essay proposes an economic and legal framework to examine the artistic consequences of copyright's regime for musical borrowing and appropriation, focusing on the issue of sampling.

A Brief History of Sampling Controversies

Sampling's roots range across jazz, blues, *musique concrète*, reggae, and early rap. Digital technology greatly facilitated the practice, which expanded in the 1980s.[9] Musically and commercially, sampling has enjoyed great success in many genres, including hip-hop, electronica, and pop, but most prominently in hip-hop. That success has led to much litigation. Over the last two decades, the courts have attempted to work out the contours of copyright's treatment of sampling.

It took until 1991 for a sampling case to reach trial and receive a judicial opinion, because previous cases had settled out of court. Gilbert O'Sullivan sued the rapper Biz Markie for sampling O'Sullivan's hit song "Alone Again, Naturally" without permission. Judge Kevin Duffy declared, " 'Thou shalt not steal' " and ruled against Biz Markie.[10] The *Grand Upright* case sent a strong message that samplers must acquire licenses. But the law of sampling remained to some degree unsettled afterward, because Judge Duffy's opinion does not offer a detailed copyright-infringement analysis. Later sampling cases gradually established that samplee plaintiffs must show that sampler defendants' recordings are "substantially similar" to the original, sampled songs to succeed on copyright infringement claims. The law also came to recognize defenses for samplers. Fair use doctrine provides samplers with a nebulous but potentially important legal defense. And courts have deemed some borrowed portions of musical compositions—say, a sample of three notes—to be "de minimis," meaning they are too small for the law to protect.

According to a 2005 case, the de minimis threshold of protection for musical compositions does not, however, apply to samples of sound recordings. In *Bridgeport Music, Inc., v. Dimension Films*, the Sixth Circuit ruled that—absent fair use—unauthorized sampling of any amount of a copyrighted sound recording constitutes copyright infringement, based on the court's interpretation of Section 114 of the U.S. Copyright Code.[11] But the *Bridgeport* court also justified its rule of "Get a license or do not sample" by asserting that such a clear rule would encourage sample licensing.[12] The music industry has developed customs and practices for obtaining licenses for samples, known as the sample clearance system.

Bridgeport has sparked protests from the public and earned the condemnation of many commentators on legal and policy grounds. It increases reliance on the arguably inefficient and inequitable sample clearance system. While the decision may not hold up over the long term,[13] for the time being its policy could affect the business practice of copyright licensing and, ultimately, the musical practice of sampling. Because many samples use both a specific sound recording and the underlying composition, the decision's stricter rule for sound recordings has real bite. *Bridgeport* makes sampling without a license much more difficult, even in situations where the use of the musical composition remains de minimis. Subsequent cases have since ordered the removal of sample-based records from stores,[14] and many more lawsuits could follow.

Assigning Rights to Music

Musicians face a complicated regime to determine when and from whom they must obtain permission to use another musician's song. This section surveys the copyright law of sampling, covers, and musical collage by discussing who gets what kind of intellectual property rights. It also addresses the limitations on those rights, such as the compulsory license for cover versions and the doctrine of fair use.

Musicians often have to acquire two sets of licenses to use one existing song. Each song can have, first, a musical composition copyright, for the detailed underlying structure, and, second, a sound recording copyright, for the particular recorded performance based on that structure. The two types of music copyrights are separate, and, like other property rights, are divisible and transferable. Songwriters and composers usually sign contracts with publishing companies in return for 50 percent of the proceeds from licensing. Recording artists typically sign contracts assigning their copyrights to a record label in return for royalties.

Both types of copyright holders receive several exclusive rights. In the context of recordings involving musical borrowing or appropriation, three of these rights are relevant: reproduction, distribution, and preparation of derivative works.[15] By definition, sampling involves reproducing parts of an existing work, and distributing a sample-based song means distributing part of the sampled work. In addition, courts often characterize sampling as creating a "derivative work," a category that includes translations and adaptations.[16] Samplers obtaining licenses should seek contract language that covers all three rights.[17]

As a default, copyright law protects copyright owners' exclusive rights in a similar fashion to the way law usually treats tangible property like cars or furniture. Copyright holders may insist on any price they wish before selling, require permission for anyone to exercise one of their exclusive rights, transfer their rights freely, and sue when others infringe on their rights. But other times copyright law recognizes rights only by requiring others to pay copyright holders for use of the rights at a rate set by Congress. For example, musical compositions are subject to a "compulsory license," outlined in section 115 of the U.S. Copyright Code. Once a song or composition has been recorded once with the permission of its copyright holder, other musicians can "cover" the song—without permission—in return for a statutory fee and adherence to certain administrative procedures. A cover must be sufficiently faithful to the original, not disrupting the "basic melody or fundamental character of the work."[18]

Some rights remain outside copyright holders' possession, leaving them to downstream creators instead. For example, copyright's subject matter includes tangible expressions of ideas but not the abstract ideas themselves. Combinations of three notes, individual chords, and I–IV–V chord progressions, to name a few examples, are closer to ideas than to expression. These musical ideas have existed for centuries, and all musicians should have the right to use them. *Newton v. Diamond* illustrated this idea.[19] The Beastie Boys sampled three notes from a James Newton song, having licensed the sound recording but not the underlying musical composition, which Newton owned. The Ninth Circuit held that the three-note sequence did not cross the de minimis threshold for copyright protection. In a sense, the de minimis threshold helps implement the boundary between ideas and expression. Although *Bridgeport* suggests that small fragments of sound recordings always qualify as protected expression, *Newton* vindicates the principle that all musicians can freely use abstract musical ideas.

Fair use is a case-by-case doctrine that recognizes exceptions to copyright protection. As an affirmative defense, fair use does not fit comfortably into a property-rights paradigm. Rather, it operates as a broad, public-law provision for the benefit of readers, listeners, educators, critics, and others. For instance, *Campbell v. Acuff-Rose* recognized that even commercial works can constitute fair use if they are "transformative," a category that includes parody. In that case, the Supreme Court vindicated rap group 2 Live Crew's unauthorized sampling from Roy Orbison's composition "Pretty Woman" as fair use. (The sound recording copyright owner was not a party.) Samplers and collagists could benefit from this doctrine if case law, industry practices, and norms of fair use developed over time, providing practical guidelines to musicians.[20] Unfortunately, the music industry has not yet done so. For now, the case-by-case nature of fair use renders it unpredictable and expensive,[21] limiting its utility for samplers and collagists.

An Economic Model of Sequential Musical Innovation

All music uses existing musical conventions, ideas, and sounds, and in this sense, all musical innovation can be considered sequential. Musicians may add new elements, but they always combine and rearrange existing elements. Copyright law overlays a system of rights onto the set of all existing songs. The rights assigned to copyright holders and downstream creators and how law protects those rights determine the relative cost of different types of musical borrowing or appropriation. Given these rights, musicians make decisions about musical production and how to engage with the commercial music industry, if at all.

Economists habitually describe the production process for any good as a function of capital (that is, the physical plant and equipment) and labor. But one can also include other things, such as land or raw materials, as inputs to production. The specific production function that converts inputs into goods represents the state of technology. Technology in this context refers to scientific, organizational, or any other variety of knowledge that applies to producing goods.

Modeling musical production under the rules of copyright requires identifying some of the raw materials that musicians use to create songs and recordings. Specifically, musicians use the already-existing musical compositions and sound recordings of other musicians. Copyright law divides musical inputs into several categories, based on the type of copyrighted work, its copyright status, and how it is used:

1. Public-domain works, meaning works that are not under copyright protection. This category includes, for instance, works that have exhausted their copyright term, works not renewed in a timely fashion, and voluntary donations to the public domain.
2. Noninfringing elements of copyrighted works, including musical ideas like notes, chords, compositional forms, instruments' sounds, and so on. This category also includes de minimis uses of musical compositions and fair uses of either musical compositions or sound recordings.

3. Entire copyrighted musical compositions, used for purposes of sufficiently faithful cover versions—that is, covers that qualify for a compulsory license.
4. Portions of copyrighted musical compositions that infringe. Primarily, this means samples that are not de minimis and do not constitute fair use. This category also includes uses of large portions of musical compositions for insufficiently faithful cover versions.
5. Portions of copyrighted sound recordings that infringe. In the Sixth Circuit, after *Bridgeport*, this means samples of any length that are not fair use.

Each category has a unique character. But a single sample can implicate two different categories at once because of the distinction between the sampled musical composition and the sampled sound recording. Each category enters a musician's production function as a separate input, alongside capital and labor. Correspondingly, each category has a different input price in the musical production function. Just as labor's input price for producers is the wage, prior songs' input prices are their licensing fees. Categories 1 and 2 have associated licensing fees of zero, although it remains useful to distinguish the categories for other reasons.[22] Category 3 is subject to the compulsory license of section 115 described above. Finally, categories 4 and 5 are distinct and separate, but both require licenses through the music industry's sample clearance system.

If musicians sought to maximize profits based on perfect information, then one could predict their behavior. Based on the form of their particular musical production function, the input categorization, and the input prices they face, individual musicians would choose what inputs to use and how much. This model of production provides a way to understand how copyright and licensing affect creativity. As licensing fees increase, musical borrowing should decrease, all else being equal. If copyright law shifted existing works into less expensive categories of inputs, however, musical borrowing should increase.

In reality, musicians must deal with imperfect information about existing works and their licensing fees. Furthermore, in addition to giving profits some weight, musicians consider artistry, enjoyment, political and social views, and other factors in their decisions, preferences that vary by individual. Finally, collectives like groups, record labels, and management teams—not just individuals—make decisions about musical production. Despite these complications, choices about usage of musical inputs and the resulting costs of musical production will be a salient factor in musicians' (and their affiliates') decision making.

Licensing fees, however, are not the only costs of musical inputs that musicians face. Each input category also comes with information costs and transaction costs. Information costs include the time and money spent verifying the status of any other musicians' works that are used and searching for the copyright holders. Transaction costs include paying a lawyer or sample-clearance professional to negotiate licenses, the time it takes to clear samples (or meet the administrative requirements for cover versions), and the hold-up costs when negotiations do not proceed easily.

Membership in some of the input categories will be more uncertain than others. Determining the category of an existing song can cost money and time—and might not result in finality or certainty. Some works, like Beethoven's symphonies, are easily identified as public-domain works, classified in category 1, because of their fame and their age. But other public-domain works are harder to identify as such, since no central directory of the public domain exists.[23] The unprotected musical elements that make up category 2 are frequently uncertain. When it comes to samples, category 2 can have a fuzzy, imperfectly predictable, and litigation-worthy boundary with categories 4 and 5. The uncertainty of some inputs' categories is an unusual feature of musical production functions. Usually, economists assume the ability to distinguish capital from labor and other inputs.

The transaction costs involved in sample clearance depend partly on a musician's position in the music industry. Recording artists signed to major record labels have access to relationships and resources (both formal and informal) that facilitate obtaining licenses. Independent artists often lack such opportunities. Still, some costs weigh heavily for all artists. As already noted, many samples require two licenses: one for the sampled composition and one for the sampled sound recording. Moreover, copyright holders can divide and sell their interests to multiple parties, further increasing the number of potential parties a would-be licensee must negotiate with to clear a sample. The complexities, pitfalls, and transaction costs of participating in the sample clearance system must also factor into decisions about musical production.

Musicians make a number of economic decisions. Before they even decide which musical inputs to use in production, musicians must allocate their time between studio recording and performing live on tour. At the same time, musicians must choose a business model with which to engage the commercial music industry—or decide to operate outside the commercial sector. Each business model will put different weight on recording versus touring. And each model entails a different approach to licensing and the sample clearance system.

Two questions divide musicians' choices into four basic business models. First, will the musician distribute recordings commercially—that is, will they sell CDs? Second, will the musician spend the time and money to obtain the proper licenses for samples and cover versions? Table 13.1 is a two-by-two matrix displaying the options formed by these questions.

Table 13.1. Musicians' business models

	Distribute recordings commercially?	
Obtain licenses?	Yes	No
Yes	Commercial	Live performance
No	Underground	Noncommercial

In commercial business models—whether with a major or an independent label—musicians who use samples or do covers pay for licenses so that they can retail their own recordings legally. Moreover, musicians adopting a commercial business model can reap licensing revenue when other artists sample or cover them. This type of business model accounts for the bulk of music industry revenue.

Yet the standard commercial model does not account for the bulk of musicians. Many musicians want to opt out of licensing transactions entirely. They can either distribute their recordings for free (the noncommercial model) or sell their recordings through small outlets (the underground model) while hoping to avoid detection, litigation, or prosecution. Musicians might adopt the noncommercial model early in their careers, perhaps taking advantage of Web distribution to develop a fan base. Sometimes fans help the noncommercial model along, as when DJ Danger Mouse's fans distributed free copies of *The Grey Album* over the Internet.[24] The underground model describes the early days of sampling. But it also describes the contemporary "mix tape" phenomenon, brought to the headlines with the arrest of DJ Drama, whose business sold albums with unlicensed samples. Ironically, he had been hired by the major record companies to promote major-label artists.[25] These recent stories illustrate the significance of business models that involve opting out of the sample clearance system.

Some musicians might also adopt a live-performance-only model, in which they create sound collages live, as many DJs do, but do not release recordings of their work. Live sampling, involving rearranging or remixing of the existing sound recordings, need not implicate the reproduction, distribution, or derivative-works rights of copyright holders, because live performance need not involve recording.[26] But live sampling would require licenses for the public-performance rights (of musical compositions only).[27] In concert venues with blanket licenses from the performing rights organizations (ASCAP, BMI, and SESAC), however, musicians who engaged in live sampling might enjoy indirect authorization to sample.

The multiplicity of available business models emphasizes that musicians have agency to react along many dimensions to the categorization of musical inputs, the licensing fees for those inputs, and the information and transaction costs of the sample clearance system. For example, when *Bridgeport* put more samples into a category subject to licensing unless fair use applies (by eliminating the de minimis threshold for sound recordings), this raised the direct cost of those samples from zero to some positive dollar amount. As the music industry absorbs the news that more samples require licenses, the overall costs of licensing might change. Fees could increase, since licensors gained leverage from courts' copyright enforcement and since demand for licenses might increase. On the other hand, fees could decrease because of increased volume, the shorter duration of samples being licensed, or reduced demand as musicians sample less or opt out of licensing. Similarly, transaction and information costs could increase because the sample clearance system becomes overburdened. Or they could decrease if, in the face of that burden, the music industry developed institutions to better facilitate licensing transactions.

In the wake of *Bridgeport*, musicians who had been employing a commercial business model can respond in a number of ways. They might stop using samples altogether; engage in more (sufficiently faithful) covers instead; use fewer samples per song; use more obscure samples that will cost less; use replays[28] more often; switch to a noncommercial or underground business model; or, finally, record less often and tour more, perhaps even switching to a live-performance business model. Assessing the effects of *Bridgeport* and other changes or clarifications to copyright law on creativity, then, requires a complex approach. The decision might or might not stifle creativity; musicians' options in the face of legal changes are too numerous to make a simple prediction.

Distorted Incentives

Copyright's regime over the use of existing music creates legal boundaries where no musical or technological boundaries exist. This could distort creativity as musicians respond to the economic incentives created by law. But changes to the background legal arrangements of the music industry might also open up new creative possibilities, which may temper the severity of the problem.

Most samples require two licenses, or more if the copyright owners have divided and transferred their interests. But from a musical perspective, the sound recording–musical composition distinction does not have the same salience. Sampling a song and covering a song involve different practices and technologies, but they are both ways of utilizing existing works in new music. Copyright's overlaid distinction between songwriter and recording artist serves a useful economic function, organizing revenue into two streams for distinct groups of people. Nonetheless, imposing a dual regime on a unitary process like sampling has consequences for creativity.

Rather than looking at existing songs in terms of the separate copyrights that inhere within them, one can look at them in terms of musical practice. Table 13.2 maps musicians' uses of musical compositions and sound recordings on two axes. Each axis runs from "none" to "all" to denote how much of the composition or sound recording is used.

When musicians do not use the sound recording of a song, there is a spectrum from originals to covers, with musical developments (a positive connotation) or rip-offs (a negative one) in between. If a musician uses some fragments of a sound recording, this usually constitutes making a sound collage.[29] But there is no sharp distinction between using none of the musical composition, a tiny amount, or a larger amount in a collage.[30] When musicians create compilations of previously recorded works or simply rerelease works in a slightly new form, this involves using an entire sound recording and, necessarily, the entire underlying musical composition.

Contrast table 13.2 with table 13.3, which uses the same axes but, rather than mapping regions of musical practice, delineates copyright's rules and licensing requirements. Boundaries appear where, musically speaking, no boundaries exist. Consider the theoretical boundary between faithful and unfaithful covers created by section 115, described above. If a musician does a cover version that reworks the original too much, then he or she will require a voluntary license to reproduce, distribute, and prepare a derivative work of the song. But if the musician covers the entire song faithfully, then the compulsory license of Section 115 becomes available, making the licensing easier and the

Table 13.2. Musical and technological perspective on using existing songs in recordings

Use of copyrighted sound recording	Use of copyrighted musical composition			
	None	Fragments	Major elements	All (i.e., faithful cover)
Some (whether all or just fragments)	Collage	Collage	Collage	Compilations, re-releases
None	Originals		Developments (and rip-offs)	Covers

Table 13.3. Licensing requirements for use of existing songs in recordings

Use of copyrighted sound recording (SR)	Use of copyrighted musical composition (MC)			
	None	Fragments	Major elements	All (i.e., faithful cover)
Fragments	1 voluntary SR license for sample	2 voluntary licenses: 1 for SR & 1 for MC	2 voluntary licenses: 1 for SR & 1 for MC	1 voluntary SR license & 1 compulsory MC license
None	Public domain & non-infringing elements	1 voluntary MC license for sample	1 voluntary MC license for insufficiently faithful cover	1 compulsory MC license (Section 115)

NOTE: In all cases, fewer licenses are required if uses of SR, MC, or both are de minimis or fair use.

fees less expensive. The bottom row of table 13.3 illustrates this incentive to mimic existing compositions more closely.

Distorted incentives arise with respect to sampling as well. Musicians who sample three notes, like the Beastie Boys in *Newton v. Diamond*, might need only one license for the sound recording. Using three notes of a composition could be de minimis, depending on the specifics of the use. But musicians who sample more notes—say, five, to create a hypothetical example—might need to acquire two licenses, if the de minimis threshold has been crossed and fair use does not apply. Musically, the distinction between a three-note phrase and a five-note phrase may exist, but it is not as stark as the difference between acquiring one voluntary license and acquiring two. Moreover, the boundaries of de minimis use and especially fair use are neither quantitative nor sharp. A thirty-second sample might be fair use—for instance, in a parody—but a one-second sample might not be—for instance, because that one second has great qualitative importance with respect to the sampled work. Case-by-case determinations of fair use and the de minimis threshold may produce rough guidelines for licensing practices but not hard-and-fast rules. So copyright creates enough boundaries to affect creativity but does so in a way that adds uncertainty, which may further deter musicians from borrowing.

The legal mapping for the use of existing songs in table 13.3 looks complicated, constricting, and even perverse compared with the looser mapping of musical practice in table 13.2. The contrast suggests that copyright law distorts creative musical activity, because activities on either side of the somewhat arbitrary lines drawn by copyright law have very different costs. Moreover, this adversely affects musicians in particular genres (like hip-hop and electronica, in which many musicians use samples) more than those in others (like country music, which involves more covers than samples).

Transgressing Boundaries

Economic theories usually assume that boundaries—what economists would term constraints, as in the mathematical constraints of a utility- or profit-maximization problem—reduce well-being. The context of musical creativity, however, requires adding some complications to this standard framework. If boundaries and constraints have benefits for those subject to the boundaries, it would temper somewhat the conclusions from the previous section about distorted incentives.

The standard economic view describes punishments for certain behaviors as constraints. They limit individuals' options if they occur, leaving individuals with less money, time, and overall well-being when they are punished. For example, Gary Becker's economic theory of crime rests on utility maximization by criminals and cost-benefit analysis by society.[31] Becker assumed that, as the severity of punishment and the probability of being punished increase, the number of criminal offenses committed should decrease. In short, when crime becomes more expensive, criminals should commit fewer crimes, all else being equal.[32] Applying Becker's approach to intellectual property crime implies that musicians who decline to obtain the proper licenses have implicitly weighed the risks and rewards of copyright infringement. Their particular expected cost of using the sample clearance system has outweighed their expected cost of a copyright infringement lawsuit against them (where the expected cost of a lawsuit incorporates its probability of occurring).

But what if boundaries paradoxically increase one's options? What if punishments are not all bad? Intellectual property crimes may present just this situation, running contrary to standard economic assumptions. Amy Adler has pointed out that "the very richness and proliferation of 'illegal art' in response to copyright law suggests that restrictive legal rules not only crush artistic production, but also stimulate it."[33] In light of postmodernism, Adler argues, boundaries have become scarce; artistic production could benefit from even the most misguided legal boundaries, whether in the context of obscenity law or copyright. If so, then violating a boundary has some positive utility for musicians, offsetting the disutility of copyright's legal penalties. Rather than refraining from using a sample because of either high licensing costs or the risk of an infringement lawsuit, some musicians would use the sample anyway. They add interest to their music, for themselves and others, by violating a boundary. Alternatively, they might have an artistic commitment to transgression, which copyright restrictions give them an opportunity to fulfill.

No one would urge Congress and the courts to craft arcane, boundary-laden, and arbitrary copyright rules on purpose. But copyright law's boundaries might have some inadvertent benefits for musicians who sample or create collages, in addition to the costs described in previous sections. *Bridgeport* set up a harsh rule but it immediately inspired artists to create hundreds of sample-based works in protest, using the very sample from George Clinton's "Get Off Your Ass and Jam" that N.W.A. infringed. Many other creative musical responses may evolve in the case's wake. This potential benefit complicates any economic assessment of copyright's treatment of sampling.

Conclusion

Musicians use existing music as an input in the production of new music. Musical borrowing or appropriation occurs through multiple and distinct practices. Copyright treats these different creative practices differently, sometimes starkly so. The sharp distinctions of copyright law—for example, requiring two voluntary licenses for many samples while requiring only one compulsory license for cover versions—can affect creativity by setting the effective input prices of using different pieces of music at very different levels. Information and transaction costs exacerbate the problem. Yet characterizing the potential distortion and the costs of thwarting certain avenues of creativity is a complicated task, because musicians have many choices in the face of copyright law's constraints. They can choose to adopt a new business model, adjust their music to avoid infringement, or violate copyright law. In doing so, musicians can turn restraints on creativity into new forms of creativity. Despite this potential for ameliorating the costs, concerns about law distorting creativity remain.

Any line drawn by the law has the potential to distort behavior. The real questions are whether the line-drawing serves an important purpose and, if so, whether law could draw a better line. Copyright aims to provide incentives for creation, balancing compensation for creators with access for the general public—and other creators. The continuing controversy over sampling suggests that copyright is out of balance in this area. While acknowledging the complications described in this chapter, my larger research project on sampling tries to assess the negative impact of copyright on musical creativity and the possibility of unjustified discrimination against particular genres or particular musical techniques.[34]

NOTES

1. I would like to thank the editors and the participants of the Con/Texts of Invention conference at Case Western Reserve University, April 2006.

2. This essay uses the colloquial term "song" as an umbrella term to refer to both the sound recording and the musical composition at once, as a unified whole as experienced by listeners. Copyright law's distinction between compositions and sound recordings is discussed further below.

3. Shakira, *Oral Fixation, Vol. 2* [rerelease with bonus track], Epic 681585.

4. Andres Guadamuz, "Shakira Don't Lie," Technollama.com, July 15, 2006, http://technollama .blogspot.com/2006_07_01_archive.html (accessed August 31, 2007).

5. Nelly Furtado, *Loose*, Geffen B0006300-02.

6. Turre Legal, "*Kernel Records v. Timbaland* Enters a Court in Florida," June 12, 2009, http:// www.turre.com/2009/06/kernel-records-v-timbaland-enters-a-court-in-florida/ (accessed June 12, 2009).

7. This essay usually uses the terms "borrowing" and "appropriation" together to highlight the tension between the positive and negative connotations of using existing musical works. Borrowing could refer to the use of unprotected elements or of public domain works, while appropriation could refer to infringing uses of copyrighted works.

8. The term "musicians" here refers to individuals who play instruments, sing, compose, produce, or any combination of those activities.

9. Mark Katz, *Capturing Sound: How Technology Has Changed Music* (Berkeley: University of California Press, 2004), 114–157.

10. *Grand Upright Music v. Warner Bros. Records*, 780 F. Supp. 182, 183 (S.D.N.Y. 1991).

11. 410 F.3d 792, 799–801 (6th Cir. 2005).

12. Ibid. at 800–801.

13. A different federal appellate court could, for instance, rule differently on the issue, perhaps leading the Supreme Court to resolve the conflict and to reject the *Bridgeport* rule.

14. Susan Butler, "The Low-Down on Damages: Juror Explains the Thinking in $4.3 Million Decision Against Diddy, UMG," *Billboard*, April 8, 2006, 14(1); Jonathan V. Last, "The Samples: A Tale of Morality, Biggie, and the Law," *Daily Standard*, March 31, 2006, http://weeklystandard. com/Content/Public/Articles/000/000/012/036sxlir.asp (accessed March 31, 2007).

15. 17 U.S.C. §106(1)–(3) (2000); see also *Jarvis v. A&M Records*, 827 F. Supp. 282, 288 (D.N.J. 1993), mentioning all three rights.

16. The derivative-work right is nearly coextensive with the reproduction right, since adapting a work generally requires copying parts of it. *Williams v. Broadus*, No. 99 Civ. 10957 (MBM), 2001 U.S. Dist. LEXIS 12894 (S.D.N.Y. August 27, 2001): 5–6.

17. For an example of licensing-contract language that arguably covers all three rights, see *Newton v. Diamond*, 388 F.3d 1189, 1191 nn.1–2 (9th Cir. 2003).

18. 17 U.S.C. §115(a)(2) (2000). No cases known to this author have ruled on the meaning of sufficient faithfulness to the original.

19. 388 F.3d 1189 (9th Cir. 2003).

20. Patricia Aufderheide and Peter Jaszi, *Untold Stories: Creative Consequences of the Rights Clearance Culture for Documentary Filmmakers* (Washington, DC: Center for Social Media, 2004), http://www.centerforsocialmedia.org/files/pdf/UNTOLDSTORIES_Report.pdf (accessed March 31, 2007).

21. *Bridgeport* suggests that parties to an infringement lawsuit have incentives to settle before the case reaches a determination regarding fair use (410 F.3d at 792). After a lengthy appeal that included a rehearing by the three-judge panel, Dimension Films lost on the de minimis issue, as discussed

above. The appellate court remanded the case to the district court for further proceedings, during which Dimension Films could have pursued a fair use defense (ibid. at 805). Instead, the parties settled before the district court had an opportunity to rule on fair use.

22. For instance, public domain works and noninfringing elements of copyrighted works will differ in their information costs—how costly it is for musicians to identify them for use.

23. Orphan works, defined as works subject to valid copyrights with unknown or hard-to-identify owners, present a related issue of uncertainty and information costs.

24. Joanna Demers, *Steal This Music: How Intellectual Property Law Affects Musical Creativity* (Athens: University of Georgia Press, 2006), 139–142.

25. Samantha M. Shapiro, "Hip-Hop Outlaw (Industry Version)," *New York Times Magazine*, Feb. 18, 2007.

26. Whether live sampling could infringe the derivative-works right without fixing the resulting musical collage in a tangible medium (by recording it, for example) is a point on which federal appellate courts disagree. For details, see Tamara C. Peters, "Infringement of the Adaptation Right: A Derivative Work Need Not Be 'Fixed' for the Law to Be Broken," *Journal of the Copyright Society of the U.S.A.* 53 (2006): 401–446.

27. Copyright only grants sound recording copyright holders a public-performance right for "digital audio transmissions," not for in-person performances 17 U.S.C. §106(6) (2000).

28. Replays are "faux samples" in which would-be samplers record their own versions of small snippets of a song. Replays implicate musical composition copyrights but not sound recording copyrights (which do not extend to "sound-alikes"). See ibid. §114(b).

29. Under this taxonomy, this category would also include other kinds of musical output, such as the backing music for karaoke performances, as noted in the table.

30. "Mash-ups," which employ large fragments of two or existing songs placed in juxtaposition and generally include no independently created sounds, also qualify as a specific type of sound collage. Some argue that mash-ups have a stronger claim to fair use than other types of sampling. Nicholas B. Lewis, Comment, "*Shades of Grey*: Can the Copyright Fair Use Defense Adapt to New Re-contextualized Forms of Music and Art?" *American University Law Review*, 57, no. 1 (2005): 267–306. But boundaries between different types of sampling, as between different types of musical borrowing, will be fuzzy at best.

31. Gary S. Becker, "Crime and Punishment: An Economic Approach," *Journal of Political Economy* 76, no. 2 (1968): 169–217.

32. Even a risk-loving (but still economically rational) criminal would not prefer a greater probability of being punished, as long as the punishment and the reward to crime stayed constant.

33. Amy Adler, "Invention and Originality in the Law of Obscenity," paper presented at the Con/Texts of Invention conference, Case Western Reserve University, Cleveland, OH, 2006.

34. Kembrew McLeod and Peter DiCola, *Creative License: The Law and Culture of Digital Sampling* (Durham, NC: Duke University Press, 2011).

IV

Old Things into New IP Objects

DANIEL J. KEVLES

14

New Blood, New Fruits
Protections for Breeders and Originators, 1789–1930

The best-known form of intellectual property protection is the common utility patent, whose requirements include the stipulations that
the invention must be man-made and useful.[1] What is patentable in
the United States according to statute dates back to the patent law of
1793, which declared, in language written by Thomas Jefferson, that
patents could be obtained for "any new and useful art, machine, manufacture, or composition of matter, or any new or useful improvement
thereof."[2] The code said nothing about whether an innovation's being
alive or not has any bearing on its patentability. However, in the nineteenth century living organisms were taken to be unpatentable. In the
United States, only one living organism was patented—a form of yeast
that Louis Pasteur claimed in connection with a beer-making process—but the claim covered the yeast only as part of the process; it did
not cover the organism as such.[3] Plants and animals were not machines
or manufactures. Improvements upon them were not identifiable new
compositions of matter. And how could one define the utility of an
ornamental plant—say, a rose exhibiting a new fragrance or hue?

　　Under the circumstances, it did not occur to early American plant
and animal improvers to seek patents on their products. Besides, they

regarded such commercialization as *infra dig*. In Massachusetts, for example, advocates of innovation comprised in the main Boston's mercantile and then industrial elite. Their fortunes made or accumulating, they embraced farming as a commitment to republican virtue removed from mere moneymaking. They bought and cultivated large farms, turning some of them into opulently improved estates. To the end of agricultural improvement, they imported fine breeds of animals and plants from Europe, built vast greenhouses for fruits and flowers, planted huge orchards with scores of varieties of the same trees.[4] They proudly exhibited their prize flowers, trees, shrubs, cattle, and sheep at meetings; offered prizes for improved livestock; and shared seeds and scions with fellow cultivating gentlemen.

However, by the mid-nineteenth century, commercial seed, nursery, and animal-breeding enterprises were burgeoning, and with the change came increasing attention to profits for innovators. Innovators did not speak of "intellectual property"—the phrase was coined in a Massachusetts court case in 1845[5]—but they were alive to the concept and eager to protect their linguistic version of it. Animal breeders talked of hereditary "blood," while plant innovators commonly mentioned where a fruit had been "originated" and, if it was not a chance find in the field, by whom. Both grew all the more eager to protect their stakes in innovation as their businesses were made more competitive by the creation of the regional and national agricultural markets that emerged with the construction of the railroads and by the increasing urban demand for meats, fruits, and vegetables, as well as ornamental plants, trees, flowers, and shrubs.[6] Given that patent protection was unavailable for living organisms, improvers sought to protect their rights in blooded stock or plant originations through a variety of alternative arrangements. The story of their efforts lies at a rich and relatively unexplored historiographical site: the intersection of pre-Mendelian craft knowledge of plant and animal improvement with law and economics.

In establishing their arrangements, the improvers recognized, at least tacitly, that they had to deal with several difficulties. They could not enforce any claim to rights in their improvements without being able to specify and warrant their identity. This was easily accomplished with a tract of land by surveying and recording its metes and bounds. In contrast, specifying the identity of a living organism—for example, a breed of cattle or a variety of fruit—was problematic, given that defining biological knowledge such as blood types or DNA sequences was unavailable. In the nineteenth century, identification of a living organism could take the form of a written description, a drawing, a painting, or a photograph, but such descriptions were by no means exact or adequate for the purposes of disputes about breeders' or originators' rights.

Then, too, the establishment of even their version of intellectual property protection also entailed reliable reproduction of the product, including its valuable characters. Absent such reproduction, the rights in the blood or the origination would be worthless. But the achievement of reproductive fidelity posed a problem for plant and animal improvers that the innovators of, say, mechanical reapers did not face. Unlike reapers, living organisms reproduce themselves. If an improved plant or animal reproduced itself faithfully—or could be made so to reproduce itself—the original improver potentially faced competition from the purchaser that in the absence of patents could not be easily forestalled.

During the nineteenth century, breeders of purebred shorthorn cattle de- vised a system for protecting their rights in the blood of their animals that was responsive to these circumstances, drawing on some of the methods pio- neered by the English breeder Robert Bakewell in the late eighteenth century. Bakewell, whose life spanned 1725 to 1795, bred sheep and cattle on a large farm in Leicestershire called Dishley Grange. He was well known in his own day as a pioneer of modern breeding, especially with sheep and cattle. He ex- ploited the methods of inbreeding to turn these animals into machines for the production of meat. Aficionados of breeding criticized him for producing animals that lacked staying power, which is a weakness of inbred lines, but the inbreeding he developed both served the end of animal improvement and enabled the protection of the blood product arising from his labors.[7]

Bakewell approached improvement by emphasizing the quality of his ani- mals, not their quantity. He focused on the production of superior males, and rather than sell them, he rented them out for stud. He was selling not just the animal's services. He was also marketing its ability to pass on its superior quality to succeeding generations. In short he was selling the hereditary blood product in the sheep and cattle he had developed.[8]

Buyers were willing to pay high prices for the services of his animals not least because the offspring would embody the male parent's desirable charac- ters. The quality of the stud animals was warranted and specified by Bakewell's reputation, but his system of improvement was far more important in making effective his strategy of licensing of the blood rights in his animals. He kept breeding records, which is to say that he bred through pedigree, selecting for valuable characters and intensifying their embodiment in his animals through inbreeding. The resulting purebreds probably tended to possess an essential feature of blood licensing: intergenerational reliability, which is to say that the products of their stud service were likely to resemble them.Bakewell protected the blood rights in his animals through a variety of complementary strategies. He kept his animals' pedigrees a trade secret so that no one could retrace his steps. Unlike other breeders he sold his animals to butchers only after infecting them with "rot," so that no one could surreptitiously appropriate them for breeding.[9]

In 1783, Bakewell also organized high-end breeders into the Dishley Society. The breeders were enticed to join in part by receipt of privileged access to each others' stocks, including Bakewell's, for yearly dues of ten guineas. But the society also operated as a self-protective cartel, providing its members with an institutionalized set of rules that addressed the problem of blood protection in creations that reproduce. Its members agreed to restrict the number of rams that could be let out to stud per season, when they could be let out, and to whom.[10] The restrictions on numbers thus imposed limits on the quantity of offspring that might themselves be deployed as breeding competitors by their owners. The restrictions on customers worked toward the same purpose, since, for example, they forbade licensing stud services to any people who themselves let or sold rams at fairs or markets.

Shrewdly, the Dishley Society's rules recognized that other breeders coveted the stud services of its members' prize animals. It allowed the provision of such services to potential competitors but imposed a system of prices that escalated in proportion to the degree of competition the purchasers might mount. Thus the society's members agreed to charge at least 10 guineas per ram per season to ordinary breeders; at least 40 guineas to breeders who themselves let rams; and at least 50 guineas for any ram let by Bakewell himself to anyone within 100 miles of Dishley, evidently a practical competitive radius.[11] This pricing system thus amounted to a blood licensing system that was graded in proportion to the likely dilution of the blood value that would arise from the reproduction and sale of progeny in proximity to Dishley.

The brothers Charles and Robert Colling, drawing on Bakewell's methods, began about 1780 to develop what would become the modern shorthorn, drawing on cattle characterized by great size, good milk production, and poor beefing qualities. Key founding animals were Duchess, a cow bought from a tenant farmer, and a bull named Hubback, which one of the brothers noticed grazing at the side of a road and bought from a bricklayer. The brothers developed their shorthorns by an intense inbreeding that they publicized and linked to Bakewell's methods. Their shorthorns caught the attention of both aristocratic fanciers and the agricultural world.[12]

Among those taking an interest was the breeder Thomas Bates. In 1810, at the Collings' dispersal sale, he purchased a descendant of the Duchess line, paying attention to her hereditary background rather than her appearance. He renamed her Duchess 1st and started on a program of intense inbreeding, using the Colling strategies and one of their bulls, Favorite. Bates produced several score of Duchesses and Dukes.[13] He would not use outside blood, even though the fertility of his stock was very limited. He thus welcomed the establishment by George Coates of a public shorthorn stud book, including ancestry, which Coates began publishing in 1822 and which Bates may have instigated. Bates saw in the public registry a means of certifying purity and thus quality of stock and, by way of corollary, a means of forestalling fraud—"the evil of false and inaccurate Pedigrees," as a preface to the *General Stud Book for Race Horses* put it in 1791.[14]

Bates of course knew nothing about the ancestry of the founding bull, Hubback, but what counted for him was the investment in his breeding line. The identification of its ancestry, even if it started only with Hubback, provided multiple advantages for the blood value he had established in his shorthorn herd. The public record of its ancestry endowed it with a kind of specificity, a warrant of its identity and quality, and an indication that it would breed true. As such, it raised the price of his shorthorns compared with other members of the breed that did not possess similar warrant and identification.

Bates appears to have supplied primarily the fancy cattle market—aristocrats who in Britain in the first half of the nineteenth century tended to be concerned in part with esthetic standards: show qualities such as beauty, stature, and elegance. But a number of the fanciers were also advocates of agricultural improvement and eager to establish models of what economically valuable animals should look like. To this end, some commissioned paintings of their shorthorns, many of which were brought out and sold widely in cheap editions.[15]

Bates's system—the combination of inbreeding and public registry—eventually spread to the United States. Shorthorns as well as longhorns had been imported into Ohio in 1817, though without publicly recorded pedigrees because they did not yet exist. But when cattlemen under the leadership of Felix Renick began importing shorthorns into the state in the 1830s, they opted for Bates's pedigreed shorthorns even though they cost more. "The value depends almost entirely upon the purity of the blood and the high pedigree," Renick explained—depended, in short, upon the guarantee of the kind of blood value in a living animal that breeders desired.[16]

The public registry system was also an advantage in the geographically expanding markets of the period, where buyers tended increasingly not to know sellers personally. It allowed Bates to warrant the quality of his cattle across the Atlantic, and it allowed Renick and his associates to warrant their animals to buyers in the rapidly expanding farming regions to the west of Ohio. Indeed, Renick's company was able to sell its stock at remarkably high prices in 1836. Advertised in an elaborate catalog that included the complete pedigrees of the animals, the cows and bulls brought an average of close to $800 each. A similar dispersal sale the next year brought an average price of more than $1,100, perhaps five times a farmer's typical annual cash income. And as the Renick group's shorthorns spread through Ohio, the demand for the unpedigreed animals imported in 1817 steadily diminished.[17]

Bates-type shorthorns caught the attention of fanciers throughout the Northeast and Midwest in the middle third of the nineteenth century. They bought them for show and investment. Prices climbed to astonishing levels, reaching more than $40,000 for a red and white cow at a sale in New York in 1871. But the laws of biology had long begun to take their toll. The intensely inbred shorthorns grew increasingly infertile. The $40,000 cow soon produced a stillborn heifer and died herself shortly thereafter. By the early 1880s, pure Duchesses were extinct.[18]

All the while, however, other breeders had rejected Bates's intensive inbreeding program, with its emphasis on the esthetics of the fancier, in favor of breeding shorthorns solely for agricultural purposes. A key pioneer in this endeavor was the British breeder Amos Cruickshank, the son of a tenant farmer. He bred more for function than for appearance. He managed to fix an advantageous type in 1859 in the bull Champion of England, which he then bred to his foundation females. Cruickshank produced a short, blocky animal that matured earlier and fattened more easily than the tall, elegant English shorthorn of the Bates type.

To accomplish this feat, Cruickshank drew on promising stock wherever in the breed he found it. At the same time, he favored purebreds, no doubt because he recognized in that strategy the inherent advantages for marketing and blood-value protection. He also relied on public registries, which enabled him to guarantee the identity and quality of his animals and to export them to buyers confident in the product. Ultimately, as Margaret Derry, a historian of animal breeding, writes, "Cruickshank beef cattle dominated all British beef cattle breeds wherever they went in the world." A Cruickshank bull named Young Abbotsburn won out as best of breed at the Illinois State Fair in 1890, the center of the beef-cattle world in the United States.[19]

The protection of blood value in shorthorns, depending heavily on the pedigree registries, was no better than their veracity and accuracy. In the United States, the registries were developed by private entrepreneurs in different states, and by the late nineteenth century the books were increasingly characterized by nonuniformity in standards, sloppiness in the records, and general unreliability. In a sense, the situation expressed the consequence of shifting from a kind of mercantilist regulation of the breeding enterprise represented by the Dishley Society to an unregulated free-market capitalist version of it.

To solve that problem, the shorthorn breeders moved in 1876 to reregulate their market by forming the American Shorthorn Association. The association bought the existing registry books and amalgamated them into one.[20] The arrangement thus advantaged genuine shorthorn breeders and protected buyers against fraudulent sellers—that is, purveyors of putative shorthorns whose animals were unregistered with the association.

This system for the protection of blood value in shorthorns probably exemplified the systems developed for other farm animals and, with some variation, for pets and racehorses.[21] It did not firmly protect the blood value developed by individual breeders, but it protected very well the collective blood value of the cartel of breeders represented by the breed association. In 1891, Liberty Hyde Bailey, the prominent plant scientist and a professor at Cornell University, noted the advantages of the system: "There is no law to compel one to register an animal, but every breeder knows that it is only through registration that he can advertise, sell and protect blooded stock. And there is no intelligent purchaser who would think of negotiating for such stock without having obtained the testimony of the herd-book."[22] In all, the breed association–stud book system provided the degree and type of protection consistent with what could be done in the then-current state of biological and breeding knowledge to specify the animal's hereditary essence, warrant its hereditary prowess, and transmit that hereditary essence to succeeding generations.

The principal protective problem for originators of plants that were reproduced sexually—for example, corn, the grains, most vegetables, and flowers— was that they did not ordinarily breed true. Sellers of their seed thus could not guarantee the quality and character of any given crop. J. M. Thorburn and Company, a prominent nursery in New York, warned buyers that it gave "no warranty, express or implied, as to description, quality, productiveness, or any other matter of any seeds, bulbs or plants they send out." Among the reasons was "*the well-known tendency of many vegetables to revert to their original types, notwithstanding the care of the seed-grower.*"[23] Then, too, farmers could save seed from their crops, and then either plant them, sell them, or both, thus undercutting the improver's control of his originator's rights in the plant. Under the circumstances, the nascent private seed industry paid little attention to the protection of such rights. It was content to rely for new varieties on importation and on the innovations produced by the state agricultural experiment stations established by the Hatch Act in 1887.[24]

Innovations and improvements in asexually reproducible plants and trees—the foundation of the horticultural industry—came partly from the hybridizing work of breeders like Luther Burbank but in the overwhelming main from chance finds in the field and orchard.[25] The finds arose from bud sports or fortunate sexual pollinations, but once found they could be reproduced virtually identically by the nurturing of grafts or cuttings. Commercial nurseries acquired the finds, tested them for characteristics such as sturdiness and fruit-bearing qualities, and then put them on the market. Stark Brothers Nursery and Orchards, based in Louisiana, Missouri, was one of the oldest and perhaps the largest such enterprise in the country. It sponsored an annual fair that encouraged farmers to submit their good fruits, including those of chance finds, for competitive judgment. In 1893, through this means, the firm learned about an apple tree that produced a luscious red fruit. The next year, it brought the tree with all propagation rights—which is to say, all its originator's value—from its owner, a farmer in Iowa, named the fruit the "Delicious" apple, and proceeded to market the tree to the world.[26]

Nurserymen and orchardists could be confident that the young trees they sold would bear fruit very much like the fruit on the trees from which they had been derived. The question for the purchaser was whether the quality of the tree—for example, its bearing abundance—and of its fruit would live up to its billing. The reputation of a well-known seller—for example, Burbank or Stark Brothers—counted for something, but in the impersonalized setting of the national market, nurserymen relied increasingly on advertising, placing ads in horticultural and gardening journals and distributing catalogs across the country. The ads tended to include what amounted to warrants of their products' quality and identity in the form of farmers' testimonials about the merits of their fruit trees, shrubs, and flowers.

Yet the ease with which, say, valuable fruit trees could be easily reproduced virtually identically, through grafting, and thus numerously multiplied facilitated theft of the originators' rights. Competitors could purchase the trees, or take cuttings of them from someone's nursery in the dead of night, and then propagate and sell them. Burbank tried to protect himself against such thieves by telling buyers that the way to judge novel fruits was to *"look to their source, and also if possible purchase direct from the originator."* He also charged high prices for his innovations—say, three thousand dollars for a new plum tree, including all "stock and control"—thus attempting to gain in the first sale revenue that would cover his costs and return a reasonable profit.[27] The pricing strategy was intended to capture what economists call the downstream revenues of which thieves might deprive him, since he would be unable to control the reproduction of the tree once he had sold it.

The trouble was that the high first-sale pricing did not work very effectively to compensate horticultural innovators for the loss of the value in their new fruit trees. Nurserymen repeatedly complained that they failed to receive just returns for all their investment of time and money. Burbank fulminated to the readers of *Green's Fruit Grower* that he had

> been robbed and swindled out of my best work by name thieves, plant thieves and in various ways too well known to the originator. . . . A plant which has cost thousands of dollars in coin and years of intensest labor and care and which is of priceless value to humanity may now be stolen with perfect impunity by any sneaking rascal. . . . Many times have I named a new fruit or flower and before a stock could be produced some horticultural pirate had either appropriated the name, using it on some old, well-known or inferior variety or stealing the plant and introducing it as their own, or offering a big stock as soon as the originator commences to advertise the new variety.[28]

Burbank as an innovator was largely in the business of selling to nurseries and orchardists, middlemen who would propagate his trees and sell them to gardeners, farmers, and other consumers. Stark Brothers, which did not breed new fruit trees but only acquired them, was in the business of mass marketing. Realizing the returns on their originator's rights by charging high prices would have been counterproductive to their business plan. To protect their rights in the fruit trees, the Starks trademarked them, using the trademark law that Congress passed in 1881. In the 1890s, the Stark catalogs included gorgeous paintings of their named fruits with a small banner beneath each declaring that it was covered by a "Trade Mark" or, in the case of the Gold Plum, that it was "Trademark Pat[ente]d. Feb. 25, 1895."[29] The trademark, however, would not prevent someone from obtaining the tree or cuttings from it, propagating the wood, and then selling the tree under a different name.

Under the circumstances, beginning in the 1880s and with mounting insistence in the 1890s, American nurserymen began urging the establishment of legal protection for originators' rights. Some of the agitation recommended the expansion of the patent system to include coverage for innovations in plants and trees. Mindful of their exclusion from the patent system, nurserymen wondered why, as the *California Fruit Grower* put it, "the writer of a book, the composer of a song, the designer of a drawing or the originator of a mechanical device should be protected in their productions, while the originator of an improved flower or fruit is denied the same privilege."[30]

The move to patentability was blocked, however, when, in 1889, in *Ex parte Latimer*, the U.S. commissioner of patents rejected an application for a patent to cover a fiber identified in the needles of a pine tree, declaring that it would be "unreasonable and impossible to allow patents upon the trees of the forest and the plants of the earth."[31] The commissioner's ruling formed the basis for what came to be known as the "product-of-nature" doctrine—that while processes devised to extract what is found in nature can be patented, objects discovered there or bred from there cannot be patented. In a report to the American Association of Nurserymen in 1891, Liberty Hyde Bailey rejected the horticulturalists' patenting initiative as in any case unwarranted. New varieties were not inventions, he noted, precisely because they were accidents found in the fields, adding, "When the time comes that men breed plants upon definite laws, and produce new and valuable kinds with the certainty and forethought with which the inventor constructs a new machine, or an author writes a book, plant patents may possibly become practicable."[32]

Bailey held that plant originators should nevertheless be protected, though he doubted that any new legislation would do the job. "It is evident that after a variety is put upon the retail trade it becomes public property, and no statute could further protect it," he observed. He proposed that the nurserymen obtain protection through a national register of plants administered by the Department of Agriculture. The originator would send the department "a specimen, description and perhaps picture of his novelty," and the department would issue a certificate, a type of trademark ensuring him "inviolable rights" in his innovation. He acknowledged that thieves could sell the variety under a different name, but he thought that "tricksters" would be discovered and in consequence commercially disadvantaged. The public would soon learn to buy only from originators who possessed a registration certificate, just as they had learned to purchase only animals registered with the breed associations.[33]

Bailey, like the Stark Brothers with their trademarked fruits, tacitly assumed that the trademark-like certificates would not only protect the name of the innovation but also secure to the originator the exclusive right to the plant or tree and to its propagation. But that assumption was severely undercut in 1895 by the ruling of a federal appeals court in the case of *Hoyt et al. v. J. T. Lovett Co.* James Hoyt and Edwin Hoyt, nurserymen in Connecticut, had sued the J. T. Lovett Nursery, in New Jersey, for selling a grape that had been found in the Green Mountains in Vermont. The Hoyts believed they had bought the grape wood with exclusive rights and they had trademarked it as the "Green Mountain Grape." The court found against the Hoyts partly on grounds that certain facts in the case contradicted the tenets of trademark law as it had been judicially interpreted. But its decision also addressed the scope of trademark protection for living products.[34]

Apparently Lovett's lawyer had raised the issue, contending, in the words of the court, "that the protection of a trade-mark cannot be obtained for an organic article which, by the law of its nature, is reproductive, and derives its chief value from its innate vital powers, independently of the care, management, or ingenuity of man." The court, while noting that the question was "novel and unprecedented," agreed, writing: "The Hoyts did not make the Green Mountain vine, nor, strictly speaking, did they produce it. It grew out of the earth, was fashioned by nature, and endowed with powers and qualities which no human ingenuity or skill could create or imitate. If such protection as that now claimed by the complainants was allowed, a breeder of cattle could with equal propriety and reason demand like protection for the natural increase of his herd. In every aspect such claims would seem to be impracticable and inequitable."[35]

Perhaps in response to the ruling, during the next decade the leading nurserymen, including Burbank and the Stark Brothers, moved to obtain legislative protection of originators' rights along the lines that Bailey had suggested, engaging a lawyer in Washington, DC, named F. T. F. Johnson. In 1906, a bill probably drafted by Johnson was introduced in the House of Representatives that would amend the trademark act by authorizing the commissioner of patents to register an originator's new variety of plant, bush, shrub, tree, or vine. Registration of the name would constitute a trademark and would include for twenty years the "exclusive right to propagate for sale and vend such variety of horticultural product under the same so registered."[36]

The bill enjoyed broad support from nurserymen, a number of whom wrote letters to Johnson that were introduced at hearings on the bill before the House Committee on Patents in March 1906.[37] Several committee members expressed sympathy for protecting the rights of the originators, but the committee leadership found the bill constitutionally dubious. For one thing, by trying to protect rights in the product by protecting rights to its name, it sought to combine the exclusivity of a patent with the coverage of a trademark. More important, constitutional authority for the granting of federal trademarks rested on Congress's power to regulate interstate commerce. The bill allowed for trademark protection of plants even if they were not sold in interstate commerce, and under prevailing interpretation of the commerce clause it was unconstitutional for Congress to regulate intrastate trade. Congressman Frank D. Currier of New Hampshire, the chairman of the Patents Committee, summarily declared: "The proposition is as clearly unconstitutional as anything can be."[38]

Although an immediate failure, the 1906 venture did lead to the formation of a lobbying group, the National Committee on Plant Patents under the American Association of Nurserymen. In 1929, Paul Stark, of Stark Brothers, became chair of the committee. Along with other nurseries, Stark Brothers had been trying to protect its propagation rights in new fruits by imposing contractual obligations upon the purchaser—for example, an agreement that he would neither sell nor give away scions, cuttings, or buds. However, the contracts were sometimes difficult to enforce, which helped energize Stark's eagerness for the stronger protection of originators' rights that a patent would provide. In 1930, not least because of Stark's lobbying effort, Congress passed the Plant Patent Act.[39]

The act covered only asexually reproduced organisms, and it authorized a patent to anyone who "has invented or discovered and asexually reproduced any distinct and new variety of plant, other than a tuber-propagated plant."[40] Given its requirement of distinctiveness rather than usefulness, it was not a utility patent law. Moreover, it did not establish the conventional legal bargain that granted the inventor a monopoly right in exchange for public knowledge of how the invention was produced so that others could innovate beyond it. In most cases, there was no such knowledge to be disclosed. Liberty Hyde Bailey may have predicted that patent protection would accompany the discovery of the laws of inheritance, but the rise of Mendelian genetics played little or no role in the work of the nurserymen who were the act's principal advocates. Even in 1930, the innovations in fruits that were their stock-in-trade continued to arise from chance variations in the field rather than breeding on Mendelian principles. As Alain Pottage and Brad Sherman note in this volume, advocates of the law held that what qualified such innovations for patents—in essence the inventive step—was their asexual reproduction, an act that required human intervention.[41]

In all, the Plant Patent Act harked back to the seventeenth century, when patents were granted as privileges in the market—royal dispensations to encourage commerce in new technologies, often from abroad, or to reward favorites. Indeed, the Plant Patent Act might well have been called the Stark Horticultural Privilege Act, not only because of Stark's role in its passage but because it granted a privilege of patent protection tailored to the practices and needs of horticultural innovators.[42] Still, for all its simultaneous restrictiveness and looseness, the act was the first statute passed anywhere in the world that extended patent coverage to living organisms. It helped pave the way for the legal protection of intellectual property in sexually reproducing plants, which Congress authorized in 1970, and for the extension of utility patents to all living organisms other than human beings after 1980, when in the emerging age of biotechnology the U.S. Supreme Court ruled that whether an innovation is alive or not is irrelevant to its patentability.[43]

NOTES

1. Part of the work on this chapter was accomplished with a grant from the Andrew W. Mellon Foundation, a Senior Scholar's Award from the National Science Foundation, and a fellowship from the Cullman Center for Scholars and Writers at the New York Public Library. I gratefully acknowledge their support and the indispensable research assistance of Karin Matchett.

2. Bruce W. Bugbee, *Genesis of American Patent and Copyright Law* (Washington, DC: Public Affairs Press, 1967), p. 152.

3. Pasteur's patent, no. 141,072, was issued in 1873. Maurice Cassier, "Louis Pasteur's Patents: Agri-Food Biotechnologies, Industry, and Public Good," in Jean-Paul Gaudillière and Daniel J. Kevles, eds., *Living Properties: Making Knowledge and Controlling Ownership in the History of Biology* (Berlin: Max Planck Institute for the History of Science, 2009).

4. See Tamara Plakins Thornton, *Cultivating Gentlemen: The Meaning of Country Life among the Boston Elite, 1785–1860* (New Haven, CT: Yale University Press, 1989), passim.

5. Catherine Fisk, "The History of Intellectual Property Comes of Age," keynote address, Wisconsin Legal History Symposium, University of Wisconsin Law School, November 13, 2004, p. 6, unpublished, copy in author's possession.

6. Cary Fowler, "The Plant Patent Act of 1930: A Sociological History of Its Creation," *Journal of the Patent and Trademark Office Society*, 82 (September 2000), pp. 623–624.

7. On Bakewell's system, see Harriet Ritvo, "Possessing Mother Nature: Genetic Capital in Eighteenth Century Britain," in John Brewer and Susan Staves, eds., *Early Modern Conceptions of Property* (London: Routledge, 1995), pp. 413–426. For Bakewell as a breeder, see H. Cecil Pawson, *Robert Bakewell: Pioneer Livestock Breeder* (London: Crosby Lockwood & Son, 1957); and Roger J. Wood and Vítězslav Orel, *Genetic Prehistory in Selective Breeding: A Prelude to Mendel* (New York: Oxford University Press, 2001), chaps. 4, 5.

8. Ritvo, "Possessing Mother Nature," pp. 416–417.

9. Ibid., pp. 415, 418–419.

10. See the Dishley Society's rules in Pawson, *Bakewell*, pp. 72–77.

11. Ibid.

12. Margaret Derry, *Bred for Perfection: Shorthorn Cattle, Collies, and Arabian Horses since 1800* (Baltimore: Johns Hopkins University Press, 2003), p. 15.

13. Ibid., pp. 15, 20.

14. Ritvo, "Possessing Mother Nature," p. 420.

15. Derry, *Bred for Perfection*, pp. 20–21; Ron Broglio, *Technologies of the Picturesque: British Art, Poetry, and Instruments, 1750–1830* (Lewisburg, PA: Bucknell University Press, 2008), pp. 167–181.

16. Derry, *Bred for Perfection*, pp. 22–23.

17. Ibid., pp. 22–24.

18. Ibid., pp. 26–27.

19. Ibid., pp. 28–29, 31.

20. Ibid., pp. 34–36.

21. Ibid., passim.

22. Liberty Hyde Bailey, Report, "Protection to the Originator of Varieties," read at the meeting of the American Association of Nurserymen, June 4, 1891, printed in *Transactions of the American Association [of Nurserymen]*, June 3–13, 1891, pp. 88–91.

23. J. M. Thorburn & Co., Catalogue [1908], copy in New York Botanical Gardens Archives, Catalogue Collection, Box. 538. Italics in the original.

24. Fowler, "The Plant Patent Act," pp. 622–623; Jack R. Kloppenburg Jr., *First the Seed: The*

Political Economy of Plant Biotechnology (2nd ed.; Madison: University of Wisconsin Press, 2004), pp. 61–65.

25. Bailey, Report, "Protection to the Originator of Varieties," pp. 88–89. The most recent study of Burbank is Jane S. Smith, *The Garden of Invention: Luther Burbank and the Business of Breeding Plants* (New York: Penguin, 2009).

26. Dickson Terry, *The Stark Story: Stark Nurseries' 150th Anniversary* (Columbus, MO: Missouri Historical Society, 1966), pp. 38–40.

27. Catalog, *New Creations in Fruits and Flowers, June 1893* (Santa Rosa, CA: Burbank's Experiment Grounds, 1893), p. 12; Catalog, *Twentieth Century Fruits, 1911–1912* (Santa Rosa, CA: Burbank's Experiment Farms, 1911), p. 1, copies in Luther Burbank Papers, Library of Congress, Box 14. Emphasis in original.

28. Burbank to Jacob Moore, May 4, 1898, published in *Green's Fruit Grower*, June 1898, clipping in Luther Burbank Papers, Luther Burbank Home and Gardens, Archives, Santa Rosa, CA, Scrapbooks, vol. 2, p. 45. See also Jacob Moore to Chas. A. Green, Apr. 20, 1898; "Protection for Fruit Evolvers," editorial, *California Fruit Grower*, n.d.; and Moore to Peter Gideon, *Green's Fruit Grower*, n.d.; all in Scrapbooks, vol. 2, pp. 44, 47, 115.

29. Copy in Scrapbooks, vol. 1, p. 141, Burbank Home and Gardens, Archives.

30. "Protection for Fruit Evolvers," editorial, *California Fruit Grower*, quoted in Luther Burbank, Burbank's Experiment Farms, *The 1899 Supplement to New Creations in Fruits and Flowers*, Luther Burbank Papers, Library of Congress, Washington, DC, Box 14.

31. Daniel J. Kevles, "Ananda Chakrabarty Wins a Patent: Biotechnology, Law, and Society, 1972-1980," *HSPS: Historical Studies in the Physical and Biological Sciences*, 25: 1 (1994), p. 111.

32. Bailey, Report, "Protection to the Originator of Varieties," pp. 88–89.

33. Ibid.

34. *Hoyt et al. v. J. T. Lovett Co.*, Circuit Court of Appeals, Third Circuit, 71 F. 173, Dec. 3, 1895.

35. Ibid.

36. U.S. Congress, House of Representatives, Committee on Patents, Arguments before the Committee . . . on H.R.113570, Authorizing the Registration of the Names of Horticultural Products and to Protect the Same, March 28, 1906, 59th Cong., (Washington, DC: GPO, 1906), pp. 3–5, 12–13.

37. Crawford to Johnson, March 19, 1906, in ibid., p. 10.

38. Ibid., pp. 4–5, 9.

39. Bailey, Report, "Protection to the Originator of Varieties," p. 90; *Hoyt et al. v. J. T. Lovett Co.*, 71 F. 173, Dec. 3, 1895; Fowler, "The Plant Patent Act," pp. 630–642; Glen E. Bugos and Daniel J. Kevles, "Plants as Intellectual Property: American Practice, Law, and Policy in World Context," *Osiris*, 2nd series, vol. 7, *Science after '40* (1992), pp. 81–88.

40. Quoted in Fowler, "The Plant Patent Act," p. 641. See Pottage and Sherman, "Kinds, Clones, and Manufacturers," in this volume.

41. The rise of Mendelian genetics similarly changed breeding practices and the system of blood-value protection for animals very little. In 1925, one farm expert noted, "Up to the present time, the new knowledge of genetics has contributed little" to advances in animal breeding, adding, "Animal breeding proceeds in much the same way as it [did] four thousand years ago." Derry, *Bred for Perfection*, pp. 12–14.

42. I am indebted to Mario Biagioli for this analogy. On patents as privileges, see Arthur R. Miller and Michael H. Davis, *Intellectual Property: Patents, Trademarks, and Copyright in a Nutshell*, 2nd ed. (St. Paul, MN.: West, 1990), p. 5; and Jessica He, " 'Hail to the Patents!' The Ethics, Politics, and Economics of the Early Modern Patent System in England," senior essay, Ethics, Politics, and Economics, Yale University, 2005, pp. 2–27.

43. For these developments, see Bugos and Kevles, "Plants as Intellectual Property"; Kevles, "Ananda Chakrabarty Wins a Patent"; and Daniel J. Kevles, "The Advent of Animal Patents: Innovation and Controversy in the Engineering and Ownership of Life," in Scott Newman and Max Rothschild, eds., *Intellectual Property Rights and Patenting in Animal Breeding and Genetics* (New York: CABI Publishing, 2002), pp. 18–30.

ALAIN POTTAGE and BRAD SHERMAN

Kinds, Clones, and Manufactures

The logic of modern patent law, which construes inventions as ideas embodied in material artifacts, emerged in parallel with the rise of industrial manufacture. The process of mechanical reproduction made the separation between form and matter, or idea and embodiment, that is so fundamental to modern patent doctrine. By extending this theory of manufacture to entities that are reproduced biologically rather than mechanically, the patenting of living organisms has exposed a hidden premise of patent law. The history of patents relating to biological inventions has been attended by the persistent question whether biological inventions resemble industrial artifacts and to what extent that resemblance matters. The debate surrounding the adoption of the 1930 U.S. Plant Patent Act offers some valuable resources for reflection on the tensions between mechanical and genealogical "manufactures" and reveals some almost premonitory early-twentieth-century discussions of "hybrid" (human/biological) inventiveness and of the peculiarities of clones.

The formal legal question in *Diamond v. Chakrabarty* was whether an organism could qualify as a "manufacture" in the sense of the U.S. patent statute.[1] The Supreme Court sidestepped this inquiry by focusing on the question of novelty rather than the question of reproducibility: the much-cited declaration that "anything under the sun that is novel and made by man is patentable" affirmed the novelty of an invention, rather than its mode of origination or reproduction, as the essential qualification for patentability. A "new" organism was every bit as "novel" as a "new" machine. More recently, the Canadian Supreme Court approached a similar issue—was Harvard's "oncomouse" a "manufacture" or a "composition of matter"?—by addressing the difference between industrial and biological reproduction. The majority opinion adopted as its starting point the commissioner of patents' distinction between two phases of transgenesis: "The first phase involves the preparation of the genetically engineered plasmid. The second involves the development of a genetically engineered mouse in the uterus of the host mouse. . . . [W]hile the first phase is controlled by human intervention, in the second phase it is the laws of nature that take over to produce the mammalian end product."[2] Whereas the federal court held that there was "no valid basis for splitting an invention between the portion that is the result of inventive ingenuity and the portion that is not,"[3] the Supreme Court held that the intervention of biological reproduction diluted the inventive contribution. Ultimately a transgenic mouse cannot be a composition of matter because although it is "composed of various ingredients and substances," it does not "consist of ingredients and substances that have been combined or mixed together by a person."[4] The inventor is therefore not—or no longer—the prime originator of the biological form of the mouse. In part, this is indicative of a more general problem that concerns us here, namely, that biological inventions imply a tension between intellectual possession and physical possession, or between two modes of invention: originating invention, which is focused on causes, and inductive invention, which is focused on effects.

Industrial Kinds

While machines were at the forefront of eighteenth- and nineteenth-century debates concerning the development of patent law, there is a sense in which machines were the focus of debate because they were a difficult, and to some degree exceptional, case. The doctrines, administrative procedures, and professional practices that composed the patent system may have been conditioned by the steady flow of a different and less troublesome kind of subject matter—namely, mechanically manufactured consumer products. The rise of industrial consumer products through the eighteenth and nineteenth centuries promoted an ideal of industrial manufacturing, namely reproduction as the mass copying of an original. In his *Principles of Industrial Economy*, Charles

Babbage observed that "Nothing is more remarkable, and yet less unexpected, than the perfect identity of things manufactured by the same tool."[5] He went on to enumerate the central techniques of industrial reproduction: printing, which produced "a similarity which no labour could produce by hand,"[6] the steel punch, "which constantly reproduces the same exact circle,"[7] and the lathe, which unfailingly turned convex forms into their concave image. These techniques illustrated and enacted the "principle which pervades a very large portion of all manufactures, and upon which the cheapness of the articles produced seems greatly to depend": "The principle alluded to is that of COPYING, taken in its most extensive sense. Almost unlimited pains are, in some instances, bestowed upon the original, from which a series of copies is produced; and the larger the number of these copies, the more care and pains can the manufacturer afford to lavish upon the original. It may thus happen, that the instrument or tool actually producing the work, shall cost five or even ten thousand times the price of each individual specimen of its power."[8]

The basic techniques of industrial copying—printing, casting, molding, stamping and punching—would have been familiar to traditional craftsmen, but Babbage's program recharacterized them as the elements of a "system of copying."[9] Of course, Babbage was particularly interested in the economies promised by mechanized standardization: the ability to measure accurately the quantities of raw materials and fuels consumed in manufacture, to reduce the wastage occasioned by traditional handcrafting, to promote an efficient division of labor, and so on. Yet these economic virtues were all premised on the ability of mechanical reproduction to turn out multiple copies with a degree of precision and consistency that would have been inconceivable in the era of preindustrial craftsmanship.

The artifacts made by artisans or guild craftsmen in the preindustrial era brought together and expressed a number of technical, cultural, and material influences: local habits of use or consumption, the incorporated know-how of a guild, or the preferences of the patrons who commissioned bespoke artifacts. But precisely for that reason they had no autonomous "form" in the sense of a reproducible quality that could be isolated and privileged over other conditions of production. In their structural configuration and external appearance preindustrial artifacts expressed a range of inputs—the "mold" from which the object was cast was the total set of local "causes" or contexts. In place of this mode of overdetermined origin, Babbage's "system of copying" isolated and idealized form or design as a singular and preeminent generative principle. This idealization was possible precisely because the social program of mechanization took the component elements of localized production, redefined them, and turned them into a mere means. The complexities of craft knowledge were superseded by a regime which recharacterized labor, skills, and materials as parts of the complex sociomechanical instrument by which an idea or design was expressed in multiple copies. For consumers, this mode of industrial origin was itself a mark of distinction; standardized artifacts were desirable precisely because they were not made by artisans. And modes of manufacture were more significant than the commonality of designs. Pattern books containing roughly standardized mechanical elements or ornamental designs had been in circulation for some time, but the decisive shift happened when pattern books became catalogs, precisely because a catalog "presupposes that the goods can be repeated exactly."[10] The novel principle of industrial origin also gave technical artifacts a distinct identity. Bespoke objects lacked what Gilbert Simondon calls "an intrinsic [technical] norm or measure"[11] because their technical elements were subordinated to other factors of production. Precision in manufacture not only enabled a distinct technical identity to emerge; it also made possible designs with a complexity of detail or shape that could not have been achieved or reproduced by artisans.

Situated in the lineage of economic-philosophical commentary that runs from Smith, Ricardo, and Hegel to Marx, Babbage's argument is hardly novel. But in describing the emergence of "industrial kinds" what matters is not so much the mechanization of labor as the identity of artifacts. Of course, these are two sides of the same question. Babbage's "system of copying" presupposed the dissolution of the system of guilds, in which technological competence was in many ways "embodied" knowledge.[12] Mechanization reversed the relation of embodiment. The replication of perfect copies turned bodies into the instruments of machines and the knowledge invested in them. But whereas most commentaries since the nineteenth century have tended to emphasize the implication of the factory system in processes of social differentiation or experiences of alienation, what is significant about Babbage's attention to economies of scale is that it focuses attention on the peculiar form or identity of industrial artifacts.

Which particular practices or techniques isolated inventive "form" and privilege it over the other elements that went into the production of an artifact (raw materials, labor or organization, anticipated functions or market shares)? First, one might say that the sociomechanical machinery of reproduction—the "production line" understood in the broadest sense—turned "invention" into a determinate value. Following the production process through from design to product, it seems that inventive designs were merely unfolded and implemented by the machinery of reproduction, but there is also a sense in which the very process of implementation delimited the abstract idea that it implemented.[13] Second, industrial artifacts were characterized by "the law of the series."[14] The whole point of industrial reproduction was that, unlike artistic performances, in which a production was allowed to be an "interpretation" of the original text or score, exemplars were supposed to be identical. By producing a succession of identical artifacts, the machinery of reproduction divided artifacts into the two dimensions of the design (form) and its embodiments (matter); indeed the sheer quantity of embodiments proved that they were subordinate or inessential by comparison with design, which was the prime mover in the constitution of the artifact.

Industrial reproduction presupposed machines and machine tools, but the objects that were reproduced were more likely to be household objects than heavy machinery. The subject matter of these patents was not mechanical innovation or the kinematical principles instantiated in machines but innovations in consumer design. And it may be that these innovations preoccupied contemporary observers rather more than the problems that attended industrial machines: "the inventors, projectors, economic policy makers of the period dwelt upon the invention of new British products, and especially consumer products, to an even greater degree than they did upon mechanical power":[15] "Products were made by new tools, even machine tools, working on new and relatively inexpensive materials, and deployed over a whole paraphernalia of hardware from stops and cocks to hinges and screws and to locks and files. But, equally significantly, they were devoted to an explosion of new, intricate consumer goods and luxuries—sugar tongs and silver-plated coffee pots, buttons and buckles, brass furniture ware, japanned tea trays and silver candlesticks, snuff boxes and watch seals."[16] Although the conception of these artifacts involved a distinct mode of invention—specifically "imitation" in the sense of translating form from one context to another[17]—the point is that the manufacturing process created an entirely new phylum of objects, which owed their essential identity to what Babbage called "copying." Substantial investments were made in the originals from which multiple exemplars were produced—steel dies and stamps for the reproduction of cutlery, blocks and looms for the production of patterned textiles or carpets, molds for china and porcelain artifacts—and these investments were often protected by patents.

In some sense, the prototypical form of industrial kind is the printed book. The printing press was "the first assembly line in the history of technology"[18] because the ability of the presses to reproduce copies of manuscripts with absolute consistency introduced a specific and unprecedented legal relation between original and exemplar. Inevitably, Babbage was keen to emphasize this connection, arguing that in mechanized printing "impressions from the same block, or the same copper-plate, have a similarity which no labour could produce by hand. The minutest traces are transferred to the impressions, and no omission can arise from the inattention or unskilfulness of the operator."[19] In stamping out multiple copies of an original text, the mechanical presses produced the first industrial artifacts. But in so doing they affirmed one of the oldest legal concepts: the distinction between form and matter.[20] So although one might say that patent law's sense of "kinds" emerged from its adaptation to new technologies, it is equally true that these technologies merely gave a new context and configuration to a conceptual form that was already innate to law. The inherited distinction between form and matter is essential to the definition of the object of intellectual property. The intangible res forms a specific intersection between form and matter. The intangible object is produced by a conjunction that interrupts and fixes the respective potentialities of form and matter in such a way that they become determinate and distinguishable. And this specific intersection of form and matter has to be repeatable, which is why the monotonous precision attributed to machinery, a precision that repeatedly imprinted an identical form into matter, was so important in the formation of the patent system.

The argument that the traditional patent system was based on a paradigm of "industrial kinds" has certain limitations. To begin with, one might ask whether this paradigm was indeed an effective force in the industrial period or an interpretive device projected back on to that period by modern observers who are familiar with mass-produced artifacts of the twentieth century. And an analysis of industrial reproduction says little about the complex networks of bureaucratic procedure, techniques of representation, and professional practices that enabled legal doctrine to make distinctions between a kind and its embodiments. Nor does it have much to say about the difficulties of making that distinction so as to identify infringement in real scenarios. But by drawing out the paradigm of kinds, it is possible to get at one of the deeper reasons biological and digital artifacts are so problematic for classical patent systems. To the extent that inventions realized in living tissues or digital media make the relation between matter and form, or kind and embodiment, provisional and open to reconstruction, they unfold an economy of production and reproduction in which it becomes very difficult to define any stable form of intangible res and hence all the more attractive to resort to open-ended criteria of patentability.

Biological Kinds

The 1930 Plant Patent Act was conceived as a response to the illegitimate copying of new varieties of fruit trees and rose bushes.[21] Using familiar techniques, "pirates" were able to market new varieties at prices that undercut the "original" breeder. It was almost pointless to impose contractual restrictions on the uses that buyers might make of new varieties because contracts only bound the initial buyer. Similarly, although trademarks may have reinforced the markets enjoyed by the larger nurseries, they gave no right to control the reproduction of plants themselves. So breeders turned to patent law in search of a remedy. The principal obstacle to extending utility patents to plant varieties was not some "ethical" reticence about ownership of living organisms; it was the more technical problem of defining the intangible object embodied in representatives of a new variety. The various elements of the patent system—bureaucratic practices, techniques of representation, jurisprudential "memory"—had adapted themselves to the paradigm of industrial manufactures. Could the inventive "principle" immanent in a new plant be identified and delimited in the same terms as a mechanical design?

Here the difference between industrial reproduction and biological reproduction was crucial. Supporters of the proposed legislation argued that patent rights should only extend to "clonal" reproductions, which, like industrial artifacts, were identical copies of an original exemplar.[22] Indeed, it was argued that plants protected under the Plant Patent Act "partake of the nature of manufacture."[23] The exclusion of sexually reproduced varieties from the aegis of the act affirmed the premise that patents were proper to manufactures. The new science of Mendelian genetics had revealed the "combinatorial" texture of heredity and essential contingency of sexual reproduction,[24] but whereas modes of sexual reproduction connoted variability and inconstant identity, "cloning," or asexual propagation, could be equiparated to industrial reproduction. Because cloning turned out multiple copies with precision and consistency, it seemed to be a biological mode of industrial manufacture.

Drawing on the analogy between plants and manufactures, proponents argued that an extension of the patent system would stimulate private investment in breeding: "nothing that Congress could do to help farming would be of greater value and permanence than to give the plant breeder the same status as the mechanical or chemical inventors now have through patent law."[25] But although it was claimed that plant breeding was becoming a "technology," there remained an important difference between plants and machines. The major sources of new varieties were nature's own "breeding experiments"—seedlings, bud mutations, and sports. Some breeders selected for new varieties by producing hybrids from which they retained "a few desirable forms and destroy[ed] great numbers of worthless individuals."[26] Others sought to provoke mutations by exposing plants to X-rays or to abnormally high levels of fertilizer.[27] But most new varieties originated in the discovery of natural "aberrations," and even where techniques of hybridization or induced mutation were employed, the results were still seen as "fortuitous events over which the discoverer has no control."[28] One might say, applying the distinction highlighted in the decision of the Supreme Court in *Funk v. Kalo Inoculants* (1948), that these aberrations were "products of nature" rather than "inventions."[29] It is more interesting, however, to notice how discussions surrounding the 1930 Plant Patent Act introduced a mode of invention that was very different from industrial invention but was made to seem similar by the rhetorical parallel between cloning and manufacturing.

How were "natural aberrations" constituted as inventions? The leading argument was that although nature could spontaneously create sports, buds, and mutations, it was unable to reproduce the resulting individuals through subsequent generations:[30] "a plant discovery resulting from cultivation is unique, isolated and is not repeated by nature, nor can it be reproduced by nature unaided by man."[31] The art of the breeder consisted in knowing "what to look for, [in] having the interest to look and in [having] the skill and persistence to make the crosses."[32] This implied two phases of invention. First, there was the art of apprehending the novelty and value of each spontaneous creation, and second, there was the art of reproducing a specific "freak or abnormality in plant life" so as to "make it useful to mankind."[33] But although these two elements seemed to instantiate the two classic phases of "conception" and "reduction to practice," it soon became obvious that the recognition of breeders as inventors represented "a drastic revision of what constitutes inventive faculty."[34]

Rather than identifying this "drastic revision" with a policy of making the "products of nature" directly appropriable, it is more interesting to return to the decision in *Funk* and specifically to the minority arguments. In his opinion, Justice Frankfurter observed that references to "products of nature" or "laws of nature" were too ambiguous to serve as exclusionary criteria of patentability: "Everything that happens may be deemed 'the work of nature,' and any patentable composite exemplifies in its properties 'the laws of nature.' Arguments drawn from such terms for ascertaining patentability could fairly be employed to challenge almost every patent."[35] Both judges argued that the problem lay not in the distinction between "discoveries" and "inventions" but in the question of description and enablement. Whereas Frankfurter considered that organisms were not properly identifiable, Justice Burton drew on the experience of plant patents to argue that the mode of description should follow the nature of the invention: "Machines lend themselves readily to descriptions in terms of mechanical principles and physical characteristics. . . . [I]t may be that a combination of strains of bacterial species, which strains are distinguished from one another and recognized in practice solely by their observed effects, can be definable reasonably only in terms of those effects."[36] But this completely changed the premise of invention: invention became an inductive rather than an originating act, so that what mattered was not form (*causa formalis*) but function (*causa finalis*). The focus of attention shifted from reproducible causes to reproducible effects, so that the question was not whether the inventor could provide an enabling description but whether he or she could "identify and use the [bacterial strains] in the manner described in the patent."[37]

According to the doctrinal theory of "disclosure" the role of the inventor was to conceive the constitutive form of a novel artifact and to define it in terms that made it reproducible by others. This was where the process of industrial manufacturing had crucial cognitive effects. Babbage's "system of copying" allowed the "inventive principle" to be apprehended and theorized as the preeminent factor that eclipsed all other causal contributions. By (quite literally) making the difference between original and copy, manufacturing privileged form (*causa formalis*) over matter, labor, and utility. The use of models and mechanical drawings in description reinforced this division by reducing the complexity of translations between design and artifact. It was not obvious that the "principle" of a new plant variety could be isolated in this way. Whereas mechanical inventors were involved at the beginning, breeders were inventors after the fact. Breeders did not originate a new genetic principle; they inductively appropriated a natural event.

But the specific mode of induction minimized the difference between manufactures and plants. By representing cloning as a quasi-industrial process of reproduction, proponents of plant patents were able to impose the doctrinal polarity of design and embodiment on a mode of "invention" that ignored those terms. Although breeders did not—and could not—"conceive" the "design" realized in a new variety, the very process of reproduction retroactively attributed a design to the variety by reproducing multiple copies from the "original" mutation. Discursively, cloning turned the original "aberration" into the equivalent of an industrial mold or template, and once that was done, it was easy to overlook (or minimize) the difference between a template and the design that informs it. If according to the logic of industrial manufacture a template is an "intermediary" between design and product, then the process of cloning drew on that logic to suggest the existence of the form or design that necessarily preceded the template. It could be assumed that a design was immanent in each original variety. In this way, the parallel between manufactures and clones made inductive invention look like a variation on an established theme, or like another way of doing the same thing. This in turn facilitated the argument that the ability to reproduce and use an organism was as good as the ability to describe it. If the inventive design could be assumed to be inherent in the original organism, then description became an incidental technicality rather than a constitutive act. Until quite recently, it was taken that as long as the description of biological inventions was as complete as possible, the statutory requirements were satisfied, the premise being that the essentials of invention were already secured.[38]

Given the same basic process of reproduction, originating invention and inductive invention could be represented as different ways of doing the same thing. But one particular doctrinal expression of the paradigm of originating invention had to be revised—namely, the distinction between conception and reduction to practice. The difficulty was addressed in the decision of the Patent Office Tribunal in *Dunn v Ragin* (1941).[39] The question was who should be recognized as "inventor" of a new variety of seedless orange. Dunn was the owner of the land upon which the parent tree had been discovered. He claimed to be entitled to a patent on the basis that he had conceived the existence of the tree by observing it over the course of seven years and also on the basis that his agent had propagated cuttings from the tree. Ragin, to whom Dunn had given permission to cut wood upon his land, identified the seedless orange tree and reproduced it through a number of generations. He showed the trees to a state nursery inspector, whose evidence affirmed that Ragin had asexually reproduced trees bearing seedless fruit by the summer 1936. Meanwhile, Dunn could only establish that his agent had reproduced the tree in 1938. What was the proper test of inventorship?

The tribunal started from the premise that "an invention comprises two main inventive acts, conception and reduction to practice." Ordinarily, the latter would follow the former, but unlike mechanical inventions, plant inventions were not the products of a prior design, so the moment of conception was "not so readily determined."[40] To resolve this difficulty, the tribunal adopted the approach pioneered in relation to chemical inventions, holding that the "conception or discovery of the new variety . . . must occur *concurrently* with the actual reduction to practice."[41] Based on this revised definition, the tribunal held that where an invention was derived by cloning a bud variation or sport, the conception of the invention "must reside in the discovery of the new variety. A new variety may popularly be said to be conceived or discovered when an individual becomes aware of its existence."[42] But given that bud variations could turn out to be either effects of environment or "inherent" and reproducible traits, the nature of what was discovered or "conceived" could be established only by reproducing the "parent" plant: the "ultimate proof" of conception was "actual propagation," or reduction to practice. So in respect of the seedless pineapple orange, the invention was deemed to have been reduced to practice at the point "when by asexual reproduction citrus trees would be established which bore fruits having all the attributes of the variety known as a pineapple orange with the exception of its habit of containing seeds."[43] It followed that Ragin was the inventor because he was the first person to reproduce the new variety asexually.[44] Again, the implicit sense was that the very process of reproduction (re)characterized the "original" variety as a template holding a design or form that was thenceforth open to "conception" by the inventor. The logic of inductive invention was complete.

The Limits of the "Clone View"

In 1912, George Shull, the coinventor of hybrid corn, observed that "the 'clones' of horticultural plants are notorious for the heterogeneity of their seedling offspring."[45] The precarious status of cloned individuals as singularities rescued from the vicissitudes of biological reproduction may have served to emphasize the factitious and quasi-industrial quality of asexual reproduction. But the parallel between cloning and industrial manufacture was more problematic than proponents of plant patents recognized. Herbert Webber, who first proposed the term "clone" in 1903, suggested that plants that were propagated vegetatively were "simply transplanted parts of the same individual, and in heredity and in all biological and physiological senses such plants are the same individual."[46] Although it was precisely for that reason that asexual reproduction could be approximated to industrial manufacture, the mode of consistency had implications that were overlooked in debates surrounding plant patents. Quite simply, cloned individuals did not fit into the categories of botanical nomenclature. In 1943, a discussion of the meaning of the term "clone" contained the observation that because clones could belong to any of the principal categories—namely, "species, subspecies, varietas, subvarietas, forma, forma biologica, forma specialis, individuum"—they had "no formal nomenclative standing."[47] The author went on to propose that clones were "actually equivalent" to the category of "individuum." So a clone might be described as an individual in serial extension. This kind of series is not structured by the distinction between a kind and its instantiations, or between genus and individual. Nor does it articulate a distinction between "original" and "copy." Clones are neither kinds nor copies.

Of course, it might be said that both cloning and mechanical reproduction set up a nongenealogical principle of identity or individuation. Although patent law drew on the consistency and exactitude of mechanical reproduction to stabilize the distinction between form and matter, it then turned forms or designs into kinds by generalizing them to encompass all equivalents of the invention—that is, all artifacts embodying (and infringing) the patented "principle" of the invention. The construction of this juridical kind presupposed a radical difference between form and matter, and the priority of the former over the latter. But clones confuse form and matter. They are neither kinds nor copies. Because they are not (just) identical copies but (also) parts of the original entity, they disrupt the coordinates that are usually deployed in determining what constitutes identity, or of what makes the difference between an original and a copy. The polarity that is essential to the conceptualization of identity and the fabrication of intellectual property—the distinction between form and matter—is collapsed. The technological knowledge that would be required to make form available as something distinct from materiality is not yet available.

A commentary on the first judicial interpretation of the 1930 Plant Patent Act criticized the "clone view" of plant patents.[48] Commenting on the court's finding that there could be no liability for infringement unless the infringing variety had been asexually reproduced from the patented variety (unless, that is, cuttings had been directly taken and reproduced without authorization), the author argued that, following the logic of this "clone view," a plant patent "represents a *biological entity* rather than a *verbal abstraction* outlined with doubtful completeness in the specification and almost defying the exact definition."[49] Unlike other patented inventions, a plant invention was not an intangible idea or design, captured and expressed in the equally intangible form of legal language, but the (tangible) thing itself. Presciently, the author argued that this approach was too restrictive because it made it impossible "to patent a 'genetic type' to be transferred at will to a number of varieties."[50] This observation highlighted an unnoticed aspect of the shift from originating invention to inductive invention. Whereas the traditional system of patents was founded on the discursive construction of proprietary artifacts and property relations—rights depended on the definition of kinds and on the appreciation of the differences between instantiations of kinds—rights in a plant invention followed possession of the material thing. Of course patent law institutions still have to delimit the rights that followed possession, but unlike industrial inventions, the ability to reproduce (or infringe) plant inventions depends on access to the biological material itself. The intangible can no longer be represented as something that is entirely contained, articulated, and circulated independently of its material embodiments. Rather, tangible and intangible become practically indistinguishable.

Although debates surrounding the introduction of plant patents presented inductive invention as a mode of manufacture, in practice the process of cloning was premised on the material continuity linking each clone to the parent plant. Implicitly, the relaxation of the description requirements conceded that "intellectual possession," or the ability to provide a recipe for the fabrication of the artifact, mattered less than physical possession of the biological "means of production." So although the representation of cloning as a mode of manufacture facilitated the integration of organisms into the patent system, the practice of cloning introduced the tension that has since made biological inventions so problematic. The difficulty is adapting the semantics of originating invention, and the accompanying rhetoric of the "patent bargain," to a form of property that is premised on physical possession, or what the dissent in *Funk* called the ability to reproduce certain "effects" from biological material. The fact that biotechnology and synthetic biology promise to reduce biomateriality to a "programmable" medium, thus making the peculiarity of biological inventions seem temporary, merely accentuates the tension. As recent cases in the United States suggest, courts remain uncertain about how to construe the written description and enablement requirements in an age when biotechnology (still) seems to be becoming the ultimate form of industrial manufacture. As in 1930, the problem is to transcribe biomateriality into law, to create a "biologio-legal hybrid,"[51] or an ideal biopolitical artifact.

NOTES

1. *Diamond v. Chakrabarty*, 447 U.S. 303, 206 USPQ 193 (1980).

2. *Harvard College v. Canada (Commissioner of Patents)* [2002] 4 S.C.R. 45, 2002 SCC 76. Comments of the commissioner reported by Bastarache J at para. 130.

3. *Harvard College v Canada (Commissioner of Patents)* [2000] 4 F.C. 528, at para. 167 (Canadian Federal Court).

4. Ibid., para. 162.

5. Charles Babbage, *Principles of Industrial Economy* (London: Charles Knight, 1832), at p. 48.

6. Ibid.

7. Ibid.

8. Ibid.

9. Ibid.

10. Michael Snodin and Maurice Howard, *Ornament: A Social History since 1450* (London: Yale UP, 1996), at p. 54.

11. Gilbert Simondon, *Du mode d'existence des objets techniques* (Paris: Aubier, 1989), at p. 24.

12. See S. R. Epstein, "Craft Guilds, Apprenticeship, and Technological Change in Preindustrial Europe" (1998) 58 (3) *Journal of Economic History* 684–713, esp. at p. 704.

13. This might be contrasted with contemporary modes of digital production, where "creative" or "productive" consumption introduces feedback loops into the process of "manufacture."

14. Bernard Cache, *Earth Moves: The Furnishing of Territories* (Cambridge MA: MIT Press, 1995), at p. 95.

15. Maxine Berg, "From Imitation to Invention: Creating Commodities in Eighteenth-Century Britain," (2002) 55 *Economic History Review*, at p. 14.

16. Ibid., at p. 6.

17. Ibid., at p. 9.

18. Walter J. Ong, *Orality and Literacy: the Technologizing of the Word* (Abingdon, UK: Routledge, 2002), 1982, at p. 116.

19. Charles Babbage, *Principles of Industrial Economy* (London: Charles Knight, 1832), at p. 51.

20. For examples from Roman law, see Daniele Conso, *Forma, Etude sémantique*, PhD thesis, Paris X University.

21. For a background see Daniel Kevles in this volume.

22. Robert Starr Allyn, "Patentable Yardsticks" (1943) 25 (11) *Journal of the Patent Office Society* 791, 816.

23. John A. Dienner, "Patents for Biological Specimens and Products" (1953) 35 *Journal of the Patent Office Society* 286, 289–290.

24. Joseph Rossman, "The Preparation and Prosecution of Plant Patent Applications" (1935) 17 *Journal of the Patent Office Society* 632, 633.

25. Edison's remarks before the Congressional Committee, H. Rep. 1129, 71st Cong., 2d sess. (1930), 3; S. Rep. 315, 71st Cong., 2d sess. (1930), 3.

26. Robert Cook, "The First Plant Patent" (1931) 22 *Journal of Heredity* 313, 319.

27. See L. Stadler, "Some Genetic Effects of X-Rays in Plants" (1930) *Journal of Heredity* 3.

28. Robert Cook, "The Administration of the Plant Patent Law from the Breeder's Point of View" (1933) 5 *Journal of the Patent Office Society* 275, 281. For a discussion of the role of bud mutations (prompted by the Plant Patent Act), see A. Shamel and C. Pomeroy, "Bud Variations in Apples" (1932) 23 *Journal of Heredity* 173 (esp. at p. 178 re impact of Plant Patent Act in fostering interest in bud variations).

29. *Funk Bros. Seed Co. v. Kalo Inoculant Co.*, 333 U.S. 127 (1948).

30. Joseph Rossman, "Plant Patents" (1931) *Journal of the Patent Office Society* 7, 18.

31. S. Rep. 315, 71st Cong., 2d sess. 1, 6–7. See also Harry Robb, "Plant Patents" (1933) *Journal of the Patent Office Society* 752, 760.

32. Robert Cook, "The First Plant Patent" (1931) 22 *Journal of Heredity* 313, 319.

33. Joseph Rossman, "Plant Patents" (1931) *Journal of the Patent Office Society* 7, 13.

34. Robert Cook, "The First Plant Patent" (1932) 14 *Journal of the Patent Office Society* 398, 400.

35. *Funk Bros. Seed Co. v. Kalo Inoculant Co.*, 333 U.S. 127, 134 (1948).

36. Ibid., 137–138 (Justice Burton).

37. Ibid., 137 (Justice Burton).

38. See for example *JEM Ag. Supply v. Pioneer Hi-Bred International*, 534 U.S. 124 (2001).

39. *Dunn v Ragin v. Carlile* (Orange Tree) Final Hearing in the U.S. Patent Office; Patent Interference no. 77,764 (6 Dec. 1940) Interference Action filed 1 March 1940 (1941, Bd Inter Exam) 50 USPQ 472.

40. Ibid.

41. Ibid.

42. Ibid.

43. Ibid.

44. Robert Starr Allyn, "Patentable Yardsticks" (1943) 25 (11) *Journal of the Patent Office Society* 791, 816.

45. George H Shull, "Genotypes, Biotypes, Pure Lines and Clones" (1912) 35 (888) *Science*, 27–29, at p. 28.

46. H. J. Webber, "New Horticultural and Agricultural Terms" (1903) 18 (459) *Science* 501–503, at p. 502.

47. William T. Stearn, "The Use of the Term 'Clone'" (1949) 74 *Journal of the Royal Horticultural Society* 41–47, at p. 43.

48. Robert C. Cook, "The First Plant Patent Decision" (1937) 19 *Journal of the Patent Office Society* 187.

49. Ibid., 189.

50. Ibid., 190.

51. Ibid.

16

CORI HAYDEN

No Patent, No Generic
Pharmaceutical Access and the Politics of the Copy

In the final days of 2001, currency devaluations, the rapid flight of foreign capital, and bank closures paralyzed Argentina.[1] Skyrocketing pharmaceutical prices, medication shortages, and hospital and clinic closures were instrumental in bringing the 2001–2002 economic crisis to a head.[2] Following the collapse, among the priority recovery measures established by President Néstor Kirchner's health minister, Ginés González García, were two initiatives meant to ensure or at least improve people's ability to acquire medicine, from antibiotics to insulin and beyond. Programa Remediar, established in 2002, distributes free medicines to the poorest Argentines.[3] This stopgap measure was accompanied by a 2002 law promoting the prescription of cheaper, copied drugs over more expensive, dominant brand-name medications. This law, formally entitled the Law of Prescription by Generic Name, was meant to drive medication prices down by requiring that prescriptions contain the generic name of a drug—that is, the name of a molecule, such as enalapril—rather than a specific brand name (such as Merck's brand of enalapril, Renitec). The goal of this law was to stimulate both a supply of and demand for less expensive medications by prying open the monopolylike hold that leading brands have maintained on physicians' prescriptions and (thus) on patients' consumption.

Argentina was certainly not alone in pursuing measures of this kind. In 1997, the Mexican government had similarly turned to the generic as the country continued to recover from its own economic crisis and peso devaluation of 1994–1995. As in Argentina, the centerpiece of the Mexican measures to combat spiraling medication costs was a prescription decree targeting physicians' common practice of prescribing by brand name. This move, and associated regulatory shifts, ushered in a new market for generics and paved the way for the emergence and growth of pharmacy chains that traffic exclusively in lower-cost, copied medicines. The effects have been tangible: beginning in 1999, pharmaceutical prices finally dropped following more than four years of precipitous escalation (Hayden 2007).

The idea that generics might come to the rescue in an economic and public health crisis has become an increasingly familiar and important dimension of health politics in Latin America and globally. In the terms used by the World Health Organization, "multisource" or generic drugs are copies marked by two defining features: they are "pharmaceutically equivalent" to the original, and they come into circulation when the original patent has expired or has been modified such that the drug may be manufactured and commercialized by labs other than the original patent holder (see Homedes and Ugalde 2005: 65). More colloquially, we might say that generics are copied drugs that circulate at the end of the patent.

With the ascendance of intellectual property as a central (if not contested) feature of international trade and pharmaceutical production and distribution globally, and particularly with the rise of global AIDS epidemics, generic drugs have come to prominence as a crucial, often lifesaving alternative to expensive patented medications (see Petryna, Lakoff, and Kleinman 2006; van der Geest and Whyte 1988). Generics configure campaigns for access to medicine in two related ways. First, there is the often spectacular and conflictual matter of "compulsory licensing," a legal instrument now sanctioned by the World Trade Organization's Doha Declaration (2001), in which national governments can, within particular circumstances, contract with generics manufacturers to obtain cheaper versions of specific still-patented drugs.[4] Thailand and Brazil, for example, have issued compulsory licenses on Merck's antiretroviral drug Efavirenz in their efforts to combat HIV/AIDS.[5] Such moves are not, of course, exercised solely by nations of the global South. In 2001, the U.S. government signaled to Bayer that the company would be asked to "relax" the patent on the antibiotic Cipro (thus allowing other labs to manufacture and sell it) in the case of a widespread anthrax attack.[6]

Second, there is the ostensibly more prosaic matter of "off-patent" generics: medicines that are or can be manufactured and commercialized widely (that is, nonexclusively) after the expiry of the original patent. Off-patent generics thus come into circulation at the arbitrarily "natural" death of the patent (the lifespan of a patent in U.S. law and most multilateral trade agreements is now twenty years) rather than with its hastened and selective relaxation through compulsory licensing. These are, for example, the many ibuprofens one finds vying for shelf space with Advil in U.S. pharmacies. Efforts to promote the prescription, consumption, and domestic manufacture of off-patent generics intervene in the question of pharmaceutical access by reconfiguring or, to adapt Michel Callon's language (1998), reformatting national pharmaceutical markets in a broad sense. That is, easing the entry of (legal) copies into the market is meant to stimulate competition and thus reduce medication costs overall.[7]

That parenthetical qualification—the generic as *legal* copy—signals one of my central concerns in this chapter. The two initiatives mentioned at the outset, in Mexico and Argentina, are at first glance markedly similar, and they both fall very much in line with moves to promote off-patent generics as noted above. Yet their similarities to each other and to received definitions of a politics of the generic are less stable than they may seem. In Mexico, the turn to generics has, in many ways, been framed as we might expect: that is, as a way to counter the dominance of expensive foreign-made patented drugs. Generics have emerged there as a new and distinctive kind of product, in commercial, regulatory, and legal terms, and domestic generic manufacturers and commercial outlets have vaulted to newfound visibility in the market.

But in Argentina, the generics question is configured differently. The powerful purveyors of dominant brands in question have largely been Argentine drug companies, which have flourished since the mid-twentieth century by making unlicensed copies of drugs patented elsewhere (the U.S. government calls these drugs "pirated"). Indeed, Argentina effectively does not grant or enforce pharmaceutical product patents. This fact has important implications for the ontological status not just of "original" drugs but also for generics. As I shall suggest in this chapter, in the absence of an enforced pharmaceutical patent law, we are hard pressed to think of the generic as a distinctive kind of thing. As many people working within the Argentine pharmaceutical landscape argue pointedly, without the patent, there simply is no generic. This is not a rhetorical flourish but a consequential legal-technical diagnosis that both unmoors a number of fundamental liberal assumptions about the ontology of drugs as objects of intellectual property and provokes some important reorientations.

No patent, no generic: this provocation, with its refusals and reconfigurations (which I will lay out in more detail throughout this chapter), certainly throws into question the definition of the generic. It also provokes us to think again about the problem to which "the generic" is a solution. For the turn to cheaper drugs known by their generic names in Argentina takes its force not primarily against foreign-made, patented "original" pharmaceuticals, but in many ways, against domestic copies.

These pointed classificatory matters open up a thicket of questions about the promise, limits, and specificities of "the generic" more broadly. Drawing on my research in both Argentina and Mexico, this chapter explores the complex and remarkably different pharmaceutical taxonomies that emerge in efforts to bring generics into new economic and regulatory landscapes. As we consider the multiple processes unfolding in the name of the generic, the specificities of a U.S.-centered perspective on intellectual property come into sharp relief and, with them, an easily assumed legal and political vocabulary organized around the axis of private (the patent) and public (the generic). We must in fact open up this language a bit in order to think, again, about the politics (plural) of the copy.

For at stake in the rise and expansion of markets for generic drugs is not simply a David and Goliath relationship between the (cheaper, accessible, democratizing) generic and the (expensive) patented original; also fundamentally gathered into a politics of the generic, as we shall see, is the relation between the *licit* and the *illicit copy*. This is a point to which international health organizations, pharmaceutical companies, and many national governments are intensely attuned, as multilateral and bilateral trade agreements extending patent rights on drugs into new national contexts have also brought with them restrictive and highly contested redefinitions of what shall count as a legal copy. Yet this point is often lost in the liberal vocabulary that animates many discussions of pharmaceutical access, in which the template for imagining access ricochets between only two possible horizons: if not patented drug (private property), then legal generic (public domain). This formulation is not, as I will argue below, a descriptive or adequate one; it is a normative one. Among many other iterations of "illicit" copies worldwide, Argentina's domestic *copias*—neither patented originals nor legal "generics"—vividly demonstrate the limits of this simple either/or proposition (see also da Costa Marques 2005: 139–140). What, then, are the implications of configuring a political language of access around the terms of intellectual property itself?

Argentina: Before the Generic, There Was the Copy

Though Brazil is perhaps the better-known Latin American pharmaceutical giant, Argentina is home to one of the region's most powerful domestic pharmaceutical industries. While the Brazilian industry has largely been funded by the state (Biehl 2004),[8] "domestic companies" in Argentina are funded by private Argentine capital (Katz and Burachik 1997). Throughout the period of import substitution industrialization (the signature economic strategy of mid-twentieth-century Latin American nationalist populism and, in Argentina, from the 1930s to the late 1960s), the domestic industry flourished under a set of conditions characterized by a high degree of state protectionism: regulation favoring national companies in the processes of authorizing and launching new products, high import tariffs, and the "weak" protection of international intellectual property standards (Katz and Burachik 1997: 87). Indeed, as a product of the era of import substitution, the Argentine pharmaceutical industry was explicitly and proudly built on the manufacture of copies, precisely in a context in which pharmaceutical patents were not recognized (see Lakoff 2004: 195–197). Argentine firms have thus risen to domestic dominance by copying drugs developed elsewhere and marketing them under their own brand names. Domestic labs—the *industria copista*—have consistently commanded over 50 percent of the pharmaceutical market in the country; in 1999, the Argentine laboratory Roemmers was the overall market leader (ahead of U.S., European, Brazilian, and other Argentine companies).[9]

Argentina's long-standing sanctioned politics of copying has generated accusations of piracy from the U.S. government and transnational pharmaceutical firms, particularly since the 1990s, when expanding multilateral trade accords (particularly through the Uruguay Round of the General Agreement on Tariffs and Trade [GATT] in 1988) placed a premium on the protection of intellectual property rights as a trade priority. That is, following the Uruguay Round, signing onto Trade-Related Aspects of Intellectual Property Rights (TRIPS) accords became a central condition for developing nations joining the GATT and the World Trade Organization (WTO). Thus, signatory nations must "harmonize" their copyright, trademark, and patent legislation to what are effectively U.S. standards. To quote former Argentine trade negotiator Carlos Correa, the ascendance of TRIPS has transformed dramatically many developing nations' abilities to exercise what was once a "relative or total freedom to imitate" (Correa 1998: 1).

Following attempts to privatize aspects of the economy during Argentina's military dictatorships (1976–1983), the radical experiments in market liberalization and deregulation initiated by President Carlos Menem in the late 1980s and 1990s indeed seemed poised to put an end to Argentina's practices of copying on several fronts. With Menem's election in 1989, the U.S. government thought it had finally found a willing partner in its project to "open" the Argentine economy to foreign investment, competition, and intellectual

property protection in a number of arenas, with the large prescription pharmaceutical market—ranked twelfth in the world in 1999, with a value of $3
billion U.S. dollars—serving as a key object of U.S. desire. Consonant with
Menem's stated willingness to implement pharmaceutical patents, Argentina
signed onto the TRIPS accord of the GATT in 1994, and the legislature subsequently passed a national patent law in 1996 that included pharmaceutical
product and process patents. Yet strong pressure from the powerful domestic industry has kept at bay the implementation of *pharmaceutical* patents
in particular (other domains of patenting have been less controversial). The
U.S.-based Pharmaceutical Research and Manufacturer's Association, which
has led the charge against what it calls "local pirate firms," has been pointed
in its criticism of exceptions written into Argentina's patent law, including,
prominently, the right not to grant patents in order to protect "public order"
and "morals." These exceptions are understood specifically to signal a long-
standing construction of (copied) pharmaceuticals as essential to the Argentine "public good" (see Katz and Burachik 1997: 87–89; Lakoff 2004).

Such wranglings over pharmaceutical patents animated rather vicious trade
disputes between the United States and Argentina throughout the 1990s.[10]
Argentina consistently featured in U.S. State Department and U.S. trade representative assessments as Latin America's most egregious pharmaceutical "pirate" (and though a copyright law is also on the books, these complaints were
peppered with references to music and film piracy as well). The Clinton administration levied trade sanctions in 1997 precisely over the pharmaceutical
issue. Much has happened in the interim, including the disastrous economic
crisis of 2001, largely understood as a direct result of Menem's failed neoliberal
"reforms." As matters now stand, Argentina technically has a patent law, but
effectively *does not grant pharmaceutical patents*; that is, the law is not enforced
for pharmaceuticals.[11]

This refusal of the pharmaceutical patent does not, however, constitute a
blanket rejection of all forms of intellectual property. Brands and trademarks
hold an important place in the structure of the domestic drug market.[12] This
point is relevant to the fact that one of the key effects of market deregulation
in the early 1990s in Argentina was a sharp rise in domestic "leading brand"
drug prices (Lakoff 2004: 196). As Andrew Lakoff notes pointedly, with the
removal of state-managed price controls, "domestic firms took advantage of
the value structure of the transnational pharmaceutical industry, which is
based on patent protection, while at the same time defying such protection"
(2004: 196). Implied here is that the "value structure" of the transnational
industry is reliant not just on the patent but on the value of the recognized
brand name. Domestic labs, relying on the latter (the brand name) but reject-

ing the former (the patent), have not only managed to block the implementation of pharmaceutical patents; they were also instrumental, until González García's postcrisis measures in 2002, in blocking the emergence of a generics market as well. The (absent) patent, the (blocked) generic, and the (dominant) unlicensed copy thus served, until 2002, as the triangulated coordinates of the Argentine prescription pharmaceutical marketplace.

Mexico's New Generics

In many respects, Argentina's contrast with Mexico could not be more stark. Mexico's tight economic and political "integration" with the United States has made an Argentina-like stance on pharmaceutical patents nearly impossible to contemplate. Strong patent, copyright, and trademark legislation was introduced in the early 1990s, as President Carlos Salinas de Gortari's administration paved the way for Mexico's entry into the North American Free Trade Agreement (NAFTA). Moreover, Mexico does not have a domestic pharmaceutical industry with anything like the strength of the Argentine *industria copista*. There are, in contrast, a number of relatively small generics labs that, from 1950s to the late 1990s, had as their consumers the state-funded public health sector. Following regulatory moves in 1997 to foment a wider market for generics, these labs now have new commercial outlets for their products, in the form of domestic pharmacy chains selling cheaper generic drugs to the wider public (see Hayden 2007). Nonetheless, in the late 1990s and early 2000s, over 90 percent (in value) of the pharmaceutical market in Mexico was controlled by transnational firms.

Efforts to make generics more widely available there in 1997 and 1998 took shape in a pharmaceutical marketplace essentially divided in two. The largest part of the state's investment in health goes to the state- and employer-funded health insurance and pension program known by its acronym, IMSS, covering those with formal employment. There is a similar program for employees of the state, the military, and the nominally state-run oil company; a network of poorly funded hospitals for those without recourse to any of the above; and a new insurance plan, the Seguro Popular, which seeks to enroll this latter category of the "uncovered" in a hybrid form of health coverage drawing on individual contributions and decentralized state funding. With the exception of the Seguro Popular (a relatively new experiment), these state institutions have their own pharmacies, which for the most part distribute unbranded, off-patent generics.

Many people—those who can afford to do so, those who for contested reasons of patronage have been kept out of IMSS, those who do not have access to IMSS because they work in the "informal" sector, or those who feel they cannot take an entire day off of work to wait for an appointment—instead pay for private care, which in turn directs patients to private (not state-run) pharmacies. Until the late 1990s, the majority of drugs prescribed and sold in these corner pharmacies and other commercial outlets were relatively pricey name-brand "originals" or *inovadores*; generics were simply not available commercially. This situation was identified as a source of increasingly untenable out-of-pocket costs for the many consumers who, for one reason or another, bought their drugs in commercial pharmacies. The problem became particularly acute in the years between 1995 and 1997, when the public-sector pharmacies began experiencing shortages of many of the drugs in their basic pharmacopeia; these patients also turned to private pharmacies. The move to generics in Mexico was thus designed to channel a wider range of cheaper, off-patent generics into regular corner pharmacies and thus, presumably, into consumers' hands.

The travel of the generic out of Mexico's public-sector pharmacies and into the public sphere of the marketplace—that is, as a new commercial and regulatory category—has produced a flurry of controversy, public-relations and media battles, and contested claims about the site and source of a drug's "quality." Indeed, the generic emerged as a novelty that required some explanation, not to mention promotion. The secretary of health and domestic pharmacy chains launched public-relations campaigns promoting the idea that a drug *can* be decoupled from its (best-known) brand name and can be reimagined as one of many possible vehicles for delivering a key substance or active ingredient. The dominance of foreign drug companies such as Roche and Merck has fueled a fair amount of nationalist marketing on the part of emergent pharmacy chains such as Farmacias Similares (Hayden 2007). For their part, transnational companies and their domestic affiliates have put up a fierce fight in an effort to stem this insurgent tide of cheaper competitors, placing the idea of "quality" (and its ostensible attachment to the recognized name brand) at the center of their efforts to redefine these legal copies as somehow less than licit.

Contested as it may be, this ongoing reconfiguration of the pharmaceutical marketplace in Mexico has been defined around the operative terms of two kinds of intellectual property law that, as in the United States, function in a closely related manner to convey priority to the original drug: the "brand" is associated with the "patented original," and the legal or licit copy emerges both chronologically and semiotically as a cheaper "second." Here, the generic and its many siblings (interchangeable generics and branded generics) step in as the other(s) to the original, patented, or brand-name drug. Though the proliferation of *kinds* of copies does not map easily onto U.S. or European pharmaceutical taxonomies, the structuring division of prior patented drug versus copy (or copies) is the same; it is, after all, the division conventionally understood to be embedded in intellectual property law itself. But this opposition is difficult to sustain in Argentina.

Argentina and the Multiplicity of the Copy

What is the landscape in which "generics" are meant to intervene in Argentina? As noted above, it is a landscape (already) dominated by copied drugs. *Copias* are copies in a few senses. First, they are often reverse-engineered from the drugs developed and patented by foreign companies such as Merck and Eli-Lilly. Thus, high-profile Argentine companies such as Gador, Roemmers, and Bagó launch products in the domestic market under their own brand names, often even *before* the originating brand makes its appearance, *if it appears at all*.[13] For example, in several of the top-selling pharmaceutical niches (such as hypertension drugs and certain classes of psychopharmaceuticals), the two or three top-selling drugs are made by Argentine companies, with the "originator" trailing behind (see Lakoff 2004). Already, then, in terms of both temporality and a predicted period of "market dominance," *copias* wreak havoc on the conventional notion of the copy's secondary relation to the patented original.

Indeed, just as feminist and poststructuralist interventions prompt us to think about an "original" itself as an iterative copy (Butler 1990: 137–138), in the Argentine pharmaceutical market, *copias* join presumably "original" brands (which have no purchase as such) in an often astonishingly large, horizontal field of *like* products.[14] Consider the best-selling pharmaceutical in Argentina, the hypertension drug enalapril (the name of the molecule, not a brand name). In 2006, there were *thirty* brands of enalapril on the market, including Roemmers's Lotrial, Bayer's Baypril, Merck's Renitec, and the Argentine lab Raffo's Enalafel. Each of these products is considered *a* brand, but none is *the* brand in the sense that is assumed and enforced in the United States or that has been in operation in Mexico since the early 1990s—that is, privileged as the original, patent-holding, brand-name drug.

While the effect in some senses is a remarkably level field where the patent is (not) concerned, we might also note that in the midst of all of this likeness, hierarchies do emerge. One of these thirty drugs is likely to stand out from the field as the best-selling or leading brand, *la marca líder*. How do these two measures of distinction—a patent-centered notion of originality or priority and a trademark-centered notion of the leading brand—relate to each other? In this context, there is no necessary correlation between them. The U.S.-based pharmaceutical company Merck, Sharp and Dohme was the original developer and patent holder on enalapril, which it markets as Renitec. In the two years before the expiry of its U.S. patent (in February 2000), Renitec was Merck's second-best-selling drug worldwide.[15] But in Argentina, the leading brand for the last *twenty-five years*—that is, from the time enalapril was patented and marketed in the U.S. and elsewhere—has been Roemmers's Lotrial (González García 2004).

Everything a Copy, Everything a Brand

This decentering of patent-protected "originality" makes the Argentine pharmaceutical market similar to the many other arenas in which intellectual property rights are an oddity and a threat rather than a naturalized form of social, legal, and technical relations (see Vann 2006). Yet we would do well to note the particular dimensions of this decentering in Argentina. As we have seen, at work is not the wholesale absence of intellectual property but rather a reorientation of the relationships between different forms thereof. As Daniel Maceira described the scenario to me, in Argentina, the brand is "divorced" from the patent (interview, 2006), thus flattening out and rewiring the temporal horizon that, in other contexts, purifies the "original" as distinct from and prior to the copy.

This decoupling of the brand from the patent has a number of important corollaries that, together, help set the stage for a consideration of what a generic drug is—and is not—in this context. First, in the Argentine market, as my interlocutors noted repeatedly, *all* drugs are, from the outset, brands. Thus, simultaneously, all are copies, in the sense of being one of many. *Todos son de marca; todos son copias.* Second, as noted previously, leading Argentine *copias* are not necessarily cheaper than other brands, including those made and commercialized by foreign companies. For example, as the long-standing leading brand (*marca líder*), Roemmers's Lotrial ranks with Merck's Renitec among the more expensive brands of enalapril, while Bayer (a German company) and Duncan (from Argentina) are among the labs offering sometimes markedly lower prices for the same presentation.[16]

Third (and therefore), very much unlike in Mexico, hierarchies of value, credibility, and even price are *not* primarily organized around the axis of the original versus the copy, or even the foreign versus the national. Rather, when I asked pharmacists how they narrow the field of potential products in order to make a recommendation, especially in a well-populated class such as the enalaprils, they routinely made a distinction between the reputable "big labs"—a list in which the domestic and the foreign mix easily (Roemmers,

Bagó, Merck, Duncan, Bayer)—and the "little labs" that "no one has heard of." In the case of enalapril, these were smaller Argentine laboratories and a few Brazilian labs.

Without doubt, the bigger Argentine drug laboratories have had a tremendous hold on "brand recognition" among physicians, pharmacists, and consumers. This hold is achieved through various means, from engaging in the kind of direct-to-physician marketing often associated with transnational labs (Lakoff 2004) to their tight relationship to the *obras sociales*, the mutual associations that are a major form of social insurance for many people in Argentina. *Obras sociales* provide medication coverage and health plans for most people with formal employment; these associations contract with particular pharmacy networks and offer 40 percent discounts on drugs to their members. For the most part, the covered drug in any given category will be the *marca líder*, which is often a national product. The power of regulating such access should not be underestimated: the *obra social* for retirees, known by its acronym PAMI, accounts for almost 50 percent of the prescription pharmaceutical market in the country (Federico Tobar, interview, May 19, 2006).

No Patent, No Generic

Where does the generic fit in this picture? Most pointedly, what room is there for the generic when the brand is unmoored or divorced from the original and when there is, indeed, no patent? Many people argue that generics do not actually exist—in fact, they cannot exist—in Argentina. For the physicians, policy makers, and pharmacists whom I interviewed in 2006, the point is simple: without patents—the horizon against which the generic is defined—there is simply no such thing as a generic. *Sin patente, no hay genérico*. This elegant double refusal draws our attention directly to the defining and limited status of the generic drug as a juridical object, often described or assumed to be the "opposite" of, or the outside to, the patented molecule. It thus draws our attention to the specificities of a U.S.-centered perspective on intellectual property, unsettling some easily assumed legal and political vocabularies that place their limits at the organizing axis of private (the patent) and public (the generic).[17] Clearly, the generic is anything but "generic"—generalized, or undifferentiated (see Homedes and Ugalde 2005; see also Hayden 2007). It is a highly specific, legal, technical object, which is defined in its strongest and clearest sense in the context of an enforced patent regime. If the generic requires and assumes the patent, then in Argentina, it is a non sequitur.

However, although "there is no such thing as a generic" in Argentina, there *are* pharmacies that advertise generic medicines, pharmacists who sell them, and people who consume them, in all senses of the word. What is circulated, then, under the name of the generic? It would be more accurate to say "under the generic name," for the generic does not operate in the Argentine context at the level of ontological or legal thing-ness. Rather, it operates through signi-fication—that is, through the process of renaming existing pharmaceuticals.[18] As I was told emphatically by Federico Tobar, the energetic and thoughtful pharmaco-economist who currently directs the secretary of health's Programa Remediar, the unique approach of Argentina in this matter is precisely that it did *not* create a new market for a new thing called generics. Here, the contrast with Mexico surfaces again, and this time the question of copying versus inno-vation surfaces, playfully, at the level of national policy. Tobar argues:

> Mexico was a copy. That is, the Mexican policy is a copy of the American policy, right? The only pharmaceutical politics (or policy) that was truly innovative was ours. In what sense? Well, the United States created an additional market, we could say. It created two markets: one market for original drugs under pat-ent protection, and one market for generic medicines. Argentina's innovation was that the law we passed, 24C49, does not produce a market in generics, like what the United States, Mexico, and Brazil did. It only decrees that you must use [prescribe] drugs by their generic name. . . . So, we didn't create *a market in* generics. What we did, *by decree and by force*, was *turn all medicines into generics*. (interview, May 19, 2006; emphasis added)

All drugs are copies, all are brands—and, in Tobar's assessment, in one fell swoop, all became "generics" as well. That is, all drugs on the market already have a generic name (the name of the molecule on which the drug is based), and it is this name that now must be prescribed. The 2002 law is thus meant to enable and encourage physicians, pharmacists, and consumers to rename (or we might say retroname) existing products and thus to rethink their relation to each other. This move reembeds "leading brands" in a field of similarity and substitutability.[19]

While mechanisms of " genericization" in Mexico and Argentina differ sub-stantially, in many ways their rationales are not radically divergent. Despite its formal, legal impossibility in Argentina, the generic is a concept that does in fact intervene in a way that one might expect and that falls in line with the in-tentions signaled by the secretary of health, Ginés González García. That is, as in Mexico, relatively expensive brand-name drugs *do* dominate the Argentine pharmaceutical market, and physicians and consumers alike have been effec-tively made aware of dominant brands. The project around which the generic (name) is organized in Argentina, as in Mexico, is to enable and encourage consumers to enter a pharmacy and ask for enalapril (the compound) and not Lotrial, the leading brand. This reformulation of the commonplace, formulaic question, "Do you have [insert molecule here] . . . ?" is precisely the moment of substitution on which a promise of improved access to "health," at least in the form of pharmaceuticals, is seen to rest.

Yet of course the key difference between Argentina and Mexico on this front is that in the former, many (but not all) of the expensive, dominant brands are also already copies. In my research in Buenos Aires in 2006, I asked a wide range of pharmacists, including those who work in new pharmacy chains that specifically sell generics, to help me understand the difference between a copied brand that sells as a brand and a copied brand that sells as a generic. In Villa Lugano, a working-class neighborhood on the outskirts of Buenos Aires, one pharmacist explained: "Well, the thing is, they're all the same—everything on these shelves [all stocked with generics] is a brand. What happens is that if people don't recognize a drug from TV [he gestured toward the television mounted high in the corner of the small storefront], then it must be a generic" (interview, May 31, 2006).

This rule of thumb actually holds in many ways. The pharmacies that exclusively sell generics are selling drugs made by the small labs that "no one has heard of," with very little marketing budget. These drugs sell more cheaply than many of the well-known *copias* made by the bigger Argentine labs, most of which have a vivid presence on billboards, on advertisements in the subway, on television and radio, and in physicians' offices. In a context in which all medications are brands and all are copies, it is the combination of price, reputation, and marketing presence that, for now at least, differentiates the brand from the generic. In other words, the concept of the generic in Argentina emerges not out of patent law but out of marketing.[20]

Languages of Access

I argued above that the Argentine double refusal—no patent, no generic—draws our attention to the specificities of a U.S. perspective on intellectual property, unsettling a vocabulary both organized and limited by the axis of private property (the patent) and public domain (the generic). It is only within this framework, of course, that we might automatically define a generic as that which is not patented and branded by a Merck or a Wyeth (Maceira, interview, May 29, 2006). With Argentina's *copias* firmly in view, we must note the degree to which this formulation seamlessly naturalizes the generic (and by extension, the public domain) as both residual in relation to the patent and total in relation to all that is left: everything that is not patented *must* be a generic.

In the context of contested international trade negotiations and reconfigured national regulatory and commercial landscapes, this is not a descriptive statement but a normative one.

Let me explain with reference to some of the effects we might identify from recent efforts in Mexico and Argentina to improve pharmaceutical access through a turn to the generic or, at the very least, the generic name. First, in both Mexico and Argentina, the emergence of (something named) generics *has* resulted in documented decreases in pharmaceutical prices and the broader availability of cheaper medicines (Espicom 1999; González García 2004). "Access," understood specifically and, arguably, problematically, as an increase in private consumption particularly among the poor, may indeed improve with efforts to bring cheaper, lesser-known drugs into a market dominated by expensive, better-known brands.

At the same time, the notion of the generic does not only "open up" access through the enhanced circulation of (some) copies. Its regularization also disciplines and closes down the circulation of (other) copies. This, we might say, can be a second effect of processes of genericization. Consider the wide range of terms for copied prescription pharmaceuticals currently operating in Mexico and Argentina: "similar" drugs, interchangeable generics, regular generics, and branded generics in Mexico and "*copias*," "*genéricos*," drugs made by big labs, drugs made by little labs, and drugs made by the state, in Argentina. The arrival of a particular kind of copy called *the generic*, within such heterogeneous pharmaceutical taxonomies, can have powerful disciplining effects. The argument is particularly pointed in Mexico, where federal health regulators and transnational industry associations have worked together to institute new regulations that will eliminate all kinds of legal (off-patent) copies from the market *except* the most restrictive category of generic, the "interchangeable generic." This designation signals not only that a copied drug is based on the same active substance as the patented original but that it has also been subject to relatively costly "bioequivalence" trials on human subjects to test the rate of absorption of the drug into the bloodstream. Such trials are not required for other categories of generics and copies in Mexico (Hayden 2007). The move to name interchangeable generics as the only legitimate kind of copied drug within a field of *legal* copies is complex, to say the least. It is made in the name of "quality"—itself a highly charged political as well as public health matter—but, as the directors of several domestic generics labs have noted, it also produces a costly obstacle to the entry of domestic companies into the generics market (see Hayden 2007). In Mexico, the interchangeable generic figures strongly in efforts to subject the unruly world of copied pharmaceuticals to standards and terminology that are, as the business intelligence community likes to say, "internationally compliant."

But what of Argentina, in which the generic (name) enters a field of like products in such a way that the kinds of domaining effected in Mexico seem almost irrelevant or at least—for the moment—impossible? This temporal qualifier is important, for the classificatory universe sketched above should not necessarily be expected to remain static for long. Referring to the distinctive feature of current Argentine pharmaceutical patent law, which exists but is not enforced, Federico Tobar told me: "We have a patent law, but we don't give [pharmaceutical] patents. It's brilliant. It's also a bit like spitting into the air; sooner or later it will come down and hit you in the face" (interview, May 19, 2006). Tobar was not alone among my many interlocutors in suggesting that an enforced pharmaceutical patent regime in Argentina is a distinct possibility within the next decade; a bit like the effects of gravity, he suggested, it may well be inevitable.

In this case, we might expect the generic to do and *be* different things as well. Consider the current situation in India, whose powerful drug industry has long been a key supplier of cheaper "generics" for Brazil, Thailand, and other nations in the global South as well as the global North (see Sunder Rajan 2006; Shadlen 2007). As in Argentina, the Indian industry was forged in the absence of a pharmaceutical patent regime, and the leading brands have tended to be domestically made copies (Ecks, pers. comm., January 30, 2007). Yet on January 1, 2005, India's ten-year period of exemption from TRIPS came to an end and a new pharmaceutical patent law entered into force. Stefan Ecks notes what might be expected in the coming years, as he has observed the simultaneous emergence of a notion of original drugs and consequently of "generics": "The increasing entry of patent-protected 'originals' for the first time *creates* the perception of 'generics' [as a distinctive kind of drug] among Indian patients" (Stefan Ecks, pers. comm., 2007; original emphasis).

Indeed, as pharmaceutical patent regimes do come into force (with all due regard for the considerable contestation and heterogeneity thereof) in nations such as India and—possibly—Argentina, we may have to pose a question about *corollary* forms of expansion. In India, and perhaps in Argentina, the categorically distinctive object called the generic arrives not *against the patent* but in a neatly bundled package *with* it. For the legally sanctioned public domain travels only as far as does intellectual property. It is in this sense that I am interested in both the promises and the limits of a politics of access, equity, and distribution tethered to the language of intellectual property itself. This point is relevant not only to the matter of copied pharmaceuticals but also to a wide range of arenas of knowledge—and technological production—in which alternative strategies for ensuring equity of access and distribution have come to be configured through the idiom of the public domain. I would thus urge a critical awareness of the implications of ever-expanding commitments to "securing" the public domain or "commons." In many progressive political-technical projects in the United States and Europe, these idioms have come to stand for the only possible antidotes to the excesses of privatization. But does the legally sanctioned public domain constitute the only idiom or mechanism through which to rethink access, equity, and a politics of copying?

This query does not necessarily make the "illicit" copy the answer to problems of (pharmaceutical) access. This chapter is organized, after all, around the fact that the absence of the patent and the prevalence of unlicensed copies in Argentina have not helped "access" in the form of a proliferation of cheaper drugs; it was the high prices of unlicensed copies that prompted Argentina's 2002 generic prescription decree in the first place. Rather, I am concerned with a too-easy reification of the public domain as both the universal and constitutive "outside" or antidote to the patent and to other forms of intellectual property. We have been reminded in other contexts—particularly in indigenous and postcolonial critiques of renewed interests in bioprospecting and biogenetic collection—that the public domain is *made* and *not found*. If pharmaceutical access is to be configured around the question of what may count as a viable politics of the copy, then it is both analytically and politically important that we not lose sight of this point and its incitement to analyze the domaining effects of intellectual property and its corollary, the public domain.

NOTES

1. A modified version of this essay was published in Portuguese in the journal *Sociologias* (Brazil) in 2008: special issue, *Conhecimentos, redes e sociedade, Edição semestral* 10 (19): 62–90. I gratefully acknowledge the thoughtful engagement, comments, and assistance of Andrew Lakoff, Daniel Maceira, Federico Tobar, Horacio Sívori, Carlos Forment, Sylvia Hirsch, Mario Biagioli, Ivan da Costa Marques, Stefan Ecks, Ken Shadlen, and Hélène Mialet.

2. The relationship between the roiling crisis and medication shortages is not a straightforward one; it is not just that prices skyrocketed and therefore people could not afford them, though this certainly happened. Argentine human rights organizations and other chroniclers of the crisis have also documented acts of financial speculation and hording by the *droguerías*, the powerful distribution committees that act as intermediaries between laboratories and pharmacies. The accusation is that the *droguerías* fueled shortages by not releasing drugs to pharmacies unless each previous delivery

was paid off in full. Given the devaluations, such payments became increasingly difficult for many pharmacies, leaving these commercial outlets without inventory. In particular, shortages of insulin led well-organized diabetes advocacy and patient groups to force the government to declare a medical emergency. I am grateful to Sylvia Brunoldi of the Liga Argentina de Protección al Diabético for her perspective on these questions (interview, May 22, 2006).

3. In this program, the government buys medicines at low cost from transnational firms. These medicines are distributed for free (and in packaging that does not display a commercial name) through primary care centers located throughout the country (Tobar 2004).

4. The Doha Declaration is formally entitled the Declaration on the TRIPS Agreement and Public Health (November 14, 2001), doc. WT/MIN(01)/DEC/2 (November 20, 2001). For a helpful overview, see Abbott 2005.

5. See the press release posted on the Web site of the organization Knowledge Ecology International, http://www.keionline.org/index.php?option=com_content&task=view&id=46&Itemid=1, accessed May 15, 2007.

6. For an excellent discussion and links to resources, see the Web site of the Washington, DC–based organization, Center for the Project on Technology, http://www.cptech.org/ip/health/cl/cipro/.

7. There has been precisely such a reconfiguration in the United States following the 1984 Hatch-Waxman Act, which removed some of the previously existing barriers to generics' entry into the market once a drug patent expired.

8. It should be noted that in Brazil, state financing of the biomedical and pharmaceutical sectors has been accompanied, since 1996, by what João Biehl calls a dynamic relation to transnational firms, which have remained highly involved in the Brazilian market for antiretrovirals (Biehl 2004, 2005, 2006).

9. As Andrew Lakoff notes, the Argentine pharmaceutical market is, in this sense, "a peculiar one": Argentina joins the United States, Germany, Switzerland, and Japan in a list of "the only countries whose domestic producers have a greater market share than foreign ones" (2004: 196).

10. See the excellent, extensive time line of this dispute posted on the Web site of Center for the Project on Technology, http://www.cptech.org/ip/health/c/argentina/argentinatimeline.html.

11. There was a flurry of activity in 2000 in which eighty-two patents were granted in a market that comprises thousands of products.

12. Though not always to the degree that foreign companies would like. One might consider here the *etiqueta* (label) shops in Buenos Aires selling labels and tags with names and logos ranging from those of neighborhood community groups to Wrangler and other transnational brands.

13. Consider Lipitor, the brand name of Pfizer's blockbuster cholesterol-lowering drug atorvastatin, which is still under patent (but as we know through the distinctive medium of spam, something called "generic Lipitor" is widely available online; Pfizer is pursuing legal action against Internet merchants). In Argentina there are three atorvastatin products on the market, two made by Argentine laboratories (Northia and Bioquímico Argentina) and the third by the Brazilian lab Richet. Pfizer itself does not directly market Lipitor or atorvastatin in Argentina.

14. We might also usefully think in terms of seriality. Theorists of a markedly different realm of intellectual property and industrial production—Anglo-American copyright regimes regarding literature, works of art, and other cultural productions—have made amply clear that certain kinds of products (mass-produced cultural works) do not always or fundamentally revolve around their relation to a presumably foundational "original" (Lury 1993: 43–44). As Celia Lury notes, drawing on Umberto Eco, a notion of seriality (such as in the TV series) can overshadow the straw idea of the copy as a replica of and therefore deviation from an authentic original (Lury 1993: 42–43). Though we are indeed talking about quite different objects and forms of production, circulation,

and consumption, this analytic shift of emphasis to the copy as part of a regime of seriality is intensely germane to the context at hand.

15. *Current Patents Gazette*, February 18, 2000.

16. As of May 2007, sample list prices for a package of thirty pills at 10 mg each were as follows: Merck's Renitec, $a26.89 (Argentine pesos); Roemmers's Lotrial, $a19.79; Bayer's Baypril, $a17.42; and Duncan's Enaldun, $a14.81. http://www.alfabeta.net.

17. It also, not incidentally, recalls anthropologist Marilyn Strathern's pointed double refusal, "no nature, no culture" (Strathern 1980), on which I draw with some poetic license here. Strathern's essay by that title drew on work in Melanesia to argue against easy recourse to familiar and linked chains of oppositions (public/private, male/female, nature/culture) in ethnographic analysis. Needless to say, "Argentina" and "Melanesia" serve as placeholders for different kinds of difference vis-à-vis Anglo-American technical, legal, and epistemological norms and forms. But as noted in the text, the double refusal works analogously here.

18. Lakoff articulates the point well in his discussion of the Argentine pharmaceutical market in the late 1990s, when he notes that "key developments were taking place in terms of crafting brand-consumer relationships rather than at the level of making new things" (2004: 196). His reference was to the production of copied drugs rather than "new" or "innovative" drugs (and the importance of the branding relationship to the former), but the same could be said of the emergence of a move toward "generics."

19. We might note that this is a kind of branding or marketing in reverse, in which "interchange-ability" and similarity become, themselves, marks of distinction. This is a point worthy of elabora-tion; space constraints prevent me from doing so here.

20. See Nathan Greenslit (2002) for an inverse account of the degree to which marketing techniques are, in the United States, being used to justify extending patents on essentially the same molecules whose patents are on the verge of expiration.

REFERENCES

Abbott, Frederick. 2005. "The WTO Medicines Decision: World Pharmaceutical Trade and the Protection of Public Health." *American Journal of International Law* 99: 317–358.

Biehl, Joao. 2006. "Pharmaceutical Governance." In Adriana Petryna, Andrew Lakoff, and Arthur Kleinman, eds., *Global Pharmaceuticals: Ethics, Markets, Practices*, pp. 206–239. Durham, NC: Duke University Press.

———. 2005. *Vita: Life in a Zone of Social Abandonment*. Berkeley: University of California Press.

———. 2004. "The Activist State: Global Pharmaceuticals, AIDS, and Citizenship in Brazil." *Social Text* 22 (3): 105–132.

Butler, Judith. 1990. *Gender Trouble: Feminism and the Subversion of Identity*. London: Routledge.

Callon, Michel. 1998. Introduction. In Michel Callon, ed., *The Laws of the Markets*, pp. 244–276. Oxford: Sociological Review.

Correa, Carlos. 1998. "Implementing TRIPs in Developing Countries." Third World Network. Available at http://www.twnside.org.sg/title/ment-cn.htm. Last accessed July 15, 2010.

da Costa Marques, Ivan. 2005. "Cloning Computers: From Rights of Possession to Rights of Cre-ation." *Science as Culture* 14 (2): 139–160.

Espicom Business Intelligence, Limited. 2003. *Report on Mexico*. World Pharmaceutical Markets Series, April 11.

González García, Ginés. 2004. "Presentación de la Política Nacional de Medicamentos en la República del Perú." 29 March. Available at http://www.msal.gov.ar/htm/site/discursos_des.asp?ID=39. Accessed May 15, 2007.

Greenslit, Nathan. 2002. "Pharmaceutical Branding: Identity, Individuality, and Illness." *Molecular Interventions* 2: 342–345.

Hayden, Cori. 2007. "A Generic Solution? Pharmaceuticals and the Politics of the Similar in Mexico." *Current Anthropology* 48 (4): 475–495.

Homedes, Núria, and Antonio Ugalde. 2005. "Multisource Drug Policies in Latin America: Survey of 10 Countries." *Bulletin of the World Health Organization* 83 (1): 64–70.

Katz, Jorge, and Gustavo Burachik. 2007. "La industria farmacéutica y farmoquímica argentina en los años 90." In Jorge Katz, ed., *Apertura económica y desregulación en el mercado de medicamentos*, pp. 81–123. Buenos Aires: CEPAL/IDRC, Alianza Editorial.

Lakoff, Andrew. 2005. *Pharmaceutical Reason: Knowledge and Value in Global Psychiatry*. Cambridge: Cambridge University Press.

———. 2004. "The Private Life of Numbers: Audit Firms and the Government of Expertise in Post-Welfare Argentina." In Stephen Collier and Aihwa Ong, eds., *Global Assemblages: Governmentality, Technology, Ethics*, pp. 194–213. New York: Blackwell.

Lury, Celia. 2004. *Brands: The Logos of the Global Economy*. London: Routledge.

———. 1993. *Cultural Rights: Technology, Legality, and Personality*. London: Routledge.

Petryna, Adriana, Andrew Lakoff, and Arthur Kleinman, eds. 2006. *Global Pharmaceuticals: Ethics, Markets, Practices*. Durham, NC: Duke University Press.

Shadlen, Kenneth. 2007. "The Political Economy of AIDS Treatment: Intellectual Property and the Transformation of Generic Supply." *International Studies Quarterly* 51: 559–581.

Strathern, Marilyn. 1980. "No Nature, No Culture: The Hagen Case." In Carol MacCormack and Marilyn Strathern, eds., *Nature, Culture, and Gender*, pp. 174–222. Cambridge: Cambridge University Press.

Sunder Rajan, Kaushik. 2006. *Biocapital: The Constitution of Postgenomic Life*. Durham, NC: Duke University Press.

Tobar, Federico. 2004. "Políticas para promoción del acceso a medicamentos: El caso del Programa Remediar de Argentina." Technical Paper 002/2004 presented to the Interamerican Development Bank, Washington, DC, January.

van der Geest, Sjaak, and Susan Reynolds Whyte, eds. 1988. *The Context of Medicines in Developing Countries: Studies in Pharmaceutical Anthropology*. Amsterdam: Het Spinhuis.

Vann, Elizabeth. 2006. "The Limits of Authenticity in Vietnamese Consumer Markets." *American Anthropologist* 108 (2): 286–296.

17

Inventing Race as a Genetic Commodity in Biotechnology Patents

A new phenomenon is emerging in biotechnology research and product development—the strategic use of race as a genetic category to obtain patent protection and drug approval.[1] A dramatic rise in the use of
race in biotechnology and related patents since the completion of the
first draft of the human genome in 2000 indicates that researchers and
affiliated commercial enterprises are coming to see social categories of
race as presenting opportunities for gaining, extending, or protecting
monopoly market protection for an array of biotechnological products and services. Racialized patents are also providing the basis for
similarly race-based clinical trial designs, drug development, capital
raising , and marketing strategies that carry the construction of race as
genetic out to ever-widening and consequential segments of society.

The introduction of race in the field of patent law as an adjunct
to biotechnological inventions is thus producing a new political geography of intellectual property. As patents are racialized, racial identity itself is becoming a patentable commodity whose value is being
appropriated to solidify market control and extend the market life of
products. The people capitalizing on race are not necessarily those who

belong to the racially identified groups but rather corporations that are literally investing their patents and products with race to gain commercial advantage in the research, development, and marketing of new biotechnology products. This commercial dynamic treats social categories of race implicated in biomedical research as a sort of raw material that the patent process refines into a "novel" and "useful" manufactured product composed of genetic race. In patenting race, biotechnological inventions actually produce (or reproduce) race as genetic. Patenting race may thus have profound implications both for the equitable distribution of benefits derived from biotechnology and for broader social understandings and mobilizations of race.

Part 1 of this chapter introduces broad themes and issues concerning the relation of race and genetics in biotechnology in the context of a brief discussion of BiDil, the first drug ever approved by the Food and Drug Administration with a race-specific indication—for the treatment of heart failure in African Americans. Part 2 discusses the rise of the new phenomenon of racially marked biotechnology patents. Part 3 considers some of the broader theoretical implications of racial biotechnology patents and explores an emerging political geography of intellectual property law. The chapter concludes with the observation that biotechnology corporations are mining the raw material of race as a social category and using the patent process to refine it into a natural construct in order to gain patent protection and market advantage. The new commodity value of patented race depends on its ultimate relation to living people who identify with particular racial groups. In the end, though, it is biotechnology corporations who are appropriating race to their own benefit.

1. BiDil: Portent of Things to Come

Since the inception of the Human Genome Project much time and attention has been devoted to ensuring that biological knowledge emerging from advances in genetic research is not used inappropriately to make socially constructed racial[2] categories appear biologically given or "natural" (see, e.g. Lock; Marks; Reardon; Zalinskas and Balint). Race is not a genetically coherent concept (Collins; Goodman). Rather, race is best understood as a complex and dynamic social construct (AAA 1997, 1998). Since the 1970s, scientists have understood that race will statistically explain only a small portion of human variation (Lewontin). As a 2001 editorial in the journal *Nature Genetics* put it, "Scientists have long been saying that at the genetic level there is more variation between two individuals in the same population than between populations and that there is no biological basis for 'race'" ("Census").

Despite this general understanding of the relationship between genes and race, on June 23, 2005, the U.S. Food and Drug Administration formally approved the heart-failure drug BiDil to treat heart failure in "self-identified black patients" (FDA). Widely hailed throughout the media and professional journals as the first "ethnic" drug, BiDil has become a focal point for debates over the appropriate use of racial categories in biomedical research, drug development, and clinical practice.

The FDA approval was based on results from the African-American Heart Failure Trial (A-HeFT) that were published the previous November in the *New England Journal of Medicine* (Taylor et al.). A-HeFT was funded by NitroMed, BiDil's corporate sponsor. The trial design, approved by the FDA, was itself pathbreaking because it included *only* self-identified African Americans. The results therefore give the impression that BiDil works *only* in African Americans. This is not the case. The trial investigators themselves concede that BiDil will work in people regardless of race. Without a comparison population, the investigators cannot even claim that the drug works differently in African Americans than in any other group (Kahn 2004, 2005a).

Underlying the trail design, however, is a race-specific patent that is premised on a biological or genetic definition of race. The Patent and Trademark Office (PTO) issued the patent on October 15, 2002 (U.S. Patent no. 6,465,463). It confers intellectual property protection for the method of using the drug to treat heart failure in African Americans until 2020. This is thirteen years longer than a previous patent issued in 1987 to the same inventor for the same method of using the same drug in the general population without regard to race. In this case, bringing race into the patent system allowed the inventor to gain a substantial extension of the intellectual property monopoly. With a projected annual revenue stream of $1–$3 billion, the additional thirteen years amounted to a potential windfall for NitroMed. BiDil's race-specific patent provided the underlying support that drove NitroMed's subsequent development of a race-specific trial design, its campaign to raise capital (first through private venture funding and later through a public offering of stock in 2004), the approach to the FDA for race-specific approval, and its massive marketing campaign to third-party payers, individual doctors, and the public at large (Kahn 2004; Sankar and Kahn).

As biotechnology patents become racialized, they are coming to drive broader scientific, political, and public understandings and uses of racial categories. As scholars such as Cheryl Harris and Richard Thomson Ford have noted, American law has a long tradition of characterizing property and physical spaces in racial terms—often to devastating effect (Harris; Ford). Whether in the most egregious and obvious form of race-based slavery or in subtler identifications of neighborhoods or even names with race making it more difficult to obtain mortgages or jobs, the nature and value of property has long been profoundly influenced in and through its association with race.

Previous associations of race and property have generally devalued racial minorities. Certain more recent legal classifications of race, as in affirmative action, have the potential to offer challenges to exclusionary conceptions of racialized property rights (Harris). Indeed, since the 1960s, new civil rights and fair-housing laws, combined with the ebb and flow of affirmative action initiatives, have provided for American minorities a substantial, if tenuous, counterpart to what George Lipsitz has termed "the possessive investment in whiteness" (Lipsitz). The racialization of BiDil's patent appears to be more in line with such assertedly "benign" uses of racial categories and has in fact added commercial value to the drug—hence the readiness of such groups as the Association of Black Cardiologists and the Congressional Black Caucus to support A-HeFT (Kahn 2004). In this regard, BiDil has gained cultural capital by being characterized as a means to redress an important health disparity in a historically underserved population. Certainly, the underlying patents and commercial market value of BiDil have given new meaning to a concept of a "possessive investment" in "blackness." In the case of BiDil, the investment is being made by NitroMed. It is also NitroMed that is reaping the commercial benefits of appropriating race to mark its product.

2. The Rise of Racial Patents

A modern patent is a "government issued grant which confers upon the patent owner the *right to exclude* others from 'making, using, offering for sale, or selling the invention throughout the United States or importing the invention into the United States' for a period of 20 years ending from the filing date of the application" (Chisum et al.: 2, citing 35 U.S.C. §154). All patent applications must meet several statutory requirements. The most prominent of these are known as "useful[ness]" (or utility) (35 U.S.C. §101), "novelty" (35 U.S.C. §102), "non-obvious[ness]" (35 U.S.C. §103), and "specification" (35 U.S.C. §112).

The usefulness, or utility, requirement can be met by a showing that the claimed invention has a specific, substantial, and credible utility. Specificity requires the use to be specific to the character of the claimed subject matter. (An oft-cited negative example is the failure to meet the requirement by specifying the utility of a genetically engineered mouse as "snake food.") A use is "substantial" if it involves a real-world use that represents an end in itself. A "credible" utility is one that would be believable by a person skilled in the field of the invention (Elliott). The novelty requirement is met if the invention is not "anticipated" (described in its relevant particulars) in a single reference of "prior art," (e.g., another patent or a published scholarly paper). The non-obviousness requirement is met if "the differences between the subject matter sought to be patented and the prior are such that the subject matter as a whole" would not be perceived as obvious to a "person having ordinary skill in the art" (PHOSITA) (35 U.S.C. §103[a]). Specificity requires a written description of the invention that is adequate to enable a PHOSITA to make and use the invention (Elliott).

DNA is patented in order ultimately to bring some DNA-related product to market. When that product is based on clinical trials, federal guidelines mandate that data be collected with reference to social categories of race and ethnicity that are promulgated by the Office of Management and Budget (OMB) (OMB 1997; NIH; HHS 1997, 2003a, 2003b). The OMB standards set forth five minimum categories for data on race: American Indian or Alaska Native, Asian, Black or African American, Native Hawaiian or Other Pacific Islander, and White. There are two categories for data on ethnicity: Hispanic or Latino and Not Hispanic or Latino. These categories provide the basis for the classification of all federal data on race and ethnicity, most notably, the census. The OMB standards, however, contain an important caveat: "The racial and ethnic categories set forth in the standards should not be interpreted as being primarily biological or genetic in reference" (OMB 1997).

Biomedical professionals may link race to genetic categories with the goal of somehow facilitating their research or practice. Such uses are generally premised on loose (often uninterrogated) understandings of potential correlations between the frequencies of certain genetic variations ("alleles") and certain racial groups. In this context, biomedical professionals often speak of using race as a "surrogate" for underlying genetic variation, while acknowledging that race itself is not genetic (Bonham, Warschauer-Baker, and Collins). But when a gene-related race-identified patent is issued, it legally marks race as, at least in part, a genetic category—i.e., *to the extent that the patent is premised on a direct connection between race and genetics, it takes the social category of race and transforms it into a "natural" category grounded in genetics.*

Patent law is supposed to promote the invention of new and useful products. In recent biotechnology patents, race and ethnicity are being exploited in new ways that do not spur the invention of new products but rather the reinvention of existing products as racial or ethnic. In so doing patent law both racializes the space of intellectual property, transforming it into a terrain for the renaturalization of race as some sort of "objective" biological category, and commodifies race and ethnicity as goods to be patented and subjected to the dictates of market forces.

A review of "Claims" and "Abstract" sections of gene-related patents and patent applications[3] filed between 1976 and 2007 indicates a significant trend toward using race in gene-related patents, with a marked increase in just the past few years. A typical patent is divided into several sections. The claims section presents a primary focus for investigation because is the legal heart of a patent. The claims specify the legally operative scope of the patent, defining the formal legal territory covered by an invention. The abstract is the basic summary presentation of the central purpose of the patent. Other sections typically include a "Background" or "Description of Invention" along with drawings or other technical support data. An overview of the claims or abstract sections of patents that employ OMB Statistical Directive 15 categories of race and ethnicity[4] in a manner that implies or asserts a genetic component to or basis for race[5] is presented in table 17.1.

The results indicate a remarkable trend toward the increasing use of racial and ethnic categories in relation to patenting gene-related biomedical innovations. The first use of racial and ethnic categories in a published gene-related patent did not occur until 1998. Pending patent applications indicate a more than fivefold increase in the use of racial or ethnic categories over existing published patents. Among pending patent applications almost 60 percent of the usage of racial and ethnic categories occurs in patents filed between 2005 and 2007. This is not because race has not previously been used in biomedical research but because it is taking on increasing significance in the commercial world of biotechnology patenting. While there are some overlapping references (i.e., patents that use more than one OMB category), the trend remains powerful and clearly parallels the availability of vast new amounts of genetic information being produced and classified in federally sponsored databases.

Race is being used both offensively and defensively in these patents. In cases such as BiDil, patents employ race affirmatively to revitalize or extend the reach and force of a patent. In many other patents, the applicants appear to be invoking race in a strategically defensive manner to provide added protection against possible patent challenges. The structure of a typical claims section of a patent begins with the first claim being as broad as possible. Successive claims generally provide narrower and narrower focus to the territory covered by the patent. The idea is that if the broadest claim is struck down by the patent examiner or a subsequent challenge, the narrower claims may still survive. Patent claims are thus structured something like a medieval castle, with an outer ring encompassing the most territory with successively smaller rings providing additional layers of protection back to the core area of the castle keep.

Table 17.1. Gene-related patents and patent applications mentioning race or ethnicity, 1976–2007

Category	Issued patents		Patent applications
	1976–1997	1998–2007	2001–2007
Race	0	2	15
Ethnic	0	9	39
African American/Black	0	7	14
Alaska Native	0	0	0
Asian	0	1	17
Caucasian/White	0	6	44
Hispanic/Latino	0	3	7
Native American	0	1	14
Pacific Islander	0	0	1
Total	0	29	154

A patent application for the "Detection of susceptibility to autoimmune diseases," filed on July 1, 2004, exemplifies the use of concentric rings of race to provide maximum protection for its claims. Its first three claims are as follows:

1. A method for determining an individual's risk for type 1 diabetes comprising: detecting the presence of a type 1 diabetes-associated class I HLA-C allele in a nucleic acid sample of the individual, wherein the presence of said allele indicates the *individual's* risk for type 1 diabetes.
2. The method of claim 1, wherein the individual is of *Asian* descent.
3. The method of claim 1, wherein the individual is of *Filipino* descent. [emphasis added] (U.S. Patent Application 20040126794)

Claim 1 is not race-specific, referring only to an "individual's" risk. Claim 2 takes a smaller subset of humanity, which it marks as "Asian." Claim 3 takes yet a smaller subset of the group "Asian," which it marks as "Filipino." In each case the categories are clearly linked to genetic alleles, forcefully implying a genetic basis to the specific racial groups. The legal and commercial imperatives of effective patenting have thus promoted the transmutation of variable genetic frequencies across populations that nonetheless all share common alleles into bounded genetic categories that are marked as distinct and functionally different.

3. The Emerging Political Geography of Racialized Intellectual Property

To more fully appreciate the dynamics of strategic reification of race as genetic in the world of racialized patents, it is useful to explore (1) how basing patents on race changes the concepts and claims that can be made for, about, or on behalf of race; and (2) how patenting race changes the terrain of intellectual property.

Racializing Patents: What Does Race Add?

Racializing biotechnology patents racializes the basic criteria of patent validity: utility, novelty, nonobviousness, and specification.

Utility

The requirement of utility is generally regarded as fairly de minimis, demanding only that the invention achieve some sort of pragmatic result. Often, the concept of utility is conflated with marketability—if someone is willing to pay for it, it must be useful (Schecter and Thomas; Kahn 2003). It is apparent that invoking race is deemed "useful" by patent applicants, in both the colloquial and formal legal sense of the term. Race is most commonly useful as a defensive claim, adding another ring to the battlements of patent protection. But race can only buttress a patent to the extent it is deemed relevant to the utility of the invention. A racialized biotechnology patent typically links race to presumed group-based genetic differences underlying different responses to drugs or disease susceptibility. While it constructs race as useful, it also invariably constructs it as genetic. In a curious tautology, race becomes commercially useful precisely because it is patentable—and it is patentable as useful because it is reified as genetic. The primary utility of race, however, is not scientific but legal and commercial.

Novelty

To meet the requirement of novelty, an invention must not be "anticipated" in a single prior art disclosure that contains every element of the claimed invention (Schecter and Thomas: 363–364). Almost any biotechnology invention can be made to appear novel through the simple addition of race. This is what happened in the case of BiDil. Jay Cohn, the holder of the BiDil patents, first filed in 1987 for a non-race-specific patent to use the generic components of BiDil to treat heart failure in the general population. This patent expired in 2007. After the FDA turned down the first new drug application for BiDil in 1997 (on the grounds that the statistics submitted in support of the application were too muddled to make a finding as to whether BiDil worked), Cohn filed a reformulated race-specific application in 2000. The resulting patent does not expire until 2020. It provided the basis for licensing the rights to BiDil to NitroMed. In turn, the race-specific patent enabled NitroMed to raise over $30 million in venture capital to fund the A-HeFT trials, which provided the basis for the FDA's ultimate approval of BiDil as a race-specific drug in June 2005 (Kahn 2004; Kahn, 2005b). For Jay Cohn and NitroMed, the patentable "novelty" of race added time and money to their invention—to wit, an extra thirteen years of monopoly market control over the use of BiDil and essential venture capital needed to get A-HeFT off the ground.

Nonobviousness

Explicitly marked race becomes nonobvious when the unstated norm is white—it being nonobvious that unmarked population groups would contain nonwhites, or its being assumed in retrospect that the unstated white norm did not comprise nonwhites. Ironically, this dynamic works in the context of biotechnology patents in part because of the hard work done by social scientists to mark race as a social category (see, e.g., AAA 1998; ASA). It is precisely because patent applicants and PTO examiners are willing to accept the "obviousness" of social race that race as genetic can be construed as " nonobvious." To solidify the definitive boundaries of a biotechnology patent, surrogate markers and correlations become naturalized into fixed racial categories, thereby producing a hitherto unappreciated, purportedly "genetic" component to race.

Specification

The written description of the invention must be sufficient to enable a person skilled in the art to make and use the invention (Schecter and Thomas: 393–394). Whereas nonobviousness relies on a previously unseen genetic basis for race, enablement relies on the obviousness of race as a social category to facilitate the later use of the invention by other PHOSITAs. Thus, for example, a reference to "Asians" or "Blacks" or "Caucasians" is deemed enabling precisely because those categories are not seen as problematic. Rather, they are "merely" social and hence obvious. Social scientific constructions of race as complex, difficult, and problematic categories cannot be allowed to enter this realm because they would challenge the assumptions underlying the patent's racial enablement.

Roger Schecter and John Thomas note that in so-called unpredictable arts, such as biotechnology or some branches of chemistry, courts are often stricter in reviewing whether a particular written description of an invention is sufficiently enabling because "small changes to the structure of the invention may lead to vastly different behaviors." They provide the example of "a very minor alteration to a functional chemical compound that may render it inert for a particular purpose" (Schecter and Thomas: 397) Given the contingent, socially constructed, and temporally variable nature of race, one might argue that race itself should be considered a sort of "unpredictable art." If so constructed, racial patents would require far more careful and elaborated definitions of race than are currently employed. Existing biotechnology patents, however, employ race as an unproblematic, fixed, and "predictable" construct. Thus these patents also "enable" a simplistic conception of social race in order to produce a reified conception of race as genetic.

Patenting Race: The Political Geography of Racialized Patents

Refining Social Race into Genetic Race

A "product of nature" cannot be patented. To be rendered patentable, it must be "purified and isolated" through human interventions to produce a substance that does not otherwise exits. Historically, this involved complex chemicals such as adrenaline (see, e.g., *Parke-Davis & Co. v. H. K. Mulford Co.*, 189 F. 95 [S.D.N.Y. 1911]). In the genomic era, however, it has come to encompass engineered complementary DNA (cDNA) that is synthesized in vitro by using an enzyme (reverse transcriptase) that produces a molecule containing only those nucleotide sequences from the original DNA that code for proteins (exons). While clearly scientific and technical in origin, isolation and purification are distinctively legal concepts when it comes to granting a patent (Kahn 2003). The PTO has asserted that "the inventor's discovery of a gene can be the basis for a patent of the genetic composition *isolated from its natural state* and processed through *purifying* steps that *separate* the gene from other molecules *naturally associated* with it" (66 *Federal Register* at 1093; emphasis added).

Sheila Jasanoff observes that "biotechnology . . . renders continually problematic the boundary between the natural and the unnatural" (Jasanoff: 895). The authoritative discourses of science and law, however, are rendered precarious by such uncertainty. Those seeking the legal recognition of patentability for biotechnological achievements work hard to resolidify and naturalize the boundary between natural and unnatural. Thus the PTO recognizes arguments that scientific intervention creates a patentable object by severing it from its "natural associations." The PTO constructs cDNA as isolated, not only in the sense of separating out exons, but more powerfully, in the sense of separating the genetic material itself from nature. This is not a scientific process but a legal one. Scientists may create cDNA, but the PTO draws the line between nature and artifice. Similarly, purification involves stripping the genetic material of its identity as a part of nature—purifying it of its "natural associations."

In contrast, race enters the world of biotechnology as a social construct. It serves as an admitted surrogate for presumed underlying genetic variations in particular populations. The patent process takes race as a social category and recodes it as "natural" by according it legal force as a component of a biotechnological invention. As corporations and markets come to attach commercial value to race as genetic, there will be increased incentives to produce more examples of race as genetic in a commercial context. Social race here becomes analogous to a sort of raw material that the patent process refines (i.e., purifies and strips of its "social associations") into a "novel" and "useful" manufactured product composed of genetic race. In patenting race, biotechnological inventions actually produce (or reproduce) race as genetic.

The Segregated Genome

It is useful to compare the genome as racialized through biotechnology patents to the legally managed production of racially identified neighborhoods in residential communities. John Calmore refers to the "racialization of space" as "the process by which residential location and community are carried and placed on racial identity" (Calmore: 1236). Through a series of legal and regulatory interventions ranging from racially restrictive covenants to zoning laws and sanctioned redlining, specific social and residential spaces in the United States have become racially marked and segregated over time (Ford; Aoki 2000). In a similar manner, racialized patents are using the legal system to inscribe portions of the genome (usually identified as areas of differing allele frequency) with distinct racial identities. Such inscription, in effect, creates a segregated genome with "black," "white," "Asian," "Hispanic," etc., neighborhoods.

Patents that exploit such racialized neighborhoods of the genome literally capitalize on race. Unlike residential segregation, biotechnology patents have the added convenience of being able to make use of racially marked genes without having to deal with the inconvenient presence of actual human bodies who might raise objections to being exploited. In the context of biotechnology patents, race becomes a statistical concept based on correlations and frequencies—not on the embodied experiences of living people walking in real time through physical space. In the new statistically informed legal schemes of biotechnology patents, such correlations provide the basis for claims that segregate the genome into racially identified neighborhoods. Some of these racial neighborhoods, in turn, may be marked as genomic "ghettos," areas associated with blight, disease, or weakness. But, as in contemporary dynamics of urban gentrification (Aoki 1993), a blighted neighborhood may also present a distinctive opportunity for development—as NitroMed discovered with BiDil.

Genomic segregation thus keeps races separate in order to develop and market products. It manages relations among haplotypes and allele frequencies rather than housing patterns or school enrollments. The racialized patent divorces race from the body, reducing it to a function of correlation and allelic frequencies. Thus molecularized, race is more readily susceptible to scientific and commercial manipulations to appropriate its value in a manner that both naturalizes it and inhibits interference from individuals who represent embodied claims to a particular racial identity.

This is made abundantly clear in a patent application for "Methods for obtaining and using haplotype data," filed December 21, 2001 (U.S. Patent Application 20040267458) by scientists from Genaissance Pharmaceuticals. This application begins with a broad claim to "a method of generating a haplotype database for a population." It goes on in claim 8 to specify that the reference population may include an "ethnic population," thereby directly connecting ethnicity to genetics. In describing the "field of the invention" after the claims section, the patent marks pharmacogenomic uses as primary, noting that genetic haplotype information can be used "to predict an individual's susceptibility to a particular disease and/or their response to a particular drug." To this point, the Genaissance patent uses race and ethnicity broadly, without singling out any particular group. Strikingly, however, in the "Detailed Description of the Invention," the patent elaborates on one particular embodiment of the invention, declaring: "Analysis of the candidate gene(s) (or other loci) requires an approximate knowledge of what haplotypes exist for the candidate gene(s) (or other loci) and of their frequencies in the general population. To do this, *a reference population is recruited, or cells from individuals of known ethnic origin* are obtained from a public or private source. The population *preferably* covers the major *ethnogeographic groups in the U.S., European, and Far Eastern pharmaceutical markets*" (U.S. Patent Application #20040267458; emphasis added). This description, whether intentionally or not, is a brazen declaration that ethnicity only matters where markets matter: the United States, Europe, and the Far East. The rest of the world, including Africa, South America, the Middle East, and South Asia, apparently is irrelevant. The patent invokes ethnicity not solely as a shortcut to finding genetic correlations with particular population groups but also, and inextricably, as a basis for developing drugs for major markets. In this context, the reference to "ethnogeographic groups" invokes a quasi-genetic category conflating ethnicity with geography as a basis for identifying lucrative markets. Ethnicity here becomes a function not only of genes but of markets.

Drawing on the work of critical geographers such as Edward Soja and David Harvey, Keith Aoki notes that "spaces are produced and maintained by a dynamic set of factors.... [I]nvestment capital may be distributed unevenly to certain neighborhoods.... Particular nations, regions, cities, and areas within cities prosper and thrive, while others decline and whither" (Aoki 2000: 918–919). The racialized spaces of intellectual property patents provide a basis for shaping research priorities and directing the flow of capital to the patent holders. Significantly, however, the added value provided by race is appropriated by the patent holder—the landlord, so to speak—rather than by the community whose race has been commandeered into the service of producing the relevant product. Indeed, to the extent that a patent is conceived of as a right to *exclude* others for use of a particular invention, a racialized patent gives the patent holder the right to exclude members of the identified races from access to of control over the terms through which the patent process appropriates and commodifies their racial identity.

Conclusion

The implications of the striking rise of race in biotechnology patents have yet to be fully played out. In cases such as BiDil we see explicitly how racialized patents are coming to play a central role in the biotechnology research, development, and marketing. BiDil involved technologies that were already and in use. Adding race to the patent did not change the technology so much as it provided an added incentive to market and extend monopoly control for the product. The striking rise of racialized biotechnology patents indicates that cases such as BiDil are paving the way for a new proliferation of patents and drug approvals that are producing new and highly problematic understandings of race as genetic. BiDil obtained its commodity value from the rebiologization of race in the regulatory process. Additional racial patents, for products not yet as prominent as BiDil, have secured the imprimatur of the state for using race as a genetic category. Like more traditional extractive industries, biotechnology corporations are mining the raw material of race as a social category and using the patent process to refine it into a natural construct that lends legal utility and novelty to their inventions. The patents are in place and proliferating, ready to be invoked to protect a product or extend a market. In the context of gene patents, genetic race literally is becoming a commodity as race-specific patents allow biotechnology corporations to raise venture capital and develop marketing strategies that present a reified conception of race as genetic to doctors, regulators, and the public at large. In the process, racialized biotechnology patents are also marking neighborhoods of the genome with racial identities as they both produce and appropriate a new genetic commodity value in race.

NOTES

1. Work on this article was supported in part by the Ethical, Legal, and Social Implications Research Program, National Human Genome Research Institute (Grant number R03-HG004034-02).

2. In the interests of economy and manageable syntax, in the remainder of this article I will often refer only to "race" when speaking generally of racial and ethnic categories. I am assuming both to be socially constructed categories that nonetheless have come to have biological implications as they play out in real-world biomedical contexts.

3. Issued patents have been formally approved by the PTO. Patent applications are currently pending before the PTO for review. Under new policies applications are made available to the public while pending review.

4. The results are from searches of the U.S. PTO patent database conducted between August 25 and September 15, 2005, and between September 1 and September 9, 2007 using the Web-based search engine available at www.uspto.gov. The search terms used included race, racial, ethnic, ethnicity, Caucasian, Caucasoid, African, African American, Negro, Negroid, Asian, Oriental, Mongoloid, Hispanic, Latino, Native American, Alaska Native, and Pacific Islander. The terms "black" and "white" alone were too broad to be useful and so were qualified with the additional terms "gene" or "genetic" or "nucleotide."

5. The categorization of patents that imply or assert a significant genetic component to race or ethnicity is meant to exclude those patents that use racial/ethnic categories as one or more of a longer list of general demographic characteristics, usually employed for information organization rather than for identifying or treating a particular physiological state. The categorization is meant to include those patents that use racial/ethnic categories as a basis for asserting a distinctive prevalence or etiology for a physiological condition, genetic variation, and/or drug response.

REFERENCES

American Anthropological Association (AAA). 1997. "Response to OMB Directive 15: Race and Ethnic Standards for Federal Statistics and Administrative Reporting." http://www.aaanet.org/gvt/ombdraft.htm.

———. 1998. "Statement on Race." http://www.aaanet.org/stmts/racepp.htm. Accessed November 8, 2005.

American Sociological Association. (ASA). 2003. *The Importance of Collecting Data and Doing Social Scientific Research on Race.* Washington, DC: American Sociological Association. http://asanet.org/galleries/default-file/asa_race_statement.pdf. Accessed November 8, 2005.

Aoki, K. 1993. "Race, Space and Place: The Relation between Architectural Modernism, Post-Modernism, Urban Planning, and Gentrification." 20 *Fordham Urb. L. J.* 699–830.

————. 2000. "Space Invaders: Critical Geography, the 'Third World' in International Law and Critical Race Theory." 45 *Vill. L. Rev.* 913–958.

Bonham, V., Warschauer-Baker, E., and Collins, F. 2005. "Race and Ethnicity in the Genome Era." 60 *American Psychologist* 9–15.

Calmore, J. 1995. "Racialized Space and the Culture of Segregation: 'Hewing a Stone of Hope from a Mountain of Despair.'" 143 *U. Pa. L. Rev.* 1233.

Chisum, D., Nard, C., Schwartz, H., Newman, P., and Kieff, F. S. 2001. *Principles of Patent Law*, 2d ed. New York: Foundation Press.

"Census, Race and Science." 2000. Editorial. 24 *Nature Genetics* 97–98.

Collins. F. 2004. What We Do and Don't Know about 'Race,' 'Ethnicity,' Genetics and Health at the Dawn of the Genome Era." 36 *Nat. Gen.* S13–S15.

Elliott, G. 2002. "A Brief Guide to Understanding Patentability and the Meaning of Patents." 77 *Academic Medicine* 1309–1314.

Food and Drug Administration (FDA). 2005 "FDA Approves BiDil Heart Failure Drug for Black Patients." *FDA News*, June 23, 2005. http://www.fda.gov/bbs/topics/NEWS/2005/NEW01190 .html. Accessed July 5, 2005.

Ford, R. T. 1994. "The Boundaries of Race: Political Geography in Legal Analysis." 107 *Harvard Law Review* 1841.

Goodman, A. 2000. "Why Genes Don't Count (for Racial Differences in Health)." 90 *American Journal of Public Health* 1699–1702.

Harris, C. 1993. "Whiteness as Property." 106 *Harvard Law Review* 1707.

Jasanoff, S. 2002. "The Life Sciences and the Rule of Law." 319 *J. Mol. Biol.* 891.

Kahn, J. 2003. "What's the Use? Law and Authority in Patenting Human Genetic Material." 14 *Stanford Law & Policy Review* 417–444.

————. 2004. "How a Drug Becomes 'Ethnic': Law, Commerce, and the Production of Racial Categories in Medicine." 4 *Yale Journal of Health Policy, Law & Ethics* 1–46.

————. 2005a. "'Ethnic' Drugs." *Hastings Center Report*, January/February, 2005.

————. 2005b. "From Disparity to Difference: How Race Specific Medicines May Undermine Policies to Address Inequalities in Health Care." 1 *Southern California Interdisciplinary Law Journal* 105–129.

Lewontin, R. 1972. "The Apportionment of Human Diversity." 6 *Evol. Biol.* 381–384.

Lipsitz, G. 1998. *The Possessive Investment in Whiteness: How White People Profit from Identity Politics*. Philadelphia: Temple University Press.

Lock, M. 1999. "Genetic Diversity and the Politics of Difference." 75 *Chicago-Kent Law Review* 83–112.

Marks, J. 1995. *Human Biodiversity: Genes, Race, and History*. New York: Aldine de Gruyter.

National Institutes of Health (NIH). 2001. "NIH Policy and Guidelines on the Inclusion of Women and Minorities as Subjects in Clinical Research—Amended, October, 2001." http://grants2.nih .gov/grants/funding/women_min/guidelines_amended_10_2001.htm. Accessed June 10, 2004.

Parke-Davis & Co. v. H. K. Mulford Co., 189 F. 95 (S.D.N.Y. 1911).

Reardon, J. 2004. *Race to the Finish: Identity and Governance in an Age of Genomics*. Princeton, NJ: Princeton University Press.

Sankar, P., and Kahn, J. 2005. "BiDil: Race Medicine or Race Marketing?" *Health Affairs*, October 11. http://content.healthaffairs.org/cgi/content/full/hlthaff.w5.455/DC1.

Schecter, R., and Thomas, J. 2003. *Intellectual Property: The Law of Copyrights, Patents and Trademarks*. St. Paul, MN: West Group.

Taylor, A., et al. 2004. "Combination of Isosorbide Dinitrate and Hydralazine in Blacks with Heart Failure." 351 *New England Journal of Medicine* 2049–2057.

U.S. Department of Health and Human Services (HHS). 1997. "Policy Statement on Inclusion of Race and Ethnicity in HHS Data Collection Activities." http://aspe.os.dhhs.gov/datacncl/racerpt/appendg.htm. Accessed April 16, 2002.

———. 2003a. "Guidance for Industry: Collection of Race and Ethnicity Data in Clinical Trials." http://www.fda.gov/cder/guidance/5054dft.doc. Accessed November 10, 2004.

———. 2003b. "Guidance for Industry: Pharmacogenomic Data Submissions." http://www.fda.gov/cder/guidance/5900dft.doc. Accessed November 10, 2004.

U.S. Office of Management and Budget (OMB). 1997. "Revisions to the Standards for the Classification of Federal Data on Race and Ethnicity." http://www.whitehouse.gov/omb/fedreg/ombdir15.html. Accessed December 5, 2005.

Zilinskas, R., and Balint, P., eds. 2001. *The Human Genome Project and Minority Communities: Ethical, Social, and Political Dilemmas*. Westport, CT: Praeger.

PATENTS AND PATENT APPLICATIONS

U.S. Patent 6,465,463. Methods of treating and preventing congestive heart failure with hydralazine compounds and isosorbide dinitrate or isosorbide mononitrate. Issued October 15, 2002.

U.S. Patent Application 20040126794. Detection of susceptibility to autoimmune diseases. Filed July 1, 2002.

U.S. Patent Application 20040267458. Methods for obtaining and using haplotype data. Filed December 21, 2001.

PAMELA SAMUELSON

The Strange Odyssey of Software Interfaces as Intellectual Property

Interfaces are important parts of computer programs because they enable the exchange of information between programs so that programs can work together to achieve particular tasks.[1] In order for an operating system program, for instance, to retrieve data from a computer's memory and make that data available to an application program for processing, the application program must request the data in the precise format for which the operating system was designed to receive it. Interfaces are informational equivalents of the familiar plug-and-socket design through which appliances, such as lamps, interoperate with the electrical grid.

Consumers greatly benefit from interoperability when, for example, they are able to use the same information resources (say, MP3 files of music) on multiple platforms in a "plug-and-play" fashion and when they are able to use information resources developed on other people's computer systems on a different kind of computer (e.g., reading on an Apple computer a Microsoft Word document written on a PC). Interoperability doesn't just naturally happen. It has to be carefully designed. To achieve interoperability requires considerable skill and access to information about the interface's design.

This chapter considers the strange odyssey that program interfaces have made through various modes of protection. Initially, they were not protected by intellectual property rules at all. Later, they were treated as trade secrets and made subject to licensing restrictions. As software became a mass-market phenomenon, proposals were made to protect them through copyrights, patents, and a possible new sui generis (of its own kind) form of IP protection. In recent years, some governmental and private ordering initiatives have sought to blunt the potency of IP protections for interfaces. Interface protection thus nicely illustrates the making and unmaking of IP.

In the early days of computing (before the 1970s), developers of hardware and software usually published documents containing interface information (known as "interface specifications") without IP or other restrictions.[2] Firms had incentives to publish interface specifications to make it easy for customers to develop software to run on their new computer systems to do the tasks that the customers had purchased the computers to carry out. Publishing interfaces also made it easier for outside developers of software or peripheral equipment to make or adapt products to operate on particular computer systems. The availability of software and peripherals for a computer system made that platform more attractive to prospective customers.

As IBM became a dominant firm in the computer industry, it came to realize that interfaces were commercially valuable in their own right. It then began to treat interface specifications as trade secrets and licensed them on restrictive terms. This not only gave IBM control over development of compatible software and peripheral equipment; it also impeded development of competing platforms capable of interoperating with applications written for IBM computers, such as those Fujitsu was developing. Other developers of computer hardware and software, such as Apple Computer, Nintendo, and Microsoft, also treated interfaces as trade secrets as they sought or attained market power.

Unlicensed firms were sometimes able to develop compatible programs even without having access to trade secret interface specifications by purchasing a copy of the program with which they wanted their program to interoperate and undertaking the tedious and time-consuming process of reverse engineering the other firm's program to extract interface information. To block this form of unlicensed access to program interfaces, many software developers made their products available through mass-market licenses that included anti-reverse-engineering clauses. Doubts have long existed about whether anti-reverse-engineering clauses in mass-market licenses are actually enforceable, given the long-standing trade secret policy in favor of reverse engineering of mass-marketed products.[3]

Prior to 1980, it was unclear whether either patent or copyright protection would or should be available to protect either computer programs or their interfaces. Doubts about the patentability of program innovations arose because programs are texts and because many information innovations embedded in programs are "mental processes" (that is, processes that can be carried out in the human mind or with the aid of a pen and paper).[4] Patent law had long considered printed matter, such as texts, and mental processes, such as numeric calculations, to be unpatentable subject matter, even though printed matter is literally a "manufacture" and mental processes are literally "processes," and these are two of the four categories of inventions for which patents may issue.[5] Twice in the 1970s, the Supreme Court ruled that program-related inventions were ineligible for patent protection.[6] In *Gottschalk v. Benson*, for instance, the Supreme Court ruled that an algorithm for transforming binary coded decimals to pure binary form was ineligible for patent protection and suggested that processes were eligible for patent protection only if they transformed matter from one physical state to another.[7]

No one doubted that computer programs were copyrightable in human-readable source code form or as depicted in flow charts. But once transformed into machine-executable form, programs became functional processes. Copyright law has long excluded useful arts, such as machines and mechanical processes, from copyright protection.[8] As the Supreme Court once observed: "To give to the author of the book an exclusive property in the [useful] art described therein, when no examination of its novelty has ever been officially made, would be a surprise and a fraud upon the public. That is the province of letters-patent, not of copyright."[9] U.S. courts have generally made a sharp distinction between the domains of copyright and utility patent law, perceiving no overlap in their subject matters.[10]

During the 1980s, there was so much doubt about the appropriateness of patent and copyright protection for computer programs that some proposed creation of a new form of IP protection for computer programs.[11] In 1983, for example, the Japanese Ministry of International Trade and Industry issued a report recommending a sui generis form of protection for software.[12] It resembled copyright in some ways—for instance, in protecting programs from unauthorized copying—but it was shorter in duration and took into account the importance of interoperability, which copyright law could not readily do. The European Commission also expressed interest in a sui generis form of IP protection for software in the late 1980s.[13]

A turning point in the evolution of IP protection for computer programs came in 1979 when the National Commission on New Technological Uses of Copyrighted Works (CONTU) issued a report to Congress.[14] CONTU had been asked to consider the implications of several new technology issues for copyright law, such as photocopying journal articles and inputting the texts of books into computers. CONTU went beyond its initial charter in recommending that copyright protection should be available for computer programs as "literary works."[15]

CONTU expressed confidence that copyright law could evolve to make appropriate distinctions between program ideas (which of course would not be protected) and program expression (which would be). Perhaps because the CONTU commissioners were mostly copyright lawyers who knew very little about computer programs, the report did not meaningfully address important scope-of-protection issues, including whether program interfaces were protectable.

Even after Congress amended copyright law as CONTU recommended,[16] some vestiges of doubt about the copyrightability of programs remained. Two appellate courts snuffed out these doubts in the early 1980s.[17] Makers of clone computers claimed, among other things, that copying Apple II operating system programs was justifiable because it was necessary to enable their computers to achieve interoperability with programs written for the Apple platform. One court observed: "Franklin may wish to achieve total compatibility with independently developed application programs written for the Apple II, but that is a commercial and competitive objective which does not enter into the somewhat metaphysical issue of whether particular ideas and expressions have merged."[18] This did not augur well for future defenses to claims of infringement based on copying of interfaces.

Even more worrisome for compatible program developers was the *Whelan Associates, Inc., v. Jaslow Dental Lab., Inc.* decision.[19] *Whelan* involved a dispute about the development of a dental laboratory business program. Jaslow had initially worked with Whelan on a software project but, after a falling out, decided to develop his own program to perform the same functions. Although his program and Whelan's were written in different programming languages and used different algorithms, the overall structure of the programs was similar, as were some data and file structures, and the two programs performed some of the same functions in the same manner. The court ruled that Jaslow had infringed Whelan's copyright.

The court in *Whelan* agreed with CONTU that computer programs were literary works. It reasoned that since copyright law had long protected nonliteral elements (i.e., structure, sequence, and organization [SSO]) of other types of literary works, such as novels and plays, it should protect the SSO of programs. *Whelan* deemed all program SSO to be protectable as long as there was more than one way to structure a program to achieve the program's functions.

Whelan also endorsed extending copyright protection to the "look and feel" of programs, which seemingly included the manner in which the programs behaved (i.e., how they performed their functions). Without broad copyright protection for computer programs, and in particular, for aspects of program SSO that were costly and difficult to develop as well as commercially significant, the court worried that there would be too little protection to provide proper incentives to develop computer programs.

The first case to address directly whether copyright protection extends to program interfaces was *Computer Associates Int'l, Inc., v. Altai, Inc.*[20] The case arose after Altai decided to convert its major product, the Zeke scheduling program, so that it could run on two different IBM operating systems, not just the one for which it had been initially developed. The programming team included Claude Arney, a former employee of Computer Associates (CA), who had worked on the CA Scheduler program, Zeke's main competitor, and who was thus familiar with the tasks that scheduling programs performed.

Shortly after joining Altai, Arney persuaded James Williams, the team leader, that the smartest way to redesign Zeke to make it compatible with both IBM systems was to build a new compatibility component for Zeke, a subprogram (given the name Oscar) that would transpose Zeke's commands for specific tasks into the appropriate format for interacting with the two different operating systems. This new design would avoid the need to customize each module of Zeke for each operating system, and if Altai wanted to adapt Zeke in the future to be compatible with additional operating systems, Altai would only need to rewrite parts of Oscar, not the whole of Zeke. Unbeknownst to Williams, CA had adopted the very same approach in the latest version of CA Scheduler, a project on which Arney had worked when he was in its employ.

Arney completed Oscar's compatibility component in only four months. Altai then shipped the Oscar-enhanced version of Zeke until Computer Associates sued it for copyright infringement and trade secret misappropriation, alleging that Oscar contained code misappropriated from CA Scheduler. Upon learning of the lawsuit, Williams called Arney into his office to ask if the charges had merit. Arney confessed that he had taken a copy of his former employer's source code when he left the firm and had directly copied portions of this code when developing Oscar.

Altai's management decided that the company should take immediate steps to purge Oscar of the tainted code. Williams determined which parts of Oscar had been copied from CA Scheduler and assigned a new team of Altai programmers to revise Oscar. Williams also provided them with a list of Zeke's services and directed them to analyze how to make the services compatible with the IBM systems, after which they were to write new noninfringing code.

Six months later, the team produced a new version of Oscar. Altai then began offering a free "upgrade" of Zeke to its existing customer base as well as selling the revised Zeke to new customers.

Altai accepted liability for copyright infringement of the code literally copied from CA Scheduler but believed the rewrite of Oscar had immunized it from further liability. CA, however, asserted that the revised Oscar program was still substantially similar in SSO to the compatibility subprogram of CA Scheduler, particularly in the manner in which the program interfaces were structured.

CA relied heavily on *Whelan* and its progeny in arguing that the revised Oscar program infringed its copyright in CA Scheduler.[21] It pointed to substantial similarities between the compatibility components of Zeke and CA Scheduler, especially as to their parameter lists (i.e., lists of information that needed to be sent and received by subroutines of the affected programs). These elements of program SSO had been carefully and precisely designed, making them costly to develop and commercially significant parts of programs. CA argued that incentives to invest in software development would be undermined if competitors such as Altai could appropriate program SSO without fear of liability. Parameter lists and other SSO elements of program interfaces are, moreover, complex and detailed, not abstract in content, which under *Whelan* made them protectable expression. In view of the SSO similarities, CA argued the revised Oscar still infringed the copyright in CA Scheduler.

Altai faced a daunting challenge to overcome Computer Associates' arguments. The *Apple* case was easy to distinguish because Franklin had not even tried to rewrite the Apple OS programs but had instead copied the code exactly, bit for bit. Altai, by contrast, had spent hundreds of man-hours and many months developing a new implementation of Zeke's interfaces to the IBM programs. *Whelan*'s SSO analysis, however, could only be elided by developing a strong counter-rhetoric.

A key step was to persuade the court to conceptualize computer programs as utilitarian works, which are meaningfully different from novels and plays and which enjoy, at most, a "thin" scope of copyright protection (that is, protection against only exact or nearly exact copying). Even more important was getting the court to recognize that external factors sometimes constrain the design choices of programmers. This includes not only the mechanical specifications of the computer hardware on which a program was designed to run but also interface details, such as the protocols that enable programs such as CA Scheduler and Zeke to exchange information and interoperate with the IBM operating systems. Of course, the parameter lists of CA Scheduler and

Zeke were similar; both aimed to provide the same scheduling services to their customers and both were trying to interoperate with the same IBM systems.

Altai won the rhetorical war before the Second Circuit Court of Appeals in New York and established an important precedent. The *Altai* decision not only rejected claims of copyright protection in interfaces but also adopted a now widely used test for assessing claims of copyright infringement in computer programs.

The *Altai* test excludes from copyright protection aspects of programs that are dictated by efficiency. Also excluded are design choices that are constrained by external factors, such as the hardware or software with which the program was designed to interoperate, demands of the industry being served, and widely accepted programming practices. Elements of programs that are in the public domain, such as commonplace programming techniques, ideas, and know-how, are also excluded from copyright. Later decisions have extended *Altai* by directing courts to filter out functional design elements, such as procedures, processes, systems, and methods of operation.[22]

The court in *Altai* asserted that its test for software copyright infringement "not only comports with but advances the constitutional policies underlying the Copyright Act."[23] In response to CA's arguments that "thin" copyright protection for programs could undermine incentives to invest in program development, the court observed that similar incentive-based arguments had been "flatly rejected" in a recent Supreme Court decision.[24] To extend broad copyright protection to program SSO would "have a fundamentally corrosive effect on certain fundamental tenets of copyright doctrine."[25] Because copyright seemed ill-suited to protecting program innovations, the court in *Altai* suggested that Congress consider whether programs needed additional IP protection; it also suggested that patents might be a more suitable form of IP protection for program SSO.[26]

The *Altai* decision may not initially have induced software developers and their lawyers to start thinking seriously about patenting interfaces and other program SSO, in part because it took some years for *Altai* to defeat *Whelan* in the subsequent case law and emerge as the leading decision for judging claims of software copyright infringement.[27] However, the patent option became more salient after the Ninth Circuit Court of Appeals issued its ruling in *Sega Enterprises, Ltd., v. Accolade, Inc.*[28] less than a month after *Altai*.

Sega was important in the IP-in-interfaces odyssey for at least four reasons. For one thing, it embraced *Altai*'s conceptualization of computer programs as utilitarian works eligible for only a thin scope of copyright protection.[29] Second, *Sega* followed *Altai* in ruling that program interfaces were elements of programs that copyright law did not protect; indeed, *Sega* spoke of interface information as "functional requirements for achieving compatibility with other programs."[30] Third, the court ruled that copying program code in the course of reverse engineering for a legitimate purpose such as extracting interface information to make a compatible program did not infringe any copyright in that code. The court reasoned that "if disassembly of copyrighted object code is per se an unfair use, the owner of the copyright gains a de facto monopoly over the functional aspects of his work—aspects that were expressly denied copyright protection by Congress. In order to enjoy a lawful monopoly over the idea or functional principle underlying a work, the creator of the work must satisfy the more stringent standards imposed by the patent laws."[31] Fourth, it indicated that even copying some exact code from another program would not be infringement insofar as that code was essential to achieving interoperability.

After *Sega*, developers could no longer hope to protect interfaces through copyright law. And because *Sega* allowed unlicensed reverse engineering of code to extract interface information,[32] it imperiled developer efforts to protect interfaces as trade secrets. *Sega* signaled that the only reliable means for protecting the functional requirements for achieving interoperability was by patenting them. Patents had at least one advantage over copyright law in protecting interfaces because, unlike copyright law, patent law has no "merger" doctrine. Hence, if there is only one way to carry out a particular function and a developer has patented that one way, it can exercise its patent rights to stop unlicensed uses.

Altai and *Sega* contributed to the eventual shift away from reliance on copyright protection for program SSO and interface innovations and toward reliance on patent protection. But developments on the patent side also made this form of protection for program SSO more plausible than in the 1970s. Especially important was the Supreme Court's 5–4 decision *Diamond v. Diehr* in 1981, which signaled a new receptivity to patenting computer-program-related inventions.[33] Diehr claimed to have invented a new method of curing rubber that used a computer program to calculate when the temperature inside rubber molds had reached the perfect curing point. The Patent and Trademark Office rejected Diehr's claim because its only novelty lay in program calculations, which the office thought was ineligible for protection under *Gottshalk v. Benson*.

In *Diehr*, the Supreme Court rejected the "point of novelty" test and ruled that Diehr's process was patentable subject matter. Because the Court was so deeply divided, because the majority opinion did not repudiate the Court's earlier rulings on the unpatentability of program innovations, and because the case involved a traditional manufacturing process (i.e., curing rubber), the

Diehr decision was initially perceived as a modest change in the patent landscape for program-related inventions.

Certain language in *Diehr*, however, reflected a broad conception of patentable subject matter.[34] In the decade or so after *Diehr*, the appellate court that hears patent cases developed a very broad conception of patentable subject matter under which virtually all computer-program-related inventions were patentable subject matter.[35] By the mid-1990s, there was a substantial surge in the patenting of software innovations, in part owing to the "thinness" of copyright protection after *Altai, Sega*, and their progeny.[36]

Software developers often seek patents for program designs, such as algorithms and data structures. Such patents are, however, generally more useful for defensive than for offensive purposes. That is, developers tend to seek patents on such internal designs to assure themselves of having freedom to operate in their fields as well as to build a portfolio of IP assets so that the firms will have something to trade (e.g., by cross-licensing) if a competitor asserts patent claims against them.[37] Patents on program internal designs are often difficult to assert offensively (that is, to stop competitors from using them) because such elements are typically difficult to discern in commercially distributed object code. Insofar as infringement is difficult to detect, patents on program internals are difficult to enforce.

Patents on interface designs, by contrast, are more likely to be useful for offensive purposes.[38] They may confer on their owners an exclusive right to control the development of not only competing but also complementary products, because the interface defines the boundaries between programs. It is generally easy to detect infringement of interface patents because if unlicensed products successfully interoperate with the patentee's products, they almost certainly infringe. Interface patents are among the most valuable patents that software developers can own, in part because such patents can be impossible to work around. Even a narrowly drawn interface patent may preclude interoperability of a key component of the program.

Software interfaces are so essential to achieving interoperability that some have argued that they should be unpatentable, or if patented, their use should be deemed noninfringing insofar as there is no equally efficient or effective way to achieve interoperability.[39] (The latter approach would, in essence, create a merger doctrine in patent law.) A policy akin to this was adopted by the World Wide Web Consortium (W3C). W3C requires member firms, which include major industry players such as Microsoft and IBM, to agree that if they own patents that "read" on a standard adopted by W3C that is essential to Web interoperability, those patents will be licensed on a royalty-free (RF) basis.[40] The Organization for the Advancement of Structured Information Standards

(OASIS) does not mandate RF licensing of Web-services interface patents but offers two widely used RF licensing options for technical committees to adopt.[41] RF policies do not, of course, make such patents unenforceable, but they do substantially reduce the leverage that such patents would otherwise provide as well as their economic value. This in turn dampens incentives to acquire such patents. Some commentators have, moreover, called for abolition of software patents,[42] in part because interface patents pose such risks to open source programming.

Another policy response is to allow interface patents to issue but to limit the remedy for infringing them to reasonable compensation. Under the Supreme Court's ruling in *eBay, Inc,. v. MercExchange, L.L.C.*,[43] for instance, courts have discretion to withhold injunctive relief in cases involving interfaces essential to interoperability and order payment of a reasonable royalty. In addition, the U.S. government has power to practice patented inventions and to authorize others to do the same as long as it provides reasonable compensation for the use.[44] Antitrust authorities could also require licensing of interface patents.[45]

Japan has been considering a proposal to require licensing of patents on essential interfaces.[46] The European Parliament considered a similar proposal to oblige owners of patents on essential interfaces to license them on reasonable and nondiscriminatory (RAND) terms during the contentious debate over the proposed directive on software patents.[47] Some standard-setting organizations require participating firms to agree in advance to license on RAND terms any patents that may be implicated by a standard adopted by those organizations.[48]

The widespread practice of cross-licensing of software patents among large and medium-sized firms in the software industry may also lessen the exclusionary impacts of interface patents. It is important to recognize that firms with interface patents often have incentives to license these patents in order to enable other firms to make compatible products that will make their platforms more attractive to customers.

This chapter has related the tortuous journey through which the law has evolved in response to efforts to protect interfaces. It is a separate question whether software and interfaces might be better protected through another regime. This question was addressed in "A Manifesto Concerning the Legal Protection of Computer Programs," which reported the results of a collaboration among Lotus Development Corporation founder Mitchell Kapor, computer scientist Randall Davis, law professor Jerome Reichman, and me.[49] The manifesto challenged the prevailing conception of computer programs as literary works and characterized programs as machines that happen to be constructed in text. It pointed out that the most valuable aspects of programs lie not in what they say or how they say it, as traditional copyrighted works do, but in what the programs actually do and how well they do it. The "industrial compilations of applied know-how" in computer programs, including their behaviors, are in need of protection against market-destructive appropriations.[50] But such compilations are only in need of a short term of exclusive rights to stop others from cloning, perhaps followed by a term in which others could use the industrial compilations subject to a right of compensation.

Interfaces are among the elements of programs that are best understood as industrial compilations of applied know-how. Because they are carefully drafted precise and detailed compilations of information, interfaces resemble copyright subject matter. Like copyright subject matter, they are relatively cheap and easy to copy, especially in digital form and so seem amenable to the ban on unauthorized copying that is copyright law's principal hallmark. However, copyright law does not protect industrial compilations, such as interfaces, rule sets, recipes, and systematic organizations of information; nor does it protect know-how.[51] It is consequently unsuitable as a form of protection for interface specifications.

Although some firms do patent interfaces, they cannot patent the entirety of their program interfaces but only specific components tied to particular functions. The textual nature of interface specifications and their information-intensive component parts make patents unsuitable for protecting interface specifications as such. A sui generis regime that focuses on protecting interfaces as industrial compilations of applied know-how would be a more suitable regime for interface protection than patents.

Whatever the merits of a sui generis approach, the IP odyssey passed it by. Software developers now use copyrights to protect program code and expressive aspects of audiovisual displays (e.g., video game animation). Distributing programs in object code generally provides effective trade secret protection for internal designs, including interfaces. Reverse engineering remains a difficult and sometimes impossible way to get access to interfaces.[52] By licensing programs on terms that forbid reverse engineering, developers have some reason to hope for a contractual bypass of the *Sega* decision, although the enforceability of mass-market restrictions on reverse engineering remains controversial.[53] And sometimes they patent interface techniques.

No other intellectual artifact has had a comparable journey through IP law. Interface specifications began as public domain documents and then as trade secret documents. For a time, it seemed that sui generis protection would be the best way to deal with the interoperability challenges posed by programs, but then copyright became the norm for software protection. *Whelan* made it seem that interface specifications would be protectable by copyright law as program SSO. *Altai* and *Sega*, however, dashed those expectations. Software developers then shifted to patent protection for interfaces and pinned their hopes on the enforceability of anti-reverse-engineering clauses in software license contracts or the difficulties of reverse engineering to gain access to interface information. Recent developments give hint of a new shift toward regulated licensing of patented interfaces.

This strange odyssey of interfaces through various forms of IP law offers some insights worthy of inclusion in this volume. Interface specifications for software are a type of information innovation that does not fit neatly in traditional copyright and patent bins.[54] Those who sought to protect interfaces by copyright law emphasized their resemblance to other copyright subject matters (i.e., compilations of information, part of program SSO). Those who fought against copyright protection for interfaces had to convince courts that interfaces were functional requirements for achieving interoperability, akin to electrical plugs and sockets, which seemed more appropriate for patent protection. Because interfaces are so important to competition and follow-on innovation, some have argued against giving patentees a free hand in exercising their rights under this law to stop the development of compatible products.

Notwithstanding several decades of controversy about interface protection issues within legal circles, the software industry seems to have surmounted these difficulties. The making and unmaking of various forms of IP protection for software and interfaces has not stopped this industry from being highly competitive, highly innovative, and increasingly interoperable. Go figure.

NOTES

1. For a more extensive discussion of interfaces and interoperability, see, e.g., Pamela Samuelson, Are Patents on Interfaces Impeding Interoperability? 93 *Minn. L. Rev.* 1943 (2009).

2. The relevant history is related well in Jonathan Band & Masanobu Katoh, *Interfaces on Trial: Intellectual Property and Interoperability in the Global Software Industry* 19–28 (1995).

3. See, e.g., Mark A. Lemley, Beyond Preemption: The Law and Policy of Intellectual Property Licensing, 87 *Cal. L. Rev.* 113 (1999).

4. See, e.g., Pamela Samuelson, *Benson* Revisited: The Case against Patent Protection for Algorithms and Other Computer Program-Related Inventions, 39 *Emory L. J.* 1025 (1990).

5. 35 U.S.C. sec. 101.

6. See *Parker v. Flook*, 437 U.S. 584 (1978); *Gottschalk v. Benson*, 409 U.S. 63 (1972).

7. *Gottschalk v. Benson*, 409 U.S. at 64–70.

8. *Baker v. Selden*, 101 U.S. 99 (1880). For a discussion of *Baker* and its progeny, see, e.g., Pamela Samuelson, Why Copyright Excludes Systems and Processes from the Scope of Its Protection, 85 *Tex. L. Rev.* 1921 (2007).

9. *Baker*, 101 U.S. at 102.

10. See, e.g., Pamela Samuelson, *Baker v. Selden*: Sharpening the Distinction between Authorship and Invention, in *Intellectual Property Stories* (Jane C. Ginsburg & Rochelle C. Dreyfuss, eds. 2005).

11. See, e.g., Pamela Samuelson, CONTU Revisited: The Case against Copyright Protection for Computer Programs in Machine-Readable Form, 1984 *Duke L. J.* 663 (1984) (proposing sui generis protection).

12. See Dennis S. Karjala, Lessons from the Computer Software Protection Debate in Japan, 1984 *Ariz. St. L. J.* 53, 63.

13. Green Paper on Copyright and the Challenge of Technology—Copyright Issues Requiring Immediate Action, Document COM (88), 172, final, June 7, 1988. Although the EU ultimately decided to protect programs with copyright law, its exclusion of interfaces from the scope of this protection and legalizing reverse engineering for purposes of acquiring interface information were sui generis provisions in copyright. See Council Directive 91/250/EEC of May 14, 1991, on the legal protection of computer programs, Art. 5–6.

14. See National Commission on New Technological Uses of Copyrighted Works, Final Report (1979).

15. Ibid. at 1, 9–26.

16. Pub. L. no. 96-517, 94 stat. 3007, 3028 (codified at 17 U.S.C. §§101, 117 [1982]).

17. See *Apple Computer, Inc., v. Franklin Computer Corp.*, 714 F.2d 1240 (3d Cir. 1983); *Apple Computer, Inc., v. Formula Int'l, Inc.*, 725 F.2d 521 (9th Cir. 1984).

18. *Franklin*, 714 F.2d at 1253.

19. 797 F.2d 1222 (3d Cir. 1986).

20. The facts in this and succeeding paragraphs are derived from *Computer Associates Int'l, Inc., v. Altai, Inc.*, 775 F. Supp. 544 (E.D.N.Y. 1991), aff'd, 982 F.2d 693 (2d Cir. 1992).

21. See, e.g., Reply Brief for Plaintiff-Appellant, in *Computer Associates Int'l, Inc., v. Altai, Inc.*, 1991 WL 11010234 (relying heavily on *Whelan*).

22. See, e.g., *Gates Rubber Co. v. Bando Chemical Indus., Ltd.*, 9 F.3d 823 (10th Cir. 1993).

23. *Altai*, 982 F.2d at 711.

24. Ibid., citing *Feist Pub., Inc., v. Rural Telephone Service Co.*, 499 U.S. 340 (1991) (rejecting "sweat of the brow" copyright claim in white pages listings of a telephone directory).

25. *Altai*, 982 F.2d at 712.

26. Ibid.

27. *Altai* has been followed in at least forty-nine subsequent decisions.

28. 977 F.2d 1510 (9th Cir. 1992).

29. Ibid. at 1526. ("Under the Copyright Act, if a work is largely functional, it receives only weak protection.")

30. Ibid. at 1525–1526.

31. Ibid. at 1525.

32. Prior to *Sega*, some commentators had argued that reverse engineering of object code should be treated as both copyright infringement and trade secret misappropriation. See, e.g., Allen Grogan, Decompilation and Disassembly: Undoing Software Protection, *Computer Law*, Feb. 1984, at 1.

33. 450 U.S. 175 (1981).

34. Ibid. at 181 (everything under the sun made by man is patentable subject matter).

35. See, e.g., *AT&T Corp. v. Excel Comm'ns, Inc.*, 172 F.3d 1352 (Fed. Cir. 1990).

36. See Josh Lerner & Feng Zhu, What Is the Impact of Software Patent Shifts? Evidence from *Lotus v. Borland* 10 (Nat'l Bur. Econ. Res. Working Paper no. 11168 2005) (presenting evidence of surge in patenting of software in the mid-1990s).

37. See, e.g., Gideon Parchomovsky & R. Polk Wagner, Patent Portfolios, 154 *U. Pa. L. Rev.* 1 (2005). Software patents may also be useful to firms in obtaining financing from venture capitalists. Ronald Mann, Do Patents Facilitate Financing in the Software Industry? 83 *Tex. L. Rev.* 961, 972 (2007).

38. See, e.g., *Atari Games Corp. v. Nintendo of Am., Inc.*, 30 U.S.P.Q.2d (BNA) 1401, 1414 (N.D. Cal. 1993) (granting summary judgment to Nintendo because Atari had infringed an interface patent).

39. See, e.g., Band & Katoh, at 332–334.

40. W3C Patent Policy, Feb. 4, 2005, available at http://www.w3.org/Consortium/Patent -Policy-20040205/.

41. See OASIS Intellectual Property Rights Policy, http://www.oasis-open.org/who/intellectual property.php. Robert J. Glushko, who serves on the OASIS board, reports that virtually all of the technical committees now use one of the two RF policies. Conversation with Robert J. Glushko, March 2, 2008.

42. See, e.g., Brad Feld, Abolish Software Patents, FeldThoughts, Apr. 10, 2006, available at http://www.feld.com/blog/archives/2006/04/abolish_softwar.html.

43. 126 S. Ct. 1837 (2006).

44. 28 U.S.C. sec. 1498.

45. See, e.g., Robert P. Merges & Richard R. Nelson, On the Complex Economics of Patent Scope, 90 *Colum. L. Rev.* 839 (1990) (giving examples of licenses induced by antitrust oversight).

46. Ministry of Economy, Trade, and Industry, press release, Interim Report of the Study Group on the Legal Protection of Computer Programs and Promotion of Innovation, Oct. 11, 2005, available at http://www.meti.go.jp/english/information/data/051011SoftInnove.html. ("Industry could consider the propagation of some concept along the lines of 'Creative Commons.' Action should be taken to popularize, through agreements among enterprises, the business practices of mutual non-assertion of rights to such patented inventions as relating to certain categories of software, such as OSS, or to interoperability of software, thereby making this concept the standard in the public domain by utilizing the current patent office. Moreover, the compulsory licensing system and the enhanced application of the antimonopoly law are considered as further issues to be studied.") See also Interpretative Guidelines for Electronic Commerce (revised Mar. 2007), 192–193, 201 (to assert patent rights to defeat interoperability may be considered an abuse of right), available at http://www .meti.go.jp/english/information/data/IT-policy/interpretative_guidelines_on_ec070628.pdf.

47. Foundation for a Free Information Infrastructure, Plenary Amendments: Interoperability, Sept. 16, 2005 (on file with the author).

48. Mark A. Lemley, Intellectual Property and Standard-Setting Organizations, 90 *Cal. L. Rev.* 1889 (2002).

49. Pamela Samuelson et al., A Manifesto Concerning the Legal Protection of Computer Programs, 94 *Colum. L. Rev.* 2308 (1994).

50. See also J. H. Reichman, Computer Programs as Applied Scientific Know-How: Implications of Copyright Protection for Commercialized University Research, 42 *Vand. L. Rev.* 639 (1989).

51. See, e.g., Samuelson, Why Copyright Excludes, at 1928–1952 (discussing case law and policy rationale for exclusion of these innovations from the scope of copyright and legislative history on statutory exclusion).

52. Developers of operating system programs, such as Microsoft's Windows and Vista, benefit by the sheer complexity of their programs and the large number of interfaces they contain, which makes reverse engineering to discover them virtually impossible.

53. See Lemley, Beyond Preemption.

54. Synthetic biology, XML schemas, and computer languages are three other kinds of information innovations that also do not neatly fit into the patent and copyright bins. See, e.g., Sapna Kumar & Arti Rai, Synthetic Biology: The Intellectual Property Puzzle, 83 *Tex. L. Rev.* 1745 (2007); Douglas E. Phillips, XML Schemas and Computer Program Language Copyright: Filling in the Blanks in Blank Esperanto, 9 *J. Intell. Prop. L.* 63 (2001).

IV

Doing and Undoing Collaborative IP

EVELYN LINCOLN

19

Invention, Origin, and Dedication
Republishing Women's Prints in Early Modern Italy

Sixteenth- and seventeenth-century Italian paintings by Raphael, Michelangelo, and Caravaggio are firmly situated in the pantheon of Western art history as illustrious examples of creative genius. Italian prints from the same period, however, are infamous today for their reliance on the ideas of others. Deemed "reproductive" or "prints of interpretation," they are typically pictures of famous works in other media, or even direct copies of other prints. At the bottom of each image the authors of the works from which the prints were made were designated as their *inventors*, and their names were joined by those of engravers, draftsmen, dedicatees, and publishers, all signature effects (or authorial inscriptions) that seemed to clamor for their share of credit for the final publication.[1] Today we privilege the role of the inventor, which we have come to understand as the single person without whom the print could not exist. But the perception of authorship at the time a print was made was far less direct in the sixteenth and seventeenth centuries, and credit for the authorship of a print could oscillate productively between several of the figures whose names appeared on it.

This chapter looks at prints made by some of the few women who found a way to claim authorship for printed images in this period.

The case of early modern women printmakers is particularly intriguing because they operated under the additional social and legal pressures of having to adjust declaration of their authorship to the decorum appropriate to their gender. As I will show, these pressures led them to take advantage of evolving conventions in printing and publishing to sign and dedicate images invented by others rather than developing what we would today call "original" ones. In so doing, they constructed an authorial role that literally upends modern assumptions about what is an author.

Since the nineteenth century, authorship has most often been located in a work's point of origin, which, in the case of prints, directs attention to the gap between the designated inventor of an image (the role that is most often understood as authorial) and the engraver. Problems arise from the modern privileging of the presence of the artist's hand in the work as proof of authorship. This is related to the importance in art history of connoisseurship: an expert's largely subjective skill in recognizing key traits of facture or representation that could not be rendered by any hand other than the artist's, thereby attributing authorship and value to a work of art.[2]

Looking at women printmakers allows us to shift our attention to the overlooked relationship between dedicator and dedicatee, both of whom could be seen in the role of author, allowing us to understand how choosing the proper destination for a print was seen as an act of authorship in the sixteenth century. In fact, making this choice bore an authorial weight similar to invention for people involved in the creation and marketing of reproductive prints in the early modern period.

Early modern conventions of signing distributed the sense of a print's authorship among many of those responsible for its making. This generous sense of those necessary for a print to be produced could even extend to a designated reader in the person of the dedicatee. Print dedications and signature effects work closely with the choice of an image to form the social and economic networks fundamental to the survival of would-be authors under the patronage system that governed most intellectual and artistic labor in the early modern period.

Women, Printing, and Publishing

Many more male than female engravers and publishers profited from the pictorial inventions of others and sent them forth hoping they would carry the proof of their skills to the most efficacious markets for them. Women benefited more from the dispersion of responsibility in the many signatures, as well as the indirect formality of courtly address that became conventional in dedications on prints, as it was in books.[3] While the signature effects that normally appeared in the margins of prints are noted in terms that appear to us to be authorial inscriptions, they bear little relation to modern signatures. In the precise place at the foot of the image where we are accustomed to look for a clear declaration of authorship, a constellation of multiple readers and makers is brought into play. This important space, where relationships were forged between the people who caused the print to be made and centers of patronage at which the print was aimed, was especially vivid for women printmakers, for whom it was the most proper sphere for this kind of collaborative work to take place.

The women who engraved with or without signing their work probably did so at home or in convents. The portability of the copper plates and wooden blocks that allowed them to be engraved in a protected domestic setting without specialized machines or equipment was a property of printmaking that made it possible for women to make the printing matrices—items of real commercial value—without having to be present in a public workshop. However, this also meant that valuable plates and blocks could easily come into the hands of different publishers who not only had no scruples about changing the text so carefully inscribed there, but made it their business to acquire old plates and blocks with proven sales records specifically in order to do so.

Republication and Rededication

When a publisher acquired a printing matrix, he could alter the information on it in any way he liked. Book publishers commonly did this, issuing later editions carrying new dedications from a publisher or translator to vastly different patrons than those whose protection was invoked the first time around. When the new publishers changed the information on the prints, particularly the dedications, they changed the social networks that governed the economy of the print in its original market in order to suit their own patronage needs. In keeping with practices in early modern book publishing, these later interventions of publishers and booksellers took advantage of the previous success and associations of the print while also taking credit for giving it new life through its republication as a worthy gift for a powerful patron.[4]

Like other publishers, Mauritio Bona, a Roman bookseller who specialized in republishing books originally printed by others, including many originally issued by women, made changes to plates or blocks that he acquired. He never tried to change the name of the designated inventor or engraver but changed instead the dedicatee. The Renaissance practice of dedication has little in common with the modern one. Signaling favors received or hoped for, the name of the dedicatee on a print is also a public invocation, a mantle under which, as dedications often say, the work dares to appear. Nothing could be less familiar or less modern than these named readers and viewers, trailing with them both history and biography, and intended neither to be the sole recipients nor the sole viewers of these multiple images. Each republished print bears echoes of previous titles and associations that continue to be meaningful into its next incarnation.[5] Exactly how the previous associations were handled and new ones brought into play was up to the publisher, who was himself entering into the role of inventor in matching the preexisting image and its history with a new patron, as we will see in the case of Bona.[6]

Invention

To better differentiate between what are today the undistinguished acts of copying, republishing, and rededicating and the more privileged act of invention, it is helpful to understand how invention came to carry the connotation of originality it now has in the arts and how it was used in the early modern period. Since much has been written about this, this explanation will necessarily be condensed and illustrated in the cases that follow in order to show how the concepts of invention and multiple authorship played out in printmaking.

The Renaissance convention of attributing a pictorial work, or even part of one, to a named inventor comes from the use of invention in rhetoric. Invention taught rhetoricians how to find subject matter for their own oratorical compositions from things already done and to provide a plan for structuring their work well.[7] Unlike today's notion of an invention as something new and never before seen, the concept did not carry implications of originality in antiquity. It began to assume that meaning only by the late sixteenth century. Understanding the use of the word "invention" as it occurs in rhetoric and how it was assimilated into the conventions of early pictorial printmaking requires routing through the issue of the respective authorial roles of early modern patrons and artists in the production of pictures at the end of the sixteenth century.

In 1982, Michael Baxandall treated the topic of shared credit for works of art with his usual sensitivity: "The renaissance sense of who was responsible for works of art and their quality is agile and elusive: renaissance observers can glide between a sense of the patron as author and a sense of the artists as author in a way that is hard to follow. There is no good reason to suppose that this was equivocation. It seems more likely that the sense of human cause in such matters as the making of buildings, sculpture and pictures was structurally a little different from ours."[8]

Baxandall was explaining a discussion of causality in a popular work on dialectic written by Rudolph Agricola, an amateur painter and musician, but most importantly a professor of rhetoric in Heidelberg and a court rhetorician at Ferrara. Agricola asserted that each person whose work could be seen to assist in a particular outcome should be considered in as many different roles as possible vis-à-vis its final goal. For instance, in the case of Agostino Chigi's commission to Raphael for the fresco of *Galatea* in the Villa Farnesina in Rome, both Raphael and his patron, Chigi, would be efficient causes of the fresco having been made—that is, sharing the work that got it done. The final cause is "that for the sake of which it is done.... The final cause is the most important cause."[9] A patron's desire to have a work done, and the funding of someone to do it, would be seen as the important final cause. According to Baxandall, Chigi can be understood as the cause of the fresco to be painted by hiring Raphael. The artist/craftsman was the patron's means toward the final end of the fresco being painted, and he could also be understood as one of the causes of the painting though not the final and most important cause. According to Baxandall, "This was not an esoteric or even a scholastic line of thought; it was implicit in, and in the grain of, the relaxed Aristotelian sense of cause current in Agricola's time."[10]

Rhetorical handbooks were an integral part of a book-driven education.[11] However, in using Agricola's late-fifteenth-century explanation of causes to explain the transfer of authorship in Renaissance patronage, Baxandall recognized that it could not take into account developing views (views that would eventually become full blown as the idea of the "romantic author") that tended to see aspects of the artist's role as similar to a final cause. Apropos of this he cited Raphael's famous letter to Baldassare Castiglione of 1514, written during the period when he was working on the *Galatea*, in which he mentioned an "*idea che mi viene nella mente*" (idea that came to my mind), or "a personal mental image improving on any one particular offered him by nature."[12] In this case, that idea could also be seen as a cause of the work—not the artist, but an idea that resided in the artist and embodied the artist in the work.[13] In late-sixteenth-century prints, this idea can be attributed to a named person and tagged with the word *invenit*.

As the painting's inventor, Raphael was associated with the creative, and according to Renaissance rhetoricians, the most important part of its composition. This helps to explain how the tag *invenit* eventually came to resonate with particular notions of agency and imagination when it appeared among the other important causes of a print having been made: the dedicatee, the dedicator, the publisher, and the engraver. Because of the rather recent importance that the modern period places on the role of originality in the demonstration

of creativity and genius, in visual art the privileged role of "inventor" was credited with the same responsibilities in the final work as was a literary "author."[14]
In sixteenth-century practice, however, this played out in a much more complex way. In accordance with the best practices of Agricolan rhetoric, different figures whose names appeared at the bottom of images were able to as-
sign themselves credit for the appearance of a print, as becomes clear in what
follows.

Credit, Copying, Invention, and Dedication

A papal printing privilege of 1575 protecting Diana Mantuana's right to profit
from her prints for a period of ten years named only compositions invented by
others.[15] The privilege clearly affirmed in legal Latin that Diana had engraved
in copper "the *Story of the Adulteress*, the *Feast of the Gods*, the *Horse Race*, or,
the *Triumph of Caesar* by Giulio Romano; *The Nativity of our Lord Jesus Christ*
by Giulio [Clovio], the *Image of Saint Jerome* from a model and invention of
Danielle da Volterra . . . [and] others by celebrated painters and sculptors" and
that she alone had license to profit from the sale of these images. The people
given credit for each named image in the privilege—who were most certainly
not final causes of the print having been made—are noted as inventors on the
prints, although today we would call these people their authors. In reality, the
final cause of any of the narrative prints could be the engraver, the publisher,
or the patron who might desire such a print or provide the financial support
for it.

Taking into account the responsibilities of all active agents in the production of a print, the dedicatee (the patron) can also be considered as having a
decisive role in its final creation. In architecture we still use a similar formulation; the famous Chrysler Building in New York is a good example. The patron (Walter Chrysler) caused the building to be built, and his ownership of
an automotive business made it appropriate for the architect to give the tower
its distinctive hood-ornament and radiator-cap decorations, in spite of the
fact that the building did not house offices related to the Chrysler automobile
company itself. We think of the way the building looks more as a product of
Chrysler's patronage than of the aesthetic preferences of the architect who designed it (William van Alen) or the skill of the steel workers who constructed
it. In this case, the role of the patron outweighs that of the artist.

An example of contested copying, invention, and the attribution of authorship can be seen in engraved versions of an image of St. Lawrence that was understood to have originated—in the modern sense—from the ideational activity of the sculptor Baccio Bandinelli (fig. 19.1).[16] His drawing for a fresco of the

F*igure 19.1.* Diana Mantuana (Diana Scultori), *The Martyrdom of Saint Lawrence* (B. 28, st. iii) engraving after Marcantonio Raimondi. © Copyright the Trustees of The British Museum.

saint's martyrdom was made into a print by Marcantonio Raimondi. Diana Mantuana, who may never have seen Bandinelli's Florentine fresco that she mentions in the print's dedication as being in ruinous shape, used Raimondi's print as the source for her own engraving. She is open about this in her dedication to Cardinal Ferdinando de'Medici, which appears at the lower left corner of the print, where she refers to her own work as "reengraving." Diana includes Marcantonio's "MAF" monogram ("Marcantonio fecit") near the center, to the left of a marker on which Bandinelli is credited with the invention of the image ("Baccius/Brandin/Inven"). Diana's full name and the word "incide-bat," or "engraved it," appears in block capitals beneath the foot of the soldier at the lower right.

While Diana's print accurately reproduced her model, which was Mar-cantonio's engraving, it probably did not as faithfully reflect the inventor's schema. Giorgio Vasari reported that when Marcantonio's print first appeared with Bandinelli's name on it as "inventor," Bandinelli complained to the pope that it was full of errors and therefore represented his work inaccurately. In medieval literature the attribution of authorship to a named person was done as much to avoid inferior works' being attributed to the author as it was to credit the author with a work.[17] The problem of works being falsely attributed to well-known authors was more often before the courts in the early modern period than the problem of plagiarism, that is, not having inventions credited to authors at all.[18] In the case of Bandinelli, who did not want to be seen as the author of a work that he felt looked different from his invention, the pope's reported response sidestepped the issue of improperly attributing work to an artist: he thought that the print was an improvement on the drawing and corrected design errors in the original, and he refused to give the artist satisfaction on that point.[19] Neither Bandinelli nor Marcantonio was alive to complain when Diana reengraved Marcantonio's engraving, putting herself in the role of engraver and dedicator.

When making a case for Diana's agency in her printing practice, scholars sometimes try to emphasize unimportant differences between her print and her models, but it was clear in this case that any differences in copying the picture were unintended. Instead, the print differed from its model primarily as a consequence of redirecting it to a specific person through her dedication, an act that bound her to the Medici by her (re)presentation to them of the family's patron saint.[20] This (re)presentation of an image is more unusual for its long dedication than for the overt reuse of another print, which was a perfectly acceptable way of obtaining both style and subject matter for her own image. The long, epistolary dedication played an important role in establishing both the engraver and the dedicatee as shared creators of the print.[21] Unlike Marcantonio, who issued his print without any dedication, Diana added a very courteous and flowery one in vernacular Italian, engraved in cursive script in the form of a letter, with an address, a message, a date, and a signature: "Knowing the devotion of the House of Medici to St. Lawrence, and how pleasing to it is the story of his martyrdom made in the past by Bandinelli and today almost in ruin, I wished to reengrave it to preserve it for a long time, and to dedicate it to your Most Illustrious Lordship with the service of my own house. December 1582. Diana Mantuana."

The Case of Mauritio Bona

Diana's dedication was one way of claiming primary responsibility for her act of reengraving, a matching of dedicatee and image that was as skillful as her own handiwork and, more importantly, was her own creative act. Claims of an engraver's authority could also be accomplished visually in the placement of her signature. The fortunes of the matrix for a rare woodblock print in the collection of the Art Institute of Chicago show how that might work.[22] A woodcut battle of soldiers and centaurs (fig. 19.2) was made by the Roman Geronima Parasole, who carved her own name into the block as well as the name of the painter and printmaker Antonio Tempesta, who had made the drawing she used as a model for her print (fig. 19.3). Latinizing her name to carve the words "Hieronima Parasolia incid[it]" on a banderole spread prominently in a clearing at the front and center of the battle scene, she claimed the act of cutting the block for herself. She noted Tempesta's role as "inventor" in the lower right corner, stamping "Anto[nio]. Tempest[a]. Inven[it]." on the broken strap of a cartouchelike shield. Casual detritus of armed struggle, it unfurls to reveal Tempesta's partially obliterated name between the fallen shield and the sword lying next to it, relinquished by a fallen centaur who has also lost his hand. Parasole's agency in the production of the print is magnified by the framing of the fully extended banderole bearing her name beneath the centaur's amputated forearm and his folded equine leg, so that the abbreviation for "incidebat," denoting Geronima's strong and nimble carving, is extended between the mute hoof and disabled stump of the vanquished and disarmed centaur.

Geronima Parasole took advantage of the popularity of Tempesta's inventions, which consisted equally of rousing battle scenes in an antique style and his particular way of portraying these scenes, when she had her interpretation of Tempesta's drawing published in multiple impressions. The year after she died, her print received a new dedication when it was reissued by Mauritio Bona: in the second state of her print, Bona addresses a single adulatory line in lapidary capitals to a Roman senator named Baldo Massei (fig. 19.4). "This print of Figures having fallen into my hands," writes Bona, "*notable for its engraving as well as for its invention*, I thought to take advantage of the opportunity to publish it under the patronage of your most Illustrious self, as one who has always taken pleasure in rewarding virtue. I beg you to accept the gift together with the devotion of my soul, which desires nothing else than to be honored by your wishes, and I end hoping for your every happiness, and making you my most humble bow."[23]

Mauritio Bona's choice of works to responsor must have ensured that he did a thriving business: he attached his name to editions of the most well-known Roman guidebooks (*Le cose maravigliose dell'alma città di Roma* and *Le antichità dell'alma città di Roma*), whose popularity had been proven between the late sixteenth century, when they appeared under the names of their original publishers, and 1621, when he picked them up and kept them in print through many editions. He also maintained sequential editions of an elaborate pattern book of lace designs, the *Teatro delle nobili et virtuose donne*, by Isabella (or Elisabetta) Parasole, Geronima's sister-in-law.[24] (fig. 19.5).

Figure 19.2. Geronima Cagnaccia Parasole, *Battle of the Lapiths and Centaurs* st. i, ca. 1600, woodcut on cream-laid paper, 415 × 672 mm, Amanda S. Johnson and Marion Livingston Endowment, 1999.684, the Art Institute of Chicago. Photography by the Art Institute of Chicago.

Figure 19.3. Antonio Tempesta, *Battle of the Lapiths and Centaurs*, n.d., ink and wash drawing with graphite and red chalk on ivory wove paper, 409 × 651 mm, the Leonora Hall Gurley Memorial Collection, 1922.2169, the Art Institute of Chicago. Photography by the Art Institute of Chicago.

Figure 19.4. Geronima Parasole, *Battle of Men and Centaurs*, st. ii, woodcut after Antonio Tempesta, published by Mauritio Bona, 1623. © Copyright the Trustees of The British Museum.

Figure 19.5. Francisco Villamena, title page engraving from Elisabetta Catanea Parasole, *Teatro delle nobili et virtuose donne* (1616). © Copyright Biblioteca Angelica, Rari I 2.5. By kind permission of the Ministero per i Beni e le Attività Culturali.

Many editions of Parasole's designs were printed under her name by publishers in Venice and Rome, combined with images from other, older model books whose woodblocks the publishers kept in stock. When they included them in Parasole's book, they added the rubric "with new additions." By the end of the sixteenth century Isabella's name was synonymous with modern needlework patterns and helped sell the often recombined selections of images put together by the publishers (an instance of other work being attributed to her). The first, 1616 edition of the *Teatro* was dedicated to Elisabetta de Bourbon, "Princess of Spain," with a long and flowery address by Isabella, calling herself, too, Elisabetta, in a gesture of self-identification with her dedicatee. This sort of dedication made prints by women—like Diana Mantuana's *Martyrdom of Saint Lawrence*—work like an exchange of letters, another kind of writing with which women created social networks.[25]

There are many good points in her long, courteous dedication that deserve close attention, so I include a translation of the entirety:

> In dedicating, which I am doing myself, these poor labors of mine to Your Serene Highness, I am well aware of the impudence, and the lack of proportion that there is between the humbleness of the donor and the loftiness of the royal persona to whom she gives, doubting, however, in the example of the brave Arachne, imitated by me in these designs. But the infinite kindness of Your Highness gives me the courage to show my devotion and observance with this testimony, since I, a poor woman, have no other trumpet with which to sound the heroic prizes of Your Highness than these rough trifles in which, as in a theater of womanly virtue, they can see themselves overshadowed by the infinite talents and endowments of your highness; and [with] my most humble servitude, begging you to accept in this little gift the pure affection of my soul in the way that the great Lord accepts a bit of the smoke from perfumed incense, such that one who is favored by the graces of your Highness receives the spirit to carry on serving, and continually divulging excellent praises, and the virtue of Your Highness, which may our Lord God keep for many, many happy years as I wish; from Rome, Elisabetta Catanea Parasole.[26]

Isabella Parasole insists that with painstaking persuasion a woman could both exhibit her virtue and openly claim a measure of fame through weaving her decorative work into the intricate fabric of early modern patronage structures.[27] At the beginning, Parasole emphasizes her act of dedication because it was unusual and important: "In dedicating, *which I am doing myself*, these poor labors of mine." Diana Mantuana, too, mentioned the share of the print that was her own work and volition in her dedication to the Cardinal de'Medici, writing: "I wished to reengrave it." And Geronima Parasole's gambit of literally foregrounding her role as engraver of the Tempesta battle scene paid off in Mauritio Bona's representation of his gift to the Roman senator, in which he claimed that the print was "as notable for its engraving as for its invention."

Unlike Isabella or Diana, Bona was dedicating something that "fell into his hands," not something he himself had made. He could draw attention to the fineness of his gift in different aspects of its making, but he could not, as the others had, claim credit for his creative labor. The best description of his intervention would lie in rematching a ready-made image with a recipient, which necessitated prying apart the pictorial and textual terms of the original print. Like an emblem, the print was composed of a tightly bound relationship between a picture and the words ("a knot of words and images," as one theoretician described it, in which neither element bears full meaning without the other) that transform it into a certain idea.[28] As an emblem, the text and image would never again be so seamlessly wound.

As opposed to Bona's blunt declaration, Isabella's dedication appears from behind a screen of smoke and shadows, softening the daring act of publishing her work. Fame was one fruit of Parasole's labor, alluded to verbally in the dedication and visually on the title page, in such a way as to seem to accrue to the dedicatee and not to the dedicator: "I, a poor woman, have no other trumpet with which to sound the heroic prizes of your Highness." In her dedication, Parasole turns the word "fame," from the Greek *pheme*, into "voice"; the Latin word, *fama*, means "report, rumor, reputation." Comparing herself to the industrious Arachne, the skilled mortal weaver who dared to challenge the gods, Parasole dared to be the spokeswoman for the womanly virtue of a famous princess from whose patronage she stood to benefit. In the frontispiece to her book, the figures of winged fame support the coat of arms of the new queen, under which Parasole's name appears. Parasole's intricate and impressive inventions (she alone of this group was the inventor of her images) bring fame to the virtues of the queen, whose name in return brings fame to the inventions and designs of Parasole. The circulation of benefits in this exchange relies, like the other emblems of relationship, on an understanding of the value of the image to the recipient and as registering the labor of the donor—a labor that is both material and intellectual.[29] In selecting their dedicatees and composing their dedications, women engravers demonstrated their ability to make the imaginative leap necessary to grasp the expectations of the recipients; their nuance in selecting the right gift displayed the engraver's ability to recognize and fulfill the desires of the recipient.

In 1620 Mauritio Bona issued another edition of the *Teatro*, changing the title page to bear the coat of arms of the aristocratic Roman Aldobrandini family, signaling a new dedication to the powerful niece of Clement VIII, Olimpia Aldobrandini (fig. 19.6). This time, the dedication on the inside page was signed by Verginia Bonvisi de Boni, Mauritio Bona's wife, a woman who stood in a very different relationship to the book than did Parasole.[30] The book of embroidery designs, without having been changed in other ways except for the addition of a few new pages attributed to Parasole by way of their inclusion in her book, was rededicated and became a gift of republication. No longer a collection of "rough trifles," the book was recast in its dedication as a gift that originally had been fit for a queen, now being made over by the publisher's wife to the local princess she had always admired: "My husband Mauritio Bona, having to newly republish at his expense the prints of the *Treasure* [*sic*] *of Noble and Virtuous Women*, with the addition of some new examples, because this work is wholly concerned with womanly virtue, has conceded to me the authority to send it forth under the shadow of some celebrated and noble person, these prints having the first time been dedicated to the Princess Elisabetta of Austria, now the most Christian Queen."

A last example of a print's being republished by Bona with a new dedication that changes the relationship between the original subject matter and dedication of the print is Diana Mantuana's engraving of *Christ and the Adulteress*. The print was a variation on an image from the Sistine Chapel tapestries designed in Raphael's workshop by Giulio Romano, the named inventor of the print, and others. Diana dedicated the print to the Duchess of Mantua, who owned a set of the tapestries and presided over the court to which the inventor had moved after Raphael's death (fig. 19.7). Diana's dedication here, as usual, flattered the tastes and patronage of her dedicatee while also emphasizing her own attachment to those things her patron valued: Diana's father had worked at the court that had been formed during Giulio Romano's residence, and she was therefore a legitimate heir to his greatness. Her choice of an image complemented the Duchess' collection and visually affirmed her own connection to the Mantuan court. Soon after Diana's death the plate was owned by the publisher Antonio Carenzano, who added his address and the date 1613 to the writing already on the plate. Sometime after that, the plate fell into the hands of Mauritio Bona, who scraped away Diana's graceful dedication and, noticing the convenient visual preponderance of columns (*colonne*) in the imagery, rededicated it to the Roman nobleman Pompeo Colonna, adding the Colonna arms—a column—at the upper right, and the date 1633 (fig. 19.8). In this period the Colonna family was strongly allied to that of the Barberini pope, Urban VIII, and in 1633 different members of the family were the focus of several honorific publications praising their military skills, some of them featuring columns.[31]

Figure 19.6. Francisco Villamena, title page engraving from Elisabetta Catanea Parasole, *Teatro delle nobili et virtuose donne* (Rome: Mauritio Bona, 1620). Typ 625.20.674F, Department of Printing and Graphic Arts, Houghton Library, Harvard College Library.

Figure 19.7. Diana Mantuana (Diana Scultori), *Christ and the Woman Taken in Adultery*, engraving after Giulio Romano, 42.1 × 57 cm (image), ca. 1575 (B. 4, st. ii) © Copyright the Trustees of The British Museum.

Figure 19.8. Diana Mantuana (Diana Scultori), *Christ and the Woman Taken in Adultery*, engraving after Giulio Romano, 42.1 × 57 cm (image), ca. 1575 (B. 4, st. vi), Fine Arts Museums of San Francisco, Achenbach Foundation for Graphic Arts, 1963.30.37649.

Bona's new dedication is pompous, punning, and obsequious: "I was pressed by the ancient service that I profess to Your Excellency to [im]press the lines of this sheet at the center of your glorious name, which was always at the center of my devotion. Therefore recognize this page [*foglio*] as the child [*figlio*] of my observance, and my observance for part of its merit, and devotedly I pay my respects, Dedicated by Mauritio Bona." Bona seemed to specialize in "re-entitling" the more popular inventions of Roman women, which kept them in circulation, making them even more popular, although on his own terms. The print still bore the original attributions of authorship in the lower left margin, attributing the subject matter and its pictorial disposition to Giulio Romano as inventor and the act of engraving to Diana.

Thinking about Bona's widely distributed posthumous state of *Christ and the Adulteress*, one of the prints specifically mentioned in Diana Mantuana's privilege, we should turn to Roland Barthes: "The reader is the space on which all the quotations that make up a writing are inscribed without any of them being lost; a text's unity lies not in its origin but in its destination."[32] These lines were never intended to make Barthes's readers envision a late, worn-out, rededicated impression of an old-fashioned block or plate, replete with a pa-limpsest of multiple publisher's names. But thinking in terms of Agricola's *destinatum*—the goal attained by final causes, and the many effects toward that goal—we can see how a culture of printmaking developed in such a way that it allowed the production of a physical unity in which authorship was sufficiently parsed and distributed for a woman to assume an important role, both causative and discreet, in the authoring of a print. In this way she could be present in the print and yet constantly chaperoned by more active or public causes. The success of these prints and the creative ways in which they achieved their goals seemed to suggest to Bona, a publisher of no great importance in his lifetime, a way to navigate a system in which sophisticated supplication and the formation of patronage networks was necessary for survival.

The examples of authority I discuss here are not uniquely female in the early modern period. But the discourses of invention and re-presentation, the conventions of multiple effects signed on the page, and the generous and fluid definitions of authority and entitlement made it possible for some women to insert their names into the list of possible causes in ways that did not threaten to turn the trumpets of Fame into the hoarse voice of Rumor as these prints were sold openly in bookshops and cried by peddlers through the streets.

NOTES

1. By "signature effects" I am referring to printed attributions of responsibility on the prints that may or may not look as though they were signed with the hand of the person named, unlike the signatures that appear in pencil on the bottom of prints made from the late twentieth century on, and are meant to certify authorship—in terms of invention of the image—by the person signing.

2. Jaynie Anderson's contribution on the development of connoisseurship in the Western world provides an excellent background for its emergence in the nineteenth century as a science meant to distinguish originals from copies, based on the presence of the artist's hand. See Jaynie Anderson in Enrico Castelnuovo et al., "Connoisseurship," in *Grove Art Online*, at *Oxford Art Online*, http://www.oxfordartonline.com/subscriber/article/grove/art/T019062 (accessed January 30, 2010). Also see Richard Wollheim, "Giovanni Morelli and the Origins of Scientific Connoisseurship," in *On Art and Mind: Essays and Lectures* (London: Allen Lane, 1973).

3. Wendy Wall, "Authorship and the Material Conditions of Writing," in *The Cambridge Companion to English Literature, 1500–1600*, ed. Arthur F. Kinney (Cambridge: Cambridge University Press, 2000), 68, on women and the responsibility for individual authorship, and 74–75, on the dangers of women placing their works in the public eye.

4. Wall, op. cit., 85.

5. Roger Chartier, "Princely Patronage and the Economy of Dedication," in *Forms and Meanings: Texts, Performances, and Audiences from Codex to Computer* (Philadelphia: University of Pennsylvania

Press, 1995), 34–42; and Victoria Kirkham, *Fabulous Vernacular: Boccaccio's Filocolo and the Art of Medieval Fiction* (Ann Arbor: University of Michigan Press, 2001), 80–82.

6. Wall, op. cit., 85, for the idea that "authorship emerged from the reader's experience with the book's form and not only its content."

7. Peter Mack, *Renaissance Argument: Valla and Agricola in the Traditions of Rhetoric and Dialectic* (Leiden: Brill, 1993), 2.

8. Michael Baxandall, "Rudolph Agricola on Patrons Efficient and Patrons Final: A Renaissance Discrimination," *Burlington Magazine* 124 (July 1982): 424–425.

9. Mack, op. cit., 157

10. Baxandall, op. cit., 425.

11. Agricola's book was printed in numerous editions, at both the popular level as well as at the most specialized, throughout the sixteenth century in France, Germany, Switzerland, Spain, and Italy, with the most editions printed between 1530 and 1540, peaking again between 1550 and 1560. Mack, op. cit., 272.

12. Raphael, "Lettera al Castiglione," in *Scritti d'arte del Cinquecento*, ed. Paola Barocchi, (Torino: Einaudi, 1979) 1529–1531; and Baxandall, op. cit., 425.

13. Baxandall, op. cit., 425.

14. For the difference between medieval and modern value placed on originality, see Mary Carruthers, *The Book of Memory: A Study of Memory in Medieval Culture* (Cambridge: Cambridge University Press, 1990), 2–4.

15. Evelyn Lincoln, *The Invention of the Italian Renaissance Printmaker* (New Haven, and London: Yale University Press, 2000), 189.

16. Lisa Pon, *Raphael, Dürer, and Marcantonio Raimondi: Copying and the Italian Renaissance Print* (New Haven and London: Yale University Press, 2004), 37–38.

17. Kirkham, op. cit., 82. In his *Little Treatise in Praise of Dante*, Boccaccio wrote that he wanted to record all of Dante's works so that no one else could either claim title to them nor attribute (Kirkham uses the term "entitle") to him works that he did not write.

18. Roger Chartier, "Foucault's Chiasmus," in *Scientific Authorship: Credit and Intellectual Property in Science*, ed. M. Biagioli and P. Galison (London: Routledge, 2003), 21.

19. Giorgio Vasari, *Le Vite*, ed. R. Bettarini & P. Barocchi (Florence: Sansoni, 1966–), vol. 5: 13, lines 34ff.

20. Aafke E. Komter, *Social Solidarity and the Gift* (Cambridge: Cambridge University Press, 2005), 6, 76–97.

21. Victoria Kirkham and Roger Chartier have already outlined how both authors and dedicatees could be considered the creators of dedicated books in this period. See Kirkham, op. cit., 82; Chartier, 1995, op. cit, 34–35.

22. Lia Markey, "The Female Printmaker and the Culture of the Reproductive Print Workshop," in *Paper Museums: The Reproductive Print in Europe*, ed. R. Zorach and E. Rodini (Chicago: Smart Art Museum, 2005), 58.

23. Michael Bury, *The Print in Italy, 1550–1620* (London: British Museum, 2001), 42–43.

24. For the Parasole family, see Marco Pupillo, "Gli incisori di Baronio," in *Baronio e le sue fonti; atti del Convegno internazionale di studi, Sora, 10–13 ottobre 2007*, ed. L. Gulia (Sora: Centro di Studi Sorani "Vincenzo Patriarca," 2009), 839–865.

25. Marina D'Amelia, "Lo scambio epistolare tra Cinque e Seicento," in *Per lettera: La scrittura epistolare femminile tra archivio e tipografia secoli xv–xvii*, ed. G. Zarri (Rome: Viella, 1999), 83; Komter, op. cit., 76–97.

26. Isabella Parasole, *Teatro delle nobili et virtuose donne* (Rome, 1616).

27. Much has been written on women's capacity for virtue in the Renaissance, or rather, the lack of it, but see Margaret L. King and Albert Rabil Jr., "Editor's Introduction to the Series," in any book from the series The Other Voice in Early Modern Europe, for example: Moderata Fonte, *The Worth of Women: Wherein Is Clearly Revealed Their Nobility and Their Superiority to Men*, ed. and trans. V. Cox (Chicago: University of Chicago Press, 1997), vii–xxvi. Also see Mark Rose, "The Author in Court" in *The Construction of Authorship*, ed. M. Woodmansee and P. Jaszi (Durham, NC: Duke University Press, 1999), 225–226.

28. Robert Klein, "The Theory of Figurative Expression in Italian Treatises on the *Impresa*," in *Form and Meaning* (Princeton, NJ: Princeton University Press, 1979), 7; and Karen Pinkus, *Picturing Silence: Emblem, Language, Counter-Reformation Materiality* (Ann Arbor: University of Michigan Press, 1996), 23–25.

29. Lee Anne Fennell on "empathetic dialogue" stresses that "a true gift embodies and perpetuates empathetic dialogue between giver and recipient, facilitating and documenting each party's imaginative participation in the life of the other." Lee Anne Fennell, "Unpacking the Gift: Illiquid Goods and Empathetic Dialogue," in *The Question of the Gift: Essays across Disciplines,* ed. M. Osteen (London: Routledge, 2002), 93.

30. Arthur Lotz, *Bibliographie der Modelbüche*, 2nd ed. (Stuttgart: A. Hiersemann, 1963), 245–246.

31. See Christina Strunck, "Old Nobility versus New: Colonna Art Patronage during the Barberini and Pamphilj Pontificates (1623-1655)," in *Art and Identity in Early Modern Rome*, ed. J. Burke and M. Bury (Aldershot, UK: Ashgate, 2008) 138–144. I thank Dr. Strunck for pointing this out to me.

32. Roland Barthes, "The Death of the Author," in *Image, Music, Text*, trans. Stephen Heath (New York: Hill and Wang, 1977), 148.

TIM LENOIR and ERIC GIANNELLA

20

Technological Platforms and the Layers of Patent Data

Technological Platforms

The primary asset of any technology company is its technological plat-form.[1] A technological platform is a foundational technology consist-ing of an ensemble of technology components, subsystems, and inter-faces that form a common structure from which derivative products can be efficiently developed and produced. Within a technology platform one or more of the components might be an especially critical "core technology," sometimes a scientific or technological breakthrough that enables the creation of the platform or provides its main competitive advantage. The platform is the technological system a company uses to produce its primary products and bring them to market; indeed, small and large companies alike direct their research and development ef-forts toward building platform technologies and diversifying them in ways capable of securing recurring product and service revenue from a range of customers.[2]

Technological platforms are so central to the industrial landscape that it makes very real sense to consider that a single invention is not by itself significant until it has been successfully incorporated into a technological platform either as the core or one of the key component technologies of a technological platform. No matter how critical a single technological breakthrough may be, it is typically necessary to create ancillary supporting technologies around it that capitalize on the innovation and shape it into a marketable stream of products or processes. The importance of technology platforms in the dynamics of the industrial marketplace is evident in the behavior of technology managers and the legal teams of major firms who invest significant portions of their time and resources in protecting their technology platforms by filing patents, creating legal thickets of licensing and cross-licensing arrangements to ensure the viability of their core technologies, and either threatening or directly engaging in legal action when their core technologies are infringed. The behavior of university technology transfer officers (TTOs) similarly underscores the importance of platforms: while TTOs proceed cautiously in incurring the cost of filing a patent on a single invention, they immediately invest in filing on what they perceive as a platform technology.

The perception that firms invest heavily in acquiring and protecting the intellectual property represented in their platform technologies leads us to focus on patent data as a means for probing the formation of novel technological systems and their applications. Our goal in this chapter is to use patent data to track the emergence of platform technologies and map them in the competitive industrial landscape. There are, to be sure, precautions to be taken in relying on patent data to investigate innovation. Patents are not transparent documents. Individual inventors and firms have a variety of motivations and strategic objectives in making use of the U.S. patent system for laying claim to a specific piece of intellectual property. Sometimes a patent is just what it appears to be: a straightforward description of an original invention or process complete with an honest and accurate description of the prior art and science upon which it depends. However, the intentions behind many patents are not so transparent. Moreover, as recent studies have revealed, the checks and balances built into the system to ensure the originality of an invention and guarantee the citation of prior and relevant art are flawed in many ways. The context of technical invention and the context of establishing and defending intellectual property are quite different. Recent studies have shown that patents can be the source of divergent and even misleading signals because of the variety of strategies deployed by corporate actors in using the patent system to protect their intellectual property. Transparency is not always a motivating factor in filing a patent,[3] and techniques abound for gaming the system to protect competitive advantage.[4] In addition to these problems, concerns have been raised about the U.S. Patent and Trademark Office's (USPTO's) practices for checking and assigning prior art, adding further obstacles to treating patents as straightforward windows onto the innovation process.[5] While these critics correctly warn that the multiple interests woven into patent data create obstacles in their utility as indicators of innovative activity, we believe that with the appropriate methodological strategy the "noise" can actually create an opportunity for using patents as a vehicle for studying the coevolution of social and technical phenomena embodied in technological platforms. Despite these and other problems discussed in greater depth below, patents remain a rich source of information that can be queried in ways useful for identifying technological platforms. Our reason for this optimism is that while lots of noise may be introduced in the system by players seeking to protect the competitive advantage of a platform or discourage others from encroaching on their territory, with the techniques we will demonstrate it is still possible to identify the emergence, stabilization, and adaptation of the ensemble of individual component technologies that make up a platform. The trick is in finding tools robust enough to identify the platform elements and observe them sticking together over time in tightly coupled mutual dependencies as they evolve through the patent landscape. We propose to demonstrate an approach to this problem. We begin with an analysis of what constitutes a technology platform using illustrative examples and then move into some of the common ways that patent data tend to capture a variety of social and business phenomena. We conclude with a case study on radio-frequency identification (RFID) technologies, which we chose for their widespread applicability, heavy patent coverage, and the many forms an RFID system can take in its implementation.

Because of its emphasis on systems, our definition of a platform resembles Thomas Hughes's classic discussion of the elements of large technological systems.[6] Hughes emphasized that systems rather than single inventions ought to occupy central stage in analyses of the history of technology. Thus, in his discussions of Edison's powerful invention of the electric lamp, Hughes emphasized that the carbon filament lamp was not invented separately by Edison but as an economically feasible element to be conjoined with other elements, such as the pump for evacuating bulbs, the DC generator, and insulated copper wiring in sufficient diameter to provide lighting for a one-square-mile area in New York City at a cost competitive with then-existent gas lighting. The environment of economic and engineering constraints was crucial to the invention. Hughes's model emphasized the socially constructed character of technological systems by pointing to the interdependencies between engineering, economic, political, and social factors and by putting them all on near equal footing in the construction of large technological systems.[7] Another key feature of Hughes's model was the role of reverse salients in the expansion and adaptation of a technological system. As a system advanced, it invariably encountered obstacles that required a technical, economic, or political solution.

Although he did not experiment with patent analysis, Hughes surmised that technological reverse salients would be attractor sites of most intense inventive and patenting activity. When Hughes first made this conjecture, work on patent citations by Zvi Griliches, Manuel Trajtenberg, Adam Jaffe, Rebecca Henderson and other pioneers in the use of patent data was in its infancy. Since they are born at the interface between scientific and technical invention on one hand and business, economic, and regulatory activities in the marketplace on the other, technology platforms as reflected in patent data are in many ways the fossil artifacts of the evolutionary forces shaping Hughes's large technical systems.[8] Of course the quantitative picture is not the entire story. As we have argued elsewhere in dealing similarly with the emergence of new technologies such as DNA microarrays, text mining and visualization tools can provide proxies of sites to pursue in-depth ethnographic and historical studies.[9]

A classic example of a technology platform is the inkjet printer, first introduced by Hewlett-Packard (HP) in 1984.[10] The components of the HP 500 Inkjet Printer, a revolutionary printer that launched an entire family of HP inkjet printers, fell into three broad categories: mechanical elements (the drive train and key panel), electronics (including a disposable print head, chip, and memory), and instructions embedded into chips that controlled printing and communications with a PC. The core technology of this first platform was a disposable printhead that used a heating element to heat liquid ink to form a vapor bubble, which forced the ink droplets onto paper through a print nozzle. A large family of different inkjet printers was based on this platform. The next generation of HP printers—the HP 600—took advantage of new ink technology invented by HP engineers that provided better-quality color and allowed HP inkjet printers to rival laser-jet printers by printing at resolutions of 600 dots per inch in rich black and 300 dots per inch in color. This novel ink became the core technology of the new HP 600 series, but implementing it forced the complete reengineering of all the other major components.

Similarly, the key components for radio-frequency-based identification and tracking systems have been around for quite some time, but it was not until the actual tracking devices could be manufactured cheaply that these components were made applicable to inventory tracking and supply chain management. As one might expect, their use in crucial manufacturing and distribution functions subsequently drove improvements and further cost reductions in RFID systems that could make them even more broadly useful. The actual RFID tracking devices, often called tags or transponders, can be passive or active. Active tags can transmit information farther but are typically larger and much more expensive because they require a battery or internal power source. In the case of passive tags, the incoming radio wave provides enough energy for the tag to transmit a response signal. These tags may merely contain a unique se-rial number, or they might contain a host of tracking information that can be updated as they move through an inventory and distribution network.

Scanners or readers can be interconnected and placed in multiple locations, such as factories and shipping yards to track items as they move through a manufacturing or transportation process. Many types of RFID readers can simultaneously receive information from multiple tags. Because tags often contain patient, consumer, or other sensitive information, much effort has been dedicated to making their data secure through encryption and other means. As a result, some readers are fairly sophisticated, containing software for decoding the information received from tags and sending it to a database or other centralized repository. The use of networked and geographically dis-persed readers with a centralized database to track an entire supply chain is fairly common. Table 20.1 presents the basic components of an RFID system. We would expect most of these components to be deployed in an installation of an RF-based tracking infrastructure:

The Use of Patents in Researching Platforms

Before we explain our approach to platforms, it is useful to think about the creation of patents and their limitations as a source of information. Many scholars of technological change are initially eager to view patents as markers of technical advance. But patents are in fact poor proxies for innovations.[11] An example of the disconnect between patents and technology is the finding that in large, diversified technology companies often less than one-third of the active patent portfolio pertains to products on the market.[12] Of the patents that may protect inventions embodied in saleable products or services, an even smaller percentage represent inventions that enabled significant performance

Table 20.1. RFID technologies

Reader	Transponder/tag
Software	Data/IC
Communications protocol	Encryption
Antenna	Antenna
	Power source[a]

[a] A power source in active tags is typically a battery, but it can take other forms as well. We did not include the manufacturing process as a feature of the stack, but it is considered as a patented area that reflects the growth of the RFID platform. There are many variations of RFID systems that we included, some with inexpensive, disposable tags, others using much more sophisticated transponders.

improvements or the realization of a new product. Indeed, patents typically cover quite minor differences in technological components or designs.

A novel invention is merely a necessary condition for obtaining a patent, but desire for intellectual property is sufficient if an applicant is willing to receive a patent with very narrow claims. In many cases, such as in software algorithms or particular manufacturing processes, trade secrets might be the best means of protecting the results of a firm's innovative labor. Yet if a software startup company were to seek venture capital funding, it might be advantageous to obtain patent protection on some aspects of its product in order to have demonstrable assets. Large companies engaged in building patent thickets to "wall off" product spaces or that are concerned with the terms of cross-license agreements often establish incentives to promote patenting. These incentives may take the form of public recognition, a financial bonus, or satisfaction of a prerequisite to promotion. These organizational practices, which often result from industry and legal contexts, strongly influence the propensity to patent, or the willingness of a firm to seek a patent on an invention of given quality. For example, industry executives explain that the dramatic increase in semiconductor patenting between 1982 and 1992 (moving from .3 to .6 patents per \$1M of real R&D spending) was a result of court decisions strengthening patents in the early 1980s and a subsequent increase in litigation and cross-licensing.[13]

Another important factor affecting the decision to patent is the trade-off between patenting and other forms of appropriating intellectual assets. Several excellent studies by economists have outlined frameworks for generating revenue from the fruits of research and development, including the consideration of factors such as complementary assets (e.g., manufacturing capability, distribution channels), strength of intellectual property protection, the nature of the technology, its strategic importance, and the expected time to market of resulting products.[14] The manner in which a firm protects and commercializes a technology, whether through means such as patenting and licensing or trade secrets and in-house manufacturing, is often the result of careful consideration of various appropriation strategies.

The nature of the underlying technology, the resulting market conditions, and the ability to effectively protect inventions and prevent workarounds through the distorting lens of patent claims have a very strong impact on the characteristics of patent data from a particular industry. In surveys of R&D managers, those involved with discrete technologies, such as chemical compounds (e.g., pharmaceuticals), patent protection is viewed as a more effective means of protecting intellectual property, whereas in complex product industries, such as semiconductor production (in which nonexclusive patent

cross-licenses are common because of widespread infringement), manufacturing, secrecy, and lead time are seen as more effective than patents.[15] In Japan,
patent claims must be narrower by law, forcing companies to file more patents
than their U.S. counterparts to protect a particular technology and encouraging more cross-licensing across all technology sectors.[16]

As this might suggest, for the most part an individual patent provides fairly
uncertain and typically narrow exclusionary rights in a product market. In
order to use patents effectively in litigation or negotiation, many companies
group them to account for their limited scope and frequent shortcomings in
enforceability. Rather than equating one patent with an invention or a single
technology, a more accurate way of thinking about patents is to imagine companies filing a large number of incremental patents along with the very rare
patent on a truly breakthrough invention, with only a fraction of the total reflecting some aspect of an actual product on the market.

To complicate matters further, there are significant challenges to searching
for and interpreting patents. Surprising variations in terminology across organizations and geographies make it very difficult to retrieve even a majority of
relevant results using terms that conceptually encapsulate a field. In some cases
this variation in language is intentionally designed to assist with patent prosecution, and in others it merely reflects different perspectives on a technological domain. Furthermore, the classifications used by various patent authorities
to assist examiners in reviewing prior art during the patent examination process are applied inconsistently and cut across technologies in unintuitive ways
that reflect the organic and historical legacy of the classification systems.

Putting aside the difficulty of interpreting the relationship between patents
and technologies, the first significant challenge in attempting to use patent
data as a source in studying technological platforms is in identifying components as reflected in the patent literature. In order to deal with this issue, we
make several basic assumptions about the nature of a technological component and the ways it might be captured through the characteristics of patent
data. Although many patents do not clearly map to a particular technology,
they can be placed into manageable conceptual units in order to be useful in
the study of technological advance. Here we propose that in some cases, the
patents relating to technological components can be identified and grouped in
a manner that reflects the key parts of a technological platform. This grouping,
often termed clustering, can be performed using citation networks, in which
patents are associated with one another on the basis of having made references
to similar types of background material. Another commonly used approach to
clustering patents is to identify unique sets of words in documents that are only
shared within small groups across the entire corpus. We use both strategies.

The other aspect of a platform, which distinguishes it from a technological system, is that it is applied in different forms in a variety of settings. We illustrate this aspect of the RFID platform by matching patent assignees, or the organization owning the patent when it was issued, to their standard industrial classification (SIC) codes, which were created by the U.S. government for the purpose of tracking industry financial activity.[17] We believe that by demonstrating the interest of companies in different industries in improving the key components of a platform (rather than just purchasing them) we can infer that a degree of customization and invention has taken place in using the platform in a particular setting. By tracking the patent citations between these components over time, we believe that, as illustrated here in the case of RFID, it is possible to map the development of a technological platform.

Patents and RFID Technology

We chose to focus on RFID technologies in our case history because of their applicability in a variety of industries and the recognizable components needed to implement an RFID system. We began with roughly 7,800 patents that were related to RFID technologies. Figure 20.1 contains data on the number of patent applications filed and patents granted in nearly the last quarter century with some relation to RFID technologies.[18] RFID patent applications

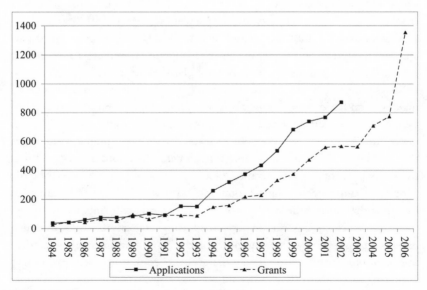

Figure 20.1. Patent applications and grants in RFID data set (1984–2006).

began to increase in the early to mid-1990s as the price of manufacturing transponders dropped—the price of tags was a key impediment to wider adoption of RFID tracking. The number of patent applications increased steadily to roughly 872 in 2002, after which we truncated the line because the time between applying for and receiving a patent makes the chart misleading beyond this year. The number of granted patents went up rapidly from roughly 700 in 2004 to 1,360 in 2006.

Analysis of RFID Patents

We placed patents into each of the nine component categories (plus manufacturing) shown in the RFID stack in table 20.1 using their most frequent key words, assignees, and the citation patterns. We manually removed patents that had been incorrectly clustered because of some patents' citing too much unrelated background material and, more legitimately, because of tight interlinking of RFID components within companies that target multiple parts or all of the vertical market. We were left with approximately 2,500 patents in the nine component categories. These patents were on RFID technology itself, whereas many of the patents that were captured in the broader query simply made claims over applying RFID to a particular problem.

In the case of RFID technologies, we would expect companies that had become providers of particular components or solution providers to have the most intellectual property in the space. There was a mix of medium and large companies in the top ten most common assignees for the RFID patents we studied (table 20.2). These companies tended to cite one another's technology fairly frequently. Figure 20.2 illustrates citations between these companies as a percentage of total citations made by that company's RFID patents. The thinnest lines represent 1 percent of total citations made by an organization, while the thickest represent 5 percent.[19] The area of each circle represents the number of patents each company had, with Micron having the most at 202 and Battelle and Toshiba having just 32 in our data set.

Most of the top twenty-five organizations in our set had fairly strong associations with one another; only two did not make at least 1 percent of their citations to the patents of another organization.[20] Companies that made a significant investment in RFID technologies tended to cite and be cited by other top organizations more broadly, displaying a high connectivity even on a percentage basis relative to organizations that had fewer patents in the space. This might suggest that the highly patenting organizations were not simply displaying a high propensity to patent compared to other organizations but actually were covering different parts of RFID systems with their patents. Some

Table 20.2 Most common corporate assignees in RFID data set

Company	No. of assignments
Micron Technology	202
Motorola	199
Sensormatic Electronics	152
International Business Machines (IBM)	148
Symbol Technologies	140
Intermec IP	119
Hewlett-Packard Development Company	65
Texas Instruments	64
3M Innovative Properties Company	60
General Electric	49

companies, such as Hitachi, Sony, HP, and Avery, were highly connected despite their small portfolios, meaning that it is likely their portfolios covered a broader spectrum of RFID technologies than those of companies that were less connected. Organizations like the U.S. Navy, Toshiba, and Eastman Kodak may have only had patents covering some aspect of RFID technologies in our data set, or they may simply have made reference to a different group of technological antecedents.

Connections between RFID Components

The basic technologies to create RFID systems had been around well before the increase of patenting in the space examined. The area only became a subject of more research and patenting as the cost of tags (i.e., manufacturing cost) dropped to the point that it was feasible to use RFID in inventory and supply chain tracking. The tags are still prohibitively expensive for widespread adoption in some areas, such as pharmaceuticals, but many experts hope the cheapest tags will someday reach a price of five cents.

Because the price of tags was so important to the further development of the system, we have modeled the citation patterns among RFID components with tag patents as the core technology in the platform. The citation map (fig. 20.3) demonstrates the increase in RFID patenting from 1987 through 2006 and the disproportionate increase in citations between various RFID component technologies over the same period. As in figure 20.2, the area of the nodes represents the number of patents relating to a component in a particular time

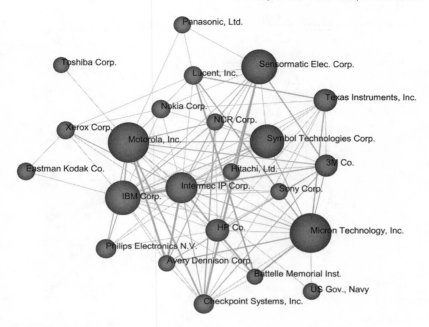

Figure 20.2. Citations among top organizations patenting RFID technologies.

period. The lines should be read from right to left, as they reflect references to previous patents. The thickness of the line indicates the percentage of citations made to that node among the total number of citations. The thinnest line represents 1 percent of citations, while the thickest represents 7 percent. As reference points, the largest cluster had 279 patents (tag 2000–2002), while the smallest had just one (software 1987–1990, manufacturing 1991–1993). In 2003–2006, the software group had forty patents. The slight vertical offset for each component in alternating time brackets is simply used to reduce confusion about the origin and destination of citation lines.

Prior to the early 1990s, there was little patenting in this space, and none of the patents in our component data set in this time period seem to have attracted a large share of citations from RFID patents in subsequent years. In the mid-1990s patenting increased substantially, with the designs of tags being more relevant, as indicated by citations, to future RFID components. As patenting continued to increase in the late 1990s and after 2000, patents on RFID transponders continued to be the most consistently cited patents by other components, suggesting, perhaps unsurprisingly, that the technology's trajectory was heavily influenced by characteristics of its core technology, the tags.

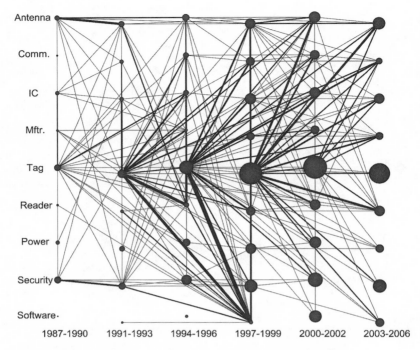

Figure 20.3. Patent citations among key RFID technologies (1987–2006).[21]

The RFID Platform

We have shown that RFID was based on components that can be identified in the patent literature, but we have not explained what characterizes this particular system as a platform. In order to demonstrate the increasing relevance of RFIDs to various industries, we analyzed patent citations to the nine component technologies. We believe that if companies in a particular industry are citing most of the components of the RFID platform, the platform has become relevant (or is in the process of being applied) to that industry. While we recognize that most RFID systems are manufactured by dedicated RFID and IT companies and deployed by systems integrators or consultants, there is a great deal of customization for each user. These unique company and industry requirements often result in modifications to the parts of the platform and new patents being filed. To discover which industries were citing RFID patents, we identified all the patents that cited the set of 2,600 component patents and matched the owners of those patents (approximately 21,000) to SIC codes created by the U.S. government to track publicly traded companies.

Table 20.3 presents SIC codes along with the number of times patents owned by public companies in that industry cited each RFID platform component.

The number of patents for each component is given in the bottom row. The total number of citations for each component is provided in the row immediately above. Semiconductor, communications, and computer hardware companies understandably dominated the group of companies citing RFID patents. Several industries cited *every single RFID component*, making their association with RFID much less tenuous than if they had simply cited a narrow slice of RFID patents.

Beyond the first few rows, the list of industries closely associated with RFID technologies becomes much more unexpected and interesting. Paper and box makers developed their own inexpensive RFID technologies and deployed the systems extensively in manufacturing and shipping operations (including paper-based tags). Defense companies and the military use RFID chips to identify and track particular weapons and materials. Tire manufacturers designed RFID technologies to monitor tire pressure and wear. Additionally, other industries became providers of technologies to the RFID platform rather than adopters or user innovators. Software and network hardware providers created products for analyzing and efficiently transmitting massive amounts of RFID data. Large information technology and electronics companies helped integrate RFID with other types of sensor and tracking technologies, such as GPS and optical scanning. As these examples indicate, the nature of the interest generated within each industry around RFID technologies was slightly different, but as a group they serve to reinforce the transformation of RFID into a versatile technological platform.

Generalizing and Automating Large-Scale Analysis of Platforms: New Tools for STS

Our intention in this paper is to use the case of the RFID platform to sketch a programmatic vision for using quantitative analyses of patents and scientific and engineering literature combined with techniques for visualizing the results in order to map the landscape of both existing and emerging technologies. While initially enamored with quantitative approaches, such as citation analysis, the field of science and technology studies (STS) has focused more on local historical studies of particular inventions, scientists, inventors, and especially ethnographic studies of laboratories. Despite the professed commitment of many STS researchers to "actor network theory" and "trading zones" as models for capturing the dynamics of science and technology, STS researchers have by and large eschewed applying quantitative economic and sociological approaches to very large data sets in which network effects involving

Table 20.3 Industries citing RFID technologies

Industry	Antennae	Comm.	Integrated circuit	Mfr.	Power	Reader	Security	Software	Tag	N
Semiconductors and related devices	146	191	254	92	245	190	152	40	1154	2464
Communications equipment	186	13	48	11	38	21	265	0	280	862
Radio and TV broadcast communication equipment	93	33	81	27	136	48	85	41	251	795
Computer peripheral equipment	23	28	28	20	29	100	37	6	221	492
Computer programming, data process	8	17	24	3	22	26	126	21	145	392
Converted paper and paperboard excluding boxes	49	13	47	31	14	7	45	1	183	390
Computer integrated system design	38	31	22	17	24	31	44	15	144	366
Calculating and accounting machinery excluding computers	10	3	14	5	5	40	71	4	144	296
Search, navigation, and guidance aero systems	44	12	5	4	12	5	24	1	114	221
Computer and office equipment	20	5	17	8	15	11	40	6	59	181
Electronic components	7	7	34	16	3	6	11	0	69	153
Public-building and related furniture	19	0	32	0	4	2	3	0	92	152
Prepackaged software	0	11	3	0	11	1	73	8	16	123
Electronic computers	11	8	18	1	19	4	41	3	12	117
Photographic equipment and supplies	5	5	7	4	3	9	17	2	58	110

continued

Table 20.3 Industries citing RFID technologies (*continued*)

Industry	Antennae	Comm.	Integrated circuit	Mfr.	Power	Reader	Security	Software	Tag	N
Electromedical apparatuses	29	0	4	0	62	0	3	1	10	109
Conglomerates	13	8	4	8	6	7	15	0	44	105
Tires and inner tubes	4	0	12	11	1	3	1	0	73	105
Computer communication equipment	2	2	2	0	8	21	53	4	10	102
Household audio and video equipment	6	7	8	2	13	3	24	8	25	96
Motor vehicle parts and accessories	8	2	12	0	7	10	15	0	34	88
Office machines	6	6	3	3	4	2	20	8	32	84
Phone communication and radiotelephone	11	5	4	1	4	2	20	13	7	67
Commercial physical and biological research	3	0	6	0	4	4	3	0	37	57
Motor vehicles and car bodies	1	1	4	1	4	2	20	13	7	57
Air conditioning, heating, and refrigeration equipment	4	0	3		36	2	6	0	4	55
Petroleum refining	0	0	1	5	10	0	6	0	32	54
Telephone and telegraph apparatuses	9	4	1	0	12	3	8	4	10	51
Electronics, other electrical equipment excluding computers	8	1	0	2	19	1	6	0	8	45
Total citations per item	763	413	698	272	766	563	1241	186	3286	8188
No. of component patents	275	136	220	112	231	183	417	135	938	2647

economic transactions are central objects of investigation and have instead followed limited numbers of links among a handful of individual actors. We are not advocating abandonment of traditional STS methods. Rather we are encouraging an expansion of the STS agenda to include quantitative methods of citation analysis, text mining, and visualization as a means for mapping the broad-stroke dynamics of the evolution of technology. The technological landscapes generated by our approach can provide an itinerary for subsequent investigation using STS ethnographic and historical research techniques.[22]

A number of factors recommend the approach we are advocating. A salient feature of the recent history of science and technology noted by a number of recent studies is the increasing globalization of scientific knowledge production and the internationalization of the R&D workforce.[23] Countries such as South Korea, Singapore, China, India, and Brazil are no longer sites for offshoring manufacturing operations of U.S.-, Japanese-, and European-based international firms. Increasingly firms based in countries such as China are moving up the value chain by becoming premier indigenous centers for research rather than merely manufacturing centers for products controlled by others. For instance, recognizing the availability of high-quality researchers and state-of-the-art infrastructure for research facilities, pharmaceutical firms such as GlaxoSmithKline, Sanofi-Aventis, and others have opened their own dedicated research facilities in China as well as collaborative operations with several key science centers, and companies such as Intel and Microsoft have recognized that Chinese-educated and -trained scientists, engineers, and managers "are capable of doing any engineering job, any software job, and managerial job that people in the US are capable of doing."[24] In high-tech research and development areas such as information and communications technologies and in areas related to renewable energy, Chinese firms, like their counterparts in other developing nations, are forming mergers with and acquisitions of firms in the United States, Europe, and other countries to increase their ownership share and control of key technologies. China has recently emerged as the leading producer of scientific articles in nanotechnology and ranks third in total patents filed with the World Intellectual Property Organization (WIPO) in 2008. Similar stories can be repeated for other national research infrastructures. The monopoly on research and development once held by the United States and leading countries of the EU is broken, and what was once a one-way street of knowledge production and diffusion is now a highly distributed network with feedback loops into different levels of global value chains worldwide.[25] As STS researchers whose recent work has focused on the development of contemporary genomics, biotechnology, and nanotechnology, we are acutely aware of the challenges in charting new clusters of innovation that may lead to stable research areas. The inter- and multidisciplinary nature of contemporary research; the vast number of scientists and engineers in academe, industry, and government working in these areas; and the increasing internationalization of research efforts in a global economy introduce problems of scale and complexity for which quantitative approaches are attractive. Our claim is that the multiply intertwined efforts of scientists, engineers, government funding agencies, strategic managers of technology-intensive firms, and intellectual property experts to build, extend, and defend technology platforms provides a window onto the dynamics shaping technoscience. Despite the complicated stakes, intentions, and strategies embodied in patents, the rich layers of information embedded therein can be mined for purposes of tracing the evolution of technology platforms.

The case of the RFID platform presented above is offered as a proof of concept of the sort of data acquisition and analysis involved in identifying a technology platform, the evolution of its key components, and the major commercial firms involved in developing and exploiting it. However, the RFID case is just a handcrafted version of the larger-scaled data- and computational-intensive approach we believe is required to yield robust results for STS with potential policy implications. In the final part of this essay we would like to illustrate our strategy for expanding the RFID case. There are a number of areas we want to improve upon. Our RFID case was constructed by using the Delphion search engine working on patents from the USPTO. We used Delphion because it is a standard tool familiar to most researchers who work with patent data. Like most patent and scientific literature search engines, Delphion utilizes the categories defined by the USPTO. A number of researchers have criticized the ontologies of the USPTO as being based in frequently outdated historical precedents and not sufficiently refined to capture very recent technological activity. The effect of this can be seen in Delphion search results, where in most cases a well-formed query returns literally thousands of patents that are not structurally related to one another, requiring patient reading and sorting to be useful. Even if the ontology of the USPTO were an accurate representation of technology space, the use of prescribed ontologies delimits the items being explored to already existing categories, making it difficult to identify potential new directions of innovation and the emergence (in the cases that interest us most) of new technological platforms.

The need for a different approach becomes evident when we consider the recent interest in nanotechnology. Unlike some fields where a core set of discoveries lead to a branching structure of scientific and technical innovation—for example, the core techniques of gene replication, splicing, polymerase chain reaction (PCR) amplification, green fluorescent protein marking, and related techniques for genomics—nanotechnology covers a diverse spectrum of fields. The USPTO, for instance, includes nanotechnology in 214 different classifications. In October 2004 a separate category for nanotechnology (Category 977) was created at the USPTO, but it is not deemed likely by most researchers to capture a large part of the most interesting work. The issue here is that for purposes of creating useful detailed search results, the standard approach is to begin by constructing a robust ontology of key words, concepts, processes, etc., that are agreed upon by the relevant communities to capture the essential information of the field.[26] Constructing these ontologies is for the most part a work of love infused with a lot of political committee work.

In order to address these issues our approach is to avoid the use of externally generated preassigned ontologies and instead use relationships among patents based on the internal contents of the documents themselves and the ways they reference one another. Implementing this "bottom-up" approach entails examining the interrelationships among the entire set of patents (approximately 4 million patents currently in the USPTO database in force since the 1970s). Since the relationships among documents in the set change as new documents are added, it is necessary to repeat the computational exercise on a regular basis (e.g., quarterly). Furthermore, in order to address the increasing globalization of research and knowledge production, it is necessary to merge the U.S. patent set with the patents filed at the European Patent Office (EPO), the Japanese Patent Office (JPO), and the World Intellectual Property Organization (WIPO).

We approached this problem by applying algorithms developed for mining the link structure of the Web. Just as Internet researchers have been interested in mapping the nodal structure of the Web, we are interested in the structure of the entire USPTO data set since 1970, WIPO, EPO, and JPO. In the present case we explore RFID technology as a possibly dense subgraph of this massive graph. In particular we adapted methods known as "shingling" developed by several researchers but most effectively for our purposes by a group of researchers at IBM Almaden.[27] The methods we have adapted are the basis for the search engine developed by SparkIP, Inc., of Atlanta.[28] Our method, incorporated into the SparkCluster engine, for generating densely related clusters of patent documents is based on a restrictive criterion of co-citation, where the same two documents (patents) are referenced (cited) by two separate documents (patents), forming a "shingle" (fig. 20.4). The assumption is that the chances are extremely low that two unrelated documents (barring that they share the same authors or organization) have exactly the same pair of citations.[29] For each patent there are $n!/2(n-2)!$ shingles, where n is the number of references in the patent. This means that for a patent with 40 references, 780

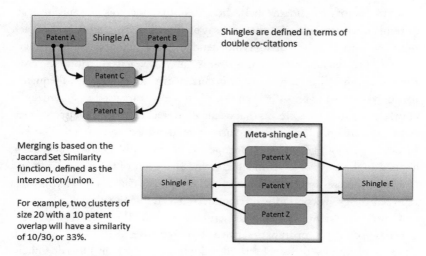

Figure 20.4. Hierarchical clustering of patents.

shingles (i.e., $(40 \times 39)/2$) are generated. All patents sharing the same shingle are grouped into a cluster as being conceptually similar. This is obviously a very small set, so our next step involves forming groups of clusters sharing overlapping shingles and then merging groups of clusters into hierarchies. The merging process we employ is based on the well-accepted Jaccard set similarity function, defined as the intersection/union. For example, two clusters of size 20 with a 10-patent overlap will have a similarity of 10/30, or 33%. In order to accommodate the merging of clusters that exhibit a significant difference in their number of patents—for example, a large cluster with 95 patents and a small cluster with only 10 patents with a 5-patent overlap between the two clusters gives a 5 percent similarity ranking on the Jaccard set similarity function, which most would consider a low similarity ranking despite the fact that half the smaller cluster is contained in the large cluster—a similarity function was developed that is proportional to the overlap expressed by the smaller cluster but decays exponentially as the size disparity grows. This decay prevents a cluster from reaching a certain mass and absorbing smaller clusters because of the thematic breadth afforded by containing vastly more patents.[30]

As explained above, our goal is to extract meaningful relationships among patents from the bottom up without taking recourse to predefined ontologies. This entails automatically generating labels describing the shared content of each of the clusters generated by the citation linkage methods described above. Labeling is based on text-mining the full text of documents in our clusters. In order to identify candidate labels, the system first analyzes *n*-grams, or a set of terms with *n* members in the full text of every patent in a hierarchy. Each *n*-gram is scored on the basis of its independence (or whether it consistently appears next to particular words or is context insensitive), its distribution across the patents in a cluster, number of occurrences, and its length.[31] Frequency lists of co-occurring terms in each document cluster are used to organize the cluster into subclusters. Terms that occur all over a hierarchy of clusters versus terms that are unique to specific clusters are identified, resulting in a ranked hierarchy of more general to more specific labels, with specific labels being applied to the clusters lower in a hierarchy. The result of these clustering and labeling processes is a global map of 44,000 patent clusters of varying sizes representing groups of tightly interconnected technologies.

Our RFID example provides a useful illustration. The SparkIP search engine based on the algorithms described above returns 3,585 patents and 5,000 patent applications for RFID-related technologies located in 1,016 document clusters in the global SparkCluster map. The entire RFID map is broken out into thirty-four landscapes, where each landscape maps patents focused on specific fields of application generated by the full-text naming algorithms discussed above. The most densely populated map is where we would expect the core technologies of the RFID platform to reside. Searching on "radio frequency identification" produces a map with a central cluster containing 986 tightly linked patents and 709 pending applications. The map of RFID technologies in the global SparkCluster map closely related to our selected cluster is shown in figure 20.5. The largest cluster of patents in the neighborhood (frequency, identification, transponders) contains 1,584 patents and 1,484 applications. The other clusters contain fewer patents, as indicated by the size and brightness of the cluster icons. In figure 20.5 the largest cluster, number 1 (frequency identification transponders), contains 1,584 patents and 1,484 applications; number 2 (radio frequency identification) contains 986 patents and 709 applications; number 3 (identification RFID tag) contains 285 patents and 167 applications; number 4 (identification RFID tags) contains 269 patents and 257 applications; and number 5 (identification RFID tag) contains 208 patents and 212 applications. Opening the "Patents" tab, as shown in figure 20.6, gives the detailed view of all the patents, patent history, inventors, and assignees in the cluster.

The elements of what we are calling the RFID platform are embedded within these cluster maps, and the combination of citation and text-mining techniques we have outlined for generating different levels of labels can be used to extract the component parts of the platform and trace the genealogy of its formation. We see that our maps, which represent the state of the RFID

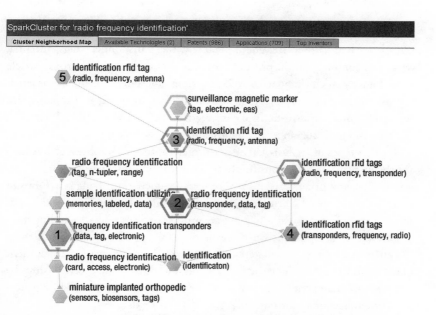

Figure 20.5. Graph for "radio frequency identification." The number labels of the largest clusters (1–5) have been added. (Source: PriorIP.com.)

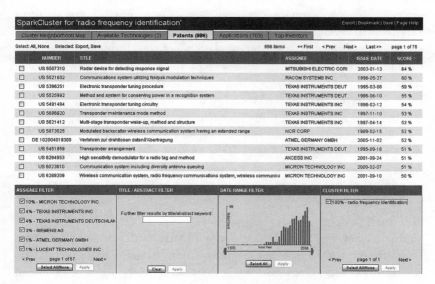

Figure 20.6. Detailed view of "Patents" tab for "radio frequency identification." (Source: PriorIP.com.)

platform in 2008, pick out the core technologies of the platform identified in our earlier handcrafted treatment—namely, the transponders/tags, antenna, data, and communication protocol components. Although electronic article surveillance markers/readers as well as various emerging techniques for labeling biological and pharmacological materials are included in the map, size limitations prevent us from displaying readers/writers, which branch off from cluster 3 in figure 20.5 in related landscapes not displayed here.

Further types of analysis can be performed on the subgraphs, such as tracking the institutional relationships between authors and inventors, assignee relationships, and other relationships of interest, such as evolving portfolios of patents held by specific firms and their relationships to other firms in the platform space. It is also possible to generate profiles of researchers, including their past, current, and possible future projects from the data contained in these document sets. Our current research effort is directed toward development of the tools to extract these social networks and institutional relationships by creating integrated data sets with published scientific literature, white papers and conference presentations, and research funding data.[32]

Figure 20.3 maps the genealogy of the core elements of the RFID platform based on working through citation links and reading documents on a year-by-year basis. Because of the nature of the "bottom-up" process we have adopted, the clustering and labeling algorithms generating our cluster maps need to be refreshed on a regular basis (e.g., weekly or quarterly) to capture newly granted patents and applications. Each new set of entries, however, leads to shifts within existing clusters and frequently the emergence of entirely new clusters (approximately seventy new clusters per week). By drawing upon a time sequence of the clusters leading to the RFID platform in figure 20.6, for example, it is possible—although too detailed and extensive a procedure for this context—to track the evolution of the RFID platform since the early 1990s, including the major teams of inventors and the companies involved in building the platform. In our view, taking into account all the caveats necessary for using the incredibly "noisy" data of intellectual property, our approach offers STS a powerful set of tools for examining actor networks.

Prospects

In this chapter we have sought to make the case that technology platforms constitute a natural unit for quantitative investigations of evolving technical domains. The technology platform is the site where invention, research and development, user feedback, modification, and adaptation to specific market segments all come together. We have argued, and tried to demonstrate in the case of the RFID platform, that patent data can be used to identify the component technologies and their coadaptation over time into the technology platform. Thus, whereas some analysts despair that the variety of business, legal, and social interests configure the meaning of patents differently from one major industry to another, we have attempted to show that it is possible to disambiguate the "noise" by focusing on technology platforms. Here we have illustrated that patent data can be used at a high level to identify components and their importance and relationships within a technology platform. In addition we have looked at broad shifts in interest from various industries in a particular technology platform by tracking patent citations to the platform's components over time. Increasingly, as our tools improve, more granular studies will be possible as sociologists and economists uncover additional concerns motivating the filing and uses of patents in different markets and technological domains.

If the approach we have outlined here is robust enough to be more generally applicable, technology platforms offer a particularly promising tool for analyzing emerging technologies. STS has traditionally been critical of approaches that import quantitative measures, arguing that such approaches tend to reify actors as rational agents, thereby missing the real action of the field, which is always political, highly contextual, and dependent on accident and the uncanny ability of users to shape technology. The field has tended to favor ethnographic studies that cut closer to the "real" lives of technologies and actors. While professing agnosticism about rationality, we think that technology platforms, born in the complex dynamics of actor networks, are the stable (if fragile) sediment of marketplace dynamics.

NOTES

1. This chapter is based upon work supported by the National Science Foundation under Grant no. SES 0531184. Any opinions, findings, and conclusions or recommendations expressed in this material are those of the authors and do not necessarily reflect the views of the National Science Foundation.

2. M. H. Meyer et al. (1993), "The Product Family and the Dynamics of Core Capabilities," *Sloan Management Review* (Spring): 29–48; D.-J. Kim and B. Kogut (1996), "Technological Platforms and Diversification," *Organization Science* 7(3): 283–301; M. H. Meyer and A. P. Lehnerd (1997), *The Power of Product Platforms: Building Value and Cost Leadership* (New York: Free Press); M. V. Tatikonda (1999), "An Empirical Study of Platform and Derivative Product Development Projects," *Journal of Product Innovation Management* 16: 3–26.

3. In fact, in newly developing areas such as nanotechnology, where terminology and classification is in flux, patent applicants may omit specific nanotechnological terminology, making it difficult for competitors to access key parts of the innovation. See G. Clarkson and D. Dekorte (2006), "The Problem of Patent Thickets in Convergent Technologies," *Annals of the New York Academy of Sciences* 1093(1): 180–200.

4. In areas where large numbers of patents are issued and it is difficult to search and review all relevant patents to guard against infringement, firms respond by filing even more patents (sometimes hundreds) in order to have something to trade in cross-licensing negotiations. See Federal Trade Commission (2003), *To Promote Innovation: The Proper Balance of Competition and Patent Law and Policy* (Washington, DC: Federal Trade Commission).

5. J. Alcacer and M. Gittelman (2006), "Patent Citations as a Measure of Knowledge Flows: The Influence of Examiner Citations," *Review of Economics and Statistics* 88(4): 774–779; I. M. Cockburn et al. (2002), "Are All Patent Examiners Equal? The Impact of Examiner Characteristics," National Bureau of Economic Research Working Paper Series no. 8980; B. N. Sampat (2004), "Examining Patent Examination: An Analysis of Examiner and Applicant Generated Prior Art," National Bureau of Economics Summer Institute, Cambridge, MA; B. N. Sampat (2005), "Determinants of Patent Quality: An Empirical Analysis," Columbia University; M. A. Lemley (2005), "Patenting Nanotechnology," *Stanford Law Review* 58(2): 601–630. R. Bawa (2004), "Nanotechnology Patenting in the US," *Nanotechnology Law and Business* 1(1): 31–50.

6. T. P. Hughes (1987), "The Evolution of Large Technological Systems," in *The Social Construction of Technological Systems: New Directions in the Sociology and History of Technology*, ed. W. Bijker, T. P. Hughes, and T. Pinch (Cambridge, MA: MIT Press), 51–82; T. P. Hughes (1983), *Networks of Power: Electrification in Western Society, 1880–1930* (Baltimore: Johns Hopkins University Press).

7. See especially T. P. Hughes (2000), *Rescuing Prometheus: Four Monumental Projects That Changed the Modern World* (New York, Vintage Books); T. P. Hughes (2005), *Human-Built World: How to Think about Technology and Culture* (Chicago: University of Chicago Press).

8. Our notion of the platform also differs from Alberto Cambrosio and Peter Keating's development of biomedical platforms in their *Biomedical Platforms: Realigning the Normal and the Pathological in Late-Twentieth-Century Medicine* (Cambridge, MA: MIT Press, 2006). Cambrosio and Keating's notion of a platform is that of a large-scale sociotechnical system. Our notion of the platform is more consistent with approaches within the economics of science and technology and is more amenable to quantitative treatment.

9. T. Lenoir and E. Giannella (2006), "The Emergence and Diffusion of DNA Microarray Technology," *Journal of Biomedical Discovery and Collaboration* 1(11): online http://www.j-biomed-discovery.com/content/1/1/11.

10. See M. H. Meyer and A. P. Lehnerd (1997), *The Power of Product Platforms: Building Value and Cost Leadership* (New York: Free Press), 24–35; D. Packard (1995), *The HP Way: How Bill Hewlett and I Built Our Company* (New York: HarperBusiness), 117–121.

11. Innovations being defined as commercially realized inventions—for example, a component in a product that consumers can purchase. On the relationship of inventions (represented by patents) and innovations, see Z. Griliches (1991), "Patent Statistics as Economic Indicators: A Survey," *Journal of Economic Literature* 28: 1661–1707; B. H. Hall et al. (2001), "The NBER Patent Citations Data File: Lessons, Insights and Methodological Tools." NBER Working Paper 8494.

12. Japanese Patent Office (2004), *Results of the Survey on Intellectual Property–Related Activities, 2003* (Tokyo: Japanese Patent Office).

13. B. H. Hall and R. H. Ziedonis (2001), "The Patent Paradox Revisited: An Empirical Study of Patenting in the U.S. Semiconductor Industry, 1979–1995," *RAND Journal of Economics* 32(1): 101–128.

14. D. J. Teece (1986), "Profiting from Technological Innovation: Implications for Integration, Collaboration, Licensing and Public Policy," *Research Policy* 15(6): 285–305.

15. W. M. Cohen et al. (2000), "Protecting Their Intellectual Assets: Appropriability Conditions and Why U.S. Manufacturing Firms Patent (or Not)," NBER Working Paper 7552.

16. W. M. Cohen et al. (2002), "R&D Spillovers, Patents and the Incentives to Innovate in Japan and the United States," *Research Policy* 31(8): 1349–1367.

17. B. H. Hall (2006), "The Patent Name-Matching Project," retrieved July 6, 2010, from http://elsa.berkeley.edu/~bhhall/pat/namematch.html.

18. We apply a combination of key word and cocitation analysis as a method for organizing patents related to RFID into meaningful technological groups. We began by identifying a set of key words and patent classifications that are relevant to RFID technologies and cast a fairly broad net, with the expectation that our clustering and subsequent textual filtering would reduce the amount of unwanted data in the study. The query we used in the Delphion patent database was

((RFID) <in> (TITLE,ABSTRACT,CLAIMS)) OR ((RFID) <in> DESCRIPTION) OR ((radio frequency identification) <in> DESCRIPTION) OR ((RF ID) <in> DESCRIPTION) OR ((((" RF " OR "radio frequency") <in> (TITLE,ABSTRACT,CLAIMS)) AND ((code OR "EPC data" OR commands OR authentication OR "encoded data" or "encrypt") <in> (TITLE,ABSTRACT,CLAIMS)) AND ((tag OR label OR identification OR passive OR active) <in> (TITLE,ABSTRACT,CLAIMS))) OR ((((" RF " OR radio OR "electromagnetic wave") <in> (TITLE,ABSTRACT,CLAIMS)) AND ((reader OR locator OR interrogator OR scanner) <in> (TITLE,ABSTRACT,CLAIMS)) AND ((transponder OR transmitter OR "inductor coil") <in> (TITLE,ABSTRACT,CLAIMS))) OR ((3405721) <in> NC) OR ((3400101) <in> NC) OR ((3405727) <in> NC) OR ((3405728) <in> NC) OR ((3405724) <in> NC).

19. There is one line that should represent 14 percent, but we were unable to render this with our visualization software.

20. These two companies are not shown in the graphic.

21. The result of our algorithm densely clustered all the closely related patents representing the RFID platform in the same region. In order to better display the relationships among the subcomponents of the platform over time, we assigned each component coordinates in the x-y plane of the figure.

22. The type of qualitative work that would complement the kind of mapping of the platform space we have in mind is illustrated by the excellent interviews reported on the case of the Intel microprocessor platform by Annabelle Gawer, Michael Cusumano, and Rebecca Henderson. See A. Gawer and M. Cusumano (2002), *Platform Leadership: How Intel, Microsoft, and Cisco Drive Industry Innovation* (Boston: Harvard Business School Press); A. Gawer and R. Henderson (2007), "Platform Owner Entry and Innovation in Complementary Markets: Evidence from Intel," *Journal of Economics & Management Strategy*, 16(1): 1–34.

23. OECD (2008), *OECD Reviews of Innovation Policy: China.* (Paris: Organization for Economic Co-Operation and Development); A. Saxenian (2007), *The New Argonauts: Regional Advantage in a Global Economy* (Cambridge, MA: Harvard University Press).

24. Craig Barrett, CEO of Intel, 2004 statement quoted in N. Kshetri and N. Dholakia (2008), "The Evolution of Broadband Industry in the Developing World: A Comparison of China and India," in *Handbook of Research on Global Diffusion of Broadband Data Transmission*, ed. Y. K. Dwivedi, A. Papazafeiropoulou, and J. Choudrie (Hershey, PA: Information Science Reference), 841–852.

25. G. Gereffi (2005), "The Global Economy: Organization, Governance, and Development," in *The Handbook of Economic Sociology*, ed. N. J. Smelser and R. Swedberg (Princeton, NJ: Princeton University Press and Russell Sage Foundation), 160–182; Lux Research (2004), *Sizing Nanotechnology's Value Chain* (Boston: Lux Research).

26. For examples of the work of generating ontologies and useful search queries that capture the literature of nanotechnology, see the excellent work of Alan Porter and his colleagues and the work of Ronald Kostoff and his colleagues: R. N. Kostoff, J. S. Murday, C. G. Y. Lau, and W. M. Tolles (2006), "The Seminal Literature of Nanotechnology Research," *Journal of Nanoparticle Research* 8(2): 193–213; R. N. Kostoff, R. G. Koytcheff, and C. G. Y. Lau (2008), "Structure of the Nanoscience and Nanotechnology Applications Literature," *Journal of Technology Transfer* 33(5): 472–484; A. Porter, I. Rafols, and M. Meyer (2008), "The Cognitive Geography of Nanotechnologies: Locating Nano-Research in the Map of Science," in *NBER Conference on Nanotechnology and Nanoindicators, Cambridge, Massachusetts, 1–2 May 2008*; A. Porter, J. Youtie, P. Shapira, and D. Schoeneck (2008), "Refining Search Terms for Nanotechnology," *Journal of Nanoparticle Research* 10(5): 715–728.

27. D. Gibson, R. Kumar, and A. Tomkins (2005), "Discovering Large Dense Subgraphs in Massive Graphs," *Proceedings of the 31st Very Large Data Base Conference, Trondheim, Norway*, 721–732.

28. While this volume has been in progress, Spark IP has been dissolved, and the patents and methods we are describing here have been assigned to Prior IP of Atlanta. In their new incarnation, the search tools are freely available and open source. See http://www.prior-ip.com/.

29. To ensure that our citation patterns are based on the strongest signals possible, we take into consideration the points raised above about factors that create "noise" in the system. Three issues are particular foci of attention: citation spamming (where the authors of a patent will include hundreds of citations to works that may not be relevant), overciting of key works, and self-citations (where patents cited share an inventor, patent examiner, assignee, or attorney). In our first pass we drop these patents entirely from consideration. They are not necessarily unimportant, however. Accordingly in a later step we introduce functions for estimating the probability that a citation is legitimate despite the citing and cited patents sharing particular characteristics and using this probability as a weight for reintroducing the "noisy" patents into our map.

30. The description provided here is a condensed sketch of the set of algorithms for clustering and labeling large collections of documents. For details see V. J. Dorie and E. R. Giannella, USPTO Application 20090043797, System and Methods for Clustering Large Databases of Documents, July 28, 2008.

31. Details of the procedure can be found in Dorie and Giannella, cited in note 30.

32. For a suggestive example of this type of data integration, see A. Mogoutov, A. Cambrosio, P. Keating, and P. Mustar (2008), "Biomedical Innovation at the Laboratory, Clinical and Commercial Interface: A New Method for Mapping Research Projects, Publications and Patents in the Field of Microarrays," *Journal of Informetrics* 2(4): 341.

DOTAN OLIAR and
CHRISTOPHER SPRIGMAN

21

Intellectual Property Norms in Stand-Up Comedy

In this chapter, we examine the intellectual property norms of stand-up comics and how these norms help comedians assert ownership of their material and discourage joke stealing.[1] Although joke stealing does not occur with great frequency, it does occur often enough to be a persistent concern. Nonetheless, comedians are not suing rivals who they believe have stolen their material. This is not because comedians are angels who object to litigation on principle. Nor do they view their work product as public property. Comedians work hard to come up with and perfect original comedic material and are not amused—to say the least—to see it stolen.

Why are comedians not using the legal system? Copyright law does not provide comedians with a cost-effective way to protect their expression. The cost of federal court litigation is too high, and the expected benefits of copyright lawsuits are too low. Copyright law protects original expression but not ideas, and much alleged joke stealing involves telling the same comedic idea in different words. Copyright plaintiffs further bear the burden of proving that the defendant copied their expression rather than creating it independently. Since jokes and comedic routines often reference common experience or the events of the day, it would not be easy in many cases for comedians to negate the possibility of independent creation (also known among comedians as "parallel thinking").

Rather than formal law, comedians use a system of social norms to assert ownership of jokes and comedic routines, regulate their use and transfer, and impose sanctions on those who do not play by the rules. These sanctions include bad-mouthing, refusals to work together, and threats of (rarely used) physical violence. Documenting this norms system, which we have done by, among other things, interviewing comedians, is this chapter's first major purpose. Part 1 thus contains a static description of comedians' norms system as it operates today. This exploration challenges the conventional wisdom in intellectual property law—which has been repeated in the specific context of stand-up comedy[2]—that formal legal protection is necessary for intellectual production to exist.

Part 2 addresses the second major aim of our research. It provides a dynamic analysis of comedians' social norms over time. In the vaudeville and the post-vaudeville eras, literal appropriation was the industry norm, and humor tended to stick to well-worn genres (mother-in-law jokes, ethnic humor, etc.). With the rise of antiappropriation norms during the 1950s and 1960s, humor has changed and become more personal, observational, and point-of-view driven. Our dynamic analysis leads us to two arguments. First, while conventional IP wisdom sees protection as mainly affecting how much creative work is produced, we suggest that it also affects the kind of content produced. In comedians' case, the emergence of social norms did not bring about a greater supply of "rim-shot" jokes but rather a new kind of comedy. Second, we provide insight into why comedians' proprietary norms emerged over the past half century. We trace an evolution in the culture and economics of stand-up comedy that tracks a corresponding evolution in the norms of stand-up comics, away from a regime that treated jokes as a commons and toward informal property rules that limit appropriation. We suggest that these are interrelated.

1. Social Norms Regulating Appropriation among Stand-Up Comedians

We have conducted nineteen lengthy, structured interviews of working comics at various levels of the industry. These interviews were conducted by telephone; interviewees were promised anonymity and told that the names and details sufficient to indentify participants in specific incidents of joke stealing would be kept confidential. Our findings from these interviews align closely with what we observed independently through the writings of comedians and comedy experts as well as publicized instances in which comedians accused or shamed other comedians for joke stealing.

The Norm against Appropriation

The major norm that governs the conduct of most stand-up comedians is a strict injunction against joke stealing. Our interviewees agreed that appropriating jokes from another comedian is the major no-no in the business; many of our interviewees referred to joke stealing as a "taboo." This norm is so fundamental that a popular guide for new stand-ups, *The Comedy Bible*, puts the following as the first of its Ten Commandments to the novice: "Thou shalt not covet thy neighbor's jokes, premises, or bits."[3]

Our interviewees were adamant that instances of joke stealing, and the confrontations that often follow them (on which more below), are not very prevalent. From our interviews we got the sense that a comedian is unlikely to be a party to more than a very few confrontations in her entire career. When they occur, confrontations are, for the most part, brief, civil, and effective in putting an end to the dispute. Interviewees told us that recidivism is rare, and persistent joke stealing is limited to a few bad actors who are identified as such in the community.

One comedian's characterization of the norms system was representative of what we heard throughout our interviews:

> In terms of sheer numbers, it's a pretty small fraternity of people who make their living telling jokes. And so we kind of run into each other and see each other on TV and pass each other in clubs and hang out in New York together and, you know, so there's nothing more taboo in the comedy world, there's no worse claim to make against somebody than "Oh, he's a f——king thief." . . .
>
> You know, there are a handful of guys [who] just have a reputation for being thieves, and for the most part it's amazing to me, actually if you think about it, how rarely it happens, because it's so professionally useful. . . .
>
> The development of [jokes] is a lot of work, and when someone comes along and sort of lifts that idea from you and uses it, it's aggravating—it can't be described how aggravating it is. The thing that's amazing to me about it is it doesn't happen more often. Because the fraternity of comedy and the people who book comedy, they feel like a vested interest, and so they also don't want to book someone who would steal jokes. Even once you're already really famous, you really can't successfully run around and steal jokes and have a career. It's amazing that's there's enough sort of self-policing within the system.

Given the significant investment that comics make in producing new material and the importance of good material to their success, the existence of a strong and generally applicable norm against joke stealing is not surprising. What is perhaps surprising is the lengths to which comics will go to punish rivals who transgress the antiappropriation norm. Repeatedly we were told by our interviewees that stand-up comedians monitor each other and, when they detect an instance of apparent joke stealing, enforce a sort of "prison-gang justice." As one interviewee put it, "They police each other. That's how it works. It's tribal. If you get a rep as a thief or a hack (as they call it), it can hurt your career. You're not going to work. They just cast you out. The funny original comics are the ones who keep working."

The most common and most socially acceptable thing for a comedian to do when he thinks another has taken his bit is to confront the alleged appropriator directly, face to face. As one comedian explained to us,

> What you learn as a child is if you have a problem with someone you go and you talk to them. . . . Now what happens is if someone takes a joke from me it's so obvious because it's—everything I do has a gay slant to it—so a straight guy is never going to write this joke because they don't think the way that I do. So if somebody has a joke that sounds like mine, it's typically another gay comic and I'll just go up to the person and say, "Hey, listen, I do this joke, that joke sounds a little bit similar," and then we talk it out. And they'll say blah, blah, blah. And then one of us will say, "All right, I'll stop doing it." And that's that. It's done.

If at the end of such a confrontation a comedian is left unsatisfied, he may seek to punish the perceived joke stealer. There are several strategies that comedians use to punish joke-stealing rivals. One comedian pithily summarized the most common strategies: "The guy [who thinks he's been stolen from] is going to try to get the [other comedian] banned from clubs. He's gonna bad mouth him. He is gonna turn other comics against him. The [other comedian] will be shunned." Another interviewee echoed these views: "If you steal jokes, [other comedians] will treat you like a leper, and they will also make phone calls to people who might give you work. You want to get a good rep coming up so that people will talk about you to the bookers for the TV shows and club dates. Comics help other comics get work on the road."

In addition to shunning and bad-mouthing, many of the comics we interviewed told us that they will refuse to appear in a comedy club on the same bill with a known joke thief. This can be, for the accused joke stealer, a painful sanction. There are as many as eight stand-up comedians most nights on a bill in urban comedy clubs and three comedians on an evening's bill in most clubs outside of major urban markets. If more than a trivial number of comedians refuse to share a bill with a perceived joke stealer, it would severely hamper the latter's ability to work, as our interviewees made clear:

> The guys who book clubs, with a few exceptions, for the most part they want to book good comics doing good original jokes. . . . They don't want to book a guy who has stolen a joke. Very often, people associated with the comedy business either used to be comics or they think of themselves as funny people, and they like the business. There's not a lot of money for the most part in booking comedy or running a comedy club or doing some of the things that are associated with stand-up. And so for the most part those people do it for the love of the craft. And so again, there's sort of a built-in network of folks who are trying to do the right thing.

There are also, as we have mentioned, occasional instances of physical violence. Physical violence as a response to joke stealing is an outlier—even repeatedly aggrieved comedians rarely resort to it. Yet the comedic community's reactions to reported incidents of violence are telling. The attackers apparently feel morally justified, and many of the comedians we spoke with are accepting (sometimes grudgingly, sometimes with more enthusiasm) of violent reprisal.

Before we move on to a description of other norms, we should state here one important caveat regarding comedians' norm against appropriation: we do not mean to suggest that the antiappropriation norm is always observed. But this is true also of formal property law: the fact that there are laws protecting personal property does not mean that no cars, for example, are ever stolen or that punishment deters all theft. All it means is that the vast majority of comedians adhere to the norms in the vast majority of cases.

The "Own the Premise /Own the Joke," "Sponsorship," and "Alienation of Ownership" Norms

In addition to the general norm against appropriation, our respondents described several related norms that supplement and together help structure enforcement of the general norm against appropriation. These norms sometimes mimic but often depart from the rules of formal copyright law.

One of these norms governs the question of authorship when more than one person is involved in creating a joke. Comics spend time together in clubs and on the road, and they often work out new material in these settings collaboratively. Our respondents stated that, absent some agreement to the contrary, a comic establishes ownership of a joke when he establishes a premise—even if the rest of the joke, including most importantly the punch line, is supplied by another comic.

This "own the premise / own the joke" norm produces a default rule of ownership different from the one in formal copyright law governing the creation of authorship interests. U.S. copyright law provides for a default rule of *joint authorship* when two people create together. If joint authorship exists, the authors of the "joint work" are recognized as the co-owners of the copyright in that work. In contrast, comedians' norm concentrates ownership in one contributor.

Our respondents detailed two related but distinct norms within the stand-up comedy domain regarding ownership of works created for payment. First, comedians agreed that writers hired to create jokes for a comedian understand, absent an explicit arrangement to the contrary, that they have no ownership interest in the work created. This norm differs from the formal "work-made-for-hire" rules in U.S. copyright law. Under those provisions, copyright in a work arises in its author unless the author is an employee acting within the scope of his employment or the work is in a limited category of "sponsored" works and the parties have expressly agreed in a contract signed by both of them that the sponsor is the copyright owner.

In contrast to the formal rules of copyright law, the norm at work among stand-up comics treats all works created for use by another comic as the property of the sponsor rather than the author. This is true regardless of whether the writer is a formal employee (rare) or an independent contractor (the more usual case). This is also true regardless of whether the transaction is memorialized by a written contract signed by both parties. The formal copyright rule is structured as a strong default rule preserving the independent author's ownership of copyright, even for works sponsored by another. The norm among stand-up comics, on the other hand, is structured as a default rule establishing property rights in the sponsor—in effect treating as employees a large number of authors who would never qualify as such under the rules of copyright law. For these reasons, we refer to this as the "sponsorship" norm.

Relatedly, our respondents agreed on another norm governing transactions in jokes—namely, that in selling a joke to a rival the originator divests himself of the joke and retains no right to perform it or to otherwise use it (e.g., by creating a derivative work). We call this the "alienation of ownership" norm. And again, this norm operating among stand-up comedians is quite different from the default rules of formal copyright law. Under the copyright law provisions structuring transfers, transactions transferring an interest in a creative work are construed as nonexclusive licenses unless the transfer is denominated in a written instrument (signed by the transferor) as a transfer of the entire copyright interest or as an exclusive license.[4] These copyright law arrangements are, again, structured as a strong default rule preserving ownership in the work's author. In contrast, the norm among stand-up comics appears to follow a default rule favoring alienation of ownership. In the words of one of our interviewees, "[When I buy a joke,] it's mine—lock, stock, and barrel. [The writer] can't perform them, and my . . . oral agreement with my writers is you can't even tell anybody that you wrote the joke. You can say on a résumé that you write for me, but you cannot say specifically what jokes you have written for me."

We believe that the explanation for the divergence between copyright law and the "own the premise / own the joke," "sponsorship," and "alienation of ownership" norms may be found in the inherent limitations of the norms system, as compared with formal law. One important difference between formal IP law and comedians' IP norms is the relative diversity of both property rights and contractual arrangements that are cognizable under the formal law in contrast to the virtual uniformity of both property rights and contractual arrangements recognized by the norms system. Comedians' norms system imposes a unitary ownership property regime. The "own the premise / own the joke," "sponsorship," and "alienation of ownership" norms all work to concentrate ownership in a single rights holder and sharply limit the choices comedians have in structuring property rights. This is because enforcement in the norms system depends on the maintenance of the clearest possible rules regarding ownership. To the extent that joint ownership involves the possibility of two owners telling the same joke, the functioning of the norms system would be frustrated: comedians monitoring for appropriation would detect false positives, and the enforcement regime might become inefficient enough to break down. The same defect would attend any attempt at nonexclusive licensing of jokes: to the extent that two rights holders attempt to exploit the same property, the norms system would come under threat because it lacks any ability to distinguish between authorized use and unauthorized appropriation. The cost of false positives, in terms of enforcement actions against nonappropriating community members, could disrupt the norms system. And the informal system has responded by constructing property rights as an all-or-nothing proposition—a joke is owned by one or none; it cannot be owned by some or many, which lends itself to effective enforcement.

2. The Emergence of Social Norms in Stand-Up Comedy

The norms just depicted did not always exist. Rather, and as we detail below, they came into being over the last half century. We would therefore like to explore two questions: How did the development of a norms system affect comedians' creative practice? And why did these norms emerge?

Protecting Creativity: Affecting "How Much" and "What Kind"

Copyright law is conventionally viewed as trading off two important but contending values. First, copyright attempts to spur creative output. It does this by establishing property rights that help authors control the copying of their works and prevent the dissipation of profits that uncontrolled reproduction and distribution would otherwise threaten. Second, copyright limits the property rights that it creates, in order to encourage the wide dissemination of existing works as well as the use of existing works as building blocks in the creation of new works. In pursuing these competing goals, copyright law must strike a balance. If protection is too low, existing works will be disseminated widely, but authors may be unwilling to invest enough in the production of new works. Obversely, if the level of protection is set too high, we might expect more new works, but dissemination of existing works will be restricted, and other potential authors will not be able to build upon protected works freely in order to create new ones.

The debate over the optimal level of copyright protection is framed as an inquiry into how to induce the production of an optimal level of creative output. The debate is about how much creativity we will obtain. If we get the level of protection just right, we will optimize creative output. Our research suggests a new and separate set of concerns that should inform debates over copyright policy. Changes in IP rules do not just affect how much stand-up comedy is produced. They also play a role in determining *what kind* of stand-up comedy we see.

To understand this point clearly we must look back at earlier phases in the development of stand-up comedy—the vaudeville and postvaudeville eras stretching from the late nineteenth century to the middle of the twentieth century. These periods were characterized by a regime of relative free appropriation among stand-up comedians and the absence of any strong norm against joke stealing.

We see evidence of joke stealing dating from the very beginnings of vaudeville (though sharing or collective authorship might be better terms for the practice then), and we see no significant evidence during this formative period of any powerful norm against appropriation. Rather, we see many instances of performers appropriating material from other performers. Indeed, vaudeville performers and companies felt free to appropriate popular material even from within the vaudeville form itself. One of the first records to have sold over a million copies, a comedy record titled *Cohen on the Telephone*,[5] was based on burlesque routines revolving around misunderstandings that stem from a heavy, stereotyped Yiddish accent. The initial release was followed by a flock of exact imitations and derivative works (for example, *Cohen Phones the Health Department* and *Cohen Becomes a Citizen*) released by competing labels, and even two "Cohen" movies, all within about a decade. Although we can find no evidence of licensing, no lawsuits were filed or, as far as we can tell, threatened, although it is unimaginable that the record companies and film producers did not know about the existence of these other versions.

Comics like Milton Berle, Henny Youngman, Jack Benny, and Bob Hope represent the transition from vaudeville, in which comedians played a relatively minor role in the greater variety show, to a new form, in which stand-up comedy was offered and consumed, not mixed with other forms of entertainment, but as a stand-alone performance. These performers told strings of jokes that ranged over a wide variety of topics and had little narrative or thematic connection to one another. This style of humor was the dominant form of stand-up between the late 1920s and the 1960s and remains a secondary but still significant form of stand-up today.

In this postvaudeville era, direct appropriation as well as the "refinement" of other comedians' materials was still prevalent, but we find the first signs of some concern with joke stealing, although we have seen little evidence that the practice was viewed as a serious threat. Bob Hope was widely accused of stealing and later moved to hiring writers to ensure a constant flow of new material. Ed Wynn gave Milton Berle the nickname "Thief of Bad Gags." Berle openly admitted to a penchant for joke stealing, and he made jokes about it—for example, Berle's famous gibe, made onstage at the Friars Club of Beverly Hills, that the prior act "was so funny I dropped my pencil."

In the late 1950s and into the 1960s, stand-up comedy made a significant turn: a new generation of comedians began a less inhibited exploration of politics, race, and sex as part of a more general move toward an increasingly personalized form of humor. Many comics shifted from the postvaudeville "rim-shot" joke style to original monologues with a narrative thread linked to the individual comedian's distinctive point of view.

Along with this shift in comedic practice we find a concomitant shift in the salience of joke stealing as an issue within the community of stand-up comics. Moreover, comedians who rely, as the vaudeville and postvaudeville comics did, on generic joke telling are derided as "hacks." Originality is prized—indeed, it is arguably the first criterion by which comedians judge other comedians—and stealing is condemned.

Thus, over the history of the form we have seen two major modes of stand-up comedy. In the postvaudeville era comedians were telling largely inter-changeable generic jokes. They differentiated themselves from each other by their individual performance style. These comedians competed mostly on technique: who delivered the joke better, timed the audience better, was able to compile and assemble from a repository of jokes a subset that fitted the particular audience. The text was easily appropriable, and as a result many co-medians based their acts on a blend of stock jokes and appropriated jokes. We see some investment in the creation of new jokes, and we see many comedians purchasing jokes from other comedians and from joke writers. Overall, how-ever, stand-up material, from whatever source, tended to stay close to stock themes and topical humor. We do not see, in the postvaudeville period, much investment in the kind of personalized or otherwise original material that is prevalent in the market today. Given the regime of free appropriation gov-erning the postvaudeville form, this makes sense. Text was the appropriable element of the comedic form; delivery, however, was relatively more difficult to steal. Postvaudeville comedians were incentivized to invest in the latter ele-ment in preference to the former.

Compare postvaudeville stand-up with the modern incarnation of the form. Appropriation in stand-up is now regulated by an informal IP system. Under the current community-based regulation, the text is protected—not perfectly, but the norms system does raise the cost of appropriation. And in line with what we might expect when the cost of appropriating text goes up, we find that comedians invest more in innovation directed at the text. Come-dians today invest in new, original, and personal content. The medium is no longer focused on reworking of preexisting genres like marriage jokes, ethnic jokes, or knock-knock jokes. Following the rise of the norms system, comedi-ans did not simply invest in creating more of the same kinds of material they had produced before. Rather, they changed the content of their material and diversified the types of comedy on offer. At the same time, it seems to us also true that comedians today invest less in developing the performative aspects of their work; indeed, many stand-ups today stand at a microphone, dress simply, and move around very little compared with the more elaborate costuming, mimicry, musicianship, and playacting that characterized the postvaudeville comics.

The Interdependence among Economic Change, Property Forms, and Creative Content

In vaudeville and postvaudeville, jokes were free for all to take. Today, they are protected by a system of social norms. What factors are likely to contribute to the emergence of intellectual property norms? And why have they emerged recently, but not before? We believe that the beginning of an answer lies in Harold Demsetz's theory explaining the emergence of property rights.

Demsetz posited that property rights emerge when economic change makes the internalization of negative externalities worthwhile.[6] According to Demsetz, economic change drives change in property forms. That much seems to be true in comedians' case. For example, technological change has increased the benefits of having property rights in jokes and comedic routines. In vaudeville, the harm from joke theft was limited. If a comedian-thief lifted a joke off the vaudeville stage and told it traveling east, the originator could still use it traveling west. Today, if a joke thief tells a joke on radio or television or if an audience member posts it to a heavily trafficked Web site, it may consume the national market for the joke. The benefits from establishing and enforcing a property system in jokes in the new technological age are thus greater in terms of ensuring return on investment.[7]

Contrary to Demsetz's hypothesis, however, comedians' case makes us doubt that causality is strictly unidirectional. As we saw, Demsetz's theory would suggest that economic change may have contributed to the emergence of (norms-based) property rights. Additionally, and as we have shown, the norms system emerged and won increasing adherence contemporaneously with the transformation of the comedic product from generic to original. But it also seems plausible that causality also runs in the other direction. The more original humor is, the lower the cost of detecting joke theft and enforcing property rights in jokes. In the postvaudeville era, many jokes were generic and therefore difficult to associate with a particular comedian. Upon hearing a stolen joke, the listener could not be sure if she had heard it before, especially since comedians tended to work in myriad variations on the same limited number of themes. Today, when comedic material is more distinct, it is easier for listeners to detect copying. The costs—social and private—of enforcing property rights in jokes are thus lower when humor is original. Our interviews suggest that comedians have at least a tacit understanding of the relationship between norms, the personalized comedic form, and the cost and possibility of enforcement. One of them captured this beautifully as follows:

> Yes, I must say I got at least three occurrences where I've seen people do one of my jokes, and it happens less frequently now because I've become a comedian who's hard to copy. As I've grown as a comedian myself, I have become more and more original. So if someone were to steal it nowadays it would be more obvious. Whereas I used to talk about more boring topics, like let's say I was making fun of being on the subway train and I then see someone do my subway train joke. It's very tough to say they're stealing because everybody talks about

the subway. It's one of those hack themes. But nowadays I'm talking about social issues that came up last week that were in the news, and I'm talking about them in a way that if someone were to copy my joke it would be very obvious. I could go up and say, "Hey, you did my joke word for word."

The number one reason that I think I did it was, well, maybe two reasons, was to be unique. Because in order to be successful in stand-up comedy when you're fighting against a thousand other guys who all want the same—they want to be on the same shows. . . . I realize if I'm telling the same topic, if I go onstage and I talk about the subway train and the next guy goes onstage and talks about subway trains, what's going to make me get that TV show and not him? And, so I realized that in order for me to be successful I needed to start talking about things that not everyone was talking about. And as a side effect, that also makes it more difficult for people to steal from me and made it more difficult for someone to accuse me of stealing some topic.

So it mainly was because I wanted to be unique and I wanted to be different, and a good side effect was it made it quite difficult—like now my jokes are longer too. They used to be closer to one-liners, meaning just setup [and] punch line, and so if someone steals a setup / punch line, it's one sentence. If they steal one sentence it's tough to say whether they stole that sentence from you because it's just one sentence. But now my jokes are much longer. They generally are two or three minutes long and made up of several paragraphs, and so if someone were to steal it word for word, it would be quite obvious. It would be incredibly obvious that they had stolen three paragraphs out of my act.

The more entrenched the norms system, the more it makes sense for comedians to produce point-of-view-driven content, and the more unique comedians' material is, the easier it is to enforce and maintain a norms-based property system. In emphasizing the way IP rules affect content, we are not denying causality in the other direction—we believe the relationship runs both ways.

Relatedly, the story of stand-up comedy suggests that our choices regarding which IP rules will govern a particular creative industry often will implicate delicate normative judgments. We can see this in the comparison between the postvaudeville and modern styles. In the postvaudeville era, creativity in jokes was more limited, but the form was also perhaps more accessible and communal. Postvaudeville-era mother-in-law jokes, one-liners, and puns are the type of jokes that one is likely to share with friends and family. The postvaudeville form was therefore less personal and inventive but probably more social. The social aspect of postvaudeville stand-up is not insignificant, because the sharing of jokes creates value (for instance, giving and receiving pleasure and cementing social relationships) for both tellers and recipients. Today, stand-up is more innovative, but it is also less inclusive; modern stand-up is consumed by the audience alone and less often redistributed by them to others. The audience does not participate in the form in the same way they did when the post-vaudeville comedians produced and reproduced jokes accessible to all.

Which environment is better? It is hard to say, in part because the role that stand-up plays in our culture has changed over time and is linked to the type of creative output prevalent in the stand-up market in a given period. Nevertheless, our study suggests that the choice of IP regime governing stand-up is a factor that helps to shape both the type of material produced and the role of the art form in our society. Over the history of stand-up comedy, different IP regimes—free appropriation in postvaudeville versus an informal property system in modern stand-up—have contributed to the production of markedly different forms of stand-up and have also changed the way in which comedy is produced and consumed. If these observations generalize to other forms of creativity, then our discussion of desirable IP rules has become more complex. We would need to update our thinking about IP rules in a way that recognizes that they may change the nature of the creative practices that they are regulating, that different people are likely to create and consume at different levels of protection (good performers versus original writers), and that different content is likely to be presented under different production processes.

Conclusion

Intellectual property law does not protect effectively the intellectual creations of comedians. Conventional wisdom would have us believe that this entails a tragedy of commons and suboptimal supply of jokes. Our research makes us pause. We see an operating market. It seems to us that the stand-up industry has economized on the costs of the formal copyright system and substituted an informal norms-based property regulatory system in its stead.

Is norms-based ordering of stand-up comedy superior to the extant legal system? From comedians' perspective, the answer seems to be yes. Comedians rely on the norms system, and they choose not to rely on the legal system.

Is norms-based ordering superior to any conceivable legal regime that might apply to stand-up comedy? That question does not admit of a definitive answer. Our description of comedians' norms system suggests, however, that before recommending the reconfiguration of legal doctrine, we must compare the costs and benefits of the two modes of regulation or any combination thereof.

The tale of stand-up comedy at least cautions against the careless expansion of legal protections without consideration of the informal norms operating within a particular creative community and without a good idea of the effect that legal protections would have on the norms system. Bolstering formal protections might reinforce comedians' existing norm against appropriation. Alternatively, it might erode norms that currently do much of the work in governing appropriation. Contrast the regulation of appropriation in stand-up comedy with that in popular music. Owners of music copyrights rely heavily on formal rights yet face a widespread appropriative ideology and practice. Stand-up comedians have little legal recourse yet operate within a norms system that punishes thievery. We do not suggest that what works for stand-up can necessarily work for other forms of intellectual property. We only suggest that formal IP law is not necessarily right for stand-up or for every creative practice.

NOTES

1. This chapter is based on two previously published articles: Dotan Oliar and Christopher Sprigman, "There's No Free Laugh (Anymore): The Emergence of Intellectual Property Norms and the Transformation of Stand-Up Comedy," 94 *Va. L. Rev.* 1789 (2008); Dotan Oliar and Christopher Sprigman, "From Corn to Norms: How IP Entitlements Affect What Stand-Up Comedians Create," 95 *Va. L. Rev.* 57 (2009).

2. See, e.g., Allen D. Madison, "The Uncopyrightability of Jokes," 35 *San Diego L. Rev.* 111 (1998); Andrew Greengrass, "Take My Joke . . . Please! *Foxworthy v. Custom Tees* and the Prospects for Ownership of Comedy," 21 *Colum.-VLA J. L. & Arts* 273, at 274–275 (1997).

3. See Judy Carter, *The Comedy Bible: From Stand-Up to Sitcom: The Comedy Writer's Ultimate How-To Guide*, 56 (2001).

4. *See* 17 U.S.C. §204(a).

5. See, e.g., Tim Gracyk with Frank Hoffman, *Popular American Recording Pioneers 1895–1925*, 10 (2000), suggesting that over 2 million copies were sold).

6. Harold Demsetz, "Toward a Theory of Property Rights," 57 *Am. Econ. Rev.* 347 (1967).

7. For a fuller account of how comedians' case corresponds to Demsetz's theory, see Oliar and Sprigman, "There's No Free Laugh," at 1859–1862; Oliar and Sprigman, "From Corn to Norms," at 64–66.

FIONA MURRAY

22

Patenting Life
How the Oncomouse Patent Changed the Lives of Mice and Men

In 1984 scientists at Harvard University published an article describing their success "engineering" the oncomouse, a transgenic mouse predisposed to cancer.[1] Four years later the U.S. Patent Office granted Harvard a patent with extensive property rights over the oncomouse, touching off a whirlwind of controversy.

In the courtroom and the popular press the controversy centered on "patenting life"—whether to grant patents on mammals (Kevles 2002). For the scientific community, the controversy was more practical. Mention the oncomouse patent, and a mouse geneticist did not expound the dilemmas of patenting mouse life; he talked about the dilemmas of the patent for his laboratory life. When the oncomouse first entered academic laboratories in 1984, it forced scientists to change their material culture: what was considered an important research question and the types of credit given to particular research activities. In other words, it changed the cycles of credit in the academic economy. But its potential to change these dynamics became much more powerful in 1988, when it gained a patent. DuPont, which controlled the patent, was attempting to use the intellectual property rights in ways consistent with a commercial economy but antithetical to an academic one. For over a decade, academics prevented the wholesale capture of their academic economy but did not reject patenting as a whole. They came instead to incorporate patents into their academic cycles of credit, impart them with symbolic meaning, and use them to reshape the dynamics of credit, control, and collaboration.

My inquiry into the oncomouse focuses on the boundary between academic science and the commercial sphere (Dasgupta and David 1994; Gieryn 1995; Shapin 2007). It recognizes that academic laboratories increasingly choose to inscribe their knowledge not only in publications (Latour and Woolgar 1979) but also in patents. By doing so, they produce so-called patent-paper pairs (Murray 2002)—ideas that are captured in two entirely distinctive documents that are traditionally associated with quite separate economic spheres. Certainly, these distinctive literary forms can initiate a distinctive "cycle of credit" (Latour and Woolgar 1979)—a cycle through which scientists use material resources to gain credit, which they in turn transform into further material resources such as grants. Initially considered to describe an academic cycle of credit based on publications—in which academics accumulate reputation, grants, and experimental resources—a patent-based commercial cycle can also be built on the accumulation of financial resources. By articulating the transformation of resources into credit, each cycle thus establishes its own distinctive economy (Biagioli 2007) with its own "operating rules" shaping access, credit, and control. Nonetheless, the two *can* intersect and resources can move between them. By granting patents equal status with publications and treating them symmetrically, I move beyond functional assumptions that patents simply map to the commercial economy. I explore how the two economies interact and the two cycles intersect as a window into the question of how patents have changed scientific life. This formulation allows me to move beyond a simple portrayal of patents and the commercial economy as either totally irrelevant to or destroying (e.g., Kohler 1999; Krimsky 2003) the traditional academic economy. I examine how the initiation of a commercial cycle based on the oncomouse changed the delicate dynamics of the academic cycle of credit. In doing so, I show how patents become entwined in the academic economy on terms negotiated not by lawyers but by the scientists themselves.

The Case of the Oncomouse

The development of the oncomouse, its publication and patenting, and the response of academic scientists is a strategic research site in which to study the different roles of patenting in the academic and commercial economy. The four-year gap between publication and the grant and licensing of the patent provides a "natural experiment." We can start by looking at how the onco-mouse shaped the material culture, cycles of credit, and local economy of the mouse community when it entered the lab unpatented, and then move on to explore how its patenting changed the life of both the mouse and the mouse men (as they were known in the 1930s).[2]

Well before the arrival of the oncomouse, the mouse men formed a tight-knit community whose cycles of credit were based on the informal exchange of mouse strains and the formal role of the Jackson Laboratory (JAX) (Rader 2004). Their culture remained stable until the advent molecular biology in the late 1970s (Judson 1996; Morange 1998; Fujimura 1987). Mouse geneticists studying cancer were among the first to recognize the potential of molecular biology. By injecting foreign DNA into mouse eggs they could create "trans-genic" offspring and thus monitor the gene's function in the whole organ-ism rather than a single cell.[3] Ken Paigen, a director of JAX, described these changes: "At the end of 1980, in a period of a few months, an entirely new era in mouse genetics began, with the creation of the first transgenic mice, initi-ated by the abrupt and then continuing entry of molecular biological tech-niques into what had, until then, been a classical genetic system. What ensued was an explosion of knowledge when a myriad of new biological and molecu-lar insights appeared over the following years. Although certainly built on the past, the new science quickly developed a life of its own and deserves its own chapter" (Paigen 2003, pp. 6–7).

While many genes might be used, building a mouse from cancer-causing "oncogenes" provided new insights into cancer. As the process required both transgenic and cancer genetics skills, few labs attempted these experiments. However, in 1982, Timothy Stewart—coauthor of one of the first transgenic mouse publications (Wagner et al. 1981)—joined Philip Leder, a leading ge-neticist at Harvard, and together they created a viable oncomouse. Leder came to recognize that "it could serve a variety of different purposes, some purely scientific, others highly practical" (Kevles 2002, p. 83). Recognizing the dual-ity of his new experimental knowledge led Leder to develop two quite differ-ent texts about his mouse, its novelty, and its relevance—a patent-paper pair. In 1984, both Leder and a competing team published the results of their onco-mouse work in the prestigious journal *Cell*, with the two teams reporting the incorporation of different oncogenes (Brinster et al. 1984; Stewart et al. 1984). But two months before submitting the manuscript to *Cell* Leder produced another text about oncomouse, one that turned into Harvard's patent applica-tion on June 22, 1984 (ultimately U.S. Patent 4736866).[4] This decision can be traced to late 1983, when Leder approached the Harvard Office of Technol-ogy Licensing at the medical school to discuss the patentability of his research

(Kevles 2002). DuPont was involved in these discussions, as Leder indicated: "The work that we did was supported, actually, by an industrial concern, Du-Pont. They made a significant investment in that research and this is one of the products that could emerge from it, and did emerge from it, and they are incentivised to make further investments in this process by virtue of the return that they will receive [from the patent]. That is our system. You may like it—you may not like it" (Lasker Foundation 1987).

Establishing and Defending Separate Economies

With the patent yet to be granted and its future implications unimaginable, the mouse community started to reshape academic cycles of credit around the opportunities created by the oncomouse. Researchers recognized that mice "carrying specific cancer-promoting genes opened an exciting new era in oncology" (Cory and Adams 1988, p. 25), but only those able to incorporate oncomice into their laboratory's research practices could actually produce publications. To do so, they initiated a series of intricate exchanges with originating labs that maintained their "competitive edge" through the difficulty of these techniques and the shortage of researchers who has mastered them.

Control of key transgenic expertise brought significant credit. One such lab "got an uptick in applications from people wanting to do post-docs and learn methods that could take them elsewhere and gain fame and fortune" (interview with author). Some went on to set up independent labs (taking mice with them), building their own cycle of research, publication, reputation, and exchanges. However, stable credit cycles and practices for sharing mice and expertise were hard to establish because of the instability of the materials themselves. Unlike the drosophila flies that were so instrumental in establishing the early genetics community in the United States because of the ease with which they could travel and be shared, and unlike the traditional laboratory mice anyone could buy from JAX, transgenic mice posed serious material challenges with direct implications for the scientific economy: "I had a few requests for mice and offers of coauthorship. But I did not send them the mice. I sent a long and detailed explanation of the implausibility of the request. The mouse line died very young. Over the period, I was having to slow my own work down because they were breeding very poorly and so it was impossible to ship them around" (interview with the author from leading embryologist).

Drawing from genetics, where the scarcity of genes shaped competition (Atkinson et al. 1998), laboratories that possessed transgenic skills used collaboration with other scientists and laboratories to retain their prominence. They incorporated valuable molecular biology tools into their cycles of credit by choosing coauthors who could contribute new elements to their skill sets. The novelty of these techniques, however, did not change the community's expectations about the possibility of collaboration, as shown by the "punishment" that the scientific press imposed on those who failed to abide by those norms. For instance, a scientist unwilling to share mice for any form of credit saw his "transgression" documented in *Science* (Cohen 1995). And as the transgenic economy stabilized, scientists recognized that a prerequisite for progress was to cede control of the mice to an efficient breeding and distribution facility like JAX. In the words of one scientist, "We needed an ambitious and well-supervised operation" (interview with the author).

At precisely this moment, DuPont appeared with the oncomouse patent, and laboratory life changed dramatically for the entire mouse genetics community.

The commercial cycle of credit was initiated by Harvard itself, when the oncomouse patent was granted and then licensed to DuPont in 1988, thus giving the firm an exclusive license to the sweeping transgenic landscape embodied in the patent. With that license, DuPont could start the transformation of property rights into financial revenues. Traditionally, industrial owners or licensors of scientific materials, techniques, or instruments sought to develop this cycle by extracting financial rewards from other for-profit firms through either contractual or more informal agreements (Gans and Stern 2000). There was no legal reason, however, to prevent them from seeking the same financial rewards from academic scientists as well. DuPont did just that. Up to this point there was a widespread assumption among academics that they were not required to play by the rules of the commercial economy when they wanted to use patented inventions—a tool, technique, or material such as a mouse. That assumption was based on the so-called experimental use exemption—a legal exemption intended to protect those who used a patented invention merely "out of curiosity" or for "amusement." The scope of this exemption has recently been challenged in the *Madey v. Duke University* decision, which states that universities do not engage in research for curiosity but rather as part of a commercial mission to raise research funds—a view that fails to appreciate the different role that resources play in the production of academic and commercial credit.

In the economy that DuPont envisioned, academics would no longer be able to establish an independent academic economy for oncomouse—an economy in which the control of the mice could be translated into academic credit in the form of prestige or coauthorship. The prevailing currency in the new oncomouse economy would be financial. Not only did DuPont set a high price for oncomouse—its fifty-dollar price tag was ten times the price of a JAX mouse (Anderson 1988)—but it also expected the scientists or their institutions to sign a license whenever they used any oncomouse. The license included three terms:

- DuPont forbade scientists from following their traditional practices of sharing or breeding oncomice, thus precluding the incorporation of oncomice into an academic economy where mice were exchanged for other materials, credit, etc. This applied not only to scientists who bought an oncomouse from DuPont but also to those who generated oncomice on their own.
- While DuPont did not impose strict prohibitions on the licensees' publications, it still exerted control on them by contractually requiring an annual disclosure of their research plans and results to the company. While not disruptive of the academic cycle of credit, this control did shape another core aspect of the academic economy, namely individual control of the academic agenda, the timing of publication, etc.
- DuPont required that scientists give them control over future inventions made using oncomice. Such requirements are called reach-through rights (common in contracts between biotech and pharmaceutical firms) and give the patent holder (or its licensee) a share in any proceeds from a future product developed using the patented technology. This was the first time a company had imposed such a provision on academic life scientists.

DuPont imposed even more stringent conditions on commercial scientists, with tighter reach-through rights and higher licensing fees on the oncomouse. Few industrial scientists, however, were interested in the oncomouse or had the skills to use it. In the late 1980s, that expertise only existed in the academic community.

Academic scientists fought to ensure that their traditional academic cycle of credit was not trumped by a commercial cycle. They did not object to DuPont's imposing a commercial economy on commercial scientists, but they opposed the notion that the contractual operating rules and values of that economy would dominate how scientific resources were accumulated and how scientists collaborated with one another.

The annual Mouse Molecular Genetics summer conference at Cold Spring Harbor, New York—a gathering that had been central to the development of the mouse genetics community—became an organizing point of the resistance. According to observers, "the grumbling reached insurrection proportions after a meeting at Cold Spring Harbor" in August 1992 (Anderson 1993). In an impromptu session led by Harold Varmus—a prominent member of the community and a Nobel Prize winner—over three hundred researchers shared their grievances, raising objections to the controls that DuPont sought to exercise over the oncomouse. In the words of one scientist, "It was an enormous obstacle to free and open distribution of information and materials. . . . [I]t was a whole new way of doing science . . . [and] it really affected the way the mouse research community works" (Rajewsky quoted in Jaffe 2004). The notion of commercial reach-through rights was particularly disturbing. On one hand this is perplexing; scientists have long negotiated something akin to control rights when they negotiate the complex expectations of authorship versus citation when translating and accumulating their resources (Biagioli and Galison 2003). On the other hand, the imposition of rights on an ongoing research stream on the basis of intellectual property (rather than continued collaboration) was an alien concept to scientific practice. As one scientist put it (in an interview with the author), "In science we always try and appreciate a new idea and give credit. People with something new hold onto it for a while and we collaborate with them, but over time these rights weaken and ideas become mainstream. No one monopolizes them forever. If they do, they just won't reach the sort of widespread acceptance that is so vital to our field."

Whatever their opinion of DuPont, scientists were in a bind. Most could not simply drop oncomice from their research agenda. As the success of the research line over the prior five years had shown, oncomice were a valuable tool for scientists accumulating new insights into the role of cancer in whole mammals. They chose instead to operate in the shadow of the commercial credit cycle, maintaining their academic cycle within the now "underground" academic economy (de Mequista and Stephenson 2006), while others were determined to flout the law "and simply breed their own oncomice, effectively boycotting the company" (Anderson 1993). Feeling very frustrated with the constraints imposed by the patent, Ken Paigen announced (much to the dismay of his legal counsel) that JAX would ignore the law and distribute the mice without a DuPont license. Many of these stances appear to be consistent with recent survey results documenting that scientists rarely consider patents in designing experiments (Walsh et al. 2003), which seems to reflect a willful insurrection rather than an inadvertent neglect of the details of patent law. In the end, while some scientists vocally resisted and proceeded without any compliance with DuPont's requirements, others lived under a cloud of fear (Smaglik 2000).

While some scientists opted for a less confrontational tactic and attempted to circumvent the patent by "inventing around" it, a few scientists tried to use the legal system, hoping to bring a law suit against DuPont to either invalidate or narrow the scope of the patent: "I have been contacted over the years by two or three lawyers on behalf of other academic labs who wanted me to join them to challenge the patent so that they could avoid the licenses and void the patent. I didn't join them—it just seemed like an exercise that would be costly and time consuming. I preferred to get on with what I was doing, breed my mice and ignore the patent" (interview with the author).

These actions, however, never gained momentum. Instead, the scientists turned to their most powerful and prestigious institution to put pressure on DuPont. In 1995, Harold Varmus (who had since become director of the NIH) entered into protracted negotiations with DuPont, arguing that the company's patenting practices should not interfere with the norms of academic science. As a result, toward the end of 1999 DuPont and the NIH signed a memorandum of understanding (MOU) under which NIH-funded academic scientists could use oncomice at no cost for noncommercial purposes, including research sponsored by a commercial firm. Press coverage at the time announced that researchers could now freely exchange the mice (Smaglik 2000), but while the arduous terms of the license had been eliminated, the MOU explicitly stated that a material transfer agreement was still required for exchanging oncomice with colleagues at another nonprofit institution. Despite these qualifications, the agreement between DuPont and the NIH signified as a return to the previous status quo: the boundary between science and the commercial world had been defended.

How Patents Entered the Academic Economy

If the story ended here, it would be a conventional account of the endurance of academia, even in the face of strong patents and an aggressive licensor. However, it would be a "thin" account of the community to argue that they rejected patents wholesale. In reality, the oncomouse patent paved the way for future patenting opportunities on other mice (Kevles 2002). Many of the same scientists who were furious at DuPont for patenting and imposing a commercial economy on academics took advantage of that precedent and started patenting their own mice. One geneticist remembers: "I was chairing yet another session [at Cold Spring Harbor in the late 1990s] on the problems of patenting in mouse models. . . . Everyone was complaining about the patent restrictions, what the licensing requirements were, how arduous they were and how they stopped them from acting independently. . . . Then I asked, 'Would all those in the room with a patent please stand up?' Suddenly half the room stood up" (interview with the author).

So why did they patent? And why didn't their patenting contradict the outrage they felt? How do we account for the fact that scientists in the mouse community, like so many of their peers in other academic fields, opposed patents but ended up producing both publications and patents themselves? The answer is that these scientists redefined the meaning of their patents. Whereas DuPont had exercised patent rights to seek monetary rewards, the mouse community stripped patents of much of their direct economic role. They developed many ways of using patents to shape credit and control *within* the academic economy, not outside of it.

While it remains something of a taboo to acknowledge the role of commercial instruments such as patents in the academic economy, interviews suggest that patents influenced mouse geneticists' and other academic scientists' notions of control and credit. First, patents emerged among mouse geneticists as a new means to transform experimental knowledge claims into a traditional form of professional prestige. Gaining a patent established the priority and the importance of a particular idea in a different sphere and with a different judge, but it could still bring prestige. As one scientist noted about patents in her own calculus of credit, "A patent is different from consulting. You see, it's really more like a publication. It has to meet certain hurdles, and there is a high bar I think (I've never tried it but I would like to). You . . . have to be inventive and useful and someone really has to think that it's new" (interview with the author). While gaining patents might be a source of pride, producing useful products was for many scientists the currency that really brought "enormous personal satisfaction" and prestige not just from peers, "but also from friends and family, and from the outside world." Many mouse geneticists thus came to see patents not as a "necessary evil" but as an "important step" in fulfilling the sense of obligation they felt: that their "research has a long term impact on health, on diseases like cancer, and on finding a cure." In other words, it allowed for an even greater repertoire of credit in the already rich cycle of credit of academia. At the same time, academic scientists in mouse genetics and beyond checked the degree to which patents could replace publication as *the* form of credit for establishing a reputation within academia. At least among the top-ranked research universities, the tenure decision among mouse geneticists (and other biologists) still relied on publications and impact, not patents.

Patents also gave scientists an additional tool for exercising control over their assets. By increasing the control that an inventor had over key scientific resources, patenting had the potential to reshape social relationships between academics, recentering them on scientists with patents. The features that defined patents—strong control rights and the legal rights to exclude—shifted the balance of competition versus cooperation toward a stronger and "legally" sanctioned form of competition. Arising in the shadow of the patent (rather than in court), this shifting dynamic was most clearly seen through its impact on academic collaboration. It was exemplified by the story of one mouse scientist criticized by colleagues in *Science* for his track record in mouse exchange. He lamented that "everybody and their brother would like to get my mice, and if they don't get it in 3 months, they badmouth me" (qtd. in Cohen 1995, p. 1717) but went on to argue that an Amgen lawyer had to approve every exchange, so he was in a difficult position when it came to compliance. He could, however, collaborate because this circumvented the legal issues. Thus collaboration provided scientists with a (gracious?) way out of the dilemma of whether and when to cede control of an asset and under what terms. For some this was a competitive benefit, for others an unfortunate outcome of clumsy licensing, but it was difficult for the mouse community to make this judgment and to sanction those who used patents for personal gain. One geneticist complained that the mice "should be part of our communal resources. Patents on mice cause problems for the community and just make bad people worse, and they seem to make the rich get richer if you know what I mean—not so much financially—I mean how much could Phil have made on the mice, but they do give him power" (interview with the author). Again practices to check the ability of scientists to use patents strategically within the academic mouse economy have emerged. An academic exemption (based on contracts rather than judicial fiat) has become a key aspect of negotiations around the licensing of transgenic mice and is expanding to other arenas of academic patent licensing. While controversial, this seeks to carve out a protected arena in which these more strategic actions become less viable and the shadow of the patent over the academic economy recedes.

Conclusion

Scholarship in the law and economics tradition has focused on the legal purpose of patents, their scope and value, and their impact on economic growth. While important, this perspective largely ignores the impact of patents on the daily life of scientists. Assigning patents a status equal to publications and treating them symmetrically within the academic and commercial spheres makes it possible to see how patents are far more than mere legal texts that allocate property rights. For academic scientists in mouse genetics, patents became a flexible instrument through which they could subtly transform their own academic economy and cycle of credit within which they operated. Over a two-decade period, scientists incorporated patents into academia but on their own terms. They changed the meaning of patents, but they also subtly shifted the ways in which they controlled their assets and regarded their sources of credit. In order to accomplish their daily work, scientists came to master a more complex calculus of credit and control. Patenting played an important role in this new boundary work. Perhaps the most important lesson from this episode is not so much what patents did to change academic science but that it was the scientists and scientists' own organizations and leaders, not the law courts, who determined the way that patents shaped laboratory life.

NOTES

1. My thanks to Scott Stern, Mario Biagioli, and Jason Owen-Smith for their advice on this paper. Kenneth Huang and Kranthi Vistakula provided excellent research assistance. All errors are my own. This research was funded in part by a Sloan Foundation Fellowship and an MIT Provost's Award.

2. My analysis is based on a rich historical study of the oncomouse and the mouse genetics community in which it was discovered and used. The study is described in more detail in Murray (forthcoming) but includes archival sources in addition to primary interviews with key scientists. In the interests of confidentiality, quotes from these interviews are not attributed to specific individuals.

3. The groups included Frank Ruddle at Yale (Gordon et al. 1980), a collaborative effort between Ralph Brinster and Richard Palmiter at the University of Pennsylvania and the University of Washington (Brinster et al. 1981), Frank Constantini (Constantini and Lacy 1981) at Oxford (later Columbia), Beatrice Mintz at Fox Chase Cancer Center (Wagner et al. 1981), and T. E. Wagner's group (Wagner et al. 1981).

4. The patent and the paper are very different in the breadth of their claims. The publication abstract describes a modest set of experiments: "We have produced 13 strains of transgenic mice that carry an otherwise normal mouse myc gene in which increasingly large portions of the myc promoter have been replaced by a hormonally inducible mouse mammary tumor virus promoter" (Stewart et al. 1984, p. 627). The legal claims of the patent are sweeping in their scope, establishing property rights over "a transgenic non-human mammal all of whose germ cells and somatic cells contain a recombinant activated oncogene sequence introduced into said mammal, or an ancestor of said mammal, at an embryonic stage" (U.S. Patent 4736866).

REFERENCES

Anderson, Alum. 1988. "Oncomouse Released." *Nature*, 336(24): 300.

Anderson, Christopher. 1993. "Researchers Win Decision on Knockout Mouse Pricing." *Science*, 260: 23–24.

Atkinson, Paul, Clair Batchelor, and Evelyn Parsons. 1998. "Trajectories of Collaboration and Competition in a Medical Discovery." *Science, Technology & Human Values*, 23(3): 259–284.

Biagioli, Mario. 2007. *Galileo's Instruments of Credit: Telescopes, Images, Secrecy*. Chicago: University of Chicago Press.

Biagioli, Mario, and Peter Galison, eds. 2003. *Scientific Authorship: Credit and Intellectual Property in Science*. New York: Routledge.

Brinster, Ralph L., H. Y. Chen, M. Trumbauer, A. W. Senear, and R. Warren. 1981. "Somatic Expression of Herpes Thymidine Kinase in Mice Following Injection of a Fusion Gene into Eggs." *Cell* 27: 223–231.

Brinster, Ralph L., H. Y. Chen, A. Messing, T. Vandyke, A. J. Levine, and R. D. Palmiter. 1984. "Transgenic Mice Harboring SV40 T-Antigen Genes Develop Characteristic Brain-Tumors." *Cell* 37(2): 367–379.

Cohen, J. 1995. "Share and Share Alike Isn't Always the Rule in Science." *Science*, 268(5218): 1715–1718.

Constantini, Frank, and E. Lacy. 1981. "Introduction of a Rabbit Beta-Globin Gene into the Mouse Germ Line." *Nature* 294: 92–94.

Cory, S., and J. M. Adams. 1988. "Transgenic Mice and Oncogenesis." *Annual Review of Immunology*, 6: 25–48.

Crane, Diana. 1969. "Social Structure in a Group of Scientists: A Test of the 'Invisible College' Hypothesis." *American Sociological Review*, 34: 335–352.

Dasgupta, P., and P. David. 1994. "Toward a New Economics of Science." *Research Policy*, 23(5): 487–521.

De Mesquita, Ethan Bueno, and Matthew Stephenson. 2006. "Legal Institutions and Informal Networks." *Journal of Theoretical Politics*, 18(1): 40–67.

Ding, Waverly, Fiona Murray, and Toby Stuart. 2006. "Gender Differences in Patenting in the Academic Life Sciences." *Science*, 313(5787): 665–667.

Fujimura, Joan H. 1987. "Constructing 'Do-Able' Problems in Cancer Research: Articulating Alignment." *Social Studies of Science,* 17(2): 257–293.

Gans, Joshua, and Scott Stern. 2000. "Incumbency and R&D Incentives: Licensing the Gale of Creative Destruction." *Journal of Economics and Management Strategy* 9(4): 485–511.

Gieryn, Thomas F. 1995. "Boundaries of Science." In S. Jasanoff et al. (ed.), *Handbook of Science and Technology Studies*. Thousand Oaks, CA: Sage Publications, 393–443.

Gordon, J. W., G. A. Scangos, D. J. Plotkin, J. A. Barbosa, and F. H. Ruddle. 1980. "Genetic Transformation of Mouse Embryos by Microinjection of Purified DNA." *Proceedings of the National Academy of Sciences of the United States of America*, 77(12): 73807384.

Hughes, Sally Smith. 2001. "Making Dollars Out of DNA: The First Major Patent in Biotechnology and the Commercialization of Molecular Biology, 1974–1980," *Isis*, 92: 541–575.

Jaffe, Sam. 2004. "Ongoing Battle over Transgenic Mice." *Scientist*, 18(14): 46–49.

Judson, Horace Freeland. 1996. *The Eighth Day of Creation: Makers of the Revolution in Biology*. 2nd edition. Cold Spring Harbor, NY: Cold Spring Harbor Press.

Kevles, Daniel J. 2002. "Of Mice and Money: The Story of the World's First Animal Patent." *Daedalus*, 131(2): 78.

Kohler, Robert E. 1994. *Lords of the Fly: "Drosophila" Genetics and the Experimental Life*. Chicago: University of Chicago Press.

Kohler, Robert E. 1999. "Moral Economy, Material Culture and Community." In M. Biagioli (ed.), *The Science Studies Reader*. New York: Routledge, 243–257.

Krimsky, Sheldon. 2003. *Science in the Private Interest: Has the Lure of Profits Corrupted Biomedical Research?* Lanham, MD: Rowman-Littlefield.

Lasker Foundation. 1987. "Philip Leder: Interview Transcript." Accessed at http://www.lasker foundation.org/awards/kwood/leder/transcript.shtml.

Latour, Bruno and Steve Woolgar. 1979. *Laboratory Life: The Social Construction of Scientific Facts*. Los Angeles: Sage.

Merton, R. 1973. *The Sociology of Science: Theoretical and Empirical Investigations*. Chicago: University of Chicago Press.

Morange, M. 1998. *A History of Molecular Biology*. Cambridge, MA: Harvard University Press.

Murray, Fiona. 2002. "Innovation as Co-evolution of Scientific and Technological Networks: Exploring Tissue Engineering." *Research Policy,* 31(8–9): 1389–1403.

Murray, Fiona. Forthcoming. "The Oncomouse That Roared: Hybrid Exchange Strategies as a Source of Productive Tension at the Boundaries of Overlapping Institutions." *American Journal of Sociology*.

Paigen, Ken. 2003. "One Hundred Years of Mouse Genetics: An Intellectual History. I. The Classical Period (1902–1980)." *Genetics*, 163: 1–7.

Rader, Karen. 2004. *Making Mice: Standardizing Animals for American Biomedical Research, 1900–1955*. Princeton, NJ: Princeton University Press.

Scott, Pam, Evelleen Richards, and Brian Martin. 1990. "Captives of Controversy: The Myth of the Neutral Social Researcher in Contemporary Scientific Controversies." *Science, Technology & Human Values*, 15(4): 474–494.

Shapin, Steven. 1994. *A Social History of Truth: Civility and Science in Seventeenth-Century England*. Chicago: University of Chicago Press.

Shapin, Steven. 2007. "Science and the Modern World." In, E. Hackett, O. Amsterdamska, M. Lynch, and J. Wajcman (eds.), *The Handbook of Science and Technology Studies*, 3rd ed. Cambridge, MA: MIT Press, 433–448.

Smaglik, Paul. 2000. "NIH Cancer Researchers to Get Free Access to 'Oncomouse.'" *Nature*, 403(27): 350.

Stewart, Timothy A., Paul K. Pattengale, and Philip Leder. 1984. "Spontaneous Mammary Adenocarcinomas in Transgenic Mice That Carry and Express MTV/myc Fusion Genes." *Cell* 38(3): 627–637.

Wagner, E. F., Timothy A. Stewart, and Beatrice Mintz. 1981. "The Human Beta-Globin Gene and a Functional Viral Thymidine Kinase Gene in Developing Mice." *Proceedings of the National Academy of Sciences*, 78: 5016–5020.

Walsh, John, Ashish Arora, and Wesley Cohen. 2003. "Science and the Law: Working through the Patent Problem." *Science*, 299(5609): 1021.

Weaver, D., M. H. Reis, C. Albanese, F. Constantini, D. Baltimore, and T. Imanishi-Kari. 1986. Altered Repertoire of Endogenous Immunoglobulin Gene Expression in Transgenic Mice containing a Rearranged Mu Heavy Chain Gene. *Cell*, 45(2): 247–259.

23

Is There Such a Thing as Postmodern Copyright?

Back in 1992, artist and entrepreneur Jeff Koons suffered a humiliating setback when the U.S. Court of Appeals for the Second Circuit repudiated the suggestion that his reuse of objects from public culture might constitute a "fair use" defense to a copyright infringement claim.[1] Fourteen years later, in a case that again involved a photographer's claim of copyright infringement, Koons triumphed in the same judicial forum.[2] What had changed? This chapter explores, in particular, one among a variety of alternative explanations: Koons may have caught the very leading edge of a profound wave of change in the social and cultural conceptualization of copyright law—specifically, the emergence of an understanding that is at least incipiently "postmodern" in nature.[3]

It would be a dangerous undertaking for one trained only in the law to venture a definition of a term as protean as *postmodernism*.[4] Nevertheless, I suggest below that several related elements, characteristic of what might be termed a postmodern cultural attitude, are beginning to seep into copyright theory and jurisprudence:

- rejection of claims based on "authority" and "expertise," including claims relating to interpretation;

- suspicion of "grand narratives" designed to justify eternal verities;
- skepticism about hierarchical claims about art and culture, especially those couched in terms of distinctions between "high" and "low," coupled with a preference for ironic juxtaposition of unlike materials;
- a turning away from values of stability toward an embrace of flux and change;
- recognition that discussions of information access and regulation are inherently and profoundly political in nature.

Copyright Law and Culture

Law has always lagged in its assimilation of new theories and their associated rhetorics. So it would be news of a kind if a close reading of some recent decisions revealed an emergent postmodern take on copyright. To be clear, the contention here is not that today's jurists are literally disciples of Jean-François Lyotard (any more than judges of previous generations pronounced themselves devotees of Johann Fichte or William Wordsworth); rather than being self-conscious trend followers, lawyers and judges who work on copyright are participants in a larger cultural conversation, and what they derive from it ends up influencing copyright discourse in various ways—for good and ill.[5]

Before proceeding further, here is a brief recap of the story so far, starting with the self-evident observation that there was no such thing as premodern copyright on a systemic level. The institution of copyright and its basic conceptual structures are preeminently "modern," in a historical/chronological sense. Although this body of legal rules certainly has a rich prehistory, the institutions and mechanisms that regulated information production before 1710 (patronage, printing patents, and so forth) were rooted in understandings of social life that assumed the primacy and stability of hierarchical authority and (accordingly) did not reflect the emergence of "possessive individualism"[6] and, with it, modernity. The conceptual move that gave us copyright as we know it was the introduction of the rights-bearing individual into the scheme of the law. An obvious marker for this development was the somewhat mysterious appearance of the "author" as the entity in whom rights initially vested under the Statute of Anne.[7] The emergent figure of the Romantic author-genius rapidly took over a dominant role in thought and discussion about copyright law in Great Britain and on the continent—and, ultimately, beyond Europe as well.[8]

If the rise of the authorship concept is historically and chronologically linked to the emergence of modernity, its durability has been attributed, at least in part, to a subsequent and mutually supportive encounter with literary and artistic modernism. In the Romantic era, one of the specific roles assigned to creative and scientific genius was the work of imposing a comprehensible pattern on the evidence of experience, once religion (and other traditional sources of authority) could no longer be depended upon for this purpose.[9] In the later nineteenth and twentieth centuries, modernism tightened culture's embrace of individual self-consciousness as a source of stable meaning in a world destabilized by migration, global war, and new science and technology, among other disruptions.

Michel Foucault observed that authorship is a structure that works to discipline and limit the meaning of particular texts and discourses.[10] Under conditions of modernism, the author function increasingly served to hold together the elements of an entire information environment that threatened to fall disastrously apart.[11] Critical consumers of culture celebrated individual painters and writers for their ability to communicate a coherent understanding of otherwise incoherent happenings.[12] Some sense of this is captured in T. S. Eliot's famous *Dial* review of James Joyce's *Ulysses*—one giant of modernism commenting (perhaps somewhat self-reflexively) on another—praising Joyce's "method" (that is, his personal take on Greek mythology) because it had the effect of "controlling, of ordering, of giving a shape and a significance to the immense panorama of futility and anarchy which is contemporary history."[13]

This extreme valorization of the individual point of view, associated with both romanticism and modernism, helped to further shape a set of legal attitudes about literary and artistic property. Most specifically, it contributed to the development of a theme in copyright discourse that associates the assignment of rights in works not with political choice but with a preexistent (and therefore invariable) set of natural rights enjoyed by entitled authors to whom publishers and other "intermediaries" have successfully assimilated themselves, often to the exclusion of the interests of the consuming public.[14] In effect, belief in the claims of authorship emerged as the grand narrative that justifies and explains this branch of intellectual property law.

If copyright theory and doctrine grew up in conversation with a particular world view, then the proposition that legal understandings of copyright could change as that dominant vision is displaced should not be particularly controversial. But it may prove to be, nonetheless, precisely because its underlying premise has yet to achieve general acceptance. The general notion that law is derivative of cultural attitudes is not revolutionary in itself. Many would accept that our notions of crime are rooted in religious and ethical beliefs or that the emergence of human rights law was abetted by the ethos of post–World War II decolonialization. But among intellectual property scholars, there has been some resistance to claims of cultural influence in the copyright field—at least in the United States. This is traceable, I think, to a collective, proudly disillusioned position that copyright, unlike other bodies of law, is really all about the money; that IP law is simply a machine to generate innovation through economic incentives; and that lawyers are merely engineers called on occasionally to tweak or tinker with the mechanism.[15] Such scholars celebrate when (from their perspectives) the machine works well, and they lament when it runs poorly—but it's all just gears and switches either way. To some extent this economic/mechanistic perspective on copyright may have been overtaken by recent events. More and more, scholars are paying attention to the roles that rhetorics (whether of "authorship" or "piracy" or even "property" itself) have played in forming legal discourse—and therefore, law itself.[16] Certainly, the "copyright wars" of the 1990s have given us new reason to appreciate how effectively the emotive tropes of individualism can be mustered in support of particular policy objectives. After all, the present account of "postmodern copyright" may find favor where the original "critique of authorship" did not.

Rogers v. Koons

In any event, the objective here is not to refight old battles but rather to suggest that, once again, copyright law has struck up a conversation with the general culture and that there are signs that this new discursive connection may prove consequential. And that brings the focus back to Jeff Koons, his art, and his litigations—beginning with *Rogers v. Koons*, about which I first wrote seventeen years ago[17]—a decision that tells the story of an image's rise from humble beginnings as a homely semiposed photo of a couple and their dogs to its apotheosis as a somewhat disquieting larger-than-life sculpture, included (along with other monumentalized kitsch) in Jeff Koons's highly successful "Banality" show.[18] In what follows, I will offer a modest revision of my previous take on that fascinating case. Back in 1992, my commentary on the Second Circuit decision emphasized the importance of the case as it demonstrated the persistence of "Romantic" authorship—the influential conceptualization of the deserving creator of culture as an inspired original genius entitled not only to ownership of, but also to a broad scope of protection over, his or her productions.[19]

I argued then that Jeff Koons lost on his fair use defense in large part because he failed, or refused, to conform to the stereotype of the serious, dedicated creator around which our copyright law increasingly came to be organized from the early nineteenth century on.[20] By contrast, artist-photographer Art Rogers, who was bracketed with Ansel Adams by Second Circuit Court of Appeals judge Richard Cardamone, was portrayed as a complete artist who "makes his living by creating, exhibiting, publishing and otherwise making use of his rights in his . . . works."[21] Conversely, Koons came off as a money-mad opportunist (with a background in commodities trading, no less) who did not even personally execute the projects he conceived.[22] Technically, the argument was framed as a case about the applicability of "parody" fair use, but in fact, I argued then, something rather different was going on.[23] The judge left no doubt about how he viewed the defendant's moral and aesthetic fitness: "The copying was so deliberate as to suggest that the defendants [Koons and his dealer] resolved so long as they were significant players in the art business, and the copies they produced bettered the price of the copied work by a thousand to one, their piracy of a less well-known artist's work would escape being sullied by an accusation of piracy."[24] In other words, Koons was not qualified to invoke a defense that was, at its base, rooted in a twist on Romantic authorship.

In retrospect, it seems possible that something more (or, at least, slightly different) may have been at work as well, and that the opinion also could be understood as evidence of the persistent influence of modernist thought on copyright law of the late twentieth century. Art Rogers is a recognizable modern maker with a gift for creating real art from common materials.[25] By contrast, according to Judge Cardamone, all the earmarks of modernist high culture—the seriousness, the integrative stance, the suspension of temporal morality—were conspicuously absent from Koons's insouciant and even trivial "performance" in *String of Puppies*: Jeff Koons was not just a nonauthor, the court's opinion suggests, but a "bad boy" disgrace to modernist values and attitudes—although, we suspect, one who is (or was) proud of that stance.[26]

In arriving at his characterization of Koons, Judge Cardamone relied on a *New York Times* article by Michael Brenson.[27] The pertinent part of that article declared that Koons's "art is largely strategic. Images have been appropriated from photographs of popular culture and collaged together into spanking new commodities. They were made collectively, even anonymously, by workshops in northern Italy. What seems to matter is not the originality of the artist, but rather images that belong to an entire culture and that everyone in that culture can use."[28] Clearly, this view of the source material was not shared by the judge![29] But that was then, and this is now. In this moment, postmodern sensibility is no longer the special province of cultural critics, if it ever was. Instead, it is being enacted (often in ways enabled through new technology) by way of the hacker ethic; hip-hop, remix culture, and other forms of bricolage; and the DIY movement, to mention only a few examples. This outlook is so pervasive that it would be surprising if it had no implications for legal thinking about information regulation. When this chapter returns to the Jeff Koons story, it will be to suggest that seventeen years later, copyright discourse has begun to reflect, however tentatively, an attitude of postmodernism.

To be clear, the suggestion is that attitudes have begun to change in the last several decades; it is not that some aspects of postmodernism were anticipated in classic twentieth-century copyright doctrine, although this may well be the case. In Justice Oliver Wendell Holmes's famous 1903 dicta in *Bleistein v. Donaldson Lithographing Co.*, he pointedly declined to discriminate between conventional fine art and the very mundane advertising posters involved in that litigation, which can be understood as a gesture of premature postmodernism.[30] Jane Gaines and Brad Sherman, respectively, are right to note that copyright can be a "great cultural leveler," and that it "refuse[s] to distinguish works of high and low authorship."[31] Generally speaking, however, copyright has held tightly onto other kinds of modernist hierarchies—especially the scale along which more and less "original" artistic productions are valued.[32] Conventionally, copyright law has given a special place of pride to work that originates from either the fertile mind of its maker or as a result of that mind's interaction with the raw materials of nature.[33] The result, of course, is that merely "derivative" works—those that take preexisting culture for their material—have been systematically undervalued in the copyright scheme. This attitude, of course, is on prominent display in *Rogers*. Koons's defensive arguments fail, at least in part, because the culturally referential nature of his sculpture contrasts unfavorably with the straightforward artistry of Rogers's photo.[34] Whatever the postmodern potential of copyright may have been, the case demonstrates how far the copyright system was, in the early 1990s, from its realization.

Blanch v. Koons

In 2006, however, the Second Circuit Court of Appeals decided *Blanch v. Koons*, which concerned the artist's incorporation of a portion of an image known as "Silk Sandals," which had earned the fashion photographer/plaintiff a $750 commissioning fee, into *Niagara*, a Koons painting in the widely exhibited $2 million, seven-painting "Easyfun-Ethereal" series.[35] Once again, Koons's defense was fair use, but this time it received a far more respectful treatment. The real indicator of change, however, is found in the specific language employed by the court on its way to a finding that the use was "transformative" in that it added value to and fundamentally repurposed the original photograph.[36] On his way to a conclusion, Judge Robert Sack noted: "The question is whether Koons had a genuine creative rationale for borrowing Blanch's image, rather than using it merely 'to get attention or to avoid the drudgery in working up something fresh.'"[37] The court continued (with considerable deference) by noting Koons's own explanation of why he used Blanch's image:

Although the legs in the *Allure Magazine* photograph ["Silk Sandals"] might seem prosaic, I considered them to be necessary for inclusion in my painting rather than legs I might have photographed myself. The ubiquity of the photograph is central to my message. The photograph is typical of a certain style of mass communication. Images almost identical to them can be found in almost any glossy magazine, as well as in other media. To me, the legs depicted in the *Allure* photograph are a fact in the world, something that everyone experiences constantly; they are not anyone's legs in particular. By using a fragment of the *Allure* photograph in my painting, I thus comment upon the culture and attitudes promoted and embodied in *Allure Magazine*. By using an existing image, I also ensure a certain authenticity or veracity that enhances my commentary—it is the difference between quoting and paraphrasing—and ensure that the viewer will understand what I am referring to.[38]

This self-justificatory statement may or may not make sense as an explanation of why *Niagara* is a critical commentary on popular media culture. Ultimately, however, its coherence may not matter. What clearly does matter is that Judge Sack takes Koons's self-expressed claims as an interpreter and repurposer of existing content very seriously—so much so that he is willing to agree that "these are not anyone's legs in particular," but limbs available for appropriation by someone with a new angle. He concludes, with a bow to *Bleistein*: "Although it seems clear enough to us that Koons's use of a slick fashion photograph enables him to satirize life as it appears when seen through the prism of slick fashion photography, we need not depend on our own poorly honed artistic sensibilities. . . . We conclude that Koons thus established a 'justif[ication for] the very act of [his] borrowing.' Whether or not Koons could have created "Niagara" without reference to "Silk Sandals," we have been given no reason to question his statement that the use of an existing image advanced his artistic purposes."[39] Clearly, Judge Sack was prepared to cut Jeff Koons a good deal of slack.[40] So what explains this reasoning and result? What changed over the years from *Rogers* to *Blanch*? Several explanations suggest themselves.

Telling a Tale of Two Koonses

By far the least interesting is that Jeff Koons has not actually escaped the grid of modernist author-based copyright reasoning at all but (always an accomplished self-publicist) has merely succeeded in slotting himself more firmly into it. In other words, the decision represents the persistence of Romantic authorship rather than hinting at its senescence. Back in *Rogers*, Koons was a "player," not an author.[41] Now, he's claimed that privileged status, with work in the collection of the Metropolitan and a solo exhibition in the summer of 2008 at the Palace of Versailles.[42] Koons has become fully credentialed as a creative genius, and that makes all the difference. The fatal shortcoming of this explanation is that it does not account satisfactorily for much of the opinion's actual rhetoric. In fact, the opinion hardly discusses "authorship" and "originality."[43] It certainly does not suggest that fair use analysis is just a matter of weighing competing authorship claims.[44]

The most technical explanation focuses strictly on shifts in copyright doctrine during the period between the two lawsuits. When *Rogers* was decided, the transformativeness-based approach to fair use analysis was still a personal project of Judge Pierre Leval and not yet the law of the Second Circuit or the land.[45] Today, transformativeness figures as a kind of metaconsideration arching over fair use analysis. The determination of whether a use is transformative or not strongly inflects (if not dictates) the outcome of at least three, if not all four, of the statutory factors to which section 107 of the Copyright Act directs judicial attention.[46] It was born in the context of factor 1 (the nature of the use) but has its most dramatic implications for factor 4 (the effect on the market), with courts (up to and including the U.S. Supreme Court) suggesting that copyright owners are not entitled to expect licensing revenues from "transformative markets."[47] However, the rise of transformativeness is far from being a self-explanatory or an autonomous phenomenon. It does not so much explain as it correlates with the court's approach in *Blanch*.[48] Or, to state the matter differently, both the hegemony exercised by this legal standard in general and the mode of its application to Jeff Koons in particular may reflect shifts in the cultural positioning of copyright.[49]

Postmodern Copyright

And that brings the argument to what may be the most interesting explanation of the Second Circuit's revised take on Jeff Koons: that the rhetorical structure of the *Blanch* opinion represents a significant move away from the modernist author worship and an early signal of a perceptible shift in how courts will increasingly understand the relationship between author and work in years to come.[50] It represents, in fact, a rejection of the grand narrative of authorship and "author-ity" in favor of an approach that distributes attention and concern across the full range of participants in the processes of cultural production and consumption.[51] As such, it may signal a general loosening of authors' and owners' control over, by now, not quite so auratic works, allowing greater space for the free play of meaning among audience members and follow-on users who bring new interpretations.[52] If so, this is a change of potentially profound importance, undermining the stability of the two concepts at the heart of modern copyright.[53]

Viewed in this way, the *Blanch* decision suggests that as old attitudes have been displaced or supplemented by new ones in the domain of culture, law is (however belatedly) beginning to follow suit. Specifically, law may be absorbing an attitude of skepticism about fixed identity and stable point of view— recognizing what has been clear for some time in arts practice and aesthetic theory: that, much like the natural world, constructed culture is fair game for reinterpretation as "fact[s] in the world," to quote Jeff Koons once again.[54] If so, as Laura Heymann has suggested, these developments will be consequential in the law of fair use.[55] Among other things, how they play out will profoundly influence the copyright position of the growing community of fan fictioneers, vidders, remixers, and mash-up artists who are currently running afoul of the online content platforms' take-down policies.[56]

Obviously, it is risky to take one decision (or even a group of related decisions concerning a topic such as fair use in appropriation art) as a marker for a trend in copyright thinking. Fortunately, the evidence of *Blanch* is not uncorroborated. Consider, for example, recent developments in the law regulating the liability of technology providers, beginning with the Supreme Court's 1984 decision in *Sony Corp. of America v. Universal Studios, Inc.*, which embodies a skeptical attitude toward claims of authority that impinge on audience choice.[57] There, the Court ruled that home recording and "time shifting" of television programming constituted fair use—and went on to immunize technology providers from liability for supplying the necessary VCR equipment. It reasoned:

> The distinction between "productive" and "unproductive" uses may be helpful in calibrating the balance, but it cannot be wholly determinative. . . . Copying a news broadcast may have a stronger claim to fair use than copying a motion picture. And, of course, not all uses are fungible. . . . A teacher who copies to prepare lecture notes is clearly productive. But so is a teacher who copies for the sake of broadening his personal understanding of his specialty. Or a legislator who copies for the sake of broadening her understanding of what her constituents are watching; or a constituent who copies a news program to help make a decision on how to vote.[58]

Making a copy of a copyrighted work for the convenience of a blind person is expressly identified by the House Judiciary committee's 1976 report on copyright reform legislation as an example of fair use, with no suggestion that anything more than a purpose to entertain or to inform need motivate the copying. In a hospital setting, using a VTR to enable a patient to see programs he would otherwise miss has no productive purpose other than contributing to the psy-chological well-being of the patient. Virtually any time-shifting that increases viewer access to television programming may result in a comparable benefit.[59]

In other words, the decision puts the controls, so to speak, in the hands of the end user, a gesture of empowerment made in defiance of the received "grand narrative" of copyright law that concentrates authority in the copyright owner. The Supreme Court's discussion, quoted above, makes it clear that its analysis is driven by an understanding that its decision is a necessary interven-tion into the politics of authority over information—an essentially postmod-ern stance.[60]

Cartoon Network LP v. CSC Holdings, Inc.

More recently, the Second Circuit decided *Cartoon Network LP v. CSC Hold-ings, Inc.*, a case that determined whether a cable system's operation of a virtual digital video recorder (RS-DVR) on behalf of its subscribers involved various violations of copyrights in broadcast content.[61] At first blush, this is hardly promising material for a close reading aimed at detecting a possible shift in underlying assumptions about the nature of copyright. Certainly, it is a highly technical decision, addressing (1) whether buffer copies are infringing repro-ductions, (2) whether transmission of those copies to users at a time of their choosing constitutes "public performance," and (3) whether the company has legal responsibility for longer-enduring "playback" copies made on its own servers.[62] But in setting aside the district court's conclusions on each of these issues, the Second Circuit ran a gauntlet of seemingly applicable precedents, driven forward by its apparent awareness of what amounts to core postmodern themes or concerns.[63]

For example, the panel of judges disposed of the public performance is-sue by noting that each performance served by the cable system to subscrib-ers was made by means of a separate copy—finding significance in the fact that each subscriber's experience of the recorded work was both formally and substantively distinct from those of others.[64] And in addressing the question of responsibility for the making of the playback copy, the court opined: "In most copyright disputes, the allegedly infringing act and the identity of the infringer are never in doubt. These cases turn on whether the conduct in ques-tion does, in fact, infringe the plaintiff's copyright. In this case, however, the core of the dispute is over the authorship of the infringing conduct."[65] The court concluded: "In the case of a VCR, it seems clear—and we know of no case holding otherwise—that the operator of the VCR, the person who actually presses the button to make the recording, supplies the necessary element of volition, not the person who manufactures, maintains, or, if distinct from the operator, owns the machine. We do not believe that an RS-DVR customer is sufficiently distinguishable from a VCR user to impose liability as a direct infringer on a different party for copies that are made automatically upon that customer's command."[66] With this new variation on the theme of "authorship," directed not to the works involved but to the challenged "conduct," the Second Circuit reenacted the rationale of the Supreme Court's 1984 *Sony* decision, with its emphasis on safeguarding private choices about information consumption.[67]

The *Cartoon Network* decision has had its detractors. In particular, critics alleged, with some justification, that in arriving at its result, the Second Circuit took liberties with statutory concepts such as the requirement that an infringing copy must exist for "more than transitory duration."[68] Noting that there are no applicable precedents to guide a determination of how stable a copy must be in order to infringe, the court continued: "No bit of data remains in any buffer for more than a fleeting 1.2 seconds. . . . [E]ach bit of data here is rapidly and automatically overwritten as soon as it is processed. While our inquiry is necessarily fact-specific, and other factors not present here may alter the duration analysis significantly, these facts strongly suggest that the works in this case are embodied in the buffer for only a 'transitory' period, thus failing the duration requirement."[69] The liberatory effect of this analysis is considerable. And reasonable as it may sound, it represents no small exercise of creativity on the part of the court. The quoted language clearly suggests the possibility that there exists a range of short-lived information phenomena (some trivial and others significant) that fall outside the scope of copyright regulation. In particular, data flows may escape its web of control—an outcome that reflects a postmodern appreciation and understanding of the instability and contingency of information objects.

Conclusion

Both the method and the outcome of *Cartoon Network* were highly controversial.[70] But the decision seems here to stay. What it and the other recent decisions discussed here may signal for the future is another question. It is too soon to pronounce the death of the modernist conception of authority in copyright or the desuetude of the related concept of the fixed work. But change may, nevertheless, be under way.

NOTES

1. *Rogers v. Koons*, 960 F.2d 301 (2d Cir. 1992).

2. *Blanch v. Koons*, 467 F.3d 244 (2d Cir. 2006).

3. It may be noteworthy that Koons was claimed early as an icon of postmodern art practice. According to Colin Trodd, it was widely believed that his early work "was part of a postmodern engagement with the role of culture within post-industrial society, an economic order where leisure and consumption became processes of great symbolic and material importance." *The Routledge Companion to Postmodernism* 252 (Stuart Sim ed., Routledge 2d ed. 2005).

4. Ibid., at xii; Gary Aylesworth, "Postmodernism," in *Stanford Encyclopedia of Philosophy*, http://plato.stanford.edu/entries/postmodernism.

5. Felix Guattari, who dismisses postmodernism as "no philosophy at all," is quoted as characterizing it instead as "just something in the air." See *Routledge Companion to Postmodernism*, note 3, at 18.

6. See C. B. Macpherson, *The Political Theory of Possessive Individualism: Hobbes to Locke* 1–3, 270–71 (1962).

7. Ronan Deazley, *On the Origin of the Right to Copy: Charting the Movement of Copyright Law in Eighteenth-Century Britain (1695–1775)* 9–10 (2004); Statute of Anne, 1710, 8 Ann., c. 19 (Eng.).

8. Peter Jaszi, "Toward a Theory of Copyright: The Metamorphoses of 'Authorship,'" 1991 *Duke L. J.* 455, 459.

9. See Richard Holmes, *The Age of Wonder* xv–xvii (2008). Holmes draws out the connections between the romantic sensibility in nineteenth-century literature and the ethos of a new science, based on the systematizing "genius" of figures like William Herschel and Humphrey Davy, that emerged during the same period. See generally ibid. at 163–210, 337–381.

10. See Michel Foucault, "What Is an Author?" in *Language, Counter-Memory, Practice* 113–138 (Donald F. Bouchard ed., Donald F. Bouchard & Sherry Simon trans., 1977).

11. Not only is the "author" a structure well suited to the concerns and premises of modernism, but the same assumptions and preoccupations also are reflected in copyright's own concept of the integrated "work" as a stable object of protection that reflects authorial sensibility. See ibid. Because the original is an object that enjoys authority derived from its maker, it can stand on its own. By contrast, as Walter Benjamin observes, "What withers in the age of the technological reproducibility of the work of art is the latter's aura." Walter Benjamin, *The Work of Art in the Age of Its Technological Reproducibility, and Other Writings on Media* 22 (Michael Jennings et al. eds., Edmund Jephcott et al., trans., 2008).

12. T. S. Eliot, "Ulysses, Order and Myth," 75 *Dial* 480–483 (1923), reprinted in *James Joyce: The Critical Heritage* 268–271 (Robert Deming ed., 1970). Paul K. Saint-Amour points out that Joyce himself was less than consistent on this point, "oscillat[ing] between embracing collective authorship and wrapping himself in the mystique and privileges of the individual genius." *The Copyrights: Intellectual Property and the Literary Imagination* 159 (2003).

13. Eliot, "Ulysses," in *James Joyce*, at 270.

14. Martha Woodmansee, "The Genius and the Copyright," 17 *Eighteenth-Century Stud.* 425 (1988), reprinted in *The Author, Art, and the Market: Rereading the History of Aesthetics* 49–55 (1994); Jaszi, "Toward a Theory," at 455.

15. See, e.g., Mark Lemley, "Romantic Authorship and the Rhetoric of Property," 75 *Tex. L. Rev.* 873, 894–904 (1997) ("[Romantic authorship does not] tell us very much at either a theoretical or a predictive level about intellectual property law. . . ."). Lemley proposes as an alternative that the ills of the field are the result of an inappropriate application of Chicago School law-and-economics movement theory to mental productions. Ibid. at 897–898.

16. See Woodmansee, "Genius," in *The Author*, at 42–47, and her chapter as well as that by

Lawrence Liang in this volume; Neil W. Netanel, "Why Has Copyright Expanded? Analysis and Critique," 6 *New Directions in Copyright Law* 3 (Fiona Macmillan ed., 2008); Justin Hughes, "Notes on the Origin of Intellectual Property: Revised Conclusions and New Sources" (Benjamin N. Cardozo Sch. of Law Jacob Burns Inst. for Advanced Legal Studies, Working Paper no. 265, 2009), available at http://ssrn.com/abstract=1432860.

17. Peter Jaszi, "On the Author Effect: Contemporary Copyright and Collective Creativity," in *The Construction of Authorship: Textual Appropriation in Law and Literature* 28, 41–48 (Martha Woodmansee & Peter Jaszi eds., 1994).

18. Ibid.

19. Ibid. at 42–44.

20. *Rogers*, 960 F.2d 301, 303–304 (2d Cir. 1992).

21. Ibid. at 304.

22. Ibid. at 303–304.

23. Jaszi, "On the Author Effect," at 44–48.

24. *Rogers*, 960 F.2d at 303.

25. Ibid. at 304.

26. Ibid. at 311.

27. Michael Brenson, "Greed Plus Glitz, with a Dollop of Innocence," *New York Times*, Dec. 18, 1988, Gallery View §2, at 41; see also Jaszi, "On the Author Effect," at 43 n.50.

28. Brenson, note 27, §2, at 41.

29. *Rogers*, 960 F.2d at 309–311.

30. 188 U.S. 239, 251 (1903) ("the act however construed, does not mean that ordinary posters are not good enough to be considered within its scope"); see Diane Leenheer Zimmerman, "The Story of *Bleistein v. Donaldson Lithographing Company*: Originality as a Vehicle for Copyright Inclusivity," in *Intellectual Property Stories* 77–108 (Jane C. Ginsburg & Rochelle Cooper Dreyfuss eds., 2005).

31. Jane Gaines, *Contested Culture: The Image, the Voice, and the Law* 64 (1991); Brad Sherman, "Appropriating the Postmodern: Copyright and the Challenge of the New," 4 *Soc. Legal Stud.* 31, 56–57 (1995). The further implications of postmodernism for copyright (and IP in general) were memorably foreseen in Rosemary J. Coombe, "Objects of and Subjects of Property: Intellectual Property Laws and Democratic Dialogue," 69 *Tex. L. Rev.* 1853 (1991); and Margaret Chon, "Postmodern 'Progress': Considering the Copyright and Patent Power," 43 *DePaul L. Rev.* 97 (1993).

32. See Jaszi, "Toward a Theory," at 460–464.

33. *Rogers*, 960 F.2d at 312.

34. Ibid. at 309–311.

35. *Blanch*, 467 F.3d 244, 247–249 (2d Cir. 2006).

36. Ibid.

37. Ibid. at 255.

38. Ibid.

39. Ibid. (internal citation omitted).

40. Ibid.

41. *Rogers*, 960 F.2d 301, 307–310 (2d Cir. 1992).

42. See Jeff Koons Versailles, http://www.jeffkoonsversailles.com/en/ (last visited Oct. 20, 2009). In announcing this coup, Koons sounds at least somewhat authorial: "It is an honor to represent contemporary culture within the walls of the Palace of Versailles." Ibid. For the controversy surrounding the exhibit, see also "Kitsch Trumps Baroque: Koons' Versailles Show Ruffles Feathers in France," Spiegel Online (Sept. 10, 2008), http://www.spiegel.de/international/europe/0,1518,577388,00.html.

43. See generally *Blanch*, 467 F.3d 244.

44. In the *Blanch* district court opinion, the judge actually seemed to take a similar approach, dismissing the "Silk Sandals" photo as (interestingly) "banal rather than creative." *Blanch*, 396 F. Supp. 2d 476, 481–482 (S.D.N.Y. 2005). But the Second Circuit firmly rejects this qualitative "comparative" technique. See *Blanch*, 467 F.3d at 247–248 (respectfully describing Andrea Blanch and her work).

45. The transformativeness-based approach was introduced by Judge Pierre N. Leval in "Toward a Fair Use Standard," 103 *Harv. L. Rev.* 1105, 1111–1117 (1990). Since that time, it has evolved into the generally accepted metacriterion in fair use analysis. But see Mitch Tuchman, "Judge Leval's Transformation Standard: Can It Really Distinguish Foul from Fair?" 51 *J. Copyright Soc'y* 101 (2003). For the evolution of the standard since 1990, see Peter Jaszi, "Copyright, Fair Use and Motion Pictures," 2007 *Utah L. Rev.* 715, 718–722 (evolution of the standard since 1990); Pamela Samuelson, "Unbundling Fair Uses," 77 *Fordham L. Rev.* 2537 (2009) (systematic analysis of fair use as applied in a wide range of contexts).

46. Jaszi, "Copyright, Fair Use," at 720, 725; 17 U.S.C.A. §107 (2009).

47. Ibid., at 722 (quoting *Bill Graham Archives v. Dorling Kindersley, Ltd.*, 448 F.3d 605, 614–615 [2d Cir. 2006]).

48. See *Blanch*, 467 F.3d at 251–253.

49. See the interesting discussion in Laura Heymann, "Everything Is Transformative: Fair Use and Reader Response," 31 *Colum. J. L. & Arts* 445, 460–462 (2008) (contrasting *Rogers* and *Blanch* and suggesting that courts might determine whether a claimed fair use is transformative by considering whether the defendant's work engages with a different discursive community from the plaintiff's work). Heymann's prescription for the improvement of transformativeness analysis is that courts take into greater account the insights of reader-response criticism; she finds in *Blanch* (and other cases cited in her footnote 90) an indication that such a refined approach may already be at work. Ibid.

50. See generally *Blanch*, 467 F.3d 244.

51. Ibid.

52. Ibid.

53. For some of the difficulties attending the concept of the "work," see Robert H. Rotstein, "Beyond Metaphor: Copyright Infringement and the Fiction of the Work," 68 *Chi.-Kent L. Rev.* 725 (1993).

54. *Blanch*, 467 F.3d at 255. An extended critique of the *Rogers* decision as failing to recognize the nature of "postmodern" appropriation art can be found in Lynne A. Greenberg, "The Art of Appropriation: Puppies, Piracy and Post-Modernism," 11 *Cardozo Arts & Ent. L. J.* 1, 23–33 (1992).

55. Greenberg, note 55, at 33; Heymann, note 50, at 460–462.

56. For a description of these issues, see Elec. Frontier Found., Fair Use Principles for User Generated Video Content, http://www.eff.org/issues/ip-and-free-speech/fair-use-principles-usergen (last visited Oct. 12, 2009); Ctr. for Soc. Media, Code of Best Practices for Fair Use in OnLine Video (May 2009), http://www.centerforsocialmedia.org/resources/publications/fair_use_in_online_video.

57. 464 U.S. 417, 454–455, 464 (1984).

58. Ibid. at 453–456.

59. Ibid. at 454–455. *Sony* displayed a streak of postmodernist self-consciousness in both its substantive analysis and in the technique of that decision—relying as it did on statutory bricolage to introduce the patent concept of "staple item of commerce" into copyright. See also Heymann, note 50, at 457 (concluding that under the proposed refinement of transformativeness analysis, time-shifting might not qualify although it might be considered fair use on other grounds).

60. See *Sony of Am. v. Universal Studios, Inc.*, 464 U.S. at 455–456.

61. 536 F.3d 121 (2d Cir. 2008). Copyright owners receive extra revenue when their content is accessed through cable systems' "on demand" features but not in cases of viewer-initiated time-shifting. Ibid. at 124. Interestingly, the parties undertook not to contest the issues of whether the cable system's activities could give rise to "secondary" (contributory or vicarious) liability and whether the "fair use" defense was available. Ibid. Instead, by agreement, the focus was placed on whether any activities might constitute direct infringement (as, for example, by reproduction) on the cable system's part. Ibid. On June 29, 2009, after a failed effort by copyright owners to persuade the new solicitor general to weigh in, the Supreme Court declined to hear a further appeal, and the courts of appeals' analyses are now settled. *CNN, Inc., v. CSC Holdings, Inc.*, 129 S. Ct. 2890 (2009).

62. *Cartoon Network LP v. CSC Holdings, Inc.*, 536 F.3d at 129–130.

63. Ibid. at 134–140.

64. Ibid. at 137–139.

65. Ibid. at 130 (emphasis added).

66. Ibid. at 131.

67. Ibid. at 132–133; see also *Sony*, 464 U.S. 417, 437–442 (1984).

68. Oliver A. Taillieu, "*Cartoon Network v. CSC Holdings*: Remote DVR Does Not Violate Copyright Protections Afforded to Television Program Copyright Holders" (Sept. 18, 2008), http://www.lawupdates.com/commentary/icartoon_network_v_csc_holdings_i_remote_dvr_does_not_violate_copyright_pro; see also Posting of Jeff Neuburger to New Media & Tech. Law Blog (Aug. 20, 2008), http://newmedialaw.proskauer.com/2008/08/articles/copyright/ram-copying-an-issue-of-more-than-transitory-duration.

69. *Cartoon Network*, 536 F.3d at 129–130.

70. Some sense of how controversial the decision was can be gleaned from the Amicus Brief filed by the Copyright Alliance, an umbrella organization of major copyright industry companies and associations, urging the Supreme Court to hear the case. Brief for Copyright Alliance as Amicus Curiae Supporting Petitioners, *CNN, Inc., v. CSC Holdings, Inc.*, 536 F.3d 121 (2d Cir. 2008) (No. 08-448), 2008 WL 4887717, at *17–23.

CONTRIBUTORS

YOCHAI BENKLER is Berkman Professor of Entrepreneurial Legal Studies at Harvard and faculty codirector of the Berkman Center for Internet and Society. In the 1990s he played a role in characterizing the centrality of information commons to innovation, information production, and freedom. In the past decade, he has worked on the sources, economic determinants, and political significance of radically decentralized individual action and loosely coupled peer collaboration in networked production of information, knowledge, and culture. His books include *The Wealth of Networks: How Social Production Transforms Markets and Freedom* (Yale University Press, 2006). His work can be freely accessed at benkler.org.

MARIO BIAGIOLI is Distinguished Professor of Law and Science and Technology Studies and director of the Center for Science and Innovation Studies at the University of California, Davis. Prior to joining UCD, he taught at Harvard, UCLA, Stanford, and the Ecoles des Hautes Etudes en Sciences Sociales (Paris). He is the author of *Galileo, Courtier: The Practice of Science in the Culture of Absolutism* (University of Chicago Press, 1993) and *Galileo's Instruments of Credit: Telescopes, Images, Secrecy* (University of Chicago Press, 2006) and of articles on scientific authorship and the history of patenting practices. He has edited *The Science Studies Reader* (Routledge, 1998) and, with Peter Galison, *Scientific Authorship: Credit and Intellectual Property in Science* (Routledge, 2003).

ROSEMARY J. COOMBE is Tier One Canada Research Chair in Law, Communication, and Culture at York University in Toronto. In 1992 she received her doctorate at Stanford University, where she was trained in anthropology and in law. She teaches in the Communication and Culture graduate program. Her award-winning book *The Cultural Life of Intellectual Properties* was published in 1998 and reprinted in 2008. Her current research focuses upon the global proliferation of cultural claims under conditions shaped by informational capital and the intersections of neoliberalism, indigeneity, and human rights. A complete list of her publications may be found at http://www.yorku.ca/rcoombe.

PETER DICOLA is an assistant professor at Northwestern University School of Law. He received his JD and PhD in economics from the University of Michigan. His research focuses on copyright law and media regulation. In 2011, he and coauthor Kembrew McLeod will publish *Creative License: The Law and Culture of Digital Sampling*, an interview-based, interdisciplinary study of the process for licensing digital samples in the music industry.

ERIC GIANNELLA is a PhD student in the Department of Sociology at the University of California, Berkeley. He is interested in economic sociology and the sociology of the law. His current work investigates how IP considerations affect interorganizational knowledge sharing and the day-to-day experience of research among industry scientists. Along with Woody Powell, he is coauthor of the chapter "Collective Invention and Inventor Networks" in the 2010 edition of *Handbook of the Economics of Innovation* (Blackwell), edited by Bronwyn Hall and Nate Rosenberg.

TARLETON GILLESPIE is an assistant professor in the Department of Communication at Cornell University, with affiliations in the Department of Information Science and the Department of Science and Technology Studies. He is also a fellow with the Center for Internet and Society at the Stanford School of Law. His book *Wired Shut: Copyright and the Shape of Digital Culture* was published by MIT Press in 2007. His current research on the "politics of platforms" examines how content sharing and social networking sites set norms and policies that shape online public discourse.

CORI HAYDEN is an associate professor of anthropology at the University of California, Berkeley. Publications include "The Proper Copy," *Journal of Cultural Economy*, 2010; "A Generic Solution?" *Current Anthropology*, 2007, "Taking as Giving: Bioscience, Exchange, and the Politics of Benefit-Sharing," *Social Studies of Science*, 2007; and *When Nature Goes Public: The Making and Unmaking of Bioprospecting in Mexico* (Princeton University Press, 2003). Her current project is an ethnography of generic drugs in Latin America and beyond.

PETER JASZI directs the Glushko-Samuelson Intellectual Property Law Clinic. He is a coauthor of *Copyright Law* (Lexis, 8th ed., 2010) and, with Martha Woodmansee, he edited *The Construction of Authorship* (Duke University Press, 1994). In 2004, he helped organize the Digital Future Coalition, and in 2007, he received the American Library Association's L. Ray Patterson Copyright Award. Since 2005, he has been working with Patricia Aufderheide to promote the understanding of fair use by creative communities. In 2006–2007, he led a research team funded by the Ford Foundation on the connections between intellectual law and the traditional arts in Indonesia.

ADRIAN JOHNS is a professor of history and chair of the Committee on Conceptual and Historical Studies of Science at the University of Chicago. He is the author of *Piracy: The Intellectual Property Wars from Gutenberg to Gates* (University of Chicago Press, 2009), *The Nature of the Book: Print and Knowledge in the Making* (University of Chicago Press, 1998), and *Death of a Pirate: British Radio and the Origins of the Information Age* (W. W. Norton, 2010). He has written widely on the histories of intellectual property, science, reading, and the book.

JONATHAN KAHN is a professor at the Hamline University School of Law. Holding a PhD in history from Cornell University and a JD from Boalt Hall School of Law, he writes on issues in history, politics, and law and specializes in biotechnology's implications for our ideas of identity, rights, and citizenship. He has published in the *Yale Journal of Health Policy, Law & Ethics, Seton Hall Law Review, Stanford Law & Policy Journal, American Journal of Bioethics, American Journal of Public Health*, and *Nature Genetics*. He is also the author of *Budgeting Democracy: State Building and Citizenship in America, 1890–1928* (Cornell University Press, 1997). His publications can be viewed at http://ssrn.com/author=180388.

CHRISTOPHER M. KELTY is an associate professor at UCLA. He has a joint appointment in the Center for Society and Genetics, the Department of Information Studies, and the Anthropology Department. His research focuses on the cultural significance of information technology, especially in science and engineering. He is the author most recently of *Two Bits: The Cultural Significance of Free Software* (Duke University Press, 2008), as well as numerous articles on open source and free software, including its impact on education, nanotechnology, the life sciences, and issues of peer review and research process in the sciences and in the humanities.

DANIEL J. KEVLES is Stanley Woodward Professor of History at Yale University. He is completing a history of intellectual property in plants, animals, and people (to be published by Knopf) and teaches a course on this subject in the Law School. His writings include "Genes, Railroads, and Regulation: Intellectual Property and the

Public Interest," in Mario Biagioli and Jessica Riskin, eds., *Worldly Science: Instruments, Practices, and the Law* (Palgrave Macmillan, 2010); and "Ananda Chakrabarty Wins a Patent: Biotechnology, Law, and Society, 1972–1980," *Historical Studies in the Physical and Biological Sciences* 25, no. 1 (1994): 111–36.

TIM LENOIR is University Professor and Kimberly Jenkins Chair for New Technologies in Society at Duke University. He has published several books and articles on the history of biomedical science from the nineteenth century to the present and is now involved in digital archiving and Web-based collaborations with Stanford University, MIT, and the NSF-sponsored Center for Nanotechnology in Society at the University of California, Santa Barbara. His current research centers on the use of text-mining and visualization tools for mapping the recent history of bio- and nanotechnology, the use of computers and digital imaging in biomedical research, and the history of interactive simulations and video games. He is a recipient of the MacArthur Foundation Digital Millennium Award.

LAWRENCE LIANG is a Bangalore-based legal researcher known for his legal campaigns on issues of public concern. He is a cofounder of the Alternative Law Forum. Liang's key areas of interest are law, popular culture, and piracy. He has been working closely with Sarai, New Delhi on a joint research project, Intellectual Property and the Knowledge/Culture Commons. Liang is a keen follower of the open source movement in software and has been working on ways of translating the open source ideas into the cultural domain. He is author of "Sex, Laws and Videotape: The Public Is Watching" and "Guide to Open Content Licenses," published by the Piet Zwart Institute in 2004. He is currently working on a book on law, justice, and cinema.

EVELYN LINCOLN is an associate professor in the departments of History of Art and Architecture and Italian Studies at Brown University. Her book *The Invention of the Italian Renaissance Printmaker* (Yale University Press, 2000) discusses the stylistic and legal conventions that defined printmaking as a new career in Renaissance Italy. She has written about printed pictures and authorship for the *DePaul Law Review* (2003). Her current research looks at the role of pictures in printed illustrated books for early modern readers and authors.

FIONA MURRAY is an associate professor of management in the Technological Innovation, Entrepreneurship, and Strategic Management Group at the MIT Sloan School of Management. She received BA and MA degrees from the University of Oxford in chemistry and her doctoral degree from Harvard University's School of Engineering and Applied Sciences. Her research highlights science commercialization, the organization of scientific research, and the role of IP at the boundary of the scientific and commercial communities. Her research is published in the *American*

Journal of Sociology, Science, New England Journal of Medicine, Nature Biotechnology, Research Policy, Organization Science, and the *Journal of Economic Behavior & Organization.*

DOTAN OLIAR is an associate professor at the University of Virginia School of Law. He received his LLB and BA from Tel Aviv University and his SJD from Harvard Law School. He currently researches the effect of technological change on copyright law. In previous work, he studied the framing of the U.S. Constitution's intellectual property clause. His research lies at the intersection of intellectual property law, property law, cyberlaw, and law and economics.

MARC PERLMAN is an associate professor in the Department of Music at Brown University. His research interests include Indonesian music, the psychology of music, the history and ethnography of music theory, intellectual property law, the variety of musical taste cultures, the cultural impact of music technology, the social history of American music education, and the historical performance movement in Western art music, Irish music, and Burmese music. He received his PhD from Wesleyan University. His scholarly writings have appeared in the journals *Ethnomusicology, Asian Music, Musical Quarterly, Postmodern Culture, Music Perception, Indonesia,* and *Social Studies of Science* and in the *New Grove Dictionary of Music and Musicians, Rhythm Music Magazine,* and the *New York Times.*

ALAIN POTTAGE holds degrees from the University of Edinburgh and the London School of Economics. Before joining the Law Department of the LSE, he was a researcher at the Law Commission and a lecturer in the School of Law at King's College, London. He has been a visiting professor at the Ecole des Hautes Etudes in Paris, the University of Sydney, and Cornell Law School. He is the coauthor (with Brad Sherman) of *Figures of Invention: A History of Patent Law* (Oxford University Press, 2010) and the coeditor (with Martha Mundy) of *Law, Anthropology, and the Constitution of the Social: Making Persons and Things* (Cambridge University Press, 2004).

WILLIAM RANKIN is completing a dual PhD in history of science and architecture at Harvard University; he will be an assistant professor of history at Yale University beginning in 2011. His research focuses on the importance of space and visuality in science, such as in drawings, maps, laboratories, and territorial engineering. His dissertation, "After the Map: Cartography, Navigation, and the Transformation of Territory in the Twentieth Century," is a history of the mapping sciences, sovereignty, and U.S. military globalism in the decades surrounding World War II. He has recently published in *Critical Inquiry* on modernist laboratory design and the history of knowledge production.

PAMELA SAMUELSON is Richard M. Sherman '74 Distinguished Professor of Law and Information at the University of California, Berkeley, and a director of the Berkeley Center for Law and Technology. She has written and spoken extensively about the challenges that new information technologies pose for traditional legal regimes, especially for intellectual property law. Among her recent publications are "High Technology Entrepreneurs and the Patent System: Results of the 2008 Berkeley Patent Survey" (with Stuart J. H. Graham, Robert P. Merges, and Ted Sichelman), 24 *Berkeley Technology L. J.* 1255 (2010); "Google Book Search and the Future of Books in Cyberspace," 94 *Minn. L. Rev.* 1308 (2010); and "Are Patents on Interfaces Impeding Interoperability?" 94 *Minn. L. Rev.* 1943 (2009).

BRAD SHERMAN is a professor in law in the School of Law at Griffith University. Prior to joining Griffith University, he worked at the University of Queensland, the London School of Economics, and Cambridge University. He is currently working on a history of information-based inventions in Anglo-American patent law. He is the coauthor, with Lionel Bently, of *Intellectual Property Law* (Oxford University Press, 2008) and *The Making of Intellectual Property Law* (Cambridge University Press, 1999).

CHRIS SPRIGMAN teaches intellectual property law, antitrust law, competition policy, and comparative constitutional law at the University of Virginia School of Law. His scholarship focuses on how legal rules affect innovation and the deployment of new technologies. Following graduation from the University of Chicago Law School, he clerked for the Honorable Stephen Reinhardt of the U.S. Court of Appeals for the Ninth Circuit and, from 1999 to 2001, served as appellate counsel in the Antitrust Division of the U.S. Department of Justice, where he worked on *U.S. v. Microsoft*. He then joined the Washington, DC, office of King and Spalding LLP, where he was elected a partner. In 2003, he left law practice to become a Residential Fellow at the Center for Internet and Society at Stanford Law School.

MARILYN STRATHERN, emeritus professor of social anthropology, Cambridge University, has recently been made life president of the (United Kingdom and Commonwealth) Association of Social Anthropologists. An interest in property and transactions runs through several branches of her work, whether in Melanesia (Papua New Guinea Highlands) or Great Britain, where research has included the technologies of assisted conception. Her writing on IP rights sprang from a collaborative research project that brought a reengagement with Melanesia in a new area.

KARA W. SWANSON, JD, PhD, is an associate professor at Northeastern University School of Law in Boston, Massachusetts, where she teaches intellectual property and property law. She has published several articles on the patent system in the United

States, including "The Emergence of the Professional Patent Practitioner," 50 *Technology & Culture* 519 (2009), and "Biotech in Court: A Legal Lesson on the Unity of Science," 37 *Social Studies of Science* 357 (2007), and is currently writing a history of biobanking in the United States.

MARTHA WOODMANSEE is a professor of English and law at Case Western Reserve University. From 1990 to 2008 she was director of the Society for Critical Exchange, and she is a founding director of the International Society for the History and Theory of Intellectual Property. She has published widely at the intersection of aesthetics, economics, and the law. Her books include *The Author, Art, and the Market* (Columbia University Press, 1994), *The Construction of Authorship: Textual Appropriation in Law and Literature* (with Peter Jaszi, Duke University Press, 1994), and *The New Economic Criticism: Studies at the Intersection of Literature and Economics* (with Mark Osteen, Routledge, 1999).

CITATION INDEX